J R McNutt

D1431833

STONEWALL JACKSON
AT CEDAR MOUNTAIN

Especially for Bob McNutt,
with best wishes from the
author.

Robert K. Krick
June 22, 1991
— at Connecticut

STONEWALL JACKSON

at Cedar Mountain

Robert K. Krick

The University of North Carolina Press

Chapel Hill and London

© 1990 The University of North Carolina Press
All rights reserved

Library of Congress Cataloging-in-Publication Data

Krick, Robert K.
  Stonewall Jackson at Cedar Mountain / Robert K. Krick.
    p. cm.
  Includes bibliographical references.
  ISBN 0-8078-1887-9 (alk. paper)
  1. Cedar Mountain, Battle of, 1862. 2. Jackson, Stonewall,
1824–1863. I. Title.
E473.76.K75 1990
973.7'32—dc20   89-36158
                                                     CIP

The paper in this book meets the guidelines for
permanence and durability of the Committee on
Production Guidelines for Book Longevity of the
Council on Library Resources.

Manufactured in the United States of America
94 93 92 91 90   5 4 3 2 1

CONTENTS

Contents

ILLUSTRATIONS

MAPS

ACKNOWLEDGMENTS

ORIGINAL HISTORICAL research requires ingenuity, but to a far greater degree it entails simple, methodical hard work. The most careful and energetic historian, however, cannot alone locate the multitude of ephemeral sources that may pertain to his subject. For that he must rely on colleagues willing to file a mental note on his behalf as they go about their own tasks.

I spent many years building the research base for this book so several dozen colleagues had ample time to learn of my goals and to turn up leads to my benefit. Michael P. Musick of the National Archives must stand at the head of almost any such listing for Civil War subjects. It is literally impossible to do adequate research for a serious Civil War book without Mike's collaboration. Keith S. Bohannon of Smyrna, Georgia, traveled indefatigably across his home state in successful quest for arcana that enabled me to unravel the heretofore obscure roles of the Twelfth Georgia and of Edward L. Thomas's scattered regiments. John J. Hennessy of Niskayuna, New York, the unequaled expert on Second Manassas, unearthed dozens of Cedar Mountain references in the course of his own exhaustive research. Waverly K. Winfree served, as he has for so long and so well, as a gracious and efficient gatekeeper to the treasures of the Virginia Historical Society. Mrs. Carlin Inskeep, matriarch of the clan that owns much of the battlefield today, welcomed or at least tolerated my ramblings across the family farm for nearly two decades; so did her neighbor, the late Taylor Wiseman.

I owe three individuals a debt of gratitude for their work on mapping Cedar Mountain. The late David A. Lilley first turned my painfully maladroit charts into recognizable terrain studies. Larry E. James of Spotsylvania County subsequently produced an uncluttered topographic base on which I was able to sketch the raw data for thirteen of the maps in this book. George F. Skoch of Cleveland Heights, Ohio, skillfully turned those primitive sketches into the polished finals that appear here.

Other individuals who supplied information or support also deserve acknowledgment: Lee A. Wallace, Jr., Falls Church; Lewis Leigh,

Fairfax; Dr. Walter L. Powell, Gettysburg, Pennsylvania; Judy Anthis, Richmond; Robert A. Hodge of Fredericksburg, a veritable oracle on local history as far afield as Culpeper; Vicki Heilig, Germantown, Maryland; Ruth Ann Amiss Moore, Manassas; Robert J. Younger, Dayton, Ohio; Mike Andrus, Richmond; Raymond W. Watkins, Falls Church; Robert E. L. Krick, Fredericksburg; H. E. Howard, Lynchburg; Brian Pohanka of Leesburg, for details about General Winder; Greg Coco, Gettysburg, Pennsylvania; Marshall D. Krolick of Chicago, who never forgets the battle's anniversary; Rick Sauers and William D. Matter, Harrisburg, Pennsylvania; Jim Moody of Charleston, South Carolina, and his beloved Citadel; C. Bud Hall of Fairfax, a good, and patient, photographer and a noted preservationist; Ed Gentry, Culpeper; Gary W. Gallagher, Pennsylvania State University; James H. Ogden III, Fort Oglethorpe, Georgia; Noel Harrison, D. Ray Brown, and Mac Wyckoff, all of Fredericksburg, for repeated reference help and in Mac's case, for research tasks during North Carolina trips; Peter Carmichael, Indianapolis; Lowell Reidenbaugh of St. Louis, for reference assistance in the Midwest and especially for an incomparable opportunity to see Bill Walsh's last outing; Stuart G. Vogt, Springfield, Massachusetts; A. Wilson Greene, Fredericksburg; and Gary D. Remy, Madison, Wisconsin.

The professional historians and archivists associated with institutions other than those cited above who proved particularly helpful include the following men and women: Philip Shiman and Robert L. Byrd, Duke University; Richard J. Sommers, U.S. Army Military History Institute, Carlisle Barracks; Bruce Cheeseman and David J. Olson, North Carolina Department of Archives and History; Diane Jacob, Virginia Military Institute; Suzanne Christoff, U.S. Military Academy; Ann Effland and George Parkinson, West Virginia University; Thomas E. Camden, University of Georgia; Marylin Bell Hughes, Tennessee State Library and Archives; Oliver H. Orr, Library of Congress; Gary J. Arnold, Ohio Historical Society; John T. Hubbell, *Civil War History*; Bill Meneray, Tulane University; Karen Stewart, Maryland Historical Society; Charlene Alling and the late (and incomparable and sorely missed) Eleanor Brockenbrough, Museum of the Confederacy; and Conley Edwards, William H. Gaines, Jr., and Louis H. Manarin, Virginia State Archives.

Trudie Calvert of the University of North Carolina Press proved patiently and skillfully that she is all anyone could ever want in an editor.

Robert K. Krick
Fredericksburg, Virginia
January 1989

STONEWALL JACKSON
AT CEDAR MOUNTAIN

PROLOGUE

IN THE MIDSUMMER OF 1862, Thomas J. Jackson was perhaps the most famous man in North America. His nom de guerre, "Stonewall," rolled sweetly on Southern tongues and was invoked by Northern nannies to frighten bumptious youngsters. When Charles M. Blackford, twenty-eight years old and a captain of cavalry, went to see mighty Stonewall in late July, the young man must have been filled with curiosity and awe.

Blackford had been running some clever and fruitful scouting ventures into the central Virginia countryside west of Fredericksburg, where Stonewall was heading to confront a Federal army. The cavalryman's work had pleased Jackson, who invited the young officer in to give a full report and maybe to get some kind words by way of thanks. The audience took place in a spartan headquarters tent. Jackson, totally innocent of social graces, immediately asked for a report, and Blackford eagerly launched into one.

After a few minutes of careful reporting, Blackford noticed to his chagrin that the general "was fast asleep." There seemed to be little point in continuing, so Blackford stopped. After several minutes Jackson woke up and calmly ordered his visitor: "Proceed." After he had talked a short while more, the captain noticed that his audience was once more unconscious. The silent vigil lasted longer the second time. When Stonewall stirred to life, he said without preamble or explanation, "You may proceed to your quarters."[1]

One-half of the Confederate Army of Northern Virginia was in the hands of this brilliant but wonderfully eccentric genius. Jackson's job was to halt the advance into Virginia of a newly created Federal army under General John Pope.

1

CHAPTER 1

John Pope's Difficult Adjustment

JOHN POPE FOUND NOTHING but trouble in Virginia in 1862. The general was a forty-year-old career soldier, a graduate of the United States Military Academy, and a veteran of the Mexican War. Pope graduated seventeenth in the remarkable West Point class of 1842, which produced nearly a score of men who became general officers during the Civil War. During the war's early days Pope had stumbled into easy success in the western theater. His brightest ally was his political record—he was a staunch Republican at a time when the radicals of that party were wielding enormous power in Washington. Pope had actually been court-martialed for political impudence against Democratic President James Buchanan before the war.

Three distinguished Northern military writers, collaborating in a paper about Pope's Virginia campaign, offered a synoptic view of the man: "Personally, Gen. Pope was of quick temper, impatient of contradiction, rude in manner, and gifted with a vivid imagination." The new Federal hope in Virginia clearly was not gifted in the field of human relations. Men said that his orders were pretentiously datelined from "headquarters in the saddle."[1] As soon as the men of both Union and Confederate armies heard of the dateline they jocularly derided the general as a man who did not know his headquarters from his hindquarters and kept one where the other should have been.

Northern jokes about Pope contained some bitterness, and Southerners would soon be bitter as well. Pope issued a patronizing circular to his troops in a maladroit effort to heighten their morale. "I have come to you from the West," he wrote, "where we have always seen the backs of our enemies." Confederate successes in Virginia, he felt sure, had resulted from timid soldiering by the Federals. "Let us discard such ideas," Pope exhorted, as "taking strong positions . . . lines of retreat [and] . . . bases of supplies."[2] His new subordinates of all ranks growled and glared.

A series of draconian general orders which tumbled from Pope's

3

pen sent a wave of outrage through the South and offended many in his own army as well. The first ordered his men to "subsist upon the country," taking from Southern civilians without reimbursement. Another declared that Virginia families would be held responsible for any damage done by Confederates in their neighborhoods; any damage to Federal troops or supplies would be assessed against all civilians within a five-mile radius. Some offenders would "be shot, without awaiting civil process." All citizens unwilling to take the oath of allegiance were to be sent outside the army's lines, their property confiscated. Execution without trial awaited any civilian who violated this stringent oath.[3]

This was very strong stuff indeed. Two years later, when chivalry had been thoroughly emasculated, the Union's most prominent officers behaved in about the same fashion. Human savagery in war has since come to know no bounds, and in the twentieth century everyone behaves in this manner. In July 1862, though, Pope was a man ahead of his time (as well as immune to conscience). Pope's bravado disgusted his own army. At a grand review, some of the troops exhibited blatant disrespect for their new leader. A gathering of officers, some of them wearing generals' stars, brought forth "cuss words of such vigor" against Pope that observers were "appalled." "Ordinary words being totally inadequate to express one's feelings, swearing became an epidemic," reported one blue-clad general. An English correspondent for *Cornhill Magazine* interviewed Pope on the eve of the battle of Cedar Mountain and recorded a vivid impression of the general. The Englishman's account is vivid and detailed:

> Tall, corpulent, and athletic, with keen dark eyes, and beard and hair black as midnight, Gen. Pope had all the air of a commander. Vain, imprudent, and not proverbially truthful; but shrewd, active, and skilled in the rules of warfare, Pope could be great and little too. He was clothed with scrupulous neatness, his hair and beard carefully dressed, his cigars exquisite in flavor. He spoke much and rapidly, chiefly of himself; swore roundly at intervals, was petulant at trifles, and sanguine of impending success.[4]

John Pope was not a man of great capacity, and it is easy to imagine that his blustering style might have covered a great uneasiness and confusion. The Civil War he had known in Missouri was much different from that in Virginia. In the West, divided sentiments led to brigandage and irregularities, including savagery not only between contending armies but also between civilians. One of Pope's apologists reported that the general was amazed at the unanimity of Confederate sentiment in Virginia. The effects of this civilian hostility on his own military security, and on his knowledge of Confederate movements, were obviously large and negative.[5] An aide to Pope later defended his chief in an unpublished memoir that portrays the officer corps and enlisted men of the army as so thoroughly cowed that shock tactics were necessary and suggests that Pope directed his bombastic general orders toward that goal. In a pungent reaction, one of Pope's fellow Union generals summarized the prevailing attitude when he said: "I don't care for John Pope a pinch of owl dung."[6]

Pope's grumbling army was about forty-five thousand men strong, including sixty-five hundred cavalry under the competent leadership of John Buford and George Bayard.[7] The infantry was arranged in three corps, commanded by Franz Sigel, Irvin McDowell, and Nathaniel P. Banks. Sigel was a German immigrant of very limited military attainments, but he had well-placed political friends and enjoyed the admiration of his troops. McDowell had commanded the Federal army that was routed at First Manassas. He was an uninspiring but solid officer, but his politics were suspected by paranoid Washington politicians.

General Banks was the man against whom Stonewall Jackson actually fought at Cedar Mountain. The two were old adversaries, and the results were always the same. It is easy to sympathize with Banks because Jackson overmatched everyone. The Northerner was forty-six years old and had spent his life in politics and railroading. Banks was far more aggressive than most Union commanders. At a "sham-fight" shortly after Pope's arrival, Banks "was with difficulty restrained by his staff from charging one of his infantry squares at the head of his cavalry escort." Vast personal bravery and ambition of the same dimensions made Banks formidable.[8] Banks was not nearly so inept as his critics were wont to declare, but he was beyond question more politician than soldier. His main claim to fame was a career as Speaker of the House of Representatives while representing Massachusetts in that body.

In early August, Pope's command threatened Lee's left and rear from an arc centered on Gordonsville. Although Pope's force included about twice as many men as Jackson could muster, they were spread from Fredericksburg to the foothills of the Blue Ridge. These far-flung Union detachments were also suffering from more than

Major General John Pope: "tall, corpulent . . . vain, imprudent, and not proverbially truthful." (Harper's Weekly)

simple unhappiness with their new general. The weather raged brutally hot and sickness ran rampant. As a result of "imprudence in eating unripe fruit, and . . . neglect of sanitary precautions, many of the men were ill, and many died."9 John Pope and forty-five thousand sweating, muttering subordinates were about to come up against Stonewall Jackson, and they would not be equal to the task.

CONFEDERATE COMMANDER R. E. Lee was prompted by Pope's shenanigans to write to Stonewall Jackson: "I want Pope to be suppressed." In an official document, Lee referred to the new Federal leader as "miscreant Pope," and in other correspondence Lee was atypically blunt in his comments. Months later, after Pope had been thoroughly suppressed, Lee's official report noted that he had sent Jackson toward Gordonsville on July 13 from the environs of Richmond to "restrain, as far as possible, the atrocities which [Pope] threatened to perpetrate upon our defenseless citizens."10

Less than two weeks before Jackson left Richmond on Pope's trail, Lee had fought and won the Seven Days' battles, pushing George B. McClellan's Northern army from the outskirts of the Confederate capital. Jackson reached Gordonsville on July 19 and assessed his enemy's strength and intentions. He told Lee that Pope was too strong to be driven. Since Lee could not afford to reinforce his lieutenant, he directed him "to observe the enemy's movements closely, to avail himself of any opportunity to attack that might arise." McClellan's languorous behavior gave Lee the chance to send A. P. Hill's strong division from Richmond to Jackson's assistance on July 27.11

Even after the addition of Hill's six big brigades, Jackson could not count more than half the strength that Pope had at hand. He determined nonetheless to find an opening for the sort of hard, quick offensive thrust that was his trademark. A successful sally would disconcert Pope and delay the unfolding of his campaign. As the situation developed, Jackson conceived the notion of defeating Pope by moving rapidly to Culpeper, interposing himself between pieces of the Northern army, and defeating them by turns.12 Stonewall's most recent independent operations, precisely two months before around Cross Keys and Port Republic, had been based on an identical premise. His tactics had not worked particularly well at that time.

When Jackson made his headquarters in Gordonsville on July 19, he took up residence temporarily at the home of the Reverend D. B. Ewing. The general, it was noted, appeared jaded and unwell, as Captain Blackford would have gladly attested. Jackson complained that he had not suffered so much since his Mexican War days—but then Jackson always savored the chance to complain about his health. The small Ewing daughters cheered Stonewall's spare moments; children always amused the general. The fresh fruit available in this agricultural country refreshed him, as did the relatively bracing climate (anything is better than the Richmond swamps in midsummer). The Ewing girls eventually wangled uniform coat buttons from Jackson, and great treasures those were, then and now alike. Near the end of July, Jackson carried his army down into Louisa County to make use of the superb pasturage for which that locality has always been justly famous.[13]

The moving army, as usual, had no idea where it was going or why when the move began on July 29. One of Jackson's headquarters entourage marveled: "It seems strange to see a large body of men moving in one direction and only one man in all the thousands knowing where they are going. . . . They will go until ordered to stop." During the march on July 30, the same bemused officer wrote: "The General . . . has very little to say to anyone." No military man has ever been more secretive than was Jackson, as any number of witnesses have reported. A Southern general who watched Jackson in his renowned Valley campaign summed up crisply: "If silence be golden, he was a 'bonanza.' "[14]

While the men and animals of Jackson's army enjoyed the lush Green Springs area of Louisa County, the Southern cavalry kept busy along the line of the Rapidan. Most of the Confederate horsemen belonged to the famed Laurel Brigade, which had its origins in the loosely organized Shenandoah Valley command that had been Turner Ashby's. When Jackson left the Valley in June 1862, the cavalry brigade stayed behind and successfully screened the movement. Now the Valley horsemen were back with Jackson, east of the Blue Ridge and spread between Gordonsville and Orange.

The Laurel Brigade was now commanded by General Beverly H. Robertson. Robertson was thirty-five years old, a career officer, and a West Point graduate—and Jackson disliked him very much. When Lee's cavalry chief, J. E. B. Stuart, showed up in the midst of the Cedar Mountain fighting, observers in the army interpreted his arrival as a fortuitous coincidence. Historians have accepted that interpretation.

Two members of Stonewall's staff knew better. One of the witnesses was Jackson's medical officer, Hunter Holmes McGuire. During the first days of August, Jackson found McGuire eating a raw Bermuda onion in a desperate effort to dispel dusty heat and thirst. The general was teasing McGuire about his taste, in the heavily humorless way that Jackson sometimes exhibited, when Robertson rode into the cheerful tableau. Stonewall immediately asked the question he always had ready for his mounted arm: "Where is the enemy?" When Robertson calmly replied, "I really do not know," the glee vanished from Jackson's face, his countenance turned black, and he abruptly moved away without speaking further. Jackson immediately telegraphed to Lee, asking for Stuart's services. Lee suspected that his subordinate was demanding too much from Robertson, but he sent Stuart up to look around.[15]

Quarreling between contending cavalry pickets gained momentum and on August 2 a hot little fight erupted in the streets of Orange Court House. Three Federal cavalry regiments—the First Vermont, First Michigan, and Fifth New York—crossed the Rapidan River at Raccoon Ford and moved against Orange from the north. In the northern outskirts of the village one company of the Eleventh Virginia Cavalry met the Yankees. The Northerners easily drove the Virginians through town and beyond, but help was on the way. The Seventh Virginia Cavalry galloped into action led by its colonel, William E. Jones, who was known to one and all by the well-earned sobriquet of "Grumble."[16]

The main Federal column was enjoying "a stillness like that of death," according to one man in its ranks, when Grumble Jones burst upon them. Screaming horse soldiers soon jammed the streets, firing carbines and pistols, slashing and stabbing with sabers. "The fight was furious in the narrow streets," reported a member of the Fifth New York.[17] There was hardly room to move or to breathe, and men reacted differently. Strong men from both sides pushed into the fray; their timid cousins withdrew from the concentrated mayhem. Someone heard Grumble Jones say frankly that "half of his men charged and half discharged."[18]

At this pivotal moment Major Thomas Marshall (grandson of the great Chief Justice John Marshall) led a squadron of the Seventh Virginia in by the railroad depot in a flank attack. Before Marshall's little column could swing the balance, it was in turn struck inopportunely in flank by a Federal force riding to the sound of the guns. His retreat cut off, young Marshall emptied his pistols into his adversaries and then was knocked unconscious by a saber stroke. Grumble Jones was winning his way through the streets and personally shot dead a Yankee who was about to kill Marshall. Yet another Northern detachment stumbled upon Jones's right rear, and in the renewed confusion Marshall was dragged away, an unconscious prisoner.[19]

Jones finally managed to defend his flanks and cleared the town, only to find the fields to the north swarming with mounted Yankees. Grumble had taken a saber wound, but that had not made him mad enough to lose his sense: he fell back south of Orange and watched the Federals from a distance.[20] One rallying point was in the yard of a house south of town owned by the Willis family—part of an old and populous clan in that vicinity. An unmarried young female Willis cheered the men on, looking "pretty and noble" to an interested male observer. When the fiery girl cried, "Oh, I wish I was a man!" she found ready answer from a cavalryman who had been down in the caldron and retorted: "If you was, you would wish you was a gal again mouty soon." The same crowd of horsemen received sterner encouragement from Captain John H. Magruder of the Seventh Virginia Cavalry, who promised that he would kill anyone failing to renew the advance when ordered.[21]

The hostile cavalry glared across the fields at each other for perhaps an hour. Jones did not have many more than two hundred troopers on hand; Jackson styled his stand a "show of resistance." The show of force succeeded; the Federals soon fell back toward the Rapidan. The Sixth Virginia Cavalry came up in time to help the Seventh pursue the Northerners back to the river. Jones had little cause to grumble about the outcome of this uneven fight, but Jackson may have wondered what it boded for the future of his campaign. Confederate losses were reported as ten wounded and forty missing, with an estimate that enemy losses had been similar. Federal official reports suggested that things had gone far better than that for them.[22]

Three days after the flareup at Orange, Jeb Stuart soundly thrashed a Federal force near Massaponax Church just below Fredericksburg. At the cost of merely two casualties, Stuart captured eighty-five Yankees and a mountain of spoils.[23] That was the sort of cavalry advantage Jackson had been wanting. He must have reveled in his secret knowledge that the daring Stuart was on the way to help suppress Pope.

Jackson's seasoned infantrymen were accustomed to having their way with hostile armies, and they relished a role in defeating Pope. A member of Jackson's own doughty old brigade reported that "we could hear it remarked in camp, 'Just wait 'till Old Jack gets a chance at him; he'll take some of the starch out of him.'" Stonewall's ranking subordinate, crusty Dick Ewell, seethed with determination to "paralyze this Western bully."[24] Richard Stoddert Ewell was a forty-five-year-old professional soldier, pop-eyed and bald-headed. He must be counted as one of the great eccentrics in an army full of unique personalities, but in the summer of 1862 he was a fine executive officer. Later summers would find his efficiency drastically reduced.

Stonewall himself heard Pope's unpleasant pronouncements when his aide Alexander S. "Sandie" Pendleton read them to the assembled staff. Another staff member reported that Jackson's wholly typical reaction was simply "a quiet smile and a frown." A clergyman visiting headquarters solicited Jackson's comment on the orders, suggesting, "here is a new candidate for your favor." Jackson—always deeply and demonstratively devout—replied: "Yes, and by God's blessing he shall receive my attention."[25]

Devout though he was, mighty Stonewall simply could not stay awake in church during these steamy summer days. A Virginia chaplain with the army in early August reported that he was "very much amused" to see Jackson "fast asleep at preaching" on several occasions. Since all eyes focused on the general, everyone noticed the habit. Ewell commented, in his saucy fashion: "What is the use of General Jackson's going to church? He sleeps all of the time."[26]

Jackson worshiped on Sunday, August 3, in the camp of Alexander R. Lawton's Georgia Brigade. The orator, a famous Georgia divine, "prayed that there might be no straggling when we again went forth to battle." An impressed observer noted that the old preacher "was eloquent and his voice thrilled like a trumpet and perspiration rolled down his face." If Jackson was awake at the height of the lengthy prayer, he surely must have seconded the preacher's plea: "O Lord, when we go out again to fight give us the biggest kind of a victory."[27]

Many of Jackson's officers spent that Sunday in the civilian churches throughout beautiful Green Springs. Captain Blackford of the Second Virginia Cavalry (the same man who had reported to a drowsy Jackson a few days before) turned out for church in a brand-new uniform wearing brightly blacked boots and glittering sword and spurs and astride a gaily caparisoned horse. Because he was so carefully gotten up, and because he knew a number of local families, Blackford felt certain of a dinner invitation. Things turned sour when the parson preached "a very trashy sermon," and then communion was made uneasy by the clanking of officers' swords against the chancel rail. The captain shook hands all around after church and

Thomas Jonathan "Stonewall" Jackson commanded the Confederate forces at Cedar Mountain with the rank of major general. His final promotion lay just more than three months in the future.

helped any number of women into their carriages but was snubbed in regard to dinner invitations by one and all, including a dear family friend. So he stole some corn from a Green Springs field and roasted it in splendid isolation in camp.[28]

Stonewall Jackson never suffered such snubs from citizens, at Green Springs or anywhere else. Adulatory matrons came from miles around bearing delicacies, unaware that the object of their admiration was indifferent to luxuries. One of Jackson's staff suggested that his attitude was typical of diet enthusiasts. "He liked a great many things he did not eat, and ate some things he did not like." The vibrant young men on the general's staff carefully steered their chief into feasts and fetes by a variety of "admirable devices." As one of them said, the staff lads "did not believe that good food affected their official usefulness."[29]

Blackford, a line officer who spent some time in Jackson's presence about this time (an "acquaintance that might be likened to that of a glowworm with the moon," he noted), left a vivid description of that extraordinary man with the ordinary appearance. The general "was poorly dressed," although on closer examination the material could be seen to be good—Jackson just exuded a certain indefinable shabbiness. "His shoulders were stooped and . . . his coat showed signs of much exposure to the weather." Jackson's sword—soon to be waved in passion at Cedar Mountain—was very ordinary, without a sash. His face "is not handsome or agreeable, and he would be passed by anyone without a second look." Even a casual glance, though, found "determination and will in his face . . . much I would say to fear but not to love."[30]

A relative stranger riding with Jackson and some of his staff during the first days of August had occasion to notice the general's peculiar behavior. After a quiet five-mile ride Jackson suddenly stopped at about 2:00 P.M. and without a word "dismounted at the foot of a tree, unbuckled his sword and stood it by the tree, then laid down with his head on the root of the tree and was asleep in a second, or appeared to be so." The amazed observer threw a startled glance at the other mounted men, but they did not seem much surprised. The Southerners sat quietly on their horses. Jackson napped for five or six minutes, then buckled on his sword and rode away, still without uttering a syllable. The witness to this episode and others like it wrote a letter home two days later, having obviously given some thought to the matter. Jackson evidently "has no social graces but infinite earnestness. . . . He is a zealot and has stern ideas of duty." Perhaps no better summation of the bizarre incident and its bizarre central figure could be supplied than that of the same witness, who concluded: "He is a curious, wonderful man."[31]

Near midday on August 4 the Confederate army began to prepare for a march. The black servants around headquarters spread the word first, basing their intelligence on the fact that General Jackson's personal servant was rapidly bringing in the commander's washing. The chief of Jackson's staff learned the news himself in that unorthodox fashion. On the fifth, army headquarters moved four miles beyond Gordonsville, arriving after dark at a familiar campsite on the Magruder farm. Everyone slept under the trees except Jackson.[32]

As the gray-clad infantry uncoiled from camps and pressed northward toward the Rapidan, some cavalry forces moved farther ahead into Culpeper County. Another of the Valley cavalry regiments (the Twelfth Virginia) arrived on August 5 to bolster Jackson's mounted arm. The Virginia troopers relished the idea of dealing with Pope. "The boys begun to have ideas," one of them wrote, "that the man with the movable headquarters had better commence moving."[33]

The reason Jackson moved north may have been simply that he had a court-martial to attend, and it was to be held at Dick Ewell's headquarters at Liberty Mills, right on the Rapidan west of Orange Court House and north of Gordonsville. The trial became one of the most famous in the Confederacy's military annals, not because it decided anything but because of the delicate points involved and because of Jackson's earnest involvement. For almost five months, General Richard B. Garnett had stood accused by Jackson of seven counts of misbehavior at the battle of Kernstown. Garnett had commanded the old Stonewall Brigade at that difficult fight—Jackson's first as an independent commander.

Several of the charges against Garnett were either patently absurd, greatly exaggerated, or inaccurate. Garnett, scion of a proud old Virginia family, was a professional soldier of some accomplishments. The charges against him burned and rankled with a wrenching pain. In Mighty Stonewall, Garnett came up against one of the most litigious officers on the continent. (Jackson inevitably waged his endless legal proceedings against subordinates. Many of his fellow Confederate officers indulged their penchant for quarreling by doing so with superiors, to the detriment of their cause.)

When Jackson took the stand on August 6, Garnett avidly attacked his foe. Every one of the regimental commanders in the brigade firmly supported Garnett and refuted any of Jackson's allegations that related to their experiences. At least one of the colonels had been eager to take the stand in person, but that did not happen. Garnett pinned down his accuser about his mistakes in estimating Federal strength at Kernstown and in putting the Southern army at considerable risk.

A few weeks before the court-martial convened, Garnett had written to the War Department that Jackson's actions "should arouse *grave doubts* as to the *motives*, and *truthfulness*" of his superior. Now that he had Jackson on the stand, Garnett maneuvered to make Jackson's duplicity apparent. Stonewall denied having made a number of statements and orders cited by Garnett. The copy of the hearing transcript which belonged to Garnett has survived. It is on blue legal paper, ironically bearing the heavily laid watermark of the U.S. eagle. All along the margin of the transcript, opposite responses by Jackson, is the word "Lie" written in pencil in Garnett's hand. To highlight those points, Garnett also penciled in oblong asterisks. There are many of them, and it would be difficult to say after a century and a quarter that Garnett was mistaken, for he apparently was not.[34]

When the court-martial recessed for the night of August 6, there was no indication that a major battle loomed just a few days ahead. One of the best-informed members of Jackson's staff wrote in his diary that night: "All quiet; not even a rumor of news." Over in Orange, quiet reigned too at the headquarters of General Ambrose Powell Hill, the thirty-six-year-old West Point graduate who commanded Jackson's largest division. Hill had set up in the yard at Mayhurst, the home of John Willis.[35] Hill was proud, short and slight, sensitive, and good at his job. A couple of those characteristics would land Hill in trouble with Jackson before two days had slipped past. R. E. Lee had specially enjoined Jackson to treat Hill well, in the interest of unified action; Lee knew that Jackson was terribly prickly and that Hill would not stand much prickling.

The Garnett court-martial reconvened on the seventh with Jackson's aide Sandie Pendleton on the stand. Sandie was loyal to his chief and testified accordingly, but it seemed evident to him that Jackson was going to lose his case. In the midst of this rebellion within a rebellion, Jackson ordered his army to move across the Rapidan River against the Federals.[36]

The Garnett court-martial was suspended in midstream during the day of August 7 and never resumed. Dick Garnett fell dead at the forefront of Pickett's charge at Gettysburg, eleven months later.

There is, of course, no evidence that Jackson consciously moved into action to terminate a court martial that was slipping away from him. Such a response runs counter to all of Jackson's well-known characteristics. It would have been much more in character for him to redouble his efforts and levy new charges. It is hard, however, not to postulate that his frustration over the court-martial was not far below the surface when Jackson fell to wrangling with A. P. Hill just a few hours later, virtually in the shadow of the court-martial chamber.

The opportunity that Jackson sought to exploit across the river in Culpeper County apparently came to his attention by way of a mixture of reports from spies and cavalry scouts. The general's own report was typically reticent: "Having received information that only part of General Pope's army was at Culpeper Court-House." The situation was precisely what Jackson had been looking for.[37]

Some of the credit for the exciting intelligence belonged to Benjamin Franklin Stringfellow, who was roaming behind Federal lines in company with the redoubtable scout Redmond Burke. Stringfellow, a wiry little man, nearly rode his horse across a Yankee scout who lay "sprawled against a tree, snoring heavily." The Southerner stealthily approached the sleeper and pressed his pistol's muzzle against his temple. Stringfellow's caution was wasted—it took several healthy pokes from the revolver to end the nap. The startled Federal lunged for his musket and Stringfellow thumped him with the butt of the pistol.

When he emerged from his second nap, the Northerner identified himself as Private Jenkins of a Pennsylvania regiment. Jenkins grumbled about the blow to his head because he was a peaceable man and had not been going for the gun so much as he had just generally been startled. He was too old for this foolishness, Jenkins said, and had joined the army to get away from his wife, "who was enough to run a man out of his mind." Stringfellow rendezvoused with Burke, who had gotten himself shot, and carried back to Jackson the information he had garnered from Jenkins (presumably omitting the details of the poor fellow's marital ordeal).[38]

Another hint about the sources of information reaching Jackson comes from a document of uncertain provenance in which one Phillip Bradley supplied fairly accurate intelligence about Pope's doings. Bradley signed himself as an "Operative Military Secret Service" reporting from Washington, Virginia, which was squarely in the midst of Pope country. "Since July 29, Gen Pope has given his personal attention to field operations," Bradley reported on an unnamed date. "He has stationed all his infantry and artillery force, number about twenty eight thousand men, along the turnpike from Culpepper to Sperrysville." Buford operated from Madison Court House with five regiments, Bradley claimed, with pickets along the Rapidan from Barnett's Ford to the Blue Ridge; Bayard was near Rapidan Station. The spy concluded that a great many Yankees had "lately arrived in these parts," and he not unreasonably was leaving in search of a safer spot.[39]

The orders that uncoiled Jackson's army inevitably took time to reach their destinations. Perhaps the orders moved less rapidly than they would otherwise have done because Jackson's headquarters cavalry detachment had been ordered away the night before on business close to Jackson's heart—a "whiskey-spilling expedition." When mounted men delivered the marching orders to bivouacs all across northern Orange County, the various Confederate units moved out without much delay. Even so it was "quite late in the p.m." when Jedediah Hotchkiss of Jackson's staff "packed up and went over to Orange C.H., going through the plantations by a way I selected, by order of the General, that was concealed from observation of the enemy." Hotchkiss had Jackson's old division, now commanded by Charles S. Winder, in his wake, "secretly led by me, to Orange C.H.," as he told his diary.[40]

The First Virginia Battalion of that division had been encamped "about five miles from Gordonsville" on the road to Madison Court House that afternoon. The battalion marched toward Orange at 5:00 P.M. and halted for the night within a half-mile of the courthouse village. The Tenth Virginia of another brigade in the same division also marched at 5:00 P.M. or soon thereafter and covered seven miles to a new bivouac some two miles west of Orange. Some of the marching was by moonlight, and one of the Tenth Virginia lads thought the night was a "lovely" one, with "the boys . . . all in high spirits."[41]

Ewell's division moved up near Liberty Mills, and at least part of it crossed the river into Madison County on the evening of August 7. So close to the enemy, Ewell's men were not permitted cooking fires. William A. McClendon of the Fifteenth Alabama was disgruntled by the stricture because it was his eighteenth birthday and it seemed hard to go without cooking on so festive an occasion; but he acknowledged the need "to conceal our advance."[42]

Few of the marching Southerners were inclined to grumble about the absence of fires because the weather was furnace-hot. At 2:00 P.M. on August 7 the temperature at a weather station a few miles northward was 92°. For the preceding six days, the lowest temperature at 2:00 P.M. had been 88°. The sort of heat that feeds on itself day in and day out in the Virginia summer always is hard to stand; in active campaigning it must have been virtually unbearable. At 8:00 P.M. on August 7 the thermometer still hovered at 83°, even though darkness had settled firmly across the landscape. Fortunately, the sweating soldiers could not know that even worse weather lurked just ahead.[43]

That environmental factors affect military affairs, sometimes decisively, is hardly a new idea. The struggle at Cedar Mountain would be shaped by terrain and ground cover and other features, but none

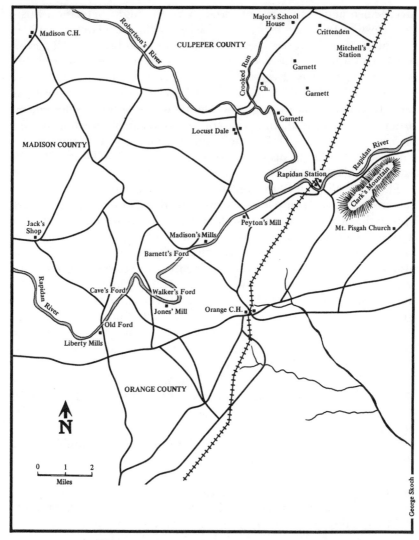

The Theater of Operations, August 7–12, 1862

of these exceeded in importance the brutal constant verity of the broiling sun. On August 7 the march began well past the height of the day and lasted a relatively short time. Even so, Lieutenant John D. Summers of the Fifty-second Virginia Infantry noted in his diary: "The weather so hot men faint and die on the march." Jed Hotchkiss

18

told his wife in a letter that the march on August 7 consisted of "poking along."[44]

Federals were moving on August 7 also, and the same relentless sun was making them miserable. In Nathaniel Banks's column there rode a clever and capable general from Massachusetts, George H. Gordon, whose trenchant published comments generally are worth noting. His men marched this day through the central Virginia oven amid choking dust. When they camped near Washington, Virginia, "the atmosphere . . . was like that of a pest-house, from the number of dead animals lying about." As many as eight or ten men died each day in some regiments, and the dead march that accompanied their burials made each evening solemn. "If we were not conforming to Pope's order to live on the country," Gordon reported with chagrin, "we were doing the next thing to it,—we were dying on it."[45]

One of the key actors at Cedar Mountain was thirty-two-year-old General Charles Sidney Winder (rhymes with finder), a native of Maryland and graduate of West Point with successful battle experience against Indians in the Northwest. The general had been sick for several days and still was "in an enfeebled condition." The men of his brigade generally were content to see Winder sick because his strict discipline had enraged them. John O. Casler of the Thirty-third Virginia, whose irreverent memoir won him immortality of sorts, went so far as to suggest that Winder was "spotted" by some of the men for being "very severe, and very tyrannical" and would not survive friendly action in the next battle even if the Federals missed him.[46]

The movement orders on August 7 reached Winder and his brigade (Jackson's famous old Stonewall Brigade) at a camp about three miles south of Liberty Mills around the O. H. P. Terrell house. The order, of course, supplied no hint of the purpose of the move. Winder was under orders from his brigade medical director to stay out of action, but he planned to ignore the doctor if battle loomed imminent. To get some idea of the prospects, Winder ordered McHenry Howard of his staff to go ask Jackson "if there would be a battle and, if so, when, and where the army was moving to, so that he might be up in time." The idea made Howard understandably uneasy: Jackson was anything but communicative about such matters. Winder insisted. Howard went, "with a good deal of unwillingness." The uneasy staff officer found Jackson at the home of Dr. John T. Jones and reported on Winder's uncertain health. Jackson expressed his concern. Then, in a rush, Howard blurted out his mission. After a pause and "with one of his diffident smiles," Jackson suggested that a battle might be expected in two days at a point somewhere across the Rapidan. Howard left marveling at his good fortune, and Winder accepted the news with relief. The Marylander remained at rest that night and started forward the next morning, although the Stonewall Brigade moved with the rest of the division on the seventh.[47]

Stonewall Jackson did not rest as well as Charles Winder. The army commander "slept part of the night on a stile in the street of Orange C.H." Sometime during the night Jackson and some of his staff went to the home of a Mr. Willis.[48] Perhaps it was the same Willis place where the patriotic girl had encouraged Grumble Jones's cavalrymen five days earlier.

CHAPTER 2

Jackson and Hill Clash

BOTH ARMIES MOVED toward Culpeper Court House on Friday, August 8. Jackson's columns moved north into Culpeper County (at least they were supposed to), and Pope's advance elements under Banks moved south on a converging course. Franz Sigel, a native German of decidedly limited military talents, added to the legend that hovered around his eccentric head during the Federal march on August 8. General Sigel was at Sperryville and had orders to march to Culpeper. There was (and is) only one practicable way to cover that ground, but Sigel equivocated at length and finally at 6:50 P.M. sent to Pope for instructions about which road to use. With some restraint, Pope tore up an angry rejoinder and eventually referred in his report to Sigel's "singular uncertainty as to what road he ought to pursue." One of Sigel's colleagues made the point more piquantly when he suggested that Sigel "remained like the ass between two bundles of hay, in a state of perfect rest." Pope ordered his inept subordinate to march hard all night in an attempt to make up for the lost day. There was some sentiment in Pope's staff that not even Sigel could be *that* stupid, and therefore he must have been consciously malingering.[1]

The rest of Pope's units moved in more conventional order on Friday. Banks's corps started near the Rappahannock River in the morning and encamped near Hazel River by night. James B. Ricketts's division marched through Culpeper and out on the road to Madison Court House to resist any Confederate threat from that quarter; Federal cavalry reported the possibility of such danger. As the Thirteenth Massachusetts marched through Culpeper it had its flags unfurled and its bands playing. Although the Northerners were hardly surprised by the palpable hostility of the populace, it still jarred them. Many of the women shed bitter tears, Austin C. Stearns of Company K noticed, and "none were glad to see us if we except the colored." One woman knelt by an open window with her arms outstretched and her eyes turned heavenward. The expression on her face convinced Stearns that she was calling on God to rain fearful punishment on the invaders. The New England soldier kept his eyes riveted on the kneeling women, held by a dreadful fascination, and "a chill of horror" rippled through him. A foreign observer in town at the same time spoke of the women as "unusually outspoken and mischievous."[2]

The militant Southern woman at her Culpeper window was emblematic of a change in the nature of the war in Virginia. Virginians had not been fond of Yankees for some time, and Northerners reciprocated with bitter feelings toward Rebels. The ugly business of internecine war, however, had been conducted within relatively "civilized" and accepted channels. The American Civil War, first and last, escaped much of the worst of the excesses that usually mark civil and religious conflicts. But the savagery of some men dragged down the standards. John Pope was not the worst of these by any means, but he was the first to find authority in the Virginia theater. (Fortunately for the soldiers on both sides—but unfortunately for the postwar South—the worst of such creatures lurked in Congress and the executive departments in Washington.)

The battle of Cedar Mountain was fought in the midst of this first major hubbub about war on civilians. Some idea of the problem is a necessary prerequisite for understanding the feelings of the men shouldering muskets on either side. General Marsena R. Patrick was admirably situated to comment on the effect on Northern troops of Pope's new way of warfare. Patrick was a professional soldier in his early fifties, West Point–educated, and accustomed to dealing with discipline. Most of Patrick's Civil War service was as provost marshal of the Army of the Potomac; he was, in essence, the head Federal military policeman in the East. Despite that stern task he was a mild man, so gentle that vindictive Northern leaders cashiered him soon after the war for treating vanquished Southerners too gently. Pope's orders mightily upset Patrick's sense of discipline. The "general license to pillage, rob & plunder" had "completely demoralized" the command. "I am afraid of God's Justice," Patrick wrote in his diary, "for our Rulers & Commanders deserve his wrath & curse. . . . I have never seen anything like it."[3]

The catalog of horrors actually was mild enough by the standards established two years later in the Shenandoah Valley and elsewhere. No civilians were killed; no private houses were burned, even by accident; and the incidents almost exclusively involved movable property. To a modern world inured to Dresden and strategic bombing of population centers, war on citizenry that was limited to thievery and insulting language seems almost commendable. In the summer of 1862, though, Southerners reacted with outrage.

John S. Pendleton, a prominent sixty-year-old Whig who had served as a diplomat in South America before the war, reported that "drunken ruffians . . . could not understand the prayers and entreaties of helpless women" who pleaded for their property. Pendleton and others were particularly incensed by the thorough destruction of Calvary Church just below Cedar Mountain, which had been built by Philip Slaughter at his own expense. The Slaughter house also was vandalized. A Louisiana chaplain came across a farm south of Slaughter's that had lost not only all of its corn, wheat, pork, and cattle but also the fences necessary to grow and protect new farm products. The fences were destroyed maliciously, it seemed, and the looters had threatened to shoot the protesting farmer.[4]

Women who faced the crisis with fortitude came to be legendary in the county, their demeanor no doubt burnished by passing years and repeated retellings. Edmonia Major, whose house became one of the most prominent landmarks on the battlefield, preserved one box of valuables by sitting on it boldly and at length, defying the physical abuse which in the summer of 1862 would not be offered. General A. P. Hill's sister-in-law (Mrs. Edward Hill) hid her silver behind a tall mirror and moved some of it under the traditional cover of a hoop skirt. Mrs. William Mason Yowell saved the contents of her meat-house by good fortune: she threw all of its contents out in the garden, perhaps to deflect interest from the house, and invited the Federals to help themselves. This unusual behavior left the foragers worried whether the proffered meat was poisoned, and they avoided it. The two grown daughters of Latin teacher Albert Simms had no bravado to report. The men who went through Simms's home were "so threatening and licentious in their behavior" that the girls fled into a cornfield and spent the night listening to shouted threats "which told of outrages."[5]

Not all Federal officers thought that the license to loot had a negative effect on morale in their ranks. Several accounts speak of high spirits in Northern units, and Banks insisted that his troops "panted for a fight." Walt Whitman's brother arrived soon after the battle and noted with ill-concealed glee that "the way the cattle and sheep have suffered . . . is a caution to secesh farmers," whose only recourse was

23

"some tall cussing." Another Northerner who visited still later guyed an unsuspecting civilian about his travails: "'Did they really burn fences?' said we with feigned surprise."[6]

David Hunter Strother was a renegade Virginian who later served on the staff of General David Hunter when Hunter was savagely burning the Shenandoah Valley. In Culpeper County in August 1862, though, Strother was so aghast at the destruction of fine old classical libraries and antique furniture that he managed to convince himself that the damage had been done by Confederate soldiers. When General John P. Hatch brought his brigade of McDowell's corps into the vicinity in August, he "was violently opposed to General Pope's system," disapproved of "such vandalism," and personally routed some silverware thieves with his sword. Other Federals noted the defiant spirit of civilians. The men of the Fifth Connecticut heard boasts: "Old Jack will give you all you want," and "You will come back tomorrow on the double-quick if you come at all."[7]

The response of Confederate soldiers in some instances went beyond outraged reaction to overt action. General Isaac Ridgeway Trimble carried the story of "a case of horrid conduct of the enemy" directly to Stonewall Jackson, though of course the army commander could make no productive response in the short term. Captain William Johnson Pegram, just twenty-one years old but well into a career that would make him justly famous among Southern artillerists, told his sister in a letter dated August 8 that Confederate cavalry had cornered several Federals burning down some mills. The horsemen killed a few of the arsonists in a quick fight and captured others. "I understand that two of them were very obstreperous," Willie Pegram wrote, "& our men hung one, & killed the other." During a later Federal incursion into Culpeper County, a local civilian named James W. Timberlake managed to brain a Northern soldier with a fire shovel, and then hide the body, when the looter pawed through the clothes of Timberlake's recently dead wife.[8] The war inexorably was turning up a dark and hideous face.

The not-so-subtle change in the treatment of civilians undoubtedly made Confederates in the vicinity angry and ready to close with their foe. Before August 8 was half gone, though, most of the Southerners with Jackson were wondering if they could close with anyone. G. F. R. Henderson, the English professional soldier who wrote a classic biography of Jackson, summarized that general's achievements on this day succinctly: "Jackson's soldiers never did a worse day's work during the whole course of his campaigns." Another careful authority on the campaign, perhaps with conscious understatement, described the day's progress as "remarkably slow."[9]

It was hot and there was confusion and the roads were few and narrow—but Jackson had become famous for celerity under like circumstances. No one whispered paeans about "Foot Cavalry" on August 8, and the reason was not hard to find: somber, secretive Jackson and proud, high-strung A. P. Hill went to war with each other and tied the army in knots in the process.

The turmoil had its roots in confusion of orders. Hill gave no hint of wishing to disobey; he simply did not understand. It is hard to postulate a set of circumstances under which Jackson was not responsible for seeing to it that his orders were understood. (One is reminded of Union General John Sedgwick's unique system of having his orders read to a "dunce" retained as "an important member of his staff" to read orders and certify their clarity. Hill was no dunce.)[10]

Sometime on the night of August 7 Jackson issued a set of simple written marching orders. Ewell was to lead with his division; Hill would follow; Jackson's old division, putatively under the ailing Winder, would close up the column. The march would move northward, crossing into Madison County at Barnett's Ford due north of Orange, then on into Culpeper County. The starting hour was to be Jackson's favorite: "at dawn." Hill was ready at dawn, he reported, "with the head of my leading brigade resting near the street down which I understood Ewell was to pass, and ready to take my place in the column of march." Unfortunately for all concerned, Ewell was several miles away and Jackson had changed the orders, but A. P. Hill had not been told.[11]

The change in orders was all but unavoidable. A glance at the map, which Jackson must have taken, showed Ewell due west of Orange at Liberty Mills. The course of the Rapidan River from southwest to northeast put that stream nearly north of Orange at Barnett's Ford. There was little point in moving Ewell east to Orange, then north to Barnett's Ford, around the legs of a triangle, when he could slide northeastward along the far (left) bank of the Rapidan and reach the same vicinity with much less marching. Ewell had crossed the river with some, perhaps most, of his force on the evening of August 7. It is possible (even likely) that Jackson had ordered that crossing with an eye to changing Ewell's route to the more logical configuration. In that case, the new orders probably had been framed by the time Hill received the old ones, and the failure to update those stale orders becomes even more inexplicable.[12]

Reducing the distance of Ewell's route was not the only good reason for sending him down the left bank of the river. The roads in this relatively sparsely settled region were not designed for the rapid movement of twenty thousand men. Spreading the axis of the movement made a great deal of sense, as the chaos engendered by the eventual junction onto one road soon would demonstrate vividly. Furthermore, Federal cavalry west of the Confederate line of march caused some uneasiness. Extending a portion of the infantry route westward served to screen that threat.

Jackson's state of mind on the early morning of August 8, 1862, is of course subject only to conjecture, not to substantial proof. It is not unreasonable to suppose that he was at least subconsciously determined to perform with that unquenchable energy that had characterized his early achievements but had been conspicuously absent during the recent Seven Days' operations around Richmond. Jackson also must have been anxious to learn about the marching performance of Hill's division, which was the largest of the three and was entirely new to Jackson's command.

When he reached the main street of Orange, aquiver with stern eagerness, Jackson was disappointed. Hill was not moving. He was "resting near the street down which . . . Ewell was to pass," awaiting his turn. Even Jackson's staff believed Ewell was passing. Jackson did not urge Hill to get moving. He simply ordered Frank Paxton of his staff to get the last division in line, Jackson's old division, on the road, bypassing the waiting Hill. The head of that division "had reached the town" and also was waiting its turn in the motionless comedy of errors. Jackson's division got in motion "about an hour after sunrise," by Paxton's recollection.[13]

Frank Paxton also intimated that Hill was not waiting in confusion but rather simply "had not moved." Paxton's perspective on the quarrel can be easily summarized by a glance at his background. He was a neighbor of Jackson's and a fellow communicant at Jackson's beloved Lexington church. When his subordinates threw Paxton out of office as major of the Twenty-seventh Virginia at the spring 1862 elections, Jackson took him onto the headquarters staff and eventually promoted him to the rank of brigadier general, three grades above the rank denied him by the Twenty-seventh. The promotion catapulted the former major over the heads of the Stonewall Brigade's fifteen

Confederate Major General Ambrose Powell Hill's clash with
his new commander on August 8 was only the first of many.

field officers, each of whom outranked Paxton. None was pleased by
the development. Hill himself commented on the promotion in a
letter to Jeb Stuart with obvious disgust: *"Paxton, Brig Gen!"*[14]

Jackson's endorsement on Hill's official account of the morning is
very specific about his subordinate's shortcomings. Historians, notable among them Douglas Southall Freeman, have attempted to rec-
oncile the varying accounts, but many of the details and some of the
main points are irreconcilable. Some, but not all, of the anomalies
may be attributed to the passage of seven months between the events
and their recounting (Hill's report is dated March 8, 1863, and Jackson's endorsement came eleven days later).

Paxton intimated that Hill had not moved at all, and Jackson went one step further and declared that when he rode into Orange and found Hill, he "did not see any of his troops with him." Jackson had spent the night three-quarters of a mile from the center of the village. The troops were to march at dawn (not Jackson's usually emphatic "*early*" dawn in this instance), which preceded sunrise by half an hour or so. The sun rose at 5:15 A.M. But it was after sunrise when Jackson noticed from his headquarters that troops he knew to be Hill's still remained in their bivouacs. When he reached Hill and could not see any troops with that unfortunate officer, the stage was set for the next act in the farce. During his brief and entirely unsatisfactory encounter with Hill, Jackson "understood him to say that he was waiting for Jackson's [not Ewell's] division to pass."[15] Hill never mentioned the meeting with Jackson.

It is hardly surprising that Hill viewed developments differently. He was on time, Hill declared, and his troops were with him—at least "the head of [the] leading brigade" was by his side. When troops began to file past him, Hill was content to watch them. The time? "A *little* after sunrise" (emphasis added). The troops must be Ewell's, Hill assumed, with no inkling that Ewell was a half-dozen miles away and steadily moving farther. After "one or two" brigades had passed, Hill somehow recognized the troops as belonging to Jackson's division. He then learned to his astonishment "that Ewell had taken another route." "Of this," Hill wrote with commendable restraint, "no intimation had been given me."[16]

Hill decided not to intrude into the column between the brigades of another division. For at least that decision he cannot be faulted. Control of units was fragile enough in that era of marginal staff work without snapping divisions in half. Hill waited for the division to pass and prepared to fall in in rear of it—but then along came the wagon train in the wake of infantry. The written orders had not mentioned the trains, and Hill had a verbal understanding that Jackson wanted the trains to stay with their respective divisions. Hill spent more unhappy hours waiting while the wagons passed by fits and starts.[17]

Stonewall Jackson's endorsement on Hill's official report made a few telling points, but it also stumbled at times. It is hard to argue with Jackson's suggestion that Hill did not display the initiative expected of a division commander. "He should have expected Ewell to be in front and not in rear of him," Jackson suggested reasonably, although even his aide Paxton had been confused on that point. "If he believed that the division for which he was waiting to pass was Ewell's, he could easily have sent some one and ascertained the fact."

The army commander suggested that "the better part of two hours" had elapsed since Hill's ordered time of departure before the question came up, "yet it does not appear that he had taken any steps to ascertain, but appears to have taken it for granted that the division which should have been in advance of him was in rear."[18] A. P. Hill clearly was wanting in initiative and energy that morning.

Jackson surely would have denied his failure to keep Hill abreast of the revised march order if he could have done so. He did not. Instead, Jackson offered some entirely unconvincing explanations about the relationship of Hill's march to Ewell's: "Ewell moved early in the morning, and though he did not cross at Barnett's Ford, yet he passed near that point in coming into the road." In other words, Ewell was indeed out front and he did come into Hill's route, albeit several miles away and in another county. Jackson also dumped the blame for the wagon-train jam on Hill's heavily laden shoulders. Had Hill moved on time, Jackson complained, "I could, had I deemed it necessary, have halted Ewell's train before it reached the road upon which General Hill was to move." That would have put the two leading infantry divisions and three-fourths of Jackson's infantry at the front of the advance, a good idea for a march headed on a combat— not a commissary—venture. Hill was an impossibly bad candidate, however, for indictment on a charge of responsibility for the configuration of Ewell's wagon train.[19]

The bitterness between Hill and Jackson inaugurated on this morning was nurtured by each man through the following months. Jackson found further occasions to grumble about Hill's marching, and Hill joined the legion of subordinates who found Jackson impossible to satisfy. In a letter to Jeb Stuart, written three months after Cedar Mountain, Hill expressed his feelings about Jackson with amazing vigor: "I suppose I am to vegetate here all the winter under that crazy old Presbyterian fool—I am like the porcupine all bristles, and all sticking out too, so I know we shall have a smash up before long. . . . The Almighty will get tired of helping Jackson after a while, and then he'll get the d——ndest thrashing—and the shoe pinches, for I shall get my share and probably all of the blame, for the people will never blame Stonewall for any disaster."[20]

Much of Jackson's difficulty with subordinates stemmed from his almost fetishistic secrecy. Hill himself had expressed the case nicely a couple of days earlier when an inquisitive Virginia cavalry officer asked where the marching column was headed. Hill "replied that he supposed we would go to the top of the hill in front of us, but that was all he knew." For his part, Jackson remained wrapped securely in his reticence and evidently entertained no qualms about assigning all of the blame to Hill. Early the next morning Jackson sent R. E. Lee a dispatch in which he bluntly criticized Hill's performance and concluded that "Hill's division is too large." Jackson proposed to reduce his problem with Hill by removing "at least" one brigade from Hill's control.[21]

The passage of a century and a quarter and the marshaling of all available evidence do not between them provide enough perspective to resolve the conflicting evidence about the events of the morning of August 8. Was Hill ready to march at dawn? at sunrise? an hour after sunrise? Was he alone in town, or was the head of his infantry column at hand? Did he tell Jackson he was waiting for the last division to pass, or was he actually expecting it to be Ewell's? Definitive answers cannot be found in the testimony of the two principals because their testimony is diametrically opposed, and little other evidence survives.

The one explanation that softens some of the divergence, without touching the rest of the problem, is that perhaps some of Jackson's/ Winder's division passed an innocent (if sadly indolent) Hill before Jackson and Paxton rode up. When those two found and ordered forward a brigade of that division after abandoning Hill, it was not the front of the division, as they assumed, but the front of a brigade farther down the division column. If it really was the front of the division, Hill lied bluntly. If it was not the front of the division, Jackson and Paxton were honestly mistaken. On the other matters, either someone lied or one party or the other or both suffered major memory lapses. The fragility of human memory is something to which any thoughtful historian can attest.

Which general has a better case to present before history's tribunal? Stonewall Jackson does. Hill deserves sympathy for his predicament, and unquestionably he was mistreated in any number of ways. Jackson was not much fun on the best of days. He was routinely dour, not infrequently sour, and always inflexible to a foolish degree. Jackson was narrow-minded and of painfully limited vision in many regards. He also was a military genius. The obverse sides of his limitations were virtues: secrecy carried to fantastic extremes did yield surprise; inflexibility yielded a determination that overrode the uncertainty of others; and blatantly unfair treatment of subordinates yielded unquestioning obedience, which gave Jackson the chance to play grim games with less well-ordered enemies.

While Jackson and Hill played out their peculiar contretemps in the streets of Orange, Ewell was well to the front and moving steadily. Ahead of Ewell and off his left flank to the west the Southern cavalry was leading the way. Beverly Robertson's mounted men pressed north on the road from Barnett's Ford toward Culpeper Court House. Their route led past Cedar Mountain. The troopers "routed quite a body" of Federal cavalry at Locust Dale, just south of Robinson's River and the Culpeper County line. A newspaper correspondent using the nom de plume "Massanutten" reported with glee that Pope's braggadocio did not keep the Federals from falling back: the Yankees " 'skedaddled' in the most approved fashion, illustrating beautifully Gen. Pope's complacent and grandiloquent remark that there must be no more falling back."[22]

The Federal cavalry was not intended to stand in the face of an advance of such strength, of course, and in fact was active and skillfully handled by the capable John Buford. The cavalry threat haunted Jackson through the marches of August 8 and 9. This worry led him to divide his inadequate cavalry force later on the eighth and to detail a sizable infantry complement as wagon guards during the battle on the ninth. Some of the slowness of the Confederate march on August 8 must also be credited to the specter of Buford's blue-clad horsemen. When Robertson's cavalry did close with the enemy, at Locust Dale and then farther north, they had considerable success. "Massanutten" claimed that eight Federals were killed, "mostly . . . by sabres, and several Yankees' heads were cleft wide open," and that three officers and a dozen men were captured. Jackson's more modest official claim was of three officers and five men taken prisoner. Hotchkiss reckoned the prisoner haul as "a good many . . . most of them from New Jersey."[23]

When Robertson's cavalry moved across Robinson's River into Culpeper County they quickly captured an enemy camp south of Crooked Run Church and then drove "quite a large body of Federal cavalry" beyond the church after what Jackson described as "a short stand." Jackson, always avid for supplies, reported with pleasure the capture of "quartermaster's, commissary, and ordnance" stores in the overrun camp. Southern troopers who followed Buford's fleeing men sent back word that enemy infantry was in evidence about five miles farther up the road. Some of the retreating Northern cavalry fell back westward toward Madison Court House instead of northward toward Culpeper. Colonel Thomas S. Flournoy of the Sixth Virginia Cavalry led a pursuit for five miles in that direction, accompanied by

Major William Patrick of the Seventeenth Virginia Cavalry Battalion. Flournoy had enough success to win mention in Jackson's dispatch to Lee the next morning. The brigade historian claimed the capture of twenty prisoners in a series of vigorous charges.[24]

In the wake of their advance, Confederates encountered relieved and outraged civilians who, wrote "Massanutten," "roused anew our indignation by thrilling details of the insults, cruelties, and injustice to which they had been subjected."[25]

Dick Ewell kept his infantry well closed up to the main cavalry detachment. The division had spent the night on the banks of the Rapidan (evidently straddling the river), "in hearing of the enemys drums." Ewell's chief of staff (soon to become his stepson-in-law), writing under no onus like that attending Hill's report, stated that the division marched "at sunrise." This division was the only one of the three that did any serious marching. For about three hours it moved steadily and rapidly despite weather so "oppressively warm" that "many of our men were broken down and some even sunstruck."[26]

The first leg of Ewell's march led northeastward, parallel to and on the left bank of the Rapidan. Jed Hotchkiss of Jackson's staff, who generally was a very solid witness, noted that some of Ewell's men came down the right (east) bank. At Liberty Mills, Ewell "bore to his right and formed a guard to the left flank of the main body; a part of his command came in at Barnett's Ford, marching down the east side of the river." Most of the division surely crossed the river at Liberty Mills and came back into the army's main route just north of Barnett's Ford. From that point Ewell moved north through the angle between the two rivers, past the scene of the cavalry skirmish at Locust Dale, and into Culpeper County. One of Early's men wrote that they marched "careless of roads, over wheat-fields, corn-fields, skirts of woods, &c." "Massanutten" timed the end of the march near Crooked Run Church at noon and declared it to be a necessity because of the wilted condition of the troops. G. Campbell Brown of Ewell's staff probably was more accurate in reporting the halt at 2:00 P.M. The infantry went into camp and began cooking rations.[27]

One Virginia cavalryman located the head of the advance "between Robinson River and Crooked Run" and reported that a hostile line was within visual range. There can be no question, however, that Confederate cavalry went well beyond the run and that the forward-most infantry reached north of the run to the neighborhood of the church.[28]

Most of Jackson's division, about to become Winder's when he was present, marched under arms at the early hour to which Jackson had accustomed them. The Tenth Virginia Infantry of William B. Taliaferro's brigade moved "at early dawn," according to its commander. Taliaferro's brigade probably came second in line in the division, while the brigade of Colonel Thomas S. Garnett (no relation to poor Dick Garnett) led the division and the Stonewall Brigade brought up the rear. That order of march is not absolutely demonstrable, but it is worthy of the label of solid conjecture.[29]

The First Virginia Battalion (Irish Battalion) of Garnett's brigade marched from a camp one-half mile south of Orange Court House. It moved through the village, crossed the Rapidan, and "encamped about a mile from the river." Wagons reached the camp—at the expense of A. P. Hill's right-of-way—that evening and the men received two days' rations and orders to cook them. The Twenty-first Virginia of the same brigade was up and marching "early" as well. When John Worsham of that regiment reached Barnett's Ford he noticed a "Quaker cannon" which the advancing Confederates had used as a stage prop. The Confederates, Worsham claimed, ran out this "hind part of a wagon with a black log on it" on a commanding knoll and frightened some Yankees with it. When he crossed the river with the Twenty-first, Worsham came across a friendly cavalryman whose "ear was nearly severed from his head" by a sword stroke. It was the first saber wound Worsham had ever seen.[30]

Taliaferro's brigade apparently followed Garnett's, or at least part of it did. The Thirty-seventh Virginia led the brigade, followed by the Tenth Virginia and then the Twenty-third. Two fresh and very green Alabama infantry regiments, the Forty-seventh and Forty-eighth, seem to have remained in camp most of the day. According to a letter written by Private James Preston Crowder of the Forty-seventh five days later, the Alabamians left their camps only about an hour before sundown "and marched about six miles and stop and staid there all night." Six miles was a better than average march on this sluggish day, but a start near dark by even a small part of Jackson's division further complicates any attempt to understand the August 8 march and the Hill-Jackson imbroglio.[31]

That portion of Taliaferro's brigade that did follow Garnett promptly found the going sticky. Not long after the three regiments moved through Orange the snarled route ahead forced a halt "for a few hours." Private Joseph F. Kauffman of the Tenth Virginia closely observed two Federal prisoners passing by rearward and somehow was able to ascertain that "one of them was a Cracker." It was after noon when the Tenth moved forward, waded the Rapidan at Barnett's Ford, and advanced one mile beyond the river to "a skirt of wood." There the column halted, and Kauffman wrote in his diary while awaiting distribution of rations. The Tenth received the same two days' allotment that Garnett's men did and the same orders to cook them while staying alert for marching orders. The cooking lasted until dark, and the regiment bivouacked where it had cooked.[32]

The Stonewall Brigade at the end of the division's column (presumably excluding the untried Alabama regiments) also managed to get across the Rapidan on August 8 and also camped about one mile beyond. A private in the ranks claimed that "several men dropped dead in ranks from sunstroke." "Several" is an elastic word, but the broiling private may have been accurate. Active Federal cavalry and inadequate Confederate cavalry were among the primary military determinants of the rate of march (together, of course, with Jackson's and Hill's problems); but the weather loomed larger than enemy action for the foot soldiers suffering under it. At 7:00 A.M., two hours after Jackson's marching deadline, the thermometer reached 80°. At 2:00 P.M. it hovered at 96°. At 8:00 P.M. the sun had set, but the temperature still stood at 86°.[33]

A veteran of the Sixth Virginia Cavalry who lived in Culpeper County wrote that "the intense heat and dust of the day, the confusion in which the columns of Winder's and Hill's divisions had fallen . . . and the intermingling of their trains, blocked the road." The sequence he used probably was intentional. Among the sufferers was Jedediah Hotchkiss of Jackson's staff. Hotchkiss was eager for food from home, understandably enough, and his letters in August talked at length of his hunger. Some light bread arrived, and Jackson, "who is very fond of light bread," got a loaf. Raw onions in the box "quench thirst . . . admirably" on the march. Most of the precious provisions in his early August shipment, however, were ruined by the heat. The same heat that boiled the men melted some butter in the box, which in its liquid form penetrated everywhere and then putrefied to spoil much of the contents. Hotchkiss emphasized in a postwar account that the "animals . . . suffered fearfully" as well, giving cause for both pity and military concern.[34]

Stonewall Jackson was riding through the blistering heat at the head of his old division as it closed on Ewell's rear. A Louisiana chaplain of Ewell's division, James B. Sheeran, came across the general there, "riding alone." The cleric had never seen the South's living legend before and—like many another observer—he was amazed at Jackson's unimposing image. "Such was his plain attire," Chaplain Sheeran recalled, "that, had I not been informed, I never would have taken him for a commissioned officer."[35]

George H. Moffett of the Eleventh Virginia Cavalry also came across General Jackson on the march. Moffett had helped teach the black Sunday school class in Lexington that Jackson had founded before the war. On August 8 the cavalryman skirted the edge of an infantry column moving north from Orange and when he reached its head he found Jackson, "his cap drawn down over his forehead, riding alone and apparently buried in deep meditation." Even in the egalitarian ranks of Sunday School graduates, private soldiers did not hail Stonewall Jackson with ease, so Moffett "rode by with a silent salute." Jackson recognized his fellow religionist and called him back to ride by his side and talk about the class. "It was a great gratification to him," Jackson told Moffett, "that the school was being kept up in his absence."[36]

Another alumnus of Jackson's Lexington class contributed a classic bit of lore to the general's legend in connection with this march. Jim Lewis, who had been a servant of Jackson's in Lexington and served the general in camp through the war years, was the bellwether for the move to Cedar Mountain. According to a chaplain with the army, he began to pack for the march before anyone knew anything was afoot. When some officers asked Lewis what was happening, he reported that Jackson had been praying at an even greater rate than usual: "The General is a great man for praying at all times. But when I see him get up a great many times in the night to pray, then I know there is going to be something to pay."[37]

While Jackson rode at the front of his old division, its highest-ranking current officer endeavored to catch up. General Charles S. Winder and McHenry Howard were obeying Jackson's advice to follow the army to the river and then ask for directions. Riding with the pair was another ailing officer from the division, Lieutenant Colonel Richard H. Cunningham of the Twenty-first Virginia. The three men "rode leisurely" through the "excessively hot" day. Both sick men "suffered from the heat in their weak condition." The shady yard of the Erasmus Taylor house north of Orange gave them some shelter until near sundown, when they continued slowly across Barnett's Ford. The little party found the Stonewall Brigade bivouacked a mile beyond the river in some woods on the left side of the road on the farm of the Magruder family.[38]

A. P. Hill, meanwhile, simmered in the streets of Orange and wondered why the road just would not clear. Surely now that Jackson had his own division in motion and had positioned himself at its head, the day of desuetude could not be blamed on Hill? A member of the Sixteenth North Carolina of W. Dorsey Pender's brigade, Hill's division, summarized August 8 succinctly when he wrote, "marched into town, lay around on the streets all day, camping at night at the foot of the hill beyond town."[39]

General Lawrence O'Bryan Branch, commander of another North Carolina brigade with Hill, clearly saw the problem all around him: a surfeit of wagons. In his journal, Branch emphatically denied the popular notion that Jackson traveled light: "On this trip to Culpeper we were accompanied by 1,200 wagons, but they make a column so long that we can make no use of their contents, and they had just as well be left behind entirely. It is generally supposed that General Jackson travels without baggage, but it is a great mistake. I think he carries too much. The secret of the celerity with which he moves is that he spends very little time in camps."[40]

Hill himself discovered the glut of wagons when he eventually rode forward to find the cause of the delay. Jackson's division stood motionless in the road, waiting for Ewell's troops and trains to clear a horrible traffic jam. Jackson's staff work and logistical sense never showed to worse effect than on this day. Hill "sent word to General Jackson that the trains were delaying the march . . . very much," he later reported. Did the commanding general really want the trains mixed into the column behind each division? No response is on record.[41]

The artillery accompanying the army stood the ordeal with drastically mixed fortitude. Captain William T. Poague of the Rockbridge Artillery, marching with Jackson's division, complained that the men felt rebellious over discipline ordered from on high. They became "greatly incensed" at Poague personally, and one attempted to foment a "personal altercation." The sizzling weather probably did nothing to soothe sensitive youngsters carefully attuned to personal honor. In contrast, Willie Pegram, Hill's brilliant young artillerist, might have been moving in a different hemisphere than the rest of the army. In a letter dated August 8, Willie told his sister how lovely the environment was: "My health & spirits have improved very

much. . . . I enjoy the pure air & fine scenery. . . . I have . . . not one
on the sick list."[42]

Between 4:00 and 5:00 P.M., cheery Willie Pegram and the rest of
Hill's troops halted—or perhaps it would be more apt to say that they
fell out of ranks, because there was little or no forward motion to
halt. Hill had observed that Ewell's wagons still were passing the bottleneck ahead and part of Jackson's division still had not crossed the
Rapidan. Hill received an order at this hour, he said, "to go back to
Orange Court-House and encamp for the night." Since Hill reckoned
that the head of his column had "only made about a mile," he "bivouacked the brigades where they were."[43] A strict constructionist, of
which ilk Jackson surely was the archetype, might have suggested
that bivouacking on the spot rather than returning to Orange in
conformance to the letter of the order constituted disobedience. The
subject never came up for the good reason that Jackson denied having issued the order at all, in any form.

After the earlier events, it is hardly astonishing to learn that Jackson's account of events was starkly at odds with Hill's. Seven months
later, when the official reports came to be written, Jackson asked Hill
for proof of the disputed communication. The order was verbal, Hill
replied, "and my recollection is that it was from Major Paxton—Of
this however I am not sure, only that such directions were recd by
me[.] Of this there is no doubt." Jackson's endorsement on Hill's
report categorically denied Hill's claim: "On the contrary, I sent a
verbal order to him by . . . Colonel Crutchfield, urging him forward,
and also sent a written order to the same effect by a courier." Frank
Paxton denied that he had carried Hill such an order, or for that
matter any order of any description during the entire day.[44]

None of Hill's division reached the Rapidan that night. Branch's
brigade, which probably was second in line behind Edward L. Thomas's, got about two miles beyond Orange. There the North Carolinians waited for rations from the wagons whose numbers and slowness
had so affected the march. Even this far from the front there was
talk about Federal cavalry. Branch bewailed his fate in his journal.
"This is hard service we are on," he wrote. The soldiers encamped in
the Old North State around Kinston and those up near Petersburg
knew nothing of real hardships, Branch was sure, "yet they have far
more of the public sympathy and admiration."[45]

That evening A. P. Hill, who was a native of the region, offered
Jackson the constructive suggestion that he knew of a smaller ford

by which he could slide his division past the bottleneck. Jackson responded by telling Hill in essence to do as he was told and move on the main road, which would be cleared of the trains.[46] Hill gave up and went to bed, putting an end to what must have been one of the most frustrating days of his life.

CHAPTER 3

A Slow March to Battle

STONEWALL JACKSON'S army spent the night of August 8–9, 1862, strewn across the corners of three counties. The general found quarters near Crooked Run Church at the farm of the James Garnett family. Several families of that surname lived in the vicinity, none of them close kin to either of the Garnetts who were officers in the army. Jackson abandoned his usual insistence on spartan accommodations and spent the night on the porch. Hotchkiss noted: "The grass in the yard was very long and nice and nearly everyone of us, except the General, slept on it."[1]

The army badly needed rest after a difficult day, with the prospect of more of the same on the morrow, but most units found little. The exception was the portion of the army far to the rear around and even beyond Orange Court House. R. Preston Chew's battery of Virginia Horse Artillery camped east of the village, and George Neese thought the night was idyllic. The moon, Neese wrote, hovered like a "great refulgent shield in a clear sky and bathes the dewy hills with a flood of silvery light." He also enthused over "silent stars that glow ... soft still air ... soothing and delightful ... zephyrs." At about midnight a brass band struck up, for no good or apparent reason, and played several numbers, ending with "Home, Sweet Home." Neese found the effect first soothing, then irksome, as he thought of the joys of peace while on the verge of what clearly would be more bloodshed.[2]

The detachment at the head of the army in Culpeper County included most of the cavalry together with Ewell's infantry division. The Southern cavalry occupied the Northern cavalry camp that they had captured during the day. The evicted horsemen took the opportunity provided by darkness to circle eagerly back toward the Confederates, but in the words of Jed Hotchkiss, they found that they had "caught a Tartar." Hotchkiss reported that fifteen Federals fell prisoner at one point and more at another.[3]

The advance of the army fared better than its middle layer camped

39

between the rivers in Madison County. There Winder's division (he was back with it now and more or less in command) spent a wearisome night. When McHenry Howard had arrived in company with his invalids, Winder and Cunningham, General Winder "laid down without giving formal notice of his arrival." The question of division command was peculiarly clouded in any case because Brigadier General Alexander R. Lawton outranked Winder by almost a full year of precedence in date of commission. Some of the references to Winder's command probably were informal; others resulted from Lawton's absence on details, probably by Jackson's contrivance. Jackson assured Winder's command of the division on the battlefield the next day by the transparent expedient of assigning Lawton to stay behind and guard the trains. Winder's commission antedated William B. Taliaferro's by three days, or Jackson's stratagem would have been pointless.

Winder and his party were awakened during the night, together with every other Confederate for miles, "by an irregular firing in the rear and close at hand and a number of bullets passed overhead through the trees." When Winder sent Howard to the colonels with orders to form up their regiments, disoriented men were delighted to learn that their general was at hand. "Thank God for that," muttered in a "tone of evident relief," impressed Howard with the confidence in Winder of at least some subordinates.[4] The ruckus quieted quickly and the men sought further rest.

A second alarm roused the Stonewall Brigade before much more time passed. Howard rode to the rear to investigate. In an open field not far from the Rapidan he found excited troops under arms. Yankee cavalry "had suddenly ridden in on a road from the Madison Court House" but promptly fell back westward whence they came under fire. Howard saw no signs of casualties on either side. "It was a very bright moonlight night . . . and the trees and fencing made deep shadows, causing firing to be wild and inaccurate." Coached by Winder, Lawton sent a note off to Jackson with the particulars.[5]

Taliaferro's brigade had marched just ahead of the Stonewall Brigade on the eighth and evidently camped nearby, perhaps across the road. The men cooked rations into the night hours and some had not yet retired when the first firing broke out back in the direction of the river. Two accounts from the brigade suggest that the initial ruckus came before midnight. Private Kauffman of the Tenth Virginia noted in his diary that after the first skirmishing the men had orders "to hold ourselves in readiness at a moments warning" so they sought doubtful repose with accoutrements draped around them. The second and larger uproar flared at about 1:00 A.M. Private Kauffman and Major Joshua Stover of the Tenth and Lieutenant Colonel Simeon T. Walton of the Twenty-third Virginia put the hour at "12 o'clock," "2 o'clock in the night," and "some time after midnight," respectively.[6]

Walton's Twenty-third Virginia had been at the end of the brigade column during the day's march and obviously camped in that same position because it was the only infantry regiment that reached the scene of action in time to do any fighting. The Twenty-third "double-quicked half a mile to meet the enemy," Walton reported. "There was a sharp skirmish for a few minutes and the enemy was routed." The Virginians captured one prisoner and two horses, losing two lieutenants badly wounded in the process. The regiment also lost the chance for sleep, "lying on its arms nearly all night."[7]

The Tenth Virginia followed the Twenty-third toward the sound of the guns, "but the enemy retired before we arrived on the field," which was situated between camp and the river. The regiment wearily "lay there" without sleeping until "early dawn," then marched back to camp. The men spent another sleepless hour in camp before heading north on the road to Culpeper.[8] The night had been a wretched substitute for recuperation from the rigors of August 8 and an even poorer preparation for what lay ahead.

The focus of the Federal cavalry probe, which contained vastly more noisy nuisance than it did substance, was near the north bank of the Rapidan River. As a result, the Stonewall Brigade and Taliaferro's saw the only action; the Twenty-third Virginia was the only infantry that engaged to any notable degree. The other brigade between the rivers, that of Colonel Thomas S. Garnett, lay far enough north to escape direct contact, but not far enough away to avoid the resulting confusion. A member of the First Virginia Battalion of Garnett's brigade timed the irruption at 3:00 A.M. and called it "a heavy musketry fire between our camp and the river." Only the next morning did he learn that Federal cavalry had been repulsed by Taliaferro's men.[9]

John Worsham of the Twenty-first Virginia of the same brigade awakened to the noise of musketry and the "ting" (he called it "sizzling" in another account) of spent rounds falling randomly around him. The men leaped directly from bed into ranks "more quickly than I ever saw it done," Worsham remembered. The threat faded quickly and without any direct contact. Then the laughs began.

"Those old Confederates made the woods ring with shouts," Worsham wrote. "Some of the men were in their shirt sleeves, some having on them nothing but shirts, some with one shoe . . . hardly one with a hat, but every man was in his place."[10]

A. P. Hill's troops over in Orange County were the infantry farthest from the front at Crooked Run Church, but Hill's two leading brigades (Thomas's and Branch's) were just across the Rapidan River from the Federal cavalry incursion. Branch timed the unwanted wake-up call at 1:00 A.M. He immediately put his North Carolinians under arms, and before long the tired men moved forward sluggishly. By Branch's account, their fitful march continued without a formal halt for more than twelve hours.[11]

At the end of Hill's column, near Orange, the South Carolina Brigade of Maxcy Gregg spent the night in relative calm. Gregg was an original secessionist of more martial ardor than many politicians of that stripe. His mother had just died in South Carolina, but he remained in the field with his five excellent regiments. Among Gregg's men that night there was the usual prebattle tension, evinced by "many little private talks around the fires, friends giving instructions to do so and so in case of being killed, to write to such and such a one." Without the least shamefacedness the men passed Bibles around the circle. Sergeant George Chisolm Mackay of Company H of Gregg's First South Carolina was unshakably convinced that he would be killed the next day and calmly made special preparations. In the event, the brigade remained in the rear and neither Mackay nor any other of the South Carolinians was killed (though Mackay died in 1864 at Spotsylvania's Bloody Angle).[12] The story of Mackay's mistimed prescience is a useful antidote for the more frequently remembered premonitions that happened to coincide with fatal bullets.

As Jackson's men stirred from their bivouacs—such of them as had not been up already for six hours—the general welcomed the promise of a fresh day in which to bring his army back to usefulness. Jackson was not, however, in a sanguine frame of mind. "I am not making much progress," he told Lee in a dispatch headed "near Locust Dale" at a very early hour. The plans of Mighty Stonewall as framed at that moment were uncharacteristically passive. "To-day I do not expect much more than to close up and clear the country around the train of the enemy's cavalry. I fear that the expedition will, in consequence of my tardy movements, be productive of but little good. My plan was to have been at Culpeper Court-House this forenoon." Jackson's concluding sentence belied his pessimism about catching the Federals: Confederate cavalry had told him that "the enemy's infantry . . . is about 5 miles in front."[13] Jackson, of course, hoped that the reported infantry would prove to be in small enough numbers to be thrashed in detail.

The Federals consisted of some cavalry under George D. Bayard, an active young New Yorker six years out of West Point, and a brigade of infantry under Samuel W. Crawford. General Crawford was a surgeon from Pennsylvania in his early thirties who had been at Fort Sumter and subsequently put together a solid record leading infantry. Crawford's brigade, which was to be much distinguished during this day, was one of two in Alpheus S. Williams's division of Banks's corps. Jefferson Davis insisted that Confederate brigades be homogenous by state, but obviously the Federals held no such policy: Crawford's brigade consisted of the Twenty-eighth New York, Forty-sixth Pennsylvania, Tenth Maine, and Fifth Connecticut. On August 8 Crawford had gone forward to support Northern cavalry, taking two batteries along to help. The brigade spent the night along Cedar Run at the foot of Cedar Mountain, four miles north of Crooked Run Church. On the ninth, the rest of Banks's corps moved south through Culpeper and closed on Crawford's position.[14] Jackson would find Banks there early in the afternoon.

Some of Pope's admirers told a New York newspaperman that morning that the day would see "the greatest battle of the season, and Gen. Pope . . . is going to ride right over him into Richmond." Pope himself seemed full of confidence, if his pronouncements are taken at face value. An Indiana soldier saw Pope in Culpeper "sitting on the porch, in apparent unconcern, with staff and orderlies lounging around, taking their ease."[15] The general felt uneasy at least about his right flank from the vicinity of Madison Court House, precisely as Jackson was uneasy about threats to his left flank from the same point.

General Banks operated on August 9 in the shadow of Cedar Mountain on the basis of confident orders from Pope. They came verbally by way of a staff officer named Louis Marshall, who was by ironic coincidence a renegade Northern nephew of R. E. Lee. Banks—less credulous than A. P. Hill—had a staff officer take dictation from Marshall on the spot. When Pope denied the substance of the orders later, Banks waved the copy: "General Banks to move to the front immediately, assume command of all forces in the front, deploy his skirmishers if the enemy advances, and attack him immediately as he approaches, and be reenforced from here."[16]

43

Major General Nathaniel P. Banks, USA, enjoyed marked success as a politician before the war.

Sometime during the morning Jackson's grim analysis of the effects of the August 8 march mellowed. His trusted physician and staff member Hunter McGuire asked the general if he expected a battle today. Jackson "smiled," McGuire later said, and responded: "'Banks is in our front and he is generally willing to fight, and,' he added very slowly, as if to himself, 'and he generally gets whipped.'"[17]

The Federals around Cedar Mountain did not muster enough strength to give Jackson cause for anything but optimism, although of course he could not know that with any surety. After judicious analysis, William Allan concluded in 1880 that Jackson brought somewhat fewer than 20,000 men to action at Cedar Mountain by the time the last of Hill's brigades arrived. By the same procedures (if anything, more liberal in deducting stragglers from Union tables of strength), Allan attributed 16,200 to Banks. The latter figure, however, included 7,000 men of Ricketts's division of McDowell's corps, who arrived in time only to stabilize a deteriorated Federal situation.[18] Some of Jackson's numbers were almost as late arriving as was Ricketts. A reasonable estimate of the men available to either side at the moment of decision is 15,000 for Jackson and 9,000 for Banks. Jackson had been winning big stakes for months against reversed odds. With the numbers in his favor, Jackson should have an easy time with Banks.

Some idea of Federal strength and dispositions was precisely what Jackson most wanted as he prepared to move north that morning. He knew whence that intelligence should come: his cavalry arm. Jackson's long-standing discomfort with General Robertson, which had prompted his recent secret call for a personal visit by Jeb Stuart, must have made him skeptical of success; but he prodded Robertson firmly. Hotchkiss reported that during the morning Jackson urged Robertson "to find out where the enemy was, and Gen. Robertson complain[ed] of the number of stragglers." Unfortunately, W. E. "Grumble" Jones departed first thing in the morning to reconnoiter toward Madison Court House, which for the second consecutive day seemed to be a mysterious sort of bogey country. Jones deserved complaints about his personality but few about his diligence in action. Jackson would have been well advised to use Jones for scouting to his front—but that invokes hindsight. As the day developed, Grumble Jones made a twenty-five-mile round-trip toward Madison "without incident or discovery worthy of record," reaching the battle zone on his return only at dark.[19]

Jackson had other concerns than cavalry. The endless lines of wagons that had been the army's incubus on August 8 had been shaken out of the column this morning, but the essential wheeled vehicles—cannon, caissons, ammunition wagons, ambulances—still clotted the crossing of Crooked Run right behind the army's van. Slippery mud on the steep rise above the ford's north edge grew deeper and stickier with each passing man or vehicle. Jackson's able quartermaster, Major John A. Harman, had occasion to live up to his reputation of being able to "swear at a mule team and make it jerk a wagon out of a mudhole as nothing else will."[20]

When Jackson rode back to attempt to unsnarl the mess, he found Harman "in full feather and the air was blue with his oaths." As Jackson drew nigh, Harman (probably impishly and in full awareness of the audience) "rather increased his energy." Jackson asked mildly whether the language was essential to the task. Harman said with some certainty that it was but offered to desist as a demonstration. Jackson looked vindicated when some empty wagons, perhaps ambulances, crossed Crooked Run without benefit of profanity, but Major Harman insisted that the loaded ordnance vehicles in the column would prove his point.[21]

The first big sample did indeed stall on the slippery exit ramp. Its driver strained and jerked and whipped but held his tongue in deference to the august presence he noticed at the top of the bank. Eventually he lumbered through, but a second laden wagon hung up impossibly deep, to the accompaniment of Harman's "triumphant laugh." An observer (a cavalryman sometimes given to enhancing his material) reported Jackson as "crestfallen" when he left the field to Harman. The quartermaster unleashed his "fluent damnation" before Stonewall was fifty yards away and "so startled the mules and their negro driver that the wagon was jerked out of the stream and was alongside the retreating general in half a minute."[22]

Jackson's staff members were ready to move ahead beyond Crooked Run Church for some time before they did. The delay may have been the result of the encounter at the ford in which John Harman demonstrated the efficacy of profanity. At least some of the column halted for breakfast. Jed Hotchkiss had time to set up for some letter writing at the church before headquarters started forward in earnest.[23]

When headquarters moved, it covered about two miles to the home of a thirty-four-year-old widow, Cornelia Petty. After a brief halt there while cavalry scouted ahead, Jackson and his staff went one-

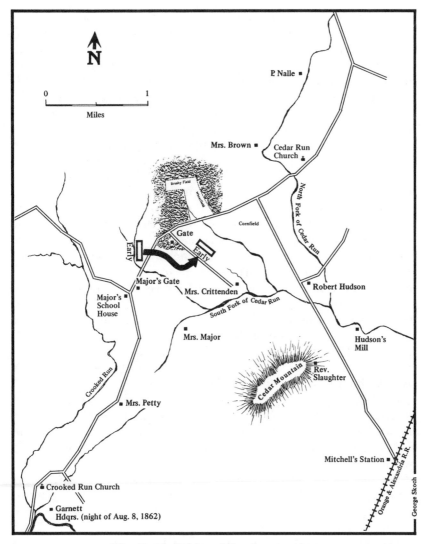

N

0 ———————— 1
Miles

P. Nalle ■

Mrs. Brown ■   Cedar Run
Church ♣

Brushy Field

North Fork of Cedar Run

Cornfield

Gate

Early   Early

Major's Gate

Mrs. Crittenden

Major's ■
School
House

■ Robert Hudson

South Fork of Cedar Run

Mrs. Major

Hudson's
Mill

Cedar Mountain   Rev.
Slaughter

Crooked Run

■ Mrs. Petty

Mitchell's Station ■

Orange & Alexandria R.R.

George Skoch

♣ Crooked Run Church

■ Garnett
Hdqrs. (night of Aug. 8, 1862)

The Battlefield and Its Approaches

half mile beyond "to a high point . . . from whence could be seen a considerable body of the enemy's cavalry." The hostile cavalry seemed to be located near the gate of the Crittenden Lane, which led off the main Orange-Culpeper Road to the Crittenden House almost a mile away. (The Crittenden Gate became the focus of enough attention to be a battlefield landmark deserving capitalization.) To the right of

47

the cavalry from Jackson's vantage point, there was evidence of infantry and artillery "in the edge of the woods." Dust clouds billowing behind the Federals gave indication of more enemy regiments on the way. Although Jackson soon went forward with his troops, and stayed forward, his formal headquarters apparently remained on the hill just north of the Petty house for hours. The general's faithful aide James Keith Boswell remained there until nearly 3:00 P.M., coordinating orders and watching the enemy.[24]

Confederate infantry pounding up the road behind the cavalry raised its own dust clouds and then choked on them. Ewell's division still led the way, but its commander knew no more of the large picture than did poor A. P. Hill. Ewell grumbled to one of his division's chaplains about being in the dark and swore: "I do not know whether we will march north, south, east or west, or whether we will march at all." That the division would march somewhere soon became evident, and apparently the direction would be northward, at least for a time. Ewell and his men soon learned, by means of inquiries they made of Federal prisoners who began to trickle rearward from the early morning skirmishing, that Banks would be their foe once more. The ragged Southerners shrieked with glee and capered about at the prospect of a reprise of their happy dealings with "Commissary Banks" in the Valley that spring: "Get your requisitions ready, boys! Put down everything you want! Old Stonewall's Quartermaster has come with a full supply for issue!"[25]

Ewell had opportunity to wonder about the day's schedule, and grouse about it a bit, because the August 9 march did not begin for the leading division anywhere near "early dawn." Jackson's favorite marching time was three hours past when Early's brigade got under way at 8:00 A.M. The weather was already all but unbearable at a time of day that should have retained a little freshness even in August. At 7:00 A.M. the temperature not too many miles away, in Georgetown, D.C., was 84° By 2:00 P.M. the mercury had reached 98°. There were no measurable breezes.[26]

The heat spread its discomfort impartially, of course, on blue and gray troops alike. H. A. Tripp of the Tenth Maine was among the men of Crawford's brigade awaiting Ewell and Jackson on the ridge beyond Cedar Run. "The heat begins to oppress us lying still" long before noon, Tripp wrote, and wondered, "What must it be on the march?" One of his comrades in the Twenty-seventh Indiana of Gordon's brigade answered the question. The air was "as hot as a bake oven," wrote Edmund Randolph Brown of that unit, who was celebrating his seventeenth birthday inauspiciously. "Our bodies seemed to be a furnace of fire." Brown passed "many" men "lying on the ground frothing at the mouth, rolling their eyeballs and writhing in painful contortions." When the Indiana regiment crossed Cedar Run (it was "not over a rod wide"), the chance to drink and splash water on parched skin seemed like an answer to prayer. One of the men killed by the heat was a brand-new recruit in the Second Massachusetts named Carey. The regiment stopped and buried the boy, then moved on. Carey's brief career and hot death left so small a ripple in the regiment's ordeal that the chaplain could not remember the dead boy's name when he wrote the unit history just after the war.[27]

Jubal A. Early's brigade led the column of Confederates moving north toward Cedar Run on a converging course with Crawford's and Gordon's Northerners. Ewell's initial order to Early that morning was to close up to the cavalry camp that had marked the Confederate frontier overnight. The specter of Union cavalry to the westward continued strong, so Ewell ordered Early to strew troops along the road as he went, to serve as pickets "at suitable points." The Confederate high command perceived the cavalry threat to be of such import that Early's orders were to picket *both* sides of the road. (Buford and Bayard would have been delighted with their impact, had they known.) Jackson's advance northward into Culpeper County was rather tentative, viewed in this light—a gingerly projection into uncertain country. Early used up the entire Forty-fourth Virginia Infantry and six companies of the Fifty-second Virginia in this fashion before he reached Beverly Robertson's cavalry headquarters.[28]

Hindsight shows clearly that the heavy picketing to rearward on August 9 was not necessary. Early's allotment of more than one and one-half regiments for that purpose would later haunt the army. Another six or seven hundred men in his ranks near the Crittenden House late that afternoon could have made a big difference. Further, Early's one and one-half regiments were only a part of the overly cautious detachment: each of Jackson's other divisions left an entire brigade behind on like duty.

Early's leading infantry reached the edge of the valley of Cedar Run shortly after noon. Although their purpose there was a grim one, and the weather was horrible, the men cannot have been immune to the beauties of the place. The mountain looming green above the rolling country had been described as early as January 1699 as being "placed so Comedious and pleaseing as tho made by Art to View and Comand that Vaile." Captain Philip Slaughter, a

veteran of the Revolution who died in 1849, saw resemblances between the valley and the scene of one of his military experiences in
Pennsylvania in 1777 and accordingly named his farm Brandywine.
Slaughter's family connection with the area went deep enough that at
least half of the mid-nineteenth-century maps, with unconscious portent, identified Cedar Mountain as Slaughter Mountain.[29]

Confederate cavalry had moved into the valley ahead of the infantry, of course, while Beverly Robertson set up headquarters at
or near the Petty house. By the time Jackson and Boswell and the
army headquarters establishment reached that point, Ewell had been
there for some time. Members of Elijah V. White's independent cavalry company, who styled themselves "the Comanches," loafed under
trees in the yard and wished they could visit their homes in Loudoun
County. Ewell coaxed some small children onto the porch, where he
frolicked with them and made "baby-talk" to them. Stonewall Jackson rode into this indolent scene, spread maps on the floor of the
porch, and crouched over them with Ewell. Both generals were angu-
lar men, and they must have looked all elbows and knees. The two
officers agreed quickly on the options presented by the maps and
promptly "laid themselves out" for a brief rest.[30]

The Federal cavalry, which had been visible for a couple of hours,
waited restlessly along one of the rolling ridgetops perpendicular to
the main road and between the Major[31] and Crittenden houses. The
initial Confederate position on what became the battlefield was west
and a little south of the cavalry's ridge, around the intersection of the
main road with a road leading westward to Madison Court House.
The intersection formed a big crude "Y," which looked at first glance
like a strategic key (though it was not), especially since Madison had
been a focus of Confederate concern for two days.

The most notable Civil War corollary of Murphy's Law might be
stated thus: No major battle will be easy to describe in compass terms
because the primary flow never is east-to-west or north-to-south, but
rather obliquely across the landscape.*

*It is not practical to spend hundreds of paragraphs describing complex
maneuvers as being on the northwest side of a field, crossing to the southeast, then vice versa, then 90° diagonally reversed. A nominal north (and
south and east and west) is essential. The main road at Cedar Mountain and
the parallel axis of the mountain mass, which must be the polestar, run much
more west-to-east than south-to-north. The road between the Crittenden
Gate and the blood-drenched wheatfield averages no more than 30° from
due east (perhaps less) and thus is 60° or more from due north. On the other

As soon as Jubal Early arrived at Robertson's cavalry headquarters, the Federal cavalry caught his attention. Whether Early arrived before or after Ewell's brief meeting with Jackson cannot be determined, but Ewell sent his subordinate out to look at the enemy and prepare to move against them. This first Southern infantry element on the field moved north to the schoolhouse at the "Y" and lay down. The schoolhouse stood in the angle of the intersection on the left of the main road and south of the road to Madison. Early put his Thirteenth Virginia Infantry on the left of the brigade in the woods at the edge of the road beyond the schoolhouse, toward Madison. The Fifty-eighth Virginia went on the right of the Culpeper road in a clump of pines. The rest of his brigade (Twenty-fifth Virginia, Thirty-first Virginia, and four companies of the Fifty-second Virginia) Early put on the left of the road directly behind the schoolhouse. The time was something before 1:00 P.M. when Early was set.[32]

Early's men had not been around the schoolhouse long ("something less than an hour," the general wrote) when Sandie Pendleton of Jackson's staff rode up with orders. Pendleton, a brilliant and much-admired youngster, gave Early a crisp salute and said: "General Jackson sends his compliments to General Early, and says that he must advance on the enemy, and he will be supported by General Winder." Early's response, "drawled out in earnest tones," was "Tell him I will do it." The rest of Ewell's division would move well to the right of the Culpeper Road on the slopes of the mountain and Early would be widely separated from them. In Early's words, his advance would be "from the position I then occupied," but he was not to begin until he received word that Winder had arrived close behind and ready to follow him. That support was on the way was manifest from the towering pillars of dust rising behind Early, "stretching back as far as the eye could reach," according to a Connecticut boy watching with concern from near the Mitchell's Station Road.[33]

---

hand, the long-term route of the road is unquestionably close to due north, from Orange to Culpeper. Very few of its legs, including that piece on the battlefield from the schoolhouse "Y" to the Crittenden Gate, trend other than northerly. The tactical maps accompanying this narrative focus on the heart of the field and on a road running nominally eastward, so movements into action beyond the schoolhouse will be presumed to be in an easterly direction. Cedar Mountain is *south* of the road; the Crittenden House is *south* of the road and *north* of the mountain and *east* of the Major house; the road to Mitchell's Station runs *south* away from the battlefield.

While Jubal Early waited for word that his support had arrived, Confederate cavalry and artillery fired the opening rounds of the battle. The artillery of Ewell's division had kept well closed up on this morning, but there was some question about how well it might perform. Campbell Brown of Ewell's staff was disgusted with Stapleton Crutchfield, Jackson's artillery chief, for mishandling the division's guns. Brown wrote: "The Batteries of the Division had been so interfered with & so arbitrarily & uselessly transferred & re-transferred by Col. Crutchfield . . . that when Major Courtney . . . on entering upon his duties, inquired as to the Arty belonging to the Divn, he found nobody could tell him, except Col. Crutchfield—and hardly he himself."[34]

All of the long arm of Jackson's army was coming off a difficult time during the campaign around Richmond. The historian of the artillery of the Army of Northern Virginia has suggested that the successful development of the arm came about because "grave defects were recognized to exist" and commensurate efforts were being made to solve the problems. Artillery commanders undertook strenuous programs of upgrading harness, equipage, and ordnance. At the time of Cedar Mountain the average strength of batteries in the field was seventy-two men, an adequate if less than ideal level.[35]

Major Alfred R. Courtney brought Ewell's guns up to the support of the inadequate cavalry screen near the Major house at about 2:00 P.M. and fired the first big guns of the battle. Confederate horsemen had been firing the first small guns in this vicinity for several hours. With Grumble Jones off chasing the Madison Court House chimera, the only full regiment left at the head of the army was the Sixth Virginia Cavalry. That regiment, in the words of one of its captains, "was unable to dislodge" the hostile horse in front of Jackson's army without help.[36]

At least some portion of the Twelfth Virginia Cavalry also was present. An unidentified member of that regiment reported that at the opening contact between the two mounted arms, the U.S. troops were along a rail fence and the Confederates behind another, with an open field two hundred yards wide intervening. During a desultory exchange of fire, the Twelfth Virginia trooper took a musket ball directly through his hat which "just drew the blood . . . and knocked me down." When the nicked man got back to his feet, an officer examined him and suggested, with more pragmatism than pity, "that a miss was as good as a mile."[37] The skirmishing drew little, if any, more blood.

The Comanches of Ewell's headquarters detachment also swirled around the Confederate van, though not in large numbers. Captain Elijah V. White and Lieutenant Frank Myers of that command rode close to their opposite numbers and were favorably impressed by them. The Yankees were "splendidly drilled . . . the first . . . seen who performed their evolutions on the field at the sound of the bugle." The two Southern officers watched a regiment deploy "most beautifully" to the bugled commands and advance to within one hundred yards of the observers. A lone Federal approached them from some nearby woods but scampered away again despite White's bellowed order to "come here to me, you rascal."[38]

The nicely drilled Northern regiment was the First Rhode Island Cavalry, whose colonel was a professional soldier from France, Alfred Nattie Duffie. The First Maine Cavalry also was in the Northern line, farther to the Confederate right and near the foot of the mountain. Colonel Duffie had matter-of-factly explained the handling of battle's ultimate currency to his chaplain that morning. "If any officers are killed, we must rescue their bodies," Duffie said in his thick accent. "If you are shot, we will save your body and send it to Rhode Island. If I am killed, save my body and send it to my friends in New Jersey." The chaplain carefully wrote his mortuary instructions in his notebook, although on this as on most battlefields, dead cavalrymen were something of an oddity and dead chaplains just did not happen.[39]

The essentially bloodless quarreling between the two cavalry arms gave way near 2:00 P.M. to a quick, hot barrage of fire from Confederate cannon. Ewell ordered Major Courtney to drive away the enemy cavalry, and Courtney used all or parts of five batteries, which he aligned southward from the main road to the Major house and on beyond it to the foot of the mountain. The first rounds came from a two-gun section of John R. Johnson's Bedford (Virginia) Artillery, under the command of Lieutenant Nathaniel Terry. Terry posted his pieces on the right "near the foot of the mountain." Trimble's brigade of Ewell's division supported the guns from a nearby thicket. An infantryman noted disdainfully that the Southern guns "did very little execution." Even so, Terry's few rounds chased the Federal cavalry from view, but they quickly returned to their original position. Ewell concluded with his seasoned eye "that the enemy intended to make a stand at this place."[40]

The rest of Courtney's guns were ready to Lieutenant Terry's left by the time the Federal cavalry reappeared. Part of William F. Dement's (two guns) and William F. Brown's batteries, both from Maryland, were positioned "on a small knoll on which there were growing pines," just behind the Major house. Louis E. D'Aquin's Louisiana guns went into the line closer to the mountain, and so did a single rifled piece of Joseph W. Latimer's Virginia battery; the rifle soon rejoined its company on the mountainside farther to the front. When this array of firepower opened, Northern guns beyond the cavalry responded and shells arced over the horsemen in each direction. One of Dement's men wrote that the two guns of his battery fired "with fatal effect" on the Federal cavalry and "it was a beautiful sight." To Early, watching from afar, it seemed that the main line of Courtney's artillery ("in front of General Robertson's headquarters") went into action almost at once after Terry's opening salvo. The return artillery fire from Federal guns near the road to Mitchell's Station "lasted only for a few minutes," and the exchange quickly guttered out.[41]

The historian of the First Maine Cavalry was disdainful of the artillery fire when he wrote of the battle. It seemed fierce, he noted (the regiment had never before been under fire), but it did the regiment no harm. The First Rhode Island Cavalry was closer to the muzzles and equally as green as the Maine regiment, and some of the very fresh New England lads wavered. General Bayard rode among them and loudly insisted (not entirely inaccurately) that "shells are only thrown for moral effect." One of the Rhode Island men wrote unkindly that Colonel Duffié was an "extremely nervous man," who winced at one passing shell, then reproved himself aloud and sat tall thereafter.[42]

Federal infantry watched the exchange with interest from the rear. When the men of the Tenth Maine learned that men on horseback several hundred yards away were genuine Rebels, they disobeyed orders and crowded to the high ground to see the fearsome foes and found them to be "no great sight." One of the Maine soldiers suggested that the mounted men could not really be Confederates: "They 'looked too natural' for that!" Officers mounted a guard near the skyline to keep the gawkers from clustering there and betraying the position or calling down hostile fire, but the fascinated men kept dodging the guard to get a look at the enemy. From their vantage point the artillery fire was impressive, though not dangerous at that distance. The regimental historian of the Tenth Maine commented drolly on Pope's innocent (and apt) use of the adjective "desultory" to

*The ruins of the Crittenden House in 1989. The old building
succumbed to fire about 1970. (Clark B. Hall)*

describe the fire in some account: "I suspect that J.P. lost his dictionary as well as the uniform, at Catlett's Station."[43]

Officers and men behind each of the forming front lines breathed a little more rapidly as the roar of cannon announced a nascent battle. A New York newspaperman methodically counted the discharges and figured that the opening Confederate spurt included only fourteen rounds. Colonel Adrian R. Root of the Ninety-fourth New York of Ricketts's division was far to the rear out of the heat of action when he noted the opening guns "at about 2 o'clock p.m." in a letter to his wife. Confederate General Isaac Ridgeway Trimble used precisely the same phrase in his diary.[44]

Not all of the Southern ordnance was falling near Northern targets. Some of it, to the delight of Chaplain Frederic Denison of Rhode Island, struck around the home of Catherine Crittenden, "a high-blooded dame of the Virginia pattern," deserving clerical scorn. She had begged for permission to go to the rear toward Culpeper to escape harm, but Denison, who had set himself as arbiter of visas, "pleasantly informed her" that she must "fare as well as we did." When Denison passed by again, he gleefully noted that the mirrors in the house were quivering and Mrs. Crittenden was "in agony, as secession shells were not as pleasing to her as the theory of secession." The effect on Mrs. Crittenden of this dose of Rhode Island chivalry cannot have been pleasing. Happily for her, the frightened woman was about to run into a less hostile Alabamian.[45]

While he waited for Winder to arrive to launch the advance and while the cavalry skirmished and the artillery began to growl, Jubal Early conducted a careful and highly successful reconnaissance. August 9 was destined to be a good day for Early, one of the rising stars in the army though still a brigadier. His early afternoon scout to the front from near the schoolhouse set the stage. General Beverly Robertson accompanied Early. The two men, with perhaps a few aides or couriers, carefully examined the position of the enemy cavalry "in the fields of Mrs. Crittenden's farm." The hostile troopers were deployed almost entirely in skirmish formation with "about a squadron in reserve." The rolling countryside and the wood lines completely hid Early's brigade from enemy view at the moment, and the general obviously liked that advantage. "I determined to advance . . . if possible, so as not to be seen until within a short distance," Early reported, and promptly located a good route for that purpose. A small tributary of the south branch of Cedar Run bisected the main road less than a half a mile northeast of the schoolhouse and just a little more than that distance short of the Crittenden Gate. Heavy woods crowded most of the main road on each shoulder as far as the Gate, but there was a "long, narrow meadow on the branch" to the left of the point where it crossed the road. Early determined to form up in that long, narrow meadow and then advance obliquely to his right front through the woods until he was in position to spring on the exposed flank of the Federal cavalry.[46]

When Early and Robertson returned to the schoolhouse, they met a courier from Winder, whose division was approaching. It was time for the infantry to take a hand. Early immediately pushed his five and a half regiments (the Twelfth Georgia, normally of Trimble's brigade, spent the afternoon appended to Early) into motion. They took "a detour to the left, passing through the edge of a woods and behind a hill" until they reached the meadow he had found for his parade ground. As the main body formed up in the meadow just east of the branch, Early without hesitation designated the stalwart Thirteenth Virginia Infantry (its first colonel had been A. P. Hill in the time long before he became court-martial bait for Jackson) to lead the way as skirmishers. The general also called for eight picked men

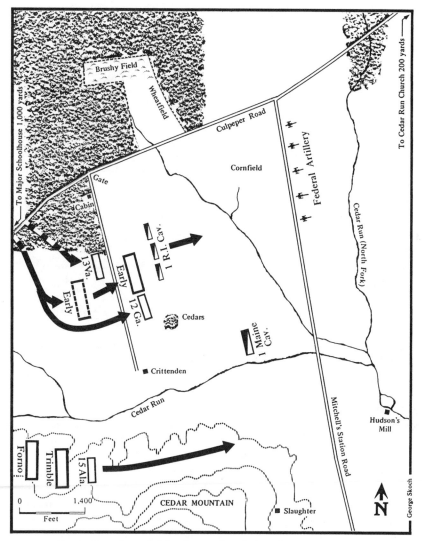

Early Brushes Aside the Federal Cavalry, 3:00–3:30

from the Thirteenth to operate as the forward point ahead of anyone else. The Thirteenth disappeared into the woods to the right front. Early said in his report with simple eloquence that whenever the Thirteenth Virginia went on skirmish duty, "I feel secure."[47]

Presently Colonel James A. Walker of the Thirteenth Virginia called back from the woods "in his ringing voice": "General Early, are you ready?" "Yes; go on," came the reply, and the Thirteenth Virginia moved to contact. Years before, Cadet Walker of the Virginia Military Institute had attempted to kill T. J. Jackson after the dour professor had driven him to distraction; now, in exquisite irony, he commanded the forward wedge of Jackson's infantry in what would be Stonewall's last independent campaign; later, in ultimate irony, Walker was transferred to command Jackson's famous old Stonewall Brigade.[48]

In his report, Early timed his advance from the schoolhouse toward the meadow at about 2:00 P.M.; it probably was at least a quarter-hour later than that. The general did not attempt to pinpoint the time he left his meadow and moved in line of battle to inaugurate the infantry fight, but several reliable witnesses agree on 3:00 P.M.[49]

Almost before the brigade began to move, a scattering of shots from the left front signaled contact. The Confederates fired "almost too soon," one of Early's men admitted. A small body of cavalry came close to Walker's left wing two hundred yards into the maneuver, but the enemy gave way quickly under the impact of the first infantry rounds fired in the battle of Cedar Mountain. The thin cavalry line in that quarter "we brushed from before us," wrote a member of the Thirteenth Virginia. The skirmishers killed two men and a horse with this first fire. The regiment on skirmish duty quickly became a left flank element as the rest of the brigade moved "obliquely through the corner of the woods" to the right of the Culpeper road and closed on the flank and rear of the Federal cavalry. While the rest of the brigade wheeled onto line, the Thirteenth Virginia "opened fire upon the main body of their cavalry in the field and kept it up . . . but the distance was too great to do much execution."[50]

Early prodded the main body of his brigade through the woods and across the road, "over fences, through cornfields, over ditches and rocks." They moved "in handsome style," Early thought. The newly appended Twelfth Georgia Infantry operated as the far right wing and went off on its own oblique, taking advantage of the ground to stay out of sight of the cavalry that was their target. The Georgians were in high good humor, "chatting about home and their sweethearts" as they advanced. When Early had the regiments where he wanted them, they all burst over the ridge together. As he watched his men "swinging around the corner of the woods and coming out into the open field in line of battle," Early's pulse beat higher and he swelled with pride. One of the Twelfth Georgia men claimed that

*Irascible but devoted Brigadier General Jubal A. Early attracted
favorable attention with his solid performance at Cedar Mountain.*

Early fired the opening rifle round at the cavalry personally. Courtney's artillery threw in a few shells from the rear, and the enemy
cavalry "scampered off" (Early's phrase) "like lightning" (Campbell
Brown's phrase). A Maryland artillerist back near the Major house
wrote that the Federals "fled in great disorder in all directions. . . ."[51]
    Colonel Duffie attempted to hold his Rhode Island regiment un-

59

der the first light fire from the Thirteenth Virginia's point elements, as befitted a French professional soldier. A Federal soldier on the receiving end identified the incoming musketry as the "one ball and three buckshot" rounds used in smoothbore muskets. That ammunition and weapon were deadly at close range but useless beyond 125 yards. In stabilizing the unsteady regiment, Duffie bellowed: "Squadrons, left wheel, form close column!" But he did not add the order for execution: "March." His flustered major went on with the left wheel anyway, and the colonel dashed up to him with an oath and screamed: "What a sickness; what a business; I be like you, I go buy one rope, I go hang myself." One of the Northern men thought that Early's troops were shooting very high and credited that traditional failing of infantrymen for the light losses in Duffie's regiment. A more likely explanation is that smoothbore rounds were not reaching their targets. A brief rally by the Federal cavalry when they reached their reserves dissolved under the impetus of two shells thrown into their midst by Latimer's cannon.[52]

When Early's regiments swung into line on their new axis, they moved parallel to the main road in the wake of the scampering Northern riders. After they covered about one-half mile, the Confederates reached the lane leading south from the Crittenden Gate toward the Crittenden House, at right angles to the main road. Early had angled south far enough before turning east (nominally east, always nominally) parallel to the road that his advance in that direction was all through open country. The woods south of the road stopped at the Gate in any event, so when Early reached the Crittenden Lane the ground in front of him was almost entirely bare of all cover but farm crops; the crop in this case was corn—acres of it. The road ran along the edge of the field to Early's left for a quarter-mile beyond the Gate, then the woods north of the road ended and gave way to a wheatfield. The Crittenden House was in the bottom to Early's right. A single notable exception to the clearing in front was a cedar-covered knoll to the left front of the Crittenden House and thus on Early's right front.

Not all of this terrain was visible when Early reached the Crittenden Lane. In fact, not all of it was visible from any one point except from the slopes of the mountain. The rolling ground in the valley is full of folds and swales and little ridges that flatten out to the eye but had room enough for unexpected regiments to lurk within them. Much of the Crittenden Lane ran behind just such a ground swell. There was a fence on the western edge of the lane behind which the brigade halted. The Thirteenth Virginia caught up on the left to make the line straight. Soon thereafter the men pulled the fence down and advanced in line to the crest just beyond. From this new vantage point Early and his men "commanded a view in front of what afterward proved to be the battle-field." The moment the Confederates emerged on the crest, three enemy batteries along the Mitchell's Station Road opened on them. Early sent the men back "a few steps" and had them lie down to avoid the shelling.[53]

While Early was advancing eastward to the Crittenden Lane, Ewell's other two brigades advanced in the same direction although on a line about one-half mile farther south, which took them across the north shoulder of Cedar Mountain. The south fork of Cedar Run separated the two movements; Early and Ewell might just as well have been in different counties. Dick Ewell manfully acknowledged to his beloved fiancée, who also was the mother of G. Campbell Brown of his staff, that he had had nothing to do with Early during the battle and little to do with anything else. "Where the printed accounts speak of Ewell, Jackson ought to be substituted. My division being in advance, movements were attributed to me that, in effect, were Jackson's. . . . Early acted separately." Newspaper accounts made much of Ewell at Cedar Mountain, but the general was quick to correct them: "In fact I have not had any more or as much to do with this as the other battles that have come off lately."[54]

Ewell had only two brigades other than Early's: Trimble's brigade, consisting of the Fifteenth Alabama, Twenty-first Georgia, and Twenty-first North Carolina; and Hays's brigade under Colonel Henry Forno of the Fifth Louisiana Infantry, which also counted the Sixth, Seventh, Eighth and Fourteenth Louisiana regiments in its strength. Trimble's brigade already was on or near the mountainside opposite the Major house, where it had supported Lieutenant Terry's guns briefly. The Fifteenth Alabama moved along the mountain slope at the head of the brigade. The route lay "along and near the base of the mountain, keeping our movements concealed until we could arrive at right angles to the enemy's left." G. Campbell Brown of Ewell's staff described the passage as "a wood road, hiding us completely from the enemy, along the side of the mountain." Forno's Louisiana regiments left the main road sooner than Trimble's did and reached the mountain south of the Garnett house. Having gotten the men forward under cover, Ewell kept them under cover as they advanced opposite Early's men, who were visible to their left and well below them.[55]

Ewell advanced along the mountain when Early's movement signaled the advance; and Early's movement became possible when Winder arrived to trigger the whole business. Not many hours before Winder arrived there had been uncertainty whether his illness would keep him out of action; apparently Stonewall Jackson had been particularly uneasy because even with Winder present, Alexander R. Lawton of Georgia was the senior officer in the division by date of commission. (Lawton's commission actually predated the secession of Virginia.) Jackson resolved the matter with a dispatch written even before "early dawn," at 4:00 A.M. The general headed the note quixotically as from the headquarters of the Valley District, as though his recent separation from the Army of Northern Virginia turned the clock back two months. The message was simple: Lawton was detached to guard the division trains from that ubiquitous Federal cavalry and Winder was to "assume command of the three remaining brigades of the Division."[56]

Jackson's reports never revealed motivations in even the least sensitive matters, and his official account of Cedar Mountain declared only the bare facts about Lawton's detachment. Winder's aide McHenry Howard suggested what everyone else guessed and what still must be presumed, that "Winder's tried character and services under Jackson's own eye preferred him for the command." The same stern discipline that made Casler loathe Winder made Jackson love the man. Howard was confident that Jackson intended for Winder to keep the division permanently, and he reported a postwar confidence from Jefferson Davis to the effect that Winder "was just about to be made a major-general."[57]

The division van under Winder and without Lawton reached the Widow Petty's farmyard, with the general looking "very pale and badly." Henry Kyd Douglas, himself a Marylander, who was at the Petty farm at the time, pronounced Winder in hindsight to have been that state's finest contribution to the Confederacy. Douglas reported that Dr. Hunter McGuire suggested that Jackson try to send the sick general to the rear, but when Douglas carried that message from Jackson to Winder the brigadier demurred. Winder looked up Jackson personally, by Douglas's account, and Jackson reiterated his assignment of division command to Winder before the two generals shook hands and parted.[58]

The Stonewall Brigade marched at the head of Winder's division on the morning of August 9, although it did not continue at that post of honor. Again there is reason to infer that the juggling resulted from concerns about the chain of command. Colonel Charles A. Ronald of the Fourth Virginia succeeded Winder in command by virtue of seniority when Winder took over the division. Ronald was a thirty-five-year-old lawyer from Blacksburg, Virginia, who had earned some limited military experience in the Mexican War. His Confederate field service ended later in the year, but Ronald survived the war's end by thirty-three years and is buried under a tombstone that says cryptically: "I Have Suffered" (whether physically, spiritually, or otherwise is not clear). It doubtless was clear to Winder in the summer of 1862 that Ronald was not made of the stuff of brigade commanders. Anyone who survived Cedar Mountain and had occasion to read Ronald's official report of the action would find it by a wide margin the most confused Confederate account extant.[59]

Winder's-cum-Ronald's brigade had had a difficult day before being bumped from the head of the column. Captain Michael Shuler of the Thirty-third Virginia noted in his diary that the regiment had been "in line this morning before day" and had "marched by sun up." Private John K. Hitner of the Rockbridge Artillery, the brigade's traditional supporting battery, wrote that after the 2:00 A.M. cavalry scare "caused quite a stir in camp," the cannoneers never returned to bed and went on the road by about 6:00 A.M.[60]

The march was an ordeal for everyone involved. Ronald reported plaintively that the brigade's progress "was frequently interrupted from causes unknown to me at the time." Winder's aide reiterated the obvious when he wrote: "The day was hot and the dust oppressive and the march was a slow one." The heat was unforgettable and often mentioned, but the dust that permeated everything got more ink on this march than any other that comes to mind. A generic depiction of dust-induced misery written by a Virginia artillerist in 1863 brings what he called the "soil-demon" into vivid focus: "Though it is seldom mentioned, and but little thought of, outside of army circles, one of the greatest discomforts of the soldier's life, and one of the severest tests of his physical endurance, is, undoubtedly, the great dust-clouds that hang over and envelop a moving army on a dry, hot day. It has to be seen and experienced to be thoroughly understood."[61]

Sometime not long before they reached the schoolhouse where Early was waiting for the division, Garnett's brigade moved around the famous veteran regiments of the Stonewall Brigade and took over the lead. Taliaferro's brigade did likewise, leaving Ronald the last in line. The Forty-eighth Virginia Infantry had been leading

Garnett's brigade all day and forged past Ronald's halted men. Jubal Early conferred with one or two other generals and then launched his movement against the Rhode Island cavalrymen. Garnett's brigade took his place with its right resting near the schoolhouse, much as Early had been deployed until minutes earlier. The Virginians near the schoolhouse soon heard "some skirmish firing to the right oblique." After Early finished his cavalry cleanup, Garnett received the obvious orders to move up on Early's left—"to move rapidly forward along the main road."[62]

The last of the three brigades in Winder's truncated division to march was that of General William Booth Taliaferro, a thoroughly aristocratic Tidewater Virginian almost exactly one year older than Stonewall Jackson. Taliaferro and W. W. Loring had been at the hub of a near mutiny six months earlier, which had resulted in Jackson's attempted resignation, so the general was not among the few officers on Stonewall's preferred list. He had put his brigade on the road at 8:00 A.M. The two raw and inexperienced Alabama regiments had caught up with Taliaferro sometime of late, and he mixed them into the column. The brigade's order of march was Thirty-seventh Virginia, Forty-eighth Alabama, Tenth Virginia, Twenty-third Virginia, and Forty-seventh Alabama.[63]

Taliaferro's brigade suffered the same environmental difficulties as did the others, of course, and with the same complete lack of recourse. The commander of the Twenty-third Virginia spoke of "a long and distressing march . . . on account of the excessive heat and scarcity of good water." A captain in the Tenth Virginia noticed "exhausted Men lying along the road through the Entire March." The brigade neared the schoolhouse at about 3:30 P.M. Its regiments spread out in the woods south of the intersection and waited.[64]

A. P. Hill's enormous division—it contained one more brigade than Ewell's and Winder's combined—began the day far to the rear spread between Orange Court House and the Rapidan River. When Jackson bluntly rejected his constructive suggestion about alternate river crossings, Hill prepared to push straight up the main road. His brigades marched in the following order: Thomas, Branch, Archer, Pender, Stafford, Field, and Gregg.[65]

Colonel Edward Lloyd Thomas of the Thirty-fifth Georgia commanded a brigade of four Georgia regiments as the senior colonel. At thirty-seven, Thomas was not much older than the average brigade commander at that stage of the war. The colonel was a Georgia planter who had served as a lieutenant of volunteers in Mexico. A

64

few months after Cedar Mountain, Thomas would win his general's wreath, but he remained a brigadier for the rest of the war. In August 1863 R. E. Lee called Thomas "a highly meritorious officer" but suggested that his promotion "might create dissatisfaction," presumably because of interstate jealousies in his division. Thomas led the Fourteenth, Thirty-fifth, Forty-fifth, and Forty-ninth Georgia infantry regiments toward Cedar Mountain at the head of Hill's column.[66]

Lawrence O'Bryan Branch, a forty-one-year-old Princeton graduate and former member of the U.S. Congress, followed Thomas with five North Carolina regiments. According to Branch's journal, his brigade remained on the road for more than twelve hours after the cavalry alarm shortly after midnight. That enervating ordeal ended only when the brigade neared action on the afternoon of August 9.[67]

James Jay Archer came third in Hill's column with a polyglot brigade made up of three Tennessee regiments, one Georgia regiment, and an Alabama battalion. Archer was forty-four years old, from Maryland, another Princeton graduate, a renowned swearer, and a veteran of Regular Army service before the war; he had been a Confederate general for just two months. Archer's brigade moved that morning at "about 8 o'clock." When the men reached the Rapidan River, one of the Tennesseeans wrote, "we waded right in like horses, holding our guns and cartridge boxes above the water." That cool interlude was their only break of the day. A Nineteenth Georgia man swore that that August 9 in Virginia was hotter than any day he ever had experienced in the Peach State: "Many fell fainting by the wayside, and large numbers fell out to hunt a shady spot to cool their parching brain." A comrade in the First Tennessee, Henry T. Childs, independently concluded that there never had been a hotter day in his home state either. Childs must have been of slender build because he emphasized that big men could not take it: "It was the hottest day I ever saw, the big men continually falling by the wayside, worn out by fatigue and oppressive heat." J. H. Moore of the Seventh Tennessee remembered the dust: "The day was remarkably hot and sultry, and the red dust of the dirt-road almost suffocating." Archer's men from three states pressed wearily onward under the spur of the roaring cannon, to which they drew ever closer.[68]

William Dorsey Pender's brigade of four North Carolina regiments choked on the dust kicked up by Archer's men just in front of them. Pender was a twenty-eight-year-old officer of great promise and one of only two West Pointers among Hill's seven brigade commanders. Although he had only eleven months to live, Pender would be the first major general among the seven and one of only two ever to achieve that rank. The general's letters to his wife reveal a somewhat querulous fellow (as personal mail so often does); they also display constant concern about Mrs. Pender's sexual health and a religious zeal akin to that of Stonewall Jackson. Pender's unquestioned bravery (he was frequently wounded) and military capacity did not endear him universally to his men, who thought he sometimes acted "unfairly" and was "pretty hard on" the troops. A lieutenant in the Twelfth South Carolina of Gregg's brigade, which later became part of Pender's division, commented on Pender's "cruel" treatment of his own brigade. The South Carolinians "had a perfect horror" of Pender and "entertained . . . fears" about coming under him but discovered that he was not so bad during the month of his tenure at their head. It is likely that Pender's harshness with his own brigade was prompted by the epidemic of desertion within it of which he complained in early August.[69]

Colonel Leroy A. Stafford, a forty-year-old sheriff from Louisiana, commanded five Louisiana regiments including his own Ninth. One of Stafford's officers called him "a most genial, whole-souled gentleman, & . . . a most cool & judicious, as well as a most fearless & dashing officer." Another styled him "a man of no special military ability . . . fond of a glass of liquor . . . also of a friendly game of cards, affable and pleasant when unopposed, but violent and somewhat tyrannical when aroused by opposition." Stafford's brigade was appended to Hill's division for only a few days bracketing the time of Cedar Mountain. A loquacious Catholic chaplain with Stafford's brigade wrote that it crossed the Rapidan "around ten" that morning to the sounds of "distant drums and bugles," which had begun at dawn. That martial noise gave way to cannon fire as the Louisianians moved north. The chaplain claimed that "the sound echoing through the valley seemed to echo also in the hearts of our men, filling them with an emotion that found expression in lusty rebel yells."[70]

Closing the infantry column behind Stafford was the Virginia brigade of Charles W. Field, consisting of three regiments and a battalion. Field was the other West Pointer among Hill's brigade leaders, in addition to Pender, and he also (hardly by coincidence) was the other man from that group who reached the rank of major general during the war.

Maxcy Gregg's South Carolinians were Hill's seventh brigade, but they did not bring up the infantry rear. While their comrades sweated and choked on dust, and later fought and died, Gregg's men remained behind and picketed around Barnett's Ford against the threat of Federal raiders. Late in the day cavalry approached from the direction of Madison Court House and Gregg's men fired into them. Their target turned out to be part of the Twelfth Virginia Cavalry returning from Madison. One of the riders "went forward with a flag of truce" and settled the confusion, in which, fortunately, "no damage was done."[71]

The Confederate artillery scattered through the column kept pace with the various brigades and divisions to which it was assigned. The infantry-clogged road did not allow for rapid deployment of artillery, but it moved steadily along. As the action heated up at the front, Hill called on his artillery chief, Lieutenant Colonel Reuben Lindsay Walker, to carry forward "all my long-range guns." When Walker endeavored to obey, he managed to push forward two batteries, but "the road was so blocked up with wagons and ambulances" that he could do no more.[72]

Artillery was very much in demand up close to the resisting Federals as the contending lines began to take shape. After Jubal Early drove back Duffie and the rest of the Northern cavalry, the opening scenes shifted to a warm artillery contest that engrossed both Jackson and Winder. Ewell was moving forward along the mountainside, Garnett's brigade had orders to move toward the enemy from the schoolhouse, Taliaferro's brigade was close behind, and Hill's van slogged forward; but in the midst of all that infantry movement, Jackson wanted guns to the front. For more than an hour, the battle of Cedar Mountain turned into an artillery showcase and Stonewall Jackson essayed the role of captain of artillery, with Winder as his lieutenant.

CHAPTER 4

Jackson and Winder as Gunners

FOUR CLUSTERS of Confederate artillery dominated attention through the formative stages of the battle of Cedar Mountain. The first cluster was just to Early's right on a conspicuous cedar-covered knoll. Another concentration of guns—the largest of the four—developed at and around the Crittenden Gate. Almost at the same moment, Southern pieces dragged by main force to a dominant shelf on Cedar Mountain came into action. A fourth artillery position near Early's left, midway between the first two, nearly came to grief. Beginning by about 4:00 P.M. and continuing until the onset of the infantry crisis at perhaps 5:45, some and then all of the two dozen guns at those four locations took center stage.

The cedars became a point of reference so important to those fighting within sight of the knoll, which included more than half of the combatants on the battlefield, that the landmark transcends the usual capitalization conventions and shall be the Cedars hereinafter. Looking across the rolling countryside toward his enemy, a Connecticut Yankee described the Cedars as standing "on the crest of the ridge beyond the cornfield . . . and just beyond the center of the cornfield on the left." Major Courtney, to whose division the occupants of the Cedars would belong, described the location as "on a little rise on the right of . . . Early's brigade, on which there is a little clump of cedars and pines." Courtney judged the distance from the Cedars to "the enemy's extreme right battery" (evidently meaning to the Confederate right) to be "about 600 yards." His estimate fell about three hundred yards short. Judge Daniel A. Grimsley, a veteran of the Sixth Virginia Cavalry and the resident battlefield expert in the county after the war (he gave President Theodore Roosevelt a tour in 1902), knew the site well and referred to it as "a little" north and east of the Crittenden House. The admirable William Allan, Confederate staff officer and historian, placed the Cedars "not far" in advance of the Crittenden House.[1] All of this attention to location results from three factors: the disappearance of the trees over time, the plethora of knolls in the neighborhood, and the usual tendency for map representations to be widely disparate.

Early's first measure after settling his men in position near the Crittenden Lane and the Cedars was to order Colonel Garnett to come up the main road on Early's left. Lieutenant Samuel Henry Early carried the message to Garnett. At the same time General Early thought to send for artillery to emplace at the Cedars and sent volunteer aide Andrew L. Pitzer on Sam Early's heels to find some. Pitzer never got the job done because there was no need to. Major Courtney had anticipated his general's wants, scanned the ordnance available in the three batteries close at hand, and hurried forward. Captain William D. Brown's Maryland battery (the Chesapeake Artillery) counted a three-inch rifle in its armament, but the other pieces were two old six-pounders and a weak howitzer. Courtney sent the rifle to the front and the others to the rear. All four guns in Captain William F. Dement's Maryland battery were Napoleons, those yeomen of bronze gunnery. The other battery was the completely untested Louisiana Guard Artillery—four guns under Captain Louis E. D'Aquin.[2]

Alfred Ranson Courtney had been promoted to major only three weeks earlier, and he welcomed this opportunity to perform while the entire army watched. It also was to be one of his last opportunities. Although Courtney became both the Grand Master of Virginia Masons and a member of the Virginia General Assembly after the war, his military career with the Army of Northern Virginia did not extend far beyond August 9, 1862: he was court-martialed for dereliction of duty at Sharpsburg the next month and disappeared into the military bureaucracy as an inspector. That unhappiness lay ahead. Beneath the shoulder of Cedar Mountain, Courtney did all that was asked of him.[3]

Between Dement's four, D'Aquin's four, and Brown's piece, Major Courtney counted nine guns as he started forward from the vicinity of the Major house toward Jubal Early's cedar-clad knoll. Before they had careened far across the "rough fields" that intervened, one of the Louisiana guns broke an axle and had to fall out. The Cedars knoll had nothing like enough room for the remaining eight. "Hub to hub" is Hollywood fiction; reality was leaping, flaming, violent recoil, which required space—so Courtney sent only three pieces to the Cedars. Brown's rifle went and so did two of Dement's Napo-

Edwin Forbes's sketch of the battle shows Williams's division (his #7) moving against the Southern line. The sketch depicts the Confederate line and its surrounding features very accurately, including

leons. Each of the Maryland captains went along to the knoll, Brown because his only gun went there, Dement because it obviously was a hotter spot than his other section would find.[4]

Early recounted the stirring arrival of the Maryland guns in his official report: "Captain Brown, of the Chesapeake Artillery, with one piece, and Captain Dement, with three pieces, came up through the fields in rear on a gallop, and were posted, by my direction, a little in advance of my right near a clump of cedars, where they had a good cover for their horses and caissons and occupied a commanding position." Writing after the war, the general had the guns come "dashing up." In both of his accounts, Early gave Dement one more gun than he had and Jackson mimicked the error in his report (as have others since).[5]

The three guns at the Cedars immediately roared into action, and

the woods west of the wheatfield sloping to the road and the cabin just south of the Crittenden Gate. (Library of Congress)

Early looked to his infantry. Courtney still had five pieces to roll into position, which he did promptly and well, though Early never mentioned them. The major found a usable piece of the ridge line "behind" (east of) the Crittenden House (the house faced away from the action), somewhat to the right and somewhat to the rear of the Cedars. Their range to the hostile artillery measured about eight hundred yards, Courtney thought, so the location obviously was two hundred yards away from the Cedars (he had estimated a six-hundred-yard range there) and about that much closer to the house.[6]

These five guns also swung into battery and opened fire at once, but one of the two Napoleons of Dement's rearward section had a comic misadventure first. The Maryland boys "went in at a furious rate" across an open field thick with bursting shells. The lieutenant in charge of the section had excitedly shouted "Forward" without

*This woodcut made from the Forbes sketch has been often
printed and probably is the most familiar depiction of the
battle. The published form includes some noticeable variations
from the original sketch that reduce its accuracy.*

remembering to order the cannoneers to mount, and the teams
dashed away leaving most of the battery personnel behind to catch
up as they could. Some of the drivers left their animals in defilade
after they unlimbered and came up to help the skeleton crews. One
of the two Napoleons, whether from the use of untrained help or
through overeagerness ("our boys . . . always wanted to have first
shot"), managed to break off a sponge head in the barrel and then
rammed home a cartridge on top of it. While the Marylanders disgustedly struggled to withdraw both, the enemy, needless to say,
shelled them furiously.[7]

A member of R. P. Chew's horse artillery battery later insisted that
his company had crossed the Rapidan at 9:00 A.M., pressed through
the jammed roads to the front, and "took position and opened fire
on the enemy right away" at about the time that the artillery fighting
erupted in earnest. If he is accurate (no official account survives for
the unit or anyone in its supervisory chain), the horse artillery must
have been firing from a point near the mountain and farther to the
rear.[8]

Jubal Early's successful maneuvering to this point deserved com-
mendation. He had found the sheltered meadow in which to form,
smoothly routed the enemy cavalry line (no great chore, to be sure,
once he was in position), pressed forward until the Federal position
was developed, forced the Northern artillery into action, and rapidly

mustered his own artillery response. The taciturn Jackson was not given to written or public applause for subordinates, but he let slip to his staff his pleasure with the affair. The general was eager to force his enemy's hand, Jedediah Hotchkiss wrote in a letter to his brother on August 14, and the artillery they fired at Early gave them away, "Gen. Jackson says before they intended to."[9]

The rectangle of countryside between the Crittenden Lane and the Mitchell's Station Road, bounded on the other two sides by the main Culpeper Road and Cedar Run, was to be Early's field of operations. He must have studied it closely as soon as he had fed his artillery into action. The landscape was beautiful, even cluttered as it was by an army with banners. The broken nature of the terrain showed an ugly side, however, for someone seeking zones of fire. A Northern correspondent much traveled in Europe wrote: "Compared to the bare plain of Waterloo, Cedar Mountain was like the antediluvian world, when the surface was broken by volcanic fire into chasms and abysses."[10]

Early's rectangle encompassed about 325 acres. The Crittenden Lane ran south from the Gate about 3,800 feet to the house and Cedar Run flowed through its banks another 400 feet beyond. From the Crittenden House to the Mitchell's Station Road was about 3,400 feet. A line diagonally across Early's rectangle from the Crittenden House to the intersection of the Culpeper and Mitchell roads covered just more than 5,700 feet. With the exception of the Cedars, the entire rectangle was cleared and much of it was in crops. To oversimplify the ground folds dramatically, consider the Mitchell's Station Road as running south along a ridge and the Crittenden Lane running south along a parallel ridge some 1,100 yards to the west. The rectangle sloped gently and irregularly southward to the drainage of Cedar Run; this slope became pronounced from the Cedars rightward to the stream.

This "beautiful field," as one of the artillery privates called it, was cultivated in several sections. Most of the crop was corn. An enormous field of tall corn covered the northeast quadrant of the rectangle. Another, smaller, field of corn grew south of the big one. Most witnesses did not differentiate between the two. A small wheatfield lay a bit north of the middle point in the rectangle, "about a hundred yards" from Early's left, which dangled not much more than halfway up the road toward the Gate. (Because a famous and much larger wheatfield east of the Gate and on the north side of the main road became the battlefield's hottest spot, Early's small and confusing

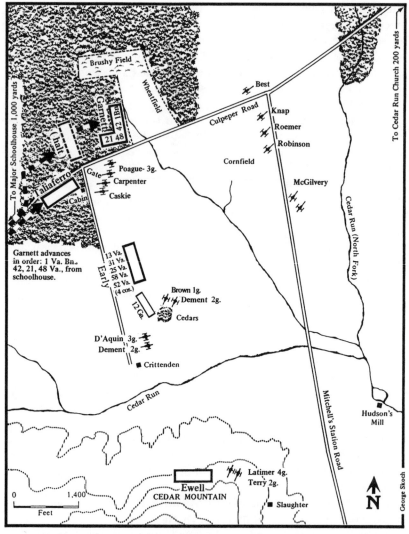

Confederate Infantry Arrives While Artillery Duels, 3:30–5:00

wheatfield will be ignored almost exclusively in this narrative in the interest of clarity.)[11]

Fortunately for Early and his men, who were in for big trouble even as it was, they had an entirely open field of fire down the slope to their front from the vicinity of the Crittenden Lane. The corn that began at the Mitchell's Station Road ran west toward the Confederates for a little more than half the intervening distance toward the Crittenden Lane. Because the men and guns fought from a point somewhat forward of the lane, thus narrowing the open space, the tall corn covered a bit more than half the space between the lines. An insignificant rivulet feeding into Cedar Run cut diagonally across Early's front through the corn, nominally from northwest to southeast, getting farther from the Confederates as it moved to their right. Early's official report also declared (with easy hindsight?) that his survey of the ground made him nervous about hostile action from the woods far to his left front across the main road and beyond the big wheatfield.[12] That zone lay, in any case, far beyond Early's sphere of influence.

General Early's infantry line initially stretched nearly as far left as the main road to Culpeper, but before long he closed it up to the right in such fashion that his left was almost halfway down the lane toward the Crittenden House. Lieutenant Sam Early had gone after Winder and Garnett for help in that direction and General Early soon went as well. He found Winder with Garnett's brigade about half a mile behind the Gate, just crossing the little stream at the meadow whence Early himself had moved an hour earlier.[13]

With Winder's leading elements coming up somewhere to his left, Early could concentrate on a new, shorter line. The space up the lane to his left remained bare of infantry for a spell, although artillery soon crowded around the Gate. Eventually W. B. Taliaferro's brigade would fill in between Early and the Gate, but Early failed to mention this development in his written narratives. As a result, several otherwise reliable accounts of the battle leave Taliaferro's brigade floating at random something like 90° and four hundred yards from its true position at the crisis. Jackson himself followed Early's report and thus added weight to the errant notion.

Even with his left drawn well down the lane, there remained a "long interval" between Early's right and the run. He sent the Twelfth Georgia to cover that interval, and it was well that he did; the Georgians saved the day soon thereafter. At the other end (the left or north) of the brigade line lay the Thirteenth Virginia. Many of its men were natives of Culpeper, and at least two of them were fighting on their home places. William D. Colvin had just enlisted in Company B, the Culpeper Minute Men, at the tender age of fifteen and never had been under fire. His family owned part of the area that was about to become young William's first battlefield. Colvin's company commander was Captain (later Major) Charles Thomas Crittenden, the twenty-six-year-old son of Catherine Crittenden, whom Chaplain Denison had so much enjoyed abusing. A local account stated that during the shelling a round crashed into her bedroom and lodged in the frame of the bed where she was huddled. Not surprisingly, she and her dependents fled from the house and ran shrieking up the slopes of Cedar Mountain, where they soon found friends. She probably had left before her officer son arrived at home to fight a battle.[14]

Before Garnett's brigade reached the Gate, General Winder and his staff arrived at that bottleneck and surveyed the scene. They could see "in the distance, across the open field" to their right front, the enemy batteries that were firing on Early and his recently deployed artillery. The Federal batteries "occupied rising ground to the right and beyond the mouth of the [Mitchell's Station] road." Winder at once directed his chief of artillery, Richard Snowden Andrews, to order up rifled pieces and get them into action in the corner of the field just beyond the Gate. Andrews was a Baltimore architect, aged thirty-one, who had just received his majority. This day would be the most memorable of his life. While Andrews rounded up some rifled guns, Winder and his staff pulled down a section of the fence near the Gate.[15] A bottleneck was about to be created.

The weapons Andrews sought were scattered among three batteries, and those batteries stretched along the road back toward the schoolhouse. Edward A. "Ned" Moore of the Rockbridge Artillery (under Captain William T. Poague) was sick and had orders to tend the wounded when they began to come in. When the battery went forward, however, Moore saw it moving at a trot and hurried to catch up. From the brow of the hill in front of the schoolhouse, the Rockbridge boys could see and hear the cannonading in front. Then the battery dropped into the bottom and crossed the stream in the meadow. As they climbed out of the bottom the cannoneers entered the woods and passed the bodies of four freshly killed infantrymen "lying side by side," the victims of a Federal shell. Soon they themselves came under what John Hitner of the Rockbridge Artillery called "a heavy fire" as they neared the Crittenden Gate.[16]

While the Rockbridge men moved past the infantry to the front, guns from William H. Caskie's Hampden Artillery and Joseph H. Carpenter's Alleghany Artillery (also called the Alleghany Roughs) did likewise; all three batteries were Virginian. The leading infantry regiment on the road, the Forty-eighth Virginia of Garnett's brigade, had to halt in place under fire while Caskie went past.[17]

Major Andrews took two of Poague's rifles and one of Carpenter's through the gap in the fence out into the corner of the field and opened with them on the guns that were shooting at Early. All three rifles were ten-pounder Parrotts with good range and accuracy. They had an oblique fire against the Federals, who reacted to the pain in short order. An onlooker recalled: "At our first shot the enemy turned his guns on us with a very heavy fire." Stapleton Crutchfield, who as Jackson's chief of artillery was Major Andrews's leader, noted that the enemy response was "immediate." Early timed the opening of this fire, which came as a blessed relief to the hard-pressed gunners at the Cedars, as being only "a short time" after his own artillery began to work. The guns at the Cedars opened at about 4:00; their support at the Gate probably began to fight between 4:15 and 4:30.[18]

Joseph Carpenter's Parrott was first through the fence and into the field, but Andrews had him wait until Poague's two guns arrived before opening fire. Carpenter's brother and ranking lieutenant, John, came up with the single gun also, as was their custom in action. John Carpenter estimated in his official report that his Parrott opened fire at a range of seven hundred yards from "five or six pieces of the enemy." The air distance from the Crittenden Gate to the road intersection at the right end of the Federal line was slightly more than thirteen hundred yards, so Carpenter was underestimating the distance some (although he was a little beyond the Gate and his foe was a little short of the intersection). Whatever the range, Carpenter noted that the fire across the field "was soon returned most vigorously."[19]

The Carpenters did not wait for more than a few moments for Poague's men and guns to arrive. One of the Rockbridge rifles remained squarely in the road; one went into battery just to the right of its mate, and Carpenter's rifle was on the right. Poague also put a Napoleon into action. Caskie's single piece fired somewhere nearby. The formation was en echelon, that is, with a staggered rather than a squared alignment, presumably with the forwardmost piece being the far left one on the road. The position was tight so the caissons and limbers and teams remained in the woods to the left of the road and "some distance" to the rear. Poague's men, like Carpenter's, reported that the enemy "replied promptly" to their fire, "getting our range in a few rounds."[20]

Almost all of the subsequent deployment by Confederates on this afternoon necessarily took place by way of the Crittenden Gate. The storm of shot and shell pouring into the area did considerable harm to Southern infantry. Colonel Crutchfield reported that after the duel began, "the enemy kept up a sharp fire at this point as one near which our troops and batteries must pass in taking position." Soon after the battle, General Trimble noted in his diary that the army was blaming Snowden Andrews for the bloody bottleneck at the Gate: "It is said the battery was placed by Major A. in a bad position drawing fire on our infantry."[21] Trimble's long-range judgment against his fellow Baltimorean cannot be sustained from the narrow perspective of responsibility: Crutchfield, Winder, and Jackson all participated in handling the guns at the Gate, and among them poor Andrews was a small fish indeed.

Thomas S. Garnett's brigade began its costliest afternoon of the entire war as it moved from the schoolhouse toward the Crittenden Gate. The seventeen hundred Virginians in the brigade started on the wrong foot by being the first infantry funneled through the maelstrom at the Gate. Not long after Early left Winder at the creek in the meadow below the schoolhouse, the Forty-eighth Virginia led Garnett's brigade up the hill ahead and into the woods that ended at the Gate. When Caskie's battery galloped past, the Forty-eighth was obliged to edge off the road to give the horses and vehicles headway. While the regiment jammed tightly together on the road shoulder, a random enemy shell burst in its midst, killing five men instantly and wounding six more.[22]

The Twenty-first Virginia followed not far behind the Forty-eighth. During the halt in the meadow bottom, the companies of the Twenty-first called the roll, and then the officers ordered the men to load their weapons. When the regiment hurried up the hill toward the woods, the men on the left of the road suddenly scurried to their right to clear the way for a solid shot "that came bounding along like a boy's ball." The enormous momentum behind the ball's apparently lazy wanderings became apparent when it struck a tree stump, glanced straight up in the air, and flew rapidly out of sight. After a few more steps, the Twenty-first Virginia men came across four dead Confederates in the road and concluded that the deadly ball had killed them. (These may well have been the victims from the Forty-eighth Virginia; it is likely that they were the same bodies seen by the Rockbridge Artillery.)[23]

Colonel Garnett prudently concluded that the fire-swept road was no place for infantry moving in column, so he ordered the Forty-eighth Virginia to march leftward into the woods for a hundred yards or so, then file right and continue forward parallel to the road but under cover. The Twenty-first Virginia cheerfully followed, leaving behind a road now "fairly alive" with incoming rounds. The detour caught the Forty-second Virginia just at the back edge of the woods. That regiment halted briefly to load and then filed off to the left, never having had to march on the road after it leveled off above the meadow. As a result, the Forty-second escaped without loss even though its commander reported that the woods "were very heavily shelled." Within the relative shelter of the forest the brigade passed "an old Confederate" who was resting against a sapling with studied nonchalance. When the advancing troops asked what he was doing there, the veteran replied: "I don't want to fight. I ain't mad with anybody." "This put all in a good humor," one of his interrogators wrote, "and amidst laughter and cheers we continued the march."[24]

Despite the detour, Garnett's brigade still was headed for the warm vicinity of the Crittenden Gate. When the brigade commander came opposite the Gate at a point one hundred yards or so to its left, he halted the column and the men stoically lay down to endure the artillery fire, which they did for about thirty minutes. (The official reports of the Forty-second and Forty-eighth time this ordeal at "near half an hour" and "half an hour" respectively.) William W. Patteson, who was entering his first battle with the Twenty-first Virginia, understandably thought it went on for more like two hours. Patteson wrote that "the shells and solid shot cut the trees down all around us."[25]

Huddling helpless under artillery fire is about the harshest medicine infantry can take, and irrational though it might have been, the men doubtless were universally glad to stand up and move forward again after the half-hour halt. Colonel Garnett had his marching orders straight from Winder, who was hanging around the artillery and playing at gunner. Garnett was "to file to the left along a by-road in the woods . . . as far as I could under cover of the woods." Once Garnett had moved as far to the left as possible, Winder said, he should get into line of battle and then hurl his brigade against the flank of the "nearest battery" of the enemy. Winder and the artillery around the Gate would keep Garnett's prey busy in the meanwhile. Winder's orders as carried out by Garnett carried the brigade to the skirt of the woods that looked east across the wheatfield.[26]

Because Garnett had not been beyond the Gate, McHenry Howard

79

of Winder's staff served as a guide. Garnett and Howard again kept the column inside the wood line by about a hundred yards, but even so some of the artillery pouring into the corner of the field at the Gate fell among them. Howard saw another shell strike down four or five men just behind him, doubtless in the unfortunate Forty-eighth again.[27]

The Virginians covered "some 400 yards" through the woods, parallel to the road, before they came to the very narrow wagon track leading north through the woods. The wagon track was roughly perpendicular to the main road and parallel to the long western edge of the soon-to-be-famous wheatfield. It lay within the woods no more than one hundred yards from the western edge of the field. When the Forty-second Virginia struck the wagon track it turned left, advanced up it for about one hundred yards, then faced right and moved in line through the woods to a fence at the edge of the field.[28]

The Forty-second Virginia covered a frontage of about one hundred yards, beginning one hundred yards north of the main road and stretching northward to a point two hundred yards north of the road. To the left of the Forty-second was the First Virginia Battalion (the Irish Battalion), which for no apparent reason was not tied in with the Forty-second's left. The front of the First Battalion rested in the woods "about twenty yards from the fence." Major John Seddon of Fredericksburg, a brother of the Confederate secretary of war, commanded the battalion. Seddon reported that "the woods were so dense that no other portion of our brigade could be seen from our position," but he did nothing to rectify that startling circumstance.[29]

The brigade's entire line lay under cover of the woods, but unfortunately for the Southerners, not all of it faced the wheatfield. The First Virginia Battalion faced east across the field and to its right the Forty-second Virginia did likewise. Half of the Forty-eighth Virginia also faced east from a position in the edge of the woods on the right of the Forty-second, but the rest of the Forty-eighth bent rightward and faced south, as did the entire Twenty-first Virginia. Garnett's brigade formed an enormous backward "L"—or perhaps it would be more apt to describe the formation as shaped like a boomerang. The Forty-eighth Virginia's position, described by Garnett in an unpublished document, "was in line, the right wing facing the road, the left at right angles, and facing the wheatfield." The published official report of the regiment expressed the same concept differently: the regiment was "so thrown into line as to cause the right and left flanks to form right angles with each other."[30]

The Twenty-first Virginia was admirably situated to witness the artillery duel and to shoot at anything that might come Jubal Early's way. The left of the Twenty-first began about 150 yards from the wheatfield and ran west toward the Gate. The regiment's main line was back in the woods "about 40 paces" from the road. A small party advanced through the forty yards of trees to the edge of the road on the far left of the regiment "to keep watch."[31] It was a good idea, but as it turned out they were looking in the wrong direction.

While Garnett obediently headed into his precarious position, W. B. Taliaferro's brigade followed the first part of his route. Taliaferro's three Virginia and two Alabama regiments were as hot (it was nearly 100° by now) and exhausted as any of their comrades. A field officer in Garnett's brigade later noted that Taliaferro's men were particularly frazzled on August 9 because the commotion the preceding night in their vicinity had left most of them with no sleep at all.[32]

Taliaferro remained at the schoolhouse when Garnett's brigade went forward to the Gate. Then when Garnett left the vicinity of the Gate and headed for his boomerang position along the wheatfield, Taliaferro advanced and took up Garnett's abandoned spot near the Gate. At least some of Taliaferro's men marched in the road rather than under cover of the woods as had Garnett. The raw Forty-seventh Alabama, for instance, apparently came straight down the road the entire distance. These neophytes had their good luck charms along. Although shells were "bursting over our heads" the whole way, most of the deadly metal fell beyond them harmlessly. In Lieutenant Colonel James W. Jackson's quaint phrasing, "as we were within the range given to their guns no damage was done to my regiment."[33]

Taliaferro himself reported that the brigade moved not in the road but "parallel to the road." He apparently used the woods south of the road, whereas Garnett had advanced on the other side of the road. Perhaps only the innocent Alabamians used the road proper, and they seem to have gotten away with it. By Taliaferro's account, those of his troops moving under cover in the woods still "were subjected to a heavy discharge of shell and shot from the enemy's artillery, thrown mostly at random into the woods." When the head of Taliaferro's column reached the vicinity of the Gate it halted, and the entire brigade faced left toward the road and lay down.[34]

The five regiments under Taliaferro were in the midst of the developing Confederate position, in fact at its very heart, but their orientation was about as far from being useful as could have been achieved by design. They huddled under the shelling "a short dis-

81

tance back in the woods and out of sight of the enemy," and squarely 90° away from either of the positions where they might have been useful. Major Henry C. Wood, commanding the Thirty-seventh Virginia, reported that his instructions were to support the batteries. Of course, the mere presence of the infantry gave some support, its orientation notwithstanding. Wood also reported that his men were "very much exposed to the enemy's shells, which were continually bursting over and around." The major was chatting at the edge of the field with Captain John V. Duff of Company C, who "was in a most cheerful mood," when an enemy round caught the junior officer and killed him. A Georgian nearby complained that nothing in his experience was "more detestable than the horrid bombshells." He claimed he could feel "the wind that the shells created as they passed over my head, and they make a most horrible noise."[35]

The noise of artillery rounds crashing and crackling through the trees overhead was nerve-racking, making the thick woods seem like an enemy instead of the friendly shield they constituted. A private in the Tenth Virginia exclaimed in his memoirs: "Oh, my! but the grape and canister hailed and crashed among the limbs and brush about our heads." Field artillery did not use grapeshot, and Taliaferro's men were far beyond canister range, but the lad's distaste for his circumstances was real enough. Another member of the Tenth Virginia crouching in the regimental line noticed Stonewall Jackson right in front of them, writing a dispatch. An uneasy officer suggested: "General, we had better get away; the enemy have a good range." The enemy made a prophet of him in an instant when a shell hit a pine tree nearby and spewed bark and splinters all over Jackson's paper. He brushed it off calmly, the Tenth Virginia boy remembered later, finished his writing, and then moved on.[36]

The report of Major Simeon T. Walton of the Twenty-third Virginia leaves room for speculation whether that regiment was away from the rest of the brigade at this juncture, in the woods south of the Gate stretching in the direction of Early's line. A much more likely explanation is that Major Walton misidentified the battery to his front and actually spent the time with the other four regiments of Taliaferro's brigade. In either case, the Twenty-third moved with the rest of the brigade after this interlude, so Walton's estimate of the time of the halt—"nearly an hour"—would apply to the other regiments as well. No one else offered a time estimate. Walton's account of what happened to the Twenty-third during those long minutes has

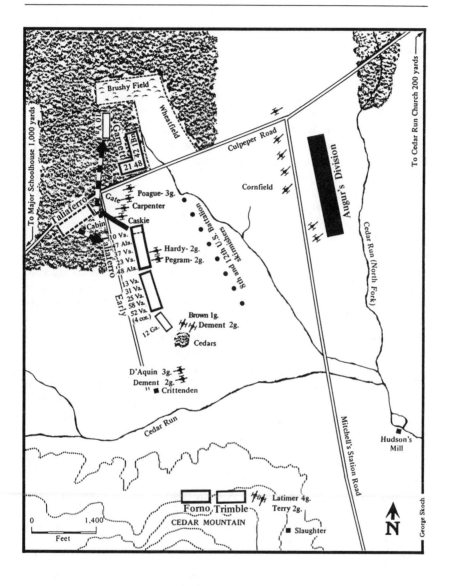

Taliaferro Takes Position, Federal Skirmishers Advance, 5:00–5:30

a familiar tone: "The shells of the enemy . . . were tearing the forest to atoms."[37]

While his brigade quailed under the onslaught with no means of response, General Taliaferro examined the ground around the Gate. His description is important for what it tells of Early at this hour. Early did not extend his left anywhere near the Gate. Taliaferro described the rectangle of open ground from a vantage at its northwest extremity, mentioning the cornfield prominently. "A brigade under General Early," Taliaferro wrote, "protected by the fall of the hills, occupied the *right* [emphasis added] of this field in line of battle, directly fronting the general line of the enemy, as far as we could make it out."[38] Before many minutes passed, Taliaferro received orders to fill the gap from the Gate to Early's left; a few minutes more and he would be under violent attack there.

Taliaferro's move southward, and the concurrent wheel through 90° to face nominally eastward, must have taken place at about 5:30 P.M. It was completed in the nick of time. During the short maneuver there came a merciful lull in the artillery fire. Taliaferro's brigade moved in line of battle, keeping the ground swell along the Crittenden Lane between itself and the enemy. The order to move "was obeyed with alacrity," according to one regimental commander, probably because of eagerness to get out of the noisy, shell-torn woods. The brigade's route was "over the ridge" near the lane, then over the fence on the east side of the lane and into the presence of enemy infantry skulking in the corn. Reporting officers variously estimated the enemy presence at three to four hundred yards in front.[39]

The formations and intentions of the enemy in the corn were unclear. William B. Taliaferro quickly encountered the same concerns about what might be hidden in the creases of the rolling terrain that plagued Early and others. "A corn field in front of this position . . . concealed the movements of the enemy," Taliaferro complained, "and the undulations of the country made reconnaissances very difficult."[40]

There can be no confusion about Taliaferro's battle position despite Early's omissions on the subject and Jackson's innocent emulation of Early's report. Several generations of historical writing have compounded those basic errors. A key witness, though not the only one, was James A. Walker, the commander of the Thirteenth Virginia Infantry at Cedar Mountain. The Thirteenth Virginia was Early's left flank regiment, and Taliaferro's brigade, Walker wrote, was "immediately on my left." Fortunately, Walker's personal set of the

Official Records survives, and his marginal annotations for Cedar Mountain include a detailed drawing of the position. Walker's sketch shows Taliaferro's brigade perpendicular to the main road and almost entirely on its south side. A tiny anchor across the road, tied in with Garnett's brigade, is hard to verify, but the general configuration is clear.[41]

The Forty-eighth Alabama stood on the right of the brigade, adjacent to the Thirteenth Virginia at the left of Early's brigade. To the left of the Forty-eighth Alabama came the Twenty-third Virginia, whose commander called its piece of the irregular ridge "the brow of a low eminence." Next to the left (nominally northward) lay the Thirty-seventh Virginia and beyond it was the Forty-seventh Alabama. When the brigade first went into the position, its fifth regiment, the Tenth Virginia, was to the left of the Forty-seventh Alabama. The Tenth was closest to the Gate and suffered from the attraction that vicinity had for Union artillery rounds. None of the other regiments complained of shelling after the move, but the Tenth was hard hit. Its commander reported that the regiment "suffered considerably." Private Tilman S. Weaver of Company K and two mates each lost a leg to a single shell. (Weaver died in Page County in 1909.) An even more deadly round wounded seven men in the same company; one of the wounded was half of the designated stretcher team for the unit. By the time the bearers came back for a third trip, the two remaining wounded, Lieutenant John W. Mauck and Sergeant James O. Wood, had died. Their comrades managed to get the two corpses to the rear at about midnight, by which time most of the survivors had gone almost two full days without sleep.[42] Before Company K pulled trigger, it had lost 20 percent of its strength to two loud explosions in quick succession.

The Tenth Virginia doubtless was glad enough to be ordered away from the Gate when that word arrived. Someone had recognized the difficult situation facing Garnett up along the wheatfield and sent the Tenth Virginia in that direction. By this time a storm was about to break against Garnett and Taliaferro and Early. The movement of the Tenth Virginia was exactly what the Confederate line needed (albeit in more volume), but the regiment was too late to be of much use. A captain in the Tenth noted that they were "Marched & Counter Marched, under Grape & Shell until the Men are Nearly exhausted the Reg having suffered a great deal from Shot & Shell."[43]

The artillery duel that began before Garnett's and Taliaferro's movements and roared accompaniment to them quickly had expanded to involve many more Confederate guns than the three at the Gate and the three at the Cedars. Major Courtney's second cluster a little behind the Cedars joined in almost simultaneously (their deployment was discussed jointly, above). The knots of guns at the Gate and the Cedars soon found help—highly effective help—from the dominating ground to their right on the shoulder of Cedar Mountain.

The guns on the mountainside necessarily were preceded by infantry to secure the ground. Trimble's brigade—one regiment each from Alabama, Georgia, and North Carolina—labored up the mountain under cover and headed toward its eastern tip. Confederate skirmishers easily dispersed the few enemy they encountered on the crest. When his regiments reached their destination, Trimble kept them concealed from detection by the Northerners far below and to their left. Dick Ewell soon arrived in person and, in Trimble's words, "decided to drag up Latimer's battery . . . and place it in position . . . which was done promptly."[44]

The difficulty of the task of getting artillery up the mountain was hardly conveyed by Trimble's simple phrase "done promptly," but "drag up" described the technique aptly. E. V. White's independent cavalry company, the Comanches, had not signed on as draymen, but that was how they spent an hour in the enervating heat of August 9. The dismounted cavalrymen pushed the guns up the hill "by hand," reported Campbell Brown of Ewell's staff, with exertion he understandably described as "immense effort." Latimer's men obviously took part too, as did some infantry from the Twenty-first Georgia. Some of the Georgians "over-exerted themselves" dragging on the guns and caissons by rope and "several suffered sun-stroke." An enemy shell exploded near one laboring group and wounded Lieutenant William D. Wright of Company D deeply in the groin. The lieutenant was apparently dead when he was carried off, but he recovered.[45]

Trimble's men and Latimer's guns gathered under cover around the hillside parsonage of the Reverend Philip Slaughter. The minister's father had long been in the area, and the family's name was the source for Cedar Mountain's ominous alternate name in the locale—Slaughter's Mountain. The Reverend Slaughter was fifty-three at the time of the battle. In 1860 his wife (aged forty-nine) and two girls in their twenties had resided with him; the family's net worth was about $13,000. A neighbor living within a few houses of the Slaughters must have taken massive doses of heckling: John Pope, a twenty-four-year-old saddler with a wife and two children, obviously was no close relation to the general of the same name known for his reprehensible attitude toward Southern civilians.[46]

Captain Joseph White Latimer, commander of the guns manhandled to cover near the Slaughter house, had been educated at Virginia Military Institute and blossomed into one of those brilliant and energetic young artillery officers with whom the Army of Northern Virginia was peculiarly blessed. Latimer was a newly minted captain in August 1862; he would be acting chief of artillery of Ewell's division within a few months; and he would be dead in less than a year of wounds suffered at Gettysburg. At Cedar Mountain he was, astonishingly, eighteen years old. One of Latimer's men wrote of the youngster: "I believe he is the very best Arty. Capt. in Genl. Lee's Army and would make the best Maj. & I know we have worse Generals by far than he wd. make."[47]

Smooth-cheeked Captain Latimer and his gunners had hurried ahead of the toiling cannon-movers in order to calculate distances and cut their shell fuses. When the weapons arrived, they were ready to load them promptly. Then, under Ewell's personal supervision, the crew hustled the guns around the Slaughter house and onto its front lawn. In the process they crunched over "at least a thousand books." A bibliophile present, together presumably with every other civilized being, was irate at the Northern vandalism that preyed on libraries. The book lover, an officer in the Twenty-first Georgia, noticed classics in Latin, Greek, and French mingled (ironically) with shattered copies of New England authors such as Longfellow and Whittier. The saddened officer professed to see a trend: whenever a library fell into enemy hands, "those barbarous iconoclasts" systematically "trampled and destroyed" it. There remained no question about the survival of the Reverend Slaughter's library after it became the platform for artillery in action.[48]

Ewell described the artillery aerie near Slaughter's as "a commanding position," which it was indeed. No guns put into action by the Army of Northern Virginia enjoyed a better one during four years of war. Stonewall Jackson's report suggested that the elevation variance was 200 feet. In fact, it was not much more than half that amount (430 to 550 feet above sea level, or thereabouts), but the difference was enormous by any calculation; more would have been too much. To heighten the effect, Latimer's position enjoyed a distinctly oblique angle of fire against the Federal guns on the Mitchell's Station Road. His guns and those of his friends far leftward near the Gate fought

The Slaughter house. (Library of Congress)

from positions more than one mile apart yet they were firing against the same targets. Ewell and Latimer had achieved for their army the cannoneer's dream: widely separated units delivered converging fire onto a concentrated foe. When Latimer's guns "blazed away" (as Campbell Brown put it), their superb position surprised the Federals far below. Jackson noted with restraint that the battery on the mountain had a "marked effect upon the enemy's batteries."⁴⁹

For its first few minutes in action, Latimer's piece operated with a most unusual crew. The Virginia cavalrymen of the Comanches who had brought the weapon up by main force helped the young captain and his few men to fire it until the rest of the battery and cannoneers came up. One of the volunteer gunners noted with pride that the very first round exploded right atop a U.S. battery on the plain. The initial Federal riposte "sent a shell within two feet of the muzzle" of the Confederate gun and struck its trail. That was not so enjoyable.⁵⁰

The remainder of Latimer's weapons arrived in short order, except for one rifle that Major Courtney had used earlier and turned loose tardily. It arrived on the mountain without missing much of the fight. Latimer also was joined by the same two-gun section of the Bedford Artillery, under Lieutenant Nathaniel Terry, that had fired the battle's opening cannon shot against Federal cavalry hours earlier. When all of the guns got going, Ewell noted with satisfaction, though it can hardly have surprised him under the circumstances, that they were punishing the Federals considerably. The hillside batteries also drew "much of the artillery fire which had been concentrated against our left wing," Ewell reported.[51]

Latimer's fire was a boon to Confederates all over the valley, but it must have seemed like the last straw to sixty-three-year-old Catherine Crittenden. The widow and a bevy of dependent females, both white and black, had abandoned their shell-torn home. The fleeing women sloshed through Cedar Run and its surrounding bogs and sought shelter in the bosom of the mountain. Now the war had found them even there. Federal shells "made a hideous noise as they passed overhead." Fortunately for the women, Captain William C. Oates of the Fifteenth Alabama, who came across them, was of a different ilk than Chaplain Denison of Rhode Island. The women "were frightened so much they scarcely knew where they were," Oates wrote. The captain directed them to a safe haven and followed their directions down the slope to find a young lady whom they had left behind in a faint. She was, Oates insisted, "as perfect a beauty as was ever reared on the soil of the Old Dominion." He helped her up the hill and out of danger, and there the story ends: "I left the young lady and never saw her again."[52]

Noncombatants of the other gender could not count on such tender treatment at the front lines, particularly from sharp-tongued Dick Ewell. The general spied a brilliantly caparisoned quartermaster on the mountain and bluntly asked for his identity and mission. When the man identified himself as a captain and quartermaster in a Virginia regiment, Ewell threw up both hands in one of his characteristic jerky gestures and squeaked: "Great Heavens! A Quartermaster on a battle-field; who ever heard of such a thing before?" The general then offered a line as old as the genus staff officer when he added, "But as you are here I will make you useful as well as ornamental." The quartermaster carried a message or two and then went back to his train, carrying along a good story on himself and on "Old Bald Head" Ewell which quickly became a standard part of army lore.[53]

Another story of noncombatants under fire came out of that afternoon on the mountain. A cluster of chaplains and surgeons sought the magnificent vantage point and relative safety of the mountainside. So many mounted targets prompted a noisy if harmless volley from Union guns far below. That was enough for the party, which fled incontinently to cover. The foremost rider in the race was a black lad in the entourage of a surgeon, who happened to be on a superb mount. When the doctor caught up, he began to abuse the youngster for riding his horse so hard. The lad responded with irrefragable logic: "I didn't like the whizzing of them things any better than the rest did—and I don't think you ought to blame me, Doctor, 'cause my horse can beat yours running."[54]

As a counterpoint to the cheerful derision for staff officers, the record must show that Major James Gavin Field went into the thickest of the fight at Cedar Mountain. Field was quartermaster on A. P. Hill's staff. His venture at Cedar Mountain cost Field a leg, but he returned to duty in less than a year. After the war the major served as attorney general of Virginia, and in 1892 he was a third-party candidate for vice-president of the United States.[55]

Some of the Confederates on the hilltop obviously took time to observe the antics of the staff tourists and record them for posterity, but most focused their gaze on the panorama unfolding far below. A Georgian watching prudently "from behind protections" called the scene "the prettiest artillery duel ever witnessed during the war." He professed to know that Latimer and Terry were throwing shells captured from Banks in the Valley, which added spice to the entertainment. The tremendous advantage in elevation gave the Southerners the advantage of plunging fire, which they used to pound their opponents with relative impunity. The Louisiana infantry of Forno's brigade joined the audience but with less caution than the Georgians. Some of the bayou boys lay on the lip of the mountain in front of Latimer's guns. When incoming rounds tore the ground, the Louisianians dashed to the spot and "cooly" sat there, citing the principle about lightning never striking twice. Unfortunately, "some of them lost their heads by the operation in spite of the proverb."[56]

The virtually unopposed occupation of Cedar Mountain by Southern men and guns produced consequences difficult to exaggerate. The absolute dominance of the position there must have been apparent to the rawest private in either army. In Cedar Mountain, the Confederates held an impervious flanking bastion for defense and a formidable artillery emplacement to support the offensive.

Latimer's gun platform was the third Confederate artillery concentration to come into action. Courtney's pieces at and behind the Cedars were first up; the group at the Gate followed quickly; then came Latimer and Terry. The fourth and final Southern artillery deployment came about halfway between the Cedars and the Gate, in front of Early's left and therefore east of the Crittenden Lane. The group

A 1989 view of the battlefield from Latimer's gun position on a shelf of Cedar Mountain. The Crittenden House site is in the lower left and the Gate lies just below the central horizon. (Clark B. Hall)

contained two rifles each from the batteries of the redoubtable Willie Pegram and the Middlesex Artillery under Lieutenant William B. Hardy. These two last sections did not arrive until the duel was well along, but in the interest of clarity this narrative will deposit them in their appointed place before discussing the artillery fight in detail.[57]

Lieutenant Colonel Reuben Lindsay Walker, Hill's artillery chief, led the two sections forward. Walker was a strapping, handsome, thirty-five-year-old graduate of Virginia Military Institute. A sergeant in one of Walker's batteries referred to him as "a nincompoop," but higher authority thought enough of Walker to make him one of the Confederacy's very few artillery generals. Walker generally was called by his middle name, but his daughter later wrote that his nickname was "Old Rube."[58]

Whenever Willie Pegram was at hand, higher authority had little need to provide leadership, but Walker sited the four rifles himself. The lieutenant colonel certainly went with the guns as far as the Crittenden Gate because he commented with opprobrium that Caskie's location there "had converged the fire of the enemy to a point necessary to be passed by all of our troops." The fire-swept bottleneck was not a healthy locale, although Pegram's men saw Jackson himself near there. Walker's two sections, however, headed for an even worse spot. They galloped south down the Crittenden Lane, then east across the fields and unlimbered en echelon, Pegram's section on the right, Hardy's to his left. Colonels Crutchfield (Pegram) and Walker (Hardy) later differed on which section held the forward leg of the echelon formation.[59]

Walker's report declared with some nonchalance that the guns unlimbered "within 150 yards of the enemy's skirmishers." The ensuing excitement came about because those hostile skirmishers lay hidden in the tall corn. The Confederates did not realize the danger they were in, although they could see a strong enemy line behind a fence *beyond* the cornfield. Closer at hand, a detachment of U.S. Regulars from the Eighth and Twelfth United States Infantry Battalion, commanded by Captain Thomas G. Pitcher, hunkered in the cornfield and began to shoot up the Confederates. The opportunity appealed to other Federals, who closed in as well. Early saw the danger in an instant and rushed some of his infantry up "with a shout" in support. To the Twelfth Georgia, on Early's far right, the advance seemed to reach the pieces "just in time to save them." During the summer of 1863, Early revisited the field in company with some staff officers and during his tour commented about "the enemy's rapid advance when our battery was run out." When the Federals sullenly (and temporarily) melted back into the corn, Captain Pitcher's detachment hung firm at the edge of the field and maintained its fire.[60]

Willie Pegram always made good copy, and his reckless dash into danger at Cedar Mountain received considerable attention. Two days later in Richmond, War Department clerk John B. Jones, who was destined to become the capital's most renowned diarist, highlighted the close call and its successful outcome in his entry for August 11.[61]

The gallop into action by Pegram and Hardy completed the string of Confederate artillery strong points along the longitude of the Crittenden Lane. The left anchor was around the Gate (five pieces); the right anchor was on the mountain (six pieces); between lay Pegram's cluster (four pieces) and the stronghold at and behind the Cedars (eight pieces). Some guns fell out of the exchange and others came up, but twenty-three pieces of artillery constituted the primary Confederate force. The Federal batteries opposite them enjoyed a very small edge in numbers.[62]

By the time Pegram and Hardy opened fire perilously close to enemy skirmishers, the intense artillery duel of which they became a part had been roaring for about an hour and was something more than half over. Major Courtney's guns opened from the Cedars at about 4:00 P.M., joined promptly by the guns at the Gate and then by Latimer's and Terry's. Jubal Early and Stonewall Jackson each estimated that the artillery held sway on the field for about two hours: "perhaps for two hours or more" (Early) and "for some two hours" (Jackson). A private in the ranks of the Rockbridge Artillery noted at the time that he was engaged "for about 2 hours."[63]

To put the concurrent infantry deployments into time perspective, General Taliaferro remained at the Gate for fifteen minutes after the guns there opened (and thus about thirty minutes after the first fire from the Cedars) before returning to his brigade to await the orders that eventually moved it forward to the Gate and then beyond it.[64]

The three guns at the Cedars were admirably posted. Their vehicles and teams and supernumeraries had shelter behind the knoll, and the guns themselves operated from "behind the clump of cedars." Colonel Crutchfield reported that the guns at the Cedars and their five mates just to their right rear "were capitally served, and evidently damaged the enemy severely." Courtney praised them even more enthusiastically. Only Dement's men had been under fire before, but all "behaved like veterans."[65]

The three pieces of D'Aquin and two of Dement back closer to the Crittenden House did not operate from quite so ideal a situation, but they contributed a steady fire. One of Dement's drivers, a boy from Baltimore, had carried ammunition for a time until the regular Number 5 crew member caught up. Then he "commenced cutting shell, as they said they could not cut them fast enough." As the eager youngster went about his volunteer task, a shell burst either over or under the limber and he came back to consciousness twenty-five feet away. A piece of the exploding shell had caught him firmly on the short ribs of his left side. "It made me see stars," he wrote in his diary, "and . . . it made me mad and I cursed and told the boys to do there worst."[66]

The Marylander's comrades a thousand yards to his left were in even worse shape. The configuration of the field left the artillerists at the Gate silhouetted against a tree-lined corner, where they were painfully easy targets. One of the men suffering under the heavy fire poured into the corner explained: "Our position, being at the apex of a right angle of open ground with the two sides bordered by woods, gave . . . a fair mark for . . . converging fire and soon the din of bursting shells . . . was quite appalling, made more so from the splintering of tree branches overhead." The incoming rounds seemed to consist principally of shell and case shot. One of the

Rockbridge men noticed "for the first time, a singular noise made by some of the shells fired at us . . . quite like the shrill note of a tree-frog on a big scale." He later deduced that this ominous-sounding "new engine of war" was the three-inch rifled gun, which soon became a popular weapon.[67]

That ordnance of many sorts and sounds came across the field is attested by the official Federal tabulation of rounds fired that day—3,213 of them. No one calculated net Confederate expenditure, or if so it does not survive, but the two engaged Parrott rifles of the Rockbridge Artillery gave evidence of the frenzied activity to which they were subjected. One became unserviceable within thirty minutes of rapid use because the vent became enlarged. The other Rockbridge rifle stayed in action but soon exhausted all of its ammunition in the limber chest and had to be returned to its caisson for replenishment.[68]

The 3,213 rounds expended by the Federals did not find a target much more often than 2 percent of the time. A member of the Tenth Maine who passed through the Gate after the battle as a captive noticed "several dead horses some broken artillery and wrecked caissons and some fifty yards further a row of dead men perhaps fifteen or twenty laid side by side on the grass." The bodies doubtless were those of the unfortunate Forty-eighth Virginia men and other infantrymen caught in closed ranks during their approach march. The "broken artillery" must have been the two guns reported by Crutchfield as "dismounted by the enemy's fire"; their identity is uncertain.[69]

One of the Confederate officers quoted above about the "appalling" shelling and noise went on to admit that "there was more noise than execution"—a phrase that would make a fitting epitaph for most Civil War artillery usage, excepting, of course, the deadly scything of canister. One artillerist claimed that no private soldier in the batteries was hit, although "this proved to be a very dangerous place for officers." One shell ricocheted past Captain Willie Caskie, who stood watching his single rifle perform near the Gate. The shell either brushed Caskie's backside or threw a large limb against his back with a whack that knocked him "eight or ten feet and his red cap some feet further." The impact propelled both Willie and the red artillery hat through some thick bushes. When the captain and his kepi were reunited, he staggered up to a fellow officer "in a half dazed way" and displayed the marks of his very close call on the back of his uniform. Caskie escaped with a whole hide, but at about the

*Brigadier General Charles S. Winder seemed to many observers to
be among the brightest prospects in Jackson's army and perhaps
the most distinguished Marylander in Confederate service.*

same time Lieutenant Archibald Graham of the Rockbridge Artillery
received a painful wound and Captain Joe Carpenter suffered a
head wound that eventually proved to be mortal.[70]

One of the 3,213 Federal shells had General Charles S. Winder's
name on it. The general had been moving his infantry around, apparently without adequate attention, while concentrating most of his
energies on the opening stages of the artillery duel at the Gate. For
those details Winder was, to use a modern bureaucratic phrase, over-
qualified. After his graduation from the U.S. Military Academy,
Winder had served as a regular officer in two artillery regiments for

five years. He was in his element at the Gate, afoot and jacketless, intently spotting the rounds of his ad hoc battery through field glasses. Poague's two guns were just in front of the Gate, the left one squarely in the main road. Winder took up position near the left gun ("right beside" it, Poague wrote) and actively directed the fire of both pieces. As he did so, there flew over his head "a constant stream of shells tearing through the trees and bursting close by."[71]

At about 4:45 there came a lull in the Federal response. Both Rockbridge rifles were still in operation (which means that no more than half an hour had passed since they opened, and the gun with the enlarged vent had not yet left). Garnett's brigade recently had passed in the direction of the wheatfield, and McHenry Howard was in the same vicinity guiding the infantry in the proper deployment. The lull was occasioned by some rearrangement of the Federal positions that Winder could see through his glasses. In vain he yelled an order at the gunners to his left: the cacophony overwhelmed the general's words, even during a period of slightly decreased fire. The nearest artillerist was Ned Moore, who walked toward Winder to catch what he was saying. The general cupped his hand to his mouth and leaned toward Moore to shout. The shout never left his lips. The inexorable fate that had Winder leaning to his left had put him in the path of a Federal shell, which went between his left side and arm and mangled him horribly before passing on.[72]

As the horrified men around the Gate watched, Winder "fell straight back at full length, and lay quivering on the ground." The deadly shell had torn all the flesh from the inside of Winder's left arm, but amazingly he retained some use of the arm. The left side of the general's chest cavity, however, was shattered beyond repair. From Carpenter's nearby gun, C. A. Fonerden could see "a tremendous hole . . . torn in his side." Ned Moore, at the distance of a few paces, noted that the general's side had been mangled "fearfully." Moore remembered clearly the orders from Winder a few hours earlier that only specifically detailed men should leave their posts to carry off the wounded, so he turned back to his gun and "went to work."[73]

Snowden Andrews and Fonerden and one or two others put the general on a stretcher and carried him behind the Gate a short distance to escape the most "withering" of the fire. Andrews then rode hastily beyond the Gate and came across McHenry Howard, who had pointed Garnett's brigade toward its position and was riding back to find Winder. Howard found his general "not suffering as much pain as he would have suffered if the shock had not been so great." The aide leaned over and asked if Winder recognized him? "Oh, yes." The fatally stricken general's mind wandered to home scenes. He spoke sadly of his family and paid little heed to the well-wishers around him. Surgeons confirmed, though it was hardly necessary, that "there was not the slightest hope," and a chaplain offered comforting words. Then some men lifted the stretcher and carried General Winder down the road toward the schoolhouse, away from his last battlefield.[74]

McHenry Howard and John Francis O'Brien, another of Winder's aides, accompanied the stretcher bearers. Almost at once they met Keith Boswell of Jackson's staff, who rode back and secured a better stretcher. The mournful party also passed the Stonewall Brigade somewhere near the schoolhouse as the men were forming up to move forward. Jackson met Boswell soon after Boswell came across Winder's party and learned the details of his protégé's mortal wound then if not before. William B. Taliaferro assumed command of the division even though he was in complete ignorance of the plans of either Jackson or Winder. In his report Taliaferro referred to Winder as "brave, generous, and accomplished," but he also gave evidence of dismay over the spot in which he had been placed.[75] In fact, Winder had been so preoccupied with the artillery duel that Taliaferro probably knew about as much of the big picture as Winder had known.

Not long after Winder's wounding, the Rockbridge rifle with the excessively large vent went to the rear. It had been belching flame and smoke for some time. The men called Poague's attention to the worsening problem and fired a round to demonstrate. At the instant they fired, a tree obliquely to their front (presumably to the left of the road and toward the wheatfield) crashed to the ground, the victim of a Federal shell. Someone in authority concluded that the loose vent was yielding an enormous deflection from the target and sent the rifle away. Poague's other Parrott exhausted its ammunition and was taken for more. By the time it returned, enemy skirmishers were visible in the corn to the right front and Jackson personally ordered the crew to advance farther into the field and down the lane toward the Crittenden House.[76]

Jackson's directions to the one gun were part of an effort to clear the Gate area by moving to the right front (nominally south and east). No doubt Jackson and Andrews and Crutchfield intended both to find better offensive positions and to uncork the costly bottleneck that the Gate had become. Carpenter's one rifle took part in the move, as did Poague's Napoleon and then his returning Parrott. Caskie apparently remained near the Gate. Lieutenant John C. Carpenter, who took over from his mortally wounded brother, estimated the distance of this movement accurately at 200 yards; Crutchfield guessed 250 yards; Poague, writing late in life, stretched the distance to an impossible 400 to 500 yards. The latter two men offered the range of defensive and aggressive rationales that prompted the movement, respectively: "in order to protect the deployment of our infantry" and "to get a better chance at a Yankee battery which had been annoying us." Poague added that the obnoxious battery was the one that had hit Winder, though he hardly could have known that with certainty.[77]

The small artillery advance also owed something to the only notable fire against Federal infantry during the duel. Federals, probably only skirmishers, in the cornfield moving toward Early through the tall stalks brought down fire upon themselves from the Gate guns in their original positions. One observer estimated the Federal strength in the corn as a regiment. Andrews directed fire into the corn, including some canister, and the blue cloth melted back among the green corn. The momentum of this minor success contributed to the Confederate notion to move ahead from the Gate, even if obliquely. Poague and Carpenter made their 200-yard move sometime before Pegram and Hardy arrived in the same vicinity. Pegram and Hardy came into action no farther east than Poague and Carpenter, but perhaps 150 yards farther south.[78]

When Poague and Lieutenant Carpenter opened, Crutchfield reported, "they were excellently served" and succeeded in diverting enemy fire from the sensitive Gate region. The two-way iron storm built anew, now that all of the Confederate guns were situated, but near the climax of the duel the Southern artillerists lost another of the hands that had been controlling their work. Major R. Snowden Andrews had performed admirably on that blazing afternoon. Like his unfortunate chief General Winder, Andrews had been on sick call for an extended period, recovering from a leg wound suffered in the battles around Richmond. A colleague said of Andrews: "Anyone not of his temperament would have been away in hospital or on sick leave." The forward move by Poague and Carpenter under the major's supervision had been a success, and after a time he proposed another relocation forward. As Andrews rode rapidly behind his guns preparing this new venture, he ran directly into the path of an exploding shell and fell wounded nearly as badly as Winder had been.[79]

A jagged piece of the shell sliced open Andrews's right abdominal wall and virtually eviscerated him. The architect-cum-artillerist had the presence of mind to throw one arm across the gaping wound and grasp his horse's neck with the other, then awkwardly slid to the ground on his back. Had he fallen frontward, Andrews would have been disemboweled. Harried surgeons who glanced at his torn abdomen offered Andrews no hope. General Taliaferro gave his imprimatur to their easy forecast four days later when he lauded Major Andrews in his official report and reported him as being wounded, "I fear mortally." When Stonewall Jackson's official report finally appeared, it tendered "especial credit . . . to Major Andrews for the success and gallantry with which his guns were directed."[80]

As might be expected, the Confederates thought that all of their artillery made a considerable impact on its targets. General Taliaferro claimed that the batteries posted at the Gate and then "in the open field to the right" had a "very great" effect on their opponents, "to a great extent silencing the enemy's guns." Major Courtney thought the effect of his two masses on the enemy "was evidently terrible," although he acknowledged the tenacity of his foe. Jubal Early thought his division's guns had "considerable effect." All Confederate witnesses agreed on their success in forcing the northernmost Federal battery back about three hundred yards (most even agreed on the distance involved).[81] That notable retrograde movement coincided with the lull of sorts at about 4:45, during which Winder was wounded.

Northern accounts agree to a surprising extent with Confederate sources on the effect of the Southern fire. A newspaperman reported that the Rebel gunners' aim on this afternoon "was exceedingly correct." A single shell killed six members of General Nathaniel P. Banks's bodyguard. A Connecticut infantryman looking on noted with chagrin that Confederate batteries were "very effective" against the entire length of the Northern line. A New Jersey cavalryman was convinced that his unit's desperate bluff of an attack cowed Rebels opposite them into quiescence (none apparently noticed), but as the horsemen fell back a stray round struck down two lieutenants and several enlisted men and horses.[82]

Professional soldiers across the field from Andrews and Latimer and Courtney acknowledged the Southerners' success. General George S. Greene held his brigade of two small regiments under shelter behind the Mitchell's Station Road ridge, supporting Captain Freeman McGilvery's Sixth Maine battery. Greene's manuscript report announced that the Maine guns killed "the rebel Genl Winder" and lauded the accuracy of the return fire, "their round shot striking the top of the ridge & falling among the men & horses of the command."[83]

Captain Clermont L. Best, Banks's chief of artillery, was more grudging in his praise, but it shone through his complaints. Best's unpublished report announced, without any apparent discomfort, that his guns were spread around where each battery could be supported by its accustomed brigade. The Confederates' nascent and growing battalion system, which would revolutionize the use of artillery, had not yet become popular in Federal artillery service. Best insisted that not only the guns on the mountain but each Southern cluster commanded his own and that even his opponents at the Gate were "pretty well masked." The plunging fire from Latimer and Terry on the mountain "was, evidently, of heavier metal." (It was not, but the advantage of elevation must have made it seem so.) Captain Best joined Jackson and Early and others across the valley in timing the duel's duration as two hours. Best reported the loss of thirteen men killed in the artillery alone, twenty-three wounded, and forty-eight horses killed. Those losses—at least three times as high as the Confederates suffered—he offered as evidence that Southern "practice was not of a superior order judging from the large amount of shot hurled at us."[84]

According to local lore, Yankees were not the only victims of the Confederate barrage. George Curtis, who lived in a small frame cottage over which shells screamed, sought a safer haven in the basement of a neighbor named James Inskeep. The move was a bad one. A "spent cannon ball" found Curtis in Inskeep's basement and killed him.[85]

About half a mile north of the intersection of the Mitchell's Station Road with the Culpeper Road stood another house containing frightened civilians, the home of a Mrs. Brown. General George H. Gordon, whose Second Massachusetts surrounded the place, described it as a "little cottage" that made "a pretty picture . . . with its green turf enclosed by a fence, and . . . an inviting grove of forest-trees." The New England soldiers had a great view of the semicircle of blazing Confederate guns. They credited the group at the Gate with the most effective fire. Women and children in the house had been fran-

The Brown house in 1912. (Gould Papers, Duke University)

tic at the arrival of enemy troops but refused to accept advice to leave. One of the Massachusetts men noticed that all during the artillery's roar, "a beautiful boy of eighteen months . . . had slept through the heavy artillery-thunder, while his mother always stood between her child and the guns as though her body could shelter him."[86]

Southern civilians all the way back in Culpeper were frightened by the man-made thunder, many of them with the certain knowledge that their loved ones huddled at the eye of the storm. A Federal staff officer commented that the windows and porches of the county seat were crowded with "pale, anxious faces of women, children, and grandsires." Even at that distance the noise reverberated loudly and seemed very close.[87]

As the fireworks display neared its end and infantry prepared to take center stage, the participants in the noisy and extended long-distance duel probably remained too busy to reflect on lessons learned or to attempt an analytical balance sheet. From afar it is easy to judge that Confederate ordnance shortcomings kept their success on August 9 from escalating into absolute dominance. Jackson had twice as many available guns as Banks. The Confederates, however, of necessity employed relatively few long-range pieces and too many weak howitzers and six-pounder guns. When all of Jackson's suitable cannon reached position, they were a couple of guns short of parity. Had the all but worthless small stuff in Jackson's arsenal been instead rifles or even Napoleons, his artillery success between 4:00 and 5:45 P.M. would have been redoubled.

By coincidence, August 9, 1862, was the day on which the Tredegar Iron Works in Richmond cast its very first bronze Napoleon. By further coincidence, one of the two technical wizards most badly needed by Tredegar to keep that essential industry functioning was stuck in the army—Private W. L. Flaherty of the First Virginia Battalion. The First Virginia Battalion was about to be shattered at Cedar Mountain.[88]

An artillery duel between even numbers in the summer of 1862 normally could have been expected to develop in favor of the men with the heavier, longer-range, more accurate guns, the men with ordnance that exploded approximately as intended—the men in blue uniforms. But Jackson's artillery had the upper hand at Cedar Mountain, not because of the ardor and skill of his artillerists, although they displayed both (and were directed by general officers acting like captains), but because of the superb positions available to them, particularly on Cedar Mountain's foreslope, and the breadth of their far-flung line, which resulted in a classic instance of converging fire. Credit for both of those decisive advantages belongs in a general sense to Jackson, whose driving spirit prodded the army to the sites and lashed the batteries forward. The tactical credit seems to go to fate, however, for no one had crafted a careful plan.

For some mysterious reason, postmortems have tended to give the artillery laurels to the Federals on this field. Such judgment came without recourse to Clermont Best's report, which remains unpublished, and probably without use of other Federal sources. Even so, it is impossible to justify the assertion of the standard history of Confederate artillery that Banks "had gotten somewhat the best of the artillery duel." That historian, Jennings Cropper Wise, then proceeded to supply an entirely lucid explanation of why Jackson did as well as he did. It is good enough to stand as an explanation of why Jackson did even better than Wise's judgment admits. Confederate artillery was "employed . . . in masses, small though they were, in order to secure from them the benefits of a cross fire." Jackson knew that "with long-range guns concentrated fire did not necessarily require massed guns." Cedar Mountain, Wise concluded after his faint beginning, witnessed "by far the best tactical employment of field artillery up to that time exhibited by the Confederates."[89]

CHAPTER 5

Confused Preparations in the Woods

DURING THE NEARLY two hours of artillery action, Stonewall Jackson had been everywhere on the field. Everyone who wrote down personal experiences of Cedar Mountain and saw the general mentioned the particulars: when great events are written of, living legends stand out above the rest of the scene. Jackson established a headquarters of sorts not far south of the Gate. He apparently spent almost all of his time on the right half of his line. And he was, like Winder, inordinately interested in artillery matters.

General Jackson's first destination on the battlefield lay to the right of the main road. His attention would remain directed to the right until Federal actions abruptly and violently forced a reorientation. At about the time that his artillery fired the opening rounds, Jackson rode south toward the Crittenden House. Catherine Crittenden and the young women still were present, but they were about to have cause to flee up the mountain. They hardly could believe that Stonewall Jackson was on their farm so soon after Rhode Island Chaplain Denison had acted ugly toward them. The general and his entourage attracted unfriendly attention in the form of "several shots" thrown by Federal artillery. Jackson remained more concerned about enemy cavalry, as he had been for two days, and thought he saw "large bodies" of it in the wheatfield across the road.[1]

Before the action was well joined, Jackson moved to his left and set up headquarters in one of the Crittenden tenant houses. The building stood vacant in 1860 when the census taker came around, but it was occupied by the farm overseer, a man named Newman, in 1862. The little house stood not far south of the Gate and on the west side of the Crittenden Lane.[2]

The small structure designated as army headquarters was situated in a zone that was anything but placid. Jackson probably did not spend much time in or near it—no contemporary eyewitness account puts him inside—but he was in the vicinity of the Gate and its artillery duel more than once. No doubt he was drawn to the artillery

*Nineteenth-century captions call this structure the house
where Winder was killed or the house where he died. It
probably depicts the cabin along the Crittenden Lane where
Jackson had a forward headquarters a few yards from where
Winder fell mortally wounded. (Library of Congress)*

action by his fondly remembered experience in that arm before the
war, just as Winder was drawn to it. The Gate clearly was a hot spot.
One mounted member of Jackson's headquarters group wrote that
his own horse was hit twice, dirt was "dashed over" him "several"
times, and stricken men nearby splattered him with blood. During
the second phase of the duel, while Taliaferro's men lay parallel to
the road just behind the Gate, a member of the Tenth Virginia observed Jackson at close range as the general ignored shells, which at
one point threw debris on his writing utensils.[3]

A Virginia cavalryman who reached Jackson from the rear with a
message wrote, perhaps with some embellishment, that he found the
general "entirely alone, sitting on the ground at the root of, and
leaning against a small tree." Jackson was holding his horse's bridle.
His eyes were shut, the dispatch carrier reported, and his lips were
moving "while the battle raged."[4]

Jackson's wanderings away from the center always, with one exception, took him south toward Early's end of the line. At about 4:30 the

general rode away from the Gate to the right, leaving behind a cavalry officer with orders to direct any of A. P. Hill's troops who showed up in the same direction. Jackson's orientation focused steadily toward his right. The ground down the Crittenden Lane was not being battered by so heavy a barrage as that around the Gate (nor were there trees down the lane to magnify the noise). Even so, Samuel D. Buck, a member of Early's left regiment, remembered lying "in an open field under an August sun without shade or water for hours while shell after shell plowed up ground about us." One of those shells exploded "almost under" Jubal Early's horse and bathed both mount and rider with dust.[5]

A cavalryman named John Blue, who was assigned to Jackson for the day, employed almost the same language as did Buck to describe the fire on that part of the line: "Every few seconds the sod was being plowed up around us." Blue could tell that the size of the general's mounted party was provoking aimed fire. The fire roared over too high at first, but then a round just missed one man's head and the next narrowly missed a horse. Jackson sat through this storm "as immovable apparently as a statue," his right leg thrown across the pommel of his saddle, field glasses trained on the hostile guns. One of the staff suggested aloud what all had been thinking—that discretion suggested a relocation. Jackson turned and, with what Blue took to be a smile, remarked that the Confederate artillery was "making it pretty warm" on the enemy. As soon as the general had spoken, a shell exploded "a few paces" in front of the group, wounding three horses. Jackson then led the group away from the hot spot—farther to the right, of course. When he stopped, the general suggested that the rest of the caravan drop back out of sight: "They will hardly aim at a single horseman." The staff obeyed Jackson's suggestion with utmost alacrity.[6]

While Jackson watched his enemy through magnifying lenses and his staff watched their health behind the ridge's crest, someone rode down the lane from the Gate with the news that Charles Winder had just been mortally wounded. Jackson reacted to the news initially in a predictable manner: he "raised his arm for a few seconds in silent prayer." Almost immediately thereafter an excited aide on General Early's staff reached Jackson with another report. Early had been looking far across the corn and wheat to his left front and thought he saw good prospect for moving a force from the left around Banks's right. He sent an aide to tell Winder so but soon thereafter thought he saw signs of a Federal threat in the same vicinity. Another aide

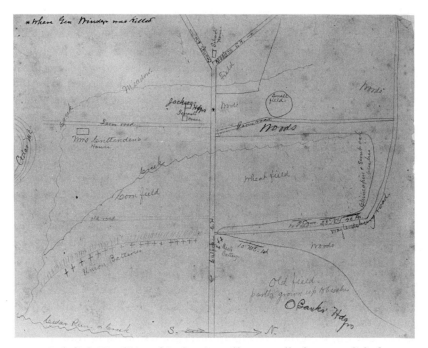

*Jedediah Hotchkiss of Jackson's staff eventually drew a polished
map of the battlefield. This crude preliminary sketch from his
papers shows the general's headquarters just west of the Crittenden
Lane and just south of the Gate. (Library of Congress)*

went toward Winder with that intelligence. Before the second message reached him (and probably before the first one did), Winder
fell. The second aide found Jackson on his way back to Early and
excitedly reported his news.[7]

Jackson's sole visit to the left of his line, beyond the Gate, came as a
result of this meeting with Early's aide. He first sent a message off to
Colonel Garnett to watch his left and then followed it with a quick
personal inspection. Garnett had word of Winder's wounding before
Jackson arrived. By that time his three regiments and one battalion
had assumed their boomerang-shaped position facing the wheatfield
and then bending rearward along the road. Jackson and his staff
found Garnett hard at work. Garnett reported that Jackson left him
with orders "to look well to my left flank and to report at once to
General Taliaferro for re-enforcements."[8]

While he was en route to Garnett's position, or perhaps after he arrived there, Jackson ran across Keith Boswell of his staff, who had been maintaining the rear headquarters near the Petty house. Boswell had come across Winder and given him succor in the form of a better stretcher. Jackson promptly detailed his topographic engineer "to go off on the left and reconnoitre to find out whether it would be practicable to turn the enemy's right." Boswell took Lieutenant Thomas T. L. Snead of the staff with him and headed for Garnett's far left outposts.[9]

The crew of Poague's replenished Parrott rifle met Jackson near the Gate when they returned from their caissons with fresh ammunition. The general personally ordered the gun to displace farther to the right as part of the movement in that direction being made by Major Snowden Andrews. The Parrott had fired for some time after Winder's wounding and then made its round-trip for ammunition, so this must have occurred after Jackson's exploration on his left. The time probably was 5:15 or so. At about the same time Pegram and Hardy arrived on the field. Two members of Pegram's battery reported seeing Jackson at or near the Gate as they rode past. One of them, Albert Sidney Drewry, wrote that while R. L. Walker positioned the guns "in an old stubblefield on a little knowl," Jackson personally directed the placement of Pegram's opening rounds.[10]

As the artillery duel ran down, and Jackson's grasp on the tactical initiative expired concurrently, the general turned his attention from the guns to the prospect of making use of A. P. Hill's infantry as it began to arrive. Thomas's brigade of Georgians first received orders to support Taliaferro, and part of the brigade briefly formed "immediately in rear" of that unit. Jackson soon ordered Thomas onward to the right to Early, and much of Thomas's strength eventually reached Early's far right. By that time, however, events were breaking so fast that one of the Georgia regiments failed to complete the journey.[11]

Far to the left of Thomas and Early and Taliaferro, the Virginians of Garnett's brigade lay nervously inside the wood line at the western edge of the wheatfield. Colonel Garnett's vague orders had been to slide far enough up to the left to attempt flanking and capturing the northernmost elements of the Federal artillery with which Winder was dueling so single-mindedly. That notion proved to be chimerical. Garnett's reconnaissance found the hostile guns protected by ample infantry on high ground and screened by cavalry (the latter being the New Jersey boys, who decided they had saved the Union by thwarting Garnett). Garnett also was taken aback by the nature of the

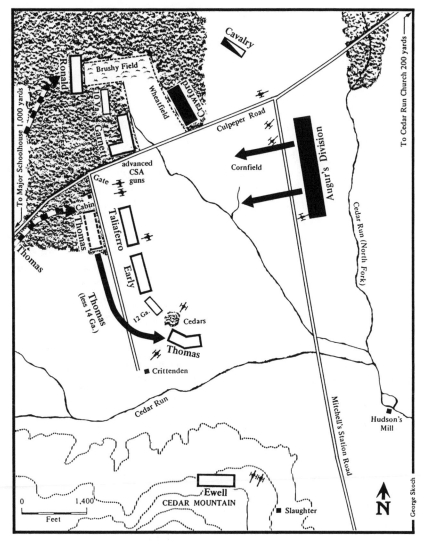

Thomas Arrives, Augur Begins to Move, 5:30–5:45

wheatfield, which was devoid of cover and must be crossed to reach
the assigned point. He sent word of all this to Winder, who responded with orders, Garnett reported, "to remain where I was for a
few moments." Winder was busy playing at gunner for the moment.
Garnett never heard from him again, doubtless because the general

was desperately wounded before he found time to turn his mind back toward his infantry.[12]

While Garnett waited for guidance, his men grimly bore a shelling. The units on the brigade left—the First Virginia Battalion and Forty-second Virginia Infantry—were closest to the Federal infantry threat from across the field. The Twenty-first Virginia and that portion of the Forty-eighth Virginia which faced south toward the road were farther from the wheatfield but closer to the Gate, which remained a magnet for enemy artillery. Captain William A. Witcher of the Twenty-first reported that enemy shells came in "with great vigor," so he ordered the men to lie down for protection. John H. Worsham of the same regiment used the word *terribly* in describing how the enemy shelling affected his unit. Among the casualties in the Twenty-first was a brilliant young officer, Captain William H. Morgan of Company F, who was killed by a fragment that went clear through his body. Worsham called Morgan not only "a splendid soldier" but also "the best informed man on military matters that I knew during the war."[13]

Although Winder paid little attention to Garnett and soon was beyond helping anyone, every other general officer within reach offered advice. Fairly early during the artillery duel—before Winder was hit—Jubal Early thought he saw the chance to turn the Federal guns through the wheatfield. Winder already had suggested that to Garnett, of course. Almost immediately after having that duplicate of Winder's idea, Early thought he saw "the glistening bayonets of infantry . . . moving stealthily to our left, through the woods." He sent that word to Winder on the heels of the first suggestion, but his aide arrived "just" after Winder was hit and instead gave the information directly to Jackson.[14]

It was then that Jackson made his foray to the left and saw Garnett and ordered him "to look well" to his left and to solicit help from Taliaferro. To help Garnett "look well" to his left, Jackson sent Boswell and Snead of his own staff up that way. Major John Seddon of the First Virginia Battalion on the far left told Boswell that he had seen enemy behind a fence across the wheatfield. To meet the second half of Stonewall's injunction, Garnett dispatched Captain Robert N. Wilson and Lieutenant Oscar White of his staff in different directions in quest of General Taliaferro "to insure an early interview" with the new division commander.[15]

Wilson and White never did find Taliaferro and had not returned by the time the Federals attacked through the wheatfield, but in the meantime Taliaferro looked up Garnett on his own and was full of good ideas. When he heard of Winder's mortal wound, Taliaferro "at once rode to the front" and examined Garnett's position. While Wilson and White searched for him, the general had passed them en route and gone out into the wheatfield in front of the First Virginia Battalion. He reported that he "could discover no evidences of the enemy in front," although to the right oblique across the road they were much in evidence. Taliaferro thought that the Federal strength over in the corn might be hidden from Early "by the undulations of the country."[16] While Early was looking far to his left and finding need to warn Taliaferro (vice Winder), Taliaferro was looking far to his right and finding need to worry about Early. Luke 6:41 comes to mind: "And why beholdest thou the mote that is in thy brother's eye, but perceivest not the beam that is in thine own eye?" Both generals, in fact, were about to find ample to concern them on their own fronts.

Taliaferro's preoccupation with the right of the division, where his own brigade lay, was manifested by the orders he left with Garnett. The colonel must pay special attention to the protection of the guns around the Gate, "on our right and some 400 yards to the rear," in Garnett's words. This injunction applied particularly to the Twenty-first and Forty-eighth Virginia because of their positions. Garnett assigned a courier to stay near Major Seddon of the First Battalion and report at once if any hostile movements developed on that flank.[17] What became of the courier is not on record.

That the last-minute transfer of command contributed to confusion is beyond question. A conventional but unconvincing interpretation of Confederate misfortunes at Cedar Mountain suggests that the change in command resulted in uncertainty that Winder's presence would have overcome. Sandie Pendleton, Stonewall Jackson's clever and competent young staff officer, summarized that school of thought in a letter to his mother: "Owing to bad management of some of the officers, incident upon the loss of Winder, some confusion resulted."[18] That judgment assumed that Winder would have protected his left flank if he had not been wounded, which is a decidedly doubtful premise (albeit as impossible to disprove as to prove). Winder's absorption in the artillery affair might have ended abruptly; he might have done more subsequently than he did initially when he sent word back to Garnett to stay where he was awhile.

The attention that did reach Garnett's misshapen position, with its too-short left flank, actually came about as a result of Winder's wounding. The new division commander went directly to the left, and so did Stonewall Jackson. Taliaferro (whom Jackson and thus Pendleton disliked intensely) did about as well as he could have done. Winder could not have done more and very likely would have done less. Winder and Jackson and Taliaferro all spent the day oriented rightward, toward the dominant mountain and the readily visible arrangements in the big open field. Winder and Jackson also expended considerable thought and energy on artillery matters, and Jackson remained much concerned about Yankee cavalry. The crisis headed squarely for them had nothing to do with either artillery or cavalry, and its most ominous features were not oriented to the Confederate right.

As the artillery duel wound down, the soldiers manning Garnett's left began to sense, then feel, then see, pressure opposite them across the wheatfield. Skirmishers went out from each Southern unit "with orders to fire as soon as the enemy came within range." Those advanced men soon discovered enemy counterparts across the field, with solid lines of infantry behind them. Garnett's skirmishers probably went across the field after Taliaferro's visit (when, it will be remembered, nothing was visible from in front of the First Battalion). Major Seddon reported that the battalion took up position at about 4:15 P.M. and was attacked at 5:45. The first time may be a few minutes early; the last time is accurate. Several accounts confirm the feeling that the Confederate skirmishers had not been posted long before the Federal movement began, so they probably went to work in support of Taliaferro's orders sometime after 5:00. The Federal line taking shape opposite the First Battalion outflanked that farthest left of Garnett's units by "two or three hundred yards"—bad tactical news indeed. To remedy the potential for such a threat (which had not then yet developed), Taliaferro had ordered the Tenth Virginia Infantry from his own brigade to move to Garnett's left.[19]

The final element in or near the Confederate front line as zero hour approached was the old Stonewall Brigade. That seasoned and valiant body had been shunted to the rear of the division column, almost certainly because of the ineptitude of its ranking colonel and acting commander, Charles A. Ronald. Before the artillery duel commenced at about 4:00 P.M. the Stonewall Brigade had reached the schoolhouse and gone into line perpendicular to and just to the left of the main road. The men waited near the edge of the woods that opened out onto the meadow where Early had formed up before his first advance. To their right was Garnett's brigade, which was about to go forward toward the Gate. The Twenty-seventh Virginia was on the Stonewall Brigade's right; on the left of the Twenty-seventh was the Thirty-third Virginia and then the Fifth Virginia.[20]

The roar of cannon in their front told the Stonewall Brigade veterans that their services soon would be requisitioned, inept commander notwithstanding. Almost as soon as the artillery started firing, they noticed Poague's and Carpenter's rifles rushing forward. A member of the Second Virginia, on the brigade left, also noticed the familiar figure of Willie Pegram riding up from the rear. Pegram was wearing a long linen duster and a visored hat. The role of the Stonewall Brigade in the artillery duel was entirely typical of infantry in such straits: the men lay under the randomly striking "overs" which Federals had aimed at the Gate, without any means of protecting themselves or fighting back. The shells "rattled through the woods over our heads very lively," one of them remembered.[21]

The orders that moved the Stonewall Brigade to the front must have arrived near 5:00 P.M. because Colonel Ronald reported that the brigade had not moved at the time that Winder was "borne from the field." McHenry Howard, who accompanied Winder's stretcher, wrote years later that he saw the Stonewall Brigade "moving to attack" when its wounded commander passed. Perhaps the events were nearly congruent. Howard described the brigade officers as filled "with sincere sorrow" as they gathered around. John Casler's cronies in the Thirty-third Virginia were less than sorrowful. In fact, Casler "firmly" believed that the Federal shell that hit Winder only saved some of the infantrymen "the trouble of carrying out their threats to kill him."[22]

The same hard-bitten men who had won such fame with (and for) Stonewall Jackson, and then had every intention of shooting their own brigade commander, indulged a timid superstition as they prepared for battle around the schoolhouse. A cavalryman watching them saw men running to the roadside and hiding something under leaves and in fence corners. He discovered that they were divesting themselves of their packs of playing cards, "being superstitious about taking them into battle." The same observer noticed, for the first time in his experience, a more practical preparation for action: some men were pinning pieces of paper to their coats with information that would identify them to strangers if they were killed or seriously wounded. As a final preparation for the march the men loaded their weapons.[23]

The Stonewall Brigade did not use the road in its advance in the direction of the wheatfield. The lesson learned during the earlier advance by Garnett and then, more cautiously, by Taliaferro, led to this reasonable expedient. Even so, the Fifth Virginia lost six men killed or wounded to a single shell that exploded near the regiment's commander, Colonel W. S. H. Baylor. The Fifth was the brigade's largest regiment at the moment, with 519 muskets in the ranks at the beginning of the action. In response to the deadly shell, Baylor "was as calm as if nothing had happened, and merely said, 'Steady men, steady! Close up!' "[24]

Staying in the woods, once past the meadow, reduced the danger from artillery fire and also kept the movement secret. Lieutenant Colonel Edmund G. Lee of the Thirty-third Virginia reported that the brigade directed its movement through the woods "to avoid raising the dust." But marching in the woods was tricky business for the commanders, who needed to maintain cohesion in order to have tactical unity when they reached the threshold of action. The Stonewall Brigade did not maintain cohesion during its half-hour or so of jerky, confused movement in the woods. The forest in question was by no means a pleasant glade. It was "dense . . . with heavy undergrowth of brush and much fallen timber," according to the official report of the Twenty-seventh Virginia. That the participants reported their progress as slow is hardly surprising.[25]

Colonel Ronald's report of his journey through the woods is interesting but confusing reading. The brigade had been more or less in line perpendicular to the road long before it received orders to move forward. Ronald dressed that line and led it into the woods a short distance, "but," he reported, "in a few minutes I was ordered to put the brigade in column of regiments." That difficult undertaking in the woods surely took some time and frayed some tempers. Enemy artillery rounds continued to crash all around. It seems likely that Ronald went through that maneuver as a result of some misunderstanding because before the reconfigured brigade advanced another step, Ronald "was ordered to deploy the column and advance in line of battle."[26]

The wanderings of the Stonewall Brigade in the woods on the left of the road included a sizable amount of sheer thrashing about. In reporting on the peculiar sequence of formations—from loose line into battle line into column of regiments and back into battle line—Colonel Ronald never identified the origin of the orders he was struggling to obey. Twice he used the passive phrase "I was ordered." The unavoidable suspicion that Ronald was rattled is strengthened by the fact that the distances he cited vary from known givens and his narrative displays clear signs of confusion.

As the Stonewall Brigade neared the end of the woods, Ronald sent an aide off to ask Taliaferro what to do. Taliaferro said to keep going toward the front. When the aide left, the five regiments had reached a fence at the edge of a brushy field that adjoined the wheatfield at its northern end. The men leveled the fence and lay down. Captain John Hall Fulton of the Fourth Virginia, who was the aide Ronald sent to Taliaferro, accomplished his task in good time; he was gone only twenty minutes.[27] The delay was as brief as it could have been, and it was an understandable effort by an overmatched colonel to find out how to proceed. From the Confederate perspective, however, the delay was well-nigh fatal.

Colonel James A. Walker was admirably situated to comment on the brigade's performance at Cedar Mountain. He had no direct vested interest because at the time he commanded the Thirteenth Virginia Infantry on Early's left, almost a mile away. A year later, though, Walker would be promoted to brigadier general and become the last regular commander of the Stonewall Brigade, winning the nom de guerre "Stonewall Jim." Walker's personal copy of the *Official Records* volume for Cedar Mountain contains marginal notes tartly critical of Ronald's halt at a crucial moment. "This untimely halt at this fence left the left-wing of the 2d brigade [Garnett's] exposed, and caused the disaster which nearly proved a defeat," Walker observed. Next to the mention of the halt in the report of the Thirty-third Virginia, Walker reiterated his point: "Here again we have this unfortunate halt of 20 minutes: a *very* long time in a battle."[28]

The field beyond the leveled fence was not under cultivation. Some of the men who described the field in August 1862 called it a brushy field, and that is how I will refer to it. The brushy field was rectangular and not as large as the wheatfield. Its long axis was roughly parallel to the main road, which is to say that its long axis was at right angles to the long axis of the wheatfield. The eastern half of the brushy field was a continuation northward of the wheatfield (though some maps show a few trees separating them). The western half of the brushy field ran back into the woods, away from the Confederate front lines. The two fields combined described an inverted and backward "L" or a "T" of which the right half of the horizontal top bar was missing.

The dismantled fence had stood at the western edge of the brushy field. The long brigade line overlapped the field on both sides. The

Twenty-seventh Virginia on the far right would march entirely in the woods when the brigade advanced from the western edge of the field. Next left of the Twenty-seventh came the Thirty-third Virginia, its right elements in the woods and its left companies in the field. Leftward beyond the Thirty-third came the Fifth Virginia, then the Second, then the Fourth on the extreme left. The Twenty-seventh and Thirty-third regiments on the right came under desultory small arms fire from invisible skirmishers before the infantry fight opened. Their comrades farther to the left were free of that nuisance, but all of them dodged a sharp fire of shell and case shot during the twenty-minute halt. Some stray Federal cavalry probably stirred up a few of the Virginians at some point because the Northerners reported falling back from this vicinity under infantry fire after suffering "some few" killed and wounded.[29]

At about 5:45 P.M. the artillery duel gave way to a desperate infantry fight. When that fight opened, the Confederate line ran from Ewell on the mountain, with Latimer's guns, leftward to Early's brigade and its two clusters of artillery at and near the Cedars. The Georgia Brigade under Edward L. Thomas was arriving on Early's right, or at least most of it was. Taliaferro's brigade tied in with Early's left, extending along the Crittenden Lane with Pegram's and Hardy's guns in front and Poague's, Caskie's, and Carpenter's near its left. Garnett's men faced south or east along the two faces of his boomerang line. The Tenth Virginia was groping through the woods in the direction of Garnett's left. And the Stonewall Brigade lay beyond and behind—too far beyond and too far behind—Garnett's short and dangling left.

An outmanned and outgunned Federal force, attacking from a weaker position, was about to pounce upon Jackson's patchwork quilt of a line and shiver it from end to end.

CHAPTER 6

Augur's Attack

THE FEDERAL INFANTRY poised opposite Taliaferro and Early near the Mitchell's Station Road consisted of ten regiments and one battalion. Taliaferro and Early between them mustered nine regiments and one battalion (figuring the truncated Fifty-second Virginia's companies as equivalent to a small battalion). Any resultant Federal advantage—if indeed there was one because regimental strengths varied widely—was far less than was usually necessary for an attacking force.[1] Further, Confederates in considerable numbers were streaming toward the front, while Federal reserves did not lend a hand to the Federal attackers. Tall corn, thickly planted, offered the Northerners the opportunity for concealment and surprise, which they used skillfully, but they had little else going for them but bravery and tenacity.

Brigadier General Christopher C. Augur (he would win promotion to major general to date from this afternoon) commanded the three-brigade division along the Mitchell's Station Road, which would fight the left half of the Federal battle unaided. John W. Geary's brigade of four Ohio regiments formed Augur's right, the brigade right resting on the main road to Culpeper. To Geary's left was the brigade of Henry Prince, a seasoned veteran of Indian fighting who was in his fifties. Prince had under him the Third Maryland, 102d New York, 109th and 111th Pennsylvania, and a detachment of regulars known as the Eighth and Twelfth U.S. Infantry Battalion. To Prince's left and rear was a tiny brigade—the First District of Columbia and Seventy-eighth New York—under George S. Greene. Nearly thirty pieces of artillery dotted the Federal line. As Augur's infantry prepared to advance into the corn the artillery around them had just become quiet.[2]

Nathaniel P. Banks posted himself just across (north of) the main road to Culpeper, opposite Geary's right. The general had survived another close call during the artillery action in addition to the one when a single shell hit six of his entourage. While Banks leaned

117

Harper's Weekly, *the popular Northern news source, printed this sketch by A. R. Waud soon after the battle. More people saw this sketch at the time than any other depiction of what*

happened at Cedar Mountain. Federals along the Mitchell's Station Road in the foreground prepare to attack toward Taliaferro and Early. (Harper's Weekly)

against a stout tree, "a cannon-ball struck it about 18 inches above his head, passing entirely through." During a mounted reconnaissance of his own lines, Banks galloped so energetically that his hat flew off. An irreverent company officer with the battalion of regulars suggested that Banks "had also lost his head, but did not know it."[3] In fact, Banks did as well as he could have done and came within an ace of a remarkable coup.

The first of Augur's infantry into action was the regular battalion, which had made its presence felt to the Confederates from first-rate skirmishing positions in the cornfield. The regulars were the men who had so frightened Pegram and Hardy when those Southern gunners dashed too close to them in ignorance of their presence. A member of Pope's staff, T. C. H. Smith, later criticized Banks harshly for using so few skirmishers to develop the Confederate position. Smith suggested that one-third of Banks's force would have been the standard usage for the purpose and insisted that Banks displayed "insane ignorance" when he ordered an advance without having clearer knowledge of his target.[4]

Smith was himself either ignorant or hyperbolic when he suggested the routine use of one-third of the available force as skirmishers. Doctrine at the time dictated use of one company per regiment (10 percent of strength), and Banks was close to that norm. Yet Smith's hindsight is irrefutably clear in noting that Banks was biting off more than he could hope to chew. Banks's greatest weakness, as seen by a succession of timid superiors, was rashness. The New England politician was anything but a Great Captain, to be sure, but his aggressive demeanor was not an unmitigated curse in an army overflowing with sluggards.

The corn that sheltered the men of the Eighth and Twelfth United States Infantry Battalion when they went out to cover Augur's entire division front was their principal ally. It was fully grown but, fortunately for them, uncut and "dense." The regulars elicited admiration from the Confederates opposite them for their apt performance as gadflies throughout the action. They remained at the front from beginning to end, acting as regulars were supposed to do. A Northern commentator suggested that Southern artillery "wasted" much canister on them. Jubal Early identified the regulars to his front and commented to a staff officer that they held firm until Confederate fire "gradually melted away" their strength. The battalion reported sixty casualties.[5]

The performance of the battalion drew enough favorable attention to make it a benchmark for the unit. To this day the coat of arms of the Twenty-first U.S. Infantry (which traces its origins to the Twelfth Regular Battalion) features a cedar tree "eradicated proper" in recognition of August 9, 1862.[6]

The one recorded exception to the doughty showing of the regulars was a green captain—"a mere youth"—under fire for the first time. Tender officers traditionally have difficulty winning the respect of the seasoned noncoms and men in regular units. This unnamed boy captain never did win his spurs. He held his portion of the battalion in a reserve line under cover of a swale and adamantly refused to go forward. Eventually, the rank amateurs of the Fifth Ohio passed over this line in the attack and called the men cowards. The boy captain ran away and his embarrassed men hurried off to join their better-led comrades.[7]

The Ohioans who ran over the reluctant captain were part of Geary's brigade, which lunged into the corn and toward Taliaferro's brigade beyond the field. The Seventh Ohio formed the right of Geary's line, and the Sixty-sixth Ohio advanced on its left; the other two regiments followed in support. Prince's brigade advanced concurrently in the direction of Early's Confederates. A soldier in Geary's second line remembered the beginning of the charge as being triggered by "a given signal" and launched "with defiant yells." When the men of the Seventh Ohio on the right topped the last corn-covered knoll protecting them from Taliaferro's view, they came under "a most murderous and tremendous fire from artillery and infantry." A friendly reporter from Cincinnati watched the Ohio men fall: "Oh! It made my blood run cold," he wrote. He had heard and read of "leaden hail" but until that afternoon had presumed that figure of speech to be an exaggeration.[8]

One of the Seventh Ohio soldiers, Lapham by name, came away less hurt than many of his mates, having had three fingers shot away. Lapham complained to the civilian who dressed the hand: "I don't care a darn for that third finger, for it warn't of no account, no how; but the 'pinter,' and t'other one, were right good 'uns, and I hate to lose 'em."[9]

General Augur was wounded early in the advance and taken from the field. A bullet hit the general in the back while he was turning on horseback to yell encouragement to his men. Geary also was hit, twice. A bullet shattered his left arm and another hit him in the foot. Before much time had elapsed, three of the four general officers in Augur's division became casualties.[10]

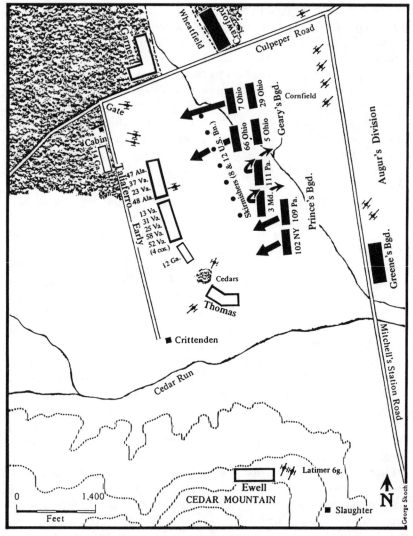

Geary and Prince against Taliaferro and Early, 5:45–6:00

The Sixty-sixth Ohio, Geary's second front-line regiment, advanced to the left of the Seventh Ohio. It seemed to the men that they were alone and uncoordinated—"on our own hook," one of them said. This regiment did not even learn of Geary's wounding until well after dark. As the Sixty-sixth took casualties, the men instinctively closed up to their right, knowing they were on the left of the brigade. Every man on the field suffered from the heat but none of them more so than the troops moving through the close, dusty corn rows. A veteran of the Sixty-sixth's attack named Charles Candy recalled it as "the hottest day I ever experienced in the field." During his decades of service in the army, Candy "never knew troops to suffer more for water." The temperature in Washington at 2:00 P.M. had reached 98°. "It was," Candy concluded simply and inarguably, "a trying day."[11]

The sergeant-major of the Sixty-sixth Ohio was particularly distinguished in the attack, although his motivations were judged by an uncharitable comrade to be mixed. William H. Tallman of the Sixty-sixth described Sergeant-Major Robert Murdoch as young, rather "womanly looking," and apparently "in doubt about the respectability of . . . soldiering." Tallman convinced himself that by August 9 Murdoch "had become so anxious" that he was willing to be killed or wounded in order to escape the service. Murdoch proved the point to his detractor's satisfaction by making himself "unnecessarily conspicuous on a gray horse all the afternoon."[12] Confederate fire hit Murdoch hard, and he died of his wounds in Washington later in the month. It is hard to feel any empathy with Tallman's bizarre analysis of his comrade's behavior.

Before he was wounded, General Geary pushed his second line up to the first in support. The Fifth Ohio had been behind the Sixty-sixth, but the rightward sidle by the shrinking line of the Sixty-sixth left a gap into which the Fifth moved. That left the Fifth Ohio as Geary's left regiment. No good evidence survives about what linkage, if any, the Fifth Ohio maintained with Prince's brigade to its left. The Twenty-ninth Ohio advanced from the right of the second line and closed with the Seventh Ohio in front. The regimental historian claimed that the regiment lost "several" men who died of sunstroke during the day. In the cornfield they found even sterner danger, and most of the men went to ground among the dead and wounded "left thick around. . . . It was scarce possible to tell the living from the dead." Alonzo H. Sterrett of Company E of the Twenty-ninth wrote four days later that "the roar and din of battle was terrible, far exceeding anything I ever heard before."[13]

The Twenty-ninth evidently did not perform particularly well, though most of Geary's men did some good work. Casualties in the Twenty-ninth amounted to barely one-third as many as those of the Seventh Ohio, on which the Twenty-ninth closed for support.[14] The regiment's shortcomings can be traced to its command. Captain Wilbur F. Stevens of Company B was the ranking officer present at Cedar Mountain. It takes an unusual captain to step three ranks above his commission and acquire instant competence. Captain William F. Brown of the Twelfth Georgia was one such, as we will soon see; Captain Stevens was made of different stuff, according to the testimony of Lieutenant James B. Storer of the Twenty-ninth, who had a distinguished career with the regiment, rising to its adjutancy. When Captain Stevens, who left the regiment soon after Cedar Mountain, later applied for a pension, Storer filed a revealing deposition which firmly and bitterly accused Stevens of rank cowardice.

Stevens made an attempt to take the regiment forward, Storer deposed, but he quickly "petered out." The captain "dropped into a ditch and staid there." The next day he returned to take command, claiming that he now felt much better. Storer adduced evidence from another captain in the Twenty-ninth, who also saw Stevens "drop into a dry ditch as we were going into battle." To complete the bill of particulars against Stevens, he was "an immoral man, a gambler, prided himself upon being a 'bad man' after women." Storer concluded his testimony with a sentence that deserves enshrinement as the quintessential example of damning with faint praise: "He didn't drink excessively so far as I know, however, & never personally knew him to have any venereal disease." Storer and his colleagues clearly were right about Stevens's behavior at Cedar Mountain because the captain did not try to refute the demonstrable facts. Instead, he supplied a new interpretation to them and attempted to parlay them into a disability claim. By Stevens's account, the responsibility of commanding an entire regiment had "completely worn out and prostrated" him, to the point that he had "suffered from Nervous Debility and Prostration ever since."[15]

While Geary's men advanced on the right (most of them, at least), the four regiments of Henry Prince's brigade attacked westward from their position at the far left of the Union line. They were headed for Jubal Early and the Cedars. About half of Prince's route lay through corn, as did Geary's, but the shallow, dry streambed across the Federal front drew in close to Prince's left and gave him a different set of knolls as obstacles and (or) protections. The general described the corn as "very high" and emphasized the resultant disorientation of his troops. Confederates beyond the corn grumbled that it made a "splendid screen" for the Yankees. Each of those analyses had some validity.[16]

*View from the Mitchell's Station Road in 1989 toward
Early's position in the distance. (Clark B. Hall)*

Prince put the 111th Pennsylvania on the right of his front line
and the Third Maryland on the left. The fences between the cornfields interrupted the advance of the Marylanders more than the
Pennsylvanians, and the former fell somewhat behind. When the
front ranks reached the far (western) edge of the corn, they found
themselves under fire from an arc of musketry stretching around
toward their left. This punishing fire came from the aptly placed
Twelfth Georgia and Thomas's brigade. The two Northern regiments
remained in the corn while, according to the Pennsylvania regiment's historian, "the standing corn about them was cut down as with
knives." When the battalion of regulars had gone out onto skirmish
duty, its officers had exhorted their men to behave well as a good
example to the volunteers. Now the volunteer officers recalled that
admonishment to their men as a sort of reverse encouragement.[17]

A member of the Twenty-seventh Indiana who watched Geary and
Prince attack through the corn offered interesting comments about
the struggle and its context. The Indiana men were themselves no
more than a half-hour short of a similar effort. Their regimental
historian later wrote (with his own regiment's experience in perspective) that the amphitheaterlike setting below Cedar Mountain let everyone see everyone else and everything that was going on. As a
result, "many considerations urged every man to do his utmost," that

is, the whole world was watching. The Indiana soldiers also noticed that "musketry scarcely ever sounded . . . so intense and wicked" as it did at Cedar Mountain. The regiment fought amid torrents of gunfire at Sharpsburg and Gettysburg within the next year, where more men were firing, "but this evening at Cedar Mountain the firing seemed unusually energetic and terrifying."[18]

Perhaps the most crucial of the many volleys of musketry affecting Prince's brigade was one delivered by two of the brigade's own regiments. Before General Prince had completely shepherded the two front regiments through the corn, he received orders to throw his entire brigade into action as soon as possible. To that end he aligned his other two regiments, the 109th Pennsylvania and 102d New York, en echelon to the left rear of the Third Maryland and sent them forward. The second line was Prince's best hope to quench the fire on his left, and he accordingly sent it in on that flank. The general took "great care" to explain to the echeloned regiments that they must fire to their left front only because friends were ahead to the right front. Unfortunately for Prince's plan, the Marylanders reacted with terror when an unexpected fire broke out to their rear. The front line later claimed that the "friendly" volley struck among them. Prince insisted otherwise but admitted that after the first volley some of the second line became confused in the corn and "came to an aim" to the right front. Wherever the bullets of the second line actually struck, the first line was demoralized by the noise and the perceived danger and streamed to the rear, most of them rallying only when they reached the Mitchell's Station Road.[19]

The 102d New York and 109th Pennsylvania stuck to their position in the corn. Lieutenant Aaron P. Bates of Company D of the New York regiment had had a bad day before he received orders to go in, and he believed the situation would be worse down in the corn. Bates (and many another Northerner) thought the day "hotter than anything I have seen north" and proved his point by swooning from heat exhaustion. When he came to, he found that someone had stolen his sword. The lieutenant advanced with his company when it followed Prince forward "over the brow of the hill" and over three fences. The men of the regiment "were fearfully mowed down," wrote Bates, by bullets that "came in perfect sheets around us." The Southern artillery on the mountain above them tore steadily at their exposed flank. To Bates's astonishment, his company lost not a single man although the regiment was battered to the extent of 115 casualties—the most in the brigade by one more than the 109th Pennsylvania suffered.

The death angel chose victims capriciously that afternoon. The reward of the two regiments of Prince's original first line, which left the scene early, was a casualty rate appreciably lower than that of the two regiments that stayed to the end.[20]

While Geary and Prince sweated and bled in the corn and on the slopes beyond it toward their enemies, General George S. Greene's tiny brigade remained near the Mitchell's Station Road in support of the Federal guns there. No doubt it won that role because of its size: Greene had only 372 men in his two regiments.[21] Some Federal presence in the rear was dictated by the Confederate infantry on the slopes of Cedar Mountain, who had the potential to sweep down behind Augur's division if given the chance.

The brigade opposite Geary's advance was Taliaferro's. When General Winder fell, William B. Taliaferro acceded to command of the division. That meant that the ranking colonel among Taliaferro's regimental officers assumed command of the brigade. Fortunately for the sake of clarity, if not necessarily for the men in the ranks, brigade command remained in the Taliaferro family. The senior field-grade officer in the brigade was fifty-three-year-old Colonel Alexander Galt Taliaferro, the general's uncle, who had graduated from the College of William and Mary before the vast majority of his infantrymen had been born. Before the war the colonel had practiced law in Culpeper County; he was fighting on his home turf. Colonel Taliaferro also was kin by marriage to another famous Virginia family. His wife was the granddaughter of Chief Justice John Marshall.[22]

Some Confederates were skeptical about the caliber of the Taliaferro-Taliaferro brigade. Jackson did not like General William Taliaferro, and Jackson's staff man Jed Hotchkiss did not like the brigade as a whole. "We did not consider Taliaferro's brigade made up of the best men we had," Hotchkiss wrote, "especially under his leadership, for although an exceedingly brave man and in many respects and [sic] able general, he was rather deficient in some of the particulars essential for an attacking leader."[23] Hotchkiss's negative opinion doubtless was inspired in part by the fact that half of the four regiments with Taliaferro were completely untried—the Forty-seventh and Forty-eighth Alabama. The solid Tenth Virginia, from the Shenandoah Valley, fought in limbo away from the brigade on this day. The two remaining Virginia regiments, the Twenty-third and Thirty-seventh, had acquitted themselves admirably in the Valley campaign of recent and glorious memory. Withal, though, Hotchkiss's sour analysis was not without basis; Taliaferro's probably was the least reliable Southern brigade on the field.

Whether by design or by accident, the two raw Alabama regiments were situated on either flank of Taliaferro's four-regiment line. The Forty-seventh lined up on the left and thus was the infantry nearest to the Gate although still some distance from it. The Forty-eighth was on the right, its right tied to the left of Early's left regiment, the stalwart Thirteenth Virginia. Between the Alabamians, Taliaferro posted the Thirty-seventh Virginia to the left of the Twenty-third Virginia.[24]

The four regiments had not been in position along the Crittenden Lane long when they received orders to advance. As inevitably happened in such cases, some of the participants exaggerated the nature and extent of the advance. The distance involved did not exceed one hundred yards and probably was closer to fifty yards. The brigade simply moved across the last major ground roll short of the corn and went to work from the vicinity of the military crest. Early's brigade made about the same move at about the same time just south of Taliaferro. Taliaferro's men could see Geary's men in the corn at the comfortable range of three hundred yards, so they began to shoot at them. The four regiments had, on balance, more than enough strength to handle Geary, and for about twenty minutes they fought the Federal advance to a standstill.[25]

General William B. Taliaferro was not overstating the case inordinately when he reported that his old brigade under his uncle "advanced in fine style and the enemy gave way before the severity of its fire." The four Southern regiments surely were capable of holding off Geary's four Ohio regiments alone, given the advantages of the defensive, but they had some highly efficient help as well. The Twenty-first Virginia was facing south across the road from the right half of Garnett's unusual formation. Their muskets pointed directly down Geary's exposed right flank, and General Taliaferro ordered the Virginians to open fire. Taliaferro claimed that he also ordered the Twenty-first Virginia to advance from the wood line against Geary. Fortunately, the regiment did not advance. The men, however, "poured a destructive fire" on Geary.[26] The sharp enfilade fire must have played havoc with the Ohioans.

The two virginal Alabama regiments stood their first combat test well. Enemy fire was hot and they suffered considerably, but the situation was well defined and the men loaded and fired with determination for about twenty minutes of stand-up slugging. A youngster in the Forty-seventh Alabama fired off a very creditable thirty rounds at the enemy and escaped unhurt "tho the bulets past me as thick as hale." Others in that regiment were not so lucky; barely more than one hundred of them were hit during the battle. Captain Michael Jefferson Bulger of Company A was one of the casualties. Bulger, at the age of fifty-six, was unusually old for his role. Two weeks after being badly wounded at Cedar Mountain, Bulger won promotion to the rank of major. Captain Albert Menefee of Company D was killed. One of his men remembered Menefee fondly as "a good man at home as well as in the army. . . . He was loved by all."[27]

On the other end of the brigade, Colonel James Lawrence Sheffield of the Forty-eighth Alabama held his men firmly to their duty. Sheffield had been "very much indisposed" for several days but refused to miss the battle. After serving in the Alabama Secession Convention, the colonel had outfitted the regiment by spending $60,000 of his own money, and he was not about to miss its first trial by fire. Sergeant John D. Taylor of the Forty-eighth called this first fight by his regiment "one of the most terrific of the war for the time it lasted." Sheffield went down wounded and so did his major and the regimental adjutant. The wounded major was Enoch Alldredge, who had been a member of the Alabama legislature in 1837, before many field officers in the army were born. Alldredge's wound drove him out of the army, leaving an opening into which his son Jesse J. Alldredge was promoted.[28]

One of the casualties in the Thirty-seventh Virginia was a sadly peculiar one. Samuel Combs of Company G was a "vigorous and strong" young fellow "of fine physical appearance." He was a newcomer to the regiment and had never been under fire. A ball passed just under the skin of his calf for no more than two inches and came out the back of his leg. Little blood flowed; no artery had been touched; and "no reason could be assigned for serious results." Nevertheless, Combs "was greatly excited and died in a few minutes."[29]

Federals watching Augur's attack from near the Brown house about a mile to the northeast gauged the casualties it was generating by the volume of gunsmoke that billowed up until "everything [was] enveloped in smoke." They also noted somberly the "constant lines of ambulances" hurrying into and out of the smoke.[30]

Stonewall Jackson watched his men's successful resistance with relish from a position near Taliaferro's brigade. Lieutenant John Blue, who was with Jackson, later wrote an extremely detailed account of the general's behavior during Augur's attack. Jackson's vantage point gave him "a fine view" of the advancing Federals. The corn just in front of Jackson ran parallel with the main road and he could see down between the rows. When the Confederate infantry opened on the Federals (Blue had not known that Taliaferro's men were there and was getting "a little shaky") from their position beyond Jackson's view, the "terrific roar" of the volley made Blue's horse squat to the ground and prick up his ears "in amazement."[31]

Blue watched Jackson closely with the notion that they would be leaving rapidly and soon. Unlike Blue, Jackson knew that friendly infantry waited in front of them, and he sat eagerly listening for their fire. The general put away his field glasses, reined up his horse, sat straight and alert in his saddle, and gazed steadily to the front. After the first volley, "the rattle of musketry was continuous along the whole line," Blue wrote, "which extended perhaps a half mile to our right, toward Slaughter's Mountain." Smoke rapidly obscured everything, but the excitement transformed Jackson, who became "a different person altogether." His nervous tension made Blue think that the general only by "the greatest exertion" restrained himself from riding directly into the action. Jackson's first official reaction to the outbreak was to write "a few lines on a leaf of a blank book" and send them to the rear in the hands of a courier. "Carry this to General Hill," Jackson barked, and added, unnecessarily, "be as expeditious as possible." The general then wheeled and rode rapidly to the right toward the junction of Early's and Taliaferro's brigades.[32]

Willie Pegram's guns and their companions under Lieutenant Hardy were firing as rapidly as they could. They "did heavy execution this day." J. W. D. Farrar of Pegram's battery remembered his gun's role: "We fired round after round of shell and then cannister, but still on they came in grand style." Farrar's comrade Albert S. Drewry told the same tale: "Changing from shell to shrapnel and canister, we turned our entire attention to this column; but they continued to come on without a waver. Finally we doubled the charges of canister, and then they broke and went back over the hill."[33]

Jackson's gallop along the Crittenden Lane ridge brought him opposite the guns. "The musket balls were flying over and around us pretty thick," Blue reported. The projectiles filled the air with "that sizzing, hissing sound peculiar to the Minnie ball, a music which any old soldier will tell you is not pleasant at any time, more especially when compelled to sit quietly and listen to their singing with nothing to do except almost break ones neck by jerking his head from one side to the other whenever one of those little messengers fanned his

*View south down the Crittenden Lane in 1989. In
1862, Taliaferro and Early stood along the lane,
facing left (eastward). (Clark B. Hall)*

cheek or brushed his nose." After that vivid description of the miseries of holding still under fire, Blue concluded, no doubt entirely aptly, "but a person must experience these things to understand them thoroughly." As the most famous of the Confederacy's leaders, Stonewall Jackson was not allowed to fret about mere bullets. He had, in any case, larger tactical worries. Blue noticed the general "looking . . . anxiously to the rear." Soon Jackson turned to an aide and directed him to ride over to the right to Jubal Early and "say to him, stand firm. Gen. Hill will be with him in a few moments."[34]

Early and his men had been stoutly resisting Prince's advance for as long as Taliaferro had been resisting Geary's. Early always showed to good advantage in tense tactical situations. He was in his element in the heat of action at the brigade and regimental level. (The general's stout spirit would stand him in good stead later in the war, when he was required to lead far larger units in difficult situations beyond his control.) By the time close infantry action developed at Cedar Mountain, Early had been at the front for four hours. For much of that time he commanded as much of the field as he could see and reach. Early's largely successful exertions that afternoon came at a time when he was unwell. His problem was not fever or disease, such as Winder and others suffered during Virginia's notorious "dog days in August." Early's problem was continuing debility from a five-month-old wound he had suffered while winning considerable glory at Williamsburg on May 5, 1862. The general had returned to duty at the beginning of July, but Ewell's report of Cedar Mountain asserted that Early "was still so enfeebled . . . as to be unable to mount his horse without assistance."[35] Early's long, hot, tense afternoon was far from over at 5:45, when the artillery duel wound down.

The timing of the onset of Prince's attack, vis-à-vis the arrival of Pegram's and Hardy's guns and the excitement about their danger at the hands of Federal skirmishers, is impossible to establish definitively. There can be no doubt that Prince and Geary attacked in unison; that Taliaferro and Early moved forward a short distance in tandem to meet them; that the Federal attack across the wheatfield was about fifteen minutes behind that of Geary and Prince south of the road; and that Thomas's Georgia Brigade moved behind Taliaferro to Early's right just as the action was opening. The timetable used in this study puts the start of the artillery duel at 4:00 P.M. and the onset through the corn against Early and Taliaferro at 5:45. A number of contemporaries suggest a steady, almost instantaneous, progression from the arrival of Pegram and Hardy, to Early's reflexive reaction to their danger, and then at once to the main Federal infantry attack. General Trimble, watching from the mountainside, was one such witness. Early's official report and postwar memoir also suggest that telescoped chronology, the latter account going so far as to place the opening of the wheatfield fight at the same time as the rescue of Pegram's guns.[36]

Several nuances in the record contribute to the conclusion that Pegram and Hardy were in place for some time before Augur attacked, but two considerations particularly stand out. First, the United States Regular battalion formed a skirmish line in the corn that was active through much of the artillery duel; it was that battalion which threatened the arriving Southern guns. The thoughtless conclusion that the guns were threatened by the first wave of a coordinated attack was easy to reach in the excitement and in retrospect, but it was not true. Second, some observers suggest that Taliaferro arrived after the action opened, which is absolutely untrue. Early failed to mention Taliaferro's brigade in most instances. James A. Walker's report, from the vantage point of Early's far left, clears up the Taliaferro chronology in resounding fashion.

At 5:45 Taliaferro was in position just to Early's left, tied in with Walker's Thirteenth Virginia. The rest of the brigade on to the right of the Thirteenth was in this order: Thirty-first Virginia, Twenty-fifth Virginia, Fifty-eighth Virginia, four companies of the Fifty-second Virginia (the other six had been left behind to picket crossroads in the morning), and the Twelfth Georgia.[37]

When the Federal skirmishers began to pester Early and the general examined the infantry supports to their rear, he began to worry about his right. The enemy seemed to overlap him in that direction, so he sent a request for help to Jackson and received a promise of support in return. General Early's concern for his right was intensified by the nature of the ground there. His line did not extend far south beyond the Cedars, and just beyond that point "the hill there falls off rather abruptly to the right." The fear that hostile infantry might come up under cover of that uneven ground contributed to Early's decision to call for help from Jackson.[38] As the affair developed, the uneven ground at that point caused Early trouble in the reverse of his expectations: he was on the right at a critical moment and could not tell what was happening to his left, rather than vice versa.

Early used the Twelfth Georgia Infantry to shore up his right. In doing so, the general made skillful use of the terrain. Early described the regiment's position as running "along the crest of a ridge, which made a curve in front, affording it a very good natural defense and enabling it to give the enemy a flank fire." That official contemporary description was augmented by the wording Early used in his postwar memoir, in which he identified the same small ridge as "leading out from the main one around in front of the clump of cedars." The Georgians' own historian used almost precisely the same language; he probably lifted his account nearly intact from Early's.[39]

The right of the line would be well served by the Twelfth Georgia and its brave commander, Captain William Frederick Brown. Early's left rested in the similarly competent hands of Colonel Walker and the Thirteenth Virginia. His difficulties would develop between those anchors. While Early began to think about his right, Walker and the left and center of the brigade came under heavy fire from Prince's advancing regiments. The Virginians advanced a short distance at the outset, in tandem with Taliaferro's brigade to their left, and then settled down to fire from the crest they had reached. Their targets—Prince's men—were coming through the corn, but at first fire these enemies were still "beyond the branch." The difficulties that Prince's regiments encountered, as recounted above, were not apparent to their opponents, which is hardly surprising. Colonel Walker thought the Federal advance came forward "slowly but steadily."[40]

In the exchange of musketry Lieutenant Colonel Alfred Henry Jackson of the Thirty-first Virginia fell wounded as his regiment fought on the right of the Thirteenth. Jackson was a kinsman of Stonewall, on whose staff he had served. Martin Mulvey of Company I of the Thirty-first Virginia carried A. H. Jackson off the field. The colonel lingered for fifty-one weeks before dying at Lexington, where he had attended Washington College, on August 1, 1863. Sergeant James Edward Winston of the Thirteenth Virginia was luckier: he had his clothes "pierced by several balls" and was slightly wounded, but survived to be killed twenty-three days later at Ox Hill. Another member of the Thirteenth Virginia, Sam Buck, had just returned from extended sick leave and did not have a weapon. Federal bullets that struck down his comrades solved Buck's armament needs. He picked up "any number of guns" dropped by stricken Confederates and fired their loads from them—ramrod and all, if the ramrod was lodged in the barrel.[41]

The two knots of artillery at the Cedars and near the Crittenden House fired rapidly, even frantically, against Prince's advance and in support of Early's infantry. One of the Marylanders with Dement's guns near the house claimed that they had to cease firing for a time to cool the guns. He calculated the Yankee advance not as coming "slowly and steadily," as Walker styled it, but rather as a series of assaults: "The Yankees . . . charged us nine times. . . . they where [sic] repulsed with great slaughter." An enemy officer on a conspicuous white horse rallied his lines again and again until Corporal George T. Scott of Dement's battery knocked him over with a well-aimed round. Colonel Crutchfield saw the deed and told Scott in front of his peers that he was "the finest shot in the service." Stonewall Jackson and R. S. Ewell both personally applauded the gunners near the house. Jackson's visit came at the height of the action. He told the Marylanders with more excitement than originality "to give the Yankees a little more grape," but by then they had expended all their canister and shell so the battery "was then useing round shot."[42]

Casualties among the men of both Brown's and Dement's batteries left them so shorthanded that both Brown and Dement each were obliged to assist personally with "loading and firing their pieces." Not all of the casualties were inflicted by the enemy, although there were more than enough of those. The merciless heat, abetted by the exertion of combat, left numbers of the cannoneers exhausted and prostrate around the guns. The artillerists were "almost famishing for water," and when a volunteer or two went after some the crews were further depleted. At least two of Dement's men were killed; one had an arm entirely severed and bled to death and the other lost both legs to a shell. Eleven other men were wounded—a total loss of one-fourth of the battery's active complement.[43]

As the Confederates plastered the cornfield with both small arms and artillery fire, and Early pushed the Twelfth Georgia into its forward oblique position, reinforcements from A. P. Hill made a timely appearance. The four Georgia regiments of Edward L. Thomas's brigade had covered ten miles under "the hottest sun you ever saw" by the time they neared the schoolhouse. They dashed forward at the double-quick for the last mile and then turned right to cross the field toward Early. A. P. Hill ordered Thomas to turn right off the road, and Stonewall Jackson personally placed the Georgians in the edge of the woods just short of the Crittenden Lane. As Jackson rode up to the Georgians, cap in hand (perhaps so they would recognize him), Thomas's men "yelled as only Johnnies could yell at sight of their beloved leader." Jackson reined in and sat bareheaded watching his reinforcements deploy. The halt was brief in this moment of intense action, then Jackson sent Thomas toward the right of Early.[44]

Thomas could see evidence of strain in Taliaferro's brigade in front of him, and as a result he either ordered (by his own account) or events dictated (by their account) the Fourteenth Georgia at the rear of the brigade to stay at that troubled spot. Thomas continued with the Thirty-fifth, Forty-fifth, and Forty-ninth Georgia regiments to the extreme right of the line, beyond Early's Twelfth Georgia, with orders Thomas described simply as "to hold that position."[45]

A captain in the Forty-fifth Georgia described the scene as the brigade hurried across "half a mile under a terrible fire of large and small arms" to reach the assigned post:

> The field we passed through was an extensive one, and presented to our sight, as we entered it, almost innumerable bodies of troops fighting, with nothing to protect them save the hand of God. Friend and foe were in open field, and such fighting is seldom witnessed. Troops of all descriptions—horses in every direction, with empty saddles—wounded and dead in all quar-

ters. But I am proud to say that with all this before us, the Forty-fifth Georgia went into it with as much spirit and determination as old soldiers, and fought like veterans.[46]

The Georgians' arrival inspirited the men they came to reinforce. A member of Jackson's headquarters cavalry detachment remembered with obvious relish how the line of gray-clad soldiers "broke from the woods to our . . . rear, [and] came at a double quick across the pasture field." The observer rethought his description and concluded that the advancing regiments really were not in line but "more like a drove or flock, for there was no regularity about it." Orderly or not, they were a welcome sight. Jackson sat near them on horseback as the Georgians broke from the woods.[47]

The Forty-ninth Georgia, one of the three regiments scurrying across the broad open field behind the Crittenden Lane, had started that morning with 213 men in the ranks. "Several" had succumbed to the heat en route. The rest started bravely through the field under the command of Lieutenant Colonel Seaborn M. Manning, the only field officer with the regiment. (The colonel and major had been wounded and captured, respectively, around Richmond.) Manning had not moved far out of the woods before he went down, severely wounded in the right arm, leaving the regiment without clear command in a moment of crisis. He died precisely one month later. Captain Samuel T. Player assumed command eventually by right of seniority, but one wing of the regiment remained under the control of Adjutant Mark Newman, who had been given that assignment by Manning.[48]

Early did not see Thomas coming to his assistance as soon as he would have had he been behind the center of his brigade. The general was aligning the Twelfth Georgia at the right of his line when Thomas led his regiments onto the scene. Their presence, he wrote, came "very unexpectedly to me." It was as though Thomas had arrived on cue, "just as" Early got the Twelfth Georgia set. The brigade formed line as it arrived along a fence overlooking the cornfield. Its field of fire pointed at Prince's southernmost troops. Thomas was, therefore, nearly at right angles to the Twelfth Georgia, which tied into his left. The brigade lay "behind the crest" of the same ridge that sheltered the Twelfth Georgia. The ridge "was so shaped that Thomas's line had the general direction of the main line," Early wrote, "but was in advance of it."[49]

The leading regiments of Hill's division had arrived in a most timely manner and moved raggedly but bravely and with reasonable efficiency to a critical point. Hill wrote proudly and accurately in his official report: "Much credit is due Thomas' brigade for the admirable manner in which they acted under very discouraging circumstances." Prince's men quickly felt the unpleasant impact of the fire of the Twelfth Georgia and of Thomas, which raked their flank viciously. Thomas probably opened fire at just about the time Prince's echeloned second line deployed because Early was worried about being overlapped to the right and enthused about the "timely arrival [which] rendered my right secure." An officer in the 102d New York remembered the bitter fire from his left from Rebels who seemed to be "right alongside of us," some of them even climbing up a tree for a better angle. The Georgians commenced picking off the New York regiment's officers "and took every company till they got to the third from the right."[50]

Thomas's men and the Twelfth Georgia were not immune to incoming fire by any means, but they enjoyed at least some cover, and they had the incalculable advantage of firing obliquely—sometimes directly—into a hostile flank. The Georgians maintained a "deadly fire," Early wrote, "strewing the ground with the killed." Although they arrived after the beginning of the fight, Thomas's men fired so rapidly that many of them ran short of rounds. The Forty-ninth Georgia ran out of cartridges, scrounged more from their own wounded and dead, and then found a few on Federal bodies near their line. Some of them eventually stood or lay in place with fixed bayonets. The men of the Forty-fifth Georgia expended from twenty-five to forty rounds apiece. They too exchanged their guns and cartridge boxes for those of the dead and wounded. One account insisted that some of the Forty-fifth's muskets grew so hot that they had to be cooled with water, presumably from the branch of Cedar Run immediately to the brigade's right.[51]

The Georgia press reported that Colonel Thomas was under fire for the twenty-fourth time at Cedar Mountain. He led the brigade from in front in the densest of the fire, which was dense indeed. An artillerist wrote that on the right of the line "the musketry raged with terrifying fury. The surrounding air was full of flying messengers that gathered in with a dull thud many inhabitants for the silent city of the dead." The Forty-fifth Georgia took 156 officers and men into the fight and lost 7 killed and 41 wounded—more than 30 percent. The Forty-ninth lost 9 killed and 41 wounded.[52]

The Thirty-fifth and Forty-fifth stood intact through the fight, but the Forty-ninth moved about in fragments, doubtless because of the absence of its field officers. The alignment of Thomas's three regiments cannot be precisely established. The right of the Forty-ninth tied to the left of the Thirty-fifth, but whether the Forty-fifth fought to the right or the left of that two-regiment block remains unclear. In either case, the junction between the Thirty-fifth and Forty-ninth became a pressure point. Adjutant Mark Newman of the Forty-ninth had been detailed to command of the regiment's right wing by Manning and retained it. Newman directed the company officers to scavenge for ammunition among the fallen of both sides while the infantrymen kept up the fire. Captain John Haynes Pate of Company K led his own and another company to support Newman's right and "directed the fire of his men with such precision that the effect was visible to the men in the ranks." Captain James T. Chappell of Company G took up a wounded man's gun and poured out a steady fire with it. Captain James Y. Willcox led Company B with distinction until he fell with a wound that eventually killed him.[53]

While the cornfield below Cedar Mountain seethed and boiled, Ewell's two brigades and two batteries looked down from their splendid vantage point on the mountain's forward shoulder. The brigades could do little but watch the struggles of Thomas, Early, and Taliaferro, but the batteries contributed their fire with élan. A Federal on the plain below mentioned the plunging fire several times when he wrote of the battle and admitted that the Northern regiments "were severely scarred by the enemy's . . . pieces on the mountain." Eighteen-year-old Joseph White Latimer sat on horseback in the midst of the volcano near the Slaughter house and directed the fire of the guns. His "clear, boyish voice" rang out again and again: "Ready, aim, fire!" An Alabama infantry officer looking on, and writing from the perspective of an oldster of twenty-eight years, called "this beardless boy" the "Little Napoleon."[54] The exaggeration is pardonable; Latimer really was a remarkable youngster.

General Trimble was most impressed by the effect of the guns on Federal batteries along the Mitchell's Station Road. Latimer drew their attention throughout the afternoon, Trimble reported, "and thus aided materially in deciding the result of the day." The infantry along the Crittenden Lane would have disputed Trimble's analysis in preference for the impact of the guns on the Federal infantry trying to overwhelm them from the cornfield. For either target, Latimer and Lieutenant Terry's associated guns could select their range "in perfect security, and in a clear atmosphere above the smoke of the battlefield . . . with all the deliberation and skill of target practice."[55]

The degree to which Latimer and his friends were immune to incoming rounds is the subject of some gradations of testimony. The difference probably is traceable to differing backgrounds and expectations; artillery always was noisy and spectacular, even when only marginally effective. A Louisiana officer wrote of "suffering from the fire of the enemy whilst we were lying in position." His brigade commander used almost the same words—"suffered considerably." An Alabama officer vividly described the enemy's bursting shells, which "plowed up the ground . . . and filled the air with sulphurous smoke." A private in the Louisiana Brigade attempted to quantify the incoming fire. He estimated that five hundred shells came at them, but only a single one of them did any harm to his regiment, the Fourteenth Louisiana, and even that one did not explode. Even though it did not explode, and was only "a small shell no bigger than my fist," it beheaded Private Ralph Smith and wounded five other men. Those six men constituted the total loss of the Fourteenth Louisiana during the entire day.[56]

Despite the occasionally harmful rounds and the noise and pyrotechnics, the men on the mountain were relatively secure. G. Campbell Brown of Ewell's staff commented on Latimer's fabulous field of fire and noted by contrast that most enemy responses "fell short, and hardly any did much harm." Dr. Robert L. Dabney, Jackson's biographer and quondam staff member, is a more important source for Cedar Mountain than he is for most other battle action because of the circumstances under which he prepared that chapter. His summary of the invulnerability of Ewell's artillery is good: "In consequence of the elevation of their position, [Latimer and Terry] commanded a wide range of the country below, and were themselves secure from the fire of the enemy. Every shot aimed at them fell short, and buried itself, without ricochet, in the hill-side beneath them."[57]

Most of the infantrymen on the mountain near Ewell's artillery enjoyed the battle from their superb seats. They were, after all, accustomed to being the bloody grist in the maw of battles, but on August 9 they watched and cheered from afar. "It was a grand sight," Alabamian William C. Oates exclaimed. One of the enlisted men in Oates's regiment enthused about the "splendid view," and Robert H. Miller of the Fourteenth Louisiana was little short of rhapsodic: "Of all the grand sights and sounds this excelled, of all sublimity this was the most sublime sight I have ever seen or imagined. It was worth all the dangers we passed and more. Two mighty armies rush tegether [*sic*] . . . the smoke rises far above even us like indeed the smoke of a great furnace. The clash and roar of muskets and the thunder of the cannon were terrible, not frightening but it filled even the least sensitive with awe."[58]

By contrast, Federals seeking to obtain a coup d'oeil from behind their own lines looked in vain because there was no elevation there to lift them above the gunsmoke. One of them was prompted by his fruitless search to remark that many soldiers "fought a whole day without so much as a glimpse of an enemy." The billowing smoke and dusk concealed most movements from view, "and where the greatest execution is done, the antagonists have frequently fired at a line of smoke, behind which columns may or may not have been posted."[59] Ewell's aerie above the smoke and dust gave a few thousand Confederates a unique opportunity to watch a battle unfold.

Ewell himself was not among those stirred to positive enthusiasm by the view. That thorough old soldier watched the battle and was prompted to write a few days later of the "gloomy prospect": "Some 100,000 human beings have been massacred in every conceivable form of horror . . . all because of a set of fanatical abolitionists and unprincipled politicians backed by women in petticoats and pants and children." Ewell spread his deep and commendable distaste for politicians equally between abolitionists and the "chivalry . . . in Richmond," who by August 1862 seemed to him to have "played themselves out pretty completely." Dick Ewell capped his ruminations prompted by the view from Cedar Mountain with a horribly prescient statement about how wars develop their own momentum: "It opens a series of events that no one can see to the end."[60]

Faceless and unquenchable historical imperatives aside, Ewell was doing his best to win the war from his mountainside perch. At some point during the action, probably soon after Augur's infantry advanced into the corn, Latimer moved farther down the mountain's shoulder with two of his pieces for a better vantage. Lieutenant Terry's guns remained at the original site near the Slaughter house. The Federals moved a section to counter Latimer, further reducing their impact on Southern infantry on the plain. Latimer found a nice location "behind a slight rise" and soon "used up" the section aiming at him. Ewell's official report commented favorably on Latimer's "usual coolness and judgment."[61]

The prospect for an advance down the mountain and around the Federal left flank on the Mitchell's Station Road surely entered

Ewell's mind. Henry Kyd Douglas of Jackson's staff claimed that Jackson sent him up the mountain to order Ewell to attack. Ewell had assigned control of Forno's Louisiana Brigade to Trimble so that unflaggingly aggressive Baltimorean commanded all the infantry on the mountain. Even Trimble could not find a way to get his infantry into the Northern flank effectively. At the same time that Augur's advance opened the infantry action in earnest, Trimble sent the Fifteenth Alabama forward as skirmishers "with orders to advance on the enemy's flank." The Federal artillery promptly paid them considerable unwanted attention; their path also was interdicted by the curtain of Southern artillery fire coming off the mountain. One of the Alabamians felt that they "had a golden opportunity of crushing the enemy's left, but could not do so on account of our own shells." Trimble sent couriers back to Ewell asking for relief, but the crisis on the plain had reached a level at which no diminution in the artillery barrage could be considered.[62]

At about 6:00 P.M., as Ewell's guns belched fire from the mountain and the brigades of Thomas, Early, and Taliaferro blazed away along the ridge in front of the Crittenden Lane, the entire Confederate right was shocked and all but routed by an avalanche of Federals who swarmed out of the woods near the wheatfield. As Early rode back toward his left from posting Thomas, he discovered that his line was in chaos and disintegrating further with each passing moment. The Confederate left around the wheatfield had ceased to exist.

CHAPTER 7

The Confederate Left Dissolves

WHEN AUGUR'S infantry attack struck the Confederates south of the road, the Southerners' unusually shaped line north of the road remained highly vulnerable on its left. That vulnerability was about to disappear because the Tenth Virginia from south of the road was en route to extend the left, and the entire Stonewall Brigade hovered beyond the left in position to close up the line. A capricious fate decreed that the Federal attack would strike, unwittingly but fortuitously for its prospects, just before the Tenth Virginia arrived on site and just before the inept commander of the Stonewall Brigade was prodded into closing on Garnett's left. Garnett's plaintive words summarized the narrow margin: "Had re-enforcements . . . arrived ten minutes sooner no disaster would have happened."

The brand-new Confederate division commander responsible was General William B. Taliaferro, replacing the dying Charles S. Winder. The confusion attendant upon that command change seems certain to deserve some blame for the poorly aligned left flank, and indeed most historians writing of the battle have endorsed that judgment. Careful examination of the evidence suggests, however, that Taliaferro paid far more attention to that end of the line than had the unfortunate artillery-oriented Winder. Just a few more minutes of grace would have left Taliaferro with an advantage Winder had not much cared about—a solid and extensive left flank.

General Samuel W. Crawford's brigade of General Alpheus S. Williams's division was the small but potent Federal unit that generated most of the mischief for the Confederate left. Williams had commanded the brigade himself before his elevation to division command and remained understandably fond of the officers and men. Near midday on that blazing ninth of August, Williams invited his old comrades in arms to lunch at division headquarters. A dozen or so of the field officers and staff of the Fifth Connecticut, Twenty-eighth New York, and Forty-sixth Pennsylvania sat down with Williams to a menu of "coffee, ham," and a mysteriously enticing "etc."

142

They lounged under a shade tree, Williams wrote, "as unconcerned and careless as if . . . on the lawn of a watering place." Within a few hours every one of the general's guests was dead or wounded.[1]

About five hours after their officers polished off the ham and the "etc.," the three Federal regiments received orders to attack across the wheatfield against the exposed Southern left in the opposite woods. The Tenth Maine also belonged to Crawford's brigade, but it lagged behind and fought virtually alone later. So did six companies of the Third Wisconsin, which Crawford appropriated for support on his right, where they ran into isolation and difficulty. Crawford's attack by three and six-tenths regiments was a phenomenally aggressive move by General N. P. Banks. He apparently made it in almost reflexive annoyance with Confederate artillery, which was giving him a hard time. The degree to which Pope was seeking or shunning aggression from Banks on this day subsequently grew into a cause célèbre. Banks obviously came to be sensitive on the subject (although his basic position in the controversy was stronger than that of the mendacious Pope): when the meddlesome Committee on the Conduct of the War began poking around, Banks told them with a straight face that the Confederates had inaugurated hostilities when they attacked his right late in the afternoon.[2] Who could blame him, in that Jacobin chamber?

Crawford's regiments advanced into the wheatfield a few minutes before 6:00 P.M. within the relative chronology used in this study. (Original accounts offer precise times scattered over a range of more than three hours.) Augur's division by then had been "engaged in long range firing for a considerable time," according to the historian of the Fifth Connecticut. He might have been referring to the extensive skirmishing by Augur's regular battalion, which did indeed go on at length. Federals in George H. Gordon's brigade, the other brigade in Williams's division, followed Crawford's route into the wheatfield that afternoon, but they were still lounging to the rear with leisure to watch Augur's main attack when it began. Stonewall Jackson described the development of the attack on Early and his reinforcement by Thomas and cinched the chronology with this phrasing: "While the attack upon Early was in progress the main body of the Federal infantry moved down from the wood . . . and fell with great vigor upon our extreme left."[3]

The wheatfield about to become the arena for the most dramatic fighting at Cedar Mountain warrants meticulous description. Inevitably, the quantified descriptions of contemporaries vary enormously

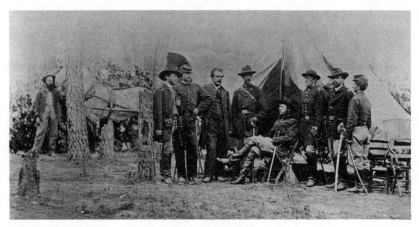

Brigadier General Samuel W. Crawford and
his staff. (Library of Congress)

(for instance, from eighty to one thousand yards for east-west width). Its salient features, however, can be well defined, and concrete facts such as dimensions are susceptible to fairly solid estimation.

The woods on either side of the wheatfield generally stood dense, particularly as they thickened away from the open space. On the Federal side, the forest was "thick with weeds, briars and under-brush, and almost impassable, and one could see but a little way to the right or left." Near their western edge, and the eastern edge of the wheatfield, "the woods became somewhat thinner." Along the fringe of the Federal woods there ran "a high log fence." The field was about three hundred yards wide, although the width varied, nar-rowing farther from the main road; it was about twice as long (north-south) as it was wide and encompassed some forty acres.[4]

Many of the Federal infantrymen looking out of their wood line could not see their goal well or at all because the wheatfield, like the rest of the battlefield, was uneven. One of the Northerners who fought across the field and then back again described the terrain with some care: "There is a swell of the ground, which falls off gently toward the enemy's side, and becomes a marsh; but as it approaches the enemy's wood, it rises again rather suddenly, and the hillside thus made is densely wooded." Another participant reported on the mid-field feature, viewed from the east: the field "was nearly level or rose gradually for about a third of the way, and then fell gradually into a slight hollow in which there was a small brook flowing towards the

144

road, which was pretty much dry at this time." The east-west contours were most pronounced, but there also was a slight descent prevailing from north to south in the direction of the road.

The stream that had cut the swale and occupied its bottom lay at least three-fourths of the way along the Federal route from tree line to tree line and probably even closer than that to the Confederate woods. A member of the Tenth Maine wrote that "the small marshy run" ran only "a few rods from the western edge of the field." A "small log shanty" stood next to the stream and a spring (the shanty probably was a springhouse) near where the stream crossed the main road.

The wheat that had grown in the field all summer had been harvested recently, and at least some of it remained in shocks. The shocks did not seem very numerous to the Northerners, so perhaps some had been removed before the armies arrived; or perhaps Southern agricultural patterns bemused the invaders. Desperate soldiers would use the wheat shocks for shelter in the coming battle, though of course they were not adequate for that purpose. The open space also was "dotted with stone heaps" accumulated over the years by farmers clearing the field. Those obviously made far better barricades than did wheat shocks and therefore were at a premium.

A second field capped the northern end of the wheatfield. This "brushy field," as it will be called in this study of the battle, was about two-thirds as large as the wheatfield and ran at right angles to it. The eastern edges of the two fields coincided, but the brushy field's western edge lay well west of the wheatfield's western edge. The configuration of the two combined fields resembled (as was suggested in Chapter 4 above) an inverted and backward "L." The northern field earned its name by virtue of ground cover variously described as "a low, bushy growth, hardly taller anywhere than a man, but so very thick as to be a perfect cover"; "brushwood the height of a man's head"; "brushwood of the height of a man's shoulders"; "low shrub oaks and brush of a couple of years' growth, rising to the height of men's shoulders"; and, "a great stretch of 'barren,' spotted with dwarf cedars." No doubt the height of the man being used for comparative purposes had something to do with the variant descriptions. Two sources identify the origins of the brushy field as being in a timbering operation of recent vintage. Anyone who has struggled through a Virginia clear cut aged two through six years is well aware of the amazingly indiscriminate fecundity with which the state's environment operates in those circumstances.

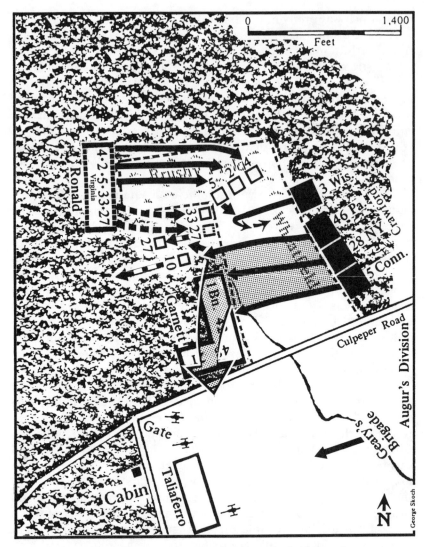

Crawford Shatters the Confederate Left, 6:00–6:15

An important feature of the brushy field's southern edge and the wheatfield's northern reaches was a gentle lateral ridge, running nominally east-west and segregating action accordingly. The initial attack by Crawford's brigade and the subsequent effort by Gordon's each would find a mixture of relief and despair in the interdicting ridge: it would block some fire from the isolated Confederate left (the Stonewall Brigade) against Northern regiments nearer the road; but it also would isolate some Federal right-flank elements from support on their left and leave them ripe for destruction.

Samuel Crawford spread his brigade along the wood line and ordered the men to fix bayonets while he made final preparations to attack across the wheatfield, about which he doubtless knew but little. Crawford put the Fifth Connecticut on his left, although not flush with the road. The Twenty-eighth New York moved up on the right of the Connecticut men, and the Forty-sixth Pennsylvania constituted the right third of Crawford's three-regiment main line. One of Banks's staff officers needlessly appropriated Crawford's fourth regiment, the Tenth Maine, to support a battery to the left and rear of the brigade. The Maine regiment went out into the field later and suffered extremely heavy losses to no good purpose. Crawford could exert little control over the last of his elements, an aggregation of six companies of the Third Wisconsin of Gordon's brigade. One of General Williams's staff officers ordered the Wisconsin companies to advance on Crawford's right, and they did so bravely but without any coordination.[5]

To rectify some of his ignorance of the ground and of enemy positions, Crawford took the logical step of sending out a scouting party under a sergeant. These inquisitive Federals moved carefully across the wide open field as far as the little hollow just below the Confederate tree line. When they reached the spring, "they discovered the gray uniforms thick among the foliage of the forest." At that range they could have hit them with a tossed pebble. Amazingly, the Confederates did not molest these enemies, though they could have killed them with ease and captured them with little more effort. The relieved Northerners concluded that the Confederates "were calmly waiting for bigger and more game."[6]

Banks ordered his chief of artillery to suspend fire when he was ready to unleash Crawford across the wheatfield. Williams ordered Crawford to attack, but Crawford first attempted to secure some close artillery support to prepare his way. Williams sent an aide with orders to go at once. The brigade's first step into the field was a false one. When Captain William S. Cogswell, acting as an aide to Crawford, brought orders to the Fifth Connecticut to attack, most of the regiment climbed the fence at the edge of the woods and rushed into the field. The rest of the main line did not yet have their orders, however, and the eager Fifth had to be rounded up and herded back

This early photograph of the battlefield bore a caption identifying the open space as the famous wheatfield, though what portion of the field it shows cannot be determined. (Library of Congress)

into the woods. There Colonel George D. Chapman took the occasion to deliver a stump speech to his men.[7]

By the time Chapman wound down, the time to attack was at hand and the three regiments went over the fence and into line. In getting over the fence, some of the men pulled sections down and others left their sections intact. The leveled stretches would become the most popular ones when surviving Federals later passed that way again in great haste. When the regiments were aligned to their commanders' satisfaction, they formed relative to one another and then "burst with loud cries" across the wheatfield "like a torrent," according to General Gordon of the reserve brigade. The officers of the Fifth Connecticut screamed at their men, "Charge, charge and yell." The bearers of the flags of the three regiments waved them steadily in the torrid air as the lines moved through the wheat stubble.[8]

Federals advancing near the road could see one of Geary's regiments moving forward to their left briefly against Taliaferro at the same moment that the wheatfield attack rolled westward. The Ohioans across the road did not have much success, though; the Fifth Connecticut saw them recoil in short order. The men in the wheatfield recognized the debt they owed Augur's men, whose cooperation kept Confederates in that quadrant from lacerating Crawford's left. Nothing could divert Ewell's guns on the mountain from this new target. Even at that considerable range the artillery on the Confederate stronghold "threw shells with beautiful exactness" into the wheatfield, according to a Northern observer.[9]

Up to Crawford's right the six companies of the Third Wisconsin scrambled to catch up to the right of the front line. When they reached the fence, they knocked it down and moved into the field on the run. Even so, the Wisconsin men moved less rapidly than Crawford because of rough ground and briars. They could not see Crawford's brigade and assumed that they had beaten it to the field. In fact, Crawford was out of sight to their left beyond the knoll.[10]

The instant the Northerners came into view in the middle of the field, the Confederate line opened on them with crashing volleys. Two Massachusetts officers in the reserve brigade back in the woods, both of them good witnesses, remarked on the instantaneous musketry. There had been no skirmishing of note in the field (witness the remarkable career of the Federal scouting party). The opening volley came "with a crash," wrote General George H. Gordon, and at once settled into "volleys so terrible that the sound of artillery was unnoticed or a relief." The notion of artillery noise as a relief from the awful sound of musketry supplies an interesting psychological footnote on the stress of combat. In the same spirit, Colonel George L. Andrews described the small arms cacophony as "the heaviest and most continuous sound of musketry that I ever heard. It was not preceded by scattering shots, but at once became a steady roar."[11]

Federal accounts speak with more grimness of the results of the first Southern volleys than do the accounts of the men who fired those volleys. That surprising result, which contravenes every basic rule of contemporary battle reporting, may have risen from the obliteration of the Confederate line thereafter. The usual tendency toward perceiving one's enemy as harmed out of all proportion to one's own hurts probably succumbed in this instance to the confusions of a very fluid battlefield. The Fifth Connecticut's historian reported that Southern musketry "opened upon them at once, vigorously," and "swept through the ranks." Another onlooker described the Confederate fire as "deadly showers of bullet and ball."[12]

Before the Twenty-eighth New York completed its trek across the field, Colonel Dudley Donnelly fell mortally wounded and was taken from the field on his horse by his orderly. Lieutenant Colonel Edwin

F. Brown of the same regiment went down with his arm shattered. By the time the New Yorkers finished their bloody work for the afternoon, seventeen of the eighteen officers with the regiment were casualties. No fewer than seven bearers of the Fifth Connecticut's colors fell dead during the advance, the regimental historian claimed, and others were wounded. By his count, three "distinct and tremendous volleys had swept through the ranks" by the time the Fifth reached the halfway point across the field and the firing became continuous. A sergeant carrying the Connecticut state flag was shot down, got up and stumbled forward, then was shot down again just as he began the ascent from the last hollow to the Confederate woods. When the wounded man regained consciousness, he wrapped the flag around his body and crawled to the rear for help.[13]

The Federal right, moving a little more slowly and under somewhat greater difficulties, went into action shortly after the Fifth Connecticut and Twenty-eighth New York. The Forty-sixth Pennsylvania came under fire "a minute or two earlier" than the fragment of the Third Wisconsin on the far right.[14]

Perhaps fifteen hundred Federal soldiers rushed across the Cedar Mountain wheatfield. They could not have gotten across without considerable élan and stubborn bravery. The survivors were immensely proud of their attack in later years, and with entire justification. One of the contemporary tributes to their bravery deserves reproduction here, at least in part, not because of its aesthetic merit but as an apposite bit of popular lore. These two verses are from *The 28th Regiment, N.Y. Vols. 1st Brig., 1st Div., 12th Army Corps, At the Battle of Cedar Mountain, Va., Aug. 9th, 1862*, an undated 128-line broadside by Charles H. Squires:

> Whizzing through the air, the bullets
>   Strew the slain upon the ground.
> Deadly rifle, roaring cannon,
>   Send a mist of smoke around.
>
> Hand to hand the conflict rages,
>   Foe meets foe, in mortal strife,
> And the herbage 'round is sprinkled
>   With the gore of human life.

The poem concludes with a mighty Federal victory and the fall of darkness.[15]

Anxious friends watching Crawford's men from the Federal woods saw some hesitation near the wood line. Some Northerners darted into the woods. Some Confederates emerged from the woods briefly and fought with pistols and clubbed muskets and bayonets. A fence at the edge of the Confederate wood line posed more of an obstacle, defended as it was, than the fence at the Federal woods had been. The "Virginia rail fence" or "high rail-fence" stood just inside the edge of the timber. The wavering at the fence cannot have occupied more than a few moments, yet Adjutant Heber S. Smith of the Fifth Connecticut was struck dead by no fewer than nine bullets as he stood next to it. Some of the Federals counted three lines of Confederates in the edge of the woods—one line prostrate in front, a second kneeling behind the first, and a third standing in the rear. Enemy they could see they could hit, and the Federals started to draw beads on targets from the edge of the woods. In a moment, though, they "sprang over the fence or flung it aside" and surged into the midst of the Confederates, now on an equal footing with them under cover of the timber.[16]

Once the Federals stormed into the woods, Garnett's left in very short order was "thrown, helpless and confused, into a disordered mass," General Gordon wrote enthusiastically, "over which, with cries of exultation, our troops poured, while field and woods were filled with clamor and horrid rout."[17]

Stonewall Jackson's army teetered on the brink of disaster as Crawford's little brigade caved in its left. When Jackson and other thoughtful Confederates came to evaluate the fiasco on the left, they must have asked themselves why Garnett's brigade folded up. Even granted the instability of the left of that brigade, how could three average-sized regiments and part of another one attack across a bare field and drive the Virginians from a covered position? Had someone collapsed with unseemly ease? Someone had indeed.

The initial hostile action taken by Garnett's brigade on August 9 actually was directed away from the wheatfield. Garnett's right wing elements that faced south—the Twenty-first Virginia and half of the Forty-eighth Virginia—gazed out across the cornfields in front of Taliaferro and Early and had an excellent enfilade angle against the Federals under Augur, who attacked in that zone. The Forty-eighth Virginia sent skirmishers to the front, and they soon became engaged.[18] Their line of advance must have been south across the road, in front of the south-facing right half of the Forty-eighth, since the Federal scouting party that came through the wheatfield all the way to the run near the Forty-eighth went unchallenged. (In fact, a southward preoccupation on the part of the Forty-eighth Virginia is the only thing that reasonably solves the mystery of the phantom Federal scouts.)

Augur's attack drew Taliaferro's attention southward for obvious reasons. Its noise filled the heavens, and everyone (except Crawford) gazed riveted on the scene. Taliaferro ordered Garnett to advance with his right against Augur's flank. Fortunately, that never happened—or perhaps it was unfortunate, because the kaleidoscope of action about to erupt would thus have had yet another interesting stray meteor in its midst. After reporting the framing of that order, Taliaferro ignored its abortion without explanation and contented himself with applause for the fire the Twenty-first Virginia hurled across the road at Augur: "The Twenty-first Virginia . . . poured a destructive fire upon the enemy and exhibited a degree of heroic gallantry rarely ever witnessed." The Twenty-first was a superb regiment, but Taliaferro's hyperbole was far from warranted for an operation so simple as flailing an exposed flank with musketry. (The Twenty-first would have a chance to earn genuine superlatives within minutes.) Colonel Garnett reported with more balance that both the Twenty-first and Forty-eighth regiments behaved with "coolness and determination" in helping to deal with Augur.[19]

A few hundred yards north and a little east of the Twenty-first Virginia lay the First Virginia Battalion under Major John Seddon. The battalion was Garnett's left flank element. It also was the left flank unit of the army's contiguous line. Well beyond the First Battalion—far enough beyond to be nothing like a continuation of the line—the Stonewall Brigade awaited obvious orders to close in on the main position. Somewhere behind the First Battalion, painfully close to reaching the place where it was needed, the Tenth Virginia Infantry fumbled in the woods. Major Seddon's official report noted that "just as the enemy advanced" he received imprecise intelligence that the Tenth Virginia lurked somewhere to his left. Seddon's introductory phrase indicated his frustration about the wretched timing and luck: "It may be proper to add that" was a mid-nineteenth-century locution signaling irritation or some other irregular form of expression.[20]

General Taliaferro had gone to the left in person and done some first hand scouting without discerning any Federal threat. By the time he reached the Gate on his return trip, an officer from the left hurried up to him with a report that, wrote Taliaferro, "the enemy were showing themselves in front of the position I had just left."

View of the wheatfield in 1910, looking northeast from a point mid-way up the Confederate wood line. (Gould Papers, Duke University)

The general's response was to hurry the Tenth Virginia in that direction and to encourage Ronald to "move . . . rapidly" thither with the Stonewall Brigade. Stonewall Jackson's own emissary on the left, James Keith Boswell of his staff, had time and inclination to look more thoroughly for Yankees than Taliaferro had done. Jackson had sent Boswell up the line toward the left in response to several stimuli, including warnings from Early about possible danger there. Boswell and Lieutenant Thomas T. L. Snead passed the First Virginia Battalion, where Major Seddon and Captain Benjamin Watkins Leigh warned of enemy "a short distance" ahead. The two men deflected farther to the Confederate left and then advanced cautiously to the edge of the clearing. They crouched there when the Federal assault surged forward.[21]

Scouts and skirmishers and general forebodings aside, every Confederate along the wheatfield's western verge received ample warning that Federals were coming at least a few moments before the opening volley. Crawford's attack achieved a tactical surprise of sorts, but it was not launched with anything like last-second stealth. The soldiers of the Twenty-eighth New York took their first steps with "loud cheers." Boswell and Snead were astonished to see the Federal line materialize over a crest less than one hundred yards away from them. As the attacking line advanced rapidly toward the left of the First Virginia Battalion, which it overlapped, Boswell hastened away in full cognizance of what was happening. He found his horse where he had left it with a courier just behind the First Virginia Battalion, yelled something of what he had seen, and galloped toward the Gate to find Stonewall Jackson.[22]

The Forty-second Virginia and the Forty-eighth Virginia both were seasoned regiments, veterans of the Shenandoah Valley campaign, which had made Jackson immortal, and of the battles around Richmond. All of the Forty-second and about half of the Forty-eighth faced the wheatfield, as did the First Virginia Battalion. The battalion was to prove inadequate for the task facing it, but even so the regiment and a half of veteran infantry should have been able to halt three regiments advancing on a naked plain. The Confederates' poor configuration played into Federal hands by accident. The impotent left was ripe for turning. Before the Federals could get across the wheatfield to reach that goal, the Forty-second men and those of the Forty-eighth who were oriented properly took a toll of their attackers. Captain Abner Dobyns of the Forty-second was the regiment's ranking unwounded survivor and wrote its official report. He reckoned that the enemy line reached the midway point in the field before the Forty-second opened fire on them "with a great deal of coolness and rapidity." Dobyns also calculated that the regiment maintained the frontal fire "for some half an hour or more." In that estimate the captain was egregiously mistaken. But the Federals complained with good cause about the fire from his regiment and his neighbors in the Forty-eighth. Those two Virginia units unleashed the "murderous fire from the front" that struck such hard blows in the Northern ranks.[23]

The fire delivered against the attackers by the First Virginia Battalion not only was less effective than that of the Forty-second and Forty-eighth: it was not effective at all. Four accounts by contemporaries looking out from the battalion's position agree on the imposing spectacle the Northerners made as they came into the Confederates' musket sights. The "beautiful" attacking formation was in either two or three lines and moved "rapidly" or "at a double-quick." Its most ominous feature was its length, which extended well beyond the left of the First Virginia Battalion; in fact, it seemed to Major Seddon "to extend indefinitely in both directions." A lieutenant in Seddon's command wrote that the Federals "extended as far as my eyes could reach ... overlapping us." Brigade commander Garnett had returned to the First Battalion's position meanwhile, arriving to find the front rank of the enemy no more than fifty yards from the wood line.[24]

Inadequately disciplined soldiers in the Confederate position had been discharging "a continual scattering fire" from the moment the Federals first broke cover, but most of the battalion's soldiers awaited the appropriate tactical moment selected by their officers for deadly volley firing. That moment came at a range of about 125 yards, which is to say with the Federals barely more than midway across the field. Major Seddon examined the leveled weapons of his men, who must have been unbearably tense, and pronounced the muskets "well leveled" and the men "perfectly cool and collected." When he bellowed "Fire," the result should have been catastrophic to the New York and Pennsylvania infantry down range. The next step logically would have been deterioration of the advance into an exchange of fire dominated by inertia and Federal casualties. When Seddon looked eastward into the wheatfield, however, he saw to his horror that "not a single shot had taken effect." That bald admission made among friends did not reach print in his official report, but even there Seddon could claim no more than that the volley achieved "very little effect." An officer in the Twenty-eighth New York on the receiving end of the First Virginia Battalion's impotent musketry agreed with Major Seddon's reading. "It went over our heads," Lieutenant William P. Warren recalled, "and I don't think a man was touched in the brigade." Seddon hurriedly—probably frantically—ordered a second volley and then a third as the distance rapidly narrowed. They, too, he thought, had "little effect." Lieutenant Warren agreed that the second fire did no harm, but by his account the bullets of the third volley "flew around and carried down many a brave boy."[25]

The Federals fired back at the First Battalion enthusiastically but without much more success. One of the few victims among the Virginians noted unhappily that his unit "was the nearest hostile object that those overlapping us had to shoot at, so we caught it a long way to our left front." Colonel Garnett, arriving in the midst of the crisis, described the Federal fire as "most galling," but in fact not a man in the First Battalion was killed by hostile action all·day long. Lieutenant

Charles Alexander, on the exposed left of the battalion, saw one man die at his feet and supposed that he had been shot; but when his friends buried him the next day they found no wound on him and concluded that the heat and stress killed him. Alexander was one of only ten men reported wounded in the battalion.[26]

Moments after Seddon's men loosed the last of their three painfully ineffective volleys, the front wave of the attackers stumbled gasping into the edge of the woods. There they came up against a physical obstacle in the form of what one of them described as "a high and strong log fence." The brief delay negotiating the fence exposed the Federals to "the hottest fire of the whole charge," and at point-blank range. Veterans of the Fifth Connecticut insisted that fully fifty men fell at the fence, either killed or wounded, in less than three minutes. Dead bodies piled up in the narrow wood line beside the fence deeply enough to hinder movement. The body of one victim bore mute testimony to the intensity of this brief, deadly exchange. Major John Seddon's horse, a beautiful gray animal of great value, fell at the first volley and caught pieces of several other volleys as well. The next day some Southerners of morbid mien took the trouble to count 165 bullet holes in the poor creature and wondered how many human targets had been unwittingly spared by the equine shield. Seddon's gray might have been the only fatal casualty in the entire First Virginia Battalion on August 9.[27]

Stonewall Jackson, that most vigorous of military men, paid high compliment to Crawford's Federals when he described their attack in his official report as falling "with great vigor." He attributed to the attack "the force of superior numbers," which it did not enjoy by any large margin. Jackson was brutally frank, however, in describing what happened to his dangling left: the enemy bore down all opposition, turned the left, and "Campbell's brigade fell back in disorder." The general's use of that long outdated name for Garnett's brigade harkened back, perhaps in nostalgia, to the days of the Shenandoah Valley campaign.[28]

What happened when the Federals poured through and over the fence and into the woods can be easily summarized: the First Virginia Battalion broke and fled.

The left of the First Battalion did not extend much more than 250 yards north of the main road and therefore only about half of the way up the wood line toward the northwest corner of the field. Although the Third Wisconsin on the Federal right and the Forty-sixth Pennsylvania next to it were stymied to some degree, the Twenty-eighth New York still extended far enough north to get around the left of the First Battalion. That unfortunate unit also suffered because its piece of the wood line grew less densely than the rest and "the thinness of the trees exposed them to view" and made them an inviting target. One of the attackers estimated that the Confederate left was "entirely overpowered" within ten minutes after entering the woods. The time cannot have been longer than that and probably was much less. Colonel Garnett was with the First Battalion moments before it collapsed and reported the event without equivocation: "The First Virginia Battalion gave way in confusion, and rendered abortive every effort of its . . . officers to reform it." A bullet knocked Major Seddon's hat off during the vain attempt at rallying, but he escaped unhit.[29]

Seddon was equally straightforward in acknowledging the chaos into which his unit dissolved. He reported that "the battalion gave way, and retreated rapidly and in great confusion." Seddon intimated, no doubt accurately, that the enemy's envelopment left his men no route to survival but flight. The battalion's lack of casualties makes clear the success of that measure. The major went on to confess his chagrin at the unwillingness of his men to rally once they had escaped their predicament. Seddon was an aristocratic Virginian from the vicinity of Fredericksburg, a brother of the Confederate secretary of war, and a member of the Virginia legislature during the war. He suffered from poor health, which the ordeal at Cedar Mountain cannot have improved any. Two months later he resigned from the army to tend to his health, apparently in vain, because he died in 1863.[30]

Two company officers in the battalion recorded their experiences, neither of them with the frankness displayed by Garnett and Seddon. One described the Federal attack at length but merely noted that the battalion "fell back to the main road" under pressure. The other reported a few wounds among the men before "the line crumpled off to rightward."[31]

The rout of the First Virginia Battalion drew widespread calumny from its brothers in arms elsewhere on the field. An artillery officer unconnected with the battalion who participated in the vain attempts to rally it wrote to his mother a few days later: "The Irish Battalion [as the First Battalion commonly was known] broke disgracefully & could not be rallied, to the untold humiliation of its officers." James A. Walker's copy of the published reports of the battle contains a penned note about the battalion that is notable for both brevity and clarity: "Behaved badly." A lonely exception to that judgment came from Irish chaplain James B. Sheeran, on the other side of the field, who claimed that that battalion "boldly" stood alone although "abandoned by their companions." Father Sheeran's defense doubtless was more readily traceable to ethnocentrism than to tactical insight lacking in other quarters.[32]

The Irish Battalion almost certainly could not have withstood the Federal tide forever, but its instant and total collapse left the Forty-second Virginia just to the right in serious trouble. Crawford's men, mostly of the Twenty-eighth New York and a few of the Fifth Connecticut, surged into the woods, pivoted to the left, and rolled down the line "charging and yelling." Colonel Garnett hurried up to Major Henry Lane, commanding the Forty-second, and ordered him to change front "to meet the enemy in this new direction." Lane was a thirty-six-year-old lawyer and newspaper editor from Floyd County who had been learning about military affairs the hard way (he had been wounded in the head in the Valley in May 1862). Lane began to try to execute the difficult task assigned him by Garnett but fell with a mortal wound before he could accomplish anything.[33]

Lane probably could not have executed the last order given to him even had he not gone down. If there was a chance for a partial reorientation of the Forty-second's line, it came about because the left of the Forty-second "was separated by a considerable ways" from what had been the right of the First Battalion and a small lateral ridge covered that ground and hid the two Confederate units from each other. It is impossible to postulate an adequate reason for failing to tie in the two flanks. The intervening ground redoubles the certainty that leaving such a gap was a dreadful mistake. But the gap was there and so was the little ridge, and the Forty-second accordingly had the briefest of moments to prepare. The cost for those moments ran dreadfully high because during them Crawford's Federals swarmed west and then south and all but surrounded the regiment. An officer of the First Battalion, noting this development as he fled, summarized the result succinctly: "Then came the forty second Virginia's turn." He also noted, apparently without recognition of the irony inherent in his comment, that the Forty-second line did not break soon enough to avoid suffering "severely."[34] In ignoring the example of the First Battalion, and suffering severely in consequence, the Forty-second Virginia did its full measure to save the day and Jackson's army.

Captain Abner Dobyns, in his official report of the Forty-second's ordeal, described with some feeling the shocking moment when the enemy "were seen suddenly advancing upon our rear." Colonel Garnett well knew what was coming, and it did—enemy fire from directly in the regiment's rear. Garnett reported the effect of that fire with what must have been a fabulous degree of understatement when he wrote that it was "producing some confusion and disorder." The Forty-second Virginia had no choice but to fight in both directions. Those men who advanced away from the wheatfield toward the threat on their rear soon tangled with the enemy "at the point of the bayonet," as Dobyns reported completely literally.[35]

In the smoky, violent melee that ensued in the woods, the Forty-second Virginia was devastated. Its Company E, the Dixie Grays from Roanoke County, was "almost destroyed," to quote the horrified words of a friend in the Fourth Virginia Infantry, Captain Hugh A. White. (White himself had precisely three weeks to live.) No fewer than eighteen men in the company were killed; that equaled slightly more than one-third of the men present for duty. Total casualties of one-third in a major battle, including killed, wounded, and missing, rarely occurred. Mortal casualties at that level are almost beyond comprehension. The commander of Company E, Captain Andrew Jackson Deyerle, fell while fighting and General Taliaferro officially lamented his mortal wounding. Deyerle was more fortunate than a painfully large number of his men: he confounded Taliaferro's report by recovering, serving in the state legislature in 1864, and living until 1907.[36]

The close-in combat on the ground defended by the Forty-second Virginia was unsurpassed for ferocity by any other engagement during the war. A Connecticut soldier described the fray as "such a hand to hand conflict with bayonet and gunbutt as was equalled by only a few contests of the war." Neither side was anywhere near out of ammunition, but there was no opportunity to load weapons. A Confederate from the other end of the battlefield reported the common understanding of the woods fight when he wrote: "The Confederates were giving ground and fighting with clubbed guns, stones, and anything they could get." A Federal at the site used almost the same words: "Clubbed muskets and bayonets were the rule."[37]

One of the Virginians in the midst of the chaos was Stovall W. Weaver of Company K. Weaver fell wounded by "a lick on the head with the breech of a musket." He passed through hospitals in Charlottesville and Lynchburg en route to a furlough, from which he never returned to service. Another, unidentified, member of the Forty-second raised his musket butt to bash a lieutenant of the Fifth

Connecticut in the head, but a New Englander with a loaded weapon shot the Confederate "in the act of striking, and he fell dead with his gun still uplifted and swinging down in front of him at arms' length." A Hollywood movie depicting such an ending would prompt us to skeptical derision of the histrionics, but in the woods at Cedar Mountain such incidents were almost commonplace. One Federal participant estimated that this close fighting lasted for fifteen minutes, but its duration probably was not much longer than half that time.[38]

The denouement of the Forty-second Virginia's struggle was a foregone conclusion: the regiment was fragmented and driven in disorder. But the delay it had imposed on the Federals was critical. So were the casualties it had inflicted and the disorder among the Northerners resulting from its sturdy resistance. Captain Dobyns reported that his regiment "was thrown in great confusion and became much scattered." In the confusion casualties mounted even higher. The Confederates were "slaughtered to a considerable extent in their retreat." Not all of the Forty-second ran rearward after the dissolution. Some men remained in the woods, in good position to rally when support came. Others made what the Fifth Connecticut's regimental historian called "a stubborn fight to the right through our ranks," which is to say northward against the tide. The casualties suffered by the Forty-second Virginia graphically highlight the difference between their fight and the First Battalion's flight. The battalion suffered none killed and no more than a dozen wounded; the Forty-second Virginia lost fifty-three men killed or mortally wounded, another fifty-eight wounded, and eight prisoners.[39]

The hugely disproportionate loss of the Forty-second in killed, by contrast to wounded, introduces an ugly footnote to the fight at Cedar Mountain. Civil wars (and religious ones) have been about the least civil of human transactions down through the centuries. The American Civil War generally offered a pleasant exception to that rule. Atrocity stories gained occasional currency in the irresponsible popular press, and radical politicians on both sides—notably in the Northern congressional committees dedicated to radical crusades— sometimes joined in. But on the whole, in the war's first years genuine atrocities were avoided to a remarkable degree. The few minutes of Federal ascendancy in the woods west of the wheatfield supplied some exceptions to that wholesome record.

John Pope had brought an unlovely new aspect to the war in Virginia with his war-on-civilian orders; the day was insufferably hot; the Federals had achieved an unaccustomed success, at heavy cost, in a highly emotional moment. Perhaps as a result of those circumstances, combat savagery extended beyond the point of surrender in some instances. There was, of course, no institutional basis for the ensuing bloodletting, but a number of Southern accounts insist with unction on its occurrence. Captain Dobyns's official report said: "A good many of the officers and soldiers of the regiment were captured by the enemy and again recaptured, and many of them severely wounded while in the hands of the enemy. Several officers and men of the regiment whom we recaptured from the enemy informed me that they were most brutally maltreated by the enemy, and saw many of our men brutally murdered after being captured."[40]

The captain's account gains some credence from an analysis of the casualty rate in the regiment. Only eight men of the Forty-second survived as live prisoners after their regiment was completely overrun. One reason for that extremely low total, of course, was that in the subsequent Southern rally many prisoners were freed. But the mortal casualties in the Forty-second mounted approximately five times as high as they should have been by comparison to net casualties. When the Federal assault moved south through the woods, more Confederates would echo the accusations of the Forty-second's survivors.

As the Forty-second fell apart at the conclusion of its brave stand, the other two regiments of Garnett's brigade clearly were in extremely serious trouble. The Forty-second had been outflanked by 90° on its left; the Twenty-first and half of the Forty-eighth were facing fully 180° from the danger, in precisely the wrong direction. Before following Crawford's lunge through the woods to the road, however, we must consider the operations of the detached pieces of the Confederate left, where the Tenth Virginia and the Stonewall Brigade struggled in separate detachments.

The Tenth Virginia had lined up originally as one of five regiments in Taliaferro's brigade south of the road. When the general acceded to command of the division and recognized the dangerous situation on Garnett's left, he ordered the Tenth to move promptly in that direction. Major Joshua Stover, commanding the Tenth, reported that Taliaferro's orders were "to prolong the line of battle on . . . the extreme left." The regiment obviously had not reached its goal of anchoring on the left of the First Virginia Battalion by the time the Federal onset made that impossible. The few minutes by which the Tenth Virginia missed that goal cost the Confederates much. It is difficult to avoid postulating a dramatic improvement in

Southern fortunes against Crawford had the Tenth extended the left of the line.[41]

The proximity of the Tenth to its goal cannot be established definitely, but the regiment surely had arrived very close to the appointed ground. Lieutenant Charles Alexander of the First Battalion was positioned at the far left of that unit on "elevated ground," but he could not see the Tenth Virginia. He heard someone say that the Tenth was somewhere to the left, but it was neither visible nor useful so far as he could tell. The commander of the battalion never saw the Tenth either, although one of Garnett's aides informed him "just as the enemy advanced from the woods that the Tenth Virginia Regiment occupied our left." The careful and well-informed William Allan declared that the Tenth was somewhere on Garnett's left, "north of and next to . . . but apparently not in close contact with it."[42]

Major Stover reported that his regiment "immediately engaged the enemy under a heavy fire of infantry" when it arrived near the scene of the Federal attack. The Tenth Virginia enjoyed a splendid position for firing into the right flank of the Federals who were routing the First Battalion, but the dense forest and the fear of firing into friends reduced its effectiveness. The collapse of the First Battalion exposed the right of the Tenth to danger. After "a very short and sharp contest," the Tenth fell straight back into the woods farther from the wheatfield. Major Stover defined the duration of his resistance as "being engaged some time." A critical officer of the First Battalion suggested unconvincingly that the Tenth "broke after firing a few rounds and retired," leaving the First Battalion exposed and without an alternative other than running.[43]

However long the Tenth Virginia fought, and wherever the location was vis-à-vis the First Battalion, the regiment became closely enough engaged to lose four times as many men as the battalion did. Captain David Coffman Grayson of Company K was one of the casualties, shot through the right lung. The surgeons who tended Grayson after his men carried him to the rear assured the captain that he would die. The infallibility of medical science was reaffirmed in Grayson's case: he did die—in June 1933.[44]

Another of the Tenth Virginia's casualties, twenty-two-year-old Sergeant Lucius Cammack of Company C, fell under interesting circumstances. Cammack was one of the thousands of Civil War soldiers who had a clear and unshakable premonition that an impending battle would kill him. He had told his aunt of his certain death and repeated the story with conviction to his superior, Lieutenant Harrison Holt Riddleberger. (Riddleberger survived the war and became a United States senator representing Virginia from 1883 to 1889.) The lieutenant ridiculed Cammack's premonition and watched him when the guns opened. Cammack behaved as if there was no danger at all. When the Tenth Virginia received orders to fall back, Cammack either did not hear them or, more probably, ignored them. The sergeant "stood in his place firing a short rifle until he was finally shot in the right side and mortally wounded." As he fell, Cammack shouted a plea back toward his comrades that they not let the enemy get his body. Lieutenant Riddleberger, Captain John W. Melhorn, and two others dashed virtually into the Federal ranks to pull Cammack back to safety. He died twenty-seven hours later after suffering "most awfully."[45] Sergeant Cammack seems to have been the victim of that surest of things, a self-fulfilling prophecy, which led him to expose his life excessively.

Two subjective analyses of the brief struggle of the Tenth Virginia deserve consideration. First, its difficulties (and by extension those of Garnett's entire brigade and Jackson's entire army) arose from the stroke of fate that left it arriving a bare few moments too late to tie in with the First Battalion and make ready to fight. Second, its casualty rate of more than six wounded to each man killed just about matched the average for the war but was about six times lower than the ratio in the Forty-second Virginia Infantry. There were several differences in their experiences, but the salient one apparently was that none of the Tenth's wounded fell into enemy hands to suffer as did the Forty-second's unfortunate prisoners.

An even more certain source of potential salvation for Garnett's left, the Stonewall Brigade, had been lurking in the woods at the west edge of the brushy field as Crawford prepared to strike. After his confusing circuit through the woods, Colonel Ronald had sent to Taliaferro to find out what to do. He obviously needed to close on the front line, and at once, but the colonel was too unsure of himself to proceed without firm orders. The Stonewall Brigade's line lay across the brushy field near its western end while it awaited Taliaferro's response. The configuration of the line was nominally north-to-south, but the left had advanced somewhat farther than the right. Each end of the line ran into the woods on the respective sides of the field.

The extent of the delay by Ronald at the western edge of the brushy field may be gauged by the fact that the same aide he sent to Taliaferro for instructions returned with those instructions. Under the prevailing conditions, Captain John H. Fulton could not have covered the ground twice and found Taliaferro (even with the best of luck) and dealt with him in less than fifteen minutes. Thirty minutes seems a better estimate, and even that may be conservative. Ronald reported Taliaferro's response in a mild phrase: "The general directed me to move on."[46]

General Taliaferro betrayed more of the urgency of the moment in his official version, which states that he ordered Ronald to "move his brigade rapidly to the support of the Second [Garnett's] brigade." The new division commander also waxed pejorative when he described the exposure of Garnett's left as "owing to the fact that the First [Stonewall] Brigade had not been moved sufficiently near originally, or that the order had not reached Colonel Ronald in time." The caveat about the order's timeliness was nothing more than a mild attempt to avoid pointing an accusatory finger at Ronald, who never again commanded the brigade in action. G. F. R. Henderson, Jackson's great biographer, eagerly accepted Taliaferro's gentle alternative and concluded that the Stonewall Brigade occupied its awkward location because it "had not received its orders" and because the woods screened it from seeing the action.[47]

The precise timing of the brigade's advance eastward across the brushy field, once Taliaferro spurred Ronald to it, is of course beyond reckoning. Ronald's advance probably began five or ten minutes before the opening volley in the wheatfield because it ended not long after that volley echoed through the field. Captain Michael Shuler of the Thirty-third Virginia wrote in his diary that the order to advance reached him "not more than 10 minutes after the musketry commenced upon our right." That musketry presumably was the roar from Augur's advance on the other side of the road, which preceded the attack in the wheatfield by about fifteen minutes.[48]

The famous old brigade advanced across the brushy field and through the woods on either side of it as soon as Ronald relayed Taliaferro's order. The regiments moved eastward, slowly closing the gap between the point where they had halted initially and the longitude of Garnett's line. Their path would not bring them far enough south to close on Garnett's left, however, unless it was adjusted about 45° to the right. Colonel Ronald did not make that adjustment for two good reasons: he knew nothing of the ground or the positions and therefore had no idea that an adjustment was desirable; and he surely had no wish to abandon the brushy field, where he could see

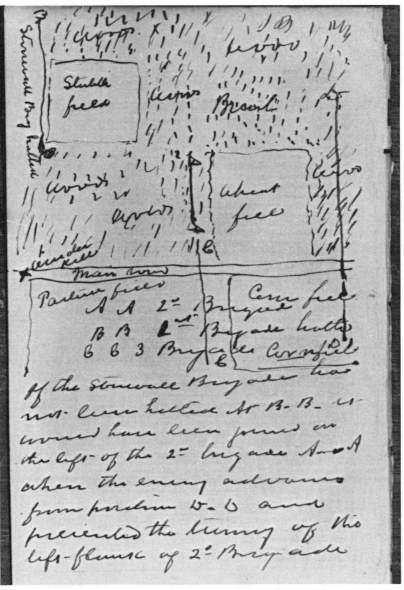

Colonel James A. Walker's crude sketch offers interesting insight on the positions of the Stonewall Brigade and its fatal pause. (Richmond National Battlefield Park)

something of what he was doing, to plunge once more into the confusing woods.

As the Stonewall Brigade advanced across the brushy field (also called the "northwest field" in some sources because it was north and west of the wheatfield), the Twenty-seventh Virginia on its far right remained entirely within the woods. The Thirty-third Virginia marched half in the woods and half (the left half) in the field. The Fifth and Second regiments on the left of the Thirty-third moved entirely in the open, and the Fourth Virginia on the far left was in the woods on the north edge of the brushy field. About halfway through the field the brigade ran across some few Federals who remain unidentified (they probably were some lost skirmishers), but the Confederates overlapped these advanced enemies with ease. The small enemy contingent fell back after exchanging a few generally harmless rounds.[49]

Charles Ronald could not be faulted for a lack of personal bravery. At some point in the advance of his brigade the colonel rode out well in front to scout his route. Ronald could see high ground ahead near the east end of the brushy field and the northwest corner of the wheatfield. He reached that elevated point just in time to see Crawford's main advance swinging through the wheat toward Garnett's line. The Stonewall Brigade had arrived minutes too late to accomplish its purpose of bolstering that line, but not too late to do some material good. The colonel hurried back to his line and shouted an order to increase pace to the double-quick. One of Ronald's subordinates wrote that the colonel "came galloping back" shouting "First brigade prepare for a charge bayonet."[50]

The left of the Stonewall Brigade had started somewhat ahead of the right, and that tendency rapidly grew more pronounced because of two considerations. Most of the left of the brigade moved through the field with far greater ease than the Twenty-seventh and part of the Thirty-third enjoyed in the thick woods to the right. Furthermore, the two right regiments were closest to the burgeoning fight around Garnett's left. That fight eventually sucked them into its maw and not only halted their progress but flung back the Twenty-seventh. The brigade's advance, therefore, featured the left regiments "coming around on a wheel," as one of the participants wrote.[51]

Lieutenant Colonel Edmund G. "Ned" Lee, commander of the Thirty-third Virginia and coincidentally General William Nelson Pendleton's son-in-law, figured that he had covered about 125 yards when he received the command to charge. That estimate seems to be entirely reasonable. Captain Shuler wrote that he "had not got far" when the command to charge reached him. Lee led the left wing of the regiment from in front, on horseback, until his mount became unmanageable under an increasing volume of small arms fire. When Colonel Lee dismounted, he noticed that each of the four other regimental commanders also was afoot. Most of the Thirty-third Virginia was in the woods on the right of the brushy field when the advance reached the wheatfield. The infantrymen halted at the fence at the edge of the woods at the far northwestern corner of the wheatfield. The Twenty-seventh Virginia pulled up to the same fence just to the right of the Thirty-third and at about the same moment.[52]

The Confederates who puffed up to the fence at the northwest corner of the field had no difficulty finding targets on the open ground in front of them. By this time the Fifth Connecticut and Twenty-eighth New York probably had penetrated the wood line closer to the road, but the Forty-sixth Pennsylvania had not kept pace with those two regiments. The six companies of the Third Wisconsin, farthest right of Crawford's units, lagged even farther behind the westward progress of the New York and Connecticut men. The same fate that left the Stonewall Brigade just minutes short of arriving in time decreed that the Forty-sixth Pennsylvania and particularly the Wisconsin troops should be minutes too late to avoid the fire of the Virginians. The Twenty-seventh Virginia promptly opened a hot fire obliquely to its right against the Forty-sixth Pennsylvania. The Thirty-third joined in that fire and also spent some rounds on the Wisconsin companies, which were more or less to their front.[53]

Major Frederick W. M. Holliday actively encouraged the men of the Thirty-third Virginia as they fought at the edge of the field. Holliday was on the mind of an Orange County girl that day, though he would not receive the letter she was writing for weeks. Mary Donaghe wrote to the major on August 9, quite likely with the roar of battle echoing across the county line to her ears. She offered Holliday a handmade "set of military stars" as the remembrance of "a friend whom he may at *any time* call upon, for the work of *anything*, in the power of my fingers to do." As Mary wrote, Holliday struggled at the eye of the hurricane, encouraging his men to climb over the fence and get into the wheatfield's corner. The firing raged "very heavy," John Casler noted, and the men were loath to obey Holliday's importunities. The major finally ordered the color-bearer to "Get over the fence with the colors and I know the men will follow." He did and they did.[54]

The brave color-bearer was shot down, but someone else grabbed the colors and waved them. Holliday also went down with a shattered arm and was carried to the rear. Surgeons amputated the arm. In a postwar era when maimed veterans enjoyed political advantage, Holliday parlayed his Cedar Mountain stump (and other admirable qualities) into the governorship of Virginia. The men Holliday had prodded over the fence could do no more good than those under the shelter of the wood line and the fence, but both groups "had severe fighting for a short time." Captain Charles L. Haynes reported that the Twenty-seventh Virginia's fire at this point "was kept up for some time with such effect that two regiments of the enemy, which immediately confronted us commenced falling back rapidly in much disorder."[55]

Haynes referred (with the usual postbattle hyperbole) to the repulse by the entire Stonewall Brigade of the tiny Wisconsin detachment on the far right. The Forty-sixth Pennsylvania, the northernmost of the three regiments in Crawford's main line but south of the Third Wisconsin, also suffered heavily from flanking fire delivered by the Twenty-seventh and Thirty-third Virginia. The Pennsylvania unit lost more men than any of the other six Federal regiments that fought at the wheatfield (including Gordon's three in the later wave). As the Wisconsin men wavered (what else could they do, facing five full regiments with six-tenths of one regiment?), a conspicuously brave officer dashed through their lines on a dark claybank horse in an attempt to rally them. Confederate rifles turned in unison in his direction, and the officer, Lieutenant Colonel Louis H. D. Crane of the Third Wisconsin, fell "riddled with bullets." Marksmanship in the Stonewall Brigade was of a higher order than that in the First Virginia Battalion. Captain Samuel J. C. Moore of the Second Virginia claimed that "a splendid shot" in his company hit Crane, but no doubt many bullets did. When John Casler of the Thirty-third Virginia later went over the battlefield, he was attracted to the dead colonel's shoulder straps—"beautiful ones, like solid gold."[56] Anyone familiar with Casler's career and writings probably will conclude that that irreverent soldier confiscated the beautiful golden souvenirs for his own.

The timing of the arrival of the Stonewall Brigade at the wheatfield's western edge may be established by the sequence of events as occurring soon after Crawford struck Garnett, probably just as Crawford's left got into the wood line, before the Forty-sixth Pennsylvania penetrated the woods, and before the Third Wisconsin came into heavy action. Colonel Lee of the Thirty-third Virginia provided ammunition for that chronology when he reported that heavy and general firing reached its height while his regiment was at the fence. Soldiers often felt that way at the core of their own crises for reasons both psychological and physiological, but Lee probably accurately gauged the roar of a battle that just now, with the arrival of his brigade, had engaged the entire length of the contending positions. The careful and invaluable Jedediah Hotchkiss, a faithful member of Jackson's staff and a fount of information on his campaigns, erred at least marginally when he placed the arrival of the Stonewall Brigade after Crawford had broken up Garnett.[57]

While the Twenty-seventh and Thirty-third Virginia harassed the Forty-sixth Pennsylvania to their right and shot up the Third Wisconsin in front, the brigade's other three regiments enjoyed a field day farther to the left. The regimental alignment to the left of the Thirty-third was the Fifth, then the Second, then the Fourth Virginia. When the two right regiments halted at the fence, the other three kept going through the brushy field above the wheatfield, where the two fields were contiguous. The Fourth Virginia operated entirely in the woods during the movement eastward, using the fence at the northern edge of the brushy field as its directional guide. The regiment soon received orders to come out of the woods and into the open. In the process, the Fourth Virginia aligned itself facing south.[58]

When Captain Hugh A. White led his Company I of the Fourth Virginia out of the woods, the scene that unfolded before his eyes struck him with awe. White's letter home (one of his last—he had three weeks to live) described the frightening but stirring sight of two armies with banners at each other's throats: "The scene . . . was more like the pictures of battles than any I had ever witnessed. As we, on the left, moved forward and gained the top of a ridge before us, we could see the line of battle extending around to the extreme right, all along which the smoke rolled up in great clouds, and fire from the two sides flashed fiercely at each other. I did not have time to look long at this scene, for a little smoke, and some fire too, nearer at hand engaged my attention."[59]

The wheel by the three left regiments through the brushy field to the northern edge of the wheatfield involved a full 90° turn. Such a maneuver under fire would have been extraordinarily difficult, if not impossible, but no Federal force was in position to oppose it. After the right-angle shift the regiments advanced nominally due south, headed directly for the right flank of the Wisconsin companies. In the process they "had to pass through a thick undergrowth" in the brushy field and over another fence, and the Fourth Virginia "became somewhat scattered."[60]

The scattered condition of the Fourth Virginia did not matter much because the left of Ronald's brigade was on the trail of an easy prey. The three regiments moving south outnumbered the six companies of the Third Wisconsin by approximately five to one. A Federal authority placed the strength of the Wisconsin companies at precisely 267, which seems accurate. The commander of the Fifth Virginia, Major Hazael J. Williams, reported 519 muskets in his regiment alone (it was the strongest in the brigade). To make matters worse for the Northerners, the lateral ridge at the northern end of the wheatfield separated them from their friends nearer the road. In their isolated arena, with the Thirty-third Virginia in front and three Virginia regiments to their right, the Wisconsin men were in serious trouble.[61]

The Fifth Virginia proved to be the most dangerous threat to the Wisconsin troops, not only because that regiment was so numerically strong but also because it was most aggressively led. The Fifth continued its advance through the wheel closer to the enemy than did the other two Virginia regiments to its left. When Major Williams ordered a charge toward the exposed enemy, his men responded "in most elegant style." Colonel Ronald cautiously ordered the Fifth to pull back to the woods at the northwest corner of the field, but not before the regiment had contributed substantially to the discomfiture of the Third Wisconsin detachment.[62]

Several Northern accounts substantiate the predictably deadly effect upon the small Wisconsin force of the fire from the vastly larger and extremely well situated Stonewall Brigade. The regimental history of the Twenty-eighth New York spoke of the "deadly fire" of the Virginians against the Third Wisconsin; that of the Fifth Connecticut blames the miseries of the Third Wisconsin on their inadvertently late start and reports that the Stonewall Brigade routed them "after very gallant fighting and heavy losses." The latter source also attributed to the Stonewall Brigade's fire the checking of the momentum of the Forty-sixth Pennsylvania. An officer of the second Federal line, which soon was to attempt to repeat Crawford's success on the same ground, credited the Confederates on the far right—the Stonewall Brigade—with crushing the Third Wisconsin. Another officer of the second wave computed the losses among the 267 men of this farthest-front Wisconsin detachment as 80 men, including both field officers present (one of those being Lieutenant Colonel Crane of the dazzling shoulder straps).[63]

Colonel Ronald claimed that "several volleys" from his regiments seemed to confuse the Third Wisconsin, which is hardly surprising, and they fell back under pressure "leaving many . . . dead and wounded upon the field." The two most complete accounts by the Wisconsin soldiers themselves confirmed all that their friends and enemies reported. One of the men on the receiving end of the Virginians' volleys described them as "the most destructive musketry fire that I have ever experienced." Another veteran used about the same emphasis when he spoke of a single volley as "one of the most effective that he ever saw delivered in battle." The Wisconsin troops could feel the fire most warmly from the Fifth and Second Virginia, closest to them, but even the fire of the more distant Fourth Virginia galled the Federals because it came most obliquely—virtually from their rear. To remain was murder, so the Wisconsin companies fell back in some disorder. As might have been expected, the right companies gave way first from their posts nearest the musketry and the pressure. The left companies soon followed. None of them felt that they had accomplished anything.[64]

The accomplishments of the Stonewall Brigade, by contrast, more particularly of its three left regiments, have been too little recognized. Their task was not a difficult one by any means, of course; in fact, it was monumentally easy under the circumstances. The timing of their arrival was unfortunately late for the welfare of Garnett's left wing, but they appeared precisely on time to swat away the Third Wisconsin on Crawford's right and in the process firmly seal the right shoulder of the Federal irruption. The Second, Fourth, and Fifth Virginia completed a 90° wheel into line looking down the rear of what had been Crawford's point of attack. When they arrived there and dispatched the Third Wisconsin companies, Crawford had moved on through the woods and the Virginians were staring down into a vacuum. In filling that vacuum, three-fifths of the Stonewall Brigade ensured the stability of Jackson's far left and guaranteed difficulty for Crawford's very small attacking force if (when) it was obliged to retrace its steps.

A Federal analyst, recognizing the solid anchor that the Virginians constituted on the north end of the wheatfield, complained under the inspiration of hindsight that a better-consolidated attacking force could have swept away that Confederate strong point. Crawford's tardy Tenth Maine and Gordon's brigade, which attacked later, might have hit those Virginians beyond the Federal right and routed them as well, he hypothesized. At the height of Crawford's success (to get ahead of the story by a few minutes and several pages), the three Virginia regiments constituted the only solid piece of Southern line for more than a mile in front. Federal grumbling about the admittedly lucky positioning of three-fifths of the Stonewall Brigade must be interpreted as a tribute to its importance.[65]

The two-fifths of the Stonewall Brigade on the right (the Thirty-third and then the Twenty-seventh on the far right) had been facing west across the wheatfield from the fence at the edge of the woods. Their role proved notably more difficult than that of their comrades of the brigade who faced across their front from farther to the left. The Federal irruption around Garnett's left flank soon shook, then crumbled, the right flank of the Twenty-seventh Virginia, and before long the entire regiment dissolved in retreat. Captain Haynes of the Twenty-seventh had been cheerfully directing fire into the wheatfield when he discovered Yankees "rapidly advancing on our right, cross-firing us and endeavoring to get in our rear." He described the fire as very heavy—but he lost only four men all day. James A. Walker wrote bluntly of the Twenty-seventh Virginia's performance: "Behaved badly—3 killed and *one* wounded—shows a good *run*, but a poor fight." Haynes admitted that his bowed but unbloodied regiment scattered "considerably" because the ground to rearward where they headed was snarled with "thick brush and fallen timber that covered the ground."[66]

When the Twenty-seventh Virginia melted away, Lieutenant Colonel Edmund Lee and his Thirty-third Virginia became the only Confederate unit facing westward in that general vicinity. Lee found himself in the unusual position of commanding his nominal superior, Colonel John Francis Neff, in action. That came about when Winder, with a flash of that fanatical discipline that made some men loathe him, had arrested Neff and confiscated his sword over some minuscule policy matter. Neff went into the thickest of the action with his men anyway, swordless and without any authority. The powerless colonel was another of the many men fighting on August 9 who had just three weeks to live because of a date with death on the plains of Manassas. Neff also had what must have been a unique background: how many sons of nineteenth-century Valley Dunkard preachers attended the Virginia Military Institute and rose to field rank under Stonewall Jackson?[67]

Lee had started the day with only 160 men in the regiment. A dozen or so of them fell out from heat prostration during the day. So the Thirty-third had barely more than half as many men as the six-tenths of the Third Wisconsin that fought in the wheatfield. The ample Confederate help farther left more than neutralized the Wisconsin companies, of course, but what of the threat from the right? Lee began to feel pressure there and noticed Federals within forty paces of his right company, Company A. He sent his adjutant out to warn the Twenty-seventh of this threat and to solicit aid from that regiment. The aide returned with the startling news that the Twenty-seventh "was not there." Lee responded to that unhappy intelligence by ordering companies A, D, and F to turn and fire into the enemy flankers.[68]

In the confused fighting on the refused right of the Thirty-third, Captain Abraham Spengler of Company F fell wounded. Spengler was a twenty-eight-year-old carpenter from Moorefield who later became colonel of the regiment and at that rank enjoyed the marginal distinction of being the shortest (at four inches more than five feet) field officer in the Army of Northern Virginia. Spengler's men and their comrades generated enough return fire to knock down numbers of Federals and dissuade them from coming closer. When Lee sent a harried message to Ronald, the brigade commander promised help soon in the form of A. P. Hill's approaching troops. The men of the Thirty-third "consumed nearly every cartridge" in their defense. Lee directed the fire of a marksman against a Yankee color-bearer and reported with relish that the man fell.[69]

The unquestioned collapse of the Twenty-seventh Virginia doubt-less affected at least a few of the men on the right of the Thirty-third Virginia. North Carolinians to the rear later reported delightedly that the entire Stonewall Brigade scampered past, which it assuredly did not. At least one contemporary Northern account is similarly severe on the right companies of the Thirty-third Virginia. James A. Walker's manuscript comments, which are candid about the behavior of the Twenty-seventh, are adamant in asserting that only that one regiment gave way.[70] Walker was correct.

When the Twenty-seventh Virginia ran and the Thirty-third Virginia did not, Colonel Ronald was directing the highly successful wheel of the left three regiments onto the flank of the Third Wisconsin. At the height of those easy pickings, Ronald received word of the difficulties with his right, perhaps from the aide Ned Lee sent to him. Colonel Lawson Botts of the Second Virginia (still another man of this hard-fighting division who would meet death at Second Manassas) moved all but one company of his regiment down toward the Thirty-third when he heard that the brigade right was "hard pressed." The Fourth Virginia pulled back from contact and reformed "for a time" under the exigency of this new emergency.[71]

The threat to the Thirty-third never was as great as it seemed in the smoking woods, nor is it likely that the Twenty-seventh had adequate cause to decamp. Federals on the right of the Stonewall Brigade were not endeavoring to turn its flank, or even to drive a well-planned wedge between it and Garnett. They simply were pouring around Garnett's left, and in small numbers in proportion to the ruckus they created. To the degree that Crawford's brave but desperate force still operated under control, it was glad to forsake the Stonewall Brigade's ground and pour leftward through the woods toward the Confederate guns around the Gate. Those guns were the raison d'être for the charge, and Crawford's Yankees had a good angle toward them.

By the time its right outriders brushed past the Stonewall Brigade, the small but determined Northern spearhead had gained impressive momentum. Its various elements had scared away the First Virginia Battalion, frustrated the efforts of the Tenth Virginia to find and anchor Garnett's line, and put down a sturdy stand by the Forty-second Virginia. Ahead through the woods lay the painfully vulnerable rear of the Twenty-first Virginia and the back of the bent line of the Forty-eighth Virginia. The aroma of victory filled Federal nostrils, and it was heady stuff. Men who had been regularly and soundly beaten by Stonewall Jackson had caved in his left wing completely and stood poised to compound the Southern hero's discomfort by many degrees more when they reached the vicinity of the Gate.

Most of the men of the Twenty-first and Forty-eighth Virginia had no idea that the dam behind them had burst. The dense nature of the woods, the din of battle coming in from an arc of 360°, and the wretched shape of the brigade's position all contributed to a nightmare for the Virginians facing the road east of the Gate. A large number of them would pay for that unfortunate combination of circumstances with their blood.

CHAPTER 8

Federal High Tide

Lieutenant colonel Richard H. Cunningham led the Twenty-first Virginia Infantry into position in the woods fringing the main road without any inkling that the woods would be the setting for a nightmare for his regiment. Before the sun set, the Twenty-first would lose more men than any other Confederate regiment on the field and more than many full brigades. The official return for the entire five-regiment Stonewall Brigade, for instance, listed precisely one-half as many casualties as the Twenty-first Virginia reported. Cunningham was a young officer (he was in his late twenties) considered to have much promise despite a lack of formal military training. His only prewar military experience had been as a member of Richmond's elite "Company F," with which he served on weekends and special events. In civilian life the colonel was a prosperous merchant.[1]

Cunningham had suffered from some ailment for several days before the battle and joined the column late, in company with fellow sufferer Charles S. Winder. His regiment had earned a fine reputation the hard way, by following Stonewall Jackson and living up to that stern man's high demands. Most of the men were seasoned veterans of victories in the Valley and elsewhere, but some green replacements dotted the regiment's ranks. One untried man clutching a musket in the Twenty-first Virginia's line was the Reverend William J. Warden, who was among Jackson's innumerable clerical acquaintances. Whatever the reverend's military utility might have been, his foray under arms raised his standing among the men: "Parson, we see that you can fight as well as preach." Another neophyte in the business of war betrayed his inexperience by saying when the artillery slowed and small arms fire began: "I am awfully glad those shells have stopped coming. I don't mind these little things." A veteran who knew better declared that the newcomer had things backward. "This I found to be true," the tyro admitted, "then for the first time, and many times afterwards."[2]

*A veteran of the Tenth Maine took this photograph in 1910,
looking east from the Confederate line near the southwest
corner of the wheatfield, "south of the line of the Confeds.
opposing 10th Me." (Gould Papers, Duke University)*

Captain Henry H. Roach of Company K, the Meherrin Grays, began this day of battle in as black a mood as any man could have
suffered. The captain's letter to his cousin Sue written on August 5
had been deeply despondent, full of awful certainty that he never
again would see his home and loved ones. Roach's remarks to Sue
stopped short of an outright announcement of his impending death,
but only barely.[3]

The Twenty-first Virginia found itself admirably situated to aid
its comrades south of the road when Augur launched Prince's and
Geary's men through the corn against Early and Taliaferro. Lieutenant Colonel Cunningham ordered his men down to the edge of the
woods from their original position forty yards back under cover.
Geary's Ohioans across the road in front of the Twenty-first and to its
left oblique made inviting targets. The regiment's official report ap-

plauded the ardor with which its men fought and staked a reasonable claim to some of the credit for Geary's difficulties. At some point in the early going Stonewall Jackson rode near the regiment, talked with Cunningham, and exhorted the troops: "Men, you must hold this line." They responded cheerfully and positively.[4]

While the Twenty-first and part of the Forty-eighth Virginia to its left rained fire on Geary across the road, their comrades of the First Battalion and the Forty-second Virginia were undergoing an ordeal by fire not far away to the north. In the noisy bedlam the Twenty-first and Forty-eighth remained oblivious to the disaster looming behind them. The survivors of two victorious Federal regiments and part of a third had pivoted around Garnett's left and now stood on the brink of an easy destruction of the rest of that brigade. The Twenty-eighth New York on the right (the west, after the pivot) and the Fifth Connecticut to the New Yorkers' left moved south through the woods "together, fairly abreast." Part of the Forty-sixth Pennsylvania also kept up with the advance, which by now counted no more than nine hundred muskets in its ranks and probably far fewer.[5]

A portion of the left half of the Forty-eighth Virginia fought as an adjunct to the Forty-second Virginia from a position facing east, next to the right of the Forty-second. That segment of the Forty-eighth fell back with the Forty-second and even "brought out with them a quantity of prisoners," according to an officer of the First Virginia Battalion.[6] The rest of the Forty-eighth—about half of its ten companies—fought beside the Twenty-first Virginia and suffered with it. The abrupt bend in the brigade line dramatically separated the experiences of the Forty-eighth's two halves.

The men of the Twenty-first Virginia learned of the dire threat to the regiment's rear in the worst fashion—by bullets fired into their backs at short range. The despondent and pessimistic Captain Roach wrote: "Our loss would have been slight but owing to some cause I don't know what the enemy got in our rear and in thirty steps of us before we found it out. I tell you they slaughtered our men for a while." One of the attackers in Crawford's brigade used precisely the same distance measurement in recounting the surprise of the Twenty-first when he wrote that the Federals "came to within 30 paces of the 21st Va., [and] gave them a withering fire in the rear."[7]

Captain William A. Witcher of Company I, who wrote the official report for the Twenty-first Virginia, recounted the terrifying moment: "The fight was raging fiercely [against Augur] and our men in high spirits, when suddenly and without any warning whatever a murderous fire was poured upon us from the rear, at least a brigade of the enemy having passed through the woods and reached within 20 or 30 paces of us." John Worsham of the Twenty-first recalled that the fire wreaked "terrible havoc" in the ranks of the regiment.[8]

Captain Witcher's first reaction as he adjusted to the painful moment was a sense of betrayal. He had been operating in the comfortable certainty that the regiment's rear was well screened, and he wrote pointedly in his official report: "Why it was not is not for me to say." Worsham's initial reaction, after ducking, was to worry about Stonewall Jackson's safety. "A great dread filled me for Jackson," he wrote, "because I had seen him at this spot only a moment before."[9]

Jackson was indeed in mortal danger to a degree surpassing any of his experiences in past battles, but before the general's personal crisis peaked, the Twenty-first Virginia faced a searing gauntlet of fire and steel. The thirty paces between the assailants and their startled quarry disappeared within moments, and the fight became hand-to-hand. The melee that ensued was of short duration but of an intensity never exceeded on the continent. Three Confederate officers who observed the maelstrom from beyond its eye commented about its savagery. The close-in struggle was "most severe," General W. B. Taliaferro reported. "The bayonet was freely used and a hand-to-hand fight with superior numbers ensued before the right of the brigade fell back." Lieutenant Charles A. Davidson of the routed First Virginia Battalion wrote of how the Twenty-first "was now entirely surrounded and suffered terribly. . . . Our whole line on the left side of the road was now in disorder." A third officer proclaimed, with understandably horrified excess, that "the most desperate hand-to-hand encounter probably ever witnessed on the battle-field took place." Bayonets and swords came into play, "and when the bayonet failed to do its work, or was broken or lost, with clubbed guns the contest was continued."[10]

The view from within the firestorm was of course even more hellish. James M. Binford of the Twenty-first Virginia's famous old elite Company F survived the ordeal by collapsing with sunstroke before he could fall prey to something worse. Binford wrote a letter four days later that exudes an atmosphere of horror and terror still hanging over him. Company F took eighteen men into the fight. "Thanks to God," Binford wrote, "I am one of the six survivors." "It was a bloody desperate fight. We were literally butchered. . . . I long to go to some quiet place where loved ones of home are, to rest body and mind." James Binford offered thanks for the simplest of privileges with something approaching wonderment: "I breathe, & have all my limbs." After four days the effect of the sunstroke had abated, but Binford's ears were "yet ringing with musketry and cannon. . . . I am sick of seeing dead men & men's limbs torn from their bodies." Company F's ranking survivor evidently shared Binford's mood; he suggested disbanding the company. In any event, Binford proposed joining the cavalry, if not to "Have a Good Time" (to use the words of Jeb Stuart's favorite song), then at least to have a less bad time. Binford received a discharge from the regiment because of rheumatism later in the year and died in 1891.[11]

Another survivor from the regiment was Adjutant Mann Page, who had started the war in Company F. Page had a close call. A Federal soldier gathered him in as a prisoner and was threatening "to blow the damned rebel's brains out" at the moment that a nearby Confederate managed to finish capping his musket and shoot the Federal dead. Page was captured again almost at once and again escaped. Corporal Roswell S. Lindsay of Company F was less fortunate, and by the barest of margins. A Northern officer fired on Lindsay with a pistol at short range, hit him in the head, and killed him instantly. Comrades coming to the corporal's assistance bayoneted the pistol-wielding Federal to death.[12]

A teenager in the Confederate line grappled over a flag with a Federal captain. The officer, armed with a multishot side arm, shot the boy and mortally wounded him. The turmoil in the smoking woods and the stress under which men fought for their lives is vividly conveyed in the secondhand account of another boy who fell in the midst of it. Lieutenant Charles Alexander of the First Virginia Battalion, who had been wounded at the outset of Crawford's attack, lay next to the youngster in a field hospital. Alexander described the lad as a handsome youth, aged about eighteen, who "told me he was suffering from a bayonet wound which extended to his hollow. This young man told me that while he had his bayonet through a Federal he felt a bayonet enter his back, and he partly turned and saw that it was his own orderly sergeant, who must have been blind with fright; he told him to pull it out; the sergeant, recognizing the voice, did so at once." The wounded boy died that night before Lieutenant Alexander had a chance to make note of his name.[13] His ordeal, horrifying and unusual as it was, doubtless was not unique.

John Worsham of the Twenty-first Virginia hurried into the main road through knots of struggling men shortly after the onset, probably in response to the impulse to get a visual grasp of the situation.

The first thing he noticed in the road was a Federal sergeant seventy-five yards to the rear, almost halfway back to the Gate. The sergeant carried a gun in his left hand and a sword in his right hand as he turned eastward and started toward the spot where Worsham stood. An enemy private soon popped out of the woods as well. The sergeant purposefully strode up to a Confederate within ten feet of Worsham, took hold of the man by main force, and started back into the woods with him. Another Southerner finished frantically loading his weapon, raised it to his shoulder, and shot the sergeant dead at the edge of the road.

The resolute sergeant's mission and his demise read like a surrealistic slow-motion dream in Worsham's account. His description of the swirling chaos that quickly replaced the clearly defined struggle of a few men virtually sizzles with the heat of battle: "By this time the road was full of Yankees, and there was such a fight as was not witnessed during the war; guns, bayonets, swords, pistols, fence rails, rocks, etc., were used all along the line. I have heard of a 'hell spot' in some battles, this surely was one." The Twenty-first Virginia's color-bearer knocked down a Yankee with his flagstaff before he was killed. Within a few minutes the regiment lost three more color-bearers killed in action in quick succession. A fifth occupant of that post of danger and honor came through, carrying a flag riddled with bullet holes.[14]

Examining the brief, bloody encounter near the road from the Confederate perspective leaves a clear but inaccurate impression of unrecompensed loss. The Federal advantage of surprise and position was so great that the Twenty-first and the Forty-eighth fragment could not stand and had no real margin for trying. The Federals pummeling the Twenty-first, however, knew that they were nearing the end of their rope. They had achieved more than anyone could reasonably have expected and would achieve more before their roll ended; but the encounter in the woods hurt them, too, as they acknowledged without hesitation. The casualties reported in Crawford's brigade tell the story. Painful as was the loss in the Twenty-first Virginia, the losses in Crawford's brigade were far greater.[15]

The regimental historian of the Fifth Connecticut described the fighting as feeling "as if the men had deliberately walked into a fiery furnace." A captain in that regiment wrote of tangling with Southerners "at the point of the bayonet and with the butt of the gun." The captain was himself "badly wounded" in the right shoulder by a violently wielded Virginian musket butt. The Twenty-eighth New York's Company D started across the wheatfield with three sets of brothers in its ranks—Sanderson, White, and Gilbert. One of each pair was killed in the woods; the other was either wounded or captured. A survivor of the Twenty-eighth New York reported that his mates gave the "grey backs," as he called them, "some rough specimens of their pugilistic acquirements" after they had fired out their muskets. Another of the same regiment mourned the "great loss" in the Twenty-eighth, which "was cut to pieces and will never be the same again. . . . The dead and wounded was everywhere." Yet another New Yorker also used the phrase "cut to pieces" in his diary and reckoned that his whole brigade had "gone up the spout."[16]

Lieutenant William P. Warren of the Twenty-eighth New York spoke of seeing several Confederates struck down with swords but claimed that the men of his own company used their muskets to good effect in the smoke-choked woods. The gunsmoke did not reach to the ground, so Warren ordered his company to get down on their knees. In that position they escaped most of the rounds flying through the air, and they could see Confederate legs under the smoke at which to shoot. If Warren's self-reported cleverness was not exaggerated, his company was one of the few that retained cohesion all the way through the woods. A Massachusetts soldier who got into the "rebel wood" later found Crawford's dead strewn so thickly that he concluded they had "melted away like snow placed in a July sun." Writing after the war, a veteran of Antietam, Chancellorsville, and Gettysburg declared emphatically that nowhere had he seen "so hot a fight for the time it lasted as this of Cedar Mountain."[17]

Federal losses notwithstanding, the hard-beset Twenty-first Virginia clearly had no choice but to get out of its death trap as rapidly as possible. Lieutenant Colonel Cunningham sought to achieve that minimal goal under the handicap of being unable to use his voice. The illness that had kept him from active service until he rejoined on the eve of battle had left him without his normal battle voice "of loud compass and great command." Cunningham, afoot and leading his horse, came upon John Worsham and said, "John, help me get the men out of this, I can't talk loudly." Worsham quickly gathered a few men around him and repeated the order. Cunningham found Captain Witcher, his ranking subordinate, near the left of the regiment and endeavored to shout a command to him. The colonel's weak voice and the din of battle conspired to leave Witcher unable to hear,

*Looking west up the slope toward the Gate from a point
in the old road trace about where Lieutenant Colonel
Cunningham was killed, 1989. (Clark B. Hall)*

but he understood enough to try to turn the nearby men around
to face the rear. Some of them were still firing across the road at
Augur's Ohioans.[18]

Cunningham again tried to order Witcher in an inaudible cross
between a shout and a whisper, pointing vigorously toward the fence
across the road at a point somewhat west of where he stood. The
captain could not make out the words but tried to obey the gestures.
After several attempts, Witcher "got the men to start in that direction." The confused mass of men moved at different speeds, "some
going fast, while others would load, turn, and fire as they went."[19]
Those hardy soldiers moving slowly and firing were of the sort that
make up the core of any efficient military force.

The fence on the south side of the road, where Cunningham was
directing his rapid withdrawal, posed a serious obstacle. The colonel
himself led his horse across the road to a point near where Winder
had fallen not long before. There he pulled down a section of the
fence by hand and moved into the field beyond. As Cunningham
thrust his foot into a stirrup and started into the saddle a bullet
knocked him backward, dead. His horse received a mortal wound at

the same moment. A member of Winder's staff mourned Cunningham as "a fine officer and much esteemed as a man," which seems to have been the universal appraisal.[20]

The bullet that killed Lieutenant Colonel Cunningham canceled any remote chance that remained for the Twenty-first Virginia to escape its trap in good order. The regiment fell apart and "stampeded" into and down the road, to use the descriptive word employed by one of the Federals. Colonel T. S. Garnett, who described the Forty-second Virginia's condition too optimistically as "some confusion and disorder," used the stronger phrase "much disorder" in connection with the retreat of the Twenty-first Virginia. John Worsham described his unit as "overwhelmed," which it surely was, and recalled the "terrible time" of the retreat.[21]

A unit losing its cohesion is a unit ripe for losing men taken as prisoners, and the Twenty-first suffered that fate. Unfortunately, numbers of the men so taken were mistreated and even killed by the frenzied and desperate Federals. Colonel Garnett's official report to Stonewall Jackson, written on August 15, called attention "to the acts of savage brutality perpetrated by the enemy upon our officers and men who fell into their hands temporarily as prisoners. Such fiendish barbarity is not to be found in the history of warfare among civilized nations." Captain Witcher's report included a specific instance of the "barbarous and brutal" behavior of the foe. Federals captured Lieutenant Thomas W. Brown of the Twenty-first just as the regiment left the woods. That evening two officers of Garnett's brigade found Brown bleeding in the woods. The stricken man told his comrades "that he was taken unhurt, but when the enemy were forced to retreat they knocked him down with their guns and bayoneted him in several places." Brown died during the night.[22]

Captain Henry H. Roach of the Twenty-first Virginia, who had been so despondent and fatalistic before the battle, escaped by the barest of margins. His postbattle letter featured a new theme. "I escaped," he wrote, "but how I cannot tell." The dangers he had escaped and the fears he had surmounted convinced Roach that God's hand hovered over him and he had nothing further to fear.[23]

The portion of the Forty-eighth Virginia joined to the left of the Twenty-first shared the unhappy fate of its neighbor. The ranking officer still on duty, Captain James Harvey Horton, reported that he and his men "were ordered to make our way out." Some of them succeeded in cutting their way out in company with portions of the Twenty-first. No doubt the path of the Forty-eighth was even more hazardous than that of the Twenty-first because it was longer, starting deeper behind the overrun point. Captain Oscar White, a staff officer serving with the Forty-eighth Virginia (he later became its lieutenant colonel) was one who made it out. In the process he came across Lieutenant Charles Alexander of the First Virginia Battalion, who had been wounded and was painfully making his way toward safety. White reached down from horseback and gave Alexander a hand up. The lieutenant barely managed to use a stirrup to hoist his bleeding body astride the horse. White's horse took a bullet through the head, but staggered off the field with its double load before collapsing. John Fletcher Bickley of the Forty-eighth Virginia was wounded but did not have Alexander's good fortune in getting out of harm's way. Federals dragged the wounded man off as a prisoner and he spent three weeks in Washington before being exchanged. A full half-century later (in 1912), John Bickley proudly displayed in his home at Yuba City, California, the bullet pried from his right arm at Cedar Mountain.[24]

Not all of the Forty-eighth, nor even all of the Twenty-first, streamed back toward and beyond the Gate when the line melted away. A small remnant of the Twenty-first, bypassed by the Federal flood, fought on. Some men of the regiment retreated somewhat north of west, rather than southwest, and reformed on high ground in the woods about 150 yards north of the road.[25]

The right wing of the Forty-eighth Virginia was better situated than was the Twenty-first to hug its ground and wait for succor rather than fleeing. That was a result of its position to the east of the axis of the Federals' primary southward impetus. Crawford's men could have cleared out every man of the Forty-eighth, of course, by wheeling farther left to close on the southeasternmost point of woods. To do so, however, would have fragmented what momentum remained to the attackers. It also would have canceled the opportunity to burst forth from the woods onto the guns at the Gate and on the flank of the Southern infantry south of the road. By this time the Federal steamroller was about out of steam and entirely out of control, so it is likely that its further progress was a reflexive strike for the Gate and the guns rather than a reasoned selection among options. Even had a guiding hand controlled the fraying charge, a calm review of alternatives would have suggested roaring on toward the Gate. Having come this far at so much cost, and with such unexpected success, why not let the momentum have its head?

The Federals who moved farther south and west left behind a substantial knot of men of the Forty-eighth Virginia anchored to their corner of woodland. Captain Horton reported that "a portion of the regiment not understanding the order [to pull out] remained at their post, continuing to fire at the enemy in front." This stout little party "clung to their position in the woods" until relief reached them.[26]

More than Garnett's regiments and the guns at the Gate stood at risk when Crawford's dwindling remnant burst forth from the woods into the main road. Stonewall Jackson himself was in the neighborhood and under fire. The general was watching Augur's attack from a point behind the left of Early's brigade when Crawford struck Garnett's left. The headquarters entourage heard the crackling of the skirmish lines from that quarter and then the sudden roar of large-scale musketry. Jackson peered down the road through his field glass but occasionally cocked his head to one side. Those who knew Jackson well recognized this as an attempt by a man almost entirely deaf in one ear to identify the direction of fire. The general "seemed to be getting a little nervous" and commented that "some hard work" was shaping up on the left.[27]

Jackson dashed off a note on a page torn from a blank book and then quickly dispatched a second note when someone pointed out Federal movement (probably the Tenth Maine trailing Crawford) visible near the wheatfield. After another pause with head cocked, the general stated the obvious: "That firing is very heavy." When a courier rode up with discouraging word from the left, Jackson dropped his leg from the pommel of his saddle where it had been resting, put his cap firmly on his head, tightened its strap under his chin, wheeled without a word, and "pressed the rowells" to his horse. Some of his staff kept close to the flying army commander, but his half-dozen couriers spread far to the rear in his wake.[28]

Jackson's gallop covered about four hundred yards before it brought him to the fence on the south edge of the road just about where Lieutenant Colonel Cunningham would be killed a few minutes later. The general found a spot where the fence was partly knocked down and leaped it on horseback. He paused long enough to order some of the artillery near the Gate to the rear. During this short pause, as we have seen, John Worsham of the Twenty-first Virginia noticed Jackson in the road—then moments later Worsham saw Federals spilling into the road in the same vicinity. By then Jackson was gone, leaping his horse over the fence on the north edge of the road and plunging into the woods. Within fifty yards he came across some men of Garnett's brigade "falling back in considerable disorder."[29]

The general also ran into Keith Boswell of his staff, who was looking for his chief to give him the bad news that the left had folded. Boswell reported that he met Jackson "just in rear" of the Crittenden Gate. The timing of their encounter is nicely fixed by Boswell's further statement, addressed to Jackson, that "soon after this, when riding with you, I met Major Holliday, very badly wounded, and carried him back and placed him in an ambulance."[30] Holliday suffered his wound after reaching the northwest corner of the wheatfield. He had covered at least five hundred yards through dense woods while wounded by the time Jackson reached the vicinity of the Gate. On an afternoon full of narrow margins, Stonewall Jackson had sliced through the Gate bottleneck with barely moments to spare before it became at least temporarily impassable.

Captain Charles M. Blackford sat on horseback near the Gate as indications mounted that serious trouble had broken out on the left. The noise approaching him soon turned into a motley horde of fleeing Confederates, "all out of order and mixed up with a great number of yankees." Blackford could not tell at first glance what was happening: "I could not understand it; I could not tell whether our men had captured the yankees or the yankees had broken through our line." At some point during his observations Blackford saw Jackson's dash across the road and felt relieved to see that trusted figure near the critical point.[31]

When Jackson plunged into the chaotic woods, his knot of headquarters people had dwindled to three or four men. One of them, William M. Taliaferro, thought it was impossible to escape and, "not fancying a shot in the back," he "turned a quarter face to left" in his saddle. To Taliaferro's amazement, he noticed that Jackson "sat upon his horse calm as a statue." The general sat stone-faced as a shell exploded near his shoulder and Confederates streamed past him. For the moment he made no effort to halt the tide. Soon Jackson turned his horse's head toward the rear and rode slowly, then in a canter, through the woods parallel to the road.[32]

Meanwhile, the crews of some of the guns in front of the Gate quickly obeyed Jackson's order to withdraw. Colonel Stapleton Crutchfield reported that the guns "were withdrawn by General Jackson's order," but in fact not all of them withdrew and Crutchfield did not identify those that did. Lieutenant Carpenter's single rifled piece was one that moved away from the pressure point, displacing "some 200 yards" to the right. Further enemy advances prompted Carpenter to abandon that new position as well. As he limbered up, a driver broke the pole, to Carpenter's disgust, and they were fortunate to be able to get the gun away, leaving its limber behind.[33]

Captain W. T. Poague's Rockbridge Artillery pieces remained silently in place, having been neutralized by friendly troops falling back into their field of fire. "My guns were rendered useless," Poague wrote, "being surrounded by our infantry." He added, with more than a touch of understatement, that the infantry "was on the verge of a panic." For the duration of the crisis Poague's guns stood quiet. In the captain's words: "No position could be gotten afterward without danger to our own infantry." While Confederates surged back around them, Poague claimed, the gunners of his famous battery "nobly stood by their pieces." Even the "two or three who in a former engagement behaved in an unsoldierly manner" stood to their duty.[34]

The Federals who overwhelmed the Twenty-first Virginia and spilled out into the corner of the field not far from the Gate found themselves in an enviable tactical position. Their comrades of Augur's division had been pounding Taliaferro's and Early's brigades from the front for about half an hour by this time. Augur's men were not making a great deal of headway, especially since Thomas's brigade had shored up Early's right, but they were keeping the Confederates busy. The appearance of Crawford's brigade on Taliaferro's left probably would have doomed that Southern position in any event. Coming as it did on top of the pressure from Augur, Crawford's entry onto the stage signaled a major disaster for Taliaferro.

Taliaferro's plight was exacerbated because one of his two green regiments, the Forty-seventh Alabama, stood on his exposed far left. The Federals who suddenly boiled up from the left poured a fire squarely down Taliaferro's line. Troops simply will not stand for that condition. Some sources suggest that Crawford's men actually debouched from the woods in the rear of Taliaferro's left. Jackson's official report and William B. Taliaferro's and that of Colonel Alexander G. Taliaferro, commanding the brigade, each mention only a flank fire. Colonel Taliaferro had every reason to be particularly careful in citing in detail the hardships inflicted on his unit (and in fact did so), but he gave no hint that the Federal onset was so far west as to come literally from behind him.[35]

That some Federals slipped west beyond Taliaferro's left flank can-

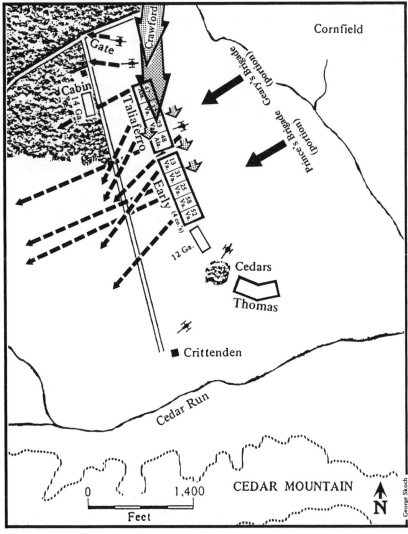

Crawford at High Tide, 6:15–6:30

not be doubted, given the chaos rampant on the scene, but the point is a fine one. Wherever the focus of the Federal advance struck, it was more than enough to unsettle even veteran troops. The raw boys of the Forty-seventh Alabama were decidedly overmatched. Many of them must have wondered if battles unfolded in this manner as a general rule. Novices in the business of war have learned and re-learned, generation by generation from the beginning of time, that battle is uglier than its pictures—uglier than can be imagined. Most have learned that lesson by increments, however, not by having their worst experience as their first experience.

Colonel Taliaferro apparently made some attempt to change front on his left to meet the onslaught. Such a move necessarily would have involved the Forty-seventh Alabama, and those green soldiers simply would not execute a 90° adjustment under surprise fire. Both the Forty-seventh and Forty-eighth Alabama, from opposite ends of the brigade, collapsed and fell back "in utter rout." A. G. Taliaferro reported gently on their fate, as befits a protective leader, noting with considerable exaggeration that the two regiments "were promptly rallied by their officers." Far less graciously, Taliaferro blamed his predicament on Garnett's brigade. The Alabama regiments fell back, he reported officially, because of the fire Crawford brought on the left and in emulation of "the example of the Second Brigade."[36]

Lieutenant Colonel James W. Jackson, who later resigned after he was disgraced at Gettysburg, wrote the official report of the operations of the Forty-seventh Alabama. "We found ourselves attacked from a very unlooked-for quarter," he wrote. The enemy had flanked them to the point of being in their rear, by Colonel Jackson's account, "and were pouring heavy volleys on us at the distance of 40 paces." The colonel promptly ordered an about face, of course, and a few of his men on the right (south) understood and attempted a new line. The men on the left, who faced the greatest danger, fled at once. Those on the right followed without delay. Jackson endeavored to rally them in vain, then "followed them across the field and over a hill that screened them from the balls of the enemy."[37]

The author of a brief memoir of the Forty-seventh Alabama made no claim of being taken entirely in the rear, writing only: "As we were busily engaged with the enemy in front of us, the Yankees flanking us on the left, opened fire." He reported the loss in his broken regiment as twelve killed and seventy-six wounded, precisely matching the official return (an almost unheard-of coincidence). Another of the Forty-seventh Alabama boys scattered in the flight wrote an account four days after the battle that tells the tale poignantly: "They say hit was the hardist fight that has ever bin yet for the lenght of hit. . . . Mother If I cold sea yo I cold tell yo more nuse than I cold right in a weeak."[38]

The Forty-eighth Alabama had far less cause for alarm than the

Forty-seventh but broke nonetheless as soon as their fellow Alabamians started rearward. The regiment was big, with 450 muskets; no doubt both of the new regiments were strong in numbers. Lieutenant Colonel Abner Hughes, age forty-six, led the Forty-eighth in this its inaugural action; two months later he resigned. In describing the regiment's withdrawal he used a pair of quaint euphemistic phrases: "We were obliged to change, which was readily done." Hughes also insisted that his retreat covered no more than "a short distance" and that his command "behaved gallantly, it being the first time they had been under fire." An unpublished history of the Forty-eighth Alabama puts its loss at Cedar Mountain at a whopping 123 men killed and wounded, although the official tabulation was 73 casualties, 12 of them killed.[39] Either figure represents a substantial toll on a regiment in its first combat.

Non-Alabamians in the vicinity were understandably—but unjustly—hard on the two regiments. Well-seasoned regiments all around them did not behave much differently all afternoon when presented with similar circumstances, although the Forty-eighth Alabama did enjoy the dubious distinction of being the only regiment that ran before feeling any direct pressure. The rookie regiments made an easy target for criticism, though, and their colleagues took aim at them. A Virginian in their own brigade blamed the mixture of conscripts in the Alabama regiments for a lack of character; conscription was a relatively new phenomenon which just then was bringing the first of its fruits into the field. "They had not been drilled," the Virginian explained, "and ran like turkeys when they got into the heat of this battle. . . . Raw men can't stand that kind of music." He tempered his criticism pleasantly by adding that the two regiments "did very well" in later battles, once they earned some experience.[40]

Another Virginian stationed with a battery somewhat to the rear noted dryly that the Alabamians decided "to do that which would permit them to fight some other day." He saw them stream rearward "in a sort of wild, conglomerate, stampedy mass." "Stampedy" may not be a proper adjective, but it seems to fit the result. Perhaps the cruelest blow of all came from Stonewall Jackson's headquarters, which issued an order to each company commander in the army to furnish a full listing of men who deserted the colors or behaved in cowardly fashion at Cedar Mountain. That unusual, if not unique, measure did not specify the First Virginia Battalion or the two Alabama regiments as its targets. In fact, the surviving copy of the circular is addressed to Richard Ewell. But the implications of that

*View south-southwest across the zone of Augur's advance,
from a vantage point on the old road at the southern
edge of the wheatfield, 1989. (Clark B. Hall)*

theretofore unthinkable order fell most heavily in well-recognized quarters.[41]

The Thirty-seventh Virginia stood next to the Forty-seventh Alabama and therefore became the left-flank regiment when the Alabamians vanished. The Thirty-seventh's major, twenty-six-year-old Henry Clinton Wood, wrote the official report for the regiment because Colonel Titus V. Williams fell wounded during the battle. In his report Wood recounted the fight against Geary's Ohioans, which lasted "for some time," during which two opposing lines gave way before the unpleasant surprise from his left flank ruined the major's day. Wood left no mystery about his opinion of the causes of his unit's retreat. When the Forty-seventh Alabama uncovered its left, the Thirty-seventh was "exposed to a fire in front, rear, and on the left flank" and had no chance to hold. Colonel Taliaferro ordered the regiment to fall back.

"It is proper to state here," Major Wood reported emphatically, "that this regiment would have been able to maintain its position had the Forty-seventh and Forty-eighth Alabama Regiments been able to have maintained theirs." The withdrawal of the Thirty-seventh Virginia began, inevitably, with the hard-pressed left companies and progressed steadily down the line. Wood insisted pridefully that the

Thirty-seventh retreated "in tolerably good order," although some companies admittedly became "a little confused." The cross fire that forced the retreat and then hounded its steps brought down "a great many" men in the Thirty-seventh Virginia, which lost about eighty men that day. Colonel Taliaferro did not mitigate the Thirty-seventh's troubles with such soothing adjectives as Major Wood used. He simply reported that part of the regiment was "thrown into confusion" and all of it was "compelled to fall back."[42]

The Twenty-third Virginia fought next right from the Thirty-seventh Virginia and fought longest and best of the regiments in A. G. Taliaferro's brigade. In doing so the Twenty-third lost fewer than half as many men as did the Thirty-seventh Virginia. That relative statistic probably illuminates two conditions: the Federal thrust was waning rapidly; and standing unified in a defensive position often proves to be less costly than running from one. The Twenty-third was Colonel Taliaferro's own regiment, from which he had moved to temporary brigade command. That left Lieutenant Colonel George Washington Curtis in charge of the regiment. Curtis was a thirty-five-year-old Mexican War veteran and a brother of Union General William B. Curtis. Like Winder and Cunningham, G. W. Curtis had been sick on the eve of battle. He had left a Charlottesville hospital on August 7 to catch up with the advancing army. Curtis's Yankee brother and western Virginia roots had cost him dearly, exiling him from home as "a refugee from the tyrants of the Northwest."[43]

George Curtis held the Twenty-third tightly under rein as the line to his left fell apart, even though the Forty-eighth Alabama to his right already had fled. A surviving officer reported that the "crossfire upon our left flank" was "very close and very destructive." The brief stand by the Twenty-third cannot have consumed many minutes, but it lasted long enough to win the applause of division commander W. B. Taliaferro, who reported officially that the regiment "deserves especial mention for its firmness and admirable conduct in the engagement." Soon the Twenty-third also fell back under orders from its brigade commander.[44]

The fallback by the Twenty-third Virginia engendered "some confusion" in its ranks, of course, and newly convalescent George Curtis rode among the men doing his best to maintain cohesion. At this critical moment a Federal bullet knocked the colonel over and inflicted a mortal wound. The parallel between his unhappy case and that of Lieutenant Colonel Cunningham of the Twenty-first Virginia is striking: each held the same rank; each had been absent sick but hurried painfully forward when action loomed; and each man fell immediately after his men had been obliged to fall back and while attempting to lead them to safety. Major Simeon T. Walton assumed command of the regiment on the spot. (Walton later won promotion to take effect from this day and held Curtis's old post until he too was killed not many miles distant in November 1863.) General Taliaferro's official report lauded both Curtis and Walton.[45]

A comrade wrote a six-stanza poem to the memory of George W. Curtis and sent it through the lines to the dead man's family of Northern sympathizers in the mountains of what later became West Virginia. In a cover note the friend mentioned Curtis's habitual weary and long-suffering expression with the suggestion that the victim had sensed his fate—"that sadness of his features in repose that seemed to betoken his early death." The poem and the letter rest today, fittingly enough, in the papers of George Washington Curtis's brother, the Yankee general. Friends buried George's body in the yard of a farmhouse near the battlefield. The body was still there in 1903 and may be there yet.[46]

In the hail of fire William Barrett Pendleton of the Twenty-third Virginia lost a leg but survived the wound and died in 1914 at Cuckoo, Virginia. Pendleton was a VMI man serving as General Taliaferro's aide. Another Twenty-third man—or, rather, boy—serving with the division commander was sixteen-year-old Private Clinton Depriest of Company H. Young Depriest distinguished himself enough to win mention for his "gallant conduct" in Taliaferro's official report. George K. Harlow of the Twenty-third Virginia expressed a relief felt by many survivors in his letter to "Dear Father and family" dated August 13: "Through the providence of the Great I am [,] I am still living. . . . have lost many a noble soldier . . . a verry [sic] hard fight."[47]

Most of the broken pieces of Taliaferro's brigade streamed directly back in the reciprocal direction from the Federal thrust, moving southwest away from both the front line and the main road in the direction of Cedar Mountain. Some of the men, however, fought by squads without any overall organization toward the woods nearer the Gate. The trees doubtless looked more inviting than did the naked plain to those Southerners within tentative reach of them.[48] Furthermore, when help came it would come from that quarter.

As the Twenty-third Virginia withdrew and completed the abandonment of the ground once held by Taliaferro's brigade, the widening gap in the Confederate line was so great that well over half of that line no longer existed. Only Early's brigade remained of the three that had faced east originally. Thomas on the right and part of the Stonewall Brigade on the left were newcomers, and most welcomed ones, anchoring the two far extremities. Now Early would feel such pressure as the fraying Federal attack could muster. It no longer boasted much potency, but it came from the flank and thus hit a most sensitive spot. The Confederate artillery under Pegram and Hardy fought from ground near Early's left, close to the now broken junction between Early and Taliaferro. Those guns obviously came directly into harm's way and attracted considerable attention from soldiers of both sides.

Willie Pegram—young, bespectacled, scholarly looking—belied his appearance by behavior that marked him as one of the bravest artillerists in the Army of Northern Virginia. Captain Pegram's cluster of four guns, two of his own and two under Lieutenant William B. Hardy of the Middlesex Artillery, had been blasting away at Federals in the cornfield for some time. Their position was such that they probably took under fire men from both Geary's and Prince's brigades. The four Confederate guns spewed out "a well-directed fire," much of it canister, and in the words of R. L. Walker, "inflicted great loss on the enemy." Artillerists who walked over the Federal ground in the cornfield the next day were gratified to see "scores of dead" exhibiting signs of being the victims of cannon fire. The flight of Taliaferro's men, however, left Pegram in extremity. Geary's Ohioans surged close to the guns and thought they had them in their grasp.[49]

As the fate of the guns teetered in the balance Pegram seized a battle flag and ran with it from gun to gun, "waving it in the very faces of the men and begging" them to hold. Albert Sidney Drewry, who was serving one of the guns, recalled that the boyish captain yelled: "Don't let the enemy have these guns or this flag; Jackson is looking at you. Go on, men, give it to them." Pegram wrote to his family about the battle, which from his vantage point seemed to be "certainly a fine sight." When his support "behaved badly" and "ran," Willie "kept a sharp look out, and played upon them with canister to the last."[50]

Lieutenant Colonel Walker, chief of A. P. Hill's artillery, watched his protégé closely as he fought off the attacking waves. It seemed to Walker that Pegram and Hardy held on beyond the point of no return and after all of their support except the Thirteenth Virginia had fallen back from their neighborhood. Walker finally "ordered the batteries to retire, the loss in both men and horses being considerable," when he saw A. P. Hill's infantry coming up from the rear. The foot soldiers would seal the breach; there was no point in sacrificing brave Pegram. "We fired until the enemy were right at the guns," J. W. D. Farrar of Pegram's battery remembered with pride. At the last possible moment the captain gave the command, "Limber to the road." Three guns raced away but the driver of the fourth was shot down at this tense moment. Pegram ordered another man into the driver's seat. When the designated new driver cringed from his task, Pegram drew his sword and raised it to strike the man. Another soldier immediately leaped onto the lead team and hustled the gun away "barely in time."[51]

A Federal observer with no vested interest in regimental claims reported that the unit that closed on Pegram's artillery knoll was a fragment of the Maryland regiment of Prince's brigade, which planted the distinctive flag of its state there briefly. Pegram left three dead horses and a caisson behind when he escaped, recovering the caisson that evening. When he found breathing space in the rear, Willie gathered the members of his battery together and delivered a short speech: "Men, when the enemy takes a gun of my battery, look for my dead body in front of it."[52] The youngster kept his promise until the war's last week, when he validated its second clause with his life. Meanwhile, within short hours on that August 9, Pegram and his guns would be in even deeper trouble than that they had escaped near the Crittenden Lane.

The left regiment of Early's brigade, and thus the first to be outflanked, was the Thirteenth Virginia Infantry. The Thirteenth was a tried and true outfit, which had begun the war under the command of Colonel A. P. Hill. Its current colonel, James A. Walker, was a fighter worthy of the regiment; nine months later he would be promoted to brigadier general and given the famous Stonewall Brigade. Although the Thirteenth was the most susceptible of Early's regiments to the panic from the left, it stood firmly even after regiments to its right had joined the rout. The loss of Lieutenant Colonel Alfred H. Jackson of the Thirty-first Virginia to a wound had weakened the resolve of that regiment. Next right came the Twenty-fifth Virginia. The Twenty-fifth's commander, Major John Carlton Higginbotham, also went down with a wound. "The panic," James A. Walker reported, "was communicated to two or three regiments on my right." Some of the Thirty-first hung close to Walker, but most of it broke, as did all of the Twenty-fifth and about half of the next regiment to the right, the Fifty-eighth Virginia. Jubal Early identified the Thirty-first and Twenty-fifth (both western Virginia regiments) as those "which chiefly participated in the disorder" and blamed that on the loss of their commanders.[53]

As the Confederate tide swept back on either side, the Thirteenth Virginia clung to its position with grim determination. Colonel Jim Walker's official report displayed well-earned pride over the stand. For some time, Walker reported, his Thirteenth Virginia and the attached segment of the Thirty-first Virginia were "the only Confederate troops in that part of the field in sight of our position." A piece of artillery in front of the right of the Thirteenth Virginia fired steadily against the approaching enemy in a clearly hopeless struggle to keep them back. Walker moved his regiment-plus of infantry about thirty yards nearer the piece and deflected the Federals until it could reach safety. During this brief struggle, Colonel Taliaferro rode up from the left and watched for a moment. Taliaferro was in his shirt sleeves under the hot sun, trying to rally his men. The colonel pointed out to them the admirable behavior of the Thirteenth, shouting a compliment variously reported as "Look at the old Thirteenth, rally on her"; or, "See, she stands like a stonewall!"[54]

Pressure on Walker's little knot of resistance soon spread to three sides. A member of the Thirteenth insisted that he and his comrades resisted to front and flank and finally were "fired upon from the rear." Walker held them there after the gun escaped for what he described as "a few moments, holding the enemy in front in check" until they had reached a point "considerably in rear of our position, and were pouring a very annoying fire into my left flank." Many of the men suffering under that fire would have considered "annoying" an irksome understatement. One of them who broke under the pressure and fled from his unit explained the next day to his company commander, Sergeant Sam Buck: "I heard you begging men to rally and heard you say to me 'for God's sake, rally' but indeed I could not stop." Sergeant Buck was a combat veteran of some sagacity and concluded judiciously that his soldier was telling nothing more nor less than the truth. "This was a fact," Buck wrote later, "he could not stop."[55]

Even Jim Walker's widely applauded stand reached its limit and the colonel ordered the Thirteenth to fall back "obliquely to the right and rear," which it did in what he described as "tolerable order." Colonel Walker and another primary source recorded the distance of the regiment's withdrawal as two hundred yards. Another eyewitness estimated the distance more optimistically as one hundred yards.

The Thirteenth's angle of retreat followed the pattern of the whole line south of the road when it flowed, in the words of a Northern witness, "down the fields towards Cedar Mountain." As the retreating men looked back over their shoulders at the ground they had just left, they saw the same Maryland flag unfurled which had caught the eye of a Federal watching from the other side of the field, a mile distant. The enemy captors of the Thirteenth Virginia's ground opened fire on the retreating men at rather short range. The regiment rallied at the end of its two-hundred-yard run and had enough organization and spark left to give vigorous assistance to the hard-pressed nearby fragment of the Thirty-first. Sergeant Sam Buck had been "horrified" when Walker ordered the retreat, feeling certain that the regiment would break apart and "stampede" in the process. The result was not as bad as Buck had feared, but he reported: "My company, indeed all were badly broken and every effort was needed to form under such a terrible fire."[56]

The central figure in the drama on the left of Early's brigade obviously was Colonel James A. Walker, not the brigade commander. That came about for the simplest of reasons: Jubal Early did not know that anything was amiss. At the moment disaster struck, General Early was hard at work on the far right of the line, beyond his own brigade's right. He placed the three Georgia regiments of Thomas's brigade well east of the Crittenden Lane. The position was as strong as it was important. So deafening was the roar of battle echoing off the mountain, and so rolling was the terrain, that Early did not know his left was assailed when it happened. While he was working with Thomas, Early wrote, "my whole left was excluded from my view." When the general rode back toward his left he came into view of a heart-stopping spectacle. His own left was gone (Walker apparently had just completed his stand) and all of the Confederates to the north for as far as Early's eye ranged had withdrawn. Augur's men "had crossed the little stream in front of where my left had been," Early wrote. "I saw at once the critical position in which we were placed."[57]

As Early emerged from the darkness imposed upon him by the devilish folds in the terrain, he quickly identified the salient facts in the chaos. Thomas stood solid behind him, as did the Twelfth Georgia. The four companies of the Fifty-second that had reached the field stood small but solid adjoining the left of the Twelfth Georgia. Part of the Fifty-eighth Virginia remained firm adjoining the Fifty-second companies. The rest of the Fifty-eighth and all of the

Twenty-fifth, Thirty-first, and Thirteenth were gone by this time. Although he never said so, among Early's first thoughts must have been a burning regret over the absence of more than one and one-half regiments of his brigade. Those seven hundred or so men, who constituted about one-fourth of Early's strength, had been needlessly strewn far to the rear as picket detachments. Their absence was not Early's fault, which if anything probably heightened his chagrin.[58]

Early did not need to study the situation long to grasp the nub of his last, best hope. The Twelfth Georgia and Thomas "were then isolated and in an advanced position, and had they given way the day in all probability would have been lost." He promptly turned away from the scene on his left and rode back to the right to hold that final bulwark with all his might, sending an aide to the left to attempt a rally. In pursuing that logical course, Early again took himself out of view of the main Crittenden Lane zone. All he saw of the fighting there, first and last, was the quick glance that informed him of the crisis and sent him scurrying back toward the Georgians.[59]

Henry Kyd Douglas found himself in a tight spot behind the Crittenden Lane during this Confederate reverse. He had gone up the mountain to see Dick Ewell and was hastening back toward the Gate in search of Jackson when he found his way sealed off by the Federal burst. Douglas reined in and turned back toward the mountain, only to find that route cut off as well. The only neutral spot on the young aide's horizon lay directly to the rear, where "a very repulsive fence" blocked his path. Bushes grew tall and thick along the fence to a degree that made it look impassable for his horse. Bullets "falling and whizzing" nearby nerved Douglas "to be up and doing." The rider's excitement and the noise made the horse "frantic with fright." The animal's desperate leap cleared the fence and threw up a tremendous shower of dirt on landing. Stonewall Jackson found the mental image of Douglas's frantic leap so amusing when he visited the site the next day that he momentarily forsook his customary dour visage.[60]

While Lieutenant Douglas ran his high-stakes steeplechase, "Old Jube" Early was weighing his Georgian helpers and finding them not wanting. At the critical moment of isolation near Cedar Run, the Twelfth Georgia Infantry and its redoubtable commander enjoyed a bright moment at center stage. The senior officer present with the regiment was doughty old Captain William Frederick Brown of Company F. Brown was forty-eight years of age, which ought not to qualify as "old," but he apparently was not a well-preserved forty-eight. Early wrote that the captain was sixty-five, and Douglas Southall Freeman tempered that estimate to "about 60." W. F. Brown owned a large plantation (he was worth $39,000 in 1860) in Dooley County, Georgia, and had served in the state senate for three years before the war. Two of his sons served in his company; one of them had died in 1861.[61]

Captain Brown and his Twelfth Georgia were perfectly situated to deal with the crisis, facing as they were across the Federal flank. One of the Georgians declared: "This was the best position we have ever had, in any fight. . . . The hill was not very high—only slightly elevated. . . . By falling back about 10 steps, we could load our guns without the enemy's bullets having any effect on us." The regiment's right anchored firmly to Thomas, and the nearby guns at the Cedars roared defiance. When General Early dashed up to the regiment and sought out William Brown, he found the captain in fine fettle. His superb field of fire and the plethora of targets scurrying across it had about exhausted the men's ammunition, but Brown seethed with ardor. To Early's exhortations to hold, Captain Brown replied eagerly: "General, my ammunition is nearly out, don't you think we had better charge them?" Early rejected the tactical suggestion but rejoiced at Brown's élan.[62] Students of the war remember the captain to this day for his spirited response to Early. Brown had few more opportunities to make his mark; he was killed in action twenty-three days later at Chantilly.

The fire of the Twelfth Georgia tilted the scales just long enough for widespread Confederate efforts elsewhere across the field to gain the momentum necessary to turn the tide. The Georgians behaved "as if we had been invited to a frolic. . . . Talking and laughing continued as long as the battle lasted." Early rode among the men of the regiment distributing well-earned plaudits. When the Virginians holding on at the left of the Twelfth Georgia yelled that the Yankees were "too many for us," Early cheerfully responded, "Go on boys; you are safe," and spoke of reinforcements coming into view. Irby Goodwin Scott of the Twelfth wrote home a few days later and reported that Early said that "the 12th Ga was his fighting regt." Lieutenant Scott felt rather more perplexed by the future implications of Early's kind words than complimented by them. "I like a good name," he concluded, "but I think we have most too much of it for our own good. It causes us to be placed in many places of danger that otherwise we would not."[63]

Another member of the Twelfth Georgia displayed a less than

*View in 1989 from the Cedars site toward
the U.S. position. (Clark B. Hall)*

cheerful spirit in looking back on Captain Brown at Cedar Mountain
on the day for which the regiment always would be remembered.
Captain Shepard Green Pryor of Company A complained a few days
later that the regiment was "allmost ruined" because of the absence
of its regular field officers. (Stonewall Jackson had both Colonel
Z. T. Conner and Major W. A. Hawkins under arrest for misbehavior
in the Shenandoah Valley three months earlier.) Captain Pryor was
eager to see them tried in order to arrange "some permanent commander." Otherwise, "being balawhacked about by such men as Capt
Brown [,] Scott [Thaddeus B. of Company E, and] Rogers [James
Gustavus of Company H] will entirely ruin it." Pryor declared—
whether ingenuously or jealously—that "the men have no respect for
them & dont try to please them."[64] All three of the men denounced
by Pryor died on battlefields within four months. Pryor resigned in
1864, leaving behind *balawhacked* as a major contribution to American usage.

Although Early did not personally witness the stand by the Thirteenth Virginia, he soon learned enough about it to pay unreserved
tribute to Colonel Walker in his official report. The musket-toting
men in the ranks who used up all of their allotted forty rounds and
more were the unquestioned heroes of the day. Captain Brown's
stout leadership put his name next to that of the hardworking infan-

try and Jubal Early put James A. Walker's on the same honor roll. "He is a most efficient and gallant officer," Early wrote, "who is always ready to perform any duty assigned him, and the men of his regiment are capital fighting men, there being none better in the army." Walker and his troops also had performed superbly as skirmishers at Cedar Mountain and elsewhere. Withal, Early concluded, he must "respectfully and earnestly recommend [Walker] for promotion to the position of brigadier-general."[65]

The astonishingly successful lunge by Crawford's brigade crested just north of the Cedars. The three and one-half Northern regiments that made the attack had shrunk to perhaps two and one-half by the time they reached the woods beyond the wheatfield. That relatively small force routed all of Garnett's brigade, all of Taliaferro's brigade, and half of Early's. It simply did not have enough men or momentum left to finish the job below Cedar Mountain. Brown's and Dement's pieces near the Cedars continued to fire, although they, like the Twelfth Georgia, were running low on ammunition; targets had been plentiful and well within reach for a long time.[66]

The Twelfth Georgia and Thomas's brigade probably numbered a few more men than Crawford's regiments had counted in their ranks when they started across the wheatfield, a mile away and several hundreds of casualties ago. Augur's men in the corn had added their weight to Crawford's from a different angle, once Crawford sprung open the Southern line, but the Federal bolt was thoroughly shot. Through all of the ebb and flow on the field below, Dick Ewell's guns from the unassailable mountain shoulder high above steadily rained iron on the Northern infantry. The physical results were considerable and the psychological results must have been even greater.

As the pendulum hesitated near its apogee in the vicinity of the Cedars, Stonewall Jackson threw himself into the balance with an enormous burst of personal vigor. The result was electric.

CHAPTER 9

Jackson Waves His Sword

WHEN STONEWALL JACKSON scampered past the Gate into the woods north of the road, missing capture by the narrowest of margins, his army lay gasping on the brink of disaster. A relatively small—almost tiny—Federal force had all but trounced Mighty Stonewall and at that moment still surged south on the way to a rout of Taliaferro and part of Early's force. Yet Jackson later pronounced the battle of Cedar Mountain "the most successful of his exploits."[1] He unquestionably based that amazing judgment not on a dispassionate analysis of opportunities lost and won, but rather on personal involvement. Jackson "saw the elephant," in the homely phrase of that war, and saw it up close with his own eyes. The hot breath of battle never blew more directly on the South's legendary hero than it did on August 9, 1862, and he remained inordinately proud of the results for the rest of his life.

When we left Jackson near the Gate he was headed temporarily toward the rear in search of A. P. Hill and the reinforcements that could save the army. Hill was between the Gate and the schoolhouse, pushing his men into line as they arrived and doing his best to stem some of the flood of retreating infantry. The fiery Virginian drew his sword as he waded into the stampede in his shirt sleeves using "urgent appeals and persuasive demeanor" on the disheartened crowd. Hill waxed more than urgent and persuasive with a lieutenant he spotted who was headed in the wrong direction.

Hill, wrathfully: "Who are you, sir, and where are you going?"

Lieutenant, trembling: "I am going back with my wounded friend."

Hill, after ripping the lieutenant's insignia of rank from his collar: "You are a pretty fellow to hold a commission—deserting your colors in the presence of the enemy, and going to the rear with a man who is scarcely badly enough wounded to go himself. I reduce you to the ranks, sir, and if you do not go to the front and do your duty, I'll have you shot as soon as I can spare a file of men for the purpose."[2]

General Hill's battle blood obviously was boiling; he sounded al-

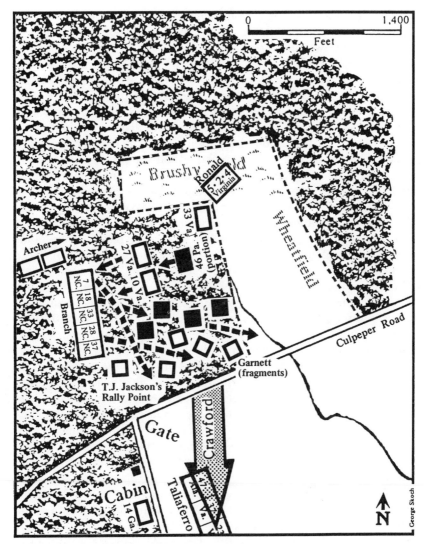

Branch Arrives and Jackson Rallies, 6:15–6:30

most like his bête noir, Stonewall Jackson, as he dealt with the poorly motivated lieutenant. Within moments Jackson found Hill and went right after him. "Jackson sharply told him he was behind time," an eyewitness reported, "and ordered him to deploy his regiments." A. P. Hill had in fact been doing just that as rapidly as his men arrived and already had reason to believe that Jackson dealt unjustly. The occasion was ripe for an angry explosion. But the exigencies of battle washed away all personal considerations, at least for Hill. He accepted Jackson's harsh remark "in entire good humor," the witness noted with apparent surprise, "and running back to the servant leading his horse, he vaulted into the saddle" and went back to work.[3]

The Georgians under Colonel E. L. Thomas who had gone around to bolster Early's right belonged to A. P. Hill's division. Behind them came the five North Carolina regiments of Branch's brigade, which constituted the first of the reserves Jackson sought so eagerly. General Branch had won renown as an orator in the antebellum United States House of Representatives and was plying his men with that elixir when Jackson reached him. The army commander galloped rapidly along the line of the brigade wearing an "unfathomable smile" and "looking the men steadily in their faces as he passed along." One of Jackson's staff members reported that Stonewall "curtly" ordered Branch to "Push forward, General, push forward!" Branch recounted a less brusque order. "General Jackson came to me," Branch recalled, "and told me his left was beaten and broken, and the enemy was turning him and he wished me to advance." In either form, Branch could not miss the nub of the message. He moved his men forward at once, even though they were not fully formed into line.[4]

As the Tarheels forged ahead, several of their officers "rushed up to Jackson and almost forced him to the rear" in an early and milder version of the protective gestures toward Lee that became famous in May 1864. Jackson was content with the results as he watched the line move past him with a yell. One observer reported that Branch's men and others moving forward on Jackson's personal prompting went into action at the double-quick shouting "Stonewall Jackson! Stonewall Jackson!"[5]

Jackson left Branch to cope with the woods and their inhabitants north of the road and headed back toward the critical situation at the Gate. As he galloped into the densest enemy fire he ever personally faced, Stonewall attempted to draw his sword. Never before had he been moved to that symbolic gesture on a battlefield, nor would the occasion arise again. Narrators of the battle never fail to mention the incident.[6] Early in the twentieth century the United Daughters of the Confederacy mentioned Jackson's unique swordplay in the text of the marker they erected on the battlefield just opposite the Gate. The episode nicely captures the drama and tension of the moment and surely deserved encapsulation on that central monument. The tale requires a slight revision, however, to its standard form.

Stonewall Jackson *tried* to draw his sword as he waded into his retreating troops, but he could not get it out of its scabbard. Jed Hotchkiss, who rode beside Jackson, described the moment in a letter to the British historian G. F. R. Henderson: "I recollect well his attempt to draw his long cavalry sabre to help him stop the rout, when he found it so rusted in from non use, that he could not withdraw it . . . so he deliberately unsnapped it from his belt holdings and used it scabbard and all on the heads of the fleeing panic stricken troops." Another member of Jackson's entourage validated Hotchkiss's image of the sword-waving as more punitive than inspirational in design. Stonewall used the weapon "to gesticulate with," he wrote, "and to arrest the tide of men rolling backward, by threatening them."[7]

Shortly after Jackson unbuckled his sword and scabbard and put them to work he also took hold of another deeply symbolic military icon to augment his armament—a Confederate battle flag. With both hands full, the general was obliged to drop his reins so that he could wave both the flag and the sword over his head at the same time (no mean physical feat, given the weight of each and the need to stay mounted). The image of the army's revered leader in that pose was enough to turn many a man back toward his duty.[8]

The setting in which Jackson played out his stirring role could not have been more dramatic or dangerous. The woods near the Gate seethed with projectiles, "a horrid fire . . . on nearly three sides of us," Hotchkiss told his brother, "the balls falling as thick as I ever saw them, reaping their harvest of death on all sides." Hotchkiss believed that God must have protected him in this "very vortex of destruction." General William B. Taliaferro, who was present, suggested that "the escape of Jackson from death was miraculous. He was in the thickest of the combat, at very short range."[9]

Lieutenant John Blue, the cavalryman whose account of this day at Jackson's side on courier duty is priceless, left the most vivid account of the melee around the Gate that had Stonewall Jackson as its centerpiece:

The rattle of musketry, the shouting, cheering and yelling was deafening. The smoke of battle and the thick foliage on the timber overhead made it impossible to see but a short distance. The

leaves and small limbs were falling thick and the bark from the
. . . timber f[l]ying in every direction, often striking a person in
the face leading him to believe that he had run against a load of
buck shot or something worse.

It appeared for a few moments as though we had struck a full-
grown tornado, loaded with thunder and lightning. This was the
most hair-raising fix I had ever struck.

Blue concluded that Jackson would have been hard to hear or to see
for long in that setting, despite the many contemporary accounts of
his inspirational behavior. The sensation of having Yankees shooting
from three sides was real enough, although perhaps it was somewhat
exaggerated. Lieutenant Blue was one of several witnesses who reported it. He described the Confederate line swirling back around
the Gate as resembling a fishhook, "doubled back until the extreme
left . . . [was] within a hundred yards of and in rear of the center."
Inside the hook, "about where [the] barb should be," stood Jackson,
surrounded by his men.[10]

Confederate soldiers who fought under Stonewall called him,
among other things, "Old Blue Light." The etymology of the phrase
apparently was dual, mixing parts of awe for Jackson's fervent Old
Testament religion with observations of the fierce light that blazed in
the general's blue eyes in battle. Many Southerners had occasion to
remark on Stonewall's blue battle light during the war, but none ever
saw it shine brighter than in the Culpeper County woods that August
9. Soldiers compared notes for the rest of their lives on "how the eye
flashed, the cheek flushed hot," when Jackson rode yelling into their
midst at Cedar Mountain. An officer who had commented on the
general's mundane appearance ("an indifferent and slouching man")
saw at first hand that when "the 'Light of Battle' [shed] its radiance
over him his whole person was changed." Jackson's normally awkward bearing became "as graceful as Lee's and his face was lit with
. . . inspiration." Even the general's undistinguished horse "seemed
endowed with the style and form of an Arabian."[11]

Those who could make out Jackson's exhortations over the cacophony heard him trading on his own name and fame. "Jackson is with
you" was his cry, according to accounts circulated around the army's
campfires from unit to unit. "Rally, brave men, and press forward.
Your general will lead you. Jackson will lead you. Follow me!" "Rally,
men! Remember Winder. . . . Forward, men, Forward!"[12] The quiet,
almost unnaturally low voice Jackson employed in everyday usage

bore little resemblance to his battle tocsin. "The voice so low and calm on ordinary occasions," wrote an acquaintance, "rose to loud and strident tones, as it called like a clarion." The level, clipped speech the general normally used sparingly turned on this afternoon into "a voice which pealed higher than the roar of battle."[13]

Stonewall Jackson stood out in bright relief to every eye within range for obvious reasons, but he did not work alone in rallying the disorganized men. Young Joseph Graham Morrison, a brother of Jackson's wife freshly arrived from seven months at Virginia Military Institute, saw his first action at Cedar Mountain as a member of the general's staff. (Nepotism at headquarters was not frowned on in that war and was in fact virtually de rigueur.) Two of the older men with Jackson commented enthusiastically upon the youngster's performance at the general's side. "Morrison . . . distinguished himself by gallantly going into the thickest of the fight and urging on the men," Hotchkiss wrote admiringly in his diary. Morrison plunged ahead of Jackson astride one of the general's horses, which took a bullet through the jaw and steadily sprinkled himself and his rider with blood from the wound. An onlooker urged Jackson to call back his "fearless and chivalric" young kinsman but the general refused. Morrison's example would be good for the troops, Jackson commented, and battle experience would teach him discretion—if he survived to learn the lesson.[14] Morrison later stood at the bedside of his dying chief and brother-in-law and survived the war despite serious wounds and the loss of a limb.

Captain William T. Poague of the Rockbridge Artillery observed the scene near the Gate and mentioned not only Jackson as conspicuous but also General W. B. Taliaferro and Private David Barton of the Rockbridge unit. Another artillerist, Lieutenant Colonel Reuben Lindsay Walker, lent a hand in the rally. Each time Walker accumulated a handful of infantry and moved on to find others the first knot would dissolve again, to Walker's immense disgust. He had his sword in hand (it apparently was better oiled than Jackson's) and was waving it and "swearing outrageously" at his current little line when Stonewall came upon the scene. The general still had his sword—and scabbard, of course—swinging in the air, so he was something to see, particularly since he had lost his hat in the woods by this time and was unaccustomedly bareheaded. Jackson's appearance silenced the artillerist's cursing at once. Apparently that was not what the general wanted because he shouted, no doubt to the astonishment of all within hearing, "That's right, Colonel, give it to them." Lindsay

Walker promptly went into action and "continued his work and in his own way."[15] Perhaps Stonewall Jackson was remembering something of his encounter with Quartermaster Harman back at the river earlier in the day.

One member of the headquarters detachment was not involved with the heroics. Lieutenant John Blue found himself caught up in the swirling chaos and became separated from Jackson. "When I began to realize the condition of affairs," he wrote drolly, "I found that I had lost the general or the general had lost one of his couriers. The confusion and noise at this time was terrible and . . . frightful, for a few moments I was almost paralyzed."[16]

Stonewall Jackson by this stage of the war had achieved a firm hold on the emotions and affections of most of the soldiers who followed him. His appearance near a camp would set off a chorus of yells audible for miles. The effect of a transformed, larger-than-life Jackson in the midst of flying bullets was manifold greater. Men stopped and looked and yelled and then began to fight anew. The rally the general began encompassed at first only "a few score men," but others steadily joined. Someone strewed spare cartridges on the ground among the men to relieve any shortages. Virginians broken from Garnett's brigade and some from Taliaferro's brigade picked up the cartridges and put them to use. Jackson's line was mending fast.[17]

Not only Confederates were impressed by Stonewall Jackson's charismatic performance. A captive Federal officer watched from near the Gate. His custodian of the moment, Captain Blackford, described the prisoner as a handsome young fellow in his early twenties clutching a broken sword. As Jackson performed his personal magic the youthful Yankee watched in amazement. "What officer is that?" he asked Blackford. When Blackford responded with about the most famous name on the continent the prisoner, "fully appreciating the magnetism of the occasion . . . seemed carried away with admiration. With a touch of nature that makes the whole world kin he waved his broken sword around his head and shouted, 'Hurrah for General Jackson! Follow your General, Boys!'" Blackford later claimed that this performance melted his heart so thoroughly that he sent the prisoner off into the woods and hoped that he escaped.[18]

Jackson's close encounter ended as did most such things in that era: a subordinate suggested the wisdom of withdrawing, which presumably would not otherwise have occurred to the leader under fire. In this instance the voice of reason belonged to William B. Taliaferro. "I rode up to him and insisted that he should retire," Taliaferro wrote, "plainly and emphatically telling him it was no place for the commander of an army." Perhaps because Stonewall and this subordinate were not on particularly close terms, Jackson responded to Taliaferro's sally by looking "a little surprised." His urgent personal mission had been discharged by this time, the tide was moving back in the right direction, and discretion clearly was the better part of valor. Taliaferro described the results: "The logic of the situation forced itself upon his mind and with his invariable ejaculation of 'Good, good,' he rode to the rear."[19]

As General Jackson rode away from the Gate those with him (if not the somewhat deaf general himself) could hear the raucous Rebel yell to the north, where reinforcements surged toward the wheatfield. By the time he reached a vantage point south of the road along the Crittenden Lane, Jackson could see Federals moving back toward and through the vicinity of the wheatfield.[20]

The drawn-sword, flag-waving episode near the Gate came to be a good deal larger than life with the passage of time, as did many things connected with Stonewall Jackson. Men who did not witness the short, tense drama in person wrote some of the most inflamed accounts of it. John Esten Cooke fought with the army in Virginia but was not on the field at Cedar Mountain. His ultraheroic account, based on reports of "those who saw Jackson" there, reflects the attitude of the contemporary army toward the episode and their general. Jackson was "mastered by excitement" and "resembled the genius of battle incarnate," with his "eyes flashing, his face flushed, his voice rising and ringing." A Confederate on the field but not within visual range summarized the impact concisely from personal experience: "To follow him was natural."[21]

Confederate interpretations of the battle's flow naturally depicted Jackson's personal intervention as the pivotal event. Jed Hotchkiss declared that his chief's presence "restored his lines and snatched victory from threatened defeat." It was the estimate of G. F. R. Henderson that Jackson's action "restored the battle." Some Federals recoiled naturally enough from this adulation for a Southerner. The historian of the Fifth Connecticut, whose account of the battle is valuable and well balanced, was quick to downplay Jackson's personal intervention. The Northern survivors all complained of pressure from the north end of the wheatfield and remembered none from near the Gate. The rate of survival for Federals was higher near the road than farther north.[22]

The Connecticut skeptic was exactly right about the substantive

Southern threat to the men of his unit and their fellow Federals. A. P. Hill's fresh brigades striding toward the north end of the wheatfield could and would do far more hurt to Unionists than Jackson's frazzled but rallying remnants. There was more of symbol than substance to the general's heroic five minutes near the Gate. To assert that Civil War leadership included far more than cold science is to launch a statement of dreadfully gratuitous proportions. Modern analyses of the impacts of Baron Antoine Henri Jomini and Karl von Clausewitz notwithstanding, Civil War leaders operated on a volatile fuel blended of mystique and willpower. Military science as taught at West Point provided an essential tincture but it was not the only (or necessarily the primary) ingredient. Otherwise, brilliant George B. McClellan would have been guaranteed immortality and plodding Cadet Tom Jackson would have had no real chance for success.

The rally near the Gate became part of a tapestry of success that bred an attitude in Jackson's followers that made them strong. In a thoughtful essay on the Jackson mystique, a Confederate staff officer explained "His men are fond of telling how he exposed himself at Slaughter Mountain and elsewhere, saying to no one 'Go on!' but 'Come on!'" The fondness in telling bore a tale of its own. None of this should be taken as suggesting that Jackson was posturing to further the growth of the legend. He was genuinely moved by battle action. Generals Fitzhugh Lee and Richard Taylor, among others, commented on Stonewall Jackson's penchant for viewing battle danger as "delightful excitement."[23]

General William B. Taliaferro, writing of the Cedar Mountain episode, rejected the notion that Jackson disdained enemy fire because of religious-based fatalism—though Stonewall was unquestionably a predestinarian. Taliaferro suggested that Jackson's forays into danger were "simply impelled by a conviction, which often carried him too far, that his duty required him to go to the front and see for himself, and he was certainly as unconscious of fear as any man I ever met."[24]

Duty, fearlessness, and conscious leadership notwithstanding, it is hard to escape the conclusion that Jackson's dour exterior concealed a liberal dose of old-fashioned warrior spirit. That spirit could lay dormant at length—and had done so, for all but a few moments during the Mexican War, through Thomas J. Jackson's first thirty-seven years. The war unleashed Jackson's phenomenal military abilities in 1861 in many areas. The personal, wide-eyed, pulse-thumping aspect of Jackson's warrior spirit shone from his eyes in battle, as any number of witnesses attested. It appeared to Dick Taylor at Port Republic. And it prompted Jackson's highly emotional and equally irrational judgment that Cedar Mountain was "the most successful of his exploits."[25]

While Jackson played out his personal drama, the North Carolinians of Branch's brigade, whom the commanding general had encouraged, plunged into the woods and headed for the wheatfield. Jackson had encountered them near the north edge of the road and perpendicular to it somewhat west of the Gate. Under Stonewall's prodding, and no doubt some from A. P. Hill as well, Branch moved his regiments forward before they were fully formed, according to most accounts (though he himself reported that the formation "was scarcely completed"). His early start would cost him the use of one of his ill-prepared regiments, but time loomed more important than any other consideration just then. The brigade was as dusty and hot and depleted by stragglers as the rest of the army that afternoon. Despite the "rapid and exhausting" approach march, however, Branch brought a solid block of infantry to throw into the balance. His Thirty-seventh North Carolina formed on the right, not far from the road. To its left were the Twenty-eighth, Thirty-third, Eighteenth, and Seventh North Carolina regiments in that order.[26]

General Branch was as unsteady on his feet (or more literally on his horse's back) as were any of his men. The North Carolina politician was another of the remarkably large contingent of sick men in authority that day. "I was so feeble that I had been riding in my ambulance all day," he wrote in his journal, "and was scarcely able to walk fifty yards." Unlike several of the other convalescents (Winder, Cunningham, and Curtis), Branch would survive the fight. He later claimed that the excitement served as a tonic—the "lead cure," if you will. "The excitement braced me up," he insisted, "and ever since I have been in better health than at any time since we started on the expedition below Richmond."[27]

A. P. Hill's report suggested that he himself, rather than Jackson, ordered his weakened but improving brigadier forward, "immediately," without any formality about alignment and flanks. By the time Branch hurried forward, Hill's next brigade, that of James J. Archer, had arrived and been about "half formed" to Branch's left. Branch quickly left Archer's men behind and plunged into woods and "thick undergrowth."[28] The Tarheels loosed their version of the dreaded Rebel yell as they sensed contact just ahead through the woods. A Louisianan a mile to the right described "a victorious hurrah" that rose above the musketry when Confederate infantry started after the enemy, and one of the Tarheels wrote home that his comrades "raised the shout [with] which they are accustomed to go into battle."[29]

After an advance of about two hundred yards (Branch insisted that the distance was less than one hundred yards), the North Carolinians came face-to-face with the disorderly retreat by the Twenty-seventh Virginia Infantry of the Stonewall Brigade. The men of that regiment doubtless had been joined by a few—a very few—men from the right of the Thirty-third and by some lost souls from Garnett's debacle. General Branch unkindly and inaccurately described the affair in his journal, which achieved wide circulation and even publication in the *Official Records*: "We met the celebrated Stonewall Brigade, utterly routed and fleeing as fast as they could run." In the much more formal forum of his official report Branch described the same affair without the sarcasm, without a specific identity, but with the same wicked relish: "I commenced meeting the men of a brigade, which had preceded me, retreating in great disorder and closely pursued by the enemy."[30]

Some of the men advancing with Branch chronicled the event in the same tones their general used, though they generally did not report the enemy in close pursuit of the Virginians. In his own journal, writing with both more vim and less calculation, even Branch did not suggest that Federals were squarely on the heels of the fugitives. One member of the Eighteenth North Carolina softened his narration of the scene somewhat by referring to the Stonewall Brigade as "that splendid body of troops" before reporting that it was "fleeing in utter rout and confusion before an exultant foe." A man in the Thirty-third North Carolina described the Virginians' condition more mildly as "retreating in some confusion."[31]

Branch's pointed criticisms and the even more barbed remarks in his journal generated the most vigorous Confederate controversy connected with Cedar Mountain. Although A. P. Hill himself hailed from Culpeper and was anything but anti-Virginian, he was not dismayed by the prospect of deriding Jackson's pet brigade. In his official report, Hill widened the schism between himself and Stonewall by reporting that the Stonewall Brigade "broke" and Branch passed "through the broken brigade" to save the day.[32] In fact, no more than one-fifth of the brigade broke. The rest fought admirably, capturing all of the Federal flags taken on the field. (A detailed analysis of the Branch–Stonewall Brigade controversy would fracture the already complicated flow of the tactical narrative at this point, so it is left for Appendix 5.)

The panicked Twenty-seventh Virginia infantrymen must have made some havoc pouring through Branch's line as it advanced through the thick forest, but Branch would not countenance anything but unsullied advance in writing his report. His regiments opened their ranks "to permit the fugitives to pass" and then, "not in the least shaken by the panic-cries of the fugitives, and without halting," Branch dealt summarily with the Federals. The historian of the Thirty-third North Carolina either reflected Branch's spirit or else literally copied his language when he wrote of how his regiment "coolly opened ranks to allow the fugitives to pass . . . in no wise disturbed by the terror-stricken cries of the runaways."[33]

Captain Walter W. Lenoir of Company A, Thirty-seventh North Carolina, offered an interesting and important counterpoint to Branch's bravado in a letter written during the war. Lenoir had been worried about how he would behave under fire and found ample occasion at Cedar Mountain to be proud of how he and his unit performed, which was well indeed. He did not, however, write in Branch's vein. The Carolinians were "pressing forward with energy and *tolerable* [my emphasis for a realistic word] order" when they came upon what the captain described as "a *portion* [my emphasis again] of Talliaferro's (Stonewall) brigade . . . falling back in great disorder." The fugitives "broke through our ranks as best they could, producing of course in places considerable disorder," Lenoir confessed, "and making with their confusion and the commands and entreaties of their officers who were striving to rally them, a clamor like a bedlam or babel." Captain Lenoir's balanced wording and sense of chaos stand out as the best account written by any of the participants in Branch's advance.[34] He also may have provided a clue to some of the bases for the dispute when he innocently identified Taliaferro's undeniably routed brigade as being the famed Stonewall Brigade.

Some few Federals lurked in the woods between Branch and the wheatfield, but they cannot have been in large numbers or even remotely organized. Most of their comrades had moved through the woods into the open near the Gate to spread havoc upon Taliaferro and Early. Hundreds more had become casualties. The Federals pursuing the Twenty-seventh Virginia were of hardy mettle but minor strength and were moving away from their friends at a wide tangent. Branch brushed them aside "quickly" and forged ahead. Later, some

Virginians criticized Branch's men a bit. One artillerist, for instance, complained that the Eighteenth North Carolina was "praised in the papers" but had "even left its arms on the field." Such a remark was merely overreaction to Branch's canard about the Stonewall Brigade. James H. Lane of the North Carolina brigade (despite being a Virginian) probably did not exaggerate overmuch when he described the advance through the woods as proceeding "cheerfully and irresistibly."[35]

The axis of Branch's movement slipped away from due east into a southeastward veer that eventually carried part of the brigade out of the woods onto and even across the road somewhat short of the wheatfield. When Archer, who advanced not too long after Branch, caught up with the North Carolinians, he saw at least some of them "in the open field on the right of the road" short of the wheatfield's western edge. Captain Lenoir, whose evenhanded account serves as a useful counterpoint to Branch's chest thumping, made clear that the same Virginians who burst through them in retreat quickly rallied to join their rescuers. "A large number" of the Virginians, Lenoir reported, formed up among the Thirty-seventh North Carolina men, "filling up the gaps which their irruption had made." These reinforcements swarmed particularly thick near the road, which served as the right guide for the Thirty-seventh.[36] Perhaps, to be charitable, Lenoir's more moderate descriptions were the result of a different geographic vantage point. Did General Branch ride on the far left of his brigade and see an anomalous zone? Or was he just ungracious and narrow-minded?

Walter Lenoir's passage through that patch of Culpeper County woods happened to be his initiation into mortal combat. He had transferred into the regiment from the unbloodied Fifty-eighth North Carolina. Like so many young men in that war, Lenoir *wanted* to fight a battle. He wanted to test his valor. He wanted to help win independence for his country. The captain had thought so much about how he would behave and what he would feel that his detailed description of the result is a curious blend of clinical detachment mixed with naïveté. In analyzing his experience, Lenoir insisted that he felt less nervous than he normally did when beginning a speech to a jury (he was a lawyer). His "very serious and uncomfortable thoughts of death" did not prevent Lenoir from noticing that the danger gave him "a disposition to chat about the battle to officers standing or passing near," as well as "an occasional sense of ludicrous, etc." This neophyte warrior concluded that, withal, "the absence of cowardly fear, and the coolness amounting in appearance almost to indifference . . . among the showering balls and dreadful sounds and sights of the battlefield, are on the whole one of the most marvelous things in human nature."[37] Three weeks after Cedar Mountain, Captain Lenoir's brief career as a combat soldier ended when he lost a leg at Second Manassas.

Branch's farthest left regiment, at the north end of his line, was the Seventh North Carolina. The Seventh had fought hard around Richmond and taken a heavy battering in the process. The state of the regimental color guard may have indicated some shortage of starch in the Seventh's composition at this stage of the war. The Richmond fights had all but destroyed that brave but vulnerable detachment, and regimental headquarters detailed a new one. Most of the men so honored, "remembering the melancholy but glorious fate" of their predecessors, "showed a great indisposition to take so dangerous a post of honor." Sergeant Joshua Washington Vick of Company E stepped forward as a volunteer, cajoled some mates into joining him, and the detailed slackers returned to the ranks.[38]

Sergeant Vick distinguished himself subsequently and won promotion to the rank of lieutenant and then captain—but at Cedar Mountain the Seventh North Carolina was not much of a factor. That result may have been traceable to confusion, to a difficult location on the dangling left flank, and to the misfortune of being last into line and still disorganized when Branch hurried forward. Whatever the cause, the Seventh wound up staggering aimlessly in the wake of the brigade. The brigade's second in command, Colonel James H. Lane, simply reported that he "did not see the Seventh Regiment after we were ordered forward." Colonel Edward Graham Haywood of the Seventh suffered a serious wound at Second Manassas so the regiment's report was prepared by Captain John McLeod Turner. The captain hinted at discontent with Haywood when he wrote somewhat obliquely that after Branch advanced, the Seventh, "for causes unknown to the writer, did not move for several minutes" and began to lose sight of the main body.[39]

When the Seventh North Carolina finally started to move, it covered no more than one hundred yards before Colonel Haywood ordered a halt to dress the lines. At that point the rest of the brigade disappeared from view. Haywood eventually started his men forward for the second time, stopped them for the second time, and dressed his line for the third time. A third start followed by a wheel to the right carried the Seventh to the main road at a point probably a bit closer to the Gate than to the wheatfield. Haywood left the regiment there marking time, figuratively, while he went in search of Branch. Captain Robert B. MacRae, the ranking captain, was about to order the Seventh toward the heavy firing in front when the colonel returned with what he represented as orders from Stonewall Jackson himself. Two completely separate accounts report that Jackson's orders directed their subsequent wanderings: one says that they sent the Seventh south of the road after retreating Yankees; the other that the orders sent the Seventh north of the road and into the wheatfield at right angles to Branch's main body. The evidence favors the former option, but in either event the afternoon exposed the Seventh to more rambling than battling. It reported net casualties of two men, whereas the average for Branch's other regiments was about twenty-five.[40]

While the Seventh North Carolina stumbled about aimlessly, the Eighteenth, Thirty-third, Twenty-eighth, and Thirty-seventh (left to right) moved steadily and effectively through the woods to the west edge of the wheatfield. In the process they drove out such Federals— doubtless mostly from the Forty-sixth Pennsylvania—as infested the woods. Jim Lane reported matter-of-factly that "the enemy's infantry were soon driven from the woods into the field beyond," but Branch thought his advance was a heroic one against stout organized resistance. Repeated volleys finally "broke" these Federals, who "fled precipitately through the woods and across the field." The North Carolinians halted at the edge of the woods and opened fire. Some of them faced south or southeast across the road, but most of them faced east across the wheatfield from its southwestern corner.[41]

The Thirty-seventh North Carolina on the brigade's far right (excepting fragments of the disoriented Seventh) fought from the fence at the edge of the woods along the main road and in the road itself. Captain Walter Lenoir's company of the Thirty-seventh had been augmented by "so large a squad of Virginians" that he was obliged to move well to the left to look after some of his own men separated from their mates by the Virginian ralliers. When Lenoir came back to the right he was disappointed to find that the Virginians had disappeared—apparently having run away. He soon found them again, however, in a better position in the road cut, "fighting bravely and effectively all the while." Some of Lenoir's own men had become exhausted by this time, and the captain went so far as to help some of them load their muskets.[42]

Other rallying Virginians fought at the edge of the woods from the ranks of the Twenty-eighth North Carolina, which adjoined the Thirty-seventh on its left. Lieutenants Thomas R. Dunn and B. E. Coltrane of the First Virginia Battalion turned up and volunteered their services to Colonel Lane. The colonel assigned them to command of companies which had been led to that point by sergeants and reported that "both discharged the duties assigned them only as brave men can do." The Federals against whom Branch was fighting included elements of Crawford's brigade, by now weakened and fleeing, and the Tenth Maine of that brigade, which had reached the middle of the wheatfield only after the other regiments had gone through the Confederate woods. Stonewall Jackson reported that after Branch reached the east end of the woods "the fight was still maintained with obstinancy between the enemy and the two brigades" of Branch and Ronald. Branch's men were engaged in that obstinate exchange when Archer's brigade arrived to their left.[43]

Branch's journal and report exaggerated his role and its circumstances in several ways. Stripped of hyperbole, the performance of his brigade was solid and workmanlike, but his sole unaided achievement was clearing the woods to the edge of the wheatfield. When Branch reached that point, the Stonewall Brigade crossed its fire with his from a position well to the left and at right angles to his own. Branch subsequently achieved no more than did the Stonewall Brigade and less than Archer or Pender.

Most of the Federal regiments under the guns of Branch and Ronald were pretty well beaten by this time. Every field officer in Crawford's three main regiments (Fifth Connecticut, Twenty-eighth New York, Forty-sixth Pennsylvania) was killed, wounded, or captured at Cedar Mountain. So too was every line officer (lieutenants and captains at the company level) in the Twenty-eighth New York and all but two in the Fifth Connecticut and all but five in the Forty-sixth Pennsylvania. The three regiments came off the field virtually destroyed in a military sense. Rufus Mead of the Fifth Connecticut wrote to the "Dear Folks at Home" on August 13 to report on the condition of his regiment—"what there is left." Mead predicted another battle soon but presumed it would not feature Crawford's brigade, "as others must take their share now."[44]

Before Crawford's three gallant regiments fell back, they had accomplished an astounding coup. The men dejectedly moving back toward and through the wheatfield knew they had done a great deed but doubtless sensed that it not only had been in vain but also that it would be diminished in retrospect by being only a prelude to defeat.

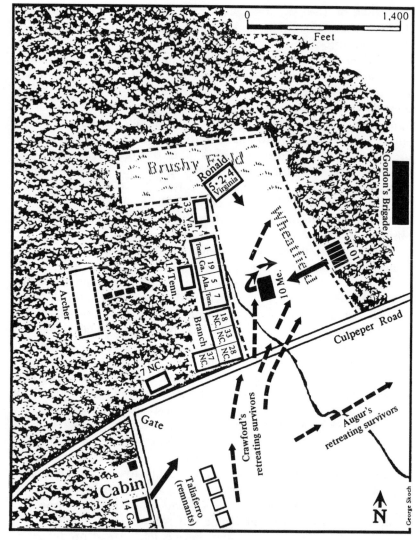

Crawford's Withdrawal, 6:30–6:45

Needless to say, not all of Crawford's men had been resolute participants in the heroic charge. As soon as the roar of small arms erupted, Pope had ordered McDowell to advance rapidly and rode ahead to see what was happening. At once they met "large numbers of disorganized troops . . . emerging from the woods in disorder."

218

One of those disorganized soldiers came to be a legend in the Thirteenth Massachusetts of George L. Hartsuff's brigade. This "great strapping fellow" passed the Bay Staters at "a two-forty pace to the rear" and shouted, "Give 'em hell, boys, we got 'em started." For a long while, that shouted phrase was a byword in the Thirteenth Massachusetts whenever stragglers appeared.[45]

Pope's first action as he neared the field posed a delicious contrast to his famous bombastic order chastising his army for thinking of lines of retreat and other such effete trappings of military science. This hot afternoon, with the din of musketry battering his ears, Pope's initial measure was, in the words of a staff officer, "selecting a position to take in case Banks should be forced back."[46]

More of Crawford's men actually did retreat stubbornly and "gave 'em hell" than raced rearward to shout about it. Their position was anything but enviable. Confederates rallying on both sides of the road and swarms of new Southern regiments from Hill's reinforcing column brought the Fifth Connecticut "under a cross-fire from various directions." The regiment's retreat gained momentum, moving steadily more rapidly and with less organization and control. Colonel George D. Chapman was wounded and captured but escaped in the confusion and organized a weak line near the spring in the southwest corner of the wheatfield. There he fell into Confederate hands again (doubtless captured by either the Thirty-seventh or Twenty-eighth North Carolina). Twenty or so of his Connecticut boys rallied and came shouting back to release their colonel. There were too many Confederates in the wood line for this effort to succeed. Almost all of the colonel's prospective saviors fell.[47]

Late in the action one of Geary's Ohioans helped save the state flag of the Fifth Connecticut. Sergeant Levi F. Bauder of the Seventh Ohio spotted two blue-clad sergeants, both wounded, "gamely but feebly" making their way toward the Federal lines. One of them carried a flag and used its staff as a crutch. Bauder ran out to them and took the flag. "They thankfully handed it to me," he recalled, "and they did not seem to worry over their own predicament." Sergeant Bauder ran back to his lines through a shower of bullets without being hit and handed the flag to General Crawford.[48]

The last of the Fifth Connecticut men to reach the wheatfield probably were those in a sizable detachment that came into the wheatfield near the spring and were astonished to find a Confederate line in the field in front (east) of them. These Southerners probably were some of Branch's men from his leftward regiments. The

Confederates turned around and fired a volley backward at the Connecticut soldiers, who promptly dodged back into the woods and scuttled northward along the edge of the field. Virginians of the Stonewall Brigade finally made prisoners of these adventurous fellows in the brushy field.[49]

The Twenty-eighth New York went into the charge just to the north of the Fifth Connecticut, but of course the retreat did not develop as a nicely modulated mirror image of the advance. The New Yorkers streamed back across the southern portion of the field intermingled with the survivors of the Fifth Connecticut. So did such men of the Forty-sixth Pennsylvania as had followed the brigade across the road through Taliaferro and into Early. Orders to fall back reached Lieutenant William P. Warren of the Twenty-eighth New York as his company was firing through dense smoke. Warren claimed that his men kept up their firing during the withdrawal, which was, not surprisingly, "the hardest of the fight." Rebels popped up everywhere, and they all seemed to be screaming. Someone pulled the regiment's flag off its staff. Lieutenant Warren was hit by five bullets, one of which passed between his carotid artery and his windpipe. He fell bleeding into a convenient shock of wheat.[50]

The retreating troops sought succor in the woods at the eastern edge of the wheatfield which they had left to launch the attack. Short of that point, midway across the wheatfield, they came upon their comrades of the Tenth Maine. That regiment belonged to Crawford's brigade but had been held back from the attack to support a battery that needed no such support. During this pointless interlude, General Banks sat nearby on horseback and Confederate artillery used the mounted men and the oversupported artillery as targets. The Maine infantrymen paid the price. Artillery fire struck among them with such vengeance that the regiment twice displaced rightward to avoid it. "Men turned pale" under the shelling, which despite the attempts to evade it "came down faster and struck nearer."[51]

When the belated orders to advance reached the Tenth Maine, it was far too late to participate with the other three regiments in Crawford's advance. Even so, the men doubtless were pleased to move out of the artillery's impact zone. T. C. H. Smith of General Pope's staff bluntly pronounced Colonel George Lafayette Beal of the Tenth as miscreant for not advancing promptly when ordered. The problem arose in large part because of an irregular chain of command. Major Louis Henry Pelouze of Banks's staff took the order to the Maine regiment. According to Smith, the troops cried

*The southeastern edge of the wheatfield in 1910, taken from
the spot where the colors of the Tenth Maine emerged from
the Union wood line. (Gould Papers, Duke University)*

loudly from the ranks "We will go forward if anybody will lead us!"
By Smith's account, Pelouze responded, "I will lead you! Forward."
General Crawford's report displayed unmistakable displeasure with a
staff officer usurping line functions. The Maine men felt that Pelouze's primary impact was to halt the regiment a little later in a bad
place in the wheatfield.[52]

John Mead Gould (1839–1930) ranked as the most important man
in the Tenth Maine at Cedar Mountain from the perspective of a
modern historian. Gould wrote the unit's history soon after the war
and worked hard for the rest of his long life at establishing historical
verities. Because he was particularly interested in Cedar Mountain,
Gould's papers are the most important Federal manuscripts about
the battle. John Gould's personal experience at Cedar Mountain began in earnest when he arrived ahead of the regiment at the edge of
the woods on the eastern boundary of the wheatfield. As the rest of
the Tenth Maine came up behind him, they could hear Crawford's

three regiments fighting in the Confederate woods across the field but could not see anything of them. Gould noticed some of Geary's Ohioans advancing just across the road. Before long he saw them come back, their rear guard fighting hand-to-hand, using bayonets in some instances.[53]

The path of the Maine soldiers into the field took them down a gentle slope, then up the midfield rise and over its top. As the regiment moved down from the rise toward the stream just below the Confederate woods, it received ample evidence of just how much too late its advance was. "The remnant of our brigade was coming back," John Gould wrote. Some of the retreating men deflected to their own left (north) to avoid the fire they presumed the Tenth Maine soon would unleash. The rearward motion by the only friendly troops anywhere near them "disturbed us much to see," Gould reported. Colonel Beal called on his men to cheer their comrades. "Give them three down-east cheers!" he bellowed, and the wheatfield rang with the nasal noise of New England yells. Officers among the routed men repaid Beal for the tribute by hollering across to him the disturbing intelligence that the woods contained too many Southerners to handle. The Maine men began to see that for themselves, especially when they looked at the woods closest to the road. Branch's brigade was up.[54]

Colonel Beal responded to the good advice from his more experienced colleagues and ordered the Tenth Maine to "about face" and head for the friendly woods behind them. Major Pelouze intercepted the regiment as it reached the crest of the midfield ridge and ordered it to halt. Beal ignored him. John Gould wrote that Pelouze "grew furious and appeared to be having a fist-fight with our Colonel, so animated were the gesticulations." That description probably constitutes a gentle Victorian circumlocution to indicate that Beal and Pelouze actually did engage in some intramural violence on the spot. Pelouze also "said much that the Colonel thought was unnecessary." The denouement of this struggle was that Beal put his regiment into line in the middle of the field near the crest of the ridge and opened fire against the woods to the west. He did so under peremptory orders and obviously unwillingly.[55]

The Maine regiment fired at an active and visible foe along the fence at the edge of the field. The New Englanders' mates in Crawford's brigade had driven Garnett's brigade from that fence not long before, but the tide had now turned and the lone regiment in the middle of the field faced a painful few minutes. The line the Tenth

Maine hurriedly laid out did not extend near the road on its left because the knoll dropped off in that direction. The men on the left crowded rightward to enjoy the protection of the high ground; that movement nudged the right well up into the northern reaches of the wheatfield. One soldier in the line remembered clearly the faces of his enemies, which he could "plainly see . . . as they peer[ed] through the fence between the rails." Although the fence afforded only intermittent protection to Confederates crouching behind it, it was a fortress by comparison to the shocks of wheat the Maine soldiers hunkered behind. The same Maine soldier noted that seven of the eight men "sheltered" behind the shock nearest to him were hit.[56]

Losses in the regiment mounted fast. Some men had to wait for the last of their friends of Crawford's brigade to clear their front before they could fire. When the field of fire lay open, the Tenth Maine loosed what its veterans always remembered as its mightiest volley of the war. The resultant smoke billowed everywhere; lengthening shadows were creeping out from the wood line; at the same time the setting sun blinded men facing west, as were the Tenth Maine soldiers. For them the scene degenerated into a bewildering tapestry of darting men and waving flags seen darkly and briefly. Confederate fire whistled among the New Englanders with alarming volume and accuracy. The unprotected men in the field melted away under it. John Gould thought that the scene, though horrible, "was ludicrous in the extreme. All were excited and were loading and firing in every conceivable way." Federals were standing, kneeling, lying down, or even "astraddle their pieces and . . . ramming the charge totally regardless of the rules on that point." Each man was swearing mighty oaths, generally unheard over the roar, until "it seemed as if bedlam was loose."[57]

H. A. Tripp of the Tenth Maine fired twenty-three rounds into the Confederate wood line from a position at the left of the regiment. He figured his range at about 150 yards, two-thirds of that downhill to the run and the rest across the "short, quite steep rise to the fence at the edge of the woods." Tripp's position obviously lay not far north of the springhouse, though well to its east. The 150-yard gauntlet Tripp described was by this time being traversed by far more eastbound than westbound rounds. John Gould described the ghoulish effects of the Confederate fire in detail. Bullets knocking men over caused "a sudden jump or shudder." So many men were being hit that "it looked as if we had a crowd of howling dervishes dancing and kicking around in our ranks." Almost every man in the regi-

*Five officers of the Tenth Maine, photographed on August 12 or 13
on the spot where the regiment made its costly stand. From the
left: Lt. Ephraim M. Littlefield, Lt. Benjamin Franklin Whitney,
Lt. Col. James Sullivan Fillebrown, Capt. William Knowlton,
and Sgt. Charles E. Jordan. (Library of Congress)*

ment "was either killed, wounded, hit in his clothes, hit by spent balls
and stones, or jostled by his wounded comrades." Some of them
"reeled round and round, others threw up their arms and fell over
backward, others went plunging backward trying to regain their balance.... Many dropped their musket and seized the wounded part
with both hands."[58]

Gould's merciless recital of horrors included attention to the sounds
of Confederate rounds of varying sorts. He concluded that the Southerners employed a diverse arsenal, judging by the unforgettable
medley of "various tunes sung by their balls"; those tunes, Gould
wrote soon after the war, he and his mates would "never confound
... with any others we have heard." An unwelcome addition to the
deadly symphony soon opened to the right front of the Tenth Maine.
Fresh Confederate troops farther north along the wood line opened
a hot fire, which came in from a 45° angle. The fierce "zip" of minié
balls from in front continued unabated, but this new sound "was
produced by the singing of slow, round balls and buck shot fired
from a smooth bore, which do not cut or tear the air as the creased
ball does." These slow but deadly messengers from a new direction
"seemed to be going past in sheets, all around and above us."[59]

*According to notations on this 1912 photograph, taken by a veteran
of the Tenth Maine, it depicts the same spot on which the five
officers of the regiment posed in August 1862. By the veteran's
calculation, the fence at the edge of the Confederate woods lay
390 feet away from the camera. (Gould Papers, Duke University)*

The new threat to John Gould and the Tenth Maine came from
the newly arrived brigade of James J. Archer, whose three Tennessee
regiments, a Georgia regiment, and an Alabama battalion pulled up
at the edge of the woods on Branch's left. Archer had been half
formed to Branch's left behind the Gate when Jackson hurled the
North Carolina brigade forward in the emergency. General Archer
counted twelve hundred men in his brigade when it marched in the
relative coolness of that early morning. He did not attempt to estimate how many overcame the intense heat and stifling dust successfully enough to be on hand when the brigade formed up west of the
Gate and north of the road. A member of the Fifth Alabama Battalion calculated that "three-fourths of our men fell exhausted on the
road." Even so, the brigade brought considerable weight into action.
Archer's men had the sobering experience of seeing the mangled

form of mortally wounded General Charles S. Winder borne past them as they neared the battlefield.[60]

The First Tennessee led Archer's column on the road. Its men noticed that Branch's troops had stripped off and piled up their knapsacks in preparing for action, so they followed suit. While his men were getting ready, Colonel Peter Turney of the First Tennessee (who would be governor of the state thirty years later) did his part by catching each of two men who fainted from the heat, easing them down and calling for a surgeon. When the colonel looked at his regiment, Private Henry T. Childs professed to hear him ask: "Where are my big men?" Childs is not a solid witness because he had a penchant for making fun of the endurance of strapping fellows, apparently being of slight stature himself. By his own account, Childs and the other small but hardy chaps responded: "Colonel, here are your boys. Your big men have broken down." Apparently the regiment did not have many small men because Childs estimated that only about a dozen men were on hand in each company.[61]

Henry Childs went beyond recounting the tardiness of large-sized Tennesseeans. The little fellow recounted in loving detail the fate of the big men when they finally reached the knapsacks piled by their wirier comrades. How he could have known the details without himself shirking the advance of the small people is hard to say, but here is his story. When the straggling and broken-down "big men" halted at the knapsacks, they began picking lice from one another's clothing. "While thus busily engaged, with their shirts pulled over their heads, a body of fifty or a hundred Yankee prisoners hove in sight. Somebody called out, 'Yankees!' Looking up to see this, everyone stampeded." Some of the louse-hunters left their hats or shoes or shirts or even pants behind. "When they ran against a bush or sapling, they would swing clear over it, the stampede increasing in volume and intensity." This ludicrous rout continued until its victims had covered two to three miles at a dead run, or so Childs insisted.[62] If such an event actually transpired, it was one of several pointless stampedes by Confederates during the campaign, which were unrelated to enemy action. The prevalence of these self-starting panics probably is indicative of nervous systems depleted by exhaustion and intense suffering from the heat.

As Archer's regiments formed to the left of the road, Branch was doing likewise just to their right. Since Branch's right was at the road, Archer's right obviously began well north of the road. When Branch hurried away eastward toward the wheatfield, Archer remained only "half formed." Archer issued orders to load weapons and prepare for immediate action. The brigade commander presumed, logically enough, that he "would be wanted in front immediately" so he emulated Branch by moving forward before his regiments had fully formed. In the process he left behind the last of his units to arrive, the Fourteenth Tennessee; in that, his experience also mirrored Branch's.[63]

The First Tennessee formed on Archer's unprotected left flank. To its right came the Nineteenth Georgia, then the Fifth Alabama Battalion, then the Seventh Tennessee. Archer left the Fourteenth Tennessee behind, "to come up onto line and overtake the brigade as it best could." As the four units from three states pushed through the thick undergrowth in the woods they raised "a shout," according to an observer—no doubt the rebel yell once again. Archer's men ran across a few Confederates still leaking toward the rear, even after Branch's advance. One of the Alabamians reported the size of this group as "a regiment" and said that they appeared when the advance neared the wheatfield.[64]

Archer's advance covered "several hundred yards," the general thought, always "obliquing toward the right in order to get near the left of Branch's brigade." Branch's rightward deflection obliged Archer to conform to avoid leaving an ever-widening gap in what was now the Confederate front line. When Archer caught up with Branch's left, he found that it consisted of a lone regiment that had become detached from the main body of the brigade. This must have been the Eighteenth North Carolina, since the putative left regiment—the Seventh North Carolina—was by now well on the road to finishing its wanderings on the far right of Branch. General Archer was glad to catch up with Branch's left, lost and bewildered though it might be, but the North Carolina regiment proved to be something of an obstacle. In passing around and through it in the dense woods, Archer's line became "somewhat broken" so the brigadier halted for a few minutes to reform it.[65]

The delay allowed the Fourteenth Tennessee to catch up. While that regiment fitted itself into the reforming line, Archer made a quick trip south through the woods to the road. Heavy gunfire from that direction made the general anxious to learn what threat or support existed there near his right flank. To his relief, Archer found that the muskets making the noise were Southern weapons in the hands of Branch's men. The North Carolinians he saw were due south of him but in and beyond the road, halted and firing at enemy to the front. Archer assumed that all of Branch's brigade was there, but in fact it only was the Thirty-seventh and Seventh North Carolina regiments. As he arrived hurriedly back with his own brigade, Archer met Murray Forbes Taylor of Fredericksburg, a member of A. P. Hill's staff. Taylor brought aggressive orders from Hill—advance! Archer did so at once and moved rapidly to the western edge of the wheatfield.[66]

Jackson and Hill spent the rest of their common lifetimes feuding over one thing and another, not infrequently including Cedar Mountain. Their difficulty over the march from Orange is common knowledge. Jedediah Hotchkiss of Jackson's staff (and one of his chief's most ardent shield-bearers) later claimed that Stonewall was dissatisfied with Hill's behavior on the battlefield of Cedar Mountain as well. If so, that aspect of the affair never reached the same level of written or oral discussion. Hotchkiss wrote after the war that Hill's "movements in obedience to orders preceding and *during* [emphasis added] the Battle of Cedar Run were not satisfactory to General Jackson as he had failed to promptly comply with orders." Hotchkiss pulled his punch a bit by adding the caveat that Hill's failings "were attributed to the intense heat that prevailed which prevented the rapid movement of troops."[67] In fact, Hill's battlefield promptness was entirely beyond reproach. Branch's early and rapid advance was followed promptly by Archer's. When Archer halted briefly and necessarily to find Branch's left, Hill put renewed aggressive orders in his hands at once. Hotchkiss simply had difficulty reining in his tar brush once it was warmed up. Whether its use was warranted in limning Hill's prebattle marching performance is a question of more legitimacy.

Archer's men covered three or four hundred yards of woods, they calculated, before they came to a halt behind the bullet-scarred fence at the western edge of the wheatfield. They quickly began to feel fire, and returned it. "Every boy leveled his gun, and the roar of battle began," a Tennessean wrote. The "rapid fire" they threw into and across the wheatfield came in upon the right front of the Tenth Maine and prompted John Gould's reflections on the variety of songs sung by Southern bullets. Archer's infantrymen could hear Branch engaging vigorously to their right and right rear, but they had more than enough to do on their own front. Federals sheltered behind wheat shocks or clinging to the midfield ridge began to break for the rear. Some arose from hugging the ground and dashed for the illusory shelter of some stacked wheat. Had the Northerners left en

*Corporal George S. Ayer of the Tenth Maine color guard, posed in
1910 next to his regiment's marker in the middle of the wheatfield.
The camera faces south. (Gould Papers, Duke University)*

masse most would have escaped, but they gave away piecemeal in
little knots of a few men each. The result was disastrous for them.
Three of Archer's men—one each from Alabama, Georgia, and Tennessee—agreed on their success with unanimity unusual for battlefield accounts: The Yankees "were always shot before reaching the
other side"; the Confederates "brought down every one who attempted to make the escape"; and, "not a Yankee got out of that wheat
field."[68] None of those Southern boys was anywhere nearly accurate
in a literal sense because the casualties of the Tenth Maine totaled
about 40 percent (a relatively enormous figure), but their accounts
accurately convey a sense of the slaughter.

The view from the other end of this firing range was bleak. The
ordeal of the Tenth Maine began when Branch reached the field and
then was punctuated and brought to climax by Archer's arrival. The

duration of the Maine regiment's engagement was something its honest veterans knotted their brows over ever after. Many thought that their fight lasted thirty minutes or more, but others—including the careful J. M. Gould—thought that about five minutes was the best estimate. "We could not have been there long," Gould concluded. By one account, the trigger for the retreat of the regiment was news brought to Colonel Beal by a stray Forty-sixth Pennsylvania soldier that there were "rebs in the chincapin bushes," which is to say that the Confederate line was becoming apparent in the brushy field well to the right.[69] That fact cannot have been startling intelligence to the colonel, nor did he need any more reason to retreat than the concentrated fire on his lone regiment of something like ten Southern regiments.

Colonel Beal's lonely Maine men actually had some help closing in just as they were breaking up. George H. Gordon's small brigade was just arriving at the eastern edge of the wheatfield, somewhat north of the rear of the center of the Tenth Maine. Gordon arrived too late to do much good, and in any event the Maine boys did not notice any dampening of enemy fire. In fact, the right of their regiment suffered more than the unsupported left because the ridge on the left was "a trifle sharper" and afforded more protection. When Beal shouted the order to fall back, the carnage in the Tenth Maine had become "terrible and altogether beyond description," Gould wrote. "There were huge gaps in our lines." The regiment lost all order in the process of getting out, and only a few men held up at the wood line. The slight relative protection to their left lured the retreating men nearer to the road in their flight; so did the heavy fire pouring from Archer's line on their right. H. A. Tripp of the Tenth Maine reported that his reentry into the Federal woods was "some distance nearer the Orange road" than the left of the entire regiment had been when it advanced from those same woods.[70]

The angle of the retreat to the southeast, rather than due east, took some of the Maine men into the woods at a point at which they entirely missed seeing Gordon's newly arriving troops. Others saw Gordon, who surely arrived in place just before the Tenth Maine fell back. The condition of the Tenth Maine was deftly summarized in connection with one of the myriad post-battle controversies. Some men of Gordon's brigade insisted that they were obliged to "close up & make room for the Tenth Maine." The Maine veterans countered with convincing self-deprecation, noting that they "went out disorganized: each man could have picked his way out without disturbing a line coming in."[71]

Inevitably, some of the Tenth Maine soldiers did not get the word to retreat immediately amid the confusion. One such stranded soul noticed some Confederate skirmishers climbing the fence and heading his way. The Southerners had seen the retreat and moved to take advantage of it. The lonely Maine man shot a "tall, lank, red-whiskered" Confederate at fairly short range and raced for the woods. In his desperate flight he noticed a few of his comrades hiding in wheat shocks, probably wounded and immobilized. When the tardy Yankee reached the woods, he hustled behind the first tree at their edge and looked back. No one was pursuing him. What caught his eye instead was a column of Federal cavalry charging headlong down the road into the teeth of the Confederate position.[72]

Every other eye on both sides soon riveted on the same spectacle, as fewer than two hundred Pennsylvania horsemen rode out on a foray as useless and relatively as costly as the celebrated Charge of the Light Brigade at Balaclava.

CHAPTER 10

The Cavalry Charge

THE CHARGE BY one-half of the First Pennsylvania Cavalry at Cedar Mountain was the stuff from which legends are made. It was pointless, or nearly so, but it was dramatic; everyone could see and hear the drama; and a large number of the daring participants fell killed or wounded.

The 164 mounted men thundered onto the scene at the southern end of the wheatfield just as the Tenth Maine was collapsing under the combined fire of Branch's and Archer's brigades, augmented by continuing pressure from the faithful Stonewall Brigade at the northern end of the field. The arrival of the charge as the Tenth Maine departed was coincidental. Its origins lay not in that current tactical development but rather in the delayed fruition of Banks's reaction to the ragged withdrawal of the survivors of Crawford's main attack. The guns near the intersection of the main road with the road to Mitchell's Station, particularly Joseph M. Knap's battery, seemed to Banks to be imperiled. The focus on artillery operations, which had driven the decisions and hypnotized the attentions of both sides, continued unabated.

An otherwise hostile observer from Pope's staff cited the danger to the guns in his account and applauded Banks in the imagined crisis by writing that his "coolness never deserted him." Colonel John S. Clark of Banks's staff spied the small four-company battalion from the First Pennsylvania Cavalry under Major Richard I. Falls nearby and suggested that his chief hurl it at the Confederates as a sacrificial offering. Banks did so without incurring serious criticism at the command level, then or later. A member of the unfortunate regiment accepted the orders as necessary "to save Knap's Battery" in a postwar unit history and again in a 1902 speech delivered on the battlefield.[1]

The timing of the charge can be established precisely by a number of sources, both Federal and Confederate, as occurring at the time the Tenth Maine fell back and before more than a few Southern skirmishers had advanced into the wheatfield. Gordon's three Federal regiments were just coming into heavy action at the eastern edge of the wheatfield north of the point where most of the Maine men were making a hasty exit into the woods. Stonewall Jackson's very general report erroneously identified the cavalry charge as a desperate attempt to blunt Archer and others in their final advance; so did some other accounts. But one of Archer's Alabamians, writing at the time, told of picking off the Maine runners and then "just at that time" here came the cavalry—with Archer's own advance opening *after* the cavalry had been routed. The careful George L. Andrews, colonel of the Second Massachusetts of Gordon's brigade, also described the chronology precisely so, as did the best of the Tennessee accounts.[2]

Charles Chase of Company G, Tenth Maine, supplied more vivid witness of the timing than he would have preferred. His hurried departure from the deadly midfield ridge coincided so precisely with the cavalry advance that he and it became tangled up. Chase was "run over, trampled on and badly bruised by the cavalry."[3]

Confederates at or near the western edge of the wheatfield got their first hint of this new development when they heard "a noise as of distant thunder." The rumble raised by the hooves of Major Falls's 164 horses rolled over the musketry to herald the attack. The major's daring column included four companies (A through D) of the regiment. Beneath Falls, Captain William Litzenberger of Company B commanded the Second Squadron. One of the Southerners watching them approach reported that the Pennsylvanians had their sabers drawn and that the earth was "fairly trembling beneath the tread of their magnificent horses." The galloping horsemen stayed out of the road itself, instead moving westward in column of squadrons parallel to the road in the southern edge of the wheatfield.[4]

A Federal officer looking on with bated breath thought that the pulse of the fight stopped to adjust to the sight of this unusual "apparition . . . coming over the ridge." Southern artillery fell silent for a moment, and Southern infantry lapsed into "a pause of expectancy." The pause was of very short duration. The great Northern war artist Edwin Forbes happened to be present and witnessed the charge. His account described how Confederate shells "raked" the cavalry "badly." The "numberless fences" in the area, most notably the one across the southern mouth of the wheatfield, fragmented the attackers and channeled them into deadly fire lanes.[5]

The Pennsylvanians claimed that they broke "three successive lines

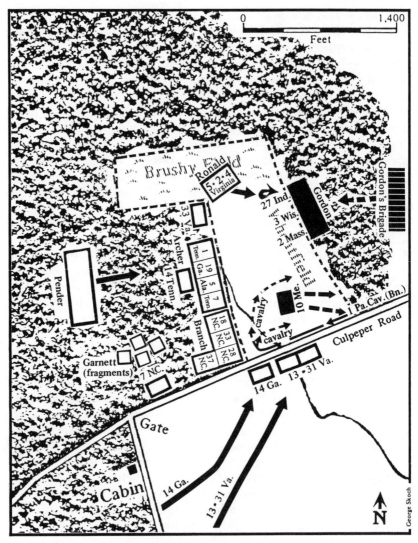

The Cavalry Charge and Gordon's Stand, 6:45–7:00

of infantry" before turning to fight their way out, with the result that the Confederate advance "was completely checked" and the battery saved. In fact, the only Confederates who fell back were those skirmishers who had been moving into the field to exploit the collapse of the Tenth Maine. The universal Southern reaction to the charge was

234

not to fall back, but rather to dash toward it as though drawn by a magnet, to get a shot at the highly vulnerable cavalry.[6] Southerners south of the road flocked with particular ardor to sample the novelty of shooting horses and riders at their ease and without noticeable danger to themselves. By this time the Confederate situation south of the road had become at least as healthy as that on Branch's and Archer's front (although this narrative left Confederates on that wing *in extremis* many pages ago and must, for the sake of continuity, postpone the story of their rally to be told many more pages ahead of this point).

Horses and cavalrymen fell by the dozens from the very beginning of the ride. Some of the Federals shot off their mounts early in the dash were mangled further or even killed when the stampede came back over them moments later during the recoil. Captain John P. Taylor came back to Federal territory battered, dismounted, and literally on his hands and knees. Adjutant William Penn Lloyd thought that the whole affair "lasted less than twenty minutes," which certainly must have been accurate. The question remains, how much less than twenty minutes? Probably much less. Lloyd declared that 92 of the 164 men were casualties. That oft-quoted casualty rate probably grew out of Major Falls's statement in his official report that only 71 of his men were present for duty after the charge. Falls, however, identified the others as including not only those killed or wounded but also those "otherwise placed *hors du combat*." The latter group may have predominated, since the final (and probably too modest) official casualty tabulation reported only 43 men lost in the First Pennsylvania Cavalry.[7]

Confederates applauded the unquestioned bravery and determination of their mounted foe, no less an authority than Stonewall Jackson extolling the "impetuous valor" of the charge. Southerners, however, did not share the notion that Knap's battery was their own primary target. They therefore presumed that the charge was the final gesture of a beaten foe—the generic delaying action by cavalry, which still was in vogue at that stage of the war. Several Southerners used almost precisely similar phrases in guessing at the genesis of the cavalry charge: Jubal Early—"attempted to retrieve the fortune of the day"; A. P. Hill—"an attempt to retrieve his fortunes"; and Major Daniel A. Grimsley—"attempted to retrieve the fortunes of the hour."[8]

Southerners facing the brunt of the charge agreed with artist Forbes about its prospects for success (writing, of course, under the soothing glow of hindsight). The charge, one of them wrote, "met with the usual luck attending such nonsense." Another summarized the charge succinctly: "Vain attempt; fatal mistake." "It almost seemed a miracle how any of them escaped with their lives."[9]

From General Branch's perspective, the charging Pennsylvanians presented a tender right flank for him to smash because their column moved diagonally across part of the Carolinians' front. Apparently the cavalry drew closer to the road as they moved westward. Some of Taliaferro's and Early's men used the head and left flank of the cavalry column for target practice at the same time. Between these converging fires the Federals "soon broke" and went "fleeing across the field in every direction."[10]

A green youngster from the Twenty-first Virginia, William W. Patteson, who was fighting from among the tangled Confederate mass around Branch's position, recalled that when the cavalry appeared, orders quickly circulated to put double charges in their guns. His ammunition all day had been a ball and nine buckshot per round. When he tried to ram down a second dose, to produce a load of truly heroic proportions, Private Patteson received a basic lesson in the effect of black powder residue on barrel dimensions: the charge stuck halfway down the begrimed bore and would not budge in either direction. A savvy comrade saved the youngster considerable grief or even harm by telling him that the gun would burst if fired in that state. The veteran hurriedly showed Patteson how to knock the ramrod down by inverting the weapon and slamming it against a rock. That left the ramrod stuck, although both charges now rested in the breech—and here came the cavalry. Patteson knelt carefully, aimed his weapon at a Yankee on a dark sorrel, called his shot to his neighbors and let fly. The gun and the boy flew in different directions and the sorrel went down. Patteson became something of a celebrity when an officer responded to the gun's explosion with the droll suggestion that "General Jackson should have had it mounted on wheels, so it wouldn't kick you over."[11]

The First Pennsylvania Cavalry recoiled "in every direction," to use Branch's phrase, but a substantial chunk of the column thundered northward up the western edge of the field before veering back east toward the Federal woods. In the process, the Pennsylvanians ran the gauntlet of Archer's brigade. The murderous fire poured into the cavalry near the road left them "so staggered," one of Archer's men wrote a few days later, "that, instead of running straight back, they inclined along our lines." The prospect of shooting such easy and

*View in 1989 from the southwest corner of the wheatfield
looking at the focal point of the cavalry charge coming
straight at the viewer. (Clark B. Hall)*

novel targets (infantry rarely got the chance to draw a bead on cavalry in large bodies) elated Archer's men as much as it had the Confederates to their right: "It did us so much good we yelled like mad
Indians." The horsemen were churning up a slight grade, and their
mounts seemed to be bent double as they raced past, flecked with
foam. A small knot of seven horses, only two of them carrying riders,
raced along ahead of the pack. As they rose up the knoll at midfield
they came into the bright rays of the setting sun and made quite a
picture. The men of the Fifth Alabama Battalion started shouting,
"Devil take the foremost," as they opened fire on this advance guard.
That many muskets could hardly miss, and the volley hit both the
first horse and its rider. The horse "turned a summerset and threw
his rider as if he had been shot from a cannon." One of the Alabamians wrote of the unfortunate Pennsylvanian: "The last I saw of him
he was about fifteen feet above his saddle."[12]

The repulse of the First Pennsylvania Cavalry did not close out
Federal efforts for the day, nor was it the only (or the last) forlorn
gesture at Cedar Mountain. Even as the cavalrymen bought fame
at high cost, George H. Gordon's small brigade was completing its

237

alignment along the fence in the woods at the eastern edge of the wheatfield. Gordon had only two strong regiments by this time, the Second Massachusetts and the Twenty-seventh Indiana. His Third Wisconsin had been split up earlier, and a bit more than half of that regiment had gone in on Crawford's right. The Wisconsin men rallied and went in again with their own brigade when it moved forward, but they had suffered losses and were hardly in a state of optimum preparedness.[13]

Gordon's troops had been in the vicinity of the Brown house under intermittent but extremely long-range artillery fire for some hours. The orders to hurry to the wheatfield to support Crawford came far too late to be timely, but their sense of urgency prompted Gordon to press his men forward firmly. After the war the historian of the Twenty-seventh Indiana recalled the physical ordeal of getting to the battlefield with marked distaste. The beastly weather and the terrain conspired to make this rapid move "more severe and trying" than anything similar during the entire war. The total distance from the line of departure to the target was just a little less than one mile, but it included a steep drop to the run and then a steep climb back out on the western edge across rocky ground cut by ravines and festooned with briars and vines. Along the way the gasping, double-quicking Federals passed a few stray armed Confederates, which gave them a vivid illustration of how thoroughly the situation in front had deteriorated.[14]

General Gordon ran across another symptom of the Federal disorder in the form of his fellow brigadier Samuel W. Crawford. That unfortunate officer was morosely contemplating the wreck of his command, "sitting quietly on his horse, with a musket across the saddle," all alone in the woods. Gordon's orders had been to go to Crawford's assistance, but as one of the Massachusetts men pointed out, they replaced rather than supported Crawford, "for that brigade had vanished." There can be no question that Crawford was "thoroughly beaten," in the words of one participant and analyst, when Gordon reached the scene of action.[15]

Gordon's regiments puffed up to the edge of the wheatfield in a less than graceful fashion. A youngster in the Twenty-seventh Indiana remembered that he arrived "red in the face, panting for breath, almost ready to drop down with heat and fatigue." In their agitation and exhaustion, some of the men did not see the fence at the edge of the woods until they literally ran into it. The two wings of the Twenty-seventh Indiana were not united, and the scene was chaotic.

The Indiana regiment struck the far northeastern corner of the wheatfield, where the field was narrow. Colonel Andrews's Second Massachusetts fought on Gordon's far left; sandwiched between those two regiments was the Third Wisconsin. Some of the Massachusetts men found themselves far enough left to be screened from the developing action at the north end of the field so they shifted rightward to participate.[16]

After their brief diversion slaughtering the First Pennsylvania Cavalry, Archer's skirmishers and perhaps some of Branch's again began to filter out into the field. Their fire against Gordon from the same midfield vicinity so recently vacated by the Tenth Maine told heavily on the Federals in the woods. The Stonewall Brigade simultaneously kept up a steady fire from Gordon's right front at an oblique angle. Many of the Northerners new to the scene were confused, a circumstance their exhaustion compounded. Some members of the Twenty-seventh Indiana straggled forward into the field for "some distance" and there "exchanged commonplace greetings with members of a Virginia . . . regiment and parted from them and returned . . . without being challenged." This mutual confusion saved the Twenty-seventh for a time because its men were tremendously outnumbered in that sector.[17]

Uncertainty about who was who in the smoke-streaked twilight was compounded by the presence of wounded Federals from Crawford's brigade between the lines and under foot of the advancing Confederate skirmishers. Lieutenant Colonel Edwin F. Brown of the Twenty-eighth New York was one such sufferer, languishing in the field with a shattered left arm. A Confederate skirmisher started with Brown toward the rear as his special prize, but a wounded Fifth Connecticut soldier sprawled nearby shot the captor, barely missing Brown's head in the process. The colonel started back through the confusion in the direction of the Federal woods. Before he reached them, loss of blood drained Brown's strength and he staggered to a halt. Colonel Andrews of the Second Massachusetts spotted Brown's plight from the edge of the woods and sent a corporal out to help him along. The wounded New Yorker had his arm amputated on August 10 in Culpeper but survived the ordeal.[18]

The confusion rampant in the wheatfield made uncertainty about targets an issue. The unwitting mixture of Twenty-seventh Indiana men with the Stonewall Brigade set the stage. The tangle of wounded Federals strewn through active knots of Southern skirmishers added to the uncertainty. Falling shadows and dust-caked uniforms contributed to the recipe. Through it all the small arms fire raged too fiercely to describe adequately. General Gordon reported: "There was no intermission; the crackling of musketry was incessant." Gordon's brigade had not operated in this devil's brew long before the cry went up among the men that they were shooting at friends. Some of the Indiana men on the right were sure that Confederates opposite them started this spurious report. Colonel Silas Colgrove of the Twenty-seventh passed the shout along to General Gordon. Colgrove later speculated that the gloaming caused the trouble because it made Confederate gray—especially dust-plastered gray—look blue. The general was decidedly skeptical. To prove his point to Colgrove, Gordon rode quickly through the corner of the wheatfield to the fence at the edge of the brushy field and managed to escape alive from the heavy volley his action provoked.[19] Historians have cause to applaud the errant Southern marksmanship in this instance: Gordon's postwar books are interesting and valuable sources.

A sidelight on this instance of mistaken identity (an astonishingly frequent Civil War episode) developed from the postwar claims of an aggressive but rather ignorant veteran of the Twenty-seventh Indiana. Sergeant John L. Files of Company H made a career of repeatedly nominating himself for the Congressional Medal of Honor for having saved his entire regiment by "one Volintry Act" at Cedar Mountain. After his self-immortalization was rejected by two different secretaries of war, Files wrote to his senator in 1897 to rectify the "grate Injustes." To that end he described "the Hole mater." Files described his initial feat as discovering that friends were the ones shooting at them from midfield, by means of spying "Our Flag in thar." When he reported this to the colonel, Files received orders to go out and make them stop. He carried his own flag on the mission (he was the "Cular Gard"). Files never finished his initial duty because he saw the heads of many Confederates peeping over the ground to his right. Rather than let them "Shoot me All too Peases," Files went back with the news of the Southern arrival.[20] There is every reason to believe that Files caused his elected representatives far more trouble postwar than his escapade caused Confederates in 1862.

Sergeant Files and his comrades of the Twenty-seventh Indiana broke and fled from the edge of the field not long after the demoralizing episode of firing at enemies who then were mistaken for friends but in fact remained enemies. This break came not under the pressure of a direct attack, but rather during a firefight at medium range. The Third Wisconsin stood firm despite the loss of its right-flank support. Captain Moses O'Brien of the Wisconsin regiment had been in the detachment that went in with Crawford initially and suffered a severe thigh wound in the process. He showed one of his men that his shoe was full of blood. O'Brien bound up the wound himself with a handkerchief and went back into action with Gordon's movement. The brave captain fell dead while fighting at the edge of the woods.[21]

Colonel Colgrove was a tough old Regular Army man, and he rallied part of the Twenty-seventh Indiana by dint of great exertion. When their colonel brought them back to the fence and the wood line, the men of the Twenty-seventh unquestionably had lost much of their organization and élan. Their ragged return probably spread these men across the front in some disarray, and that circumstance may have led to the confusion about alignment cited in note 16 to this chapter.[22]

THROUGH THE frantic period when the battle swung 180° in its momentum, four-fifths of the Stonewall Brigade anchored the Confederate left from a position in and near the brushy field at the north end of the wheatfield. When Crawford swept past, breaking the Twenty-seventh Virginia (one of five regiments in the brigade), the rest stood firm. They faced south when Branch pushed up to the west edge of the field, when Archer followed up on Branch's left, and while the First Pennsylvania Cavalry made its charge. To the discomfiture of many Federals, the Stonewall Brigade stood firmly in place, delivering heavy fire into the wheatfield when Crawford recoiled through it.

Captain Charles L. Haynes of the Twenty-seventh Virginia wrote the report of that regiment, which had formed in the woods off the northwest corner of the wheatfield and was broken there by men of the Forty-sixth Pennsylvania. Haynes noted that he ran into Branch's brigade about 150 yards to the rear. The captain did his best to rally his men behind these fresh troops. Colonel Ronald, commanding the solid portion of the brigade, watched as Branch's advance pushed Federals back through the woods and into the field. Ronald cheerfully acknowledged Branch's "vigorous fire" and its results, probably doing so in ignorance of the slander Branch was contemplating concurrently about the Virginians. The Stonewall Brigade faced 90° or so away from Branch's front, and its left was at least two hundred yards east of (as well as perpendicular to) the longitude of Branch's position. The right of the Stonewall Brigade was located more than three hundred yards north of (as well as perpendicular to) Branch's northernmost regiment.[23] Archer soon would fill most of that gap.

As Crawford's retreating men spilled out of the west woods and streamed through the wheatfield, the Stonewall Brigade became their bitter adversary. From a position sharply on the Federals' flank, the four regiments had a field day. Lieutenant Colonel Ned Lee of the Thirty-third Virginia "carried the colors of his regiment" and led them in the fight. Lee's men cleaned out the corner of the woods where the Twenty-seventh Virginia had had trouble a few minutes before and were pushing on down the wood line as Branch came into view at the far end of the field. Both Branch and the Virginians well to his north faced toward the wheatfield and settled down to generate some heavy fire.[24]

The solidarity of the Confederate far left, in the form of the Stonewall Brigade, was one of the constants throughout the seesawing fortunes on August 9, 1862. When much of the Southern army was on the run, the brigade stood fast. When reinforcements turned the tide, they crossed fire with the newcomers to lacerate the fleeing enemy. And when the pendulum accelerated down its path into a Confederate mode, the Stonewall Brigade formed the hinge and supplied a respectable part of the motive power for the final offensive maneuver. Through all these phases, that same brigade was doing the most direct and extensive damage being done to Federals. Perhaps it is for that reason that Northern accounts of their temporary success do not display the verve and optimism that characterize Confederate reports.

Anyone who has used the official reports of Civil War battles will come away amused, first, at the irreconcilable differences between the reports of opposing individuals referring to the same events. After the amusement fades, a careful student will quickly recognize the need for discretion in accepting a lone report as solid fact without substantiation. Civil Warriors always lashed their foe at minimal cost to themselves, or so they reported. If they suffered an unmistakable reverse, it came after tremendous losses and last-ditch stands. In that light, Confederate accounts of Federal success at Cedar Mountain, which left the battle swaying in the balance, are almost unique. The Confederates unquestionably won the battle resoundingly after their close call—but to an amazing degree they judged the crisis as far greater than did their foe.

Confederates who wrote of a critical situation were not echoed by proud Federals boasting of their success and lamenting what might have been. Williams, Crawford, and Gordon reported successes but did not make sweeping assumptions about near victory. They emphasized instead their brutal losses. Northern regimental commanders wrote in the same spirit but in even more negative tones. It is hard to avoid the twin conclusions that the Federal attack spent itself more quickly and completely than Confederates sensed and that the solid stand by the well-placed Stonewall Brigade (minus its routed Twenty-seventh Virginia) was one of the key determinants in that result.

As Crawford's tattered remnants spilled back into the field in retreat, the four Virginia regiments of the Stonewall Brigade fired on them from two different directions. The Thirty-third Virginia faced nominally east from the farthest northern piece of the western wood line. Its men "fought well," according to the captain of Company H. The other three regiments faced more or less south from a position that denied them a view of the field near the road. They made life miserable for those Federals within view. One of the men of the Twenty-eighth New York retreating through the field wrote in his diary that Confederates "came at us from all sides." When the New Yorker's company reassembled its fragments on the other side of the field, it discovered that every one of its officers had been hit. The regiment was so thoroughly decimated that a lieutenant from the Fifth Connecticut took temporary command of the New York company.[25]

Each of the regiments of the Stonewall Brigade took a hand in tormenting the retreating Federals, but the most effective action came from the Fifth Virginia under the aggressive leadership of Major Hazael J. Williams. While the other three Virginia regiments remained more or less static and delivered fire, the Fifth surged out into the field at just the right time to round up Federal men and flags. The historian of the Fifth Connecticut acknowledged the Fifth Virginia as the source of his regiment's greatest difficulty when the Southern regiment charged out into the field and "captured and killed many of the retreating soldiers." The retiring New Englanders who escaped the Virginians' grasp noticed the Tenth Maine still holding as they scampered to safety. Survivors of the Twenty-eighth New York similarly identified the Fifth Virginia as their most successful enemy.[26]

Major Williams reported that he had just seen the opportunity to move into the field when Colonel Ronald timidly ordered the Fifth Virginia to fall back into the woods near the Thirty-third Virginia.

Williams instead moved the Fifth Virginia across the front of the Thirty-third and into the disheveled Federal ranks. "At this juncture," Williams wrote after the war, "I discovered that I was in rear of the enemy's line." The major wheeled his regiment around, "thus bringing me in their rear." Williams immodestly claimed that his movement captured the whole of Crawford's brigade and turned the tide of battle. In his report written five days after the battle Williams claimed the capture of "a large number" of Federals. By 1897 the captives had grown to "6 or 7 hundred."[27] Major Williams and the Fifth Virginia achieved more than enough success in the wheatfield to make postwar magnifications unnecessary (although apparently irresistible).

Regimental flags meant more to Civil War soldiers than modern observers can readily understand. The beauty, symbolism, and emotional appeal of the state and national flags—and for Confederates, of their star-crossed battle flag—is obvious enough. It has been almost a century since men have gone into action beneath flags, however, and some of the understanding surely has faded. During the Civil War soldiers on both sides died by the thousands around and for their flags—not just for what the flags symbolized but for the flags themselves. On the Federal side, capturing an enemy flag was an easy way to win the newly inaugurated Congressional Medal of Honor (which at the time was dispensed with relative prodigality, including in one instance to every breathing being in an entire regiment, hero and coward alike). Chances to win the medal by that means remained scarce indeed until the final days of the war, when wholesale Confederate rout and surrenders came into vogue. Dozens of captures, and the resultant dozens of medals, came at the battle of Waynesboro five weeks before Appomattox. No one on either side did much of note in that brief dead-end mismatch, but every soldier who picked a flag out of a culvert received the Medal of Honor. Those more dutiful mates who continued the pursuit, unencumbered by trophies, got shot at for their troubles and nothing more.

The enthusiasm for flags—protecting them and capturing them alike—bore fruit only at one time and place during the battle of Cedar Mountain. That was in the wheatfield as the Fifth Virginia stormed into Crawford's unfortunate remnants. The Fifth Connecticut's flag waved in the hands of its eighth color-bearer as he stumbled desperately eastward through the field. The first seven men who bore it had all been killed. The Fifth Virginia captured the Fifth

Connecticut flag and then that of the Twenty-eighth New York as well. In 1883, Colonel Edwin F. Brown of the New York regiment addressed a gathering of Fifth Virginia veterans with recollections of the twenty-one-year-old events. "You captured our brave boys by the hundred," Brown said, "and with them [our] flag." When the Twenty-eighth's color sergeant went down with wounds through both legs, he tore the flag from its staff and tried to hide it under his coat. The flag's bulk thwarted the wounded sergeant; a Confederate saw the edges sticking out and took it.[28]

That night a New York prisoner found the chance to cut out a piece from the captured flag. He kept the fragment throughout his period in captivity and later gave it to Colonel Brown. The treasured fragment served as crucial evidence in 1882 during an effort to identify the original flag. On May 22, 1883, veterans of the Fifth Virginia returned the flag to veterans of the Twenty-eighth New York at Niagara Falls in an unusually early reunification gesture. Peaceful sentiments flowed deep and saccharine: "Unfurl it to the gentle breeze of a now peaceful heaven," and similar poetic words stated at great length. The Virginians returned home and decorated Northern war graves in Staunton the following month. In 1884 the New Yorkers reciprocated with a visit to the Shenandoah Valley during which they placed wreaths on the graves of Jackson and Lee.[29]

The Stonewall Brigade captured a third flag, in addition to those of the Fifth Connecticut and the Twenty-eighth New York, although its identity was not established. Regiments generally carried both a national flag (or battle flag in the case of Confederates) and a state flag. Perhaps the third flag was a national flag and therefore of uncertain regimental origin. Major Williams asserted that his regiment captured all three of the flags. Colonel Ronald credited the Fifth Virginia with two of the three and wrote indistinctly about the other flag being "improperly" confiscated from a private by an officer after its capture. Stonewall Jackson's official report confirmed the three flags' identities (including one nonidentity) and simply cited the Stonewall Brigade as their captor.[30]

Two enlisted men in the Fifth Virginia Infantry won special plaudits for their role in the advance that captured all of the flags taken on the day as well as so many prisoners. Major Williams left a small detachment on his left to protect his flank when he advanced, even though the Second and Fourth Virginia operated somewhere in that direction. As the rest of the Fifth moved forward, Color Sergeant John M. Gabbert hurried ahead, waving the regiment's flag in one hand and a sword in the other. Gabbert was "calling to the men to come on" when bullets hit him in the shoulder and leg and knocked him down.[31]

Private Narcissus Finch Quarles of Company E also enjoyed a memorable adventure in the wheatfield with the Fifth Virginia. Two survivors of the company reported that Quarles single-handedly captured all three flags as well as nineteen prisoners. They saw Quarles herding the prisoners across the field with the flags on his shoulder. He was taking all of these spoils to Jackson's headquarters. In recognition of the feat, someone gave Private Quarles a sword. Family tradition insists that Stonewall Jackson honored Narcissus with the gift, though that is hardly likely. Unfortunately, brave young Quarles did not have long to bask in the glory of his memorable day because he was killed three weeks later at Manassas. Captain Lycurgus Grills (who himself was dead within a year) took the gift sword home to Quarles's mother and told her of her son's great deeds.[32]

The stellar success of the Fifth Virginia became telescoped in time in the memories of some of the men who participated in it and in some resulting historical accounts. The Fifth Virginia and the brigade did *not* rush pell-mell onward from its success with Crawford's retreating men and drive everything "as chaff before the wind, with frightful loss." A member of the Fourth Virginia, behind and to the left of the Fifth, wrote of the initial success but admitted that the brigade "had to fall back for a time" and regroup.[33] During that period the First Pennsylvania Cavalry charged, the Tenth Maine completed its withdrawal, and Gordon's Federal regiments began to fight in earnest from the wood line east of the wheatfield. The Stonewall Brigade lay too far north to experience any effects from the whirlwind cavalry charge near the road. Few of the men in the brigade saw the charge, and few if any commented on it.

During the brief lull after Crawford's remnants slipped past, the Stonewall Brigade realigned itself preparatory to swooping across into the east woods, which all day had belonged to the Federals. Gordon's brigade had assumed center stage from the Northern perspective, but Confederates flooded their side of the battlefield in steadily increasing volume. Gordon's position was far enough north from the road to be much more in the sphere of action of the Stonewall Brigade than of Branch's (much as, in reverse, the cavalry charge had been too far south to be of much interest to the Stonewall Brigade). The good fortune of Twenty-seventh Indiana men who strayed out into the wheatfield has been recounted above. The Stonewall Brigade soldiers they met were too disorganized to do them any harm for the moment. The Second Virginia suffered enough confusion to require a display of gallantry by Captain Raleigh T. Colston of Company E. Colston seized the colors and in "clear, ringing tones called upon the regiment to 'dress to the colors,' which it quickly did."[34]

A member of the Fifth Virginia later regaled the regimental adjutant with a story of his exploits in the confused, smoky darkness. Three Yankees loomed up close and suddenly. The Virginian had lost his bayonet and had no cap on his gun. Grabbing his musket by the barrel, the Confederate clobbered the nearest Yankee to the ground. Here he paused in the narration until the adjutant impatiently inquired, "What of the other two?" "Why I ran away from them as fast as I could."[35] By this time, however, most of the running was flowing in the other direction.

The Confederate strength swelling on the west edge of the wheatfield and along its northern boundary clearly overmatched Gordon's three regiments on the Federal side of the field, and the preponderance continued to grow rapidly. At the beginning of the infantry action, Garnett's brigade had been the only Southern unit along the field's edge. Now Branch, Archer, and the Stonewall Brigade all fired from the fringe of the field and Pender's brigade was coming fast to help. The tide had turned and now was building to the dimensions of a Confederate tidal wave. Some of the rivulets that combined to make up that wave were composed of proud little knots of men from Garnett's brigade who grittily pulled themselves back together after their disaster and looked for places to lend a hand. Their rally probably meant more to the participants than to the outcome of the battle. Before completing the stage setting for the Confederate advance into the wheat, we must examine the experiences of Garnett's fragments.

Colonel Thomas S. Garnett described the efforts to rally his broken units in a modest and balanced manner. "Portions of different regiments were reformed," Garnett wrote, and they "assisted in driving the enemy." The colonel himself was suffering from a gunshot wound but remained in the saddle for five hours, "thus endangering his life by irritating his wound." His behavior won Garnett the compliments of onlookers, including temporary division commander Taliaferro, who wrote of his subordinate's "rare skill and courage" at Cedar Mountain.[36]

The First Virginia Battalion broke first and worst of Garnett's four units. Perhaps that unhappy distinction prompted its members and other observers to chronicle attempts at rallying to a far greater degree than any other part of Garnett's command. Major Seddon of the battalion reported that his officers without exception "made the most heroic endeavors" to rally the men. He admitted, however, that the efforts generally failed, leaving the officers and some few of the men to join with other units headed toward the front. Captain Benjamin Watkins Leigh of Company A distinguished himself within range of many admiring eyes in the endeavor to rally the battalion. Leigh "took the colors of his battalion and rode in front, directly down the road, exposed to a concentrated fire."[37]

Lieutenant John Hampden "Ham" Chamberlayne of A. P. Hill's artillery owned no vested interest in the performance of the First Virginia Battalion, but he exerted himself vigorously in attempting to halt its rout. In a letter to his mother the young officer identified himself as one of many who worked on restoring order. Although Chamberlayne "tried my best," he admitted that his efforts were "for the most part unavailing." Two years later, Colonel R. L. Walker cited Chamberlayne's Cedar Run exploits ("noticed by many, and . . . of great service") in recommending promotion for the younger man. To his mother, Ham admitted that "the minnie balls were awful" and as a result he was "more nervous than I have ever been before." Writing to a young lady friend, however, the lieutenant waxed nonchalant, describing his contentment under fire based on recollections of friends and home: "It has at least the effect of making one more quiet in danger, and so far so good."[38]

Lieutenant Charles A. Davidson of Company E, First Virginia Battalion, described his experiences after the break in a detailed letter he wrote a few days later. Davidson managed to rally only "four or five" men, but they joined a contingent of about fifty others who must have been the largest (and perhaps only) semiorganized body out of the battalion. This rump battalion fought some on the right of the road and then fell back toward the Gate. Davidson came across Stonewall Jackson during the rally and later wound up on Branch's left, sweeping through the woods toward the edge of the wheatfield from which the battalion had been driven not long before. In the process, Davidson noted that "great numbers" of prisoners lost by the First Battalion came back into Confederate hands. Eventually Lieutenant Davidson came across his colleague Captain Leigh and was relieved to see the flag of the First Battalion held aloft in the captain's hand.[39]

The Tenth Virginia had been edging toward the left of the First

Battalion when Crawford struck and paid the price for that imprecise positioning. If the Tenth rallied to any degree, it was not in large numbers. Major Stover contented himself with a brief and broad remark about rallying and helping the Stonewall Brigade. He claimed for the regiment "a number" of Federal prisoners.[40]

Captain Dobyns of the Forty-second Virginia made a strong case for the rehabilitation of his regiment after the disaster. The captain insisted that more than half of his survivors participated in the Confederate resurgence. Dobyns's wording, however, leaves the inference that this renaissance came about in the decidedly unmeasurable form of fragments mixed into other organizations. The ugly business of hurt done to surrendered Southerners by Northern captors cropped up again as the Forty-second Virginia's scattered survivors moved through their former position. An officer in the brigade wrote at the time that "in every instance" among the "good many" of which he had heard, Federals forced to abandon prisoners "attempted to shoot or bayonet them." A captain in the Forty-second asserted positively that the Federals had carried a black flag—the legendary symbol for war with no quarter given. Others echoed his story, which must have resulted from a glimpse of a furled flag or a state flag of dark hue.[41] The prevalent horror stories about harmed prisoners are more difficult to dismiss out of hand.

Garnett's two right-hand regiments, the Forty-eighth and Twenty-first Virginia, had suffered dreadfully because of their location, bent around the unwholesome angle in the brigade line. Each regiment had left a knot or two of survivors behind when the main body broke under intense pressure and the attacking Federals forged on across the road. These detachments served as ready-made rally points. The official report of the Forty-eighth Virginia claimed no more than that the unit was "partially reformed" and joined in the subsequent advance. The primary rally point for the Twenty-first Virginia was on a small knoll about 150 yards from the road. Captain Witcher of the Twenty-first reported that pieces of other disorganized units adhered to the edges of the resurgence by the Twenty-first and the whole polyglot detachment accomplished some good near the end of the battle. This "little band" was augmented steadily by Confederates who had spent a quarter-hour or less as prisoners of war before being set free and taking up arms strewn on the battlefield.[42]

The last of the broken Confederate regiments did not belong to Garnett. The Twenty-seventh Virginia of the Stonewall Brigade had dissolved under pressure, giving General Branch and others not fond of Virginia and Virginians the chance to slander the entire brigade. General Jackson himself came across this unfortunate piece of his old command near the nadir of the regiment's afternoon. Captain Haynes, commanding the Twenty-seventh, had rallied a handful, who gave Stonewall a cheer. He saluted them back with a wave of his hat and an admonition to remember they were his namesake brigade. Haynes admitted that despite the general's pep talk, "After this the regiment did not appear as a regiment but acted in detachments, some connecting themselves with other regiments, others going in with squads from different regiments, some detailed or ordered back in charge of prisoners."[43]

As the rallied fragments filtered toward the front line at the western edge of the wheatfield, they approached a scene in which Confederate strength was peaking at an irresistible level. Pender, Archer, Branch, Ronald, and the various fragments gathered in position to demolish the small Federal force across the field. Before unfolding that story, however, we must go back in chronology about half an hour to pick up the thread on the south side of the road at the point when Taliaferro's and Early's brigades lay in disarray.

CHAPTER 11

The Fourteenth Georgia
Fills the Breach

GENERAL JUBAL A. EARLY was a hard man of irascible mien who fought with the same bitter tenaciousness he brought to the rest of life's transactions. Near the end of their bold advance, Crawford's attacking Federals surged briefly against the left of Early's brigade, but they spent their last ounce of momentum in the process. Early held the far right of Jackson's line, excepting the detachment with Ewell across Cedar Run on the unapproachable shoulder of Cedar Mountain.

Early was busily slotting the newly arrived reinforcements from Thomas's Georgia Brigade into the right of his line when disaster struck his left. Rolling ground obscured those developments from Early until he rode back in that direction and discovered the crisis. Early's initial reaction must have been to spur into the fray and attempt to correct the situation. If so, he resisted the impulse and instead hurried back to his right in the clear understanding that salvation lay in assuring the firmness of that anchor. Early sent Samuel Hale of his staff to the left to do what he could. Hale and two other members of the general's staff, Samuel H. Early and Andrew L. Pitzer, each had a horse shot under him in the confused melee. General Richard S. Ewell watched Early's performance from his mountaintop vantage point without any ability to affect his subordinate's decisions. A few months later Ewell expressed warm approval of Early's accomplishments in his official report.[1]

When Early satisfied himself that his right was rock solid, he rode again to his left. This time a happier view unfolded when he neared his left. Confederates were advancing; Federals were beginning to fall back. To his joy, Early discovered that the advance consisted of pieces of his own brigade mixed with a few of Taliaferro's rallying fragments. Some of them had done stalwart work in pulling themselves together. The primary motive force for the rally came from the left, however, where a stray Georgia regiment separated from Thomas's brigade threw itself into the balance. Early acknowledged that his ralliers generally fought on in the final stages of the battle in conjunction with or behind reinforcements from A. P. Hill's division.[2]

The Thirteenth Virginia Infantry had started the battle as Early's farthest left regiment, which left it the most vulnerable to the pressure applied by Crawford from the north. Nevertheless, the Thirteenth's performance during the crisis outshone that of the rest of Early's regiments (except for the Twelfth Georgia on the far right) and won the plaudits of observers from many different commands. After the Thirteenth finally fell back some two hundred yards, it led the rally by Early's brigade and again became the focus of attention. A chunk of the Thirty-first Virginia had clung to the Thirteenth during its stand and its short withdrawal and staunchly took part in the rally as well.

One of the first things that caught Jubal Early's eye when he returned to his left was the cluster of Thirty-first Virginia men standing firm around their colors and the flag of the Thirteenth Virginia, similarly supported, nearby. "I was particularly struck by the bravery exhibited by the color-bearers of these two regiments," Early wrote, "who, with these small bodies of men around them, were waving their flags in the very front, as if to attract a fire upon them, and advancing all the while." Colonel James A. Walker of the Thirteenth had assumed control of the organized remnant of the Thirty-first Virginia in addition to his own troops.[3]

Colonel Jim Walker (he would come to be known as "Stonewall Jim" after transferring to the command of Jackson's old brigade) acknowledged in his report that the chance to reform and move back toward the enemy was won for him by the work of fresh troops on his left. When Walker moved his polyglot two-regiment demi-brigade back toward the ground he had left minutes earlier, he guided on the knoll where two hostile flags had been unfurled. The colors—one Federal, one Maryland state—faded back whence they came. Walker's movement relieved Confederate artillery, which had been endangered in that quarter. He did not sweep the field without interruption. What seemed to be a fresh Federal line in the corn held up the Thirteenth and Thirty-first for about ten minutes at a point near where they had stood when the fight began. By that time Southern successes farther to the left conspired to collapse the Federal resistance in front of Walker, and his men poured down toward the corn.

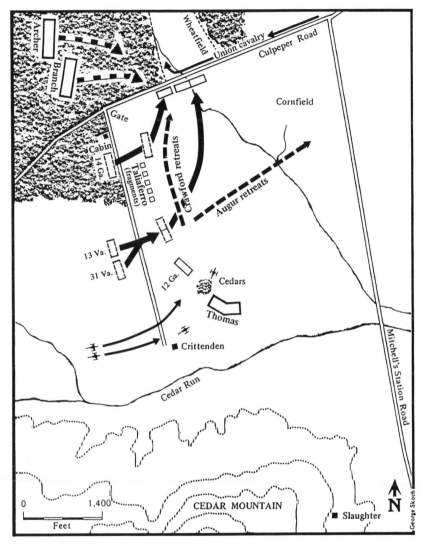

The Confederate Rally South of the Gate, 6:30–7:00

Just as Walker's little band reached the corn east of the Crittenden Lane, the men saw and heard the Federal cavalry charge heading down the road on their left. They gleefully flocked in that direction.[4]

One other piece of Early's brigade earned applause by its behavior after falling back from the Crittenden Lane. Captain Robert Doak

Lilley of the Twenty-fifth Virginia won general's stars before the end of the war, but at Cedar Mountain (and for five months thereafter) he commanded only one of the regiment's ten companies. The steps to Lilley's several promotions—four of them after Cedar Mountain—included his performance on August 9 after the Twenty-fifth Virginia fell back. Captain Lilley caught Jubal Early's eye during the rally, advancing at the forefront of a small detachment of the Twenty-fifth which included the regiment's color-bearer and his flag. According to the version of the incident that reached Stonewall Jackson's personal staff, Lilley seized the flag in his own hands and waved it vigorously in front of his line as a stimulus to rallying and as a focal point for a renewed advance.[5]

Jedediah Hotchkiss earned the reputation of being among the most careful and accurate chroniclers of Jackson's campaigns by virtue of a meticulous diary and numerous contemporary letters. Hotchkiss paid particularly close attention to weather details; so when he wrote in his diary on August 9 that "there was a hard shower in the midst of the fight," that intelligence cannot be dismissed lightly. If rain fell, it must have been a very brief shower and perhaps localized in extent. Hotchkiss mentioned his unique weather note immediately after citing Captain Lilley's exploits, which gives the only hint of the timing or location of the phantom shower.[6]

The Twelfth Georgia and Thomas's brigade stood rock solid throughout the period during which Early's Virginia regiments fell back (through dust or rain?) and then regrouped. Although the Twelfth Georgia was only a temporary adjunct to Early's brigade, the general cheerfully applauded the regiment's performance, bestowing in his official report "my especial approbation." The "gallant, fighting regiment" and its redoubtable commander, Captain Brown, won encomiums as high as those Early used for his own Thirteenth Virginia. Thomas and the Twelfth Georgia ran short of ammunition because they fired so much, but at about the same time the tide they had helped to turn swept past them and made ammunition a much less critical commodity. Palpable confusion sweeping the Federal ranks showed the Georgians an opportunity they eagerly joined, moving forward and "sweeping the fields and mowing down the Yankees before us as if they were only blackbirds before the sportsman."[7]

Early's salvation, and Taliaferro's as well, sprang in large part from the fine performance of a single Georgia regiment that broke off the end of Thomas's brigade and fought alone north of Early's left. The men of the Fourteenth Georgia supplied some Confederate presence between Early's left and the Gate. Their presence gave Walker some leeway in which to rally the Thirteenth Virginia and other remnants and get back into the fight.

When Thomas led his four regiments southward from the main road, he moved through the small body of woods south of the road and short of the Gate. Thomas and his first three regiments moved steadily to the right, where they found a fine position under Early's guidance, as we have seen, and contributed substantially to the Confederate effort. The Fourteenth Georgia was marching at the end of the brigade column and evidently was delayed. Perhaps, to indulge in the rawest speculation, Thomas had room for only three regiments in column in the woods as he awaited final orders, leaving the tail end Fourteenth to form up after the main body of the brigade headed to Early. Thomas reported that he *ordered* the regiment to hang back, but other accounts disagree implicitly. For whatever reason, the Fourteenth emerged from the woods into the open near the Crittenden Lane only after its three companion regiments had marched well beyond easy reach. "Just as the head of our column emerged from the woods," a Fourteenth Georgia participant wrote, "and attempted to cross the [lane], Taliaferro's brigade, or at least two regiments of it . . . gave way and retreated in wild disorder across the road, breaking through our ranks."[8]

The two regiments were, of course, the raw Alabamians of Taliaferro's brigade, soon to be followed by the rest of that command. The apparent misfortune that stopped the movement of the Fourteenth Georgia toward its intended destination near Cedar Run proved instead to be good Confederate luck. The Fourteenth necessarily halted where it was to dress its line and soon went to work in the emergency at hand. The regiment never did move on to the position of its brigade.

Taliaferro's fleeing men did not stand upon the manner of their going. The tremendous negative impact on the physical alignment and psychological preparedness of the Fourteenth Georgia required yeoman service by the regiment's commander, Lieutenant Colonel Robert W. Folsom. Folsom had held the command of the Fourteenth for no more than a few minutes, since Colonel Felix L. Price had been wounded by a piece of shell during the passage through the woods. Taliaferro's flying troops made Folsom's job difficult "by their exaggerated and panic stricken reports, spreading dismay among our scattered men, who involuntarily began also to give back." A participant suggested, doubtless on the basis of his own nervousness, that "a headlong rout" was imminent. To avert that result, Folsom joined the roll of Confederate officers who waved flags aloft on this afternoon to hold their men to their duty.[9]

Colonel Folsom needed the brass and technique of a political stump orator; he was, in fact, a twenty-six-year-old medical doctor. Even so, he and his flag managed to halt the dissolution of the Fourteenth Georgia. By one account, Folsom shouted "in a voice whose intonation rang far over the plain ... 'for the sake of old Georgia to stand!'" A member of the regiment supplied a more elaborate version of the appeal by his youthful physician-commander: "Folsom ... seized the colors, sprang to the front, and waving on high the glorious battle flag of the Confederacy, called on the Fourteenth in a soul-stirring appeal, adjuring them by the memories of the past, and the glories of the future to rally to them, and sustain him in this dark and trying hour." Federals closing on the Georgians' ground punctuated Folsom's impassioned appeal. Willie Pegram's guns not far from the Fourteenth Georgia seemed to be in particular danger. Without the stand by the Georgia regiment it is hard to imagine how Pegram could have escaped. Colonel Folsom concluded his application of starch to the Fourteenth's resolve by slamming the flagstaff into the earth and asking "quietly": "Boys, are you going to leave your Colonel?"[10]

In the caldron of battle, Colonel Folsom's appeal could not have been delivered very "quietly" or it would have gone unheard. Apparently it did not, because the Georgians stoutly rallied to their colonel. Some of Taliaferro's men also gradually rallied around the regiment and built up a fire base. Folsom's group soon numbered eight hundred to nine hundred men, in the estimate of one of their number, which would mean that about half of them must have been Taliaferro's resurgent troops. That many muskets delivering what was described as "a terrific, well-aimed and destructive fire" had a major effect on the tactical situation.[11]

As exhausted Federals recoiled before that sheet of fire, Folsom seized the moment and acted decisively. Still clutching the flag, he leaped in front of his line and yelled in a voice audible above the din: "Boys, follow me." Folsom turned to the front and led the way; his Georgians and their supports from Taliaferro had no choice but to follow the colonel. A member of the Fourteenth Georgia estimated that Folsom remained "from thirty to fifty yards in advance of the line" and made "a most conspicuous mark ... waving his banner aloft, and turning every now and then to encourage his men." To his troops, Folsom seemed to bear a charmed existence.[12] The route covered by brave Folsom and his followers covered about the same ground across which the Federal attack had come, only in reverse direction. It was, therefore, headed northeast or perhaps even north-northeast.

Folsom could not maintain his position at the front for the duration of the charge, but it was not for want of effort. A participant estimated, probably conservatively, that the Fourteenth Georgia (reinforced) covered about three hundred yards in the advance. Somewhere along the route, while still in front of his men, Folsom collapsed, "overcome by heat and feebleness." One contemporary account reported the case of an unidentified colonel, under circumstances that make Folsom a very likely match, who collapsed temporarily because he was suffering internally from a fall when his horse was shot. Whatever the cause of his weakness, Folsom stalwartly resumed the advance supported on either side by one of his men. Their leader's dauntless grit inspired the men, as such things always do. All eyes watched the scene as Folsom went down. One witness situated far enough away to miss some of the details reported that the incident was "only a stumble, and in an instant his tall form is again seen pressing on" next to the flag. The men supporting Folsom and the flag were supporting the spirit of the Fourteenth Georgia as it pressed on toward the main road.[13]

The steady thrust of the Fourteenth Georgia and its friends finally came to a halt at the edge of the road. A few enemy skulking in and around the road scampered away or fell easy prey to Georgian muskets. As the men caught their breath and looked for new worlds to conquer, they might well have been proud of their impact on the battle. A. P. Hill reported with understandable exuberance that Folsom had achieved a "brilliant success." The charge had carried this augmented regiment to a point near the southwestern corner of the wheatfield, not far from Branch's front. The men could see the wheatfield obliquely across the road, and noticed the small stream near them in that corner of the field. Federals remained in the wheatfield in some strength at this juncture (the Federal cavalry charge still lay in the future). The road afforded a good position from which to fire at that enemy, and the regiment began to do so.[14]

A part of Early's brigade quickly rallied in the friendly backwash of the Fourteenth Georgia's advance, as we have seen. Taliaferro's brigade obviously enjoyed the same opportunity. Those of its men and units who had not run themselves clear out of the area took the occasion to come back into action. Some of them joined the Fourteenth Georgia during its stand and subsequent advance. Taliaferro's two raw Alabama infantry regiments broke first and doubtless ran farthest. Lieutenant Colonel James W. Jackson of the Forty-seventh Alabama claimed that his men rallied "of themselves" around their flag behind a friendly hill. After the reorganization produced enough strength, the colonel ordered the colors forward, and the men followed them, "though without," Jackson admitted, "any line of battle." Jackson remained behind to encourage stragglers forward and to prevent the men in the rear from firing into the backs of their friends who had gone forward. Despite this bluntly pessimistic summary, Lieutenant Colonel Jackson claimed that his reconstituted command fought again during the evening. One of Jackson's Alabamians wrote home that he remained in action "untill after dark a whyle" and eventually "takened a good many prisoners."[15]

The two Virginia regiments of Taliaferro's brigade did not fall back so soon or so far as did their less experienced Alabamian comrades. Colonel A. G. Taliaferro reported through excessively rose-colored glasses that "the whole brigade was speedily reformed" and advanced "until darkness interposed" as an integral element in the Confederate sweep. Division commander W. B. Taliaferro routinely validated his uncle-subordinate's account and described in general terms the contribution of the brigade. General Early supplied an unsolicited testimonial to his fellow brigade commander's bravery, reporting that he personally observed "the conspicuous gallantry exhibited by Colonel Taliaferro . . . whom I saw urging his men on."[16]

Despite Colonel Taliaferro's undoubted personal bravery and the demonstrable participation of his men as individuals and small units in the Confederate resurgence, it is impossible to assign a role of any significance to their second effort. A. P. Hill's arrival in strength meant more to the large-scale tactical picture than all of the subsequent small rallies it made possible. As was the case with Garnett's brigade, Taliaferro rallied for pride and then served ably as an outrider to the A. P. Hill juggernaut. One of Hill's artillerists observing the fight wrote in somewhat unfair derogation of Garnett's and Taliaferro's misfortune, then aptly identified the secondary role those two brigades played in the battle's later stages.[17]

The spirit of the comeback was summarized nicely in the words of an officer in its midst. One bullet had nipped the poor fellow's nose; another inflicted a flesh wound on his thigh; a third shot away the toe of his boot; and a fourth hit him fairly seriously in the arm. This partly bandaged and thoroughly battered leader returned to his reforming regiment and shouted encouragement: "Come on, boys, forward! we'll pay 'em off for that last trick of theirs."[18]

To Federals facing the reinvigorated Confederates, gray-clad soldiers seemed to spring from the ground in every direction. Crawford's stalwart attackers heading back toward the wheatfield found renewed troubles awaited them. The historian of the Fifth Connecticut described the rallying enemy all around him as gathering momentum from increasing awareness of just how few Federals had caused all of the excitement. Many Southerners "had only scattered and sought cover near at hand, here and there," he wrote. They regrouped "in squads all about . . . and renewed the contest in all directions." South of the road, Geary and Prince felt the same pressure, although they were in less exposed positions and had not suffered the disorganization inherent in a long and circuitous advance. Enfilade fire from their left hurt those two brigades, and they soon had the sense that they were "nearly surrounded."[19]

Although it hardly mattered, the guns at the Cedars and near the Crittenden House ran dry at about this time. Major Courtney hurried forward three short-ranged Maryland pieces and two Parrott rifles from Captain John J. Rivera's untested battery, but no occasion arose for any of the five replacement guns to fire a round.[20]

Not long after the Fourteenth Georgia (reinforced) reached the main road, the First Pennsylvania Cavalry came roaring down it right into the setting sun and at the regiment and the Thirty-seventh North Carolina of Branch's nearby brigade. Colonel Folsom ordered his men to hold their fire until he called for it. The rapidly approaching horses seemed "magnificent" to one of the Georgians waiting to kill them and their riders. Another described the spectacle of the approaching cavalry as a "splendid" sight. Three men in the regiment recorded the affair in some detail, and their estimates of the range at which Folsom ordered the first volley agree to a remarkable extent. One calculated the distance as sixty yards, another at "fifty or sixty," and the third guessed it to be seventy-five. By the time the colonel shouted to fire, the waiting infantrymen could feel the earth "fairly trembling" beneath the thundering hooves.[21]

The same accounts display similar agreement in describing the results of the volley. Down went many horses and riders "in one confused undistinguishable mass," by one account, or "in a conglomerated tangle," according to another. Some of the mounted men reached within twenty yards of the regiment's line before swerving

*A view looking south in 1912 from a point two hundred feet
south of the Tenth Maine marker. The First Pennsylvania
Cavalry charged across the ground in the intermediate distance,
from left to right. (Gould Papers, Duke University)*

away and dashing up the west edge of the field (where Archer's brigade, as we have seen, riddled them anew). A statistically inclined
Georgian counted twenty-nine dead horses in front of the regiment
and almost as many Pennsylvanians. Captain Washington L. Goldsmith of Company K found some illusions about cavalry shattered
after helping to slaughter the attackers. He confessed to having cher-
ished "exalted ideas as to cavalry charges . . . Murat and Kellerman
. . . the iron-hearted Blucher . . . Napoleon's splendid cavalry at Waterloo." Goldsmith's experiences on August 9 thoroughly "dispelled"
those exalted ideas, to use his word.[22]

General A. P. Hill reported that the Fourteenth Georgia was one of
two regiments that repulsed the cavalry charge with "a deadly fire."
Hill evidently considered the harm done by Archer's brigade to be

post-crisis mopping up. (Archer's troops were of Hill's division, and he would not have shortchanged them.) The other regiment Hill cited as strong against the cavalry was, amazingly, the Thirteenth Virginia Infantry. General Hill was accurate in his report; the amazement is warranted by the rapidity with which the Thirteenth Virginia got untracked and moved so far north and east. Colonel James A. Walker had been enjoying a remarkable day, which he topped off with a prompt and effective reaction to the cavalry charge. Walker was prodding forward the Thirteenth Virginia and attached fragments from other units when he spied the beginnings of the cavalry movement. The colonel took off his hat and waved it with one hand while the other held his sword aloft and shouted the order, "Thirteenth left wheel!" The regiment dashed forward toward the road at a point just east of the spot where the Fourteenth Georgia awaited the attack. If the Thirteenth could reach the road in time, it would be squarely on the flank of the First Pennsylvania and within a few yards of its targets.[23]

The men of the Thirteenth Virginia knew that the cavalry posed no threat to them: cavalry never threatened infantry seriously except in extraordinary circumstances. Furthermore, fences on either side of the road intervened (the Federals were just north of the road in the edge of the wheatfield). Federal sabers could not reach the Confederates, but Southern lead could cross the road in an instant. Colonel Walker reported that his men raced toward the near fence "laughing, yelling, shouting, looking as if they were the best pleased set of chaps in the world." The Virginians did not observe fire discipline as did the Fourteenth Georgia to their left. The first scattered fire from the Thirteenth "did not do much," but the second tumbled Pennsylvanians from their saddles.[24]

The decisive volley by the Thirteenth Virginia lashed out as the cavalry "came thundering down the hill . . . immediately under our muskets." Sam Buck of the Thirteenth Virginia harkened back to the legend of Bunker Hill from the preceding century when he swore that he "could see the whites of their eyes" as his company volleyed. When the smoke cleared, Buck could see "horses and riders rolled over each other blocking the road and keeping them under our guns." Some of the Pennsylvanians had spilled into the road itself, which put them even closer to the Thirteenth's muzzles. Those who survived scampered back across the fence north of the road and galloped north into the musketry pouring from Archer's brigade. Colonel Walker's official report described the Federal difficulties more prosaically. His regiment's fire "was very destructive" and drove away the cavalry "in confusion and disorder." A member of Stonewall Jackson's headquarters entourage, watching anxiously, mentioned only the Thirteenth Virginia in describing the easy slaughter and said of the cavalrymen: "It almost seemed a miracle how any of them escaped with their lives." Colonel Walker claimed, perhaps with mild exaggeration, that in contrast to the Federal losses, "Not one of our men fell in this charge, and they seemed all the time to look on the whole affair as a joke."[25]

Sergeant Sam Buck of the Thirteenth Virginia was unarmed as he hurried up to the fence with the rest of the regiment. Buck had just returned from sick leave and had not rearmed himself on his return. In any case, he was acting as company commander and had broader duties than merely generating musketry from the ranks. During the earlier stages of the fight, Buck had fired a few rounds from weapons left on the field by men wounded or fleeing. At the height of the cavalry excitement Sergeant Buck grabbed the nearest unused weapon and noticed that a ramrod protruded from the muzzle. The Pennsylvania cavalry had turned north and was escaping by the time Buck could cap the weapon so he hurriedly fired it at the retreating horsemen, ramrod and all.[26]

Colonel A. G. Taliaferro later claimed that his own reformed brigade stood at the impact point of the cavalry charge. By his account, the Northern cavalry was fired upon "also" by three other brigades after the charge had been broken by his brigade. Some of the colonel's men took part in the affair, of course, but Taliaferro's immodest and decidedly inaccurate report went beyond the normal egocentric perspective expected in official reports. The colonel's brigade included neither the Fourteenth Georgia nor the Thirteenth Virginia, and those were the two regiments that stood squarely at ringside. Jubal Early, who rode over to the road in the wake of his aggressive regiment under James Walker, noticed the Twenty-third Virginia, which did belong to Taliaferro's brigade, in the area and gave it credit for being there. General Early's two written accounts of the cavalry charge and its repulse are wholly accurate and well balanced. The brand-new division commander, General William B. Taliaferro, also summarized the action concisely and generally accurately, albeit in a fashion that afforded his own old brigade some undue credit.[27]

Circumstances delineated in General Early's postwar account help to explain why so many units claimed large accomplishments: they were so broken apart by the moves and countermoves of the past hour that some soldiers from almost every regiment turned up in almost every corner of the battle's final phases. The Southerners who beat back the point of the cavalry charge included many tiny fragments fighting without organization and without formation. The Fourteenth Georgia and Thirteenth Virginia played the key role because they were organized and in formation and responding to intelligent leadership, but many of their friends cheerfully joined in from the wings.

CHAPTER 12

Counterattack

WHEN THE SURVIVORS of the First Pennsylvania Cavalry regained the shelter of the woods east of the wheatfield, just one Northern unit on the entire battlefield still stood firm. That lonely outfit was Gordon's brigade of three regiments. South of the road the brigades of Geary and Prince were falling back, although neither had been mauled nearly as much as Crawford's brigade had been. Gordon's three regiments faced more than six times their numbers across the field. Branch's brigade on (and even partially south of) the road was farthest right of four Confederate brigades preparing to attack through the wheat. Archer fired from the wood line on Branch's left. Four regiments of the Stonewall Brigade stood to Archer's left, though they were nearly at right angles to Archer and faced nearly south. Pender's brigade was groping toward the left of the Stonewall Brigade at the moment when all eyes turned south toward the cavalry diversion. When Pender reached his goal, he would be entirely on Gordon's flank and in a position to seal the fate of that small and desperate Federal remnant.

The four Confederate brigades moved to the attack more or less simultaneously. (Pender's lagged a little behind because it required time to find the best position and because it arrived later than the rest.) Since Gordon's line would be overlapped from the north, each Southern unit from right to left became more important than its neighbor on its right. For that reason, this narrative will follow the climactic attack into the wheatfield by stages from the right, beginning with Branch's brigade and moving around leftward to Pender's.

Branch had reached the southwest corner of the wheatfield during his initial advance from behind the Gate by a movement that deflected gradually rightward toward the road. His renewed advance into the wheatfield, which began "immediately" after the repulse of the First Pennsylvania Cavalry, started out oriented about due east. Once again he deflected rightward. This time the twist did not result from resistance or thick woods or other stray circumstances. Stonewall Jackson himself ordered the tangential movement.[1]

The brigade had not moved much more than one hundred yards when Branch ordered it to halt. The main line had reached the stream running through that corner of the wheatfield and halted facing the gentle slope ahead leading to the midfield ridge where the Tenth Maine had made its stand a few minutes earlier. General Branch's official report, and to an even greater degree his private journal, oozed bombast about every aspect of this day's work; but for this moment in the wheatfield, Branch found himself uncertain what to do. While the brigade marked time in the comfortable shelter of the ridge's defilade, the color-bearer of the Eighteenth North Carolina charged ahead with all eyes upon him. This daring fellow ran to the crest, planted his colors in full view of Federals in the eastern wood line, and stood alone "as steady as if on a parade." Not long after the color-bearer assumed his pose, the army's highest-ranking witness rode onto the scene and saw him there. Stonewall Jackson rode rapidly and all alone across the front of the brigade, halted opposite the colors, and raised his cap. The men in the ranks "wildly cheered" Jackson and called encouragement to him. Branch described their reaction as "a terrific shout." Although Jackson did doff his hat, he typically uttered not a word.[2]

In addition to saluting the North Carolina color-bearer and inspiriting his mates, Stonewall Jackson transacted some business with General Branch. The army commander could see that his developing strength north of the road was more than adequate, so he directed Branch to change front "so as to incline to the right." Branch did so, angling southeastward across the edge of the high ground and closing in toward the road. Jackson moved with the brigade for at least a short distance. Before long the Tarheels moved on beyond the road and into the cornfield on its south side. Despite Jackson's personal involvement with Branch's brigade in the wheatfield, he did not mention the unit in summarizing the attack. Jackson paid strong compliments to the brigade's earlier advance but mentioned only Archer and Pender and a "general charge" that drove the enemy, "strewing the narrow valley with their dead."[3]

One of Branch's company officers, Walter W. Lenoir of the Thirty-seventh North Carolina, remembered physical fatigue as the paramount sensation during the brigade's attack. Though he was "much exhausted" himself, Lenoir had to support physically two of his men as they tottered across the road in the direction of the cornfield "by letting them lean for a while on my shoulder." Lenoir's entirely understandable exhaustion was shared by a great many of his comrades throughout the army and did not detract from his otherwise worthwhile performance. It does, however, indicate a somewhat more ragged and fallibly human advance than General Branch painted in a decidedly immodest journal entry. "We gained a splendid victory," the general wrote, "and the credit of it is due to my brigade. . . . Other brigades were engaged that did well, but none contributed so much to gain the day as I did."[4]

Branch's brigade bent so far southward during its advance that it made little impact, if indeed any at all, on Gordon's three Federal regiments standing midway up the wood line east of the wheatfield. As a result, the Northerners were able to concentrate their entire fury on Archer's men as those Confederates charged through the naked field. The fire hurt Archer's Tennesseeans, Alabamians, and Georgians, but it did not stop them. Jackson's official report described the musketry into which Archer drove as "a heavy fire." Archer himself used precisely the same three words. A. P. Hill's report deviated by adding an emphatic adjective—"a very heavy fire."[5]

Archer's attack began within minutes after the last of the First Pennsylvania Cavalry survivors limped out of range. The Confederate regiments went over the fence at the west edge of the field and into the open with a fierce yell, then moved somewhat leftward as they advanced, to get onto line with Gordon's front. The Southern soldiers could see the opposite woods "swarming with Yankees" posted "behind the fence on the far side of the field." Archer's leftward slant made the advance appear to waiting Federals to be moving "diagonally across the field" toward them.[6]

The moment Archer's infantry stepped into the open field, heavy fire began to hit some of them. Others remained in defilade until they crossed the residual ravine in the field and reached the crest beyond. At that point the entire brigade line came under the intense fire described so uniformly by Hill, Archer, and Jackson. On that open fire-swept crest where Crawford and the Tenth Maine had suffered before them, Archer's men stumbled to a halt. A member of Archer's Fifth Alabama Battalion admitted: "It was indeed a dreadful moment." Momentum had swung totally to the Southern banner on the battlefield by this time, but Gordon's muskets extracted payment in blood from Archer's brigade for daring to stand in the open in the wheatfield. One of the Second Massachusetts men firing from

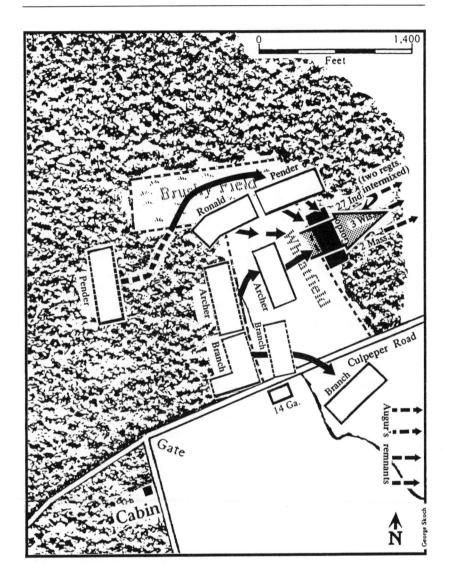

The Confederate Surge across the Wheatfield and Beyond,
7:00–7:30

the eastern wood line saw gaps open in the enemy line that was his target, then "the Rebel line wavered, and became very much broken." Another wrote of "great gaps" torn in Archer's line. An Alabamian admitted to the same result. "Our center was broken," he wrote, "and our right halted."[7]

The Federals inflicting this woe on Archer enjoyed the cover of both the fence and the woods, in which they were "comparatively safe," Archer complained. Their safety was enhanced by orders issued to the men of at least one of the attacking regiments (the First Tennessee) to hold their fire until they reached the east side of the field. Stopping to engage in a firefight was indeed the worst thing the Confederates could have done, so the orders made sense. But the advance withered under Federal fire and halted anyway.[8]

The silent First Tennessee probably began to fire during the halt despite the initial proscription against doing so. Two men of Company G of that regiment, James C. Kelso and James Cashion, suffered peculiar wounds during the unfortunate midfield delay. The two chums had enlisted side by side in 1861, standing literally as well as figuratively arm in arm to be mustered in. They were still side by side in the middle of the wheatfield at Cedar Mountain when a bullet fired by one of Gordon's men went through Kelso's left arm and on into Cashion's right arm. Surgeons eventually amputated both limbs—the same two that had been joined at enlistment—and Kelso and Cashion left the service by the same route through which they entered. (The men lived until 1905 and 1892 respectively.)[9]

The Seventh Tennessee lost two color-bearers shot dead at midfield. Enemy fire severed the staff of the regimental flag, and several officers went down wounded. Among its three dozen losses the Fourteenth Tennessee counted Lieutenant Colonel George A. Harrell, who died six days later in Charlottesville at the age of forty-six. Archer's Nineteenth Georgia also had its colors knocked down twice and lost heavily.[10]

James Jay Archer must have made a remarkably easy target during the deadly delay at midfield as he rode among the regiments trying to get them started anew. One of his men writing a few days later noted that "Gen. Archer was on horseback in the open field and did all that a commander could do." The general's stalwart efforts held the wavering regiments under fire and then prodded them into moving forward once more. An Alabamian credited the First Tennessee Infantry with being the initial firm rallying point. The rest of the brigade rallied on them and then went across the remainder of the

field "with a rush." Henry T. Childs of the First Tennessee described
the rapid assault to the eastern wood line as "a terrific dash for the
fence," made with fixed bayonets and weapons at "trail arms." The
Tennesseeans augmented that armament with their version of "the
wild Rebel yell."[11]

When the screaming Rebels reached the fence that was their goal,
"it was turned bottom side up," and the attackers surged over its
remains with blood pumping high. Bullets whistled by their ears,
but by then very few unwounded Federals remained in sight in the
"dense thicket and jungle." Archer had paid a high price for the
exhilarating opportunity to upend the fence and rout its defenders.
He reported the loss of 19 killed and 116 wounded (though the tabu-
lar loss return adds up to 3 fewer than that). The flying bullets criss-
crossing the middle of the wheatfield left Archer with about half
again as many casualties as Branch's brigade suffered in its adjacent
position during a longer period of combat.[12]

The Stonewall Brigade stood just north of Archer's brigade but
facing across its front—looking nominally south while Archer faced
(and soon advanced) toward the east. The two Southern brigades
obviously could not advance simultaneously into the wheatfield: that
would have mixed them squarely into one another's ranks. Just as
Archer launched his attack into the field, Pender's brigade was groping for the left of the Stonewall Brigade to complete the line and
overwhelm the Federal right. Pender's was the last Confederate force
to come up in time to participate in the main battle. The North Carolinian arrived beside the Stonewall Brigade "about sundown." His
brigade's position at the far Confederate left lay well behind the enemy's front. As we shall soon see, Pender's straw broke the back of
Gordon's camel. Pender's convergence with Archer's axis of advance
squeezed the Stonewall Brigade out of line and left that brigade looking for a job to accomplish, to add to the considerable laurels it already had won. The Stonewall Brigade finally moved south through
the wheatfield to lend a hand across the road in the cornfield.[13]

Before being squeezed out of the line, the Stonewall Brigade made
an attempt to participate in driving Gordon from the eastern edge of
the wheatfield. One man near the left of the brigade reported that
his initial advance began at the moment when Federal movement
into the field gave the Confederates a good target to charge. That
Federal advance cannot have been a general one and probably was
nothing more than a rearrangement in the edge of the woods that no
Southerners saw except those very close to it. Captain Hugh White of

the Fourth Virginia wrote that his unit "advanced through an open field upon the enemy, who fought under the cover of woods" until driven out of them. White was "greatly pleased with the behavior of my boys in the fight." Colonel Charles A. Ronald, commanding the brigade, described the Confederate attack as "a short but very vigorous contest." Ronald did not hint at any advance by his regiments toward the wood line. He simply identified the thrust of his attack as being "in the direction of the main road." Colonel Ronald clearly was content with the attack, noting that his brigade "charged at the proper time." Ronald attributed his modest loss on the day (ten killed, fifty-one wounded in all five regiments combined) to the timeliness of the final assault.[14]

The lot of the Stonewall Brigade doubtless led to substantial confusion. Being pinched out of line and then advancing perpendicular to the route of the rest of the Confederates, and behind them, must have been a highly irregular experience, despite Ronald's general contentment. The experiences of two small groups from the Fourth Virginia are instructive. Captain Hugh A. White of Company I and his brother, together with Stonewall Jackson's kinsman Willie Preston and a handful of others, became separated from the Fourth. Someone told Hugh White that Colonel Ronald had timidly called him back to reform with the brigade, but, White wrote, "I did not know of the order until we were so far ahead that I was unwilling to go back." White did not mention any distaste for Ronald's behavior in justifying his own blatant disregard of orders. He simply reported the episode with apparent nonchalance. By this time, "the Yankees were running, as they only can run," and the White brothers had the scent. The two Lexington men "fell in with another regiment . . . and went ahead."[15]

Young Willie Preston of the Fourth Virginia also pressed ahead into the woods, although he and one or two others lost track of the White brothers and went on alone. Preston and an unidentified lieutenant of the Fourth Virginia found themselves in the midst of a leaderless cluster of men from one of Hill's brigades (perhaps Pender's or, more probably, Archer's). The infantrymen "were very much confused," Preston wrote the next day to his father, "every man acting for himself." Confusion reigned in the dusty and smoky woods just at sundown. Willie Preston and his colleague managed to rally what seemed like a full regiment of men from various commands. The two Virginians placed themselves in front of this polyglot detachment and pressed through the woods, capturing Federals at every turn. Willie shot away every cartridge in his box and captured one Yankee personally. His first test under fire won Willie much applause.[16]

The brave but sad story of Willie Preston ended after only another three weeks of war. Willie spent much of that time around the headquarters of Stonewall Jackson, who had, to use the general's own words, "loved him since he was a little boy." Hunter McGuire wrote that the entire staff "became much attached to the boy, and Jackson in his gentle winning way did his best to make him feel at home and at his ease. The lad's manners were so modest and graceful, his beardless, blue-eyed face so manly, so handsome!" Preston was mortally hit on August 29 at Second Manassas and died during the night, still in his eighteenth year. When Surgeon McGuire brought Mighty Stonewall the news, the general completely lost his composure. Willie Preston's bright moment under the setting sun of August 9 at Cedar Mountain was his first and last military triumph. Captain Hugh White, who had burst ahead of the brigade with Willie at Cedar Mountain, outlived the youngster by one day.[17]

Adjutant Charles Steele Arnall of the Fifth Virginia won plaudits by staying at home and doing his job on the front of the main body of the brigade. Major Williams of the Fifth reported officially that Arnall's "conduct was highly commendable" in rallying the left of the Stonewall Brigade, including the Second and Fourth Virginia, and pushing steadily forward. This large body continued to advance until darkness made further movement impossible. The Second and Fourth crossed the main road to its south side before the main body of the Fifth and the Thirty-third joined them in the corn. Unlike White and Preston, Arnall survived the entire four years of war. He committed suicide in Atlanta in 1905.[18]

The confusion rampant on the field as the battle passed its climax has required many words and pages to unravel. It left some participants remembering the fighting as a complex and lengthy nightmare. Darkness was falling fast when the First Pennsylvania Cavalry charged, and the Confederate attack that immediately ensued cannot have occupied much time. The sun set that evening at 6:56 P.M. A member of the Second Virginia wrote that after the advance began, "the infantry fighting was soon over." When it ended, the entire organized portion of the Stonewall Brigade lay well south of the main road. During the few minutes of their advance, the Virginians had captured "a great many prisoners."[19]

While Archer went right at Gordon's Federals in the east wood line and the Stonewall Brigade found itself pinched out of the line, Pender's North Carolinians swung left and delivered the coup de grace. Stonewall Jackson himself met the head of Pender's column and directed it to proceed "along behind his fighting line to his extreme left," according to Samuel A. Ashe of Pender's staff.[20] This brief encounter must have taken place some time before Jackson rode up to Branch in the southeast corner of the wheatfield with orders to move rightward. Jackson recognized that he had ample resources at hand and needed to spread them wide to exploit the advantage.

Pender's march in obedience to the army commander's instructions was not an easy one. The dense woods between him and the left of the line had been the source of complaints all day long. Pender joined the chorus, citing the "thick woods" as an impediment to his advance. Colonel Ronald of the Stonewall Brigade first noticed the new arrivals as they debouched into the brushy field well to his right. Ronald sent his tireless messenger, Captain John H. Fulton, to advise Pender to deflect eastward to find his assigned spot. Pender, however, reported that he figured this out for himself, and indeed the situation was patently obvious. Fulton probably did not reach Pender in time to be of any use.[21]

A Tennessean watching Pender move into line reported that the new brigade formed "at almost right angles" to Archer's brigade. Pender obviously was to the left of Ronald's Stonewall Brigade when he attacked the Federals. Ronald reported that Pender had tied his right to the left of the Stonewall Brigade. When Pender advanced from Ronald's left, he did so against a dangling Federal flank. Had Ronald advanced simultaneously, he would have moved directly into Archer as the latter moved across the field. The result was the pinching out of the Stonewall Brigade from the front line, as described above. Even Pender had to adjust his axis of attack a bit farther to the left, and he nonetheless soon became entangled with Archer, as will be seen shortly.[22]

Before Pender launched his decisive attack, he took time to ensure the security of his own left flank. That end of his line was exposed, and the general detected enemy activity in the area. With hindsight it is easy to see that nothing could have seriously threatened Pender at this stage in the action, but he behaved prudently in taking a few moments to be certain. Without hesitation, the general detached the Twenty-second North Carolina to swing out well beyond the left of the brigade. Pender thought he saw Federal cavalry, which "scampered off" as the Twenty-second approached them. On reflection, it was a pity that Pender had not had responsibility in this area earlier in the afternoon: his careful attention to his left stood in marked contrast to carelessness in that regard by a number of other Confederates. Pender publicly lauded Lieutenant Colonel Robert Harper Gray and Major Christopher Columbus Cole of the Twenty-second North Carolina for their efforts on the brigade's left. Both men were dead within nine months—Gray of disease the next March and Cole by enemy action at Chancellorsville. Pender himself survived Cole by only a few weeks.[23]

Pender did not stand in his new position for any length of time. "Very shortly" after Pender reached the left, the attack began. Archer's men had rushed into the wheatfield a short time before Pender was ready to move, so the Federal line that was the North Carolinians' target was engaged to its front as the Confederates lunged against its right flank and rear. Archer's temporary difficulty at the middle of the field caused Pender to move somewhat farther east to be sure he would uproot the men (Gordon's) firing at Archer.[24]

Captain Samuel A. Ashe of Pender's staff left an interesting report of his chief's deportment during the climactic advance. According to Ashe, he "had been advised to keep a good lookout on General Pender himself, and try to protect him, for his intrepidity was such that it was thought that he might expose himself unnecessarily." The staff officer accordingly kept an eye on his general. "I was struck by his coolness," Ashe wrote, and by "the entire absence of excitement or emotion." A cool hand was needed on the Confederate left, and that was precisely what Dorsey Pender supplied. Captain Ashe wrote of this episode long after General Pender's death. Pender had paid him a compliment in about the same coin soon after the battle by officially noticing that Ashe "deserves notice for his conduct, being found at every point almost at the same time, cheering the men." Ashe went on to postwar prominence in North Carolina and frequently appeared in print on Confederate topics.[25]

Since Pender's brigade was advancing approximately south and Archer's was advancing approximately east, the two advances inevitably ran into each other. Between them they routed Gordon's brigade of Federals, but not without even more confusion than normally would be attendant on such a violent displacement. Pender brushed the Federal right flank from his path and started it in disarray to the rear before his leading elements came athwart Archer's line. General Archer reported that the collision and intermixing of the two brigades affected only his two left regiments and the right of Pender's brigade, "which was sweeping through from the left oblique across my course."[26]

The two brigade commanders rapidly got together for a brief conference. Archer was swearing like a trooper when Pender found him. Whether Archer was angry because of the hard time he had had in the wheatfield, or emotional and exhilarated by the success opening before them, is not clear. Archer asked his younger colleague, "Pender, do you curse in times like this?" " 'Why no,' replied the General smiling. 'Well I know its wrong, but I be damned if I can help it,' " Archer responded. That point of etiquette established, the two quickly agreed to split the tangled mixture of the two brigades into geographical halves. Pender commanded the left half and Archer the right.[27] An attempt to reorganize the commands on the spot obviously would have foolishly squandered the opportunity of the moment.

Pender's appearance on the right flank and rear of the Federal line sealed a doom that had been clearly in portent for some time. The Second Massachusetts, which was Gordon's left regiment and thus farthest from Pender's threat and the last to flee, clearly understood that its fight had ended when Pender's guns opened in that dangerous quarter. The Bay Staters had no choice but to recoil regardless of the result. The battle broke open at that point. Pender reported that Federals in his front subsequently "made but slight resistance again during the evening." Captain Ashe concurred: "Soon we had everything our own way." The minuscule loss in Pender's brigade—two killed, eleven wounded, and two missing—graphically illustrates the relatively easy time the North Carolinians enjoyed. Pender, however, sold his foe short when he wrote on August 14 to his wife: "The specimen of fighting shown us the other day by the Yankees does not compare to that of the rascals around Richmond. In fact, Pope's men did not fight at all."[28] Pender's judgment in that matter was distorted by his late arrival. Furthermore, he was writing to a wife who was then very unhappy and who held the general on a short leash at the best of times. Perhaps he was lying cheerfully for her sake.

The Federal perspective on Archer's assault and Pender's clinching hammer blow was predictably bleak. Most of the Twenty-seventh Indiana had returned from its premature retreat by the time the crisis hit Gordon's line. If the Third Wisconsin remained in place, it did so in somewhat disjointed fragments amid the rallied Twenty-seventh Indiana. The Hoosiers must have wondered why they had bothered to come back when, shortly after their return, they discovered Pender charging in on their flank at a range of only "twenty paces." Colonel Colgrove of the Twenty-seventh ordered two of his companies to change front to the right, but they did not have nearly enough time to do so before a Confederate volley blew apart resistance on the spot. The North Carolinians "charged literally into the midst" of the Twenty-seventh, according to that unit's regimental history, "and, at the point of the bayonet, demanded their surrender." The same source remembered Confederates demanding capitulation with "fierce oaths and imprecations" followed by gunfire delivered at such short range against those still resisting that some Federals suffered powder-burned faces.[29]

The two flights of the Twenty-seventh Indiana saved the regiment from suffering brutal losses. It incurred fewer than one-third as many casualties as the adjacent but more resolute Second Massachusetts. The New Englanders paid a heavy price for their stout stand as the last organized Federal regiment on the field. With the Twenty-seventh Indiana gone from their right, the Massachusetts soldiers found themselves exposed to a fire of musketry that came "like hail." The roar of musketry "was perfectly deafening" to Charles F. Morse of the Second Massachusetts: "The noise of the bullets through the air was like a gale of wind. . . . It seemed as if only a miracle could save any one."[30]

Major James Savage of the Second Massachusetts fell grievously wounded to a crashing volley of musketry. General Gordon described Pender's volleys with vividly hot imagery: a "terrible . . . dreadful and remorseless fire, that came like a whirlwind, and licked up with its fiery blast more lives than were lost to the Second Regiment and my brigade in any battle of the war." Captain Henry S. Russell hurried to the side of his prostrate major and lay down between Savage and the worst musketry his regiment would ever face. As the fight quickly closed, Private Leavitt C. Durgin also attempted to help Major Savage. Three North Carolinians intercepted him. One of them exchanged blows from clubbed muskets with Durgin before all four ran in separate directions. Durgin survived, only to be killed at Gettysburg; Captain Russell escaped with his life; Major Savage died of his wounds.[31]

One of the Massachusetts men (Charles F. Morse) professed to be astonished when he heard a yelled order to retreat. "I never was more surprised in my life," he wrote. As he fell back, though, this soldier saw the regimental flag with the eagle emblem shot off the staff top and the flag full of holes. Scenes around the unit's aid station were "very painful," and when the regiment made a feeble attempt to muster and reorganize, Morse saw so many huge gaps in the ranks that he finally understood the retreat order.[32]

General Gordon later claimed that the retreat of the Second Massachusetts was triggered by the simultaneous bolting of both the general's horse and that of Colonel George L. Andrews. In fact, the behavior of officers' horses had nothing to do with an event that had become inevitable. Andrews's horse bolted for the best of reasons: two quick wounds, in the neck and shoulder. The animal's panicked trip rearward took a toll on his rider. "The way in which he went plunging into the trees & branches," Andrews wrote, "was somewhat bewildering." The colonel complained a few days later that the buffeting he suffered during the ride left him "very stiff and sore now."[33]

In letters to his wife composed within the week after the battle, Colonel Andrews offered some pungent private comments on what he considered the misuse of his regiment and brigade: "The action was totally unnecessary and about as great a piece of folly as I have ever witnessed on the part of an incompetent general." Even Crawford's dramatic and initially successful venture seemed in hindsight to Andrews to be "an error." "The attack should not have been made on our part with so small a force," he declared emphatically. Colonel Andrews's final pronouncement to his wife had nothing to do with military affairs. With a touch of nature that makes the whole world kin, Andrews pleaded with his wife to abandon her spendthrift ways. "We *must* find a cheaper way to live," he begged.[34]

An Alabamian advancing with Archer's brigade wrote that pursuit of Gordon did not continue long nor was it executed diligently because of the heat-induced weariness of the pursuers. He concluded that Archer might have chased Gordon as far as a mile and a half, but that estimate probably was much too generous.[35] However far Archer and Pender pressed their advantage, they left behind them a wheatfield finally quiet after hours of bitter combat. The field and the surrounding battle-scarred, blood-soaked woods finally passed from center stage in the violent drama of Cedar Mountain. The only noise rising now from the rural farmland in the darkness was the heart-chilling chorus of agonized cries from hundreds of wounded men.

While Archer and Pender reaped a Confederate triumph north of the road, Ewell's infantry rolled forward more than a mile to the

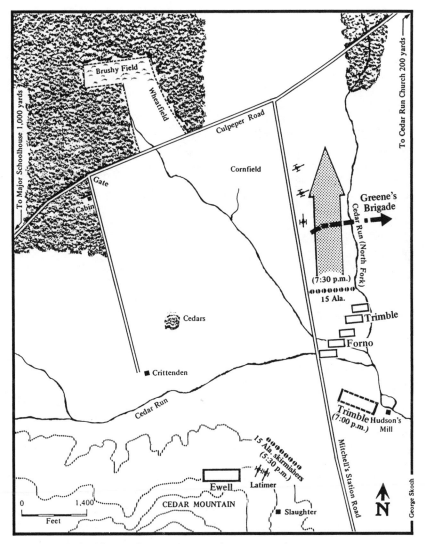

Trimble's Advance Down the Mountain, 5:30–7:30

south on the slopes of Cedar Mountain. The first advance by any of Ewell's force came when the general threw the entire Fifteenth Alabama forward as skirmishers. General Trimble, to whose brigade the regiment belonged, timed that movement at 5:00 P.M., though it may have been somewhat later. Major Alexander A. Lowther led the Fif-

277

*Trimble's route took him down the mountainside below
this point, then hooked left across the low ground
toward the main road. (Clark B. Hall)*

teenth down the hill. The entire regiment in skirmish order must
have made an enormous swarm against the Federal left flank. Their
sheer numbers, combined with the extended nature of Prince's brigade during its attack on Early, left the Fifteenth Alabama in good
position to contribute substantially to the discomfiture of the Federals.[36] Greene's small but unhurt Federal brigade never became involved in the cornfield fight, probably because of the threat posed by
the Fifteenth Alabama and other infantry hovering on the mountain
slope.

The Fifteenth Alabama in its swarming skirmish mode did not
have things entirely its own way. Every foot of elevation it lost in
moving toward the toe of the mountain slope made its men more
vulnerable to the Federal artillery mass on the Mitchell's Station
Road. The loose skirmish order of the regiment reduced the potential for harm of each incoming round, or the Fifteenth might have
been considerably damaged. Major Lowther halted the Fifteenth for
a time near the head of a ravine. During that interval, a shell exploded within a few feet of the face of Captain William C. Oates of
Company G. Miraculously, none of the iron hit Oates although some

of the powder grains from the shell's explosive charge buried themselves in the skin of his face. An Alabamian of Company F was less fortunate. "A solid shot struck [him] . . . and only some few fragments of him were ever found. He had a pair of pants rolled up, which he carried under his arm, and they were carried away and could not be found." Private W. A. Brown, "a good soldier," also fell mortally wounded.[37]

While Lowther and his men dodged shells with mixed results, Trimble's other two regiments, the Twenty-first Georgia and Twenty-first North Carolina, watched the fight from higher up the mountain. Forno's Louisiana Brigade also remained near Latimer's artillery position. At the height of the crisis below them, as all of the infantry prepared to move, the valley of Cedar Run presented a noisy and confusing spectacle. Captain James Cooper Nisbet of the Twenty-first Georgia wrote: "The whole valley was a boiling crater of dust and smoke."[38]

The hilltop infantry spectators soon headed toward the boiling caldron. The Fifteenth Alabama led the movement from its advanced position. Trimble brought his other two regiments along after the Fifteenth, and Ewell personally led the Louisiana brigade forward behind Trimble. Ewell ordered Trimble to head initially for a clump of trees about four hundred yards from the left end (the Confederate right) of the Federal position near the Mitchell's Station Road. En route to that point the two fresh regiments took the lead and the Fifteenth Alabama followed close in their wake. General Trimble would have been pleased to know that he was well enough known across the lines to warrant the spread of a false report of his death. A Washington paper reporting on the advance down Cedar Mountain announced that "Trimble was knocked dead from his horse by the explosion of a shell." The Washington paper was dead wrong. (The newspaper referred to Cedar Mountain as the "sugar-loaf eminence," which conjures up the images of other land masses referred to in that imagery in American military history, notably the costly one in the Ryukyu Islands.)[39]

Federals on the Mitchell's Station Road could easily foretell the loss of their position as they saw Trimble and Ewell sweeping toward them. To Confederates all across the battlefield, however, the sight of their comrades pouring off the hill in support was a thrilling one. "We could plainly see Ewell . . . way off to the right of our line, advancing too," recalled John Worsham, who watched from near the wheatfield. "We could see his skirmish line in front advancing down the mountain, his line of battle following, and his cannon belching forth fire and smoke. . . . It was a magnificent and inspiring sight."[40]

Trimble reached the copse of trees that was his target without difficulty. He promptly pushed two companies as skirmishers to the near side of a fence around the trees and directed them to shoot the enemy cannoneers and horses. The sharpshooters soon began to hurt their targets, but Trimble recognized that the condition of affairs all across the field gave him the opportunity to move boldly right into the midst of the Federal position. The only obstacle to a further advance was the intense "friendly" artillery fire which Latimer and Terry were pouring into the area in front of Trimble from the hillside position Trimble himself had occupied not long before. In Trimble's words, "Our batteries on the hill directing their fire at enemy's battery threw shot &c. right into the space we had to charge over." The general sent back William Duncan McKim of his staff to silence Latimer's interdicting fire.[41]

Trimble's difficulties were compounded by the existence of a mill-pond to his right front. The pond served a mill run by fifty-one-year-old Jerry Hudson and his three children. Had the pond not channeled his front, Trimble easily could have moved farther east around the Federal flank before turning north toward the main road to strike into a tender area. That route would have bypassed the zone being beaten by Latimer's artillery.[42]

Between the "friendly" artillery fire and the constriction imposed by the pond, Trimble lost twenty minutes or more of precious time. The general later expressed disgust with himself for not ignoring the artillery and dashing right ahead. The specter of wounds inflicted by friends, however, is always too ugly to bear no matter what the prospects or consequences. In any event, the nearest Federal battery fired a few rounds of canister at its impatient tormentors near the mill-pond. The canister wounded three members of the Fifteenth Alabama as they prepared themselves for the final charge in the rapidly gathering darkness.[43]

When the artillery fire across their front lifted (perhaps McKim had reached the guns on the mountain?), Ewell's two brigades surged north after the Federals. The Fifteenth Alabama performed as skirmishers yet again while the other regiments advanced en echelon. Trimble formed his two regiments on the right and in front of Forno's Louisiana regiments. The regiments of both brigades also formed en echelon: Trimble's right regiment was slightly ahead of his

*Federal artillery nearing the battlefield on August 9,
according to an original caption. (Library of Congress)*

left one and Forno's were similarly stair-stepped behind to the left
and rear. To Trimble's dismay, the coveted enemy battery "limbered
up and moved off in the darkness, just in time to escape notwithstanding our rapid pursuit," according to a Fifteenth Alabama participant. The general wore his chagrin plainly for all to see. The same
Alabama lad commented that Trimble "was on his mettle chaffing
under disappointment."[44]

Ewell's advancing men stumbled across some consolation prizes in
the darkness when they reached the Federal position. They captured
either one or perhaps two guns (accounts vary), five caissons, an
undetermined number of limbers, several abandoned ambulances,
"several loaded ammunition wagons," and many wounded Federals.
Greene's little Federal infantry brigade, which Ewell had done so
much to pin impotently in place all afternoon, lost two dozen prisoners (and three wounded) during the battle, most of them no doubt at
this juncture.[45]

Although General Trimble had not captured the enemy battery
intact, his frustration was assuaged to some degree by the chance to
make a victorious speech in the midst of the variegated spoils. One

of his North Carolinians recorded the oratorical climax of "a little speech" that Trimble made to compliment the brigade: "Comrades, I feel that I am on my way to my home in Maryland."[46]

Federal fortunes all across the field had run their course. Stonewall Jackson's official report concisely summarized the victorious picture as darkness fell: "Thus repulsed from our left and center, and now pressed by our right, center, and left, the Federal force fell back at every point of their line and commenced retreating, leaving their dead and wounded on the field of battle."[47]

The day was Jackson's, and the general had every reason to believe that the night would be too.

CHAPTER 13

Mopping Up in the Cornfield

As EWELL'S MEN loped north along and near the Mitchell's Station Road they bottled up some of the Federals who had not yet escaped from the cornfield west of that road. Geary's and Prince's brigades of blue-clad troops faced more than they could handle in that sector in the form of five Confederate brigades even before Ewell showed up behind them. Early and Taliaferro had rallied and come forward; Thomas never had fallen back and now surged forward on the right of Early and Taliaferro; Branch had crossed to the south side of the main road at Stonewall Jackson's direction; and the Stonewall Brigade eventually wound up south of the road as well. Before all of those Southerners closed upon them, the more prudent of Prince's and Augur's troops scurried out of harm's way. Ewell's advance north up the Mitchell's Station Road sealed the fate of those Federals who had put off the hour of retreat. They were too late.

We last encountered General Jubal A. Early as he cheered the fire of James A. Walker's aggressive Thirteenth Virginia Infantry from the south edge of the Culpeper Road against the First Pennsylvania Cavalry. Early had been drawn to that hot spot like filings to a magnet, but most of the troops under his command were endeavoring to reorganize back near the Crittenden House at that juncture. The general applauded Walker and his band and unleashed them to press ahead up the road. Early later proudly reported that Walker's men "contributed very largely" to the victory and advanced "as far as any of our troops were advanced until after the conclusion of the fight."[1]

According to one story that made the rounds, the general lost track of Walker's progress and lost his temper as a result. Early was not distinguished for his patience, so the story has that degree of verisimilitude. By this account, Old Jube received and foolishly credited a false report that the Thirteenth Virginia had fallen back once again. In reaction, "Old Jube was red hot, cursing!—the very air smelt of brimstone." When Colonel Walker turned up, Early assailed him harshly: "Where in the h—— is the Thirteenth?" Walker replied in kind: "Gen. Early, d—— it, if you want to find the Thirteenth, go closer to the enemy. It is a mile in front, holding on for you to come up. The Thirteenth don't stay with the wagon-train!"[2]

In the wake of the exciting repulse of the Federal cavalry charge, Early rode rapidly back to his main sphere of responsibility near the Crittenden House. There, amazingly, he discovered an organized body of Federals still standing in opposition to Thomas's brigade and the Twelfth Georgia. Prince's brigade, at least some of it, was sticking stalwartly to its assigned task. The depletion of ammunition among Early's own men and those with Thomas reduced their offensive power and made Early uneasy in a defensive sense even at this late hour. In the enclave at the southern end of the Crittenden Lane, Early did not comprehend the all-encompassing extent of the Confederate tidal wave sweeping the field. The advanced position of Thomas, relative to the rest of the line in front of the Crittenden Lane, had been a defensive boon; but it now left Early nervous about launching that brigade on an attack that might make its own left flank vulnerable. Early described the impediments to moving Thomas promptly forward as "great disadvantages and . . . great danger."[3]

While Early wavered uncharacteristically, he came across General A. P. Hill. That officer told Early that Jackson had spread the word for everyone to pursue on the Culpeper Road, which Hill faithfully was attempting to do with his scattered division. Early responded with the honest assessment that his troops were "much fatigued and in some confusion" and out of ammunition to boot. General Hill strongly advised Early to advance anyway. Perhaps Hill mentioned his own recent unhappy experience with Jackson's rigidity about rote compliance with orders. Early accepted the advice and pushed across the cornfield in the darkness with such men as he could find. Before long he ran into his own division commander, Dick Ewell, near the intersection of the Culpeper and Mitchell's Station roads. Soon thereafter Early's exhausted and disorganized men heard with relief the order to bivouac for the night. Colonel Thomas and his three Georgia regiments followed Early and also bivouacked somewhere east of the Mitchell's Station Road. The Forty-fifth Georgia, and perhaps Thomas's other regiments as well, had advanced with empty cartridge boxes.[4]

Early's experience on his right demonstrated again the degree to which the battlefield's rolling ground created an almost airtight little subbattlefield around the Crittenden House. Near the Culpeper Road, the front line had moved well east of the Lane at a time when

Early continued to face organized opposition. Although Taliaferro's brigade fought immediately to Early's left, it operated in the mainstream action zone near the road. As a result, many of that brigade's men and such of its units as retained at least partial identities were sucked into the vortex of the advance. The most notable of the units was the Fourteenth Georgia Infantry, which did not belong to the brigade. The Georgians, however, had broken from the rear of Thomas's brigade to fight in front of Taliaferro, doing much to save the Virginians in the process. After sharing with the Thirteenth Virginia the center-stage honors against the cavalry charge, the Fourteenth Georgia headed up the attack from Taliaferro's ground. Captain Washington L. Goldsmith of Company K reported that Stonewall Jackson himself led them for a short distance, "in person against the enemy's infantry." Not unreasonably, Goldsmith and the rest "were very proud."[5] Jackson seemed to be everywhere in the gathering darkness, leaving inspiration behind him at each brief stop.

The unfortunate Tenth Virginia returned to Taliaferro's position to join its brigade in the pursuit. The Tenth had spent much of the battle marching to no avail. It had been moved from Taliaferro's line south of the road to shore up Garnett's desperately weak flank—arriving just in time to do no good and to suffer some hurts in the process. After a retreat, the regiment marched back south and rejoined its parent unit after dark. Major Stover of the Tenth reported in very general terms on a pursuit through the corn, followed by orders to fall back into a ravine in the cornfield for the night. Even the Forty-seventh Alabama claimed recovery from its early and earnest flight in time to pursue the enemy "from one field to another." The brigade commander, Colonel A. G. Taliaferro, reported in contradiction of Major Stover that his command camped in advance of the battlefield somewhere.[6]

Any map or word picture that draws discrete military blocks moving through the dark in purposeful pursuit misses the mark by a wide margin. Although the tide clearly flowed eastward in the Confederates' favor, the reality on the ground consisted of knots of disoriented men swirling in the darkness. Their net progress wove a pattern, but that pattern was hardly visible to individuals carrying muskets. Lieutenant Charles Anderson Raine, commanding Company E of Taliaferro's Twenty-third Virginia Infantry, discovered this verity for himself. "In the confusion and disorder" Raine could locate only two of his men, Asa J. and George A. Green, brothers from Halifax County. The three faithfully pressed forward. They soon noticed a dozen or so men advancing in the same direction, from their rear. The Green boys ducked into some trees and busily cocked and uncocked their muskets in frantic imitation of an armed host. To the accompaniment of the Greens' racket, Lieutenant Raine negotiated the surrender of a Captain J. A. Smith from Boston and thirteen unlucky men. The captives expressed some chagrin when they saw the size of their captors' detachment, but the Virginians herded their prizes back in safety.[7]

Ewell and Trimble meanwhile were corking the cask by spearing north up the Mitchell's Station Road. The two brigades with Ewell could not snare Federal prizes with any efficiency because of the chaos and darkness, but they still found the hunting good. Ewell admitted some confusion. "It was too late to distinguish friend from foe," he reported, "and shouting was heard to my left rear of the line of battle." The general halted in the noisy darkness to get his bearings and ascertained that Early was moving at a tangent from Ewell's left toward the main road intersection. The two officers met at the crossroads, then turned right and moved slowly in the direction the fleeing enemy had taken. Ewell had orders to join Jackson in that vicinity, but Hill's division, some of it fresh, clogged the road in front of him.[8]

At some point Ewell found opportunity to use artillery against the retreating enemy. A member of the Twelfth Georgia overhead Ewell ordering the battery commander to open fire. The Georgian insisted that the general used a colorful if not entirely original phrase in the process: "A little more grape, Captain, if you please, for they travel too fast for our boys." Another indication that Ewell's progress through the darkness included further hostile contact comes from the case of Nicholas Baker of the Fifteenth Alabama. Poor Baker managed to get himself captured, presumably during this time of confusion, despite the overwhelming Confederate success all around him. Pat Clark, a twenty-nine-year-old Irishman in the same regiment, also fell into enemy hands, but in his case that result was by design. Clark "fought well for a time, but got tired, and at the battle of Cedar Run . . . deserted to the enemy."[9]

Desultory enemy contact notwithstanding, Ewell did not accomplish much with Trimble's and Forno's brigades once he reached the main intersection and turned eastward. The division commander oversimplified the end of his action when he reported tiredly that "night stopped the pursuit." General Trimble figured that the advance ended perhaps one mile beyond the enemy's original main line.[10]

Tidying up in the cornfield west of the Mitchell's Station Road yielded one very satisfying prize. Brigadier General Henry Prince had fought his brigade hard and rather well but left his own departure from the field until a bit too late. By the general's account, he was walking his horse "in the dense corn, where the ground was heavy" at about 7:45 (fifty minutes after sunset) when Confederates seized his bridle before he knew anyone was near. "I perceived that I was in the midst of enemies before otherwise discovering any person to be there," Prince recalled three months later.[11] For a man in his fifties, Prince had put in a long and difficult day, which now reached an unhappy conclusion. Pope's threats against civilians had prompted orders from Richmond to retaliate on high-ranking Federal officers, and here was a genuine general to practice on. In the event, of course, Pope was consigned to oblivion so quickly that nothing ever came of the threats and counterthreats. In the steamy dark cornfield that night, however, Prince must have reflected on the familiar saying about discretion and valor and fighting again on another day.

Almost inevitably, several Confederates claimed responsibility for snaring Prince and impugned the veracity of other claimants. No doubt several men of Taliaferro's brigade had a hand in the affair, leaving the more aggressive among them to talk about it. Private John M. Booker of Company I, Twenty-third Virginia Infantry, received (and probably deserved) the most credit. Colonel A. G. Taliaferro's official report named Booker as the soldier who brought Prince to him and then took the captive general on to General W. B. Taliaferro nearby. A volunteer aide serving temporarily on Stonewall Jackson's staff heard and recorded Booker's name. General Taliaferro confirmed the circumstances in his official report but did not cite Booker by name. More than three decades later, writing a tribute to Jackson (whom he had hated in life) for Stonewall's widow, Taliaferro embellished the tale a bit, highlighting the hostility resulting from Pope's ugly orders. The Twenty-third Virginia, he wrote, captured part of Prince's brigade and at the same time leveled "a dozen muskets" at Henry Prince. By Taliaferro's late and gilded account, "a sergeant saved his life by calling out, 'Don't shoot him, boys, save him to hang.'"[12]

Another claimant with good credentials from the same brigade was George C. Pile of Company A, Thirty-seventh Virginia. Pile saw a mounted man of obviously high rank some distance ahead and went after him. Prince identified himself by rank, and Pile responded proudly with his name and unit—"of Stonewall's Division." The reflected glory men felt from association with Stonewall Jackson stuck with them through the years and made better fighting men of them in critical moments. "I recall how proud we were to let it be known that we were with Stonewall Jackson," George Pile mused years later as he reflected on his encounter with Prince. (Modern historians working with postwar materials can attest to the syndrome: every stray cavalryman who came under Jackson's aegis even remotely for a week or two had "fought under Jackson," never mind the three and a half years with John Imboden or Samuel Jones.) After the prideful colloquy between blue general and gray private, Prince expressed the opinion that troops visible in the nearby darkness were his own. Pile felt certain they were of Taliaferro's brigade. Pile was right, and Prince was a prisoner.

Military usage required surrender to a commissioned officer. William B. Taliaferro appeared and accepted Prince's sword. When George Pile started to help himself to the revolver in Prince's holster, Taliaferro shooed the lowly yeoman away. After the war Pile offered in support of his claim the testimony of Major Henry Clinton Wood of the Thirty-seventh, an 1862 Lynchburg newspaper account mentioning his name, and the widespread local acceptance of his identity in connection with the exploit.

Both Pile and Booker probably participated in different bits of an incident played out in darkness and stressful confusion. A third vehement claimant was William W. Patteson of the Twenty-first Virginia. Patteson's account does not hold together quite as well as the other two, but it is enthusiastic enough to deserve at least some attention.[13]

Once the various soldiers from the ranks had done their part, Prince belonged to his fellow officers and gentlemen. W. B. Taliaferro held Prince in his personal custody for only a brief period, but it was long enough for the Confederate to appropriate his unfortunate opposite number's horse. That prize did not put Taliaferro in a charitable mood. In his report, Taliaferro declared both unkindly and starkly inaccurately that Prince's command "fled upon our approach with scarcely any opposition." Prince flew upon Taliaferro's approach, of course, to the same degree that Taliaferro was behind other Confederates in getting to the front. In fitting retribution for the Confederate general's canard against his master's efforts,

Prince's captured charger proved a dreadful disappointment to his new owner. The "great big beef of an animal . . . could not rise to ditches and hedges as could the thoroughbred Virginia race horse."[14]

Prince passed to the rear, presumably afoot, and was taken to A. P. Hill while bullets still "were flying briskly around." A witness reported the typically formal-turned-sassy exchange that was virtually de rigueur under those circumstances in that war. Prince: "General, the fortunes of war have thrown me in your hands." Hill: "Damn the fortunes of war, General; get to the rear; you are in danger here."[15]

Not long after Confederates south of the road started their final advance, Branch crossed the road by Jackson's personal direction and joined the enormous conglomeration of units gathering in that quarter. Their location and timing were such that the North Carolinians could contribute little of substance. They gathered up "many prisoners," most of them surrendering voluntarily. Branch advanced in a semblance of order east of the little dry streambed and then south into the cornfield, finally finding Taliaferro's left and halting there. The Seventh North Carolina, which had spent the afternoon imitating a wandering comet, finally came up with the rest of the brigade in this location and joined its four sister regiments in bivouacking for the night. The Seventh's adventures had cost it precisely two men.[16]

During the easy advance that terminated in the cornfield, Colonel James H. Lane of the Twenty-eighth North Carolina came upon a member of his Company F who had fallen out of ranks. The soldier replied to a tongue-lashing with the stout assertion that he was no coward but had succumbed to the extraordinary heat and exertions of the day. Jim Lane, who evidently was tolerant of human frailties (he later administered Virginia Tech), unsnapped his canteen, handed it to the private, and told him to take a "stiff drink" of the liquid encouragement it contained. After the Twenty-eighth and the rest of Branch's brigade had settled into line, Lane moved down the ranks of his regiment complimenting the men on their behavior. When the colonel came opposite his new-found drinking partner, that gallant stepped from ranks, saluted, and said: "Colonel, here I am. I tell you what, that drink you gave me just now has set me up again, and I feel as though I could whip a whole regiment of Yankees." The chronicler of this bacchic tale reported that "everybody was in a good humor" at the time and, not surprisingly, "of course everybody laughed."[17]

The Stonewall Brigade followed Branch's across the road and into the chaotic cornfield, which by that time must have been all but choked with shoulder-to-shoulder Confederates. Elements of the brigade advanced east of the Mitchell's Station Road and halted. Skirmishers moved several hundred yards farther and brought back prisoners, horses, mules, and other prizes. Captain Philip F. Frazer of Company E, Twenty-seventh Virginia, had rallied from the late afternoon difficulties that beset his regiment. Frazer captured a Federal officer and three enlisted men single-handed and turned them over to Stonewall Jackson in person, though they were just what the general did not need to encumber his ride through the darkness. Lieutenant Alfred Mallory Edgar of the same regiment went out hunting in company with two sergeants and a hospital steward and returned to the Twenty-seventh Virginia's lines with a Yankee sergeant and twelve privates as prisoners.[18]

After some time devoted to those forward adventures, the scattered regiments of the Stonewall Brigade fell back a couple of hundred yards and went into bivouac for the night on high ground in the midst of the corn. The Fourth Virginia Infantry of the brigade made preparations to spend the night near the Mitchell's Station Road, where Federal artillery had fought not long before. The artillery firing that soon began farther to the northeast flung some stray rounds into the regiment's ground so the men tiredly picked up and moved back into the corn toward the rest of the brigade. It is difficult to imagine how, in the confusion, brigade commander Charles A. Ronald could have been able to certify that "when the brigade was halted for the night nearly all were present." The report of Lieutenant Colonel Ned Lee of the Thirty-third Virginia implicitly contradicted Ronald. Lee reported that he collected the "somewhat scattered" fragments of several regiments until he had what seemed like half of the brigade with him, then moved this detachment half a mile eastward before finding Ronald with other pieces of the puzzle. Somewhere in the cornfield Ned Lee ran up against another wandering body, whose leader inquired brusquely, "What regiment is that?" Lee responded, with some exaggeration, that his knot of men was the Stonewall Brigade, and turned the query around to the stranger. "I am General Early and his brigade," came the reply.[19]

The final Confederates who poured into the densely populated area of the cornfield came from Garnett's brigade. The individuals of that brigade who had fought alone or in small squads eventually aligned themselves with other like knots until a semblance of order reappeared. General W. B. Taliaferro and several subordinate officers reported on the early evening movements of the brigade in phrases that suggested a smoothly swelling tide advancing across the map with precision. Such reports spoke of capturing prisoners in large numbers, but the mass of Confederates already in front cannot have overlooked many (if any) Federals. No doubt here as elsewhere prisoners disarmed in front of a fluid and advancing line were "recaptured" again and again as they wended their unhappy way rearward.[20]

A more typical experience for Garnett's men was that described by Lieutenant Charles A. Davidson of the First Virginia Battalion. The lieutenant had managed to scrape together only about twenty men from that least distinguished of Garnett's units on this day. He led the little band forward through the cornfield in the wake of the Stonewall Brigade and halted it just short of the Mitchell's Station Road. Davidson did not boast of captured Federals but marveled instead at the number of men from his own brigade who had escaped from enemy hands when the tide turned. The most meaningful transaction for Garnett's brigade that night was not capturing Northerners but welcoming home their own men they had presumed lost.[21]

By the time Thomas, Early, Taliaferro, Trimble, Forno, Branch, Ronald, and Garnett all had poured into the cornfield and its fringes, that small tract of ground contained about as many men as resided in the entire remainder of Culpeper County. The eight brigades constituted the entire army with which Stonewall Jackson had fought his battle, excepting the two late-arriving brigades of Archer and Pender. Even those two finished their advance south of the road, but at a point northeast of the cornfield. Archer and Pender conquered fresh territory as they advanced and in the process captured numbers of untamed Northerners.[22]

One prospective captive who remained untamed approached the Thirty-fourth North Carolina of Pender's brigade in the darkness on horseback. The Federal approached near enough to be identifiable as an enemy officer and asked who the Carolinians were. Before anyone could grab him, the Federal fired a pistol shot, wheeled, and spurred away. A Confederate watching estimated that as many as five hundred shots whizzed past the fleeing Yankee but without apparent effect. The moral of the story, according to the narrator, was that "the Northern army had some brave men and the Confederates some poor marksmen, especially when shooting by starlight."[23]

When the First Tennessee of Archer's brigade emerged east of the woods near the main road intersection, its men ran across the ubiquitous Stonewall Jackson. Their own officers had halted them in the open ground to make an attempt at reorganization. While the men wearily attempted to establish orderly lines, two men rode across their front. One of the mounted men yelled: "Boys, I want to introduce to you Gen. Stonewall Jackson." The famous man took off his hat yet again, as was his trademark this day. The Tennesseeans pulled off their hats, too, and "with the wild Rebel yell saluted the General." In a more businesslike vein, Jackson suggested that skirmishers move onward at once. The entire line stepped out in response, but eventually Lieutenant Colonel Newton J. George led forth a more modestly configured detachment. The dust and smoke had settled somewhat by this time and the bright moon lit the skirmishers' way as they splashed through the muddy but welcome water of the north branch of Cedar Run. The Tennessee lads captured Federals all along the way and ran into trouble only when they came across some alert Confederates of another detachment and barely averted a shooting incident with them.[24]

Long before Archer and Pender and the eight Confederate brigades in the cornfield ceased operations and settled in for the night, Stonewall Jackson had handed the initiative to fresh troops arriving at the tail of A. P. Hill's column. The brigades of General Charles W. Field and Colonel Leroy A. Stafford hardly deserved the label "fresh" by ordinary standards. They had marched just as far as any of the others and under the same brutal conditions; but they had arrived too late to do any daytime fighting. Now Jackson would push them ahead to see what he could do about compounding the Federal rout. The enemy forces ahead in the darkness were confused and disorganized and unhappy—but their numbers had been much increased late in the day and new arrivals steadily continued to augment them.

The abbreviated pursuit by Archer and Pender missed the opportunity to gather in many Federals of Crawford's and especially Gordon's commands because its direction looped so quickly around southward to the road. Gordon headed back to the Brown house when he left the edge of the fatal wheatfield. He found the house jammed with bleeding men and was loath to leave them. Archer and Pender could have corralled many more prisoners in that quarter, but no Confederates ever penetrated that far north of the road. General Alpheus S. Williams sent orders for Gordon to retreat toward Culpeper. Eventually Williams came forward in person to supervise the move. As the two Federal generals fell back they found themselves between the retiring Northern cavalry vedettes and aggressive Southern infantrymen. A heavy volley fired at Williams and Gordon and their large retinue killed two men but hit neither of the generals. Despite this close call Gordon's ranking subordinate insisted that "the pursuit . . . was very feeble." Feeble or not, Gordon retired briskly just ahead of the pursuit.[25]

Across the road, the men of Prince's and Geary's brigades likewise were getting out as and if they could. Banks's chief of artillery, Clermont L. Best, acknowledged the loss of a gun and caisson to Ewell's advance but blamed it on a small stream in which the vehicles became mired. Best claimed that the gun had been spiked and noted that the limber and horses escaped. He also asserted optimistically that he had suffered "no other loss in materiel."[26]

John W. Gilbert of Company K, 102d New York, described his adventures in returning after dark to the field where he had fought in the ranks of Prince's brigade. During the battle Gilbert suffered a freak injury when his chum, an Englishman named Brooks, was hard hit and went down so abruptly that his swinging musket clobbered Gilbert and left him stunned. Gilbert revived during the evening and accompanied one John Drummond back into the regiment's battle positions to look for wounded. Gilbert claimed that the mission was particularly perilous because "the rebels were scouring the field to rob the dead, who had plenty of greenbacks about them, having been paid off a day or two before." Gilbert's suspicion about Confederate willingness to rob corpses was very well founded, but perhaps it is not excessively skeptical to suggest that Gilbert's own foreknowledge may have made him at least as dangerous and willing to return to the field from which a dead man's musket had driven him.[27]

While John Gilbert looked around the battlefield, his highest-ranking commanders put their heads together not far to the rear. Nathaniel Banks had been at or near the front all day. Sergeant A. W. Chillson of Memphis, Michigan, spent the battle at Banks's headquarters and attested to the general's personal bravery, which hardly was in question. Chillson noted two days later in a letter home that Banks often went out to the skirmish line at points where he refused to allow his entourage to follow because of the danger. At one of them the general's horse suffered a wound from small arms fire. By the time Pope arrived and met with Banks at about sunset it was obvious to them as well as to Sergeant Chillson (though perhaps they would have expressed the thought more literately) that "we ware whiped." Why? "Segil & Mcdowel came up to slow," the sergeant thought.[28]

Captain D. D. Jones spent part of August 9 around John Pope's headquarters and recorded his observations in a letter written two days later. Jones was quartermaster of the Eighty-eighth Pennsylvania of General Zealous B. Tower's brigade, Ricketts's division, McDowell's corps. He opened his letter with a droll wordplay: "Well, we have met the enemy, and they are not ours." As Jones looked on during the afternoon, he saw Pope "laying back smoking a cigar with as much sang froid as if the country was at peace." McDowell stared at the ground and both figuratively and literally twiddled his thumbs. Occasionally a sweating and dust-covered staff officer would gallop in and report. Late in the day an orderly rode up with a dispatch that McDowell read and handed to Pope. "The effect of this dispatch was like the fragments of a bombshell falling amongst them," Captain Jones wrote, "for they sprung upon their feet in an instant."[29]

When the paper bombshell finally prompted Pope to movement, the general rode toward the thunderous sound of a battle he had been studiously ignoring. He arrived just at sunset. Pope and Banks met at once. Some undiscriminating soldiers nearby offered a few cheers for Pope (or perhaps they were in recognition of Banks's gritty bravery). The cheers seemed to attract Confederate shelling. The moon was just rising, and its silvery light, here away from the battle's obscuring smoke and dust, made the large group of mounted men feel nakedly exposed. The shells seemed to one of Pope's nervous staff officers to be arriving "half a dozen at a time, hissing, screaming, and bursting over, scattering fragments . . . in nervous contiguity, some striking within ten feet of where I lay." The high-ranking group quickly put another hill between itself and the front, then hugged the ground for what seemed like thirty minutes.[30]

Banks and his men doubtless found far less comfort in Pope's personal move to the front than in the concurrent advance of Ricketts's division of McDowell's corps. More blue-clad soldiery was just the prescription for Banks's ills. General Zealous B. Tower's brigade had been subjected to a pep talk by zealous John Pope himself during the quieter phases of the day. One of the general's audience reported that the remarks were brief and consisted of "telling us he expected great things of us etc." The brigade eventually moved at the double-quick to the edge of the battlefield, arriving just at sunset (about simultaneously with Pope). Its two Pennsylvania and two New York regiments saw almost no action. Three of the regiments did not report casualties, though they doubtless had at least a few; the fourth reported one man wounded. A member of the Ninetieth Pennsylvania described light contact with "a mere skirmish line who kept up a steady fire till midnight when they decamped."[31]

General George L. Hartsuff's brigade of Ricketts's division had stood quiet in the rear all through the day, watching troops head past to do battle with what one of the men referred to as "the 'Mountain Devil' Jackson." Hartsuff commanded four regiments, one each from Pennsylvania and New York and two from Massachusetts. When the Eleventh Pennsylvania finally hurried toward the front, it moved into a bewildering sea of utter chaos. "The scene was one of indescribable excitement," wrote Phil R. Faulk. "My own sensations were of the most peculiarly thrilling character. It was my first battle."[32]

Hartsuff's brigade found more excitement than Tower's, thanks in large part to some indiscreet musicians. As the brigade neared the front by moonlight, which glinted off barrels and bayonets, a foolish regimental band somewhere nearby broke into a loud and incongruous rendition of "Dixie." Four independent accounts from Hartsuff's brigade mention this peculiar episode. The accounts disagree on the identity of the Federal regiment whose band erred so egregiously in its timing, but all accounts easily agreed on the extraordinarily bad judgment involved. Confederate artillery focused on the band's noise, despite its congenial choice of tunes, and filled the night sky above Hartsuff's men with hissing shells. The brigade was strung across "a long naked ridge" at the time, which made the ordeal that much worse. Most of the rounds went long, however, as was typical of Confederate artillery practice that night, and casualties were not very heavy. In retrospect, some of the infantrymen thought the ordeal was fully offset by the hilarity afforded them in watching the shiny band dissolve instantaneously into a panicked mob.[33]

One of Hartsuff's regiments suffered further from "friendly" action that evening. A Confederate shell prompted by the misguided Federal band music caused some confusion in the Twelfth Massachusetts when it exploded in the midst of the regiment. Just as the men restored order, a battery headed toward the rear careened through their ranks with its horses entirely out of control. The regimental historian used a colorful (if perhaps unintentioned) euphemism for the result when he wrote that the passage of the runaway battery "temporarily detached" the Twelfth Massachusetts from the rest of the brigade.[34]

General George L. Hartsuff, a West Pointer just past thirty, did his best to hold the brigade together despite difficulties imposed on it by friends. During the shelling Hartsuff sat tall in his saddle and encouraged the men by both word and example. He even mustered an impressive array of statistics, under the circumstances, to support his point. "Men, remember that it takes a man's weight in lead, even, to kill him; and as for shells, I am not able to give the exact statistics, but they are comparatively harmless, anyway, and it is foolish to dodge." The general observed entirely accurately that dodging at the passing sound was dodging too late. Needless to say, the episode ended precisely like each of several dozen similar Civil War episodes ended (else they would not have been worth the narrator's effort). Just as the general finished his lecture, wrote a witness, "a terrible monster, with unearthly screech, whizzed by, and down he went on to his animal's neck, while the whole brigade burst out laughing." Hartsuff's rejoinder, when the merriment subsided, was: "Well, boys, I couldn't help it. I was always taught to be polite."[35]

Abram Duryea's brigade also suffered more at the hands of friends than foe. It was that sort of night. In the noisy confusion a battery of Federal artillery a half a mile to the rear of Duryea's Ninety-seventh New York "began firing without orders, alike endangering friends and foes." Its shells threatened to pummel a laden ambulance train near the New York regiment. The misguided guns managed to throw fifteen rounds among their putative friends before one of McDowell's staff with a wonderfully militant name, Captain Flamen Ball, dashed back and arrested the battery commander.[36]

The 107th Pennsylvania of Duryea's brigade also became its own worst enemy. Just after dark, when the regiment settled in not far from the front, it received the first mail call in a fortnight. Notwithstanding their proximity to hostile forces, the men exuberantly opened their long-awaited correspondence and lit candles by which to read. The regimental officers realized without prompting that the flickering sea of candles was not a good idea. One slow-witted lieutenant had his extinguished by a superior officer who kicked it out of his hand. Confederate fire poured onto the rapidly darkening target. One minor casualty came indirectly from the fire. A small black boy accompanying the regiment was hiding beneath the frame of an ambulance wagon when a shell exploded in the road. The little fellow "sprang up and struck his head against the axle . . . and fell down dazed, with a scalp wound. He always insisted that he had been hit on the head by that shell." The 107th Pennsylvania cheerfully obeyed orders to fall in and march to the rear. The regimental commander, however, soon dashed down the column and put a halt to the maneuver: a captain had unilaterally determined upon the necessity for a retreat. To complete its ordeal, the regiment later moved closer to the front and found itself trapped between the two violently contending knots of artillery whose duel capped the evening's action. The Pennsylvanians were completely disoriented by this time. They were so thoroughly bewildered that they had no idea which of the groups of belching guns was their own as they huddled inertly under the fireworks display.[37]

An itinerant correspondent recorded vividly the reaction of one Federal regiment on that night of confusion and artillery fire. The regiment had thought itself out of danger just before a barrage hit into its ground. "With a sort of intuition," the correspondent wrote, "the whole regiment rose and ran." He tried to follow, but panic had stripped his limbs of their grace and he could not mount his horse. "Panic took possession of me," the correspondent admitted with unusual frankness for one of his estate. "I grasped my camp-bed, rather by instinct than by choice, and, holding it desperately under my arm, took to my heels . . . the swift iron followed me remorselessly." Few more vivid descriptions of the terrifying effect of Civil War artillery survive. Yet few more telling examples of the relatively light physical effect of that intimidating arm can be offered than the official return of casualties in Ricketts's division. Despite all the artillery furor described in these last few pages, Ricketts reported total losses from all causes as only two dead in the entire division, plus eighty wounded and twenty missing. Although the returns no doubt are incomplete, they reflect few traces of the panic inspired by Confederate shelling and reported so vividly by its victims.[38]

Among the final Federal reinforcements on the scene that night was General Franz Sigel. Sigel finally had located the only road from Sperryville to Culpeper and moved down it as ordered. When he neared the battlefield, Sigel's warrior spirit at last took hold of him. Witnesses reported that the German general was a wild man behind the lines after dark, yelling at straggling and retreating men, getting artillery sorted out, and generally behaving with frenzied energy. Sigel berated the long-suffering Second Massachusetts, among others, for falling back, but apologized when General Gordon explained to him with some asperity the regiment's accomplishments on the field.[39]

Perhaps it was just as well for the Federal cause that Franz Sigel did not have a chance to apply his bravado to a genuine military situation. By the time Sigel stormed into the melee behind the Federal front line, the battle had run its course. The final act to be played out involved Hill's last unused brigades in a tentative advance through the darkness to see what they might run against. The probe led to an artillery duel in which the Confederates' best gunner on the field bit off far more than he could chew and suffered accordingly.

CHAPTER 14

After Dark

STONEWALL JACKSON'S unfailingly aggressive tendencies were the key to most of his successes. While his troops thronging the cornfield puffed and wheezed and counted their limbs and gave thanks for a narrow escape, Jackson thought only of pressing ahead and exploiting his advantage. The general summarized his aspirations in his official report: "Though late, I was so desirous of reaching Culpeper Court-House before morning as to induce me to pursue. . . . But owing to the darkness of the night it was necessary to move cautiously."[1]

Before he could contemplate any such renewal, Jackson faced the necessity of taking stock and reorganizing. As one observer reported, "It was now dark and the pursuit ceased for a time." An officer with Jackson's headquarters came across the general in the main road trying to sort out the tactical situation after darkness, while the "great heat" had halted the advance. The heat that had dominated men's minds and bodies all day long did not succumb easily to the darkness. At 8:00 P.M., slightly more than an hour after sunset, the thermometer still stood at 86°. There was no measurable breeze.[2]

Jackson's insistence on moving toward Culpeper prompted him to detail some of Captain Crittenden's men as guides to lead the army in that direction. The battle had been fought in large part on the captain's family's property. Crittenden's company of the Thirteenth Virginia had been known at the beginning of the war as the Culpeper Minute Men. Perhaps A. P. Hill suggested that expedient to Jackson. Hill was also a Culpeper man and the former colonel of the Thirteenth Virginia. When Captain Keith Boswell of Jackson's staff moved forward through the darkness after escorting the wounded Major Holliday to the rear, he found his chief and A. P. Hill together east of the main intersection and "near the crossing of North Fork of Cedar Creek." The two generals promptly sent Boswell back whence he came with orders to bring up Field's brigade of Hill's division.

Field's was one of the two unused brigades in the division. Jackson intended to use those units as his spearhead.[3]

Jackson also received welcome word that at least some of his cavalry was coming up and soon would be available. Charles T. O'Ferrall, who would become a Virginia politician of importance later in the century, rode in quest of Jackson in company with a squad of men. O'Ferrall had orders from the colonel of the Twelfth Virginia Cavalry to deliver a written message to the army commander. He found Jackson near the same point Boswell had, sitting by a piece of artillery, eating a raw onion and a piece of hardtack. O'Ferrall delivered his written message and received one in like format. Unfortunately, he never knew the content of either, and the originals do not survive.[4]

General William B. Taliaferro looked up Jackson to report on the location and condition of his newly inherited division. The report must have discouraged Jackson and convinced him that the division would be of no further use because he uncharacteristically issued orders "to permit the troops to rest for the night." Perhaps as a result of his encounter with Taliaferro, Jackson sent Sandie Pendleton and Charles M. Blackford back among the troops to ask the various brigadiers whether the men "were in a condition to advance after a short rest." Each responded without hesitation "that their men were too exhausted to go further." Marching, fighting, and the oppressive weather had left the troops so tired that most sprawled dead asleep on the ground when the staff officers wandered among them. "I do not believe anything short of the enemy could have revived them to action," Blackford wrote.[5]

Stonewall himself had been seen all over the front during the pursuit immediately after the battle broke open. His peripatetic wanderings put him in touch with elements of virtually every brigade on the field. At one point the general stumbled across his young friend and kinsman Willie Preston as Willie was completing his highly successful first battle. Young Preston had just suffered the discouragement of finding no one willing to volunteer to accompany him farther to the front on a scout when, as he wrote to his father, "to my joy, I suddenly found General Jackson just by me." Willie enthusiastically dashed over to his famous friend and "slapped him on the leg, and . . . slapped his horse so hard that he came near jumping from under the rider. But some allowance must be made for me, as it was the first time I had ever been under fire." The boy enlisted Stonewall as an ally in his quest for volunteers, and the general obediently followed him toward the reluctant troops nearby. "I called out that

General Jackson was coming," Willie remembered, "and I thought the heavens would have been rent with the cheers." When the noise abated and Jackson said something about volunteers, "it was hard to keep the whole regiment from springing forward to volunteer."[6] (This episode bears a resemblance to the encounter between Jackson and the First Tennessee, recounted in the last chapter; the two affairs may indeed have been one and the same.)

Jackson discovered during his moonlit reconnaissances that Cedar Run posed an impediment to his desire to advance across a broad front. Although the run was not particularly deep or wide, its banks and bottom constituted an obstacle that Confederate artillery could not negotiate in the darkness. The only place the artillery could cross either branch was on the road. That factor slowed preparations for the advance and, of course, funneled it at least temporarily into a narrow channel.[7]

When Hill's artillery splashed across the run and spread out away from the road, Jackson directed it to fire into the woods just ahead around Cedar Run Church to roust out any Federals who might be lurking there. The division's entire artillery complement shelled the woods "vigorously" and "for some minutes." Crutchfield mentioned participation by the batteries of William J. Pegram, William C. Fleet, Carter M. Braxton, and Alexander C. Latham. As Jackson watched the pyrotechnics from a position not far from the guns, an officer dashed up on horseback and began to address the general in a fashion that made it clear that he was a confused Yankee. Something tipped the lost Northerner to his mistake before he had said more than a few words and he whirled to flee. Confederates all around demanded the Federal's surrender, but he raced away heedless. Some infantrymen eventually gave up the attempt to capture the officer and shot him dead from his horse, then delivered the horse and the dead man's papers to Jackson.[8]

The two infantry brigades upon which Jackson was counting for a fresh thrust arrived at the front about concurrently with the artillery effort to feel out the woods around Cedar Run Church. A Catholic chaplain, Louis-Hippolyte Gache, who advanced with the Tenth Louisiana Infantry of Leroy A. Stafford's brigade, watched artillery bursts peppering the "rather thick forest of pine and oak" in front and thought that he detected a heavy Federal force in the woods. The militant priest found it "thrilling to watch the shells streaking through the air, then bursting against the trees with a blast as loud as that with which they had been fired; or to see them fall between trees into the air." Gache's only complaint about the show was that darkness and the thickness of the trees kept him "from enjoying the sight of Yankees fleeing in panic from the very place where they had hoped to entrap us."9

In fact, few Yankees had been lurking in the woods. The brigades of Ricketts's division were settling into a new line across a field from the woods that Hill and Jackson were shelling. (The nominal east-west road axis in use throughout this book becomes strained during the night phase of the action, which took place at a point where the road toward Culpeper had swung back to a predominantly northerly route. To stick with the nominal convention, however, Ricketts was forming up well east of the east edge of the Cedar Run Church woods while Jackson was shelling those woods from their west.) The brigades of Tower and Hartsuff formed on the Federal right of the road, extending in an arc nearly to the Brown house. The brigades of Samuel S. Carroll and Duryea formed on the Federal left of the road behind the Hudson house. Ricketts placed two batteries on his right near the Brown house and two others straddling the main road. These latter two looked down the road toward the almost empty woods crackling under Jackson's precautionary pummeling.10

Hill and Jackson were out of Federal sight beyond the woods as they aligned the two brigades that were to advance after the barrage ended. Field's three Virginia regiments and a battalion spread into line on the left (north) of the road. They had spent the day broiling and choking in a marching position that Field disgustedly identified as "the rear of the whole army." Despite efforts to hurry forward, the crush of animals and vehicles and men in the road denied the brigade any chance to move steadily. When Field finally reached the front, the main action was just ending. (For evidence that one of the regiments of this brigade may have taken part in the final assault, see note 28 of Chapter 12.) A. P. Hill formed Field's troops in the midst of the carnage and sent them ahead toward the near edge of the woods where Stonewall Jackson waited impatiently.11

Stafford's Louisiana regiments on the right formed in position before Field's came up across the road, giving Chaplain Gache time to enjoy the fire and brimstone pouring into the woods. The Louisiana troops had suffered through the inevitable marching travails of the day but apparently arrived in better shape than Field's men. Captain Henry Monier of the Tenth Louisiana wrote in his diary of a "harassing and rapid" march, but he also noted that the regiment stacked arms on the battlefield and took a rest before moving beyond it toward Jackson's advance post.[12]

Once Jackson was satisfied with the extent of the shelling, Stafford advanced into the woods ahead of Field as well as to his right. The two brigades constituted a formation en echelon. General Hill remained near his units and closely observed their progress. He reported that Stafford moved into the woods "feeling his way cautiously, skirmishing, and taking prisoners." Stafford remarked on the denseness of the woods—an attribute no doubt very much enhanced by the darkness—and reported that he pushed through against "heavy skirmishing" with Federals. A soldier of the Twenty-ninth Ohio of Geary's brigade reported that the Confederates were "yelling and cheering as they came." The Ohioan seemed disappointed when the "rebel horde" halted on the edge of the woods instead of continuing forward against the new Federal position.[13]

When Colonel Stafford reached the far edge of the woods, he found the enemy opposite him. The Federals seemed to be a "large force, much superior to my own, and in line of battle" in an open field. Although the Federal force was not yet firmly in line, it did indeed outnumber Stafford's substantially. Even after Field pulled level with Stafford across the road, the Federals outnumbered the two brigades by more than two to one. Jackson reined in Stafford at the edge of the woods and told him to form his column perpendicular to the road along a fence that separated the woods from the field. General Field's position on the left of the road lay a bit closer to hostile infantry because of the configuration of the enemy line. Field somewhat egocentrically reported the presence of the enemy on his side of the road as though none threatened elsewhere. Stafford enjoyed the presence of a portion of the Seventh Virginia Cavalry off his right flank and part of the Sixth Virginia Cavalry advanced on the road. Field's left flank had no such mounted protection and doubtless felt naked.[14]

Chaplain Louis-Hippolyte Gache had neither training nor experience as a tactician, but he and Stonewall Jackson evaluated their mutual prospects identically at the northeast edge of the woods. From his location on Stafford's far right, Gache could see Yankees several hundred yards ahead in woods beyond the Hudson house. He presumed that "our artillery . . . was soon going to do to the second wood what it had done with notable success to the first." Jackson was of like mind. The reconnaissance by artillery fire that worked for the initial advance should work again. Both men were to be sorely disappointed with the results.[15]

As Field and Stafford and their few cavalry accompaniments reached the northeastern edge of the Cedar Run Church woods, the forward elements of both armies were in a state of flux. Ricketts had not completed the formation of his division straddling the road ahead of the Confederates, and Stafford and Field remained uncertain of how to proceed. Jackson's determination to reconnoiter by artillery fire made sense at the time and still does. Federals nearby in disarray offered a tempting target. What harm could come from shooting a few of them with cannon?

Although the entire artillery complement of Hill's division had shelled the woods a few minutes earlier, only one battery stood close to the front and ready to unlimber. No Confederate at Cedar Mountain was, and no student of the Army of Northern Virginia should be, surprised at the identity of the battery pressed farthest to the front: it was Willie Pegram's. That unflinchingly combative youngster lay close at hand and eager for renewed opportunity to fight. Jackson personally ordered Pegram to the edge of the woods with his four guns, there to open "with shell and canister." The latter commodity was indicative of the short ranges involved.[16]

In the moonlit confusion, Pegram and other Confederate leaders sought to identify the nature and extent of their targets. Artillery colonel Stapleton Crutchfield described the concentration opposite Pegram as "what was thought and proved to be the enemy's camp." That peculiarly (and inaccurately) domestic label for the outer crust of a solidifying military position said something about Confederate uncertainty at the time. To penetrate the veil, Pegram made a personal scout into the no-man's land just in front of the woods. A member of the Seventh Indiana named W. S. Odell reported years later on an encounter with Pegram close to the Federal front. According to Odell's extravagant account, "a young officer mounted on a thoroughbred mare, wearing a linen duster over his uniform, with a Havelock cover over his cap" rode up with a group of Federal officers. When the rest left, the duster-clad horseman remained behind and after a time exclaimed: "You look like Yankees." Despite that suspicious remark, the Hoosiers complacently allowed the mounted man to position their outposts before he rode away. Odell reported with assurance that the horseman was Willie Pegram.[17]

James M. Hendricks of the Second Virginia Infantry of the Stonewall Brigade saw Odell's tale in print and offered confirmation.

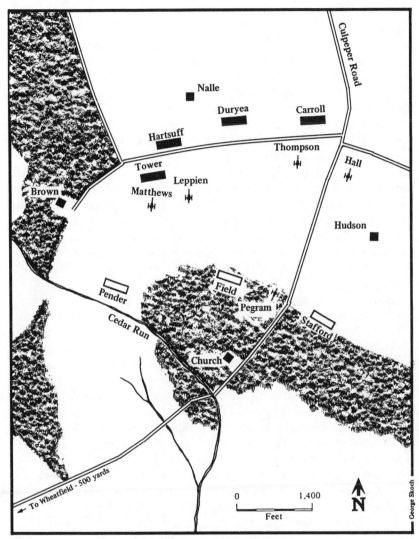

Pegram's Ordeal at Night

Pegram did indeed sport a linen duster and a visor on August 9, Hendricks asserted. Furthermore, an account circulated through the Confederate army that Pegram had ridden "into the Yankee lines, looking for a place to plant his battery, and was captured." That story lost its credence when Pegram turned up on August 10, but the currency of the rumor at the time offers substantiation for a Pegram exploit of some description.[18]

A more modest Confederate account of Pegram's adventure suggested that the captain scouted close to the Federal lines but not into their midst. In that version, Willie impulsively undertook to resolve a disagreement about the identity of some troops dimly visible through the darkness. Turning to his ranking subordinate, Lieutenant (later Major) Joe McGraw, Pegram said: "McGraw, I shall ride up close to these fellows; keep a sharp lookout, and if you see me wave my hat, open all the guns." Willie dashed across the field to within a few yards of the unidentified soldiers, who were, of course, Federals, and reined in his horse. Within moments he knew enough to signal with a waving hat and then tear back toward his guns at full speed. Pegram found Jackson in the midst of the artillery pieces. McGraw apparently had not taken literally the suggestion to shoot past and around the hat-waving captain because Pegram now "with great glee" ordered his guns to open. "Pitch in, men," he cried, "General Jackson's looking at you!"[19]

Pegram's four guns covered what A. P. Hill described as "a little knoll upon the margin of the field." The little knoll stood just to the left (northwest) of the road and slightly beyond the edge of the woods. As it emerged from the woods, the roadbed was cut into the rising ground, so when the guns pulled up out of it onto the knoll they seemed very much elevated and exposed. The knoll's height and the surprise attending the opening blasts conspired to win a brief early success for Pegram. The first round striking into the Seventh Indiana's ground hit seven men. Shells hurled into the Federal confusion, which Pegram had personally reconnoitered, scattered Northerners in every direction. Stonewall Jackson's official report, based on an eyewitness view, described the initial rounds from the knoll as a "well-directed and unexpected fire [which] produced much disorder and confusion among that portion of the Federal troops." Willie Pegram himself wrote of hearing the Federals in the field "in great confusion, the officers trying to make their men charge upon me, and the men running."[20]

Pegram's early success probably included some of the fire at incautiously lighted Federal targets, which was described at the end of the last chapter in connection with the arrival of Ricketts's various brigades. One of Geary's Ohioans reported that Pegram aimed at campfires "foolishly kindled" by teamsters, who stampeded at once. Lights in use at the Fifth Ohio's field hospital far to the rear attracted other

The view from Pegram's knoll in 1989. (Clark B. Hall)

rounds. (The Cincinnati correspondent who reported this incident pointed out with uncommon mildness that the Confederates could have had no idea that they were shooting up a hospital.) Some particularly careless Northerners on the infantry line also had built little fires for brewing an evening cup of coffee. Pegram's opening rounds cleared the area within the firelit arcs in an instant. Confederates looking across the field could distinctly see men "rushing headlong to the rear" past the fires.[21]

David Nichol of Knap's Pennsylvania Battery watched Pegram in operation with the eye of a fellow artillerist. Nichols and his battery by this time were veterans of five hours of combat during which they had fired thirteen hundred rounds—all of them that afternoon in their maiden battle. Nichols marveled at Pegram's "daring & brave" cannoneers, who hurled canister from "the edge of woods on a rising knoll, while right below them in the hollow were a Brigade of Infantry of ours." He declared that the range was so short (about four hundred yards) that Federal artillerists could distinctly hear the Confederate officers' orders.[22]

Colonel Adrian R. Root of the Ninety-fourth New York of Tower's brigade did not mention any candles or fires as target points on his front but felt that the moonlight did more than enough to make him an alluring target. The colonel wrote to his mother that the moon shone "with a beautiful clear lustre . . . showing our position to the enemy." Confederate artillery sizzling toward the New Yorkers prompted all of them except the field officers to stretch flat on the ground. "I was too proud to do it," wrote Root. Once they became acclimated to the noise, Root and his men discovered that Pegram was shooting far over their heads, and they relaxed to watch the show. They could hear Southern voices shouting orders, and sometimes they could glimpse the Confederate artillerists through the smoke. The Ninety-fourth New York lost no one to Pegram's fire. Root did not have to watch long before the spectacle before him turned in favor of his side. Federal response to Pegram was, from Root's perspective, dramatic, explosive, and exciting.[23]

Within a short time after Pegram's auspicious beginning, the Confederate artillery knoll came under a torrent of counterfire from three Federal batteries supporting Ricketts's division. Pegram had been facing somewhat leftward from the road, delivering most of his fire against the right of the enemy infantry line. From that direction George F. Leppien's Fifth Maine Battery returned a steady and accurate fire. The range was so short that now Pegram's men could hear New England voices shouting orders. Leppien's Yankees quickly picked up the precise range ("which was short") from Pegram's muzzle flashes. Far worse was fire right down the road from two other batteries, which seemed to the Confederates to come in "obliquely and . . . at our backs." The two well-served Northern batteries were James A. Hall's Second Maine Battery on the Federal left of the road and James Thompson's Pennsylvania guns on the Federal right of the road. A fourth battery at the far right of Ricketts's line, Ezra W. Matthews's from Pennsylvania, did not impress the Confederates. Jackson, A. P. Hill, and Field each mentioned the terrible concentric fire of three batteries.[24]

Thompson and Hall played havoc with Pegram despite some slight protection the Confederates enjoyed from their knoll. Thompson soon discovered that his two Parrott rifles could not hit their target with flat trajectory fire. The Pennsylvanian's two twelve-pounder howitzers, however, lobbed rounds in with dreadful effect at short range. While the howitzers looped shells over the knoll's crest, the two rifles fired at an angle into the wood line on either side of Pegram's position against the Confederate infantry they accurately guessed would be there.[25]

On Pegram's left, Field's Virginians crouched helpless in the edge of the woods. The brigade reported seven men killed in action at Cedar Mountain; presumably most or all of those fatal casualties came at this difficult spot. General Field displayed the same leftward orientation he exhibited in describing the Federal position when he reported his location as "a little to the left front" of Pegram. The only way Field was in front of the artillery was by assuming that "front" lay leftward. A. P. Hill properly described Field's passive position as "a little in rear of Pegram."[26]

Stafford's Louisianans on the right of the road had somewhat less to contend against than Field's men because the midpoint of the Federal artillery deployment was toward the Confederate left of center. Even so, Stafford's troops suffered extensively from the artillery that was battering Pegram. During the night the brigade lost four men killed and twenty wounded. Colonel Stafford felt obliged to admit in his formal report that two officers, Lieutenant Benjamin F. Jackson and Captain Alfred A. Singletary, absented themselves without leave at the height of the night battle. Despite this suggestion of cowardice, Singletary reached the rank of major in October 1863.[27]

Chaplain Louis-Hippolyte Gache of the Tenth Louisiana recorded his personal ordeal on Stafford's far right. The Tenth had advanced about fifty yards beyond the woods into the field when the artillery opened, perhaps to straighten the line vis-à-vis the Federals ahead of them. The chaplain had wandered back near the wood line to conduct his overdue personal evening prayer when a shell thundered into the trees alarmingly close. Gache led his horse over to Major John M. Legett, a twenty-seven-year-old New Orleans lawyer born in Scotland, and asked naively, "What is the meaning of this, Major?" Legett suggested reasonably enough that Gache should "lie down and keep quiet." As the intensity of the Federal fire increased, the chaplain noticed with discomfort that some rounds flew through the two-yard-wide space between him and the similarly recumbent major.[28]

Although the infantry in the wood line suffered to some degree, they were on light duty by contrast with the gunners serving Pegram's four pieces. The little knoll at the edge of the field quickly turned into hell in a very small place when three batteries converged their fire upon it from the outer edge of an arc. J. W. D. Farrar went into action with one of Pegram's pieces, probably the far left one, serving as the Number 8 man in the gun drill. Farrar's gun had fired "only . . . a few rounds" before casualties moved him up the ladder to serve as both Number 3 and 4 in an abbreviated crew consisting of only four men. Several caissons exploded under fire, horses fell shrieking on all sides, and Farrar himself went down wounded after firing only a dozen or so rounds. Farrar thought that his wound was mortal, but he recovered to tell the tale and to offer the judgment that this night ordeal "was one of the hottest actions the battery was ever in." Considering Pegram's penchant for hot spots, that judgment speaks vividly of the nature of the August 9 artillery fight.[29]

A cavalryman named Harry Gilmor, who had been supporting the center of the advance before it bogged down, curiously if imprudently moved forward through the woods toward the hot spot. There he found an old acquaintance from Baltimore, Lieutenant Mercer Featherston, serving with Pegram. The cavalryman quickly determined to leave a dangerous place where duty did not force him to stay, but as he bade Featherston farewell "a spherical case shell came thundering through the wood." The shell beheaded Mercer Featherston, tore through a horse behind him, and exploded in the body of a second animal. Gilmor helped with the frightful task of extracting his friend's remains from the caldron of torn horseflesh and then went back whence he had come. Before Gilmor got away, at least two more of the artillerists had been beheaded by shells. These mortal head shots testified to the dreadful efficiency of Thompson's howitzers lobbing rounds over the edge of the knoll.[30]

Pegram stubbornly stuck to the knoll past the time when he could hope to accomplish enough to offset his losses. In fact, he characteristically clung to the position until losses left him literally no longer able to serve the weapons. General Field reported from his vantage point just to Pegram's left that the famous battery "fully sustained the reputation made on other fields." Pegram himself described the knoll in a letter written five days later as "a very hot place." The captain credited God's mercy for his personal escape despite four bullet holes through his coat. One sharpshooter in particular fired eight or ten times "with deliberate aim," Willie calculated. Pegram concluded with a mixture of plaintiveness and renewed aggression: "If they had brought another battery by me, we could have whipped them."[31]

Why did not Jackson or Hill order up more batteries to support Pegram? Four of them had participated in shelling the woods through which the Confederates advanced to the position now so hard beset. The answer must have been that the Southern high command saw the uselessness of forcing more fodder into the meatgrinder. Another battery next to Pegram's would only serve as a larger target. Confederate artillery on the right or the left of the line would have done Pegram some good at the same time that it did the opposing Federals some harm. The only way to reach positions on that wider arc, however, was by way of the road and then the field: artillery could not move directly through the thick woods in daylight, to say nothing of darkness. To move through the woods on the road, past Pegram's dangerous position, and then through the field with a flank exposed to punishment the whole way obviously was impossible or at the very least impracticable. The question remains, however: What could the Confederates have done differently and better? Not much, other than get Pegram out of the mess more rapidly, and that ran counter to the young captain's code of behavior.

Confederates removed from the vortex of the tornado knew full well that someone was catching it ahead of them, but they had the liberty to marvel innocently at the pyrotechnical display. A cavalryman at Ewell's headquarters waxed nothing less than lyrical: "If there is anything in war that can be called splendidly beautiful, it is a night cannonade, when high overhead, in the very middle, apparently, of the black field, the hissing shells fly in curving lines of beauty, leaving behind them a track of sparkling flame, until the explosion blazes a lurid glare all around the sky, which can be likened to nothing better than to the fitful flashing of aurora in her most gorgeous masquerades."[32]

Jed Hotchkiss of Jackson's staff, who obviously was not at the front with his chief, wrote that "the whole horizon was lighted up by the flashes . . . [of] one of the most active artillery duels I have ever seen." An Alabamian named Fulton, of Archer's brigade, who apparently was closer to the front than Hotchkiss, complained that some stray rounds rustled the trees over his night bivouac. The tired infantryman "longed for a place where I could rest in peace, such rest as one gets under such circumstances being anything but satisfactory." Fulton tormented himself under the shelling with thoughts of "home, sweet home, and the comfort of a soft feather bed."[33]

Not surprisingly, the view of the artillery exchange from the Federal ground was vastly more pleasing than that of the Confederates who stared into the fiery red mouth of the monster. A staff officer in the Federal rear called the exchange "the most furious fire I ever heard. It was a steady roar, and the blazing of the guns, the bursting of shells, and the vast columns of white smoke obscuring the woods and piling up like snow mountains in the moonlight was a scene . . . dramatic and grand." General Alpheus S. Williams did not command the troops opposite Pegram but he came up to watch gleefully as the Confederate battery was "knocked . . . to pieces rapidly." General Williams quickly noticed, as everyone else on his side of the line had, that Pegram was shooting very high, so the general stood in the open and watched the "flaming pyrotechnic display" in complete safety.[34]

Zealous B. Tower's brigade actually lay between the opposing guns, or nearly so, in what should have been an uneasy location. The high Southern fire spared them any pain, however, and left them quietly waiting to repel attackers. None came. Charles S. McClenthen of the Twenty-sixth New York described the shower of shot and shell passing over as so thick "that an ordinary sized thunder storm would be but a 'tempest in a teapot' compared to it." John D. Vautier of the Eighty-eighth Pennsylvania wrote in his diary: "The thunder of the cannon were awful, while the screaming & groaning of the Solid Shot & Shells was appalling." Joseph A. McLean of the same regiment insisted in a letter to his wife that "when the rebels was shelling us it looked perfectly grand. First the fuse in the shell would be seen dashing through the air with lightning speed. Then the sharp whiz as it cut the air over us. Next the sound of the gun 'booming' in the distance, the explosion of the shell next, the shells crossing and recrossing."[35] Enchantment and danger clearly functioned in a starkly inverse ratio.

The Federal onlookers had opportunity the next day to walk across the field to the abandoned knoll where Pegram had fought the night before. Many of them commented on the chaos wrought by the three batteries on Confederate matériel, horses, and men. General Williams counted twenty dead Confederate horses and "several" dead men, including a lieutenant; evidently Pegram departed in such a crippled state that he could not even bring off Mercer Featherston's body or those of his other dead. Alonzo Sterrett of the Twenty-ninth Ohio also counted the dead horses bearing Confederate brands but found only ten of them. David Nichol of Knap's battery counted eleven. Charles McClenthen of the Twenty-sixth New York viewed the scene more qualitatively than quantitatively. He found the ground "strewn with dead men and horses" and thought it "a splendid sight, and as we seemed to be perfectly safe we enjoyed it hugely." A journalist who had been scared by Pegram's opening rounds the night before described his daylight tour of the knoll where "a signal vengeance" had overtaken his tormentors: "Some splinters of wheel and an overturned caisson, with eight horses lying in a group,—their hoofs extended like index boards, their necks elongated along the ground, and their bodies swollen."[36]

The duration of Pegram's stand on the knoll remains (together

*These dead horses on the battlefield may well be strewn
across the knoll on which Willie Pegram took a pounding
after nightfall. (Library of Congress)*

with every other time estimate from any of the war's battles) a legiti-
mate subject for debate. The most common suggestion was that an
hour or so elapsed from the battery's first round until it fell completely silent. The reported time estimates are as follows: General
Field, "an hour"; Colonel R. L. Walker, "an hour or more"; A. P. Hill,
"soon silenced"; Jackson, "for some time"; and Major D. A. Grimsley
of the Sixth Virginia Cavalry, who was the battle's leading contemporary historian, "an hour or more." One circumstantial bit of evidence
about the duration arises from a consideration of ammunition consumed. Pegram doubtless had burned all or nearly all that he had
available during the afternoon fight. It seems unlikely that he could
have refilled his chests entirely during the short lull between rounds
of the battle. After the night action began, the battery threw "about
eight rounds from each gun" in clearing the woods around Cedar
Run Church. Pegram clearly did not have adequate ammunition to
fire rapidly for more than an hour, if indeed for that long.[37]

Estimates of the hour at which the artillery exchange ended vary
much more widely than do estimates of its duration. Participants
honestly endeavoring to time the day's events regularly described a
floating window of two or two and one-half hours in breadth. It is

hardly surprising, then, to find declarations that the barrage ceased at 8:45 P.M.; began at 10:00 P.M.; ended at 10:00 P.M.; and continued "till nearly midnight." Willie Pegram himself wrote a few days later that after the enemy opened fire, "we had it until nearly 12 o'clock at night."[38]

Whenever Pegram's fire ended, it marked the suspension of Confederate offensive action for the night. No Southern infantryman or artillerist would advance farther during the campaign. As A. P. Hill declared succinctly in his official report: "No further attempt was made to advance." Pegram remained near the silent guns until early morning when they were withdrawn, doubtless with help from troops other than the battery's own battered survivors. The salvage operation apparently ignored the Confederate corpses scattered on the knoll. The cavalry detachments pulled back to the vicinity of the wheatfield at about midnight, but Field and Stafford clung to the edge of the wood line until daylight and captured several prisoners during their stay. When Willie Pegram shepherded his remnants toward the rear, he must have known that his brave efforts had not been productive of any good. He took pride in the stand nonetheless. In a contemporary letter the bespectacled captain noted with pleasure that Generals Hill and Field had each recommended him for promotion based on his work at Cedar Mountain. The promotion, Willie admitted, "I do want."[39]

At the same time that Willie Pegram was using his artillery to launch one Confederate attack and then failing in a second effort, his colleagues of the cavalry arm explored far out on the flank, advancing farther into Federal country than any other Southerners reached. In fact, they galloped right through the yard of John Pope's headquarters.

Beverly H. Robertson had given Jackson no good reason during the day to revise the negative opinion that had prompted the army commander to send out an emergency call for Jeb Stuart. The fragmentation of the available cavalry force on fugitive missions in every direction, which could not be blamed on Robertson, had left Jackson without much mounted strength on the battlefield. Some Southern cavalry did advance at sunset as Jackson swept the field, notably along the banks of Cedar Run between the Crittenden House and Cedar Mountain. Robertson was not in evidence, however, and Jackson felt the absence of an active and energetic mounted arm. Not long after the charge of the First Pennsylvania Cavalry, when it became obvious that a Confederate advance would sweep through the

dissolving Federal line, Jackson asked among his couriers for someone who knew Robertson. John Blue spoke up. Jackson wrote a note
and suggested that Blue ride out on the right in quest of Robertson.
Blue eventually found Robertson and delivered the message.[40]

Whatever response General Robertson made to the message from
Jackson did not propel him onto center stage. The cavalry commander's actions during the hours of darkness remain unknown and
apparently unimportant. Robertson's energetic if grumpy subordinate, W. E. "Grumble" Jones, however, soon arrived on the field and
promptly swung into action. Jones had spent the day out toward
Madison Court House, covering twenty-five miles on the fruitless
round-trip. When he returned late in the day to a point in the army's
wake and discovered the battle raging, Jones "moved on without a
moment's delay" to the sound of the guns. Grumble could not locate
Stonewall Jackson or, fortunately, Beverly Robertson, so he took
A. P. Hill's advice to pursue the enemy on any promising tack. Jones
slipped between Field's and Early's brigades with a sizable body of the
Seventh Virginia Cavalry and headed toward the right. Judging from
the infantry gap he passed, Jones must have moved ahead of the
Confederate main line after it had reached the Mitchell's Station
Road but before the advance into the woods around Cedar Run
Church.[41]

The extensive woods around Cedar Run Church blocked effective
cavalry movement. Even had they not, Grumble Jones needed to
swing wide to avoid hitting enemy infantry head on. The cavalrymen
felt their way through the darkness, leaving the woods well to their
left, and eventually came in view of the main Federal line from a
position northeast of the Hudson house. Grumble sent a courier
back toward the Confederate artillery he could see firing on the enemy with orders to inform the Southern gunners of the location and
extent of the potential target. This probably coincided with the lull
before Pegram's ordeal.[42]

Grumble Jones quite properly hesitated to charge into the Federal
strength he could see opposite him in the moonlight. While Jones
waited for his opportunity, one of the private soldiers in his command approached a personal crisis. The cavalryman was one of two
brothers in the regiment. One brother was very brave; the other
could not face fire and had reached August 9, 1862, without ever
once being forced to do so. In the darkness beyond the Federal left
flank, an officer prepared to remedy that cowardly behavior. When
the order to charge finally came, the Confederate officer pricked the

"mettled" horse of the coward with a drawn saber and crowded man and horse alike into the action. Federal response was limited. A ragged discharge sent a few generally harmless rounds past the Confederate cavalry. One bullet hit the coward and killed him on the spot. No one else was touched. Perhaps the unfortunate soldier had been privy to a vivid and all-too-accurate premonition when he finally was forced to face the elephant.[43]

The first and last charge of the luckless timid cavalryman swept through the shadowed moonlight against no less a target than John Pope and most of his fellow generals in blue. Grumble Jones and his men did not know at the time that their quarry was so desirable or they surely would have accomplished more than they did. No more tempting prey than John Pope existed at that stage of the war. The spectacle of Pope in Richmond on trial for his infamous anticivilian orders would have been irresistible to the Confederates. Jones simply attacked mounted men who seemed to offer an inviting target. He had no idea of their rank. In reporting on the brief affair, Grumble described it as "a gallant charge on our part" and added without any apparent sense of irony: "We killed one of their horses."[44]

Jones was doing a fine job in discharging cavalry's role in the darkness and deserves better than disparaging hindsight. It is not hard, however, to grasp the differing lot of Civil War infantry and cavalry as revealed in Jones's brief phrase. Infantry in both blue and gray uniforms lay dead in windrows a few thousand yards to the southwest as the nighttime cavalry charge gallantly reached its climax, and with what result? "We killed one of their horses."

The braid-bedizened line and staff officers on the receiving end of Jones's charge suffered through a harrowing succession of difficulties. General Gordon recalled that Pope and most of the other officers were "reclining" on the ground when they noticed the Southern cavalry about forty yards from them. A staff officer in the group wrote that his first notice of danger came when he "heard some trampling in the wood and presently a body of cavalry issued from the forest and passed along until their flank entirely covered our position." The Confederates paused, then came on in a yelling mass, pouring in "a rapid and continuous volley from carbines and pistols." A Southern witness described how the Rebel horsemen "dashed from the thicket and madly spurred towards them."[45]

The knot of reclining Northern officers dissolved as though by magic. They leaped to their feet and raced for their nearby horses "in hot haste," as one of them put it. As they ran, "bullets hissed through the bushes, sparkled in the darkness as they struck the flinty road, or singing through the tree-tops, covered Pope and his officers with leaves and twigs." None of the august assemblage stood on the order of his going. Dignity was not a priority. Pope himself scrambled on his horse, "stuck his head down and, striking spur, led off at full speed." General Banks went down in the confusion, apparently dead or wounded. In fact, he had been struck savagely by the forefoot of the horse of a mortally wounded orderly as the animal reared in terror. Banks managed to escape capture or further injury, though his hip was "badly hurt." Perhaps the general also suffered some bruises, since a sergeant detailed at headquarters wrote home that Banks was hurt "by someone riding against him."[46]

General Alpheus Williams reported on this tangled moonlight encounter from the vantage point of a front-row saddle. Williams was among the high-ranking Federal officers who scrambled energetically out of harm's way. He believed that the flying Southern bullets failed to do much execution because they all spun too high. Williams had the same experience with Willie Pegram's artillery fire this evening; the Confederate problem seemed to be universal among the arms. Alpheus Williams maintained enough poise and perspective to sense the humorous aspect of Pope's skedaddle. The undignified rout "became laughable in spite of its danger," the general wrote. The danger increased and the humor dwindled when a "friendly" regiment about five hundred yards away opened indiscriminate musketry on the noisy galloping men of both sides. As Williams put it, the Federals "opened fire with very little regard to friend or foe, and I fear killed some of our horses if nothing else." A staff officer fleeing with Williams reported that two enlisted men were killed by the misguided Federal volley.[47]

One of the speeding Northern staff officers marveled at his deliverance. "The balls struck around us so rapidly that I thought it impossible for anyone to escape," he recalled. At the moment when the "friendly" regiment to the rear also took the officers under fire, most of them were scrambling through a hollow and as a result escaped that new threat. Half a dozen of the officers ended their flight abruptly when they crashed blindly and at full tilt into a rail fence five rails high "and wound up in a cursing struggling knot." Pope turned up missing in the confusion, and for a time uncertainty about his fate was the topic of the moment.

To make matters even worse for the stirred-up Yankees, the artillery action going on intermittently to the southwest snared them as well. Some nearby Federal pieces shooting at Confederates prompted other Federals farther to the rear to shoot at their own friends nearer the front. "One of our batteries on a hill behind opened a rapid fire on our front batteries," complained a frustrated staff officer. One of the "friendly" shells landed in the midst of the generals and burst directly beneath General Gordon's horse. Outraged and unrefined shouts of "Stop him! Stop that damned ass!" and other such shrieks finally halted the barrage.[48]

The unwelcomed barrage actually did some good from the Federal perspective. Grumble Jones had kept after the fleeing enemy horsemen to the limited extent that he could control an all-but-uncontrollable night ruckus, but the enemy artillery sweeping the field convinced him "to seek the shelter of a friendly hill until they had sufficiently amused themselves." Soon thereafter Jones and his horsemen headed back toward friendly lines. They left behind some thoroughly shaken Federal commanders, who gradually relaxed and went to chatting "on a pile of fence rails under a tree." A staff officer with them soon began to rhapsodize about the silvery moonlight, shooting stars, the blue firmament, and the red planet Mars. The emergency obviously had ended.[49]

Grumble Jones accomplished more than frightening Pope during his sortie, deeply satisfying as that achievement would have been to the Southerner had he been aware of it at the time. Jones also took back with him fifteen prisoners—eleven privates, three lieutenants, and one black. The latter proved to be an invaluable prize because he was an officer's servant who knew that Sigel was arriving to reinforce Banks and Pope. When Jones learned this from his captive, he promptly communicated the important intelligence to army headquarters. Stonewall Jackson acknowledged the value of Jones's news and in his official report declared that on that basis he abandoned plans for any further attempt to advance. The men of Jones's command heard of this intelligence coup and thought they had done a good thing. Indeed they had.[50] Grumble Jones had used his cavalry well, but he had done so on his own initiative. There can be no doubt that Stonewall Jackson noticed that General Beverly Robertson had nothing to do with the brightest moment Confederate cavalry enjoyed at Cedar Mountain.

Although Stonewall Jackson told no one else at the time, the intelligence Jones uncovered about Federal reinforcement did not come as news to the army commander, but rather as confirmation. Benjamin F. Stringfellow, the Confederate scout whom we last heard from in

Chapter 1 as he knocked out a henpecked Northern soldier, was back behind Federal lines again during the afternoon's battle. Stringfellow watched from a clump of trees on the Union flank and rear as the enemy line reeled back toward him. He also watched fresh Northern troops filing steadily into the battle zone. When the scout found a chance to creep from his copse and snare a straggler, he found that the captive belonged to Sigel's corps. Stringfellow thanked his victim for the information, apologized in advance, then knocked the poor chap unconscious with the butt of his pistol and hurried for friendly lines. Jackson atypically acknowledged by name the scout who delivered this early warning of enemy movements when he cited "Farrow, my most reliable scout." John Farrow was a newly commissioned officer of irregular troops, with whom Stringfellow was working and to whom the scout apparently had reported. The reason that Jackson mentioned Farrow by name was that the partisan officer had been killed long before the general wrote his report and not long after the battle of Cedar Mountain.[51]

The Federal situation as described by the Stringfellow-Farrow scouting tandem and Grumble Jones's contraband left Stonewall Jackson no hope for further advance that night. Morning's light would not offer any brighter prospects for Jackson, but with the bit in his teeth that ever-aggressive officer doubtless hoped that his abandonment of the initiative on the night of August 9 was a temporary expedient. By the time he left the front at about 11:00 P.M.,[52] Stonewall had reached the point of physical exhaustion. The general did not display signs of the chronic long-term stress fatigue that had rendered him ineffective around Richmond six weeks earlier. The events of August 9 had simply worn out the man behind the legend. Jackson had used himself up for the day.

As Stonewall Jackson wearily made his way rearward across his blood-stained battlefield he received a peculiar tribute that testified to his fame at that stage of the war. The several hundred Northern prisoners gathered in guarded groups did not suffer from broken spirits by any means. A Virginia artillerist noted that the captives were not particularly crestfallen. Reasonably enough, the unfortunate Federals looked "as if they had done their best and had nothing of which to be ashamed." When these self-confident prisoners identified Jackson and his headquarters cavalcade as it rode past, they sent up a friendly cheer for the famous victor of the day.[53]

The general also passed some older and more constant friends on his trek back across the battlefield when he rode through the bivouac of the Stonewall Brigade. The Valley soldiers recognized their old leader in the moonlight, jumped to their feet, and filled the air with "enthusiastic cheers." For his part, Jackson applauded the brigade's exploits during the day. When the affectionate demonstration quieted down, the general asked Colonel Lawson Botts of the Second Virginia if he knew where some buttermilk could be had. Jackson always had been fond of that pungent beverage and particularly craved it during the frequent episodes when he suffered from real or imagined stomach miseries. A clever soldier muttered, "The Buttermilk Rangers have gobbled that up." ("Buttermilk Ranger" was a Southern soldier euphemism for rear-echelon people with soft jobs and a reputation for avoiding field service.) Several men volunteered to hunt for a supply, of course, just as three of King David's mighty men turned a passing phrase into a quest for water from the Well of Bethlehem (2 Sam. 23:15–17). The Confederate scavengers dodged no hostile Philistines in their quest and apparently found what Jackson craved, or so an enlisted man at the scene reported. A staff officer's account of the episode asserts that it ended in failure, but staff officers always have been prone to miss the word.[54]

With or without the soothing buttermilk, Jackson remained "excessively fatigued and terribly hungry" as he looked for a place to rest. The few roofs on and near the battlefield sheltered hundreds of wounded, leaving hundreds more outdoors. The "utterly worn out" Jackson found a likely stretch of undisturbed grass and prepared to spend the night there in the open. Someone rounded up a bit of food for the general at this point, but he rejected it: "No, I want *rest*, nothing but *rest*!" A staff officer spread a cloth on the ground and without further ado Stonewall "wrapped himself in his old cloak, stretched himself flat on his breast under a tree, and instantly fell asleep."[55]

Jackson's staff promptly followed their leader to rest. One noted that when he dismounted, his hard-used horse "laid down immediately and seemed utterly worn out"; the last three words precisely mirrored another staff officer's description of Jackson's state. C. M. Blackford and A. S. Pendleton divided a can of sardines between them, drank some malodorous but badly needed water trapped in a horse's hoof track, and fell dead asleep. In the morning Blackford awoke to find Pendleton gone, a dead man nearby, and bloody water in the horse track to which he had had recourse.[56]

Jed Hotchkiss of Jackson's staff headed farther to the rear in search of food and comfort. (The famous mapmaker waxed more militant with ink than powder through the war, as a careful examination of his writings makes clear.) Hotchkiss found General Lawton with the wagons at Crooked Run Church. During the night orders came from the front to move the wagons forward. Thousands of men were longing for the food they contained. Hotchkiss went up with the wagon train and slept under some trees on a hill near the battlefield.[57]

Stonewall Jackson and his helpers went to sleep before they heard good news arriving from the rear. After midnight the army received about the best reinforcement it reasonably could expect under the circumstances when Jeb Stuart arrived. As McHenry Howard sorrowfully accompanied General Winder's body southward toward Orange, he met a cavalry detachment coming into the main road from the east. Howard worried that the horsemen might be enemy and if so that they would refuse to allow him to go about his melancholy mission. After a few worried moments, the Marylander recognized Jeb Stuart's features. Stuart eagerly absorbed what information Howard could give him about the battle and then spurred forward toward Cedar Mountain.[58]

While Jackson slept and Stuart rode, infantry and artillery officers all across the Confederate front struggled to ready their units for the possibility of renewed combat on the morrow. Hours of intense action had emptied cartridge boxes and limber chests, which required refilling. Lieutenant John C. Carpenter, who had assumed command of his mortally wounded brother's Virginia battery, labored energetically to repair the broken pole of an abandoned limber. Carpenter promptly put that right but was forced to admit that at least two or three of his men were exhausted and unable to do further service. Private William J. Winn of the battery was a worse case. Winn had left the battery that morning when battle loomed near, a stunt he had "been in the habit of doing," Carpenter reported.[59]

The tired but proud boys of Dement's Maryland Battery scavenged through the abandoned enemy gun and accessories on the Mitchell's Station Road. In the limber they found a note left by its former owners and signed by a lieutenant: "Take this gun, and make as good use of it as I have." The Marylanders were sure the note paid grudging tribute to them and that they had played the leading part in battering the abandoned piece into submission.[60] Trimble's infantry would have challenged that view, but in fact there was credit enough to go around.

Some Confederate infantry remained alert and in a skirmishing posture all through the night. Field and Stafford held onto the wood line just behind Willie Pegram's battered knoll. Farther left, General Pender personally commanded a strong group of skirmishers drawn from the regiments of his brigade, which maintained desultory contact with the enemy through the night. These Carolinians apparently held a point not far from Field's left, beyond Cedar Run and at the edge of "an old sedge field." All through the hours of darkness Pender's pickets gathered in stray Federals and sent them to the rear. The general sternly enforced the discipline necessary to accomplish his purpose. He allowed no lights and no talking above the level of a whisper.[61]

Behind Pender the silence of the night was regularly broken by the cries of more than two thousand wounded men. A member of the Thirty-third North Carolina of Branch's brigade noted that the moon, which "was already far up when we desisted from the pursuit," shone down with ironic sweetness on a "festival of blood." Wounded men thirsted dreadfully for water: "On every side, the groans of the wounded and dying and the imploring cries for water, water, fell upon [our] ears."[62]

George Neese of the Confederate horse artillery spent the night in the horrible shambles of the wheatfield amid uncounted corpses and "the pitiful groans of the wounded and the low weakly murmurs of the dying." A band playing homely tunes had lulled Neese to sleep near Orange the night before. Tonight he longed to have it near to play a dirge loudly enough to drown out the ghastly human chorus. The same lovely moon about which Neese had rhapsodized on August 8 hung again "in an unclouded sky and bathes the plains . . . with a sea of mellow light . . . a weird silvery glow nearly as light as day . . . falls and lingers on many upturned faces that are as cold as marble and wearing the pallid and ghastly hue that can alone be painted by the Angel of death." It is hardly surprising that the experience prompted young Neese to write: "If this cruel war lasts seventy-five years . . . I hope that I will never be compelled to bivouac on another fresh battlefield."[63]

John Blue, whose record of his travels with Jackson during the day provides much of what we know about the general's activities, wound up that night in the wheatfield not far from George Neese. When Blue returned to the center of the battlefield from carrying a message to Beverly Robertson, Jackson had disappeared. The courier sat to wait for Jackson in the wheatfield, allowing his famished horse to feast on one of the shocks of grain. Blue had not slept for two nights, and his body cried for rest. Even after he "stuck a finger in each ear to drown the moans, prayers and cries of the wounded and dying," Blue could not sleep. One nearby sufferer pleaded for water until the cavalryman went and got him some from the little stream branch in the field. As he filled the canteen, Blue thought that by moonlight the water "looked as red as blood," but he admitted that his imagination might have been working too hard.

The badly wounded lad (Blue never mentioned his affiliation) fell into a coma after his drink. John Blue sat patiently beside the unconscious man, watching for Jackson on the road and watching his thirsty charge for signs of wakening. The continuing cries from all across the large field had pretty thoroughly demoralized Blue by this time. "I felt, to tell the truth, more like a baby than a soldier," he admitted. Blue rapidly nodded off to sleep and knew no more until morning. When he awoke, the man beside him was dead.[64]

Other Confederates worked steadily through the night in well-organized efforts to succor their wounded friends. Joseph Franklin Kauffman of the Tenth Virginia was one of two men in his company detailed on August 9 to carry off the wounded. The other fellow fell wounded early in the action and Kauffman carried on alone. On his third trip after darkness Kauffman located Lieutenant David C. Grayson and carried him to the rear. On two later trips the tired soldier brought off the corpses of Lieutenant John W. Mauck and Sergeant James O. Wood. Although he had slept very little the preceding night because of marching and the enemy cavalry scares, Kauffman stuck to his gruesome chores until daylight. On the evening of August 10 he finally was able to lie down and, not surprisingly, "slept soundly." Less than three weeks later he himself would find a soldier's grave on the battlefield of Manassas.[65]

Chaplain Louis-Hippolyte Gache of the Tenth Louisiana saw and described the plight of many sufferers of both sides but was unable to help them for a remarkable and peculiar sectarian reason. Gache saw with "a profound sadness: so many men only a few hours before so full of life now lying wounded, mutilated and grotesquely contorted." One agonized man thought Gache was a surgeon and pleaded with him to cut off his leg at once, and above the knee. The delirious man claimed he could feel gangrene setting in and described it as purple in color. Gache responded with spiritual counsel, but "the poor fellow was a Protestant Yankee; what I was saying meant nothing to him." Even the Southern Protestants fell outside Gache's power to help, he felt, and by some special dispensation not a single Catholic on either side came within the chaplain's view.[66]

The few wounded Federals within their own lines enjoyed better care than their mates in Confederate hands or the Confederate wounded because the Northern surgeons had far more equipment and supplies and a much smaller volume of business. Because the Confederates held the entire scene of the battle, the better-prepared medical department on the scene had little to do while the under-equipped Confederates had far more than they could manage. The large number of wounded Federals clustered in and near the Brown house benefited from Confederate ignorance, indifference, or compassion through the night. Southern skirmishers spent the night virtually in the yard but never made a move to capture the enemy wounded. The next day those suffering Federals had the good fortune to enter the Northern medical apparatus, en route home.[67]

A Northern correspondent close behind the front line described the night as a pleasant one—"fine starlight, a transparent atmosphere . . . and a fragrance of sweet-clover blossoms." His description of the staggering stream of wounded pouring past him stands in stark contrast to nature's gentle setting:

> As soon as the firing ceased, the ambulance corps went ahead and began to gather up the wounded. . . . The spectacle . . . was of a terrible character. The roads were packed with ambulances, creaking under fearful weights, and rod by rod, the teams were stopped, to accommodate other sufferers who had fallen or fainted on the walk. A crippled man would cling to the tail of a wagon, while the tongue would be burdened with two, sustaining themselves by the backs of the horses. . . . Friends who had passed me hopeful and humorous the day before, now [were] crawling wearily with a shattered leg or dumb with a stiff and dripping jaw. . . . Imagine a common clay road, in a quiet, rolling country, packed with bleeding people,—the fences down, horsemen riding through the fields, wagons blocking the way, reinforcements in dark columns hurrying up, the shouting of the well to the ill, and the feeble replies.[68]

Inevitably there were those who fell to looting as soon as the musketry quieted and darkness covered the field. Some men of the Forty-seventh Virginia of Field's brigade located four gallons of whiskey and passed it around. The whiskey was, of course, "cheerfully consumed," General Field himself helping with one of the jugs, according to an enlisted man. The same men also rounded up some abandoned sutler's goods and had their way with them. Soldiers "barefooted with bleeding feet and ragged clothing and bareheaded" found solace in stores of honey, canned goods, and "rare and delicious delicacies." Soon they were waxing eloquent about patriotism and loyalty, sentiments easier to come by when well fed and well watered.[69]

Still other Confederates circulated among the dead and wounded stealing clothes and other articles. "Their number was greater than you might suppose," wrote a witness, who reported with disgust seeing two men fighting over a corpse's canteen. Some of the dead were stripped entirely naked during the night by men who needed the clothes for their own use.[70]

Most of Jackson's army quietly slept the sleep of exhaustion, both physical and emotional, while some few of their comrades looted and stole, or tenderly cared for the wounded of both sides, or fought intermittently from vigilant posts at the front. A simple Alabama soldier described a typical experience in a letter he wrote to his mother four days later. After boasting about the Confederate success, Private James P. Crowder of the Forty-seventh Alabama told his mother simply: "I slep all a monkst the ded yankes that night."[71]

CHAPTER 15

August 10

THE HOT SUN of August 10, 1862, dawned on the ugliest sight ever witnessed in Culpeper County, Virginia. More than two thousand men lay wounded and in agony across a few acres beneath Cedar Mountain. Hundreds more corpses covered the ground among the wounded. Most of the mangled men had been in superb condition and full of spirits fifteen hours earlier.

Not many minutes after sunrise musketry echoed across the landscape again, but at a scattering skirmish level hardly reminiscent of the preceding day's mighty roar. Jed Hotchkiss wrote at the time that firing began again at 6:00 A.M. An observer in Federal country timed the opening at 5:30. The listening Northerner described the fire as "a faint rattling of musketry . . . which continued for several hours." Still another observer declared that the skirmishing turned "brisk" and that renewed battle seemed imminent.[1]

The Confederate units near the front bore the brunt of this early morning activity. Field's brigade stood near and to the left of the knoll where Pegram had suffered so heavily in the darkness. Stafford's Louisiana regiments remained in the edge of the woods across the road just to Field's right. The third Confederate group consisted of the forward elements of Archer's and Pender's brigades, somewhere to Field's left rear. Field's Virginians retired without difficulty through the woods behind him. They set up in a picketing position that probably was somewhere in the eastern edge of the woods east of the wheatfield. There they remained undisturbed until "late evening," when Field received orders for a further retirement.[2]

Stafford's brigade had more difficulty than Field in disengaging. The Louisiana troops had skirmished all night from the fence line at the outer edge of the woods around Cedar Run Church. During the morning hours Companies C and F of the Tenth Louisiana assumed picket duties. A hot localized fight flared up. The Southerners held their ground but lost four men killed and three wounded in the process. Some regiments had passed through the previous day's battle less hard hit than that. All four of the dead men—Patrick Feeny, Edward Martin, William Quinn, and Michael Slavin—were natives of Ireland. At 10:00 A.M. Stafford received orders to fall back from the fence line. He was able to do so in reasonably good order a little before 11:00.[3]

Farther to the Confederate left the skirmishers from Pender's and Archer's mixed brigades spent a nervous night and found some targets at dawn. Lieutenant George H. Mills of the Sixteenth North Carolina had about thirty men well to the front and enjoyed a surprisingly quiet night and early morning with them. At about 9:00 A.M. orders reached Mills to fall back stealthily in an hour. The last hour included some lively skirmishing, but the Tarheels held on and then cheerfully headed back away from the pressure.[4]

In that same quarter A. P. Hill established an artillery strong point to protect the Confederate left as it bent back from the front. Hill sent Lieutenant Colonel R. L. Walker out to find a position well to the left but west of the creek. Walker found a likely spot and emplaced two of his own batteries and one from Early's division at a point that "commanded the enemy's camp, somewhat to their rear." The purpose of the movement was defensive, however, and Walker's guns remained silent.[5]

A similar retrenchment on the Confederate right anchored that flank and left Jackson's front on very solid ground. Ewell described his movement on the right quaintly: "I was remanded to Slaughter Mountain." Back he went with his troops (apparently still excluding Early) up the slopes to his aerie on the mountain's shoulder. General Trimble timed the return at 6:00 A.M. and reported that its purpose was to stop a rumored enemy flanking effort. Ewell's men remained on the now familiar hillside all day.[6]

While the infantry dithered, Jeb Stuart went to work with the underused cavalry of the army. No evidence survives to establish the time at which Stuart and Jackson first met at Cedar Mountain. The cavalryman certainly arrived more than an hour after Stonewall collapsed into the deep sleep he craved, so the initial meeting of the two leaders doubtless took place early on August 10. Jackson must have been ecstatic to see his friend, who held the potential to find out just what Beverly Robertson could not: "Where is the enemy?" The circumstances of Jackson's hurried telegram seeking a visit from Stuart have been recounted in Chapter 1. Jackson also had been decidedly frank in writing to Stuart on August 7 just before the army began the march that led to Cedar Mountain. "I wish you could bring your command up," Jackson had written, offering the suggestion that an inspection of the cavalry with the army might serve as a subterfuge. The army commander hoped the inspection would take place "during active operations; as I may thereby secure your services for the time being."[7]

Jackson carried the charade into his official report, in which he declared that Stuart's fortuitous arrival was "on a tour of inspection." Given Jackson's absolutely rigid moral code about most things, his white lie about Stuart takes on remarkable dimensions. In a more straightforward vein, Jackson simply stated that Stuart assumed command of the cavalry "at my request . . . and made a reconnaissance."[8]

Jeb Stuart went about the reconnaissance his friend so badly needed with the energy that characterized the brilliant cavalryman throughout the war. An admiring Jedediah Hotchkiss, no doubt mirroring the appreciation of his own chief, Jackson, wrote in his diary that Stuart "went out on our right and nearly around the enemy's left." That is precisely what Stuart and his horsemen did, although it was appreciably harder in the saddle than Hotchkiss's simple sentence sounds. Stuart's purpose as assigned by Jackson was "gaining information respecting the numbers and movements of the enemy." Ahead of the main cavalry force went a detachment ordered by Stuart to capture the signal station on Mt. Pony, well behind Federal lines near Culpeper. Stuart would not only acquire information; he also would deny information-gathering facilities to the enemy.[9]

The mounted men followed Stuart—and Robertson, who went along—around the nose of Cedar Mountain and out onto the beautiful level plain opening eastward and southeastward toward the Orange and Alexandria Railroad. When the column struck the tracks, it turned north and followed them for about two miles. At that point the Confederates caught up with some advanced scouts and carefully went into position in support. Stern orders forbade speaking above a whisper. Some of the men fell into scrapes when they came in too close proximity to enemy troopers, but most watched silently and saw no danger. Some of Stuart's men went as far as the Stevensburg road, far in Pope's rear. Most fell back cautiously when the scout ended. The horse artillery with Stuart retired one mile, held there for thirty minutes, then fell back farther. On the return, enemy cavalry were "looking and feeling" along the track the Confederates used when outbound in the morning. As a result, at least part of the column retired as far as the saddle of Cedar Mountain and recrossed toward the main road far from any pressure.[10]

Captain C. M. Blackford of the Second Virginia Cavalry led a small scouting party toward the railroad on his own that morning. Blackford suffered through "a very poor breakfast of hardtack and stone-cold fried middling" before he departed. Despite taking time for that hard and greasy repast, the captain probably preceded Stuart's main thrust in the same direction. The Virginia horsemen rounded up a small enemy picket at Mitchell's Station on the railroad. The "very intelligent," if somewhat incautious, sergeant commanding the picket was not loath to share what he knew, so Blackford carried the man directly back to Stonewall Jackson.[11]

The loquacious Federal sergeant provided an early entry in the mass of evidence Jackson assembled about enemy capabilities and intentions. When Stuart returned with prisoners, eyewitness evidence, and matured conjectures, Stonewall knew what he had to know. From Stuart's report, "as well as from other sources of information," Jackson wrote, "I was confirmed in my opinion that the heavy forces concentrated in front rendered it unwise on my part to renew the action." The general optimistically posted his troops with an eye to repulsing an enemy advance, were Pope willing to try that approach. Major Grimsley of the Sixth Virginia Cavalry and Culpeper County judiciously described Jackson's analysis as revealing that no *decided* victory could be expected. Jackson also applied the word *imprudent* to the thought of any further attack on his part. Accordingly, the general issued instructions about caring for the wounded, burying the dead, and "collecting arms from the battle-field."[12]

Meanwhile, John Pope suffered pangs over the security of his right flank, about which Jackson apparently thought not at all, and sent out opposition to the phantoms in that quarter. At 10:20 A.M. Pope directed a dispatch to Banks postulating that troops moving on the Madison Court House road probably were friends and that Banks ought not to fire at them if they were. Perhaps that marked the end of the fright on the Federal right. During the afternoon Pope pulled in his skirmishers and widened even more the unoccupied zone between the armies.[13]

With the lines widened, Walker's artillery on the far left abandoned its post and fell back. The incomparable Fredericksburg Artillery brought up Walker's rear, retiring "by half battery" to thwart any hostile threat; none came. Some of the Southern infantry spent the day marching hither and yon, though nothing came of any of their exertions. Once Stafford and Field fell back (by 11:00 A.M.) very few men of either army found occasion to add their names to the long casualty list. Private James Bartley Stinson of the Forty-ninth Georgia of Thomas's brigade, still in his teens, was reported killed during the day.[14] Poor Stinson was, needless to say, every bit as dead as the hundreds who fell together on August 9 while the guns boomed loud.

By far the biggest uproar of the day on the battlefield erupted in midafternoon along the main road east of its intersection with the road to Mitchell's Station. The Loudoun County cavalrymen who made up Lije White's Comanches did not accompany Stuart on his venture up the railroad. Whether by design or neglect, the company remained near the forward edge of Jackson's army near its middle. At about 1:00 P.M. the men were lounging in the shade near a spring, having taken the bits from their horses' mouths and turned the animals out to graze. Most of the troopers were eagerly devouring the Northern newspapers strewn around a former Northern position. A thin line of infantry moved past this bucolic scene, headed toward the rear. An infantry officer mentioned to Captain White that the only Confederates remaining to the front were a few cavalrymen helping an ordnance officer salvage ammunition from an enemy wagon. White acknowledged this intelligence absent-mindedly, paying more attention to messages he was receiving from his wife by way of a newly arrived civilian.

A few minutes more and the relaxed horse soldiers saw vivid first-hand evidence that they had become the front line. A noisy ruckus just ahead and out of sight soon developed into a squadron of Yankee cavalry charging at full tilt, "firing, yelling, and making everything look blue." Southerners scrambled to their feet in "great consternation" and mounted if they could corral rearing and frightened horses. Lije White mounted without putting the bit in his horse's mouth. Once the Loudoun lads sat astride their horses, the situation quickly smoothed out. The Federals hurried back on the same route they had used for their surprising attack. Before the tide turned, the Comanches were amazed and amused to see one of their number, Thomas Spates, escape the threat "by literally outrunning his horse, a thing until then entirely unheard of." The staff officer attempting to collect ordnance in front of the cavalry was in dire straits when the Comanches pounded to his rescue. Federals "had him surrounded and were striking him over the head and back with their sabres" when the cavalry came to his assistance. The crackling of Southern pistols put an end to that nonsense in short order and "the old man" (to soldiers, anyone past thirty) climbed up behind a lieutenant and rode away. The Comanches never after had difficulty in securing what they wanted from the ordnance wagons so long as they asked in the right place. Two of the Confederate horses caught the spirit of the counterattack with such zeal that they hurtled within reach of Northern infantry despite their riders' contrary desires. Lieutenant Frank Myers and Sergeant Ben Conrad escaped this adventure unscathed, though Conrad's horse paid for his unwonted ardor with a bullet wound. Conrad fell back cursing the Yankees "heartily" for wounding his mount.[15]

The panic spread to wagons all across the front and involved a few fainthearted line troops as well. The Cedar Mountain campaign developed more unwarranted panics than any two other campaigns of the war combined. Perhaps the intense heat contributed an unaccustomed factor to nervous tension levels. Although Lije White and a few dozen men quelled the source of the panic, it continued rearward not only unabated but, in the nature of such things, gaining momentum. "For awhile there was a wild stampede," Jed Hotchkiss wrote in his diary, "the wagoners thinking the enemy had flanked us." Jackson himself reprised his role of the previous day on the same ground, riding into the stampede to stem it. This time he did not dodge hostile lead, only flying hooves. Jackson "soon restored quiet" and then sternly "fixed to prevent any such move again." Eight months later and only a few weeks before his death, Stonewall Jackson still exhibited disgust with Latham's Virginia Battery for participating in the panic. By then the battery had left Jackson's command and, Stonewall remarked, "it was not much loss."[16]

A member of the Fredericksburg Artillery described the rout and its origins. "With the combination of extreme heat, long and rapid march, fighting against heavy odds, scarcity of water &c, the corps was in terribly nervous condition," he explained. When the wagons came racing back at the start of the panic, they raced across a piece of road with a "very rocky" bottom. The noise their wheels made on the rocks sounded just like musketry. Hundreds of men rushed out of the bushes and headed for the rear, followed by "one or two batteries." The Fredericksburg battery served in Hill's division with Latham's and no doubt saw that unit scamper away. Captain Braxton ordered the Fredericksburg guns to the nearest crest to stand firm, which they did. Their cool reaction made the gunners proud, but of course they had nothing to shoot at.[17]

Most of Stonewall Jackson's day featured far less excitement than the stampede afforded. The general's first important order of business in the morning was to greet his most welcomed reinforcement, Jeb Stuart, and to plan with him the cavalry initiative that ensued. One of Jackson's couriers looking for the general that morning found him about half a mile behind the Gate. Jackson, Stuart, Ewell, and A. P. Hill were sitting together on a log not far from the road "holding a consultation." A little farther to the rear the famished courier came upon Jackson's headquarters establishment and secured his first food in thirty-six hours—a piece of raw bacon and two hard crackers.[18]

Among the fruits of the cavalry forays Stuart and Stonewall planned together was the talkative Yankee sergeant Captain Blackford had captured at Mitchell's Station. Blackford carried his captive directly to headquarters, where Jackson was ensconced in a tent. Several staff officers stood around the tent holding their horses. Jackson's famous sorrel horse also stood at hand, ready for the general to mount. While the assemblage awaited Jackson's appearance, the Yankee sergeant stood behind the sorrel and began pulling hairs from the poor animal's tail. Blackford thought the prisoner was behaving nervously. Just as the sergeant had a handful, one of the staff noticed him and "with some asperity" ordered him to stop what he was doing. At the same moment Jackson himself appeared at his horse's head. Jackson asked mildly, "My friend, why are you tearing the hair out of my horse's tail?" The prisoner took off his hat and with a disarming smile responded, "Ah, General, each one of these hairs is worth a dollar in New York." "Was there ever a more delicate compliment to a man's reputation?" Captain Blackford mused, and added that Jackson "was both pleased and amused" to such an extent that he actually blushed. Perhaps because he was disconcerted the general sent this talkative potential intelligence source to the rear without questioning him and with his valuable trophies intact.[19]

Jackson also dealt humorously with Kyd Douglas of his staff during a relaxed moment. Staff members were teasing young Douglas concerning his frightened horseback leap over a huge fence the day before, which he had told them about. Jackson listened in quiet amusement, and when Douglas proposed an expedition to the scene to examine the evidence, the general went along. After Jackson examined the marks accompanying the enormous leap, he turned in his saddle and said: "Gentlemen, the evidence is conclusive—that— Douglas was very badly scared!" Douglas, who recorded this story about himself, insisted that Jackson delivered this line with "what was almost a chuckle"—the equivalent of an unbridled guffaw from a less dour individual.[20]

Jedediah Hotchkiss probably did not participate in either of the two diverting encounters with the general. Hotchkiss spent the day hard at work doing what made him invaluable at the time to Jackson and later would make him famous—drawing maps. Jackson ordered the topographer to make a preliminary sketch of the field at once. Hotchkiss completed the sketch during the day. That evening Alexander R. Boteler, Jackson's friend and a member of the Confederate Congress, left for Richmond, taking the sketch with him for presentation to Jefferson Davis. Hotchkiss proposed to Jackson that the fight be named "Cedar Run." The general concurred, and that name headed the sketch.[21] To the end of his life Jackson referred to his victory on August 9 as Cedar Run. Many other contemporaries called the battle Slaughter's Mountain. Only gradually over the years did Cedar Mountain become the conventional designation, probably in part because of the inherent potential for confusion between Cedar Run and the October 1864 fight at Cedar Creek.

During the day Jackson faced up to some unpleasant unfinished business concerning the organization of his army. The improvisations that had been necessary during the preliminaries of the battle to keep Alexander R. Lawton from commanding a division cried out for a more permanent solution. On August 10 Jackson transferred Lawton and his brigade from the Jackson-Winder division to Ewell's.[22] Ewell ranked Lawton by a full grade. Jackson could not know, of course, that Ewell would be wounded seriously within a few days, leaving Lawton as the ranking brigade commander in his new affiliation. (Lawton himself was seriously wounded a few weeks later and returned to service as a competent Richmond bureau chief when he recovered. His fine Georgia brigade retained its connection with the division it joined on August 10 until the war's end.)

The lesser Confederate ranks generally spent August 10 hard at work on something, whether gathering spoils (for personal or national benefit, by turns) or tending wounded of both sides and burying the dead. Most of them realized full well that they had won a close-fought victory. Jackson's great and growing fame hushed the murmuring that might otherwise have been heard about the previous day's near-disastrous beginnings. Some of A. P. Hill's partisans doubtless muttered about the eccentric army commander. One of them, artillerist Ham Chamberlayne, told an intimate friend in a letter soon after that when they met he would have some comments to make. "I could tell you some things about Jackson that would astonish you, about Cedar Run," Chamberlayne declared.[23]

The spoils of victory rounded up and turned in to quartermasters and ordnance officers amounted to quite a pile. Stonewall Jackson the inveterate wagon hunter saw to their careful accumulation and enumeration, as was his custom. In addition to the prisoners and the one captured Napoleon, he counted some forty-three hundred enemy weapons. William Allan, a competent ordnance officer and similarly successful as a historian, estimated that about a thousand of the fifty-three hundred weapons recovered were Confederate. The early afternoon panic on August 10 probably cut into the haul at least marginally. A member of the Nineteenth Georgia of Archer's brigade, for instance, grumbled that two ordnance wagons his regiment captured during the night "we lost the next day by the cowardice of two teamsters sent for them."[24]

Efforts to succor wounded Confederates moved promptly and efficiently. Before midmorning all of the wounded along and around the Crittenden Lane had been removed. From the hillock near the Gate, where Jackson's headquarters had stood the previous day, an observer noticed the distinctive yellow flag of a hospital to rearward. Southerners made every effort to assist wounded foe as well as friends, but one of them admitted that, reasonably enough, "we had our own men to attend to first."[25]

The relentless sun that had turned central Virginia into a bake oven for several days running appeared again to torment the wounded of both sides indiscriminately. The mercury stood at 86° an hour after sunup, reached 94° by 2:00 P.M., and dropped only to 84° by 8:00 P.M. Relief apparently was on the way. It arrived late in the day when a downpour struck the sweltering battlefield. Men huddled under the pelting storm described it variously but with a common theme, as "a very heavy thunder shower," "a terrible rain," and "a very heavy rain." The problems posed by water in such volume certainly did not offset the relief it posed for parched and weary men, wounded and unwounded alike.[26]

The degree to which men on the battlefield welcomed water, even in inconvenient and immoderate doses, can be imagined through the eyes of a correspondent of the *New York Tribune*. The journalist wrote before the storm that Pope's army was "suffering terribly . . . from the want of water. If it is not moved in a few days, hundreds of

*The original caption to this photograph reads: "Head Quarter's
of Gen's Pope and McDowell. Near Cedar Mountain." Presumably
the photograph is of the Nalle house. (Library of Congress)*

horses will die of thirst and men of disease, from drinking the thick
mud."[27]

Federal field hospitals between the front lines and Culpeper quickly
filled to overflowing with stricken men on the afternoon of August 9.
Before dark hundreds of wounded arrived in the courthouse village
needing attention. "Every church and other suitable building . . . including private houses, was filled with them." Citizens of both sexes
pitched in to help the mass of suffering humanity. Although the
townspeople were universally pro-Confederate, they "were very generally vieing with each other in rendering [the Federal wounded]
every accommodation and assistance in their power." The casualty
situation probably was exacerbated because Pope's army was in the
midst of disbanding all the regimental bands. Bandsmen traditionally
served as stretcher teams during combat. As the musicians left ser-

vice, the wounded infantrymen lost their best friends. No doubt realignment of that function took some time.[28]

Compassionate Southern civilians did not abandon their cause by any means, despite displaying admirable willingness to help the wounded. An ill member of the 107th Pennsylvania taken in at "a secesh house" in Culpeper and then nursed for four days wrote haughtily, "i got tired of there talk and cleared out." The householders no doubt felt the pangs of his principled departure very slightly indeed. The sick and wounded huddled everywhere. Culpeper became literally "one vast hospital." George A. Townsend, the Northern correspondent, wrote simply: "The shady little town was a sort of Golgotha now."[29]

At the Nalle house south of town, where General Pope had his headquarters, surgeons operated until the place looked "more like a butcher's shambles than a gentleman's dwelling." An operating table stood in the parlor next to the piano, which, together with every other piece of furnishings, was covered with blood. When the house filled up, as it quickly did, orderlies carried long tables from the kitchen out into the front yard and set them up there under locust trees. The result, wrote a witness, was "blood, carnage, and death among the sweet shrubbery and roses." The women of the house bravely helped out in a nightmare they could not have imagined a few hours before. The little boys of the family "watched with fascinated horror from behind the blinds in an upper window as the surgeons operated on screaming men and the pile of shattered arms and legs grew higher and higher."[30] It is easy to imagine that their young minds never shed the vision of the dreadful scene.

Some wounded Federals received attention from the most famous nurse in American history. Cedar Mountain was the first battlefield on which Clara Barton plied her merciful arts. Barton's fame lay in the future, and she had had some difficulty cutting through red tape to reach the suffering men whom she called her "precious freights." Dr. James I. Dunn of Conneautville, Pennsylvania, wrote to his wife lauding Clara Barton's help in supplying the surgeons' needs at trying times, while shellfire still sputtered. Dunn told his wife, "I thought . . . if heaven ever sent out a homely angel, she must be one, her assistance was so timely." Dunn's letter was widely published in the Northern press, adding greatly to Barton's reputation. The surgeon was embarrassed that his private description received such wide circulation, and Barton was embarrassed by the adjective "homely." On the newspaper clippings she saved, the famous nurse crossed out "homely" and substituted "holy," as though correcting a typographical error.[31]

Wounded Northerners within Southern lines received attention before the day ended. A staff officer riding across the field wrote of the "most agonizing shrieks and groans from the many wounded Yankees that were lying exposed to the full blaze of the sun" and added that "our men moved them into the shade and ministered to them." When a Federal officer of Pope's staff had opportunity to visit the field soon after, he attested to that kind attention. He found the Northern casualties "lying under booths of gum branches, each man with a canteen of water by his side." Pope might have begrudged the tribute, but his staff officer thought that the careful Southern attention to foemen "well illustrated the humane & chivalric spirit which Jackson had impressed upon his army."[32]

Lieutenant William P. Warren of the Twenty-eighth New York left a more personalized account of his treatment in rebel hands. Warren was suffering from five wounds, a couple of them dangerous. During the morning of August 10 a sergeant from the Twenty-seventh Virginia came to Warren's aid. Both men were Masons. The Virginian "filled several canteens with water and placed them within my reach," Warren remembered, "and fixed up a rubber blanket over me that kept off the hot sun all that day." Not surprisingly, Warren, considered the Confederate sergeant "a noble fellow."[33]

Another wounded Federal who considered himself relatively fortunate made Sam Buck of the Thirteenth Virginia uncomfortable. Buck had fired a ramrod from a loaded gun he picked up off the ground at the charging Pennsylvania cavalry the preceding evening. On August 10, when they returned to the vicinity, Buck and his men found a wounded Federal cheerfully encouraging passersby to guess what had hit him. When they gave up, "he laughed and said 'a ramrod went through my shoulder and stopped at the swell in the rod.'" Buck felt almost guilty about the round he had fired and relieved that this wounded enemy had survived the removal of the ramrod in such good spirits.[34]

Field hospitals crowded wounded men into every available corner without regard to their allegiance. Two men of opposite uniforms amazed a witness by stoic discussion of their respective hurts. If the staff officer reporting the dialogue can be trusted, the Federal commiserated with the Confederate because his lost leg ruled out dancing and the Confederate responded in kind about the Federal's missing arm and its negative impact on hugging a sweetheart. Doubtless many other Confederates, wounded and whole, shared the sterner attitude toward the wounded enemy displayed by Louisiana Chaplain Sheeran, who described the field as drenched with the blood of "the victims of fanaticism, tyranny and injustice."[35]

Possession of the battlefield gave Confederates the opportunity to scavenge for food at points where they had driven Federals away from wagons and other stores. A famished Tarheel found a bag full of ground coffee (a commodity by now all but extinct in the South), sugar, cakes, and other delicacies. He and his mates feasted on that find plus mutton chops, Irish potatoes, and crackers. The Virginia boys of the Rockbridge Artillery enjoyed the contents of a large chest of delightful edibles which arrived from home soon after the battle. A little later they also came into the bounty of a cornfield full of roasting ears. One of them recalled of the corn-ears feast, "the number a young Confederate could consume in a day would have been ample rations for a horse."[36]

Confederates scouring the battlefield sought more than ordnance for their regiments and food for their stomachs. A chronicler of one unit bivouacked near the road to Mitchell's Station wrote that at daylight "their first notion was to look around for Yankees and plunder"—not necessarily in that order, no doubt—"in which interesting occupation they passed the time until noon, having secured a number of . . . trophies of the battle-field" together with prisoners and military gear. An Alabama infantryman of limited literary attainments told his mother in a letter with apparent disappointment, "I never pick up nothing but a inder [India] ruber haver sack and a canteen." Captain Charles H. Stewart of the Second Virginia Infantry intercepted a wad of counterfeit Confederate money that a prisoner tried to throw away. The *Richmond Dispatch* learned of the incident and waxed wrathful about the Yankee perfidy it illuminated.[37] A modern observer examining the range of what passed for Confederate paper money can only marvel that counterfeits were discernible.

Tattered Southern infantrymen eagerly sought better clothes from haversacks of the dead and from dead bodies as well. A member of Hill's division wrote at the time that he and his comrades had become nonchalant about "the coarsest of clothes, the plainest of shoes, and . . . the dirtiest of shirts." The chance to upgrade some items proved irresistible. An officer in Early's brigade who observed a personal rule throughout the war against even the simplest pillaging on battlefields broke his own rule at Cedar Mountain. The officer needed a hat, and a nice one lay next to a dead man. When he picked it up and put it on, he described the results with the ghoulish humor of a man inured to blood and death by the horrors of many battlefields: "At once [I] threw it away as the poor fellow had left his brains in it and while I needed brains, I did not want them on the outside of my head."[38]

Confederates described the carnage at Cedar Mountain with perhaps even a touch more of revulsion than such scenes inevitably engendered. The close-packed nature of the slaughter probably contributed to the awful impression. Greater and bloodier fights lay in both the past and the future, but yard by yard Cedar Mountain impressed Kyd Douglas, for instance, "more deeply with the horrors of a battlefield . . . after a bloody fight, than ever before or after, not excepting Malvern Hill." When John Blue rode west from the wheatfield toward the Gate early on August 10, he found that he could not use the road; it was "so blocked up with dead men and horses that it was impossible to follow it." Blue fell in with General Archer, and the two men rode over the field together. South of the Gate "there were saplings from four to six inches cut entirely off by musket balls." Marks on the timber showed that about 80 percent of the rounds fired into it had been too high to hit any human target and many of them had struck twenty feet above the ground. Even so, Blue was astonished that anyone escaped alive from musketry that left such heavy marks in its wake. In the wheatfield, Archer commented "that he had never seen such slaughter."[39]

Jed Hotchkiss of Jackson's staff, a New York–born schoolteacher of mild manner and scientific interests, could not look at the rows of dead without segregating their intentions. "My heart grieved for every son of the South that lay there . . . [having] poured out his life blood to rescue our land from a worse than Egyptian bondage. May God help them with salvation." The foe, on the other hand, Hotchkiss looked upon "without a feeling of sorrow . . . for they had come of their own will upon our soil to waste and burn, and kill."[40]

Catherine Crittenden's battered farm was a cynosure for the damage and drew all eyes to its troubles. The house was "riddled . . . a ghastly spectacle." Wounded jammed each room, and "the floors were covered with blood." The yard had been "thoroughly plowed by shell." Corn near the house lay on the ground, harvested by musketry, and an unexploded shell rested in the parlor. A Confederate lieutenant's fresh grave lay at the foot of the front steps. The Crittenden women returned to their home in stouter spirits than they had left in the day before. Dr. Hunter McGuire, who used the women's help in tending the wounded men sprawled throughout their home, reported that they took him to task for a pessimistic remark about Confederate military prospects if the fight reopened soon. "You, a man," they scolded McGuire, "and belonging to Jackson's army, and talk of him being defeated! You ought to be ashamed of yourself and learn courage from a helpless woman."[41]

Two Confederates reported independently that they noticed dead black soldiers in Federal uniforms on the battlefield. Ham Chamberlayne, a good witness, wrote to his mother on August 14 that he "saw & examined a negro soldier, uniformed & accoutred, dead in the ranks of the Yankees." A soldier in the Forty-fifth Georgia of Thomas's brigade told his fiancée in a letter dated August 11: "Several negroes were killed in the late battle, with Yankey uniforms fighting against us. What think you of that?"[42] The use of black troops in Virginia was still almost two years away. The dead men must have been contrabands or other noncombatants to whom uniforms or uniform pieces had been given; or perhaps the unbearable heat had already discolored some of the dead.

The heat soon made identification of bodies difficult, thus exacerbating the ordeal of loved ones at home who were hoping against hope on behalf of missing soldiers. A report on one such search involving a Fifth Connecticut officer concluded that "the bodies were much disfigured." Kyd Douglas of Jackson's staff supervised some of the burials and precisely one month later dealt with a Federal family as a result. During the operations around Harpers Ferry in September, two ladies in black approached Douglas, whom they knew, and solicited his help in ascertaining the fate of the husband of one. The missing man was "conspicuous for his height and person, but his body had never been found and he was not a prisoner." Douglas felt sorry for the woman, of course, and promised to do all he could for her, even though he knew that her husband had been part of a crowd that stoned to death Douglas's intimate friend D. C. Rench in a civilian sectional quarrel at the outset of the war. He never had any luck, however, in locating information about the missing corpse.[43]

The majority of the Confederate dead were buried tenderly by friends and comrades who retraced their movements for that cheerless purpose. Captain Shepard Green Pryor of the Twelfth Georgia buried William Batts and Thomas H. L. Tinsely where they had fallen. "Billy & Tom were buried as soldiers," Pryor wrote in a letter back to Georgia. "I had their graves marked. I guess they will never be moved as they have no coffins." Coffins were, of course, decidedly the exception on a Civil War battlefield. Joe Luttrell and Thaddeus White of the First Tennessee buried their comrade William P. Cooper, who was killed storming across the wheatfield. Both of the grave-diggers were killed themselves before long, and thirty-eight years later Cooper's brother advertised in *Confederate Veteran* in hopes of finding someone who knew where the grave was located.[44]

Joseph Franklin Kauffman of the Tenth Virginia finished a long night of faithful stretcher duty at sunup on August 10 and promptly went to work burying the dead of his company. Kauffman buried John W. Mauck and James O. Wood in a single grave, then found Henry Lucas and went to work digging another grave. Just as Kauffman and his helpers were about to finish filling in Lucas's grave, the afternoon stampede swept over the spot and carried them back with it. When quiet reigned again the Virginians finished closing the grave and put a "rail pen" around their graves with a board at the head of each.[45] Few graves on the battlefield received such careful attention.

Four miles or so northeast of Kauffman's customized little graveyard, the Federal high command watched burial of some of its own dead. Most of the Northern dead remained in Confederate country, but wounded men died steadily in and around the gory hospital at Pope's headquarters. A staff officer noticed how "worn and sad . . . [and] discouraged" Generals Gordon, Crawford, and Banks looked. McDowell and Pope sat under an apple tree on boxes near the Nalle house. A burial detail walked past the generals carrying five dead men; others followed with picks and spades. Pope commented, "Well, there seems to be devilish little that is attractive about the life of a private soldier." McDowell responded, "You might say, General, very little that is attractive in any grade of a soldier's life."[46]

Some Federals killed at Cedar Mountain went into mass, or at least multiple, graves dug by their late enemies. A Confederate observing the technique of the burials commented that the procedure went forward in "absolute quiet" that seemed "unnerving" by contrast to the well-remembered holocaust of noise and fire in the same place not long before. The men on burial details generally buried several men together in a ravine washed out by rains, covering them up "shallow" in the natural depressions. The choice of erosion-washed draws obviously ensured an impermanent burial; the next runoff could expose the shallow graves. A Northern chaplain discovered the shortcomings of the burial technique soon thereafter as he rode across the wheatfield. The ground was torn up in every direction, and he rode unknowingly across a huge pit grave. "My horse sank to his body among the dead," the chaplain wrote in horror, "over whom was but a thin coat of soil."[47]

Stonewall Jackson concluded this day of hospitals and burials and cavalry thrusts where he had started it and where his headquarters stood—"on the hill in rear of the battlefield."[48] This location almost certainly was either the knoll around the Major house or perhaps farther north along the same high ground near the schoolhouse. The general's second night in this location doubtless was a more comfortable one for at least three reasons: the exhaustion and hunger of the day of battle had passed; his pitched tent offered a few more amenities than the bare ground of the night before; and, most important, Jeb Stuart rode near at hand to ensure the steady screening of the army by daylight and darkness alike.

CHAPTER 16

August 11

THE BREAK IN THE weather afforded by the thunderstorm late on August 10 did not last. Within an hour after sunrise on August 11 the sun had nudged the thermometer to 80°. The 2:00 P.M. reading of 95° offered no improvement over the preceding afternoon, and the 83° recorded at 8:00 P.M. remained uncomfortably hot. Private Edward M. Yowell of Company L, Tenth Virginia, died of sunstroke during the day, offering mute testimony to the heat.[1]

One of the men working hardest in Jackson's army on this hot morning was Captain Edward Hitchcock McDonald of the Eleventh Virginia Cavalry. McDonald had drawn the thankless task of escorting four hundred Federal prisoners to the rear. His own mounted men staggered with exhaustion and the footsore marching prisoners were even more tired. McDonald gave his horse to one of the worn-out captives, and some of his troopers emulated him. As dawn broke on August 11 the column splashed through the Rapidan River. Shortly thereafter they stumbled into Orange Court House. McDonald herded his charges into the fenced courthouse yard and went in quest of food. The citizens of the town flatly refused to cooperate because of the way Federals had behaved when in town a few days earlier; the post commissary was similarly disposed. The captain finally broke into a storage bin loaded with provisions and distributed them.[2]

Back on the battlefield Stonewall Jackson entertained a flag of truce during the morning of August 11. The Federals sought permission to remove such of their dead as the Confederates had not buried. The requested truce would last until 2:00 P.M. Jackson readily granted the request. Sometime after noon it became apparent that the job was greater than the time allotted would cover, and Jackson approved an extension of the truce to 5:00 P.M. A Confederate officer looking on thought the prospect of Jackson holding the enemy at bay while they buried their dead by permission was "amusing." One of Pope's staff officers evidently recoiled from the sting of that atmosphere because he felt it necessary to claim that the *Confederates* had sought the truce to bury their own dead—who, of course, lay well within Confederate lines. This officer, David Hunter Strother, further declared that Southern dead and wounded lay helpless where they fell, presumably under Northern control, including the abandoned body of General Winder.[3] Two years later, Strother and his like-minded kinsman David Hunter would burn and pillage their way down the Shenandoah Valley (paying especially cruel attention to the homes of relatives they disliked) in one of the least savory episodes in American military history.

Incredibly, the arrival of the flag of truce triggered yet another of the needless Confederate panics of that boiling August week. As John Casler of the Thirty-third Virginia trudged slowly toward the rear with his regiment after an arms-salvage detail that morning, soldiers within sight began running and shouting that Yankee cavalry was charging. The running soldiers set off "quite a stampede," and soon wagons and other vehicles joined the panic. The mounted enemy sought only to deliver the truce message, and the Confederates quieted down again.[4]

As Federals streamed through the lines under the terms of the truce, they had opportunity to notice and record the torn condition of the battlefield. Most of the Confederate dead had been buried by this time and some of the Federal dead as well. The wheatfield and the cornfield remained a bloody shambles. A Massachusetts soldier wrote simply that "the scene . . . [was] too awful to attempt to describe." Yet many of his comrades attempted to do so. A Rhode Island officer noticed particularly that "the smell of the field was well-nigh insupportable." The square mile at the heart of the battle site was "torn, trodden, cannon plowed, bloody; fences and corn fields obliterated; trees splintered and cut off by shot; dead men, dead horses, fragments of bodies, broken wagons, remnants of arms and equippage."[5]

Another Federal officer wrote of corpses "hideously blackened and swelled, already putrefying," and of trees as large as twelve inches in diameter cut down by shells. A larger tree contained a big shell buried in its bole but it was still standing. Journalist George A. Townsend crossed the lines during the truce and wrote a vivid description of the carnage he saw:

> The road and fields were strewn with knapsacks, haversacks, jackets, canteens, cartridge-boxes, shoes, bayonets, knives, but-

Graves on the battlefield of Cedar Mountain. (Library of Congress)

tons, belts, blankets, girths, and sabres. . . . Some of the tree-
tops . . . were scarred, split, and barked, as if the lightning had
blasted them. . . . A hurricane had apparently swept the country here, and the fences had been transported bodily. . . . The
ground looked, for limited areas, as if there had been a rain of
kindling-wood; and there were furrows in the clay, like those
made by some great mole which had ploughed into the bowels of
the earth. All the tree boles were pierced and perforated, and
boughs had been severed so that they littered the way. . . . When
I passed beyond [Cedar Run], I entered the region of dead men.
Some poisonous Upas had seemingly grown here, so that adven-
turers were prostrated by its exhalations.[6]

Federals crossing the lines looked first for friendly wounded needing succor. The regimental historian of the Twenty-eighth New York
spoke of the "sufferings and horrors" of Northern wounded and
complained that Confederate surgeons had tended to their own men
and not their enemies. The New Yorker admitted that "some hu-

mane Confederates had brought water, and built shelters of boughs to protect a few of the wounded from the hot sun." Other Federals applauded with virtual unanimity the care their mates had received. Even that most virulently anti-Confederate Virginian David H. Strother admitted that the numerous wounded he met uniformly reported kindnesses from Rebels, who had "washed the gore from their faces, and given them water to drink."[7]

A soldier in the Second Massachusetts was delighted and apparently surprised by his reception by Southerners during the truce. "We met some very pleasant rebel officers," he marveled, "who were very gentlemanly and kind." The chaplain of the same regiment echoed that report, writing that the Confederates he met "were courteous and kind, and far from exultant." Chaplain Alonzo H. Quint further applauded the attitude of Southern officers toward clergymen and contrasted it favorably with the treatment to which he was accustomed. Quint met a Confederate general, whom he did not identify, and recalled with pleasure: "On learning that I was a chaplain, the general showed the greatest regard for an office which some Union generals treat with contempt." The same Massachusetts cleric also expressed gratitude for Southern treatment of Northern wounded. Confederates "had sheltered some with blankets or boughs; had brought water, and sometimes biscuits and apples." Federal dead, he added, had been stripped naked, and so had some of the wounded.[8]

The unlovely practice of stealing clothes from corpses overnight after each battle became habitual as the war dragged on among cloth-starved Southerners of unqueasy tendencies. Few of them admitted to the practice, and no doubt most shunned it, but the demand for clothing ran so high that enough men participated to leave little remaining on the field at postbattle sunrises. Northerners expressed outrage at what they considered uncivilized behavior. Complaints of stealing from wounded, at Cedar Mountain and elsewhere, were of much less frequency. No one on either side could justify that to himself so it remained the province of out-and-out scoundrels of both armies. At Cedar Mountain men of the Fifth Connecticut were particularly incensed to find the body of the popular regimental adjutant, Heber S. Smith, stripped in the wheatfield as they went about burying friends.[9]

Federal burial crews quickly emulated the techniques for mass, shallow graves that Confederates had used the day before. A Southerner looking on noted that burials proceeded "without ceremony or coffin. A long ditch for a grave and a blanket for a coffin." Connecticut men returning to the wheatfield found most of their dead "buried in trenches in one undistinguished mass, and not half buried at that, arms and feet left protruding, and . . . the horrible stench of the battlefield was truly sickening." The Twenty-eighth New York buried its dead in the same fashion, "in one large grave." Some men searching for particular missing comrades were thwarted because "many of them had become so discolored by the intense heat that they could not be recognized." The additional day with the temperature above 90° had increased that problem. Company G of the Twenty-eighth New York sought the body of Lieutenant William M. Kenyon, found it, and marked the grave aside from the mass burial. Kenyon later turned up as a paroled prisoner of war, and it developed that the body under the marker was that of Lieutenant H. Melzar Dutton of the Fifth Connecticut. Under the circumstances, those men missing in action only gradually could be presumed to have died.[10]

Peripatetic correspondent George A. Townsend watched the Northern burial parties and reported on their progress. "There seemed to be no system in the manner of interment," Townsend wrote, "and many of the Federals had thrown down their shovels, and strolled across the boundary, to chaff and loiter with the 'Butternuts.'" The journalist was astonished at the nonchalance of the burial teams toward their ghastly surroundings. "No one, whom I saw, exhibited any emotion at the strewn spectacles on every side, and the stories I had read of the stony-heartedness during the plague, were more than rivalled by these charnel realities. . . . The heat of the day and the general demoralizing influences of the climate, were making havoc with the shapely men of yesterday."[11]

Although Townsend was not at hand to witness it, young George M. Neese of New Market, a Confederate horse artillerist, exhibited ample emotion as he watched Federals "packing away their comrades for dress parade when Gabriel sounds the great Reveille." Neese had seen enough of Pope's system of war to feel nothing but relief as each individual threat to his homeland was covered with dirt. "You came down here to invade our homes and teach us how to wear the chains of subordination," Neese said to them in retrospect, "and may God have mercy on your poor souls and forgive you for all the despicable depredations that you have committed since you crossed the Potomac."[12]

Most men of both sides cheerfully eschewed bitterness and welcomed the chance to satisfy curiosity about their foe. A Northern infantryman wrote to a relative that during the truce the burial parties of quondam enemies were "all mixt up gether as frendly as brothers." Confederate cavalryman Harry Gilmor met Lieutenant Colonel Gustavus A. Muhleck of the Seventy-third Pennsylvania and Colonel Clemens Soest of the Twenty-ninth New York during the truce. Muhleck and Soest told Gilmor that they had heard of him from the ladies of Luray as a "pretty good sort of fellow." The mixed threesome rode over the field together at length, then the two Northerners invited Gilmor to come back into their lines for a drink. Gilmor left his arms with an orderly and followed his hosts into Yankee country. They spent an hour together there "very agreeably" over something refreshing and parted the best of friends.[13]

Confederate Chaplain J. William Jones also made some friends among the enemy during the truce, although the clergyman's encounter did not include strong drink. Jones and a fellow chaplain rode curiously among the peaceful truce parties and began arguing politics with some Northerners. Jones was an arguer if nothing else, as his postwar career as apologist for the Lost Cause established. One Northern field officer offered to bet Jones $100 that Stonewall Jackson would be in full retreat on Richmond within a day. By Jones's account, he had the good fortune to meet his debating prey a few weeks hence as a prisoner captured at Second Manassas and indulged himself in rubbing salt into the wounds.[14]

During the truce, general officers from both sides mixed congenially in the neutral ground. Their byplay produced some of the most famous episodes of the Cedar Mountain campaign. Several generals took part in the scene, but flamboyant Jeb Stuart held center stage. He and Jubal Early administered the truce for their side; Generals Benjamin S. Roberts and George L. Hartsuff did so for the Federals. Roberts and Hartsuff waited for their counterparts on a log at the edge of the cornfield branch of Cedar Run, ignoring the gaggle of lesser Confederate officers who arrived. Most of these latter, wrote an observer, were "young fellows in gray suits." Early rode down the slope at length and taciturnly "nodded his head" to the Federal party.

Stuart appeared on horseback soon after Early and headed for the knot of officers, stopping on the way to check correspondent Townsend's sketch pad to make sure the Northerner was not doing anything proscribed during truce periods. The close encounter gave Townsend the opportunity to inspect Stuart and describe him—"a lithe, indurated, severe-looking horseman." The Northern newspaperman generally enjoyed a strong descriptive flair, but he missed

Stuart's essence by a wide margin. Stuart was lithe, to be sure, but indurated and severe-looking? If you want to have a *good* time, 'jine the cavalry. Townsend struck closer to the mark when he later heard Stuart's conversational style and described the cavalier's personality as featuring "what is known in America as 'airiness,' and [he] evidently loved to talk of his prowess."[15]

Hartsuff and Stuart had been contemporaries at West Point and greeted each other with suitable enthusiasm. "Hartsuff, God bless you, how-de-do?" "Stuart, how are you." The two young men exchanged jocular remarks about their relative wartime ranks compared to the sluggish advancement of the prewar army, then took a brief private walk together. When they returned to the log by the stream, a thoughtful surgeon uncorked a bottle of whiskey and passed it among the group. The Federals all addressed Stuart as "Jeb." Toasts spoke of an early peace; jests focused on how well each would treat the other as a prisoner of war. David H. Strother of Pope's staff was so thoroughly the quintessential radical that he knew beyond any argument that his side had won the battle. As he watched Stuart chattering in his "cheerful, friendly manner," Strother somehow convinced himself that the Confederates actually were "very much down and the gayety was only superficial."[16]

Generals Bayard and Crawford arrived at some point, bearing a basket of eatables, and added to the party. A Confederate accompanying Stuart could tell that Bayard and Crawford were fond of Stuart and "were very glad to see him, and it was amusing to hear them talking of their exploits on opposite sides, and how that countermarch had foiled something etc." During this high-spirited and almost boyish banter (of the three, only Crawford had reached his thirtieth birthday, and that recently), Stuart declared with emphasis that Jackson's thrashing of Pope would be accounted a Northern success in the lying Yankee newspapers. (Stuart did not know, of course, that at that moment a few yards away D. H. Strother already knew as a righteous fact that it had indeed been a Northern success.) Crawford swore that not even the *New York Herald* would have the audacity to put out such a whopper. The two men bet a hat on the issue; Crawford manfully paid off in a few days when the press made a poor prophet out of him.[17] The same hat apparently was the one Stuart lost to his chagrin at Verdiersville in a famous episode on August 18.

Jubal Early drew far less mention than his garrulous cavalry colleague, but Townsend took the time to describe the infantry brigadier as resembling "a homely farmer" who remained mounted during much of the meeting and said little. Stuart lounged on the log completely at his ease, "working his jaw till the sandy gray beard brushed his chin and became twisted in his teeth." Everyone ignored the corpses in view, which in places nearby choked the little stream. A Federal surgeon mentioned relations of his near Richmond whom Stuart knew, and the general responded by relating "trifling occurrences" about them. To Townsend, the meeting seemed to take "the form of a roadside gossip, and Stuart might have been a plain farmer jaunting home from market."[18]

When the lengthy and relaxed reunion broke up, Stuart rode across the front. The general's lassitude vanished in an instant when he found a party of Federals advancing with ambulances, which he threatened to confiscate. Ewell came onto the field during the truce at least briefly and chatted with his opposite numbers. In the process he noted the need to police the field more thoroughly and bury Confederate dead overlooked the day before. Ewell ordered Early to do both chores and applauded the results. "Early returned to the field with a detachment from his brigade," Ewell wrote in his official report, "and while there removed six wagon loads of arms, besides burying nearly 100 dead left by the other divisions of the army, and which would not have been buried but for his energy."[19]

Early's salvage chore involved more than simple exertion. He discovered a "very large quantity of excellent rifles" stacked on the field, left behind by those detailed to carry them away. Perhaps they had been within the area assigned to the teamsters who started one of the panics of the past two days. One of Franz Sigel's staff officers was calmly superintending their removal under the protection of a flag of truce. Early firmly halted and then reversed this process, filling six wagons as a result. The Northern staff officer felt inclined to be contentious about the situation, but another Federal officer rode up and straightened him out. "He then cursed him and told him that Sigel had better send some one there that was not a damned fool." Early heard a Federal soldier say, "It is hard to see our nice rifles going that way," to which a fair-minded comrade replied, "Yes, but they are theirs, they won them fairly." Jed Hotchkiss told his wife in a letter that Stonewall Jackson's comment about the recovered rifles was "that is the best way to get arms."[20]

A good number of Federals deserted soon after the battle, perhaps beginning during the truce. Jackson probably considered this as good a way to reduce enemy numbers as rifle salvage was to secure arms. A round dozen Yankee soldiers from western Virginia came in together to surrender as a group. Jackson's response to these men was simply to parole them and let them go home.[21]

Early's other chore, in addition to salvaging rifles from Sigel's truce-breaker, was the unhappy one of completing burial of Confederate dead. Surprisingly, he found ninety-eight unburied bodies, or nearly half the total number killed during the battle. Most of these lay in the woods west of the wheatfield where Garnett had suffered so much and where reinforcements had taken additional losses during the rollback of Crawford. One possible explanation is that friends buried friends in that era of casual record-keeping, long before graves registry became an organized staff function. Garnett's brigade was shattered to such a degree that it probably did not have the men or energy needed for the frightful job of policing those blood-drenched woods. Even so, that many unburied friendly dead after two days of holding the field was a terrible business. Early finished his sad task late in the afternoon, after the truce expired.[22]

Long before the truce ended at 5:00 P.M., Jackson began to uncoil his army and nudge its tail—about to become its head—back toward Orange. Jackson probably had determined before the day began to make this move that night. In fact, the general doubtless had reached the decision upon receiving full news of Federal strength during the afternoon of August 10. He had done all he could do to Pope and all he had set out to do. With the river between his army and the foe, Jackson could absorb reinforcements en route from Lee and then play another tune on Pope. In the event, Jackson spent eight days south of the Rapidan before he and Lee came back at Pope with fire in their eyes. In the sparse words of Jackson's official report, "I remained in position until the night of the 11th, when I returned to the vicinity of Gordonsville, in order to avoid being attacked by the vastly superior force in front of me, and with the hope that by thus falling back General Pope would be induced to follow me until I should be re-enforced."[23]

Word of the withdrawal spread through Jackson's army near midday. The first wagons started to move back "soon after" the Federals solicited an extension of the truce's expiration from 2:00 to 5:00 P.M. That request necessarily antedated 2:00 P.M. by some time, of course, so the movement probably had begun before 2:00 P.M. A wounded and limping Maryland artillerist of Dement's battery heard the news at a hospital near the front. He was anxious to avoid capture because he knew that Maryland Yankees were "all desperadoes from Baltimore and a hard set of men" who would kill him if they had a chance. So the Maryland boy hobbled back to his battery's wagons early in the day and waited for hours for the retreat to begin.[24]

Through the afternoon the army's units fell into line and took the road toward Orange. By the time the truce ended and Early's detachments finished their work, the Confederates left on the field were hugely outnumbered; but an enemy completing a requested truce posed little threat. Jackson trotted out about the oldest trick known to retreating armies when he ordered his soldiers still in position to light and stoke blazing campfires, as though to cook rations. Even had the idea been a novel one, the broiling heat would seem to have made it an obvious ploy and worth investigation by the Federals. Just after dark what seemed like "a thousand bright beacons blazed over the plains . . . and hillsides." The youngsters of the Fredericksburg Artillery dutifully built their fires, but J. Dickson White grumbled that it was adding insult to injury to order the building of cooking fires and then supply no rations to cook. As soon as darkness descended, the battery fell into the slowly moving column, unfed.[25]

When Ewell's division moved away, the Comanche cavalry company from Loudoun County took over responsibility for keeping the fires blazing. Sam White and John Marlow piled hay on one fire, creating a brief inferno that lighted up the entire mountainside. The two troopers quickly discovered that Ewell had not followed his infantry away. That feisty and eccentric general hastened to the scene of the indiscreet White-Marlow blaze and "angrily threatened to 'throw a pistol ball among them if they did so any more.'" In the best tradition of volunteer soldiers and cavalrymen everywhere, the two "promised," more or less quietly, "to return all the pistol balls he threw them." They did not, however, try the hay trick again.[26]

While Ewell exchanged threats with private soldiers, the rest of the army slogged southward slowly—very slowly, as is the custom with night retreats. Jackson's division marched in front, followed by Ewell's and then A. P. Hill's. The Maryland artillerist who had hurried back to the wagons during the morning did not begin rolling until nearly midnight, by his estimate. The wagon seemed to move at a double-quick pace most of the time, though no doubt it halted regularly between spurts of movement. In Hill's division the foot soldiers moved slowly as well as infrequently. "Oh my! What a march that was," one of them recalled, "going five or ten steps and stops— five or ten steps again and stop and so on and on—everybody tired and hungry and sleepy, ready to drop."[27]

Sam Buck knew the campaign was over when he saw a familiar face coming toward him in the darkness and recognized his father. The elder Buck (who lived in Winchester) had located Sam's brother safe in the Seventh Virginia Cavalry and now came looking for his other son. As soon as the father approached close enough to the leading company of the Thirteenth to be recognized, some of the men told him that Sam had survived intact. "What a relief to a parent," Sam later wrote knowingly at a time when he had attained that status himself. The two generations of Bucks enjoyed a brief reunion in the dark road.[28]

The Confederate column passed one house that night in which only four girls, two of them in their teens, held down the family homestead. One of the girls, writing of the experience years later, remembered: "We didn't sleep any that night." Bareheaded and barefoot soldiers trudged past all through the hours of darkness. At about midnight an Alabama soldier known to the family dropped by and remained with the girls. The only man on the property or for miles around was an old black preacher who made barrels for the farm. When the last Southerner passed, the girls were back in the Union, to their intense regret.[29]

During the dark hours of August 12, 1862, still another panic swept through a portion of Jackson's army. This last, and perhaps greatest, of those misadventures during the Cedar Mountain campaign began in the ranks of Maxcy Gregg's South Carolina brigade. The redoubtable historian of the brigade described the stampede as the "greatest panic I ever saw." The South Carolinians had spent the past two days bivouacked near the Rapidan in woods on either side of the road. Soon after dark on August 11 the army began to stream past their position. Gregg's men picked out friends and acquaintances in the column with whom to chat, but eventually they went to sleep, as soldiers must do when they have the chance. Most of them took off their shoes and many took off their clothes.

Sometime after midnight the South Carolinians awakened suddenly amid loud and confusing voices and the rattle of accoutrements. Brigade historian James Fitz James Caldwell described the ensuing mess: "At the same moment a line of men rushed over us, crying out, 'O Lord!' and similar exclamations, stamping upon us in the dark, and, in many instances, beating us down with their guns, (which men in a panic always carry at a trail,) as we rose out of sleep." The result was predictable. Men half awake or less shouted "Yankee cavalry!" and struggled to escape a phantom foe. Caldwell watched "crowds of men dashing hither and thither, barely visible in the deep fog, running against trees, stumbling over the sleepers, and crying out everything dreadful and unreasonable." The ruckus finally quieted, of course, but one of the South Carolina infantrymen ran so fast and so far that he only rejoined at noon the next day, and then without his hat or jacket, lost in the panic. In retrospect Gregg's men concluded from various reports that the trigger of the stampede was either the rapid approach of some Confederate cavalry from the rear, the rattling of an ambulance on the rough road, or the sudden appearance of two small dogs.[30]

During the night A. P. Hill personally unsnarled one of the myriad tangles that turned the infantry march into a snail's pace. Had Jackson been present, which he was not, Hill would have risen in the army commander's estimation as a marching manager. Hill pressed to the front of the column after a delay exhausted his patience and found troops of another division avoiding the ford in Robertson's River, "a little stream not over waist-deep." The men were obliquing through a gap in the fence in order to reach a log across the stream. The log's capacity was limited to one man at a time, so the entire army languished badly in the interest of avoiding damp calves.

General Hill promptly turned the head of the column back into the road and the ford and stood watching his handiwork. The division commander was wearing his "fighting shirt" of red and black stripes, with no coat or mark of rank other than a black feather in his hat and a sword by his side. Near sunrise a weary infantryman spotted the log and decided to cross the stream dry shod. Hill ordered him to use the ford. "I'll be hanged if I do!" "Go on through the water or I'll run you through with my sword." Hill drew his sword by way of emphasis.

"Well now," the yeoman replied, "that's a game two of us can play at. You put that little 'frog-sticker' into me and I'll put a bullet through you." The infantryman unslung his weapon by way of emphasis.

Hill brusquely suggested that his adversary did not know to whom he was speaking. The foot soldier guessed, or pretended to guess, that his roadblock was "some darned cavalry-man! All they do is to get us infantry into a fight and then go back to the rear and if we poke our noses through a hole in the fence they are right there to order us back." Hill identified himself, and the two infantrymen, one famous and one obscure, commiserated together on the shortcomings of cavalry the world over. The infantryman also mustered a tale about medical reasons for keeping his feet dry, left his new friend behind, and clambered across the log.[31] Such were the vicissitudes of major generals commanding armies composed of fiercely egalitarian civilians.

Cavalry covering the rear of the column still had General Ewell to contend with. Dick Ewell had been a dragoon officer for many years before the war and was inclined to slip back into that role when opportunity offered. The unfortunate Comanches, with whom Ewell had exchanged threats about pistol balls soon after dark around the bonfires, ran into the general again late in the night. At midnight Ewell ordered a detachment of the company under Lieutenant Frank Myers to march to and hold the river crossing at Liberty Mills. They reached that point in a state of exhaustion at daylight. Thirty minutes later Myers received an order from Ewell to send ten men back to him north of the Rapidan to act as couriers. The ten tired men on stumbling mounts took the wrong turn and missed Ewell, who had a screaming raging fit when he caught up with Myers in camp. The tirade wound up with an emphatic demand for an explanation. Myers innocently began to give one, though he must have known that none would suffice. "I supposed, General," the lieutenant began—but Ewell broke in excitedly. "You supposed; you supposed, you say; what right had you to suppose anything about it sir; do as I *tell you*, sir; do as I *tell you*." That ended the explanation. Myers's three words were all he ever managed to wedge into the one-sided discussion.[32]

Maxcy Gregg's poorly rested South Carolina brigade marched soon after dawn, no doubt still discussing the night's panic. The men splashed through the Rapidan in broad daylight as the army's rear guard and soon after went to hunting for corn to steal. All of Stonewall Jackson's infantry was back in Orange County. Most of them would have sympathized with the diary entry for that day by one of Early's men, which in its entirety read simply: "Very tired."[33]

A few Southern cavalrymen remained north of the river, of course, to keep an eye on Pope's leisurely advance. The cavalry retained a couple of pieces of horse artillery for support. From time to time the guns went into battery to warn any Federals who appeared in the distance, but none ever came close enough to warrant even a single round. As the cavalry neared the Rapidan the skies opened and poured out a torrent that drenched everyone to the skin and even washed out haversacks. The soaked men and animals crossed the Rapidan at Madison Mills and dropped the curtain on the Cedar Mountain campaign.[34]

The Cedar Mountain chapter of Stonewall Jackson's amazing military career had ended for the general the evening before. Jackson had moved along byways out of the army's path to one of the Garnett places, where he took supper. After dinner around a blazing fire Stonewall and some of his staff talked over incidents of the battle. S. Bassett French of Governor John Letcher's staff, who had just joined Jackson for a month's detail, was "in the midst of a rhapsody . . . over the gallantry of our troops—a tribute to our 'noble dead'" when he discovered with some amazement that Jackson was sound asleep. "While I was dropping a tear 'to memory dear,'" French remembered wryly, "the hero was lost to 'time and sense' in the gentle embrace of Morpheus."[35]

And so we leave Stonewall Jackson just where we found him: sound asleep in the midst of a conversation.

APPENDIXES

Appendix I

The Military Aftermath

Badly wounded men suffering on the banks of Cedar Run were not the only casualties in fear for their lives. More than six hundred Federal prisoners had occasion to feel nervous. General Pope's savage anticivilian orders had prompted official as well as unofficial Southern outrage, including hints of retaliation against prisoners. On August 1 the Confederate Adjutant and Inspector General's Office promulgated its General Order Number 54 codifying the government reaction to Pope's orders. The order cited Pope and General Adolph W. von Steinwehr in particular but included "all commissioned officers serving under their respective commands." All such were "expressly and specially declared to be not entitled to be considered as soldiers." Specifically, they were to be exempt from the cartel for parole and exchange, and they were to be hanged in the event of any judicial murder by United States forces of Southern civilians. The order included nearly one thousand words in careful explanation of the Confederate position on this dreadful matter.[1]

General Henry Prince ranked at the head of the list of the splendid crop of prisoners Jackson harvested at Cedar Mountain. He reached Richmond on the morning of August 10, obviously having made a rapid trip by rail from the junction at Gordonsville. According to a government observer, when Prince reached the Confederate capital "he affected to be ignorant of Pope's brutal orders" and vigorously "vented his execrations upon Pope."[2] Happily for Prince and his brother officers, and for the tidiness of the nation's historical annals, none of Pope's threats bore fruit. No Confederate civilians fell victims to capital punishment in Pope's military courts so no Federals stood hostage as a result. The reason was simple: within a few weeks John Pope embarked on a well-earned banishment to fight Indians, or at least to garrison posts among them.

Long before the unpleasant business about war on civilians reached circumstantial resolution, an even more widespread cause of discomfort disappeared. On August 12 the heat broke at last. A Confederate civilian imprisoned in Washington's Old Capitol Prison (Pope was not the only bully abroad in the land that summer) noted with relief in his diary that the long-awaited front arrived late in the day. On August 13 he exulted: "The mercury must have fallen 20 degrees since noon yesterday. It is now uncomfortably cool."[3]

Soldiers of both sides doing duty in Orange and Culpeper counties doubtless reveled in the changed weather without any thought whatsoever that it had reached coolness that might be described as uncomfortable. The blue-clad men in Culpeper County counted noses and marveled at their loss. General Crawford inspected the thinned ranks of the Twenty-eighth New York of his brigade on August 13 and then remarked to a lieutenant of the regiment: "Out of 140 regiments from New York State I reckon the 28th will be remembered when all the rest are forgotten." Crawford soon found that he had lost his bet with Jeb Stuart. Substantial portions of the Northern press routinely elevated Pope's disaster into another rout of the rebellious Southerners. A Washington paper, in the best tradition of that city's journalistic ethic, noted that Pope "is again in motion towards Gordonsville" and added with certainty that "his men all believe him irresistible."[4]

A more judicious journalist, writing for the *New York Tribune*, filed a report in which he appropriately applauded Banks for his skill, declared that Jackson had won the fight, and predicted that false claims of a Federal victory would soon find wide circulation. Chaplain Quint of the Second Massachusetts felt similarly. Pope's postbattle bombast fell on stony ground with the chaplain, who suggested that that general's congratulatory orders were "a burlesque." Quint thought that his regiment, at the least, could well do without "such victories as being driven from the field . . . leaving their wounded in the hands of the enemy, burying their dead afterwards by permission of the enemy; while the arms captured by the rebels, lay in huge piles." "But," Quint concluded in a fit of world-weariness, "that was the way they used to write history."[5]

Some few Confederates, meanwhile, muttered about Stonewall Jackson's shortcomings and irritating quirks, but most gained even more confidence in their legendary leader in the aftermath of victory at Cedar Mountain. A Louisiana soldier compared his experience with Jackson favorably to the frustrations of the Seven Days' campaign of recent memory. "The good sense and soldierly mind of Genl. T. J. Jackson," he wrote home to his mother, "accomplished this result with a comparatively small loss on our side which shows to us [the difference] between him and the *fools* in uniform who commanded us at Richmond."[6]

R. E. Lee offered typically pious thanks to both God and Jackson for the victory. "I congratulate you most heartily," he wrote to Jackson on August 12, "on the victory which God has granted you over our enemies at Cedar Run. The country owes you and your brave officers and soldiers a deep debt of gratitude." Among the applause of the Richmond newspapers there appeared the interesting note that Northern financial markets reported increasing gold prices and dropping stock prices when the news of Cedar Mountain reached New York. A Virginia cavalryman with Jackson delivered one of the most insightful analyses of the effect of the battle. After commenting on the relative fury and destructiveness of the fight, Charles M. Blackford showed that he was beginning to discern the nature of this bloody new face of war. "The victory was decided," he judged, "but the results, beyond the moral effect on the men of both sides, will not be much."[7] Battles of annihilation and surrender, à la Yorktown, simply were not on the Civil War agenda.

Jackson's inevitable reaction to a victory (or to almost any other transaction) was to call for religious celebrations. Cedar Mountain was no exception. As the general reported his purpose: "In order to render thanks to God for the victory at Cedar Run and other past victories and to implore His continued favor in the future, divine service was held in the army on August 14." In the midst of those divine services Jackson himself unwittingly caused a serious disruption. The general attended preaching at the camp of the Fifth Virginia Infantry of his old brigade. As he rode back toward headquarters he passed Taliaferro's brigade drawn up to listen to the Reverend Daniel Blaine Ewing, a Presbyterian divine from Gordonsville. Ewing was "in the midst of a splendid curl," an eyewitness reported, when Jackson came into view. "At the sight of the old grey cap coming down the road the men all broke and marched to the road-side to cheer the Gen. as he passed, leaving Mr. Ewing in amazement at the height of his eloquence." General Taliaferro spread the word that he intended to have Stonewall "arrested for disturbing a religious meeting, and a Presbyterian one at that!"[8]

If postvictory religious celebrations were virtually de rigueur in Confederate armies, so too were personal quarrels and threatened duels. One such complex affair of honor in the aftermath of Cedar Mountain is illustrative of the syndrome as well as interesting as a reflection of the personalities of two North Carolina generals. A captain in Pender's brigade, who remains unidentified, had mentioned soon after the battle something about the disposition of Branch's wagon train. His remark was in error, as the facts developed, but it also was entirely innocent and the affair was not important in any case. About two weeks after the battle, when Pender attended church near Branch's headquarters, Branch sent a message to Pender asking that the captain come to see him. Pender blandly assumed that Branch wanted to dine with the man and sent him along.

The unfortunate captain found Branch livid with indignation. Branch "abused" the target of his wrath "severely, and told him that his sword ought to be broken." The captain, of course, responded with some acerbity and spirit of his own, then returned to General Pender and complained of having been set up. Pender "was very much astonished" and explained his casual role in arranging an apparently friendly visit. When Pender questioned his subordinate further and heard that he had countered Branch with some bitterness, the general quietly told the captain that his behavior "did not indicate the spirit" that was required in the brigade—and sent him home. A less inflexible onlooker on Pender's staff suggested what must have been obvious to all reasonable men, that the poor captain's situation "was so novel when violently assailed by a superior that he knew not what to do or say." But Pender did not stop there. He addressed a note to Branch detailing the circumstances and requiring an apology to himself and "reparation" to the victimized captain. The correspondence between Branch and Pender quickly reached an understanding that the two men would fight a duel "when peace should come and the country no longer have need of their services on the battle field."[9] In the event, neither man survived the war; in fact, Branch did not survive the summer.

Stonewall Jackson faced some staff problems in the aftermath of Cedar Mountain, though not of the sort that led to pistols at twenty paces. The general's staff was in a state of flux for at least two reasons. The Reverend Robert Lewis Dabney, who had been its inept but pleasingly pious chief through the spring, officially resigned shortly after the battle (at which he had not been present). To almost any impious observer that boded well for efficiency at headquarters because Dabney had been useless for any purpose other than assuaging the general's hyperactive religious needs. The resignation came, however, at a time when "almost all the General's staff" were "laid up" with one disorder or another.[10]

Those staff members present for duty found their leader ready to keep them from idleness and boredom, as was his custom. Jedediah Hotchkiss received orders from Jackson on August 12 to "at once make as many maps as I could of the region from where we are on to the Potomac." "Do not be afraid of making too many," Stonewall added. Jackson's further preparations for chasing his foe out of Virginia included the unhappy one of identifying those among his soldiers who had not been doing their full duty. By means of an order issued through a staff officer on August 13, Jackson directed that each captain in the army should list cowards and deserters in their companies. The lists were to include "all who absented themselves from the late battle with intention of avoiding the fight."[11]

During the week that the army fell back from Cedar Mountain, Captain Charles M. Blackford had occasion to discover that Jackson's much-mooted eccentricity lived up to its billing. One night just past sundown Blackford received orders to report with twenty men to the general for scout duty. Jackson, with Sandie Pendleton by his side, led the cavalcade "in by-paths and unused roads in places where neither friend nor foe would ever pass" all night long. The venture seemed to have no aim nor purpose. "It was," Blackford wrote, "one of those freaks which sometimes seize him and which make many people think he is somewhat deranged." As he drowsed in the saddle, the captain sometimes muttered darkly to Pendleton by his side. At one point Blackford wakened after dozing off for a moment and "said in an undertone, but very irreverently and somewhat petulantly, 'Sandy, where is the old fool taking us?'" The response from the dark figure next to the horse was an uncertain query—"What?"— in the unmistakable voice of Stonewall Jackson. Blackford reined back in the darkness, thankful for its cover, and continued the peculiar night jaunt. The entire party slept on the roadside just about daylight for half an hour, then rode to the top of Clark's Mountain.[12]

And so it went in the August of 1862, with Stonewall Jackson on the loose, making maps and plans and aimless night rides, onlookers marveling all the while. With Stonewall in top form, Northern Virginia would prove to be a poor haven for Federal armies.

Appendix II
Organization of the Contending Armies

CONFEDERATE

Ewell's Division

Early's Brigade:
13th Virginia
25th Virginia
31st Virginia
52d Virginia
58th Virginia
12th Georgia

Forno's Brigade:
5th Louisiana
6th Louisiana
7th Louisiana
8th Louisiana
14th Louisiana

Trimble's Brigade:
15th Alabama
21st Georgia
21st North Carolina

Division Artillery, A. R. Courtney, commanding
Latimer's Battery (Va.)
Dement's Battery (Md.)
Brown's Battery (Md.) [Chesapeake Artillery]
D'Aquin's Battery (La.)
Lt. Terry's Battery (Va.) [Bedford Artillery]

A. P. Hill's Division

Branch's Brigade:
7th North Carolina
18th North Carolina
28th North Carolina
33d North Carolina
37th North Carolina

Archer's Brigade:
1st Tennessee
7th Tennessee
14th Tennessee
5th Alabama Battalion
19th Georgia

Thomas's Brigade: 14th Georgia
                           35th Georgia
                           45th Georgia
                           49th Georgia

Gregg's Brigade: 1st South Carolina
                         12th South Carolina
                         13th South Carolina
                         14th South Carolina
                         1st (Orr's) South Carolina Rifles

Starke's Brigade: 1st Louisiana
                         2d Louisiana
                       9th Louisiana
                       10th Louisiana
                       15th Louisiana

Field's Brigade: 40th Virginia
                       47th Virginia
                       55th Virginia
                       22d Virginia Battalion

Pender's Brigade: 16th North Carolina
                         22d North Carolina
                       34th North Carolina
                       38th North Carolina

Division Artillery, R. L. Walker, commanding
  McIntosh's Battery (S.C.) [Pee Dee Artillery]
  Pegram's Battery (Va.) [Purcell Artillery]
  Fleet's Battery (Va.) [Middlesex Artillery]
  Braxton's Battery (Va.) [Fredericksburg Artillery]
  Davidson's Battery (Va.) [Letcher Artillery]
  Latham's Battery (N.C.)

Jackson's Division Brig. Gen. Charles S. Winder
                    Brig. Gen. William B. Taliaferro
Winder's Brigade: (Colonel Charles A. Ronald)
                           2d Virginia
                           4th Virginia
                           5th Virginia
                         27th Virginia
                         33d Virginia

Col. T. S. Garnett's Brigade: 21st Virginia
          42d Virginia
          48th Virginia
          1st Virginia (Irish) Battalion

William B. Taliaferro's Brigade: (Colonel A. G. Taliaferro)
          10th Virginia
          23d Virginia
          37th Virginia
          47th Alabama
          48th Alabama

Lawton's Brigade: 13th Georgia
          26th Georgia
          31st Georgia
          38th Georgia
          60th Georgia
          61st Georgia

Division Artillery, R. Snowden Andrews, commanding
 Poague's Battery (Va.) [Rockbridge Artillery]
 Carpenter's Battery (Va.) [Alleghany Artillery]
 Caskie's Battery (Va.) [Hampden Artillery]

Cavalry, Brig. Gen. Beverly H. Robertson
 6th Virginia Cavalry
 7th Virginia Cavalry
 12th Virginia Cavalry
 17th Virginia Cavalry Battalion
 2d Virginia Cavalry (detachment)
 4th Virginia Cavalry (detachment)
 Chew's Battery

All units in the organization chart are infantry unless otherwise designated. The battle of Cedar Mountain was the only major battle in Virginia for which a printed organization chart does not appear in the *Official Records*. A listing of casualties on pages 179–80 of the main Cedar Mountain volume of that standard work approximates a table of organization as a by-product of enumerating the casualties by unit. That table, however, contains a very large number of errors. Many units are omitted entirely. Others are placed in the wrong brigade, or in some instances even in the wrong division. The chart above, prepared for this book, reflects evidence gathered from a wide variety of sources. It may include some anomalies but is far superior to the *Official Records* version. The confusion in the *Official Records*, which enjoy a well-deserved reputation for definitiveness in such matters, doubtless resulted from the extraordinary state of flux in which the Army of Northern Virginia and its components found themselves during August 1862.

The Union table of organization that follows is, by contrast, almost precisely as shown in the *Official Records*.

UNION

BANKS'S CORPS
A. S. Williams's Division
S. W. Crawford's Brigade: 5th Connecticut
                                10th Maine
                                28th New York
                                46th Pennsylvania

George H. Gordon's Brigade: 2d Massachusetts
                                3d Wisconsin
                                27th Indiana
                                Zouaves d'Afrique
                                (Collis's company)

C. C. Augur's Division Brig. Gen. Henry Prince
                         Brig. Gen. Geo. S. Greene
John W. Geary's Brigade: Col. Charles Candy
                                5th Ohio
                                7th Ohio
                                29th Ohio
                                66th Ohio

Henry Prince's Brigade: Col. David P. De Witt
                                3d Maryland
                                102d New York
                                109th Pennsylvania
                                111th Pennsylvania
                                8th and 12th U.S. Infantry
                                Battalion

George S. Greene's Brigade: 1st District of Columbia
78th New York

Corps Artillery, Clermont L. Best, commanding
4th Battery Maine Light Artillery (Robinson)
6th Battery Maine Light Artillery (McGilvery)
1st New York Light Artillery, Battery K (Crounse)
1st New York Light Artillery, Battery L (Reynolds)
1st New York Light Artillery, Battery M (Cothran)
2d New York Light Artillery, Battery L (Roemer)
10th Battery New York Light Artillery (Bruen)
Pennsylvania Light Artillery, Battery E (Knap)
4th U.S. Artillery, Battery F (Howard)

MCDOWELL'S CORPS
James B. Ricketts's Division
Abram Duryea's Brigade: 97th New York
104th New York
105th New York
107th Pennsylvania

Z. B. Tower's Brigade: 26th New York
94th New York
88th Pennsylvania
90th Pennsylvania

George L. Hartsuff's Brigade: 11th Pennsylvania
12th Massachusetts
13th Massachusetts
83d New York

S. S. Carroll's Brigade: 7th Indiana
84th Pennsylvania
110th Pennsylvania
1st Virginia (Union)

Corps Artillery, Davis Tillson, commanding
2d Battery Maine Light Artillery (B) (Hall)
5th Battery Maine Light Artillery (E) (Leppien)
1st Pennsylvania Light Artillery, Battery F (Matthews)
Pennsylvania Light Artillery, Battery C (Thompson)

Cavalry, George D. Bayard, commanding
  1st Maine Cavalry
  1st New Jersey Cavalry
  1st Pennsylvania Cavalry
  1st Rhode Island Cavalry

  1st Ohio Cavalry (detachment)—Pope's escort
  1st Michigan Cavalry (detachment)—Banks's escort
  5th New York Cavalry (detachment)—Banks's escort
  1st Virginia (Union) Cavalry (detachment)—Banks's escort

Appendix III
Casualties

The casualty tables below include substantial revision to Confederate losses, based on research in manuscripts and other primary sources. The increase of about 150 in Jackson's net losses results in part from inclusion of some units entirely omitted from the *Official Records* tables and in part from larger returns for some of the units that were included in that standard source. Casualty returns for both sides in every one of the war's battles could be increased by detailed examination of nominal lists and service records. That is not the case because of some dark conspiracy among those reporting the losses, but rather because of administrative complexities.

The column below headed simply "Killed" includes men mortally wounded who died reasonably soon after the battle. The original tables always enumerated such victims as wounded, in some cases even if they died the same day. That refinement in the definition of *killed* applies here only to Confederate losses. Research in Federal sources obviously would yield similar results. As established in Appendix 7, more than four hundred Federal bodies were removed from the battlefield to Culpeper, even after many Northern dead had been taken home by family and friends. The total killed reported by Pope therefore must be increased by approximately one-half.

The increased precision in reporting Confederate casualties offers the potential for mistaken comparison of Jackson's losses relative to Pope's. The ratio of about two-to-one in the *Official Records* tables must remain the standard. A microscope on the Northern statistics would certainly yield the same inflation—particularly among the os-

367

tensibly casualty-free units in McDowell's corps. Accordingly, all references in the narrative portion of this book to casualties on either side, particularly when comparing units to one another, use the figures from the *Official Records* tables as a means of standing on common ground.

CONFEDERATE CASUALTIES

	Killed	Wounded	Prisoners or missing	Total casualties
Ewell's Division				
Early's Brigade				
13th Virginia	2	32		34
25th Virginia[1]	2	23		25
31st Virginia	3	17		20
52d Virginia[2]	4	12		16
58th Virginia	2	28		30
12th Georgia[3]	7	33		40
Brigade Total[4]	20	145	2	167
Forno's Brigade				
5th Louisiana	1	9		10
6th Louisiana[5]				?
7th Louisiana[5]				?
8th Louisiana[5]				?
14th Louisiana[6]	1	5		6
Brigade Total	2	14		16
Trimble's Brigade				
15th Alabama[7]	1	7	2	10
21st Georgia[8]	0	4		4
21st North Carolina	0	2		2
Brigade Total	1	13	2	16
Division Artillery				
Latimer's Battery (Va.)[9]	0	5		5
Dement's Battery (Md.)[10]	2	11		13
Brown's Battery (Md.) [Chesapeake Artillery][11]	0	1		1
D'Aquin's Battery (La.)[12]	2	4		6

Lt. Terry's Battery (Va.) [Bedford Artillery]			?
Artillery Total	4	21	25
Total, Ewell's Division	27	193	4	224

A. P. Hill's Division

Branch's Brigade

7th North Carolina[13]	1	2	3
18th North Carolina[14]	3	13	16
28th North Carolina	3	26	29
33d North Carolina	6	30	36
37th North Carolina	2	13	15
Brigade Total	15	84	99

Archer's Brigade

1st Tennessee	4	20	24
7th Tennessee[15]	7	27	34
14th Tennessee[16]	12	22	34
5th Alabama Battalion	1	8	9
19th Georgia[17]	4	27	31
Brigade Total	28	104	132

Thomas's Brigade

14th Georgia[18]	4	24	28
35th Georgia[19]	9	17	26
45th Georgia[20]	8	40	48
49th Georgia[21]	13	37	50
Brigade Total	34	118	152

Gregg's Brigade	0	0	0

Starke's Brigade

1st Louisiana				?
2d Louisiana	0	5		5
9th Louisiana	2	4		6
10th Louisiana[22]	4	4	1	9
15th Louisiana	0	2		2
Brigade Total	6	15	1	22

Field's Brigade

40th Virginia	0	4	4
47th Virginia			?

55th Virginia	o	2		2
22d Virginia Battalion	7	o		7
Brigade Total	7	6		13
Pender's Brigade				
16th North Carolina[23]	1	2	1	4
22d North Carolina[24]	o	1		1
34th North Carolina				?
38th North Carolina				?
Brigade Total[25]	2	11	2	15
Division Artillery				
McIntosh's Battery (S.C.)				
[Pee Dee Artillery]				?
Pegram's Battery (Va.)				
[Purcell Artillery][26]	3	12		15
Fleet's Battery (Va.)				
[Middlesex Artillery]				?
Braxton's Battery (Va.)				
Fredericksburg				
Artillery]	o	o		o
Davidson's Battery (Va.)				
[Letcher Artillery]				?
Latham's Battery (N.C.)[27]	o	o		o
Artillery Total	3	12		15
Total, A. P. Hill's Division	95	350	3	448
Jackson's Division (staff)	1	o		1
Winder's Brigade				
2d Virginia	1	7		8
4th Virginia[28]	3	7	1	11
5th Virginia[29]	3	19		22
27th Virginia[30]	3	1		4
33d Virginia[31]	o	17		17
Brigade Total	10	51	1	62
Col. T. S. Garnett's Brigade				
21st Virginia[32]	39	78	6	123
42d Virginia[33]	53	58	8	119
48th Virginia[34]	19	43	4	66
1st Virginia (Irish)				

Battalion[35]	1	9	13	23
Brigade Total	112	188	31	331
William B. Taliaferro's Brigade				
10th Virginia	6	37		43
23d Virginia[36]	7	22		29
37th Virginia[37]	24	56	1	81
47th Alabama[38]	12	85		97
48th Alabama[39]	15	58		73
Brigade Total	64	258	1	323
Lawton's Brigade				
13th Georgia				?
26th Georgia				?
31st Georgia				?
38th Georgia	1	1		2
60th Georgia				?
61st Georgia	1	1		2
Brigade Total	2	2		4
Division Artillery, R. Snowden Andrews, commanding		1		1
Poague's Battery (Va.) [Rockbridge Artillery][40]		1		1
Carpenter's Battery (Va.) [Alleghany Artillery][41]	1	1		2
Caskie's Battery (Va.) [Hampden Artillery]				?
Artillery Total	1	3		4
Total, Jackson's Division	190	502	33	725
Cavalry				
6th Virginia Cavalry				?
7th Virginia Cavalry	1	15	2	18
12th Virginia Cavalry				?
17th Virginia Cavalry Battalion	1	2		3
2d Virginia Cavalry				

(detachment)			?
4th Virginia Cavalry			
(detachment)			?
Chew's Battery			?
Cavalry Total	2	17	2	21
Total, Jackson's Army	314	1,062	42	1,418

The Confederate casualty statistics reveal that Jackson's own smallish division suffered slightly more than one-half of the army's losses (51.1 percent). A. P. Hill's huge division, arriving late, suffered 31.5 percent of the losses, and Ewell lost fewer than half as many men as did Hill. The most frightful result of a statistical analysis of Southern losses is the discovery that the brigades of Taliaferro and Garnett each lost approximately 23 percent of the Confederate casualties on the field. Those two small units constituted perhaps one-seventh of the force under Jackson's command, yet between them they bore nearly one-half of the August 9 burden of blood. On none other of Virginia's major battlefields did the butcher's bill fall so unevenly among the Confederate units charged with paying the price.

Although absence without leave does not count as a casualty column, the degree to which that problem plagued Jackson's army in August 1862 deserves mention. A set of morning reports for Taliaferro's division covering three days just after the battle of Cedar Mountain survives at the Museum of the Confederacy. On August 14, the only one of the three days on which all three brigades reported, 5,020 men were present and 1,914 were absent without leave —a staggering proportion of more than 27 percent. The raw data, reproduced below, show a predictable trend toward increasing strength as the battle and marches receded into the past. The First Brigade was the Stonewall; the Second, which had been under Garnett on August 9, appears as Major Seddons's at this date; and the Third was Taliaferro's own.

	August 13	August 14	August 15
Present, 1st Brigade	2,028	2,074	2,100
AWOL, 1st Brigade	904	900	864
Present, 2d Brigade	—	1,302	1,313
AWOL, 2d Brigade	—	432	433

			Prisoners	Total
			or missing	casualties

| Present, 3d Brigade | 1,523 | 1,644 | — | |
| AWOL, 3d Brigade | 614 | 582 | — | |

UNION CASUALTIES

	Killed	Wounded	Prisoners or missing	Total casualties
BANKS'S CORPS				
A. S. Williams's Division (staff)	0	0	1	1
S. W. Crawford's Brigade				
5th Connecticut	21	71	145	237
10th Maine	24	145	4	173
28th New York	21	79	113	213
46th Pennsylvania	31	102	111	244
Brigade Total	97	397	373	867
George H. Gordon's Brigade				
2d Massachusetts	40	93	40	173
3d Wisconsin	17	66	25	108
27th Indiana	15	29	6	50
Zouaves d'Afrique				
(Collis's co.)	2	3	8	13
Brigade Total	74	191	79	344
Total, A. S. Williams's				
Division	171	589	452	1,212
C. C. Augur's Division (staff)	0	1	2	3
John W. Geary's Brigade				
(staff)	0	1	0	1
5th Ohio	14	104	4	122
7th Ohio	31	149	2	182
29th Ohio	6	50	10	66
66th Ohio	10	81	3	94
Brigade Total	61	385	19	465
Henry Prince's Brigade				
(staff)	2	1	0	3
3d Maryland	12	42	16	70
102d New York	15	85	15	115
109th Pennsylvania	14	72	28	114

111th Pennsylvania	7	74	9	90
8th and 12th U.S. Infantry Bn.	8	37	15	60
Brigade Total	58	311	83	452
George S. Greene's Brigade				
1st District of Columbia	0	3	1	4
78th New York	0	0	22	22
Brigade Total	0	3	23	26
Total, C. C. Augur's Division	119	699	125	943
Corps Artillery, Clermont L. Best, commanding				
4th Battery Maine Light Artillery (Robinson)	1	6	1	8
6th Battery Maine Light Artillery (McGilvery)	4	9	5	18
1st New York Light Artillery, Battery K (Crounse)				?
1st New York Light Artillery, Battery L (Reynolds)				?
1st New York Light Artillery, Battery M (Cothran)				?
2d New York Light Artillery, Battery L (Roemer)	0	1	0	1
10th Battery New York Light Artillery (Bruen)				?
Pennsylvania Light Artillery, Battery E (Knap)	1	7	0	8
4th U.S. Artillery, Battery F (Howard)	1	4	0	5
Artillery Total[42]	13	48	6	67
Total, Banks's Corps	303	1,336	583	2,222

MCDOWELL'S CORPS
James B. Ricketts's Division
  Abram Duryea's Brigade

97th New York	o	1	o	1
104th New York				?
105th New York	o	8	o	8
107th Pennsylvania	o	3	1	4
Brigade Total	o	12	1	13
Z. B. Tower's Brigade				
26th New York				?
94th New York				?
88th Pennsylvania	o	1	o	1
90th Pennsylvania				?
Brigade Total	o	1	o	1
George L. Hartsuff's Brigade				
11th Pennsylvania	o	3	2	5
12th Massachusetts	1	7	2	10
13th Massachusetts				?
83d New York	1	1	o	2
Brigade Total	2	11	4	17
S. S. Carroll's Brigade (staff)	o	1	o	1
7th Indiana	o	43	o	43
84th Pennsylvania	o	9	7	16
110th Pennsylvania	o	o	5	5
1st Virginia (Union)	o	1	3	4
Brigade Total	o	54	15	69
Total, James B. Ricketts's Division	2	78	20	100
Corps Artillery, David Tillson, commanding				
2d Battery Maine Light Artillery (B) (Hall)	o	2	o	2
5th Battery Maine Light Artillery (E) (Leppien)				?
1st Pennsylvania Light Artillery, Battery F (Matthews)				?

Pennsylvania Light Artillery, Battery C (Thompson)				?
Artillery Total	0	2	0	2
Total, McDowell's Corps	2	80	20	102
Cavalry, George D. Bayard, commanding				
1st Maine Cavalry	0	2	0	2
1st New Jersey Cavalry	2	14	0	16
1st Pennsylvania Cavalry	5	25	4	34
1st Rhode Island Cavalry	3	4	2	9
1st Ohio Cavalry (detachment)—Pope's escort	0	0	2	2
1st Michigan Cavalry (detachment)—Banks's escort	4	2	3	9
5th New York Cavalry (detachment)—Banks's escort	1	0	0	1
1st Virginia (Union) Cavalry (detachment)—Banks's escort	0	3	3	6
Cavalry Total	15	50	14	79
Federal Total	320	1,466	617	2,403

Appendix IV

Two Mortally Wounded Marylanders:
Charles S. Winder and R. Snowden Andrews

When General Charles S. Winder fell near the Crittenden Gate during the artillery duel that preceded the infantry engagement, everyone who saw Winder knew that he could not live long. The shell that mangled the general's left side inflicted far more harm than mid-nineteenth-century medical science could repair. As careful hands bore Winder away from the front, he passed the Stonewall Brigade. Perhaps recognition of his old command stirred the dying man's military impulses because he asked his aide, McHenry Howard, how the battle was going. Winder "seemed gratified at my reply," Howard later wrote, so the aide must have lied a bit because at that juncture the battle was not going particularly well for the men in gray.

Lieutenant Howard trudged along beside the stretcher, holding Winder's hand. He noticed that the general soon became less restless. At the same time Winder's hand grew steadily colder in Howard's grasp. As the unhappy party moved across the stream in the meadow where Early had formed some three hours earlier, it passed a portion of A. P. Hill's division moving north of the road and preparing for action. Just west of the meadow at the top of the rise the general and his attendants reached the schoolhouse intersection. By this time Winder had slipped into unconsciousness. Howard stopped the party in the grove around the schoolhouse and sat with his arm around the stricken general's neck, supporting his head. At about sundown, Howard wrote, General Winder died "so quietly that I could scarcely mark the exact time of his death."

An ambulance carrying Winder's body started south for Orange Court House accompanied by Howard and Captain John F. O'Brien, also of the general's staff. Near midnight this doleful little procession collided with cavalry entering the road from the east. The strange horsemen proved to be friends—Jeb Stuart and his party heading for Jackson. Captain O'Brien went on into Orange to make arrangements for transporting Winder's body to Richmond. Howard remained with the ambulance. As the ersatz hearse crossed the Rapidan at Barnett's Ford at daybreak on August 10, Howard noticed "the purple clouds above the rising sun and the oppressive heat even at that early hour." When Howard arrived at Orange, he found that O'Brien had not succeeded in his mission. The heat forced Howard reluctantly to conclude that he must bury Winder in Orange, at least temporarily. Wounded officers in town and others arriving from the rear joined a large number of civilians in the Episcopal church for the service. The mourners made up "a long line" as they followed the casket to a burial plot provided by the Freemasons in the cemetery "on the Gordonsville road, half a mile south of the town."[1]

Winder's remains occupied the Orange grave for less than a week. On the evening of August 17 his body reached Richmond on the cars of the Virginia Central Railroad. Lieutenant Edward Scott Gay and the Public Guard, a long-established local infantry company, met the train and accompanied the casket to the capitol. There it remained in the chamber, which before the war had housed the senate of Virginia, through the night and most of August 18, wrapped in the flags of Maryland and of the Confederacy. After an impressive state funeral from Capitol Square at 4:00 P.M. on the eighteenth, the casket was carried to Hollywood Cemetery and buried near the crypt of President James Monroe. Three years later the Winder family moved their fallen soldier to an ancestral burying ground at Wye House in Talbot County, Maryland.[2]

McHenry Howard kept as a souvenir of his chief the field glass Winder had been wearing when he was hit. The device was dented on the side when Winder fell with his mortal wound. When Howard fell into enemy hands at Spotsylvania, his captors took away the souvenir, but Howard managed to regain possession with an explanation of its sentimental value. A few months after the war, however, the Marylander lost the field glass for good when some rascal stole his bag while he was changing steamboats at Norfolk.[3] At this writing the general's field glass remains missing.

Postmortem analyses of dead generals—or dead human beings of any variety, for that matter—inevitably include much fanciful nonsense. Any other result would be accounted poor taste. Commentary about Winder ranged across a wide spectrum, from the spiteful remarks of John Casler (see Chapter 1), to McHenry Howard's obviously worshipful feeling toward his chief as "the best soldier under Lee and Jackson in the Army of Northern Virginia." Confederates of rank agreed that Winder's loss was more painful than most, even as enlisted men who had felt his discipline rejoiced at its disappearance. General Isaac R. Trimble wrote in his diary that Winder's death "fills us all with deep gloom" and added the sentiment that "such losses make war sickening." Captain Hugh A. White of the Fourth Virginia called his dead brigade commander "a most gallant soldier" and concluded that Winder's much-discussed discipline was an "admirable" measure that had been making the Stonewall Brigade "better, I think, than it ever was before."[4]

Stonewall Jackson never had entertained any doubts about Winder's merits, which he evaluated very highly. The army commander's formal tribute to Winder is familiar from frequent quotation but deserves reprise in summary of what the great man thought about his dead subordinate:

> It is difficult within the proper reserve of an official report to do justice to the merits of this accomplished officer. Urged by the medical director to take no part in the movements of the day

because of the then enfeebled state of his health, his ardent patriotism and military pride could bear no such restraint. Richly endowed with those qualities of mind and person which fit an officer for command and which attract the admiration and excite the enthusiasm of troops, he was rapidly rising to the front rank of his profession. His loss has been severely felt.[5]

The last sentence might well have struck William B. Taliaferro, who took Winder's place, as insulting (not that Jackson would have cared). By the time Jackson wrote his report, however, Taliaferro was far away from the Army of Northern Virginia.

Jackson's sorrow at the death of Winder is much more poignantly evident in the intimate format of a letter to Mrs. Jackson. "I can hardly think of the fall of . . . Winder without tearful eyes," he wrote, then launched into a 130-word religious essay on the subject for his wife's edification. The general's short sermon based on the death of Winder concluded: "While we attach so much importance to being free from temporal bondage, we must attach far more to being free from the bondage of sin."[6]

MAJOR R. SNOWDEN ANDREWS, commanding the artillery of Jackson's old division (Winder's, then Taliaferro's on August 9), went down wounded about as badly as Winder soon after the general was mortally struck. As Andrews galloped behind his guns not far south of the Crittenden Gate, a piece of shell tore apart the wall of his abdomen on the right side. The major had enough presence of mind to press one arm over the gaping wound and clutch his horse's neck with the other in such a fashion that he could fall to the ground without being entirely disemboweled. Everyone who saw the mangled artillerist knew that he was dying with as much certainty as they knew that General Winder's wound was mortal. Another Virginia artillery officer who saw his bleeding friend wrote home immediately after the battle that Andrews had been killed. The same man sent another letter home on August 14 with an update: "I saw him, but thought twas impossible he could live more than an hour; yesterday twas said he was still alive." The ultimate outcome on the fourteenth remained certain: Andrews was "mortally wounded."[7]

General A. P. Hill passed Andrews on the roadside not long after the major went down. Hill promised to send help at his first opportunity and did so. Doctor Hunter H. McGuire, Jackson's staff surgeon, came by and expressed with some bluntness a hopeless prognosis.

Others had suggested a fatal outcome to Andrews already, and he responded to McGuire, "Yes, that's what you fellows all say." McGuire ordered two brothers who were surgeons in Georgia regiments to do what they could for Major Andrews and continued on his way full of doubts.[8]

The two doctors detailed by McGuire as miracle workers were Thomas B. and William H. Amiss, surgeons respectively of the Thirty-first and Sixtieth Georgia Infantry regiments. An account of their performance by Andrews himself described, with carelessness bordering on ingratitude, Doctor "Amos" as a country doctor. Thomas B. Amiss practiced in Page County, Virginia, for almost half a century after the war, and Page County counts as country by almost any geographical or demographical standard.[9]

When Thomas B. Amiss found Snowden Andrews and examined him, he described the wounded man as "completely disemboweled, his intestines covered with dust, hen-grass, sand and grit." The surgeon turned to his brother and suggested more pragmatically than sensitively that Andrews was entirely beyond their capacity to help. Andrews retorted angrily that he had been hearing that for some time, "but if you damned doctors would do something for me I'd get well. I once had a hound dog that ran a mile with its guts out and caught a fox, and I know I am as good as any damned dog that ever lived, and can stand as much." To that spirited entreaty Thomas Amiss responded by punning to his brother, "'This man is full of all kinds of grit,'" meaning physical stamina as well as literal sand.[10]

Captain Charles M. Blackford rode up at about this time and noticed the surgeons doing a bit of work, "though with little hope." Two men of Blackford's Company B, Second Virginia Cavalry, who were fond of Major Andrews also appeared and "were doing all they could to help him"—apparently very little. Another enlisted man on the scene was John K. Hitner of the Rockbridge Artillery, who served with the gun of that battery that had been forced to retire with an enlarged vent. Dr. Thomas Amiss rounded up some stretcher-bearers, including Hitner and probably the Second Cavalry pair, and ordered them to carry Snowden Andrews to the James Garnett house a couple of miles to the rear.[11]

Some twenty-four hours earlier Major Andrews had gone to sleep on the porch of the James Garnett house under much happier circumstances, sharing the porch with Stonewall Jackson and some other officers on the eve of battle. The trip back to that point on the sultry evening of August 9 cost Andrews much agony. A chaplain rode in the springless ambulance with the suffering officer and held his hand, repeating the words of familiar hymns. When the painful journey ended, willing hands carried the major into the house and placed him on the dining room table. The clock stood near midnight when the Amiss brothers went to work on the wound, which by that time was nearly seven hours old. Andrews was convinced that the doctors remained certain that they were doing no real good but would "at any rate make the body more sightly" for burial.[12]

The ghastly tear in Andrews's abdominal wall proved to be only one of two wounds once the gore was cleared away. The savage piece of shell had continued its path across the top of the major's thigh, cutting it open near the hip. Dr. William Amiss carefully cleaned both wounds, washing the mass of dust and debris from Andrews's intestines and abdominal cavity. Thomas Amiss then replaced the organs and sewed the wound shut with "Boss cotton and a common calico needle, the only instrument available at the time." Andrews helped hold the wound's edges together during the sewing. Dr. Harvey Black of the Stonewall Brigade happened upon the scene, though he did not participate in the surgery. An officer who was friendly with Andrews asked Black "if there was any hope." Black concurred in the universal opinion: "He said no."[13]

As soon as the surgery ended, Andrews began asking that same vitally interesting question. A witness in the next room marveled that the major "was perfectly cool and composed, and even cheerful, and no one . . . listening to the natural tone of his voice as he gave directions about himself could have believed that it was the wounded man who was talking." "Doctor," asked Andrews, "how many chances have I?" When he received no response, Andrews suggested that he hoped for at least one in ten or twenty. The surgeon responded gravely, and with what he probably counted as kindly optimism, "Not more than that." Andrews cheerfully announced his intention "to hold on to my one chance," which the doctor had not in fact promised him. In a more pragmatic moment the stricken man sent his seal ring away in the care of McHenry Howard, his fellow Marylander, for delivery to his wife when the worst happened.[14]

Mary Lee Andrews was staying in Baltimore with her three children in early August. She learned of her husband's mortal wounding while reading a morning paper at the breakfast table soon afterward. The soldier's wife had already received a false report of her husband's death at an earlier battle and nurtured hopes of a similar outcome in this instance. She soon received confirmation of the mortal wound from civilian sources and then by means of a telegram from Louis H. Marshall of Pope's staff. Mary Andrews hurriedly prepared to go to Culpeper County, leaving two children behind but taking along an unweaned baby and a nurse. She and her tiny party reached Culpeper at 6:00 P.M. (probably on August 16) after a difficult trip among boisterous soldiers. Marshall had an ambulance ready for her, so she set out in the darkness with the baby crying lustily. The next morning Mary and Snowden Andrews enjoyed a touching reunion. It was the first time Snowden had seen the seven-month-old baby.

Pope's men encamped all around the James Garnett house during the third week of August were forced to pack up and leave in a hurry by the renewed offensive movements of Lee and Jackson. When they had left, the Andrewses and the Garnetts had a relatively pleasant time despite the continuing near certainty that peritonitis must soon level Snowden Andrews. The Garnett family included James and his wife and a widowed daughter-in-law, all of whom doted on the Andrews baby. James Garnett had hidden his livestock successfully during Pope's tenure as lord of Culpeper so food was no problem. The inevitable peritonitis never did appear, and Snowden's vicious wounds healed within five weeks to the point that he could sit up. A few more weeks and he was gimping about on crutches. Eventually he wore a silver plate over the wound. By the spring of 1863 a miraculously healed Andrews returned to field duty wearing the second star of a lieutenant colonel. Snowden Andrews's friend McHenry Howard had the pleasure of returning the ring that had been entrusted to his care and later learned to his disgust that Andrews subsequently lost the ring in a boating accident on the Patapsco River. Howard echoed many another man when he wrote that Andrews survived "the worst wound I ever knew anyone to recover from."[15]

Lieutenant Colonel Andrews did not spend much time back in the field before another wound knocked him out of service again. This time a bullet hit Andrews near the end of the Confederate victory north of Winchester around Stephenson's Depot on June 15, 1863. At that point, someone decided that the star-crossed artillerist deserved some time on ordnance duty in Europe. When he reached the Continent, Andrews found the widely acclaimed German armed forces engaged in some fighting with the Danes and in vain sought permission to go to the front to see German artillery in actual practice. When he argued with a high-ranking German, Andrews recounted his own military experience and capped his recital with the unusual boast, "and I dare say that I bear the most desperate wound ever received by a man from which he recovered." The German was impressed and called in a surgeon. When Andrews flaunted his honorable and enormous scar, his German counterpart said, "Mein Gott in Himmell!" (what else?) and asked permission to bring the renowned Helmuth von Moltke for a viewing. By Andrews's account, his exhibition for von Moltke won him permission to go to the front and see whatever interested him while wearing a noncombatant badge.[16]

The fabulous wound and its German exposure yielded another bizarre denouement, according to an account from the successful doctors Amiss. By their account, "about the time of the breaking out of the Franco-Prussian war . . . this remarkable recovery was freely discussed . . . and the conclusion was reached that the finely-powdered dust which so completely covered the wound and intestines in this case proved an antiseptic, and this led to the use of dust as an antiseptic during the Franco-Prussian war, and the more extensive use of powdered antiseptics later."[17] There is no indication that the Amiss brothers picked up the same dirty habit, which probably accounts in part for the relatively populous condition of Page County in this century.

Andrews not only survived his dreadful wound and a second wound and the rest of the war, he also survived the nineteenth century. After the war he was a leading architect in Baltimore, where he died on January 6, 1903. A fellow Confederate veteran and Marylander wrote that for forty years after the war Snowden Andrews could be "often seen on the streets in Baltimore, with just as positive opinions on all subjects as ever." As befit a sturdy survivor of positive opinions, Andrews grew to an enormous size after the war and was ever eager to describe his unusual recovery. On a visit to Richmond's Westmoreland Club, that elite veterans' watering hole, Andrews came across one of the surgeons who had been pessimistic about his survival. When the ponderous architect reminded the doctor of their earlier encounter, the former surgeon refused to believe the story and lost a bottle of wine in a friendly wager—no doubt settled by the same means Andrews had used to impress von Moltke.[18]

The stained and torn jacket Andrews wore in the face of the guns at Cedar Mountain is on display today at the Maryland Historical Society in Baltimore.

Appendix V

Lawrence O'Bryan Branch Libels the Stonewall Brigade

When Crawford's three and one-half Federal regiments burst across the wheatfield, abruptly opening the infantry action at Cedar Mountain, they funneled into a gap between Garnett's brigade at the left of the main Confederate line and the newly arriving Stonewall Brigade, which was intended to close up and extend that left farther to the north. Garnett's brigade found itself in an untenable position and rapidly came unhinged, from left to right. At the same time Crawford's rightwardmost elements caught the dangling southernmost piece of the Stonewall Brigade and folded it up in short order. That crumpled unit was the Twenty-seventh Virginia Infantry, one of five regiments in the Stonewall Brigade.

Meanwhile, the five North Carolina regiments of Lawrence O'Bryan Branch's brigade had arrived behind the lines and begun to form into line. Before the Tarheels were entirely ready to advance, Stonewall Jackson ordered them forward into the breach. As Branch moved east through the woods toward the wheatfield, the fleeing Twenty-seventh Virginia burst through his ranks, causing some disorder. Branch's advance spiraled south while thrusting east so that his brigade reached the edge of the wheatfield at its southwestern corner. During this movement Branch entirely lost track of one of his own regiments, the Seventh North Carolina, which caromed through the woods like a stray meteor and never accomplished any good whatsoever. Under the circumstances, the loss of control of one-fifth of the brigade must be accounted something far less than an actionable offense. It is worthy of remark, however, that Branch lost the use of precisely the same portion of his brigade as did the Stonewall Brigade, and did so before having met with any hostile action.

Soon after Branch reached the wheatfield, Archer's brigade of A. P. Hill's division arrived on his left. Not far behind came Pender's brigade, which went even farther left. When the full weight of the newly constituted Confederate front line surged forward, Archer and Pender carried the day, contributing substantially more than did Branch to the ultimate success. Branch did a workmanlike job with the opportunity presented to him and had every reason to be proud of his men and of himself, despite the Seventh North Carolina's difficulties. Although Branch did not admit it, and indeed may not have known the facts, North Carolina sources remark that many of those

Virginians who had been routed quickly rallied and fought stoutly in gaps in Branch's own front line.

Through all of Branch's advance to the wheatfield and Archer's and Pender's subsequent movements to and fighting at the same point, the four-fifths of the Stonewall Brigade at the north end of the wheatfield stood firm. For a time the Thirty-third, Fifth, Second, and Fourth Virginia of that famous old brigade stood solid on the Confederate left with no supports on their right for nearly a mile. During that crucial period, the Stonewall Brigade was the army's linchpin. As Branch and then the others showed up to its right and gradually rebuilt the line, the four Stonewall Brigade regiments poured a sheet of fire obliquely into the wheatfield from the north and northwest. That strong left anchor and Early's solid hold on the Confederate right, far to the south, were the cornerstones upon which Stonewall Jackson reestablished his line.

The particulars of these actions are supplied in much more detail, supported by a flood of notes, in Chapters 9 and 10 above. Further analysis of Branch's canard, which has achieved wide attention, would have fallen clumsily into the midst of an already complex tactical flow at that point so it was delayed to this appendix.

General Branch's brief report pointed a finger at the entire Stonewall Brigade, though without mentioning it by name: "I had proceeded about 100 yards when I commenced meeting the men of a brigade, which had preceded me, retreating in great disorder and closely pursued by the enemy. Opening ranks to permit the fugitives to pass, and pressing forward in unbroken line, my brigade met the enemy. . . . Not in the least shaken by the panic-cries of the fugitives, and without halting, my regiments poured volley after volley into the enemy, who broke and fled precipitately."[1]

Branch concluded his report with the proud statement, "I was able to preserve my line of battle unbroken throughout the day." That flat statement was not accurate by any reasonable standard which might be applied to it, but it does not represent so egregious a misstatement as to warrant outraged rejection. In fact, coming from anyone other than the primly accusatory Branch, it could be accepted as the ordinary run of postbattle self-aggrandizement that was virtually de rigueur.[2]

General Branch's official statements, taken alone, would hardly prompt special comment, to say nothing of an explicatory appendix. They were seconded, however, by much more pungent commentary in a journal the general kept. In that forum Branch escalated his attack on the Stonewall Brigade and inflated his own performance. Jackson came to Branch, in this version, with the woeful tale that "his left was beaten and broken." When Branch responded to this desperate plea, his brigade "had not gone 100 yards through the woods before we met the celebrated Stonewall Brigade, utterly routed and fleeing as fast as they could run." Undaunted, Branch "quickly drove the enemy back from the woods." The battle developed into "a splendid victory and the credit of it is due to my brigade. . . . Other brigades were engaged that did well, but none contributed so much to gain the day as I did."[3] That smug claim surely could have been contested sternly and with no little merit by the brigades of Early, Thomas, Archer, and Pender, among others—not excluding the Stonewall Brigade.

North Carolina writers picked up the refrain without any real urging and even A. P. Hill swallowed the tale. Hill's digestion no doubt was eased because the brigade under criticism was Jackson's own, and he and Jackson were on the prickliest of terms. In his official report, Hill wrote simply that the Stonewall Brigade "broke" and that Branch passed "through the broken brigade."[4]

Whether the magnification of the Twenty-seventh Virginia (the smallest regiment in the brigade) into a force six or eight times its number was a conscious misrepresentation by Branch, accepted innocently by Hill, is a matter for nothing more substantial than conjecture. Branch had been in the United States Congress for six years, which is to say he had learned to abandon any native dignity or honesty with which genetic quirks may have saddled him. A reasonably good guess would be that Branch was dissembling with an easy faculty developed in Washington, while Hill was misled, albeit with some eagerness. The post–Cedar Mountain quarrel between Branch and fellow Carolinian W. Dorsey Pender gives evidence that Branch was more than a little hyperactive and querulous that weekend.[5]

A balanced and evidently entirely reliable account of the difficulties of the Twenty-seventh Virginia and the behavior of Branch's men is in a letter by Captain Walter W. Lenoir of the Thirty-seventh North Carolina, which is cited repeatedly in Chapter 9 above. Lenoir wrote of the disorder in "a portion" of the Stonewall Brigade and of Branch's advance in "tolerable" order. He also reported the almost immediate rallying of many of the fugitives, who then fought mixed up with the Tarheels.[6]

The tactical achievements of the Thirty-third, Fifth, Second, and Fourth Virginia of the Stonewall Brigade are recounted in considerable detail in the narrative chapters of this account. That the men and their commanders reported positively on their performance is hardly surprising: rarely did anyone on either side admit otherwise, including the fleeing raw Alabama regiments at Cedar Mountain. A member of the Second Virginia wrote that Jackson verbally "gave high praise for the gallantry of his old brigade" just after the action quieted. Colonel Ronald, commanding the brigade, declared that the "conduct of the troops in this brigade was, indeed, splendid. Men never behaved better in battle." Division commander William B. Taliaferro, who had been critical of Ronald's hesitation before the infantry fight began, reported that the Stonewall Brigade struck at a "critical moment" and "fully sustained its ancient reputation."[7]

Jedediah Hotchkiss of Jackson's staff came down squarely on the side of the Stonewall Brigade, a result less than surprising but one not to be ignored, given Hotchkiss's careful historical perspective. The born-again New Yorker wrote to G. F. R. Henderson after the war that the success of the Fifth Virginia at the north end of the wheatfield antedated Branch's arrival and "disconcerted the Federals before Hill got in." "It was the advance of Winder's men," Hotchkiss insisted, "that restored the battle." Writing in his diary during the war, Hotchkiss grumbled that Jackson's draft report coddled Branch by suggesting that he and the Stonewall Brigade went into action simultaneously, when in fact "it is well known" that the brigade "had charged the Yankees . . . before Branch had passed [the schoolhouse] on his way to the field."[8]

Randolph Fairfax of the Rockbridge Artillery wrote home that the Stonewall Brigade "fought splendidly" and was complimented by Jackson, "who said they had always done well, but this time gloriously." Captain W. T. Poague of the same battery remarked that the Stonewall Brigade performed admirably and suggested that A. P. Hill's report "contains strictures . . . undeserved and unjust. I can't help thinking he was a little jealous of 'Old Jack' and the old Stonewall Brigade." Others nearby on the field reported in the same vein.[9]

Popular opinion among civilians hardly constitutes a court of last resort in military matters, but for what it may be worth the local citizenry around Cedar Mountain absorbed the widely held conventional wisdom that the Stonewall Brigade had turned the tide to victory.[10]

Although the tactical details provided in Chapters 9 and 10 are the crux of the episode, a fitting capstone to the case for the Stonewall

Brigade is the matter of captured battle flags. The tenacity with which those tokens were defended and sought by either side stands out in contemporary accounts of all Civil War engagements. At Cedar Mountain the Confederate army captured three Northern flags. Each and every one of the three was captured by the Stonewall Brigade.[11] That accomplishment does not begin to mesh with Branch's self-serving picture of a "celebrated" but "beaten and broken," "routed and fleeing" brigade.

Appendix VI
Cedar Mountain Battlefield, 1862–1865

For a few days after the battle Northern soldiers and correspondents visited the battlefield and marveled at its sights. George F. Noyes rode across the field on August 14 and noticed to his amazement that even at that early date the healing hand of nature had begun to soften the traces of men's violent destruction of one another. Within the woodlands even the scenes of fiercest carnage were covered by a "summer canopy of leaves, while all through the woods the birds sang sweetly, as if their pleasant homes had never known the rude blasts of war." Noyes wandered across ground "strewn with the usual relics of a battle-field—fragments of shot and shell, caps perforated with bullets, garments dyed crimson, cartridge-boxes, canteens, and knapsacks." He picked up a few souvenirs, but within a few weeks thereafter he had some personal battle experience that quenched his enthusiasm for such things and he threw away his Cedar Mountain mementoes.[1]

Three days after Noyes examined the battlefield David Hunter Strother returned for another look at the scenes of his adventures during the battle. On the side of Cedar Mountain Strother came upon an entire company of blue-clad soldiers ardently digging up something buried in a large and freshly filled depression. The men felt certain that treasure lay in the bottom. As Strother watched, the diggers came to a dead horse in an advanced state of putrefaction. "This, instead of discouraging them," Strother wrote, "only raised their hopes afresh. The horse must have been buried to conceal the treasure. When I left them they could hear a hollow sound at every stroke of their mattocks."[2]

Among the Northern troops occupying the battlefield at the time that Noyes visited it were the men of the Twenty-third New York.

The Empire State infantrymen observed that some of the Confederate dead had been buried with "much care and taste," but that "others were hardly covered with earth." An understandably horrified member of the Twenty-third wrote: "I saw the worms crawling from the face of one man, the arm and shoulder of another were drying in the sun, while the feet of another protruded from the grave."[3]

Not many hours after Strother's encounter with the optimistic company of shovel-wielding infantrymen, R. E. Lee and T. J. Jackson relocated the Confederacy's military frontier to the northern edge of Culpeper County. That left the scene of Jackson's recent closely contested victory within Southern lines. When John B. Hood's division of James Longstreet's corps camped on the battlefield in late October and early November 1862, nature's handiwork had obliterated many of the battle's scars. Jedediah Hotchkiss visited Hood and noticed that the battlefield where he had fought "looked much changed." Hotchkiss also noted that the rowdy fellows in Hood's command had not changed. A steady stream of them passed all through the day, eagerly heading to buy apple brandy at $15 a gallon, even though some of the men were barefoot and a sleety rain pelted down.[4]

When Hood's men were not prowling after refreshments, their officers kept them busy drilling. The Fifth Texas drilled near the Gate "on the very spot" where Winder had received his mortal wound. During respites the men would fall out of ranks and "see who could pick up the most bullets without moving out of our places." The winner often picked up "as many as thirty or forty, possibly more." Despite rain and fog and generally unpleasant weather, the Texans grew comfortable on the battlefield and hoped to spend the winter in encampments there. More fighting loomed on the horizon, however, and in mid-November they moved southeast toward Fredericksburg, which was about to become a fresh battlefield.[5]

Steady cavalry use of Culpeper County as a skirmishing arena took detachments from either side through the historic area. In February 1863 a Confederate mounted column bivouacked for the night on the slopes of Cedar Mountain and observed the ground still strewn with relics, many of them beginning to rust. "The debris of the late contest lay profusely around," wrote one of the horsemen, "in broken fragments of shell; a rusty bayonet here and there, and broken muskets; scarred and crushed timber on the western slopes." Some of the men wandered down near the run at the foot of the mountain and visited Confederate graves there.[6]

The battlefield was on Stonewall Jackson's mind that late winter and early spring. By his orders it also was on the agenda of his staff members. At the beginning of April Jackson still was working on his official report of Cedar Mountain and the maps to accompany it. (Similar tardiness among subordinates would have been tolerated not a bit, of course.) Jed Hotchkiss worked hard on the map, but when Jackson saw the result it put him "out of humor . . . and he gave vent to considerable displeasure." The general eventually accepted the map after his topographer made two minuscule changes of no real interest or importance. "Strange man!" wailed Hotchkiss in his diary—"everything must conform to standard of simplicity and accuracy, severe in all its outlines."[7] The mental disorder that weighs all things as of equal value or importance had not been delineated at the time; Hotchkiss would have recognized the symptoms.

The words in the report caused even more knotted brows. Jackson went to great lengths to avoid clarity in the interest of avoiding the controversy that hard facts almost invariably engender. The general's willingness, indeed almost eagerness, to quarrel with immediate subordinates stopped at that level. The first draft of the Cedar Mountain report spoke even more highly of the dead Winder than did the final and said something about his loss being felt. Jackson struck the reference out with the thought that it might be judged as an oblique reflection on Winder's permanent replacement, Frank Paxton. After some particularly extensive quibbling over language, Jackson suggested in exaggeration that his report-writing specialist on the staff should seek out a vantage point when the next battle opened and watch events with great care. "Write it down," Jackson asked, "so we may not have so much labor and so many conflicting statements" when the season for writing reports appeared.[8] Although no one trifled with the stern general to his face, no doubt some quietly thought that writing the report a week or so after the battle would solve many of the problems that cropped up in attempting the same feat eight months later.

A month after Jackson finally submitted his final report, he lay dying as a result of wounds received at Chancellorsville. During that last of the general's campaigns, a Northern column under W. W. Averell passed through the Cedar Mountain battlefield and noted corpses lying unburied—or, more probably, washed up—on the side of the mountain. In at least one spot the Union cavalry saw an open trench full of bones.[9]

A month later Confederates moving toward the Shenandoah Valley on what became the Gettysburg campaign saw the same sights.

Two 1902 reunion ribbons. (Mrs. Lucy Robb Works)

The same Texas regiments that camped at Cedar Mountain during October and November 1862 did so again on June 13, 1863. They saw "a great many unburied skeletons, presenting a very ghastly appearance. There were forty-nine skulls in one little ditch; the bodies were torn to pieces and scattered about." Hands and feet stuck out of the ground at weird angles. Signs of hogs rooting in the area made men sick. By the summer of 1863 the two Alabama regiments routed at Cedar Mountain had become veterans and belonged to a brigade in the same division as the Texans. The Alabama men wandered over their first battlefield and "with feelings of sadness saw some of the bones of our dead comrades who fell there, which were exposed by the rains." No doubt the Alabamians knew full well that hogs as well as rains were the despoiling agents, but they drew a veil over the horrifying facts to protect the sensibilities of homefolks. Colonel James Lawrence Sheffield of the Forty-eighth Alabama sent out work parties to cover the exposed bones.[10]

Evidently the Alabama reburial parties did not finish their jobs or else hogs and rains undid their work again because during the second week of September 1863 General Jubal A. Early once more had details on the battlefield, "fixing up the graves of our fallen." Once again the problem seemed to be that "hogs had been rooting there."[11]

The mortal remains of two men escaped that final indignity in unusual circumstances. Charles H. Colley of Gray, Maine, fell mortally wounded on August 9 and died soon thereafter in an Alexandria hospital. When Amos and Sarah Colley recovered their son's body in a coffin after no little trouble and expense, they discovered that the coffin contained the body of a Confederate soldier. They subsequently straightened out the situation and retrieved Charles's body, but meanwhile the unknown Southerner had been buried in the local cemetery. To this day the lone Confederate grave in Gray, Maine, is decorated with a Confederate flag on Memorial Day.[12]

The final intensive military occupation of Cedar Mountain battlefield during the war came during the winter of 1863–64 when the Federal Army of the Potomac sprawled across Culpeper County. The Thirteenth Massachusetts Infantry camped between Mitchell's Station and the battlefield. For some reason the officers of the unit became interested in Indian projectile points they turned up on the battlefield rather than in souvenirs of more recent historical conflict. One of the Massachusetts men gathered a haversack full of "arrow-heads, hatchets, and lance-heads" from a point along what had been the Confederate lines and sent them to Philadelphia for sale as curiosities at a fair intended to raise money for charity. Since the scavenger attached an explanatory note to the Indian relics and reported that "quite a considerable sum was received from their sale," no doubt some collections somewhere still include Indian souvenirs garnered from a Confederate battleground by a Massachusetts Yankee.[13]

Appendix VII
The Battlefield since the War

Shortly after the war the Federal government moved all of its war dead who could be found in the vicinity to a national cemetery in Culpeper. By 1871 the cemetery contained 1,337 bodies. Of that total, 422 were identified and 915 were unknown. A detailed summary of the locations from which those bodies were removed was published in 1868, at which time the national cemetery held 1,321 bodies. Addition of barely 1 percent more bodies over three years suggests that the work was essentially over by 1868. Someone calculated in 1868 that of the cemetery's dead, about 351 were brought from the battlefield of Cedar Mountain.

Careful tabulation of the bodies removed from locations identified as at or near Cedar Mountain yields a total of 405 on the 1868 enumeration. The listing below includes only bodies specifically identified as moved from near Cedar Mountain. The various numbers of bodies in the tabulation represent groupings as printed in the original (a maximum of six locations, for Charles Crittenden's farm).

Location	*Total Number of Bodies*
Charles Crittenden's farm—168, 90, 36, 1, 2, 6	303
Thos. B. Nalle's farm—1, 1, 1	3
Catherine Crittenden's land—2, 24, 53, 3	82
James B. Smoot's farm—9	9
Robert Hudson's farm—3	3
Lucy D. Brown's land—1	1
Patten's land—1	1
Lucy Hudson's land—1	1
John Rixey's land—1	1
James Garnett's land—1	1
	405

*President Theodore Roosevelt visited the battlefield in
November 1902, guided by Major Daniel A. Grimsley, Sixth
Virginia Cavalry, and accompanied by Elihu Root and George
Bruce Cortelyou of his cabinet. (Mrs. Lucy Robb Works)*

Of that mass of 405 bodies from the battlefield only a single one
was of an identified soldier. He was an artillerist named N. B. Phillips, whose body came from the Nalle farm.[1]

A Massachusetts newspaperman and Federal veteran who visited
the Southern battlefields in the spring of 1869 found the area around
Culpeper the best restored from war damage of any locale he saw in
Virginia. He remarked upon the "many little openings in the wheatfields and grey spots in the cornfields . . . the uncultivated sandhills
that arose during the war . . . broken trees . . . [and] blackened remains of fence posts." Even so, the scene was a placid agricultural
one by that date four years after the war and nearly seven years after
the battle.[2]

As late as 1900 the heirs of Catherine Crittenden engaged in an
earnest but futile attempt to secure reimbursement from the U.S.
Congress for $14,000 in damage done to their property during the

war. Their attempt, which included support from Senator Thomas Staples Martin of Virginia, generated a 206-page file, which survives in the National Archives. It did not, however, yield any money.[3]

Just after the turn of the century, interest in the forty-year-old battlefield took an upswing. On the battle's anniversary in 1901 a sizable contingent of veterans met to mark positions on the field. In July, Judge Daniel Amon Grimsley (formerly major in the Sixth Virginia Cavalry) suggested to the Culpeper County supervisors that the fields of all of the Civil War battles in the county should be "surveyed, marked and platted and made a part of the records of the county for all generations." The governing body approved and, of course, designated Grimsley to coordinate the work. The major promptly issued a call through the press for veterans to meet on August 9. Among the men of both armies who appeared for the day in addition to Grimsley were General James A. Walker, Major Alfred R. Courtney, and J. G. Field of A. P. Hill's staff, who had lost a leg near Pegram on the night of August 9, 1862.

The aging warriors "went all over the contested ground" together, "locating batteries and regiments of both armies, as if the fight were but yesterday." At 1:00 P.M. the various parties met at Cedar Run Church and did justice to a mighty feast spread by local women. After lunch Grimsley called the gathering to order and introduced General Walker as the first speaker. Courtney and Fields also spoke, as did A. S. Drewry of Pegram's battery and one veteran each from the Seventh Ohio and the Twenty-seventh Indiana. A little girl recited a poem and sang a song to end the affair. Major Grimsley looked ahead to the need to mark the battlefield for posterity and urged that the veterans of each unit that fought at Cedar Mountain contribute at least $5 for a marker to be placed where they fought. Men of both sides promised to further the project.[4]

What was doubtless the largest reunion and commemoration by veterans of the battle took place on August 8–9, 1902. The assembled veterans and other interested individuals made up a good-sized throng, which unveiled a monument to the Twenty-eighth New York in Culpeper National Cemetery and then visited the battlefield. Major Grimsley presided over a large meeting on the night of the eighth at Rixey's Opera House in Culpeper. The two keynote speakers represented the opposing sides. William Penn Lloyd, on behalf of Northerners, ignored the battle and spoke emotionally of the joys of sectional reconciliation. Lloyd concluded his remarks by comparing a speech by Georgia's Henry W. Grady (of "New South" fame), entitled

"The Race Problem," to Christ's Sermon on the Mount. The Confederate orator was the same Charles M. Blackford whose account of service at the head of Jackson's couriers is a primary source on the battle. The audience of four thousand souls who listened to Blackford must have rejoiced that he eschewed Lloyd's example and spoke about the battle, including anecdotes, which resulted in a "pleasing, humorous" speech. When the oratory stopped, all hands adjourned to consume the mountain of edibles groaning on tables in a pleasant grove on the battlefield.[5]

President Theodore Roosevelt visited Cedar Mountain battlefield on Sunday, November 2, 1902, probably as a result of news accounts he had seen of the recent reunion. Secretaries Elihu Root and George B. Cortelyou of Roosevelt's cabinet accompanied the president to the battlefield. D. A. Grimsley, of course, served as guide. Roosevelt wanted to see the Twenty-eighth New York marker, about which he had read. His other premier concern was the charge of the battalion of the First Pennsylvania Cavalry. The president, after all, was "a cavalryman himself," the *Washington Post* mentioned in explaining that special interest. Perhaps it is just as well that no record survives of Teddy Roosevelt's comparisons of his own much magnified exploits at San Juan Hill to the genuine hell experienced by the Pennsylvanians in 1862. The president played the politician before and after his tour, going to the Baptist church to hear preaching and rooming overnight with a local elected official. Roosevelt carried home as a souvenir a shell dug up on the battlefield.[6]

The fiftieth anniversary of the battle attracted considerably less attention than had the fortieth anniversary in 1902. Only fifteen hundred turned up for the 1912 affair, fewer than half as many as the four thousand who listened to Lloyd and Blackford a decade earlier. The death of the energetic local expert, D. A. Grimsley, in 1910 may have left a void in the coordination and preparation department. The fifteen hundred veterans and others "roamed over the battlefield" after local citizens provided conveyance to the site. Ladies of the neighborhood served an outdoor dinner. Former U.S. Senator John M. Thurston of Nebraska spoke and so did West Virginia state senator James A. Strother. "The ladies sang war-time songs, and the veterans joined in the chorus."[7]

In the last quarter of the twentieth century much of the battlefield of Cedar Mountain is owned and farmed by the various branches of the Inskeep clan. That fertile and hardworking family operates a thriving farm, which covers several thousand acres of the historic ground where Stonewall Jackson won his last independent campaign. The Inskeeps' stewardship of the land has resulted in a scene not dramatically different than that in which thirty thousand men locked in mortal combat on August 9, 1862. The pastoral setting is nearly as aesthetically pleasing as it is historically interesting.

A formal submission of Cedar Mountain battlefield for admission to the National Register of Historic Places as a Registered National Historic Landmark went forward to Washington in June 1987. If the nomination succeeds, Cedar Mountain will enjoy thoroughly deserved recognition and at least some few marginal protections.

NOTES

Abbreviations

DU	Duke University. William R. Perkins Library, Manuscript Department. Durham, North Carolina.
EU	Emory University. Robert W. Woodruff Library, Special Collections Department. Atlanta, Georgia.
LC	Library of Congress. Washington, D.C.
NA	National Archives. Washington, D.C.
NCDAH	North Carolina Department of Archives and History. Raleigh, North Carolina.
NYSA	New York State Archives. Albany, New York.
OHS	Ohio Historical Society. Columbus, Ohio.
OR	U.S. War Department. *The War of the Rebellion: A Compilation of the Official Records of the Union and Confederate Armies.* 128 vols. Washington, D.C., 1880–1901.
RTD	*Richmond Times-Dispatch.*
SHC	Southern Historical Collection. University of North Carolina. Chapel Hill, North Carolina.
SHSP	*Southern Historical Society Papers.*
TSLA	Tennessee State Library and Archives. Nashville, Tennessee.
USAMHI	United States Army Military History Institute. Carlisle Barracks, Pennsylvania.
VHS	Virginia Historical Society. Richmond, Virginia.
VSA	Virginia State Archives. Richmond, Virginia.
WVU	West Virginia University Library. West Virginia and Regional History Collection. Morgantown, West Virginia.

Prologue

1. Blackford, *Letters*, p. 95.

Chapter 1: John Pope's Difficult Adjustment

1. Horton et al., "Campaign of General Pope," p. 35. The widely circulated story about Pope and his "headquarters in the saddle" is not supported by any of that general's printed orders, although some are datelined almost as

pretentiously, "In the Field." Apocryphal or not, the rapid and gleeful spread of the tale through Pope's own army says a good bit about his image.

2. U.S. War Department, *War of the Rebellion: A Compilation of the Official Records of the Union and Confederate Armies*, 128 vols. (Washington, D.C., 1880–1901), Ser. I, vol. 12, pt. 3, p. 474. This classic and standard primary source will be cited hereafter simply as *Official Records*, abbreviated to *OR*. The original collation of 128 thick books is arranged in four series, with volumes making up as many as four different books (which we normally would call volumes); the various books within the multibook volumes are called parts. The reference at the beginning of this note gives series, volume, and part. Hereafter the notes will ignore series entirely, assuming Series I. The notes also will not mention the words "volume" or "part," instead simply providing the volume number followed by the part in parentheses. The citation above thus would be *OR* 12(3):474. Because the vast majority of references to the *Official Records* in this work will be to volume 12, part 2, the abbreviation system for that volume goes one step further and omits volume and part identity entirely.

3. *OR*, pp. 50–52.

4. Gordon, *Brook Farm*, pp. 275–76; *New York Times*, December 26, 1862.

5. Harvey, "Cedar Mountain"; see also the response to this article in the same journal.

6. Smith Memoir, OHS; Haupt, *Reminiscences*, p. 83.

7. Numbers and losses minutiae may be argued endlessly. These figures are from Grimsley, *Battles in Culpeper*, pp. 25–26.

8. Horton, "Campaign of General Pope," pp. 37–38.

9. Andrews, "Battle of Cedar Mountain," p. 401.

10. *OR* 12(3):919; Freeman, *Lee's Dispatches*, pp. 38–39; *OR* 11(2):936; *OR* 12(2):176–77.

11. *OR*, pp. 176–77, 181.

12. Allan, *Army*, pp. 165–66; Grimsley, *Battles in Culpeper*, p. 26.

13. Dabney, *Life of Jackson*, pp. 489–90.

14. Blackford, *Letters*, pp. 95–96; Taylor, *Destruction and Reconstruction*, p. 50.

15. Hunter McGuire to Jedediah Hotchkiss, June 1896, Hotchkiss Papers, LC; Freeman, *Lee's Dispatches*, pp. 43–44. In a letter to Hotchkiss dated August 23, 1896, Colonel Thomas T. Munford commented on Robertson's assignment to command Jackson's cavalry: "'Old Jack' was mad about it I know." The Munford letter is in microfilm roll 49 of the Hotchkiss Papers, LC.

16. McDonald, *Laurel Brigade*, p. 78.

17. Beaudry, *Fifth New York Cavalry*, pp. 37–38.

18. McDonald, *Laurel Brigade*, p. 78; Humphreys, *Heroes and Spies*, pp. 102–4.

19. McDonald, *Laurel Brigade*, pp. 78–79; *OR*, pp. 181–82.

20. Cooke, *Stonewall Jackson*, p. 255; McDonald, *Laurel Brigade*, p. 79.

21. Humphreys, *Heroes and Spies*, pp. 102–4.

22. McDonald, *Laurel Brigade*, pp. 79–80; *OR*, pp. 111–14, 178, 181–82.

23. *OR*, p. 177.

24. Casler, *Four Years*, p. 145; Hamlin, "*Old Bald Head*," p. 117.

25. Douglas, *With Stonewall*, p. 123; *SHSP* 10:84.

26. *SHSP* 10:83–84.

27. Hotchkiss, *Make Me a Map*, pp. 64–65.

28. Blackford, *Letters*, pp. 97–98.

29. Douglas, *With Stonewall*, p. 122.

30. Blackford, *Letters*, p. 86.

31. Ibid., p. 96.

32. Ibid., p. 99; Hotchkiss, *Make Me a Map*, p. 65.

33. Myers, *Comanches*, p. 88; Hotchkiss, *Make Me a Map*, p. 65.

34. Garnett Papers, Museum of the Confederacy. For a more detailed discussion of the Garnett court, see Krick, "Army of Northern Virginia's Most Notorious Court Martial."

35. Scott, *Orange County*, p. 155; Hotchkiss, *Make Me a Map*, p. 65.

36. Chambers, *Stonewall Jackson*, 2:104 and 104n.; Garnett Papers, Museum of the Confederacy.

37. *OR*, p. 182; Freeman, *Lee's Lieutenants*, 2:10.

38. Brown, *Stringfellow*, pp. 153–54.

39. Phillip Bradley, Operative Military Secret Service, Little Washington, to Major General Stonewall Jackson, photocopy in the files of Manassas National Battlefield Park.

40. Blackford, *Letters*, p. 98; Hotchkiss, *Make Me a Map*, p. 65.

41. Davidson, "Letters," p. 28; *OR*, p. 210; Kauffman Diary, SHC. Kauffman served in the Tenth Virginia.

42. Hotchkiss, *Make Me a Map*, p. 65; McClendon, *Recollections*, p. 92.

43. Manuscript Weather Journal Recording Observations at Lewinsville, Virginia, and Georgetown, D.C., June 1858–May 1866. (All war entries are from Georgetown.) The journal is microfilmed with call number CL-1064 at the National Weather Records Center, Asheville, N.C. This source will be cited hereafter as Georgetown Ms. Weather Readings.

44. Summers Diary, VSA; Jedediah Hotchkiss to his wife, Aug. 9, 1862, at LC on Reel 4 of microfilmed edition of Hotchkiss Papers. Summers was a lieutenant in Company I, Fifty-second Virginia.

45. Grimsley, *Battles in Culpeper*, pp. 26–27; Gordon, *Brook Farm*, p. 277.

46. Howard, *Recollections*, p. 162; Casler, *Four Years*, pp. 142–43. Admirers of Casler's feisty memoir will be amused but not surprised to learn that he did not mellow noticeably with age. Casler entered the R. E. Lee Camp Soldiers' Home in Richmond in January 1903 and, to quote from the home's ledger, was "dismissed, Mar. 13, 1903, for bringing liquor into the Home, drunk, & cursing Commandant." The episode is recorded on page 72 of the

home's typescript ledger book, on deposit at VHS. Charles S. Winder was extraordinarily well connected. His grandfather was Edward Lloyd V, governor of Maryland and a huge landholder. General Winder's mother was Elizabeth Tayloe Lloyd (1800–1880); her brother Edward Lloyd VI had a daughter Alice (1832–1921), who married her first cousin—the general. Winder's father was Edward S. Winder, an army officer who died in 1840. Confederate General John Henry Winder was Charles S. Winder's uncle. Admiral Franklin Buchanan, CSN, married C. S. Winder's mother's sister. Winder also was related to Francis Scott Key and Confederate General Lloyd Tilghman. C. S. Winder's son Edward Lloyd Winder lived 1858–1939. A daughter of C. S. Winder, Elizabeth Lloyd Winder, died in 1862, aged thirteen months. This Winder information is summarized from a letter to the author dated October 30, 1984, from Brian Pohanka of Alexandria, an admirable historian and historic preservationist. Pohanka found much material on Winder at the Talbot County Historical Society in Easton, Maryland.

47. Howard, *Recollections*, pp. 162–63.
48. Hotchkiss, *Make Me a Map*, p. 65.

Chapter 2: Jackson and Hill Clash

1. *OR*, pp. 26, 54, 133; Horton, "Campaign of General Pope," 46; Smith Memoir, OHS.
2. Grimsley, *Battles in Culpeper*, p. 26; Stearns, *Company K*, p. 86; *New York Times*, Dec. 26, 1862.
3. Patrick, *Inside Lincoln's Army*, p. 120. This outstanding diary was very skillfully edited by David S. Sparks.
4. These and other accounts of depredations are in the following sources: Calfee, *Confederate Culpeper*, p. 10; Strother, *Virginia Yankee*, p. 81; Slaughter, *Cedar Mountain*, p. 5; Sheeran, *Confederate Chaplain*, pp. 2–3; and Miller, "Letters," p. 90.
5. Hotchkiss, *Make Me a Map*, pp. 174–75; Calfee, *Confederate Culpeper*, pp. 3–5, 10; "What a Woman Saw."
6. U.S. Congress, *Report of the Joint Committee on the Conduct of the War* (Washington, D.C., 1863–66), vol. 3 (serial 7, published 1865), p. 46 in the last of numerous paginations. This source, which suffers from typically confusing government collation, is cited hereafter as *Committee on the Conduct of the War*. High Northern spirits are described in Townsend, *Non-Combatant*, p. 249; Whitman, *Civil War Letters*, p. 60; and Conwell, *Magnolia Journey*, pp. 169–70.
7. Strother, *Virginia Yankee*, pp. 75, 81; Emerson, "A Boy in the Camp of Lee"; Marvin, *Fifth Connecticut*, p. 151.
8. Hotchkiss, *Make Me a Map*, p. 66; William Johnson Pegram to his sister, Aug. 8, 1862, Pegram-Johnson-McIntosh Papers, VHS; Calfee, *Confederate Culpeper*, pp. 12–13.

9. Henderson, *Stonewall Jackson*, 2:88; Grimsley, *Battles in Culpeper*, p. 26.

10. Steele, *American Campaigns*, 1:149.

11. *OR*, p. 214. Hill told Alexander S. Pendleton in a letter dated March 13, 1863, that "the order to me on the night of the seventh of Aug . . . was written." Unfortunately, Hill admitted, "I did not preserve it." The letter is in the West Papers, Mss2W5205b, VHS. Since we cannot see the order Hill did receive, we cannot judge how markedly it varied from Jackson's later plan.

12. Jackson denied some of Hill's contentions at great length (*OR*, pp. 216–17) but did not deny Hill's pointed complaint that the change in orders was not sent to him.

13. *OR*, pp. 214–16; E. F. Paxton to T. J. Jackson, Mar. 11, 1863, West Papers, VHS.

14. Paxton's remark is in the March 11, 1863, letter to Jackson; Hill to Stuart, Nov. 14, 1862; both in West Papers, Mss1St923C4, VHS.

15. *OR*, pp. 215–17. Sunrise on this date came at 5:13 in Richmond, according to the *Confederate States Almanac* [Crandall no. 4988].

16. *OR*, pp. 214–15.

17. *OR*, p. 215.

18. *OR*, p. 217.

19. *OR*, pp. 216–17.

20. Hill to Stuart, Nov. 14, 1862, West Papers, VHS. The letter's heading is from "Hd Qrs, Opequon, Nov. 14th [1862]."

21. Blackford, *Letters*, p. 99; *OR*, pp. 180–81.

22. *OR*, p. 182; Hotchkiss, *Make Me a Map*, pp. 65–66; "Massanutten," "Cedar Run," also printed in an unidentified newspaper clipping in the M. J. Solomons Scrapbook, Ms. 4950, DU.

23. Grimsley, *Battles in Culpeper*, p. 26; Massanutten, "Cedar Run"; *OR*, p. 181; Jedediah Hotchkiss to his brother, Aug. 14, 1862, Hotchkiss Papers, LC. The Federal cavalry involved were mostly of the First New Jersey Cavalry and the First Pennsylvania Cavalry (*OR*, pp. 92, 129–30).

24. Hotchkiss, *Make Me a Map*, pp. 65–66; *OR*, p. 181; McDonald, *Laurel Brigade*, p. 80.

25. Massanutten, "Cedar Run."

26. William P. Harper Diary, (captain, Company H, Seventh Louisiana Infantry), Tulane University; George Campbell Brown Memoir, Brown-Ewell Papers, TSLA; Sheeran, *Confederate Chaplain*, p. 3.

27. Hotchkiss, *Make Me a Map*, p. 66; Grimsley, *Battles in Culpeper*, p. 26; Hetland, "Battle of Cedar Run"; Massanutten, "Cedar Run"; Brown Memoir, Brown-Ewell Papers, TSLA.

28. Blackford, *Letters*, p. 101; Grimsley, *Battles in Culpeper*, pp. 26–27.

29. *OR*, p. 210; Kauffman Diary, SHC. Evidence scattered through the sources for the march of August 8 suggests the formation as described in the text, and there is no question that the march to battle on the next day had this configuration.

30. Davidson, "Letters," p. 28; Worsham, *Foot Cavalry*, pp. 108–9; *SHSP* 27:145.

31. *OR*, p. 210; James Preston Crowder to his mother, Aug. 13, 1862, Crowder Papers, EU.

32. Kauffman Diary, SHC; *OR*, p. 210.

33. Casler, *Four Years*, pp. 145–46; Georgetown Ms. Weather Readings.

34. Grimsley, *Battles in Culpeper*, p. 26; Jedediah Hotchkiss to his wife, Aug. 16, 1862, and to his brother, Aug. 14, 1862, Hotchkiss Papers, LC; Hotchkiss in Evans, ed., *Confederate Military History*, 3:308.

35. Sheeran, *Confederate Chaplain*, p. 3.

36. Cable, "The Gentler Side of Two Great Southerners."

37. *SHSP* 10:84.

38. Howard, *Recollections*, p. 164; Hazael J. Williams (major, Fifth Virginia), Memoir, Hotchkiss Papers, LC (Roll 49, Frame 422) is the source for the name of the farm where the brigade camped.

39. Clark, *North Carolina Regiments*, 4:159.

40. *OR*, p. 223.

41. *OR*, p. 215.

42. Poague, *Gunner*, p. 32; William J. Pegram to his sister, Aug. 8, 1862, Pegram-Johnson-McIntosh Papers, VHS.

43. *OR*, p. 215.

44. A. P. Hill to A. S. Pendleton, Mar. 13, 1863, West Papers, VHS; *OR*, p. 217; E. F. Paxton to Jackson, Mar. 13, 1863, West Papers, VHS.

45. *OR*, pp. 222–23; "Gamma Sigma" to *Raleigh State Journal*.

46. *OR*, p. 215.

Chapter 3: A Slow March to Battle

1. Andrews, *Memoir*, pp. 66–67; John K. Hitner Diary (Rockbridge Artillery), United Daughters of the Confederacy National Headquarters; Hotchkiss, *Make Me a Map*, p. 66; E. F. Paxton to T. J. Jackson, Mar. 13, 1863, West Papers, VHS.

2. Neese, *Horse Artillery*, pp. 83–85.

3. Hotchkiss, *Make Me a Map*, p. 66; Jedediah Hotchkiss to his wife, Aug. 9–10, 1862, Hotchkiss Papers, LC.

4. Howard, *Recollections*, pp. 164–65.

5. Ibid., p. 165.

6. *OR*, pp. 210–11; Kauffman Diary, SHC; Melhorn Diary, Stanford. Captain John Wesley Melhorn of the Tenth Virginia also timed the alarm at 2:00 A.M. and complained that his company had to march out and form line of battle "several times until after daylight."

7. *OR*, p. 211.

8. Kauffman Diary, SHC; *OR*, p. 210.

9. Davidson, "Letters," p. 28.

10. Worsham, *Foot Cavalry*, p. 109; *SHSP* 27:145.

11. *OR*, p. 222.

12. Krick, *Maxcy Gregg*, p. 14; Benson, *Civil War Book*, pp. 16–17. For Mackay's service record see Salley, *South Carolina Troops*, 1:331.

13. *OR*, p. 181.

14. Grimsley, *Battles in Culpeper*, pp. 26–27.

15. *New York Tribune*, Aug. 10, 1862, in Moore, ed., *Rebellion Record*, 5:327; Brown, *Twenty-seventh Indiana*, p. 195; Smith Memoir, OHS.

16. *Committee on the Conduct of the War*, seventh serial volume (third for 1865), page 45 in final supplement. Freeman, *Lee's Lieutenants*, 2:21, included half a dozen mistakes in what ostensibly is a direct quotation.

17. McGuire, *Address*.

18. William Allan, "Relative Numbers and Losses at Slaughter's Mountain," *SHSP* 8:178–83.

19. Hotchkiss, *Make Me a Map*, p. 66; *OR*, p. 239.

20. Blackford, *Letters*, pp. 101–3.

21. Ibid.

22. Ibid.

23. Jedediah Hotchkiss to his wife, Aug. 9–10, 1862, Hotchkiss Papers, LC; Blackford, *Letters*, pp. 99–100.

24. Boswell Report, LC, Roll 49, Frame 172; Hotchkiss, *Make Me a Map*, p. 66. Cornelia Petty was enumerated in the 1860 census during the month of August as a thirty-two-year-old farmer worth $11,125. A son aged thirteen and two daughters (ages ten and eight) lived with her. This and all subsequent references to census information are from the 1860 census for Culpeper County, microfilmed as National Archives publication M653, Roll 1341. Petty is on page 30, building 240, of the Southern District of the county. She died August 11, 1902, forty years and two days after the battle.

25. Hamlin, *"Old Bald Head,"* p. 117; *Confederate Veteran* 12 (1904): 174–75; *SHSP* 10:89.

26. Summers Diary, VSA; Georgetown Ms. Weather Readings.

27. H. A. Tripp (Company F, Tenth Maine), in an unidentified newspaper clipping, Hotchkiss Papers, LC, Container 70 (cited hereafter as Tripp, Tenth Maine n.p. clipping); Brown, *Twenty-seventh Indiana*, pp. 195–96; Quint, *Second Massachusetts*, p. 105.

28. *OR*, p. 228.

29. Essay by Cadwallader Jones, January 1699, *Virginia Magazine of History and Biography* 30 (1922): 333; *Richmond Dispatch*, Aug. 20, 1862.

30. Myers, *Comanches*, p. 88.

31. The Major family in the 1860 census (page 26 of the Southern District of Culpeper County) included William, age thirty-nine, a farmer worth $81,000; Edmonia, age thirty-six; five sons (ages six through seventeen); and one sixteen-year-old daughter. For the Crittenden house, see below. For an

interesting incident from April 1864, in which Mrs. Major refused to accept food from two Maine officers and also rejected "with the utmost scorn" any assistance with a brushfire, see Small, *Road to Richmond*, pp. 127–28.

32. *OR*, p. 228. Evidence about timing is, as always with such things, contradictory. See *SHSP* 10:84—"a little after noon"; Tripp, Tenth Maine n.p. clipping offers 1:00 P.M.; Ewell in *OR*, p. 227, is much too early in all of his timing but has been accepted by several writers. Backtracking from the time of the subsequent advance is similarly difficult (cf. Early in *OR*, p. 229, and in his *Autobiographical Sketch*, pp. 94–95).

33. *SHSP* 10:85; *OR*, pp. 228–29; Marvin, *Fifth Connecticut*, pp. 153–54; Early, *Autobiographical Sketch*, pp. 94–95.

34. Manuscript note by G. Campbell Brown, Brown-Ewell Papers, TSLA.

35. Wise, *Long Arm of Lee*, 1:241–42.

36. Grimsley, *Battles in Culpeper*, p. 27.

37. Manuscript account by an unidentified member of the Twelfth Virginia Cavalry, Matheny Collection, WVU.

38. Myers, *Comanches*, p. 89.

39. Denison, *Cedar Mountain*, p. 15; *OR*, p. 140.

40. *OR*, pp. 182, 226, 228, 235, 237; Hotchkiss, *Make Me a Map*, p. 175; Hetland, "Battle of Cedar Run."

41. Grimsley, *Battles in Culpeper*, p. 27; *OR*, pp. 228, 237; manuscript memoir by an unidentified member of Dement's Battery Memoir, NYSA. Courtney suggested that his line opened only when infantry skirmishers moved from the left, but this clearly was not Early's major advance.

42. Tobie, *First Maine Cavalry*, p. 80; Denison, *Cedar Mountain*, pp. 20–21.

43. Gould, *Tenth Maine*, p. 170.

44. *New York Tribune*, Aug. 10, 1862, quoted in Moore, ed., *Rebellion Record*, 5:327; Adrian R. Root to "My dear Mother," Aug. 16, 1862, typescript, Manassas National Battlefield Park; Trimble, "Civil War Diary," p. 3. Other estimates on the time cover (as usual) a three-hour range, but "about 2 o'clock" is the most accurate.

45. Denison, *Cedar Mountain*, pp. 19–20, 23. Catherine Crittenden and her daughter Anne (then aged twenty-one) lived alone at the house in 1860 (page 26 of the census, Southern District of Culpeper County, NA). Between them they declared the relatively huge net worth of $60,680 in real estate and $19,268 in personal estate. The two women were listed in the house next to the Majors (other than one intervening vacant one). Mrs. Crittenden died on July 24, 1868.

46. *OR*, pp. 228–29; Early, *Autobiographical Sketch*, pp. 94–95.

47. *SHSP* 10:85; *OR*, pp. 229, 232.

48. *SHSP* 10:85. Walker's conflict with Jackson at VMI is mentioned in several sources, but its escalation to attempted murder, with Jackson considering carrying a pistol for protection, is reported only in manuscript notes by Jedediah Hotchkiss, p. 333, Hotchkiss Papers, LC.

49. Accounts by Early in *OR*, p. 229, and Early, *Autobiographical Sketch*, p. 95; Trimble, "Civil War Diary," p. 3; Boswell Report, LC; G. Campbell Brown Memoir, Brown-Ewell Papers, TSLA; Massanutten, "Cedar Run"; Denison, *Sabres and Spurs*, p. 124.

50. Hetland, "Battle of Cedar Run"; *OR*, pp. 229, 234; Buck, *Old Confeds*, p. 44; Early, *Autobiographical Sketch*, p. 95.

51. C.W.A., "Battle of Cedar Run"; Grimsley, *Battles in Culpeper*, p. 27; *OR*, p. 229; Dement's Battery Memoir, NYSA.

52. Bliss, *Reminiscences*, pp. 10–12; Denison, *Sabres and Spurs*, p. 124; G. Campbell Brown Memoir, Brown-Ewell Papers, TSLA.

53. *OR*, p. 229; Early, *Autobiographical Sketch*, p. 96; Grimsley, *Battles in Culpeper*, p. 27.

54. Hamlin, *"Old Bald Head,"* p. 121.

55. *OR*, pp. 182, 227; McClendon, *Recollections*, p. 94; G. Campbell Brown Memoir, Brown-Ewell Papers, TSLA; Grimsley, *Battles in Culpeper*, p. 27.

56. Howard, *Recollections*, p. 165.

57. *OR*, p. 182; Howard, *Recollections*, p. 166.

58. Hotchkiss, *Make Me a Map*, p. 66; Douglas, *With Stonewall*, pp. 125–26. Henry Kyd Douglas used so many exaggerations in his memoir that it is difficult to use his material without corroboration.

59. *OR*, pp. 200, 204; Krick, *Lee's Colonels*, p. 281; *OR*, pp. 191–93.

60. Shuler Diary (captain, Company H, Thirty-third Virginia), LC; Hitner Diary, United Daughters of the Confederacy National Headquarters.

61. *OR*, p. 191; Howard, *Recollections*, p. 166; Jones, *Under the Stars and Bars*, p. 111.

62. *OR*, pp 200, 203–4; Howard, *Recollections*, p. 167.

63. *OR*, p. 210; Green, *Word-book of Virginia Folk-speech*, p. 16.

64. *OR*, pp. 209, 211; Melhorn Diary, Stanford.

65. *OR*, p. 215.

66. *OR*, pp. 219–20; Freeman, *Lee's Dispatches*, pp. 115–16.

67. *OR*, p. 222.

68. Ashe Memoir, Ashe Papers, NCDAH; Nineteenth Georgia "Participant"; Childs (First Tennessee), "Cedar Run Battle as I Saw It"; J. H. Moore, "Seventh Tennessee Infantry," in Lindsley, *Military Annals of Tennessee*, p. 234. An unlikely story in *Confederate Veteran* 8 (1900): 66–67 reported that when Archer met Jackson at about this time, he referred to their last meeting, on a dueling field in Mexico, where Archer had been an invited spectator and Jackson a second; it was said that Jackson drilled the duel participants in their roles as though they were an awkward squad of infantry.

69. Pender, *General to His Lady*, pp. 164–66 and passim; Brunson, *Pee Dee Light Artillery*, p. 20; Boyles, *Reminiscences*, pp. 33–34, 38–39. Another South Carolinian, James Fitz James Caldwell, in his classic book *The History of a Brigade of South Carolinians*, p. 102, wrote that Pender "had not been very popular."

70. Seymour Memoir, University of Michigan; Handerson, *Yankee in Gray*, pp. 28–30; Gache, *Frenchman*, pp. 128–29.

71. Gilmor, *Four Years*, p. 53; Krick, *Maxcy Gregg*, p. 14.

72. *OR*, pp. 225–26.

Chapter 4: Jackson and Winder as Gunners

1. Marvin, *Fifth Connecticut*, p. 154; *OR*, pp. 237–38; Allan, *Army*, pp. 170–71; Grimsley, *Battles in Culpeper*, p. 27. Grimsley's compass directions from the Crittenden House are 90° different from those used nominally in this study.

2. *OR*, pp. 230, 237–38; Early, *Autobiographical Sketch*, p. 97.

3. Krick, *Lee's Colonels*, p. 86.

4. *OR*, pp. 237–38.

5. *OR*, pp. 182, 230; Early, *Autobiographical Sketch*, p. 97. Grimsley, *Battles in Culpeper*, p. 27, cut through the confusion successfully and identified three guns net. So did Jennings Cropper Wise in *Long Arm of Lee*, 1:248.

6. *OR*, pp. 237–38; Grimsley, *Battles in Culpeper*, p. 27.

7. Dement's Battery Memoir, NYSA.

8. Neese, *Horse Artillery*, pp. 84–85.

9. Jedediah Hotchkiss to his brother, Aug. 14, 1862, Hotchkiss Papers, LC.

10. Townsend, *Non-Combatant*, p. 257.

11. Neese, *Horse Artillery*, p. 85; Early, *Autobiographical Sketch*, p. 96.

12. *OR*, p. 230; Early, *Autobiographical Sketch*, p. 96.

13. *OR*, p. 230.

14. Early, *Autobiographical Sketch*, p. 97; Calfee, *Confederate Culpeper*, p. 3; Culpeper County Works Progress Administration Report, Apr. 2, 1936, Culpeper Town and County Library.

15. Howard, *Recollections*, p. 167; *OR*, p. 186.

16. Moore, *Cannoneer*, p. 94; Hitner Diary, United Daughters of the Confederacy National Headquarters.

17. *OR*, p. 204.

18. Howard, *Recollections*, pp. 167–68; *OR*, pp. 186, 230; Massanutten, "Cedar Run."

19. Moore, *Cannoneer*, p. 94; *OR*, p. 213.

20. Poague, *Gunner*, p. 33; *OR*, pp. 213–14; Moore, *Cannoneer*, pp. 94–95.

21. *OR*, p. 186; Trimble, "Civil War Diary," p. 4.

22. *OR*, pp. 200, 204, 230.

23. Worsham, *Foot Cavalry*, pp. 110–11.

24. *OR*, pp. 200, 203; Worsham, *Foot Cavalry*, p. 111.

25. *OR*, pp. 200, 203–4; Emerson, "A Boy in the Camp of Lee," p. 406.

26. *OR*, pp. 188, 200.

27. Howard, *Recollections*, p. 169.

28. *OR*, p. 203.

29. *OR*, pp. 201–2, 205; Davidson, "Letters," p. 28.

30. *OR*, pp. 182, 204; Thomas S. Garnett manuscript report in Hotchkiss Papers, LC, Container 34; Grimsley, *Battles in Culpeper*, pp. 28–29.

31. Worsham, *Foot Cavalry*, p. 111; *OR*, pp. 201–2.

32. Hotchkiss, *Make Me a Map*, p. 130.

33. Howard, *Recollections*, p. 169; *OR*, pp. 207–8.

34. *OR*, p. 188.

35. *OR*, pp. 189, 207–8, 212; Wood, *The War*, pp. 86–87; Hetland, "Battle of Cedar Run."

36. Huffman, *Ups and Downs*, p. 58; typescript memoir of an unidentified soldier of the Tenth Virginia, signed "J.W.G.," Cook Papers, WVU.

37. *OR*, p. 211.

38. *OR*, p. 188.

39. *OR*, pp. 206, 208, 211; Wood, *The War*, pp. 86–87.

40. *OR*, p. 188.

41. *OR*, p. 234; Grimsley, *Battles in Culpeper*, p. 29; manuscript sketch map drawn by General James A. Walker on the flyleaf of his copy of the Cedar Mountain volume of *OR*, now deposited in the library of Richmond National Battlefield Park. Walker also marked on the margins of Confederate reports of the battle in the same volume. Many of his remarks are pungent and all are interesting. Reference to Walker's notations hereafter is as J. A. Walker manuscript marginalia, Richmond National Battlefield Park. I am indebted to Judy Anthis of that library for bringing Walker's valuable notes to my attention.

42. *OR*, pp. 210, 212; *Confederate Veteran* 17 (1909): 423; Kauffman Diary, SHC. Lieutenant Mauck's diary is printed in Strickler, *Short History*, pp. 176–81.

43. *OR*, p. 210; Melhorn Diary, Stanford. Melhorn reported the regiment's loss in killed and wounded as sixty-two.

44. *OR*, p. 235; Nisbet, *Firing Line*, p. 132.

45. G. Campbell Brown Memoir, Brown-Ewell Papers, TSLA; Nisbet, *Firing Line*, pp. 132–33; Myers, *Comanches*, pp. 89–90.

46. 1860 Culpeper County Census, Southern District, pp. 29–30, NA.

47. Krick, *Lee's Colonels*, pp. 197–98; George P. Wallace to "Dear Sister," Mar. 31, 1863, Wallace Letters, WVU.

48. Nisbet, *Firing Line*, p. 133; *OR*, p. 237.

49. *OR*, pp. 183, 227; G. Campbell Brown Memoir, Brown-Ewell Papers, TSLA.

50. Myers, *Comanches*, pp. 89–90.

51. *OR*, pp. 227, 235, 237.

52. Oates, *The War*, p. 129. In 1900 Crittenden heirs still were seeking recompense from the Federal government for looting of their place. To demonstrate the family's recidivist tendencies, the government was rounding

up evidence of such things as accepting $5 for fodder from the Confederate government in March 1862. See Crittenden Family Claim Files, War Department Record and Pension Office, File 616957, June 13, 1900, Record Group 94, NA.

53. *Land We Love* 5 (1868): 441–42; *SHSP* 10:89.

54. *Land We Love* 5 (1868): 90; *SHSP* 10:85–86. The latter version is considerably broader in caricature.

55. *SHSP* 10:89; [Wright], *List of Staff Officers*, p. 54; Richey, *Memorial History of the John Bowie Strange Camp*, pp. 47–48.

56. Nisbet, *Firing Line*, p. 133; Myers, *Comanches*, p. 90.

57. *OR*, p. 187.

58. Fleet and Fuller, eds., *Green Mount*, p. 262; application by General R. L. Walker's daughter for admission to the United Daughters of the Confederacy, on file at that organization's national headquarters in Richmond.

59. *OR*, pp. 187, 226; J. W. D. Farrar in "Our Confederate Column," *RTD*, Oct. 19, 1902; Yeary, *Boys in Gray*, pp. 197–98.

60. Gordon, *Brook Farm*, p. 290; *OR*, pp. 226, 231; Thomas, *Doles-Cook Brigade*, pp. 213–14; Hotchkiss, *Make Me a Map*, p. 175; Farrar, in "Our Confederate Column," *RTD*, Oct. 19, 1902.

61. Jones, *Rebel War Clerk's Diary*, 1:148.

62. The standard figure for Confederate guns has been twenty-six rather than twenty-three. That includes eight on the mountain (where Lieutenant Terry's strength was only a two-gun section, not a full battery) and six near the Gate (no doubt adding a later arrival, which in fact only offset one gun removed because of mechanical problems, as will be seen). Henderson, *Stonewall Jackson*, 2:91; Grimsley, *Battles in Culpeper*, p. 28.

63. *OR*, pp. 230, 183; Hitner Diary, United Daughters of the Confederacy National Headquarters.

64. *OR*, p. 188.

65. *OR*, pp. 238, 186, 239.

66. Dement's Battery Memoir, NYSA.

67. Howard, *Recollections*, pp. 168–69; Moore, *Cannoneer*, p. 106.

68. *OR* 51(1):120; Hitner Diary, United Daughters of the Confederacy National Headquarters; *OR*, p. 214.

69. John D. Beardsley (Tenth Maine) to John M. Gould, Feb. 13, 1870, Gould Papers, DU; *OR*, p. 187.

70. Howard, *Recollections*, p. 169; Moore, *Cannoneer*, p. 96; Krick, *Lee's Colonels*, p. 70.

71. Heitman, *Historical Register*, 1:1049; Moore, *Cannoneer*, p. 95; Poague, *Gunner*, p. 33. The usually reliable local authority on the ground, Major Daniel A. Grimsley of the Sixth Virginia Cavalry, reported the tradition in the neighborhood that Winder was hit "in the main road, a short distance south [west, by the nominal reckoning of this study] of the Crittenden gate." In fact, the general unquestionably was between the Rockbridge pieces, and

they, of course, were a little bit beyond the Gate in the open, nominally east [Grimsley would have said north] of the Gate. See Grimsley, *Battles in Culpeper*, p. 29.

72. Hitner Diary, United Daughters of the Confederacy National Headquarters; Howard, *Recollections*, pp. 169–70; Moore, *Cannoneer*, pp. 95–96. Hitner served with the gun with vent trouble, but Winder was "struck . . . at my side," Hitner wrote.

73. Moore, *Cannoneer*, p. 95; Fonerden, *Carpenter's Battery*, pp. 30–31; Howard, *Recollections*, pp. 169–70.

74. Fonerden, *Carpenter's Battery*, pp. 30–31; Howard, *Recollections*, pp. 169–70.

75. Boswell Report, LC; Howard, *Recollections*, p. 170; OR, p. 189.

76. Moore, *Cannoneer*, p. 96; OR, pp. 213–14.

77. OR, pp. 213–14, 186; Poague, *Gunner*, p. 33. Crutchfield's official report is a bit too immodest in claiming personal involvement and initiative beyond what the facts warrant. It also differs in small particulars from others and inevitably is in error when those differences can be resolved.

78. OR, pp. 186–87, 213, 226.

79. Howard, *Recollections*, p. 162; OR, pp. 186–87. Andrews clearly was wounded well after the advance from the Gate, but the chronology beyond that is not firm. Since the further move he proposed but never executed was again to the right front, into the locale where Pegram and Hardy set up, it is very likely that Major Andrews suffered his famous wound just before those two officers and their four guns arrived on the field. Ned Moore's account of Andrews's wound in *Cannoneer*, p. 95, is garbled both as to timing and circumstances.

80. Andrews, *Memoir*, pp. 55–56; OR, pp. 191, 183.

81. OR, pp. 188, 238, 230.

82. *Cincinnati Times*, Aug. 10, 1862, quoted in Moore, ed., *Rebellion Record*, 5:325; *New York Tribune*, Aug. 10, 1862, quoted in ibid., p. 329; Marvin, *Fifth Connecticut*, p. 154; Pyne, *First New Jersey Cavalry*, pp. 87–88.

83. Greene Report, Aug. 14, 1862, LC.

84. Best Report, LC.

85. Calfee, *Confederate Culpeper*, p. 3.

86. Gordon, *Brook Farm*, p. 285; Quint, *Second Massachusetts*, pp. 108, 116. Mrs. Brown cannot be positively identified, but she probably was Sarah Brown, age twenty-one, then childless, living with twenty-seven-year-old J. B. Brown at the time of the 1860 census (Culpeper County, Southern District, p. 27, NA).

87. Strother, *Virginia Yankee*, p. 76.

88. Dew, *Ironmaker to the Confederacy*, pp. 185, 232.

89. Wise, *Long Arm of Lee*, 1:249–50.

Chapter 5: Confused Preparations in the Woods

1. Blackford, *Letters*, pp. 103, 110; *OR*, p. 182.

2. Manuscript map in Hotchkiss Papers, LC, by an unidentified hand (not Hotchkiss's); 1860 Census, Culpeper County, Southern District, p. 26, NA.

3. Blackford, *Letters*, p. 100; typescript memoir of an unidentified soldier of the Tenth Virginia, signed "J.W.G.," Cook Papers, WVU.

4. Humphreys, *Heroes and Spies*, p. 196.

5. Blackford, *Letters*, pp. 103–4; Buck, *Old Confeds*, p. 44.

6. Blue, "Reminiscences."

7. "Our Confederate Column," *RTD*, Nov. 8, 1903; *OR*, p. 230.

8. *RTD*, Nov. 8, 1903; *OR*, p. 200.

9. Boswell Report, LC.

10. *OR*, p. 214; J. W. D. Farrar in "Our Confederate Column," *RTD*, Oct. 19, 1902; A. S. Drewry in Yeary, *Boys in Gray*, pp. 197–98.

11. *OR*, pp. 215, 219.

12. *OR*, p. 200; Grimsley, *Battles in Culpeper*, pp. 28–29.

13. Worsham, *Foot Cavalry*, pp. 111–12, 114–15; *OR*, p. 202.

14. Early, *Autobiographical Sketch*, p. 97; *OR*, p. 230.

15. Boswell Report, LC; *OR*, p. 208.

16. *OR*, p. 189.

17. *OR*, p. 200.

18. Lee, *Pendleton*, p. 203.

19. *OR*, pp. 204, 203, 205; Davidson, "Letters," p. 28.

20. *OR*, pp. 192, 197; Hazael J. Williams to Jedediah Hotchkiss, Jan. 30, 1897, Hotchkiss Papers, LC; Hendricks, "Pegram at Cedar Mountain," p. 448.

21. *OR*, pp. 192, 197; Hendricks, "Pegram at Cedar Mountain," p. 448; Casler, *Four Years*, p. 146.

22. *OR*, p. 192; Howard, *Recollections*, p. 170; Casler, *Four Years*, p. 148.

23. Blackford, *Letters*, p. 104; *OR*, p. 198.

24. *OR*, p. 192; Blackford, *Letters*, p. 104; Williams to Hotchkiss, Jan. 30, 1897, Hotchkiss Papers, LC.

25. *OR*, pp. 198, 197; Casler, *Four Years*, p. 146.

26. *OR*, pp. 192, 198.

27. *OR*, pp. 192, 195, 198.

28. J. A. Walker manuscript marginalia, Richmond National Battlefield Park.

29. Casler, *Four Years*, p. 146; *OR*, pp. 192, 197, 198; *Cincinnati Times*, Aug. 10, 1862, quoted in Moore, ed., *Rebellion Record*, 5:325. Hazael J. Williams of the Fifth Virginia, in his January 30, 1897, letter to Hotchkiss (Hotchkiss Papers, LC), claimed that the Twenty-seventh and Thirty-third Virginia regiments remained behind the rest of the brigade to support a battery when the other three regiments advanced. Although Williams gener-

ally is a reliable source, that tale does not fit any of the demonstrable facts and contradicts several.

Chapter 6: Augur's Attack

1. *OR*, pp. 137–38.

2. Grimsley, *Battles in Culpeper*, p. 28.

3. Wood, *Seventh Regiment*, p. 127; Anderson, "Civil War Recollections," pp. 386–87.

4. Smith Memoir, OHS. As an aside, it is interesting that an entire chapter of Smith's manuscript memoir is a paean to John S. Mosby.

5. Marvin, *Fifth Connecticut*, p. 153; Anderson, "Civil War Recollections," pp. 386–87; Andrews, "Battle of Cedar Mountain," p. 415; G. Campbell Brown Memoir, Brown-Ewell Papers, TSLA; *OR*, p. 137.

6. Mahon and Danysh, *Army Lineage Series*, p. 443.

7. Anderson, "Civil War Recollections," p. 387.

8. Andrews, "Battle of Cedar Mountain," pp. 430–31; *OR*, p. 161; SeCheverall, *Twenty-ninth Ohio*, pp. 52–53; *Cincinnati Times*, Aug. 10, 1862, in Moore, ed., *Rebellion Record*, 5:325–26.

9. Wood, *Seventh Regiment*, p. 127.

10. *OR*, p. 161; *New York Tribune*, Aug. 10, 1862, quoted in Moore, ed., *Rebellion Record*, 5:328.

11. Charles Candy to H. A. Tripp, June 29, 1887, from Fort Leavenworth, Gould Papers, DU; Georgetown Ms. Weather Readings.

12. Tallman Memoir, Harrisonburg Civil War Round Table Collection, USAMHI. I am indebted to Gregory A. Coco for bringing this and several other Federal manuscripts to my attention.

13. *OR*, p. 161. SeCheverall, *Twenty-ninth Ohio*, pp. 51–52; A. H. Sterrett to "Dear Innis," Aug. 13, 1862, in possession of Lewis Leigh of Fairfax, Virginia. I owe thanks to Leigh, owner of an admirable collection of manuscripts and other Civil War material, for this information and for many other such things over the years. The Twenty-ninth Ohio regimental cited in this note displays an amusing degree of plagiarism from the account published on pages 126–27 of Wood, *Seventh Regiment*.

14. *OR*, p. 137.

15. Stevens Pension File, Record Group 94, NA.

16. *OR*, p. 168; *SHSP* 27:147.

17. *OR*, p. 168; Andrews, "Battle of Cedar Mountain," p. 431; Boyle, *Soldiers True*, p. 44.

18. Brown, *Twenty-seventh Indiana*, p. 201.

19. *OR*, p. 168; Andrews, "Battle of Cedar Mountain," p. 431; Boyle, *Soldiers True*, p. 44.

20. Bates, letter, in *Second Annual Report of the State Historian of the State of New York*, pp. 101–3.

21. Greene Report, LC.

22. Krick, *Lee's Colonels*, p. 315.

23. Jedediah Hotchkiss to G. F. R. Henderson, July 30, 1896, Hotchkiss Papers, LC.

24. *OR*, pp. 207–10.

25. *OR*, pp. 189, 206, 234, 208. The concurrent advance to action by Early and Taliaferro is demonstrable (albeit of very short distance). G. F. R. Henderson in his *Stonewall Jackson*, 2:93, is one of several secondary sources that err in bringing Taliaferro into position as a relief to Early when Early already was hard-pressed. Thomas arrived in about such circumstances, but Taliaferro clearly was on hand before Augur attacked.

26. *OR*, p. 189.

27. *OR*, p. 208; James Preston Crowder to "Dear Mother," Aug. 13, 1862, Crowder Papers, EU; Burton, *Forty-seventh Alabama*, p. 1; Botsford, *Forty-seventh Alabama*, p. 4; Krick, *Lee's Colonels*, p. 64.

28. Typescript history of the Forty-eighth Alabama by Sergeant John Dykes Taylor, Taylor Papers, Alabama Department of Archives and History; Krick, *Lee's Colonels*, pp. 27, 292.

29. Wood, *The War*, p. 89.

30. Morse, *Letters*, p. 76.

31. Taliaferro Memoir, Agecroft Hall, Richmond. This account also was published in the *RTD*, November 8, 1903.

32. Blue, "Reminiscences."

33. *OR*, p. 216; J. W. D. Farrar in *RTD*, Oct. 19, 1902; A. S. Drewry in Yeary, *Boys in Gray*, pp. 197–98.

34. Blue, "Reminiscences."

35. *OR*, p. 227.

36. *OR*, pp. 235, 230–31; Early, *Autobiographical Sketch*, pp. 98–99; Grimsley, *Battles in Culpeper*, p. 29.

37. *OR*, pp. 231–32.

38. Early, *Autobiographical Sketch*, p. 98; *OR*, p. 230.

39. *OR*, p. 231; Early, *Autobiographical Sketch*, p. 98; Thomas, *Doles-Cook Brigade*, p. 214.

40. *OR*, p. 234.

41. Cook, *Lewis County in the Civil War*, pp. 113–19; Krick, *Lee's Colonels*, p. 177; Johnson, *University Memorial*, p. 262; Buck, *Old Confeds*, p. 46.

42. Dement's Battery Memoir, NYSA.

43. *OR*, p. 233; Dement's Battery Memoir, NYSA.

44. Rogers, Letter, Aug. 13, 1862; *OR*, pp. 215–16, 219; Blue, "Reminiscences."

45. Unidentified newspaper clipping by a member of the Fourteenth Georgia in an August 21, 1862, Georgia newspaper, in the M. J. Solomons Scrap-

book, DU (Ms. 4950); *OR*, p. 219. The unidentified clipping is cited hereafter as Fourteenth Georgia newspaper account, Solomons Scrapbook, DU.

46. Rogers, Letter.

47. Blue, "Reminiscences."

48. Newman, Letter; Player, Report.

49. *OR*, p. 231; Thomas, *Doles-Cook Brigade*, p. 214; Early, *Autobiographical Sketch*, p. 98.

50. *OR*, pp. 216, 233; Boyle, *Soldiers True*, p. 44; Bates, letter, in *Second Annual Report of the State Historian of the State of New York* (Albany, 1897), pp. 101–3.

51. Early, *Autobiographical Sketch*, p. 98; *OR*, p. 233; "Georgians at the Battle of Cedar Run"; Newman, Letter; Rogers, Letter.

52. "Georgians at the Battle of Cedar Run"; Neese, *Horse Artillery*, p. 87; Rogers, Letter; Newman, Letter.

53. Folsom, *Heroes and Martyrs of Georgia*, p. 129; Player, Report. The Folsom book is Confederate imprint no. 2625 in Crandall's checklist.

54. Denison, *Sabres and Spurs*, p. 124; Oates, *The War*, p. 129.

55. *OR*, p. 235; Dabney, *Life of Jackson*, p. 494. Dabney's biography is an old standard source, although much of its language, and some of its attitudes, are sententious. Its value increases markedly when firsthand knowledge informs the text. The Cedar Mountain portion deserves special respect in light of a surviving letter written by Jedediah Hotchkiss thirteen months after the battle. On September 6, 1863, Hotchkiss wrote to his wife (Hotchkiss Papers, LC, Roll 4, Frame 545): "Dr. Dabney is here on a visit, collecting information for his life of Jackson & I am going tomorrow, with him & Gen Early, to the battlefield of Cedar Run." That visit to the field with Early and Hotchkiss must have been an important part of Dabney's preparations for writing about the battle.

56. Ring Diary, (Company K, Sixth Louisiana), Tulane University; *OR*, p. 237; Oates, *The War*, p. 129; Miller, "Letters," p. 89.

57. G. Campbell Brown Memoir, Brown-Ewell Papers, TSLA; Dabney, *Life of Jackson*, p. 494.

58. Oates, *The War*, p. 129; McClendon, *Recollections*, p. 94; Miller, "Letters," p. 90.

59. Townsend, *Non-Combatant*, p. 258.

60. Hamlin, *The Making of a Soldier*, p. 114.

61. *OR*, p. 227; G. Campbell Brown Memoir, Brown-Ewell Papers, TSLA.

62. Douglas, *With Stonewall*, pp. 126–27; *OR*, pp. 184, 235–37; McClendon, *Recollections*, p. 94.

Chapter 7: The Confederate Left Dissolves

1. *OR*, p. 201; Williams, *Cannon's Mouth*, p. 100.

2. *Committee on the Conduct of the War*, Thirty-Eighth Congress, 3:44–50. This reference is to the seventh volume in the overall set and the third volume for the session; the pagination is the last of several in the volume.

3. Marvin, *Fifth Connecticut*, p. 156; Andrews, "Battle of Cedar Mountain," p. 423; Brown, *Twenty-seventh Indiana*, p. 201; *OR*, p. 183.

4. The sources cited here cover in chronological order the material used in the next five paragraphs of the narrative to describe the wheatfield. Confederate sources, which cover the same gamut, will be cited below in connection with the experiences of their authors. Marvin, *Fifth Connecticut*, pp. 154–55; Dwight, *Life and Letters*, pp. 279–80; Bryant, *Third Wisconsin*, pp. 79, 82–83; H. A. Tripp of Company F, Tenth Maine, in unidentified newspaper clipping, Container 70, Hotchkiss Papers, LC; manuscript map in Blake Papers, Connecticut Historical Society; Henderson, *Stonewall Jackson*, 2:92; Townsend, *Non-Combatant*, p. 256; Gordon, *Brook Farm*, p. 284; Dabney, *Life of Jackson*, pp. 496–97.

5. Tripp, "Charge of Cedar Mountain"; Hinkley, *Third Wisconsin*, p. 33.

6. Marvin, *Fifth Connecticut*, p. 157.

7. Best Report, LC; *OR*, p. 151; Marvin, *Fifth Connecticut*, pp. 157–58.

8. Gordon, *Brook Farm*, p. 294; Marvin, *Fifth Connecticut*, p. 158; Grimsley, *Battles in Culpeper*, p. 29.

9. Marvin, *Fifth Connecticut*, p. 156; Townsend, *Non-Combatant*, p. 256.

10. Hinkley, *Third Wisconsin*, pp. 33–35; Bryant, *Third Wisconsin*, pp. 79, 82.

11. Gordon, *Brook Farm*, p. 298; Andrews, "Battle of Cedar Mountain," pp. 423–24.

12. Marvin, *Fifth Connecticut*, p. 158; Townsend, *Non-Combatant*, p. 256.

13. Boyce, *Twenty-eighth New York*, p. 37; Marvin, *Fifth Connecticut*, pp. 159–60. The one New York officer who escaped unscathed apparently was Lieutenant John C. Walsh of Company B. A court-martial reported by AGO General Orders No. 68, dated March 18, 1863, found that Walsh "did . . . run and hide behind shocks of wheat" during the charge after having fired his pistol wildly before the battle began.

14. Bryant, *Third Wisconsin*, pp. 79, 82.

15. This broadside verse was published without a date by J. H. Murphy, Printer. A copy is in the collections of Petersburg National Battlefield.

16. Townsend, *Non-Combatant*, p. 256; Tripp, "Charge of Cedar Mountain"; Gordon, *Brook Farm*, p. 294; Marvin, *Fifth Connecticut*, pp. 160–61.

17. Gordon, *Brook Farm*, p. 295.

18. *OR*, p. 204.

19. *OR*, pp. 189, 200.

20. *OR*, p. 205.

21. *OR*, pp. 189, 230; Boswell Report, LC.

22. Boyce, *Twenty-eighth New York*, p. 36; Boswell Report, LC.

23. *OR*, p. 203; Boyce, *Twenty-eighth New York*, p. 36.

24. Lieutenant Charles Alexander (Company C, First Virginia Battalion), in *RTD*, July 17, 1904; Davidson, "Letters," p. 29.

25. "An Historic Flag," in the James Garver Collection, USAMHI; Hotchkiss, *Make Me a Map*, p. 130; *OR*, p. 205. The distances given for the first volley by these three sources are, respectively, 50, 125, and 150 yards.

26. Lieutenant Charles Alexander in *RTD*, July 17, 1904; *OR*, pp. 200–201.

27. Marvin, *Fifth Connecticut*, pp. 155–56, 160; Lieutenant Charles Alexander in *RTD*, July 17, 1904.

28. *OR*, p. 183.

29. Hotchkiss, *Make Me a Map*, p. 130; Marvin, *Fifth Connecticut*, p. 161; *OR*, p. 201; *Richmond Dispatch*, Aug. 13, 1862.

30. *OR*, p. 205; Krick, *Lee's Colonels*, p. 290.

31. Davidson, "Letters," p. 29.

32. Chamberlayne, *Ham Chamberlayne*, p. 90; J. A. Walker manuscript marginalia, Richmond National Battlefield Park; Sheeran, *Confederate Chaplain*, p. 3.

33. Marvin, *Fifth Connecticut*, p. 162; *OR*, pp. 190, 201, 203; Krick, *Lee's Colonels*, p. 195.

34. Davidson, "Letters," p. 29.

35. *OR*, pp. 203–4, 201.

36. White, *Hugh A. White*, p. 113; Roster of the Forty-second Virginia Infantry, VSA; *OR*, p. 190; Krick, *Lee's Colonels*, p. 102.

37. Marvin, *Fifth Connecticut*, pp. 160–62; Bradwell, "From Cold Harbor to Cedar Mountain," p. 224.

38. Chapla, *42nd Virginia Infantry*, pp. 20, 138, and passim; Marvin, *Fifth Connecticut*, p. 162.

39. *OR*, p. 204; Marvin, *Fifth Connecticut*, p. 162; roster tabulations from Chapla, *42nd Virginia Infantry*, pp. 59–142.

40. *OR*, p. 204.

41. *OR*, p. 210.

42. Lieutenant Charles Alexander in *RTD*, July 17, 1904; *OR*, pp. 189, 205; Allan, *Army*, p. 173.

43. *OR*, p. 210; Marvin, *Fifth Connecticut*, p. 161; Davidson, "Letters," p. 29.

44. *Washington Star*, June 27, 1933, reporting on Captain Grayson's death.

45. Cammack, *Personal Recollections*, pp. 60–61.

46. *OR*, p. 192.

47. *OR*, p. 189; Henderson, *Stonewall Jackson*, 2:93–94.

48. Shuler Diary, LC.

49. *OR*, pp. 192, 198; Casler, *Four Years*, p. 146.

50. *OR*, p. 192; Shuler Diary, LC.

51. Casler, *Four Years*, p. 146.

52. *OR*, pp. 198, 197; Shuler Diary, LC; Casler, *Four Years*, p. 147.

53. *OR*, pp. 197–98.

54. Mary Donaghe to Frederick W. M. Holliday, Aug. 9, 1862, from Spring Farm, Holliday Papers, DU; Casler, *Four Years*, p. 147.

55. Casler, *Four Years*, p. 147; *OR*, pp. 197, 193.

56. Marvin, *Fifth Connecticut*, pp. 158–59; Casler, *Four Years*, p. 147; Bryant, *Third Wisconsin*, p. 83.

57. *OR*, p. 198; Jedediah Hotchkiss in Evans, ed., *Confederate Military History*, 3:310–11.

58. Hazael J. Williams to Jedediah Hotchkiss, Jan. 30, 1897, Hotchkiss Papers, LC, Roll 49, Frame 422; *OR*, pp. 194–95.

59. White, *Hugh A. White*, pp. 113–14.

60. Allan, *Army*, p. 174; *OR*, p. 195. Allan's fine narrative is the best chronology of Cedar Mountain written to date, although he timed Branch's arrival too early relative to the movements of the Stonewall Brigade.

61. Andrews, "Battle of Cedar Mountain," pp. 426–27; Bryant, *Third Wisconsin*, pp. 79, 82–83.

62. Andrews, "Battle of Cedar Mountain," pp. 426–27; *OR*, p. 196; Hazael J. Williams to Jedediah Hotchkiss, Jan. 30, 1897, Hotchkiss Papers, LC.

63. Boyce, *Twenty-eighth New York*, p. 36; Marvin, *Fifth Connecticut*, pp. 156, 160–61; Gordon, *Brook Farm*, p. 294; Andrews, "Battle of Cedar Mountain," pp. 426–27.

64. *OR*, p. 192; Hinkley, *Third Wisconsin*, pp. 34–35; Bryant, *Third Wisconsin*, pp. 82–83.

65. Marvin, *Fifth Connecticut*, p. 168.

66. *OR*, p. 197; J. A. Walker manuscript marginalia, Richmond National Battlefield Park.

67. Walker, *Memorial*, p. 403.

68. *OR*, pp. 198–99.

69. Krick, *Lee's Colonels*, p. 305; *OR*, pp. 198–99.

70. *OR*, p. 221; Marvin, *Fifth Connecticut*, p. 162; J. A. Walker manuscript marginalia, Richmond National Battlefield Park.

71. *OR*, pp. 192, 194–95; Allan, *March Past*, p. 148.

Chapter 8: Federal High Tide

1. *OR*, p. 179; Krick, *Lee's Colonels*, p. 93.

2. Emerson, "A Boy in the Camp of Lee," p. 406.

3. Captain Henry H. Roach to "Dear Cousin," Aug. 5, 1862, Roach Letters, VSA.

4. *OR*, p. 202; Emerson, "A Boy in the Camp of Lee," p. 406.

5. Marvin, *Fifth Connecticut*, p. 160.

6. Davidson, "Letters," p. 29.

7. Captain Henry H. Roach to "Dear Cousin," Aug. 13, 1862, Roach Letters, VSA; Tripp, "The Charge."

8. *OR*, p. 202; Worsham, *Foot Cavalry*, p. 112. The 1964 "reprint" of Worsham's superb memoir, which is one of the important sources for the Twenty-first Virginia at Cedar Mountain, is not a reprint in the usual sense. The new edition includes huge numbers of editorial changes from the original for some reason, among them changes in material Worsham put in quotes as direct dialogue from individuals (such as Colonel Cunningham at Cedar Mountain). Why those gratuitous changes were made in so many places is beyond knowing. Suffice it to say that someone who wants Worsham undiluted, as he chose to present himself, will be obliged to go to the 1912 original.

9. *OR*, p. 202; Worsham, *Foot Cavalry*, pp. 112–13.

10. *OR*, p. 190; Davidson, "Letters," p. 29; *Lynchburg Republican*, Aug. 15, 1862, quoted in Moore, ed., *Rebellion Record*, 5:332.

11. James M. Binford to Carrie and Annie Gwathmey, Aug. 13, 1862, Gwathmey Papers, VHS. The note on Binford's later life is from his manuscript application for admission to the Portsmouth Camp, United Confederate Veterans, copy in the author's possession.

12. *Richmond Dispatch*, Aug. 13, 1862 (Page) and Aug. 14, 1862 (Lindsay); Chamberlayne, *Ham Chamberlayne*, p. 91; Worsham, *Foot Cavalry*, p. 113.

13. Charles Alexander in *RTD*, July 17, 1904.

14. Worsham, *Foot Cavalry*, pp. 112–13; *OR*, p. 202.

15. *OR*, pp. 137, 179.

16. Marvin, *Fifth Connecticut*, pp. 149–51, 171; Boyce, *Twenty-eighth New York*, p. 38; Reed, *100 Years Ago*, pp. 113–15.

17. "An Historic Flag"; Quint, *Potomac and Rapidan*, p. 188; Tripp, "The Charge."

18. Worsham, *Foot Cavalry*, p. 112; *OR*, p. 202.

19. *OR*, p. 202.

20. Worsham, *Foot Cavalry*, p. 113; Howard, *Recollections*, p. 164. In another account (*SHSP* 27:148, 150) Worsham described Cunningham's death as coming as the colonel began to pull down the fence, rather than afterward. Worsham also located the spot as "very near" the point where Winder suffered his mortal wound.

21. Tripp, "The Charge"; *OR*, p. 201; Worsham, *Foot Cavalry*, p. 113.

22. *OR*, pp. 201–3.

23. Henry H. Roach to "Dear Cousin," Aug. 13, 1862, Roach Letters, VSA.

24. *OR*, p. 204; Allan, *Army*, p. 173; Lieutenant Charles Alexander in *RTD*, July 17, 1904; Yeary, *Boys in Gray*, p. 55.

25. Worsham, *Foot Cavalry*, p. 114; *OR*, p. 202.

26. *OR*, p. 204; Allan, *Army*, p. 173.

27. Blue, "Reminiscences."

28. Ibid.

29. Ibid.; Worsham, *Foot Cavalry*, pp. 112–13.

30. Boswell Report, LC.

31. Blackford, *Letters*, p. 104.

32. The account by an unidentified member of the headquarters party in "Our Confederate Column," *RTD*, November 8, 1903, was written by William M. Taliaferro (no known relationship to General William B. Taliaferro). The original manuscript is in the T. C. Williams Papers at Agecroft Hall, Richmond. Taliaferro belonged to Company E, Second Virginia Cavalry, and apparently was serving as a courier to Jackson. Captain C. M. Blackford, who has appeared often in these pages, was from the Second Virginia Cavalry and was in charge of Jackson's couriers at Cedar Mountain.

33. *OR*, pp. 183, 187, 213. Jackson's report (p. 183) says that "the rear of the guns . . . were withdrawn."

34. Poague, *Gunner*, p. 33; *OR*, p. 214.

35. Tripp, "The Charge"; Grimsley, *Battles in Culpeper*, p. 29; *OR*, pp. 183, 189, 206.

36. Grimsley, *Battles in Culpeper*, p. 29; *OR*, p. 206.

37. Krick, *Lee's Colonels*, p. 177; *OR*, p. 208.

38. Botsford, *Memories of the War*, p. 6; *OR*, p. 179; James P. Crowder to his mother, Aug. 13, 1862, Crowder Papers, EU. Crowder's letter reported eleven killed and ninety wounded in the Forty-seventh Alabama.

39. Manuscript history of the Forty-eighth Alabama by John Dykes Taylor, Taylor Papers, Alabama Department of Archives and History; *OR*, pp. 209, 179.

40. Huffman, *Ups and Downs*, p. 58.

41. Neese, *Horse Artillery*, p. 86; Henry Kyd Douglas to R. S. Ewell, Aug. 13, 1862, Douglas Collection, Chicago Historical Society.

42. *OR*, pp. 212, 206.

43. Krick, *Lee's Colonels*, p. 93; *OR*, pp. 179, 207.

44. *OR*, pp. 211, 190, 206. Colonel A. G. Taliaferro also reported (page 206) that he ordered the Tenth Virginia to fall back at this point, in words that make it clear that he thought they were in his main line instead of more than half a mile away in the woods recovering from an earlier stage of the same Federal breakthrough. Either Taliaferro was phenomenally confused or some portion of the Tenth Virginia remained under him. The former alternative seems more likely.

45. *OR*, pp. 211, 190; Krick, *Lee's Colonels*, p. 333.

46. W. S. Hawkins to the Curtis family, undated letter in folder labeled "Correspondence of W. B. Curtis, 1860–1899," Curtis Papers, WVU; Hawkins, "Col. George W. Curtis," p. 466.

47. Harris, *Louisa County, Virginia*, p. 405; *OR*, p. 191; George K. Harlow to "Dear Father and family," Aug. 13, 1862, Harlow Papers, VHS.

48. Marvin, *Fifth Connecticut*, p. 163.

49. *OR*, pp. 187, 226; SeCheverall, *Twenty-ninth Ohio*, pp. 52–53; J. W. D. Farrar in "Our Confederate Column," *RTD*, Oct. 19, 1902.

50. Albert Sidney Drewry in Yeary, *Boys in Gray*, pp. 197–98; Willie Pegram to Jennie Pegram, Aug. 14, 1862, Pegram-Johnson-McIntosh Papers, VHS. A slightly variant account by Drewry is in a typescript extracted from an unidentified newspaper, on file at the USAMHI.

51. *OR*, p. 226; J. W. D. Farrar in "Our Confederate Column," *RTD*, Oct. 19, 1902.

52. Smith Memoir, OHS; Pegram to Jennie Pegram, Aug. 14, 1862, Pegram-Johnson-McIntosh Papers, VHS; Yeary, *Boys in Gray*, p. 198.

53. *OR*, pp. 232, 234; Krick, *Lee's Colonels*, p. 164.

54. *OR*, p. 234; Buck, *Old Confeds*, p. 44; Buck, "Gen. Joseph A. Walker," pp. 35–36. The mistaken first name of the general obviously was not Buck's fault but an editorial faux pas.

55. Buck, *Old Confeds*, pp. 44–45; *OR*, p. 234.

56. *OR*, p. 234; Buck, "Gen. Joseph A. Walker," pp. 35–36; Buck, *Old Confeds*, p. 45; Marvin, *Fifth Connecticut*, p. 164.

57. *OR*, p. 231; Early, *Autobiographical Sketch*, p. 99.

58. *OR*, pp. 231, 228.

59. *OR*, p. 231; Early, *Autobiographical Sketch*, p. 99.

60. Douglas, *With Stonewall*, pp. 126–27.

61. Thomas, *Doles-Cook Brigade*, p. 214. Information on William F. Brown came from the 1850 Dooley County Census, page 250, NA; the 1860 Dooley County Census, page 90 (Drayton post office, NA); and Powell and Powell, *Historical and Genealogical Collections*, 1:9, 3:85. Brown was born in 1814, married Martha Johnson (she was forty in 1860), and had four sons. The two sons who served in Company F, Twelfth Georgia, with W. F. Brown were John G., a physician (1835?–September 1, 1861) and James Monroe (died 1931). The two exaggerations of Brown's antiquity cited in the text are from Early, *Autobiographical Sketch*, p. 99, and Freeman, *Lee's Lieutenants*, 2:30.

62. Hetland, "Battle of Cedar Run"; Early, *Autobiographical Sketch*, p. 99.

63. Irby Goodwin Scott "To loved ones at home," Aug. 13, 1862, Scott Papers, DU; Hetland, "Battle of Cedar Run."

64. C.W.A., "Battle of Cedar Run"; Shepard Green Pryor to Penelope Pryor, Aug. 18, 1862, Pryor Letters, University of Georgia.

65. *OR*, p. 232.

66. *OR*, p. 238.

Chapter 9: Jackson Waves His Sword

1. Jackson, *Stonewall Jackson*, p. 313.

2. Neese, *Horse Artillery*, p. 86; *SHSP* 10:89.

3. Taliaferro Memoir, Williams Papers, Agecroft Hall. This memoir was

printed anonymously with slight variations in the *RTD*, Nov. 8, 1903.

4. Douglas, *With Stonewall*, p. 124; *OR*, pp. 222–23.

5. Douglas, *With Stonewall*, p. 123; Cooke, *Stonewall Jackson*, p. 261. The enchanting account of Jackson at Cedar Mountain by Charles M. Blackford is susceptible to criticism on a number of points, among them his description (Blackford, *Letters*, p. 105) of the arrival of Branch and Pender after Jackson had moved back toward the front. He surely was describing the arrival of Archer and Pender.

6. Blackford, *Letters*, p. 104; Grimsley, *Battles in Culpeper*, p. 30; Freeman, *Lee's Lieutenants*, 2:37–38; Dabney, *Life of Jackson*, p. 501.

7. Jedediah Hotchkiss to G. F. R. Henderson, Sept. 5, 1896, Hotchkiss Papers, LC; Taliaferro Memoir, Williams Papers, Agecroft Hall; *SHSP* 19: 314–15.

8. Blackford, *Letters*, p. 105, says that Jackson took the battle flag "from my man, Bob Isbell," implying that it was a cavalry flag. William M. Taliaferro, in his fine account of this episode, said that Jackson used the flag of the Fourth Virginia Infantry, but it is difficult to imagine what that unit's flag would have been doing at that location just then. See also Bradwell, "From Cold Harbor to Cedar Mountain," p. 224.

9. Jedediah Hotchkiss to his brother, Aug. 14, 1862, Hotchkiss Papers, LC; Hotchkiss, *Make Me a Map*, p. 66; William B. Taliaferro in Jackson, *Stonewall Jackson*, pp. 517–18.

10. Blue, "Reminiscences."

11. Cooke, *Stonewall Jackson and the Old Stonewall Brigade*, p. 14; Blackford, *Letters*, p. 105.

12. Bradwell, "From Cold Harbor to Cedar Mountain," p. 224; Dabney, *Life of Jackson*, p. 501; Blackford, *Letters*, p. 105.

13. Cooke, *Stonewall Jackson and the Old Stonewall Brigade*, p. 14; Dabney, *Life of Jackson*, p. 501.

14. Hotchkiss, *Make Me a Map*, p. 67; Douglas, *With Stonewall*, p. 124.

15. Poague, *Gunner*, p. 33; *SHSP* 19:314–15. The *SHSP* account is by the highly reliable Hunter Holmes McGuire, who quoted Jackson as addressing R. L. Walker as "General," which rank Walker attained subsequently. I have changed the rank to "Colonel" in the quote for that reason.

16. Blue, "Reminiscences."

17. Dabney, *Life of Jackson*, p. 501; Bradwell, "From Cold Harbor to Cedar Mountain," p. 224.

18. Blackford, *Letters*, p. 105. Captain Blackford's tale is almost—if not entirely—too delicious to be true, it must be admitted, though it is represented as coming from a contemporary letter.

19. William B. Taliaferro in Jackson, *Stonewall Jackson*, p. 518.

20. Blue, "Reminiscences."

21. Cooke, *Stonewall Jackson*, p. 261.

22. Jedediah Hotchkiss to G. F. R. Henderson, Sept. 5, 1896, Hotchkiss

Papers, LC; Henderson, *Stonewall Jackson,* 2:94; Marvin, *Fifth Connecticut,* p. 166.

23. Cooke, *Stonewall Jackson and the Old Stonewall Brigade,* p. 14; Taylor, *Destruction and Reconstruction,* p. 90; Fitzhugh Lee in Jones, ed., *Army of Northern Virginia Memorial Volume,* p. 320. Lee quoted Taylor's phrase in describing Jackson at Chancellorsville.

24. William B. Taliaferro in Jackson, *Stonewall Jackson,* p. 517.

25. Jackson, *Stonewall Jackson,* p. 313.

26. Clark, *North Carolina Regiments,* 2:549–50.

27. *OR,* pp. 223, 221.

28. *OR,* pp. 215, 218, 221.

29. Sheeran, *Confederate Chaplain,* p. 4; Captain Walter W. Lenoir in Hickerson, ed., *Happy Valley,* p. 84.

30. *OR,* pp. 223, 221.

31. Clark, *North Carolina Regiments,* 2:28, 550.

32. *OR,* p. 215.

33. *OR,* p. 221; Clark, *North Carolina Regiments,* 2:550.

34. Walter W. Lenoir in Hickerson, ed., *Happy Valley,* p. 84.

35. *OR,* pp. 223, 220; Chamberlayne, *Ham Chamberlayne,* p. 90.

36. Walter W. Lenoir in Hickerson, ed., *Happy Valley,* p. 84; *OR,* p. 218.

37. Walter W. Lenoir in Hickerson, ed., *Happy Valley,* p. 84.

38. Birdsong, *North Carolina State Troops in the War,* pp. 24–25.

39. Jordan, *North Carolina Troops,* 4:452; *OR,* p. 221.

40. *OR,* pp. 221, 180; Clark, *North Carolina Regiments,* 1:370.

41. *OR,* pp. 220–23.

42. Walter W. Lenoir in Hickerson, ed., *Happy Valley,* p. 84.

43. *OR,* pp. 220–21, 183, 215.

44. Marvin, *Fifth Connecticut,* p. 169; Rufus Mead to "Dear Folks at Home," Aug. 13, 1862, Mead Papers, LC.

45. Smith Memoir, OHS; Stearns, *Company K,* p. 87.

46. Smith Memoir, OHS.

47. Marvin, *Fifth Connecticut,* pp. 166–67.

48. Levi F. Bauder to his son, Dec. 4, 1912, Palmer Collection, Western Reserve Historical Society.

49. Marvin, *Fifth Connecticut,* pp. 167–68.

50. Boyce, *Twenty-eighth New York,* p. 37; "An Historic Flag."

51. Gould, *Tenth Maine,* pp. 171, 173.

52. Smith Memoir, OHS; *OR,* p. 151.

53. Gould, *Tenth Maine,* p. 173.

54. Ibid., pp. 173–74.

55. Ibid., p. 174.

56. Unidentified newspaper clipping by Tenth Maine veteran in Container 70, Hotchkiss Papers, LC.

57. Gould, *Tenth Maine,* pp. 174–75.

58. H. A. Tripp to J. M. Gould, Feb. 14, 1893, Gould Papers, DU; Gould, *Tenth Maine*, pp. 175–76.

59. Gould, *Tenth Maine*, p. 176.

60. *OR*, p. 218; C.M.H., Letter; Mockbee, "Historical Sketch," Museum of the Confederacy, pp. 24–25. The Mockbee manuscript was attested authentic by General William McComb.

61. Childs, "Cedar Run Battle."

62. Ibid.

63. *OR*, p. 218; Nineteenth Georgia "Participant."

64. *OR*, p. 218; Blackford, *Letters*, p. 105; C.M.H., Letter; Childs, "Cedar Run Battle."

65. *OR*, p. 218.

66. *OR*, pp. 218–19.

67. Jedediah Hotchkiss manuscript memorandum on A. P. Hill, Hotchkiss Papers, LC, Roll 49, Frame 455.

68. Nineteenth Georgia "Participant"; Childs, "Cedar Run Battle"; *OR*, pp. 219, 215; C.M.H., Letter.

69. Gould, *Tenth Maine*, pp. 181–82; H. A. Tripp to J. M. Gould, Feb. 14, 1893, Gould Papers, DU.

70. Gould, *Tenth Maine*, pp. 176–77; H. A. Tripp to J. M. Gould, Feb. 14, 1893, Gould Papers, DU.

71. H. A. Tripp to J. M. Gould, Aug. 14, 1891, Feb. 4, 14, 1893, and Gould's marginal notes on the last of the three letters, Gould Papers, DU; Gordon, *Brook Farm*, p. 303.

72. Unidentified newspaper clipping by a Tenth Maine veteran, Container 70, Hotchkiss Papers, LC.

Chapter 10: The Cavalry Charge

1. Smith Memoir, OHS; Lloyd, *First Pennsylvania Cavalry*, pp. 23–24; Lloyd, *1902 Address*, pp. 4–5.

2. *OR*, p. 189; C.M.H., Letter; Lindsley, *Tennessee*, p. 234; Andrews, "Battle of Cedar Mountain," pp. 429, 438.

3. Gould, *Tenth Maine*, p. 195.

4. Fourteenth Georgia newspaper account, Solomons Scrapbook, DU; Chapman, "Battle of Cedar Mountain"; W. L. Goldsmith account in Graham, *Tales of the Civil War*, p. 219; Grimsley, *Battles in Culpeper*, pp. 30–31.

5. Smith Memoir, OHS; Forbes, *Thirty Years After*, 2:257.

6. Lloyd, *First Pennsylvania Cavalry*, pp. 23–24; unidentified Tenth Maine veteran in a newspaper clipping in Container 70, Hotchkiss Papers, LC.

7. Smith Memoir, OHS; Lloyd, *1902 Address*, p. 4; *OR*, pp. 141, 139.

8. *OR*, pp. 184, 231, 216; Grimsley, *Battles in Culpeper*, p. 30.

9. Charles Alexander in *RTD*, July 17, 1904; Blue, "Reminiscences."

10. *OR*, pp. 216, 222–23.

11. Emerson, "A Boy in the Camp of Lee," p. 406.

12. *OR*, p. 223; C.M.H., Letter.

13. Marvin, *Fifth Connecticut*, p. 156.

14. Brown, *Twenty-seventh Indiana*, pp. 202–3; Gordon, *Brook Farm*, p. 303.

15. Gordon, *Brook Farm*, pp. 304–5; Quint, *Potomac and Rapidan*, pp. 188–89; Allan, *Army*, p. 175.

16. Brown, *Twenty-seventh Indiana*, p. 203; Gordon, *Brook Farm*, p. 305; H. A. Tripp to J. M. Gould, Feb. 14, 1893, Gould Papers, DU. General Gordon confused the regimental alignment on the right, declaring that the Twenty-seventh Indiana held the middle and the Third Wisconsin the far right. The letter of H. A. Tripp establishes clearly on the basis of contacts with Colonels Colgrove (Twenty-seventh Indiana), Ruger (Third Wisconsin), and Andrews (Second Massachusetts), as well as with several other participants, that the order of the units was as given in the text. Even without Tripp's careful work, the position of the Twenty-seventh Indiana on the far right stands out from regimental narratives. The collapse and subsequent return of the Indiana regiment contributed to Gordon's confusion, more than likely.

17. Gordon, *Brook Farm*, p. 308; Brown, *Twenty-seventh Indiana*, pp. 203–5.

18. Boyce, *Twenty-eighth New York*, p. 37.

19. Brown, *Twenty-seventh Indiana*, p. 205; Gordon, *Brook Farm*, p. 308; Quint, *Potomac and Rapidan*, p. 110.

20. Manuscript account of "the Sedar mounten Afair," Files file, Fairbanks Papers, Indiana University. The account is dated November 15, 1897, and was written on the letterhead of the agricultural implements firm in Hanover, Indiana, which Files owned.

21. Morse, *Letters*, pp. 76–77; Gordon, *Brook Farm*, p. 308; Brown, *Twenty-seventh Indiana*, p. 206; Hinkley, *Third Wisconsin*, pp. 35–36.

22. Brown, *Twenty-seventh Indiana*, p. 206; Gordon, *Brook Farm*, pp. 310–11.

23. *OR*, pp. 197, 192.

24. Alexander S. Pendleton to his mother, Aug. 1862, in Lee, *Pendleton*, p. 203; *OR*, p. 199.

25. Shuler Diary, LC; Reed, *100 Years Ago*, p. 114.

26. Marvin, *Fifth Connecticut*, pp. 159, 167; Buckley, *Great Reunion*, pp. 40, 45, 113–14.

27. Hazael J. Williams to Jedediah Hotchkiss, Jan. 30, 1897, Hotchkiss Papers, LC, Roll 49, Frame 422; *OR*, p. 196.

28. Marvin, *Fifth Connecticut*, p. 159; Buckley, *Great Reunion*, p. 45.

29. Buckley, *Great Reunion*, pp. 40, 46, 57, 74, 82, and passim.

30. *OR*, pp. 184–85, 193, 196.

31. *OR*, p. 196.

32. Tyler, ed., *Encyclopedia of Virginia Biography*, 3:125; Bruce, ed., *History of Virginia*, 6:627; "Souvenir of a Gallant Soldier," unidentified newspaper clip-

ping, Hotchkiss Papers, LC, Roll 58, Frame 793; "Confederate Museum," p. 3, col. 6.

33. Grimsley, *Battles in Culpeper*, p. 30; Willie Preston to his father, Aug. 10, 1862, in Allan, *March Past*, p. 148.

34. *OR*, p. 193; Marvin, *Fifth Connecticut*, p. 167; Walker, *Memorial*, p. 125.

35. Jedediah Hotchkiss to his wife, Aug. 16, 1862, Hotchkiss Papers, LC.

36. *OR*, pp. 201, 190; Walker, *Memorial*, p. 239.

37. *OR*, p. 205; Cooke, *Stonewall Jackson*, p. 260.

38. Lieutenant Ham Chamberlayne to his mother, Aug. 14, 1862, and to Salley Grattan, Aug. 19, 1862, and R. L. Walker to W. N. Pendleton, July 11, 1864, all in Chamberlayne, *Ham Chamberlayne*, pp. 90, 95, 235.

39. Davidson, "Letters," pp. 29–30.

40. *OR*, p. 210.

41. *OR*, p. 204; Davidson, "Letters," p. 30.

42. *OR*, pp. 205, 202; Worsham, *Foot Cavalry*, p. 114.

43. Jedediah Hotchkiss to his brother, Aug. 14, 1862, Hotchkiss Papers, LC; *OR*, p. 197.

Chapter 11: The Fourteenth Georgia Fills the Breach

1. *OR*, pp. 231, 233, 227.

2. *OR*, p. 231; Early, *Autobiographical Sketch*, p. 100.

3. *OR*, p. 233; Early, *Autobiographical Sketch*, p. 99.

4. *OR*, pp. 234, 232; Buck, *Old Confeds*, p. 45.

5. Jedediah Hotchkiss to his brother, Aug. 14, 1862, and to his wife, Aug. 16, 1862, Hotchkiss Papers, LC; Hotchkiss, *Make Me a Map*, p. 67; Early, *Autobiographical Sketch*, pp. 99–100; *OR*, p. 233.

6. Hotchkiss, *Make Me a Map*, p. 67.

7. *OR*, pp. 232–33; Thomas, *Doles-Cook Brigade*, p. 214; C.W.A., "Battle of Cedar Run."

8. Folsom, *Heroes and Martyrs*, p. 148; *OR*, pp. 216, 219; Fourteenth Georgia newspaper account, Solomons Scrapbook, DU.

9. Fourteenth Georgia newspaper account, Solomons Scrapbook, DU.

10. Folsom, *Heroes and Martyrs*, p. 148; Fourteenth Georgia newspaper account, Solomons Scrapbook, DU.

11. Fourteenth Georgia newspaper account, Solomons Scrapbook, DU.

12. Ibid.

13. Folsom, *Heroes and Martyrs*, p. 148; English Combatant, *Battlefields*, p. 433; Fourteenth Georgia newspaper account, Solomons Scrapbook, DU.

14. *OR*, p. 216; account by "Dixie" in the same August 21, 1862, Georgia newspaper that contains the Fourteenth Georgia account, Solomons Scrapbook, DU.

15. *OR*, p. 208; James Preston Crowder to his mother, Aug. 13, 1862, Crowder Papers, EU.

16. *OR*, pp. 206, 189, 233.

17. Chamberlayne, *Ham Chamberlayne*, p. 90.

18. English Combatant, *Battlefields*, p. 433.

19. Marvin, *Fifth Connecticut*, p. 165; Andrews, "Battle of Cedar Mountain," p. 431; Wood, *Seventh Regiment*, p. 127.

20. *OR*, p. 238.

21. Captain W. W. Lenoir in Hickerson, ed., *Happy Valley*, p. 84; Captain W. L. Goldsmith in Graham, *Tales of the Civil War*, p. 219; Fourteenth Georgia newspaper account, and account by "Dixie," Solomons Scrapbook, DU.

22. Fourteenth Georgia newspaper account, Solomons Scrapbook, DU; Goldsmith in Graham, *Tales of the Civil War*, p. 219.

23. *OR*, p. 216; Buck, *Old Confeds*, p. 45.

24. G. Campbell Brown Memoir, Brown-Ewell Papers, TSLA.

25. Buck, *Old Confeds*, p. 45; *OR*, pp. 234–35; Blue, "Reminiscences"; G. Campbell Brown Memoir, Brown-Ewell Papers, TSLA.

26. Buck, *Old Confeds*, pp. 45–46.

27. *OR*, pp. 206, 231, 189; Early, *Autobiographical Sketch*, p. 100.

Chapter 12: Counterattack

1. *OR*, p. 222.

2. Statement by Captain (later Major) Joseph H. Saunders of the Thirty-third North Carolina in an undated and unidentified newspaper clipping owned by a descendant of a member of the Eighteenth North Carolina. A copy of the clipping is in the author's files. Its style and typeface suggest a Confederate-imprint newspaper, or at least one published very early postwar. Most of the rest of the accompanying file consists of Confederate-imprint newspapers from the Statesville area, among them the *Iredell Express*. The article containing this anecdote deals primarily with Chancellorsville. Other sources on Jackson and Branch at this interlude include Clark, *North Carolina Regiments*, 2:68, 472; *OR*, p. 223; and James H. Lane in Jackson, *Stonewall Jackson*, p. 535.

3. *OR*, pp. 222–23, 183; Grimsley, *Battles in Culpeper*, p. 30.

4. Captain W. W. Lenoir in Hickerson, ed., *Happy Valley*, pp. 84–85; *OR*, p. 223.

5. *OR*, pp. 184, 219, 215.

6. Nineteenth Georgia "Participant"; Dwight, *Letters*, pp. 280–81; Childs, "Cedar Run Battle."

7. C.M.H., Letter; Dwight, *Letters*, pp. 280–81; Morse, *Letters*, pp. 76–77.

8. *OR*, p. 219; Childs, "Cedar Run Battle."

9. *Confederate Veteran* 14 (1906): 83.

10. Evans, ed., *Confederate Military History* (expanded edition), 8:478; *OR*, p. 180; Krick, *Lee's Colonels*, pp. 155–56; Mockbee, "Historical Sketch," Museum of the Confederacy, pp. 24–25; Nineteenth Georgia "Participant."

11. C.M.H., Letter; Childs, "Cedar Run Battle."

12. *OR*, pp. 219, 180; Childs, "Cedar Run Battle."

13. *OR*, pp. 195, 193.

14. Hendricks, "Pegram at Cedar Mountain," p. 448; White, *Hugh A. White*, p. 112; *OR*, pp. 193, 179.

15. White, *Hugh A. White*, p. 114.

16. Willie Preston to his father, Aug. 10, 1862, in Allan, *March Past*, p. 148.

17. Allan, *March Past*, pp. 146–57; McGuire, *Stonewall Jackson*, pp. 18–19.

18. *OR*, p. 196. The personal material on Arnall is from the French Papers, VSA, and the files of the *Atlanta Journal*.

19. Hendricks, "Pegram at Cedar Mountain," p. 448; Shuler Diary, LC. The sunset given was for Richmond's longitude, and is from *Confederate States Almanac*.

20. Ashe Memoir, Ashe Papers, NCDAH, p. 5.

21. *OR*, pp. 225, 193.

22. J. H. Moore, "Seventh Tennessee Infantry," in Lindsley, *Tennessee*, p. 234; *OR*, pp. 193, 225.

23. Ashe Memoir, Ashe Papers, NCDAH, p. 5; *OR*, p. 225; Krick, *Lee's Colonels*, pp. 82, 142.

24. *OR*, pp. 193, 225; Ashe Memoir, Ashe Papers, NCDAH.

25. Ashe Memoir, Ashe Papers, NCDAH; *OR*, p. 225.

26. *OR*, pp. 219, 225.

27. Ashe Memoir, Ashe Papers, NCDAH, p. 5; *OR*, p. 219.

28. Dwight, *Letters*, pp. 280–81; *OR*, p. 225; Ashe Memoir, Ashe Papers, NCDAH, p. 5; W. Dorsey Pender to his wife, Aug. 14, 1862, in Pender, *The General to His Lady*, p. 167. There is a hint that Field's brigade of A. P. Hill's division, or at least its Forty-seventh Virginia Infantry, arrived in time to take part in the final attack. Charles N. Barrett of the Forty-sixth Pennsylvania, in a letter to H. A. Tripp of the Tenth Maine written from Fredericksburg on January 24, 1887 (Gould Papers, DU), recounted the story of an officer named Taliaferro of the Forty-seventh Virginia. Taliaferro described vividly and not unreasonably his experience charging across the wheat field. Taliaferro believed that his unit's volley hit Lieutenant Colonel Crane of the Third Wisconsin behind the fence at the east edge of the wheat field. Barrett marveled at how friendly Southerners were to visiting Yankees and found them as interested in war stories as Northerners ("and . . . much more free to speak of their failures &c"—an interesting comment on the state of Northern historiography of that vintage). Despite this account, there is little likelihood that the passage of the Forty-seventh Virginia across the wheat field, or near to it, occurred before darkness fell.

29. Gordon, *Brook Farm*, p. 311; Brown, *Twenty-seventh Indiana*, pp. 206–8.

30. Quint, *Second Massachusetts*, p. 110; Morse, *Letters*, pp. 77–78.

31. Gordon, *Brook Farm*, pp. 311–12; Dwight, *Letters*, p. 282.

32. Morse, *Letters*, pp. 78–79.

33. Gordon, *Brook Farm*, p. 312; George L. Andrews to his wife, Aug. 12, 1862, Andrews Collection, USAMHI.

34. George L. Andrews to his wife, Aug. 12, 15, 1862, Andrews Collection, USAMHI.

35. C.M.H., Letter.

36. Trimble, "Civil War Diary," p. 3; *OR*, p. 227.

37. Oates, *The War*, pp. 129–30, 657.

38. Nisbet, *Firing Line*, p. 134.

39. *OR*, pp. 227, 236; G. Campbell Brown Memoir, Brown-Ewell Papers, TSLA; *Washington Star*, Aug. 11, 1862, quoted in Moore, ed., *Rebellion Record*, 5:323.

40. Worsham, *Foot Cavalry*, p. 114.

41. Trimble, "Civil War Diary," p. 3; *OR*, p. 236.

42. Grimsley, *Battles in Culpeper*, p. 30; *OR*, pp. 184, 227. The 1860 census for Culpeper County listed Jerry Hudson, age forty-nine, a miller, on page 30 in household number 236. Reverend Slaughter on the hilltop occupied household 239, also on page 30. The 1860 census was taken in August so its readings fell precisely two years before the battle.

43. Trimble, "Civil War Diary," p. 3; G. Campbell Brown Memoir, Brown-Ewell Papers, TSLA; McClendon, *Recollections*, p. 94.

44. *OR*, pp. 227, 236; McClendon, *Recollections*, pp. 94–95.

45. Nisbet, *Firing Line*, p. 134; G. Campbell Brown Memoir, Brown-Ewell Papers, TSLA; Clark, *North Carolina Regiments*, 2:133; McClendon, *Recollections*, p. 95; *OR*, pp. 227, 236, 138.

46. Clark, *North Carolina Regiments*, 2:133.

47. *OR*, p. 184.

Chapter 13: Mopping Up in the Cornfield

1. *OR*, p. 232.

2. Buck, "Gen. Joseph A. Walker," p. 36.

3. *OR*, pp. 231–32.

4. *OR*, pp. 232, 219–20; Francis Solomon Johnson (Company F, Forty-fifth Georgia) to Emily Hutchings, University of Georgia.

5. Washington L. Goldsmith in Graham, *Tales of the Civil War*, p. 219.

6. *OR*, pp. 210, 208, 206.

7. Raine Memoir, copy in the research collection of Fredericksburg and Spotsylvania National Military Park. As is often the case with tales of this sort, the victim of the plot is not easy to identify. The only Massachusetts regiment in the thick of the fight was the Second Infantry; the only Smith shown on its casualty list was a private bearing the given name of George, who was mortally wounded.

8. *OR*, p. 227; G. Campbell Brown Memoir, Brown-Ewell Papers, TSLA.

9. C.W.A., "Battle of Cedar Run"; Oates, *The War*, pp. 750, 763.

10. *OR*, p. 227; Trimble, "Civil War Diary," p. 3.

11. *OR*, p. 169; Boyle, *Soldiers True*, p. 45.

12. *OR*, p. 206; French, *Centennial Tales*, p. 20; William B. Taliaferro in Jackson, *Stonewall Jackson*, p. 518.

13. The various claims and countercharges by Pile and Patteson are in *Confederate Veteran* 24 (1916): 406; 25 (1917): 106, 394; and 29 (1921): 70. An account crediting the capture to "Private C. Thomas" of the Thirty-sixth Virginia (which was not present at the battle) is "The Way Prince Was Captured," *Columbus* (Ga.) *Daily Sun*, Aug. 22, 1862.

14. *OR*, p. 189; French, *Centennial Tales*, p. 20.

15. *SHSP* 19:182.

16. *OR*, pp. 220–21.

17. Clark, *North Carolina Regiments*, 2:472.

18. *OR*, pp. 195, 197; *Richmond Dispatch*, Aug. 18, 1862. Edgar's exploits were confirmed by both of the last two citations in this note.

19. *OR*, pp. 195–96, 199, 193; White, *Hugh A. White*, p. 113; Hazael J. Williams to Jedediah Hotchkiss, Jan. 30, 1897, Hotchkiss Papers, LC, Roll 49, Frame 422; Hotchkiss, *Make Me a Map*, p. 175.

20. *OR*, pp. 189, 204.

21. Davidson, "Letters," pp. 29–30.

22. *OR*, pp. 219, 225.

23. Clark, *North Carolina Regiments*, 2:584. The full moon was reported by the 1862 *Confederate States Almanac*.

24. Childs, "Cedar Run Battle."

25. Gordon, *Brook Farm*, pp. 313–14, 320; Quint, *Potomac and Rapidan*, pp. 189–91; Andrews, "Battle of Cedar Mountain," p. 439.

26. Best Report, LC.

27. Gilbert, "Cedar Mountain."

28. Sergeant A. W. Chillson to his parents, Aug. 11, 1862, copy in author's possession. Original owned (1985) by Gary D. Remy, Madison, Wisconsin.

29. D. D. Jones to John Jordan, Jr., Aug. 11, 1862, Jones Papers, Historical Society of Pennsylvania.

30. Strother, *Virginia Yankee*, pp. 76–77.

31. Frank Jennings to "My dear Brother & Sister," Jan. 7, 1867, USAMHI. Jennings served in the Ninetieth Pennsylvania of Tower's brigade. His letter to his siblings recounted at length his two-months-long marriage in 1861; Jennings had been out of touch with his family for quite some time.

32. Faulk, "Battle of Cedar Mountain." Faulk dated his article from Yankton, Dakota.

33. Jaques, *Three Years' Campaign*, pp. 91–92; Stearns, *Company K*, pp. 87–88; Davis, *Three Years in the Army*, p. 97; Faulk, "Battle of Cedar Mountain."

34. Cook, *Twelfth Massachusetts*, p. 59.

35. Article by George Kimball in "Carleton," *Stories*, p. 88.

36. Hough, *Duryee's Brigade*, p. 55.

37. William Byrnes in Graham, *Tales of the Civil War*, pp. 268–70.

38. Townsend, *Non-Combatant*, p. 261; *OR*, pp. 138–39.

39. Lyon, *War Sketches*; Gordon, *Brook Farm*, pp. 323–25. Lyon was an officer on Hatch's staff. His thirty-three-page pamphlet is primarily concerned with Second Manassas.

Chapter 14: After Dark

1. *OR*, p. 184.

2. Grimsley, *Battles in Culpeper*, p. 31; Blackford, *Letters*, p. 106; Georgetown Ms. Weather Readings.

3. *SHSP* 10:87; Boswell Report, LC.

4. O'Ferrall, *Forty Years of Active Service*, p. 44.

5. *OR*, p. 190; Blackford, *Letters*, p. 106.

6. Willie Preston to his father, Aug. 10, 1862, in Allan, *March Past*, pp. 148–49.

7. Henderson, *Stonewall Jackson*, 2:97; *OR*, p. 187.

8. Grimsley, *Battles in Culpeper*, p. 31; *OR*, pp. 216, 187; Blackford, *Letters*, pp. 106–7.

9. Gache, *Frenchman*, pp. 133–34.

10. Grimsley, *Battles in Culpeper*, p. 31.

11. *OR*, p. 217.

12. Journal of Henry Monier in Bartlett, *Military Record of Louisiana*, p. 30. This citation is to the first of several sets of paginations.

13. *OR*, pp. 216, 224; Alonzo H. Sterrett (Company E, Twenty-ninth Ohio) to "Dear Innis," Aug. 13, 1862, in possession of Lewis Leigh.

14. *OR*, pp. 224, 217.

15. Gache, *Frenchman*, pp. 134–35.

16. *OR*, pp. 217–18; Willie Pegram to Jennie Pegram, Aug. 14, 1862, from Gordonsville, Pegram-Johnson-McIntosh Papers, VHS.

17. *OR*, p. 187; Odell, "Pegram's Strategy at Cedar Mountain."

18. Hendricks, "Pegram at Cedar Mountain," p. 448.

19. Johnson, *University Memorial*, p. 717.

20. *OR*, p. 216; J. W. D. Farrar of Pegram's battery in "Our Confederate Column," *RTD*, Oct. 19, 1902; Grimsley, *Battles in Culpeper*, p. 31; Odell, "Pegram's Strategy at Cedar Mountain"; Johnson, *University Memorial*, p. 717; *OR*, p. 184; Willie Pegram to Jennie Pegram, Aug. 14, 1862, Pegram-Johnson-McIntosh Papers, VHS.

21. Alonzo H. Sterrett to "Dear Innis," Aug. 13, 1862, in possession of Lewis Leigh; *Cincinnati Times*, Aug. 10, 1862, quoted in Moore, ed., *Rebellion Record*, 5:326; Grimsley, *Battles in Culpeper*, p. 31.

22. David Nichol (Knap's battery) to his parents, Aug. 17, 1862, USAMHI.

23. Colonel Adrian R. Root to "My dear Mother," Aug. 16, 1862, typescript at Manassas National Battlefield Park. The original is in Erie County, New York, Historical Society.

24. J. W. D. Farrar of Pegram's battery in *RTD*, Oct. 19, 1902; Alonzo H. Sterrett to "Dear Innis," Aug. 13, 1862, in possession of Lewis Leigh; Grimsley, *Battles in Culpeper*, p. 31; *OR*, pp. 184, 216, 218.

25. *OR*, 51(1):121.

26. *OR*, pp. 180, 218.

27. *OR*, p. 224; Krick, *Lee's Colonels*, p. 297.

28. Gache, *Frenchman*, pp. 134–36; Krick, *Lee's Colonels*, p. 200.

29. J. W. D. Farrar of Pegram's battery in *RTD*, Oct. 19, 1902.

30. Gilmor, *Four Years*, pp. 53–54.

31. *OR*, p. 218; Willie Pegram to Jennie Pegram, Aug. 14, 1862, Pegram-Johnson-McIntosh Papers, VHS.

32. Myers, *Comanches*, pp. 90–91.

33. Jedediah Hotchkiss to his brother, Aug. 14, 1862, Hotchkiss Papers, LC; Fulton, *Family Record and War Reminiscences*, p. 68.

34. Strother, *Virginia Yankee*, p. 78; Williams, *Cannon's Mouth*, p. 102.

35. McClenthen, *Sketch of the Campaign*, pp. 3–5; Vautier Diary, USAMHI (the Eighty-eighth Pennsylvania Collection includes an excellent pencil sketch by Vautier); Joseph A. McLean to his wife, Aug. 11, 13, 1862, USAMHI.

36. Williams, *Cannon's Mouth*, p. 102; Alonzo H. Sterrett to "Dear Innis," Aug. 13, 1862, in possession of Lewis Leigh; David Nichol to his parents, Aug. 17, 1862, USAMHI; McClenthen, *Sketch of the Campaign*, p. 5; Townsend, *Non-Combatant*, pp. 271–72.

37. *OR*, pp. 218, 226, 216, 184; Grimsley, *Battles in Culpeper*, p. 31.

38. Gache, *Frenchman*, p. 136; *OR*, p. 226; Johnson, *University Memorial*, p. 717; Neese, *Horse Artillery*, p. 87; Willie Pegram to Jennie Pegram, Aug. 14, 1862, Pegram-Johnson-McIntosh Papers, VHS.

39. *OR*, pp. 216, 187, 218; Grimsley, *Battles in Culpeper*, p. 31; Willie Pegram to Jennie Pegram, Aug. 14, 1862, Pegram-Johnson-McIntosh Papers, VHS.

40. Grimsley, *Battles in Culpeper*, p. 30; Blue, "Reminiscences."

41. *OR*, pp. 239, 184; McDonald, *Laurel Brigade*, pp. 80–81.

42. *OR*, p. 239.

43. Humphreys, *Heroes and Spies*, p. 143. Humphreys identified the dead coward as Isaac Acker of the Seventh Virginia Cavalry, but Acker's Compiled Service Record, NA, and one other source show him alive much later. The story is worth repeating in any case. The Compiled Service Record has Acker present in August 1864. McDonald, *Laurel Brigade*, shows Acker alive well after the war.

44. *OR*, p. 239.

45. Gordon, *Brook Farm*, p. 320; Strother, *Virginia Yankee*, p. 77; English Combatant, *Battlefields*, p. 429.

46. Strother, *Virginia Yankee*, p. 77; Gordon, *Brook Farm*, p. 320–21; Ser-

geant A. W. Chillson to his parents, Aug. 11, 1862, copy in the author's files and original owned (1985) by Gary D. Remy of Madison, Wisconsin.

47. Williams, *Cannon's Mouth*, p. 101; Samuel L. Conde to "My dear young friends," from headquarters Army of Virginia, Aug. 15, 1862, USAMHI.

48. Strother, *Virginia Yankee*, pp. 77–78; Gordon, *Brook Farm*, p. 322.

49. *OR*, p. 239; Strother, *Virginia Yankee*, p. 78.

50. *OR*, pp. 184, 239; McDonald, *Laurel Brigade*, p. 81.

51. Brown, *Stringfellow*, pp. 155–56; *OR*, p. 184. For Farrow and his death, see *Stringfellow*, pp. 173, 182–85.

52. Boswell Report, LC.

53. Moore, *Cannoneer*, pp. 96–97; Hotchkiss, *Make Me a Map*, p. 67.

54. Hendricks, "Pegram at Cedar Mountain," pp. 448–49; Cooke, *Stonewall Jackson*, p. 265.

55. Jackson, *Stonewall Jackson*, p. 312; Cooke, *Stonewall Jackson*, p. 265.

56. Blackford, *Letters*, pp. 108–9.

57. Hotchkiss, *Make Me a Map*, p. 67.

58. Howard, *Recollections*, p. 173.

59. *OR*, p. 213.

60. Goldsborough, *Maryland Line*, p. 261; Dement's Battery Memoir, NYSA.

61. Ashe Memoir, Ashe Papers, NCDAH, pp. 5–6.

62. "Gamma Sigma," Letter.

63. Neese, *Horse Artillery*, pp. 87–88.

64. Blue, "Reminiscences."

65. Kauffman Diary, SHC.

66. Gache, *Frenchman*, pp. 130–32.

67. The story of the wounded at the Brown house is recounted at some length in the battle narratives of Quint, *Second Massachusetts*; Quint, *Potomac and Rapidan*; and Gordon, *Brook Farm*.

68. Townsend, *Non-Combatant*, pp. 258–59.

69. "Steptoe" of the Forty-seventh Virginia in Hallum, *Reminiscences*, p. 258.

70. Gache, *Frenchman*, p. 133.

71. James P. Crowder to his mother, Aug. 13, 1862, Crowder Papers, EU.

Chapter 15: August 10

1. Jedediah Hotchkiss to his wife, Aug. 10, 1862, Hotchkiss Papers, LC; Strother, *Virginia Yankee*, p. 79; Grimsley, *Battles in Culpeper*, p. 31.

2. *OR*, p. 218.

3. Journal of Captain Henry Monier (Tenth Louisiana) in Bartlett, *Military Record of Louisiana*, p. 30 of the first collation; *OR*, p. 224. Service records for the four dead Irishmen are in Booth, *Records of Louisiana Confederate Soldiers*, vols. 2–4, which include place of birth.

4. Clark, *North Carolina Regiments*, 4:159.

5. *OR*, p. 226.

6. *OR*, p. 227; Trimble, "Civil War Diary," p. 4.

7. Jackson to Stuart, Aug. 7, 1862, quoted in Vandiver, *Mighty Stonewall*, p. 343.

8. *OR*, p. 184.

9. Hotchkiss, *Make Me a Map*, p. 67; *OR*, p. 184; Grimsley, *Battles in Culpeper*, p. 31.

10. Neese, *Horse Artillery*, pp. 88–89; Grimsley, *Battles in Culpeper*, p. 31.

11. Blackford, *Letters*, p. 109.

12. *OR*, p. 184; Grimsley, *Battles in Culpeper*, p. 32.

13. Strother, *Virginia Yankee*, pp. 79–80; manuscript dispatch, "Geo. D. Ruggles, Col. & etc., By command of Maj. Gen. Pope" to Banks, 10:20 A.M., Aug. 10, 1862, original sold at auction in Chicago in April 1985, copied for the author by Marshall D. Krolick; Jedediah Hotchkiss to his brother, Aug. 14, 1862, Hotchkiss Papers, LC.

14. *OR*, p. 226; Clark, *North Carolina Regiments*, 4:159–60; Henderson, comp., *Roster of the Confederate Soldiers of Georgia*, 5:208.

15. Myers, *Comanches*, pp. 91–93.

16. Hotchkiss, *Make Me a Map*, pp. 67, 129.

17. Charles B. Fleet (Fredericksburg Artillery) memoir in Hodges, *C. B. Fleet*, p. 48.

18. Blue, "Reminiscences."

19. Blackford, *Letters*, p. 109.

20. Douglas, *With Stonewall*, p. 127.

21. Hotchkiss, *Make Me a Map*, p. 67.

22. Manuscript note by G. Campbell Brown, 1862, Brown-Ewell Papers, TSLA.

23. Chamberlayne, *Ham Chamberlayne*, p. 134.

24. Allan, *Army*, p. 176n.; Nineteenth Georgia "Participant."

25. Blue, "Reminiscences"; Hotchkiss, *Make Me a Map*, p. 67.

26. The temperature readings are from the Georgetown Ms. Weather Readings. Georgetown reported only a sprinkling rain at 9:00 P.M. Accounts of the heavy rain at Cedar Mountain can be found in Trimble, "Civil War Diary," p. 4; Buck, *Old Confeds*, p. 46; Kauffman Diary, SHC; Douglas, *With Stonewall*, p. 127; Hotchkiss, *Make Me a Map*, p. 67; and Jedediah Hotchkiss to his brother, Aug. 14, 1862, Hotchkiss Papers, LC.

27. *New York Tribune*, Aug. 10, 1862, quoted in Moore, ed., *Rebellion Record*, 5:329.

28. *Washington Star*, Aug. 11, 1862, quoted in ibid., 5:324; John Viles (Thirteenth Massachusetts) to "Frank," Aug. 9, 20, 1862, USAMHI.

29. Albert Weiser to George Miller, Aug. 24, 1862, USAMHI; Townsend, *Non-Combatant*, p. 270.

30. Strother, *Virginia Yankee*, pp. 79–80; Calfee, *Confederate Culpeper*, p. 3.

31. The ugly word *homely* must have struck home hard on Barton, a

strange and narcissistic creature given to stuffing tissue paper into her un-derfilled bodice and lauding her own appearance in diary entries. The story of Dr. Dunn's missive and much else of interest on Barton, developed from manuscript sources, is in the typescript "The Professional Angel: A Life of Clara Barton," by Elizabeth Brown Pryor. The 108-page typescript was pre-pared for Clara Barton National Historic Site in Maryland; a copy is at Chat-ham, Fredericksburg and Spotsylvania National Military Park, where Barton labored during the war. The "homely" phrase came from an Antietam de-scription, though Dunn also mentioned Barton's Cedar Mountain work.

32. Hotchkiss, *Make Me a Map*, p. 67; Smith Memoir, OHS.

33. "An Historic Flag."

34. Buck, *Old Confeds*, p. 46.

35. Douglas, *With Stonewall*, p. 128; Sheeran, *Confederate Chaplain*, p. 4.

36. Clark, *North Carolina Regiments*, 4:159–60; Moore, *Cannoneer*, p. 97.

37. Myers, *Comanches*, p. 91; James P. Crowder to his mother, Aug. 13, 1862, Crowder Papers, EU; *Richmond Dispatch*, Aug. 18, 1862.

38. Davidson, "Horrors of the Battlefield," pp. 306–7.

39. Douglas, *With Stonewall*, p. 127; Blue, "Reminiscences."

40. Jedediah Hotchkiss to his brother, Aug. 14, 1862, Hotchkiss Papers, LC.

41. Denison, *Cedar Mountain*, p. 42; Hamlin, *"Old Bald Head,"* p. 120; Blackford, *Letters*, p. 110.

42. Chamberlayne, *Ham Chamberlayne*, p. 91; Francis Solomon Johnson to Emily Hutchings, Aug. 11, 1862, University of Georgia Special Collections.

43. The Connecticut episode is recorded in a fine article by Walter L. Pow-ell, "Heaven Alone Can Soothe Hearts"; Douglas, *With Stonewall*, pp. 155–56.

44. Shepard Green Pryor to Penelope, Aug. 9[?], 1862, Pryor Letters, Uni-versity of Georgia; *Confederate Veteran* 8 (1900): 412.

45. Kauffman Diary, SHC.

46. Strother, *Virginia Yankee*, pp. 79–80.

47. Blue, "Reminiscences"; Denison, *Cedar Mountain*, p. 42.

48. Hotchkiss, *Make Me a Map*, p. 67.

Chapter 16: August 11

1. Georgetown Ms. Weather Readings; Compiled Service Record of Ed-ward M. Yowell, Tenth Virginia Infantry, in M324, Roll 497, Record Group 109, NA.

2. Davis, *Mount Up*, pp. 71–72.

3. *OR*, p. 184; Hotchkiss, *Make Me a Map*, p. 68; Blackford, *Letters*, p. 100; Strother, *Virginia Yankee*, p. 80.

4. Casler, *Four Years*, pp. 148–49. Casler may refer here to the panic on August 10, but he tied its origins firmly to the flag of truce.

5. Morse, *Letters*, p. 80; Denison, *Sabres and Spurs*, pp. 127–28.

6. Strother, *Virginia Yankee*, pp. 80–81; Townsend, *Non-Combatant*, pp. 272–73.

7. Boyce, *Twenty-eighth New York*, p. 39; Strother, *Virginia Yankee*, p. 80.

8. Morse, *Letters*, p. 80; Quint, *Potomac and Rapidan*, pp. 192–94; Quint, *Second Massachusetts*, pp. 117–18.

9. Boyce, *Twenty-eighth New York*, p. 39; Marvin, *Fifth Connecticut*, p. 172; Rufus Mead (Fifth Connecticut) to "Dear Folks at Home," Aug. 13, 1862, Mead Papers, LC.

10. Buck, *Old Confeds*, p. 46; Marvin, *Fifth Connecticut*, p. 226; Boyce, *Twenty-eighth New York*, p. 39.

11. Townsend, *Non-Combatant*, p. 276.

12. Neese, *Horse Artillery*, p. 90.

13. T. H. McBee (Unionist infantryman from western Virginia) to Zadoc McBee, Aug. 14, 1862, WVU; Gilmor, *Four Years*, p. 55.

14. *SHSP* 10:90.

15. Townsend, *Non-Combatant*, pp. 273–75.

16. Ibid., p. 275; English Combatant, *Battlefields*, p. 432; Strother, *Virginia Yankee*, p. 80.

17. Blackford, *Letters*, p. 111; Douglas, *With Stonewall*, p. 128; Blackford, *War Years with Jeb Stuart*, p. 98.

18. Townsend, *Non-Combatant*, p. 275.

19. Hotchkiss, *Make Me a Map*, pp. 67–68; Kauffman Diary, SHC; *OR*, p. 227. It probably was in these mass graves that a relic hunter sometime in the 1960s "really hit the jack pot . . . at Cedar Mountain. . . . The burial parties had thrown them in the graves with all equipment on, cartridge boxes and all. Got something like 30 plates out of 3 or 4 mass graves" (letter dated August 30, 1975, copy in author's possession, written from a nationally prominent writer about Civil War artifacts to another relic hunter. Common decency dictates omitting their names, even if it did not forestall their desecrations.).

20. Early, *Autobiographical Sketch*, p. 102; Jedediah Hotchkiss to his wife, Aug. 16, 1862, Hotchkiss Papers, LC; Hotchkiss, *Make Me a Map*, p. 68.

21. Jedediah Hotchkiss to his wife, Aug. 16, 1862, Hotchkiss Papers, LC.

22. Early, *Autobiographical Sketch*, p. 102; *OR*, p. 227.

23. *OR*, p. 185.

24. Hotchkiss, *Make Me a Map*, p. 68; Dement's Battery Memoir, NYSA.

25. Neese, *Horse Artillery*, pp. 90–91; C. B. Fleet Memoir, in Hodges, *C. B. Fleet*, p. 48.

26. Myers, *Comanches*, p. 94.

27. Dement's Battery Memoir, NYSA; Fleet Memoir, in Hodges, *C. B. Fleet*, p. 48.

28. Buck, *Old Confeds*, p. 46.

29. "What a Woman Saw."

30. Caldwell, *Brigade of South Carolinians*, pp. 27–28.

31. C. B. Fleet Memoir, in Hodges, *C. B. Fleet*, pp. 48–49.

32. Myers, *Comanches*, pp. 94–95.

33. Caldwell, *Brigade of South Carolinians*, p. 28; Summers Diary, VSA.

34. Neese, *Horse Artillery*, pp. 90–91.

35. Hotchkiss, *Make Me a Map*, p. 68; French, *Centennial Tales*, p. 13.

Appendix 1: The Military Aftermath

1. Adjutant and Inspector-General's Office, Confederate States Army, *General Orders*, pp. 66–68. This Confederate imprint is cataloged as Crandall no. 1343.

2. Jones, *Rebel War Clerk's Diary*, 1:148.

3. Broaddus Diary, p. 1006.

4. Reed, *100 Years Ago*, p. 114; *Washington Star*, Aug. 11, 1862, quoted in Moore, ed., *Rebellion Record*, 5:325.

5. *New York Tribune*, Aug. 10, 1862, quoted in Moore, ed., *Rebellion Record*, 5:328; Quint, *Second Massachusetts*, p. 113.

6. Miller, "Letters," p. 89.

7. *OR*, pp. 185–86; *Richmond Dispatch*, Aug. 18, 1862; Blackford, *Letters*, pp. 100–101.

8. *OR*, p. 185; Jedediah Hotchkiss to his wife, Aug. 16, 1862, Hotchkiss Papers, LC.

9. Ashe Memoir, Ashe Papers, NCDAH, p. 3. Ashe identified the victim of this silly affair as "Capt. Y," who "afterwards became known as one of the most gallant and staunchest field officers among the N.C. troops." No North Carolinian with a surname starting with the letter "Y" became a literal field officer in the Army of Northern Virginia after serving first in Pender's brigade. Pender had an aide, Lieutenant John Young, who never became a field officer. The only other option (a slender one) would be a line captain who later became a field officer outside the Army of Northern Virginia.

10. Johnson, *Robert Lewis Dabney*, pp. 271–72; Blackford, *Letters*, p. 112.

11. Hotchkiss, *Make Me a Map*, p. 68; Henry Kyd Douglas to R. S. Ewell, on behalf of Jackson, Aug. 13, 1862, Douglas Collection, Chicago Historical Society.

12. Blackford, *Letters*, p. 113.

Appendix 3: Casualties

1. The *OR* figure (p. 180) for the Twenty-fifth Virginia is one killed, twenty-four wounded. The postwar roster of the regiment (Rosters of Virginia Units, VSA) mentions by name two men killed; presumably one of them was mortally wounded.

2. Driver, *52nd Virginia Infantry*, p. 24.

3. A nominal list in the *Columbus* (Ga.) *Daily Sun*, Aug. 30, 1862 ("List of the Killed and Wounded in the 12th and 21st Ga. Regiments in the Battle of Cedar Run, 9th August, 1862") shows six killed and thirty-four wounded. The *OR* figure of seven and thirty-three obviously indicates the loss of one mortally wounded man. The latter figure also is used in "From Jackson's Army," *Columbus Daily Sun*, Aug. 28, 1862.

4. The two missing come from Early's report in *OR*, p. 233.

5. The presence of the Sixth, Seventh, and Eighth Louisiana at the battle is confirmed by the record-of-events entries on their original muster rolls at NA. No evidence survives, however, about their losses,which doubtless were minimal under the shelling. Only a full survey of each man's service record would yield a definitive answer.

6. Miller, "Letters," p. 89.

7. Although *OR*, p. 180, shows none killed and three wounded, ibid., p. 236, reports one killed and seven wounded. The larger loss is confirmed in part by Oates, *The War*, and in its entirety by the nominal list in Confederate States Army Casualties: Lists and Narrative Reports, 1861–1865 (NA Microcopy 836). That extremely useful, albeit fragmentary, source is cited hereinafter as CSA Casualties, M836, NA. Oates named the one killed and two missing on pages 130, 657, and 750.

8. The Twenty-first Georgia does not appear on the loss table in *OR*, pp. 179–80, but ibid., p. 236, reports three wounded, as does CSA Casualties, M836, NA. The rosters in volume 2 of Henderson's compilation of Georgia soldiers yield four wounded. The *Columbus Daily Sun* article of Aug. 30, 1862, also reported three wounded.

9. *OR*, p. 236.

10. Dement's Battery Memoir, NYSA. Goldsborough's *Maryland Line* confirms the two killed.

11. Goldsborough, *Maryland Line*, p. 328.

12. CSA Casualties, M836, NA.

13. Jordan, *North Carolina Troops*, 4:405–514.

14. Ibid., 6:305–424.

15. Lindsley, *Tennessee*, pp. 262–64.

16. Ibid., pp. 329–32.

17. *Augusta Daily Constitutionalist*, Aug. 22, 1862.

18. A letter dated August 21, 1862, in the M. J. Solomons Scrapbook, DU, reported none killed and twelve wounded in the Fourteenth Georgia. The notoriously incomplete Henderson, comp., *Soldiers of Georgia*, 2:339–407, shows no men killed and fewer than half a dozen wounded. Because of the nature of those sources, this table carries the *OR* total of four killed, twenty-four wounded. That may well be garbled, however, and too high.

19. Folsom, *Heroes and Martyrs*, p. 138.

20. *Columbus* (Ga.) *Daily Sun*, Aug. 22, 1862; *Augusta Daily Constitutionalist*, Aug. 20, 1862; Henderson, comp., *Soldiers of Georgia*, 4:839–924.

21. *Augusta Daily Constitutionalist*, Aug. 19, 1862; Henderson, comp., *Soldiers of Georgia*, 5:197–288.

22. The four killed, together with three wounded (all from just two companies) are mentioned in the Monier journal in Bartlett, *Military Record of Louisiana*, p. 30. The names of the four dead are confirmed in Booth, *Record of Louisiana Soldiers*.

23. Jordan, *North Carolina Troops*, 6:10–117.

24. Ibid., 7:10–132.

25. *OR*, p. 225.

26. Willie Pegram to Jennie Pegram, Aug. 14, 1862, Pegram-Johnson-McIntosh Papers, VHS.

27. Jordan, *North Carolina Troops*, 1:465–78.

28. CSA Casualties, M836, NA.

29. Ibid.

30. Ibid.; *OR*, p. 197.

31. Reidenbaugh, *33rd Virginia Infantry*, p. 102.

32. CSA Casualties, M836, NA.

33. Chapla, *42nd Virginia Infantry*, p. 20.

34. *OR*, p. 205.

35. CSA Casualties, M836, NA; Hotchkiss, *Make Me a Map*, p. 130.

36. Rankin, *23rd Virginia Infantry*, p. 96.

37. Rankin, *37th Virginia Infantry*, p. 47.

38. *OR*, p. 179, gives twelve killed, seventy-six wounded. CSA Casualties, M836, NA, reports twelve killed, eighty-five wounded, by name. Botsford, *47th Alabama*, p. 6, echoes the figures in *OR*, p. 179. James Preston Crowder to his mother, Aug. 13, 1862, EU, mentions eleven killed and ninety wounded. *OR*, p. 207, agrees exactly with CSA Casualties, M836, NA.

39. The total used here is from the nominal list in CSA Casualties, M836, NA, which shows three more killed and three fewer wounded than the table in *OR*, p. 179. The John D. Taylor typescript history of the Forty-eighth Alabama reports 123 net casualties, but that figure is not supportable (Taylor Papers, Alabama Department of Archives and History). *OR*, p. 207, agrees precisely with M836.

40. *OR*, p. 214.

41. Ibid., p. 213.

42. Clermont L. Best's manuscript report at LC totals his artillery loss as thirteen killed and forty-eight wounded. The figure of six missing comes from *OR*, p. 138. The losses not shown in the *OR* table that make up the difference to Best's totals probably came in the four batteries that did not report in *OR*.

Appendix 4: Two Mortally Wounded Marylanders

1. Howard, *Recollections*, pp. 171, 173–74. A manuscript note penciled by Howard in the margin of his copy of Fonerden, *Carpenter's Battery*, corrects the textual comment that Winder was killed with the phrase "lived an hour." The book is in the private collection of Vicki Heilig of Germantown, Maryland.

2. "Local Matters: Gen. Charles Sidney Winder," in *Richmond Dispatch*, Aug. 18, 1862, p. 1, col. 6; Wallace, *Guide to Virginia Military Organizations*, pp. 232–33; *Richmond Dispatch*, Aug. 19, 1862, p. 1, col. 7; Freeman, *Lee's Lieutenants*, 2:49n.

3. Howard, *Recollections*, p. 306.

4. Casler, *Four Years*, pp. 142–43; Howard, *Recollections*, p. 174; Trimble, "Civil War Diary," p. 4; White, *Hugh A. White*, p. 113.

5. *OR*, p. 183.

6. Jackson, *Stonewall Jackson*, p. 312.

7. Andrews, *Memoir*, p. 55; Chamberlayne, *Ham Chamberlayne*, p. 91.

8. Andrews, *Memoir*, p. 65; Douglas, *With Stonewall*, p. 126. According to Douglas, McGuire himself did some rudimentary stitching on Andrews on the spot, but other accounts disagree. Douglas's charming memoir makes far better reading than it serves as a footnote citation. Under ordinary circumstances, conflicting testimony must be adjudged against Douglas.

9. Andrews, *Memoir*, p. 67; Koontz, "Disembowelment in the Field with Cure," includes much detail about the Andrews case.

10. Bruce, *History of Virginia*, 5:217–18.

11. Blackford, *Letters*, p. 106; Hitner Diary, United Daughters of the Confederacy National Headquarters.

12. Andrews, *Memoir*, p. 67; Bruce, *History of Virginia*, 5:218; Hitner Diary, United Daughters of the Confederacy National Headquarters.

13. Howard, *Recollections*, pp. 171–72; Bruce, *History of Virginia*, 5:218.

14. Howard, *Recollections*, pp. 172–73. I am indebted to Ruth Ann Amiss Moore of Manassas, a great-granddaughter of Thomas Benjamin Amiss, for copies of the surgeon's letters and papers.

15. Andrews, *Memoir*, pp. 58–69; Howard, *Recollections*, p. 173.

16. "A Desperate Wound . . . How He Impressed the Germans—His Wound Acted as a Magic Talisman," unidentified newspaper clipping in Hotchkiss Papers, LC, Roll 59, Frame 303.

17. Bruce, *History of Virginia*, 5:218.

18. Krick, *Lee's Colonels*, p. 30; Douglas, *With Stonewall*, p. 126; Andrews, *Memoir*, p. 69.

Appendix 5: Lawrence O'Bryan Branch Libels the Stonewall Brigade

1. *OR*, p. 221.
2. *OR*, p. 222.
3. *OR*, p. 223.
4. Clark, *North Carolina Regiments*, 2:28; *OR*, p. 215.
5. For the quarrel and proposed duel, see Ashe Memoir, Ashe Papers, NCDAH, p. 3, and Appendix 1, above.
6. Captain Walter W. Lenoir in Hickerson, ed., *Happy Valley*, p. 84.
7. Hendricks, "Pegram at Cedar Mountain," p. 449; *OR*, pp. 193, 189–90.
8. Jedediah Hotchkiss to G. F. R. Henderson, July 30, 1896, Hotchkiss Papers, LC; Hotchkiss, *Make Me a Map*, p. 131.
9. Slaughter, *A Sketch of the Life of Randolph Fairfax*, p. 30 [Crandall no. 2605]; Poague, *Gunner*, pp. 33–34. See also Gilmor, *Four Years*, p. 54, and *RTD*, Nov. 8, 1903.
10. Hudson, "Battle of Cedar Mountain." Hudson was a nephew of Catherine Crittenden.
11. *OR*, pp. 184–85.

Appendix 6: Cedar Mountain Battlefield, 1862–1865

1. Noyes, *The Bivouac and the Battle-field*, pp. 74–76.
2. Strother, *Virginia Yankee*, pp. 81–82.
3. Maxson, *Camp Fires of the Twenty-third*, p. 71.
4. Hotchkiss, *Make Me a Map*, p. 92.
5. Stevens, *Reminiscences*, pp. 84–85.
6. Brooks, *Stories of the Confederacy*, p. 128.
7. Hotchkiss, *Make Me a Map*, pp. 123, 125.
8. Ibid.
9. Bigelow, *Campaign of Chancellorsville*, p. 228; Schenck, *Up Came Hill*, p. 155n.
10. West, *A Texan in Search of a Fight*, pp. 74–75; typescript history of the Forty-eighth Alabama Infantry by John Dykes Taylor, Taylor Papers, Alabama Department of Archives and History.
11. Hotchkiss, *Make Me a Map*, p. 175.
12. *Yankee* magazine, May 1982, p. 14.
13. Davis, *Three Years in the Army*, p. 309.

Appendix 7: The Battlefield since the War

1. *Roll of Honor, No. XXVI*, [249]; *Roll of Honor, No. XV*, pp. 116–48.
2. Conwell, *Magnolia Journey*, pp. 167–68.

3. *Culpeper Exponent,* June 8, 1900, p. 3, col. 2. The file on the claim is at the Suitland, Maryland, Branch of NA under 123 Court of Claims, U.S. Congressional Jurisd., Case File 10256. (Be advised that the penultimate digit is fuzzy and may not be a 5.) For more details on the Crittenden claims, see note 52, Chapter 4.

4. Wilson, "Cedar Mountain." Wilson was a veteran of Company D, Seventh Ohio.

5. *Richmond Times,* Aug. 10, 1902, p. 3; Lloyd, *1902 Address.* Lloyd had been adjutant of the First Pennsylvania Cavalry during the war.

6. "On Field of Battle: Visit to Cedar Mountain by President Roosevelt," *Washington Post,* Nov. 3, 1902.

7. "Reunion on Battlefield," *Fredericksburg Free Lance,* Aug. 13, 1912.

BIBLIOGRAPHY

Manuscript Sources

Agecroft Hall. Richmond, Virginia.
  William M. Taliaferro Memoir, T. C. Williams Papers.
Alabama Department of Archives and History. Montgomery, Alabama.
  John Dykes Taylor Papers.
Chicago Historical Society. Chicago, Illinois.
  Henry Kyd Douglas letter to R. S. Ewell, August 13, 1862, Douglas
    Collection.
Connecticut Historical Society. Hartford, Connecticut.
  Edward F. Blake Papers.
Culpeper Town and County Library. Culpeper, Virginia.
  Report on Crittenden family and farm, in Culpeper County Works Prog-
    ress Administration Papers, April 2, 1936.
Duke University. William R. Perkins Library, Manuscript Department. Dur-
    ham, North Carolina.
  John Mead Gould Papers.
  Frederick W. M. Holliday Papers.
  Irby Goodwin Scott Papers.
  M. J. Solomons Scrapbook, MS 4950.
Emory University. Robert W. Woodruff Library, Special Collections Depart-
    ment. Atlanta, Georgia.
  James Preston Crowder Papers.
Fredericksburg and Spotsylvania National Military Park. Fredericksburg,
    Virginia.
  George Nye letter to his wife, August 12, 1862.
  Elizabeth Brown Pryor, "The Professional Angel: A Life of Clara Barton."
  Charles Anderson Raine Memoir.
Historical Society of Pennsylvania. Philadelphia, Pennsylvania.
  D. D. Jones Papers.
Indiana University Library, Manuscript Department. Bloomington, Indiana.
  John L. Files File, in Charles W. Fairbanks Papers.
Library of Congress, Manuscript Division. Washington, D.C.
  Clermont L. Best Report, Nathaniel P. Banks Papers.
  James Keith Boswell Report, Jedediah Hotchkiss Papers.
  Jubal A. Early Papers.
  George S. Greene Report, Nathaniel P. Banks Papers.
  Jedediah Hotchkiss Papers.

443

Rufus Mead Papers.

Michael Shuler Diary.

Manassas National Battlefield Park. Manassas, Virginia.

Phillip Bradley Letter to T. J. Jackson (photocopy).

Adrian R. Root Letters (typescript).

Maryland Historical Society. Baltimore, Maryland.

Charles S. Winder Papers.

Museum of the Confederacy. Richmond, Virginia.

Richard B. Garnett Papers.

R. T. Mockbee, "Historical Sketch of the 14th Tenn. Regt. of Infantry."

National Archives. Washington, D.C.

Compiled Service Records of Confederate Soldiers Who Served in Organizations from the State of Virginia. Record Group 109.

Confederate States Army Casualties: Lists and Narrative Reports. Record Group 109.

Crittenden Family Claim Files, War Department Record and Pension Office, File 616957, June 13, 1900. Record Group 94.

Crittenden Family Claim Files, 123 Court of Claims, U.S. Congressional Jurisd. Case File 10256.

Population Schedules of the Eighth Census of the United States, 1860, for Culpeper County, Virginia. Record Group 29.

Wilbur F. and Mary E. Stevens Pension File (404051). Record Group 94.

National Weather Records Center. Asheville, North Carolina.

"Weather Journal Recording Observations at . . . Georgetown, D.C., June 1858–May 1866."

New York State Archives. Albany, New York.

Memoir by unidentified enlisted man in Dement's Maryland Battery.

North Carolina Department of Archives and History. Raleigh, North Carolina.

Samuel A. Ashe Papers.

Ohio Historical Society. Columbus, Ohio.

Thomas Church Haskell Smith Papers.

Private Collections.

Vicki Heilig, Germantown, Maryland.

Copy of Fonderden, *Carpenter's Battery*, with marginalia by McHenry Howard.

Marshall D. Krolick, Chicago, Illinois.

Copy of Dispatch by George D. Ruggles to N. P. Banks, 10:20 A.M., August 10, 1862.

Lewis Leigh, Fairfax, Virginia.

Letter, A. H. Sterrett to "Dear Innis," August 13, 1862.

Ruth Ann Amiss Moore, Manassas, Virginia.

Thomas Benjamin Amiss Papers.

Brian Pohanka, Leesburg, Virginia.

Papers Concerning General Charles S. Winder.

Gary D. Remy, Madison, Wisconsin.
Letter, A. W. Chillson to parents, August 11, 1862.
Portsmouth Public Library. Portsmouth, Virginia.
Membership Applications, Portsmouth Camp, United Confederate
Veterans.
Richmond National Battlefield Park. Richmond, Virginia.
Marginalia by James A. Walker in his copy of the printed *Official Records*
volume for Cedar Mountain.
Stanford University. Green Library, Manuscript Department.
John Wesley Melhorn Diary.
Tennessee State Library and Archives. Nashville, Tennessee.
Brown-Ewell Papers.
Tulane University Library, Louisiana Historical Association Collection. New
Orleans, Louisiana.
William P. Harper Diary.
George P. Ring Diary.
United Daughters of the Confederacy National Headquarters. Richmond,
Virginia.
John K. Hitner Diary.
United States Army Military History Institute. Carlisle Barracks,
Pennsylvania.
George L. Andrews Collection.
Samuel L. Conde Letter to "My Dear young Friends," August 15, 1862,
Civil War Miscellaneous Collection.
Albert Sidney Drewry Memoir.
James Garver Collection.
Frank Jennings Letter to "My dear Brother & Sister," January 7, 1867,
Civil War Times Illustrated Collection.
Joseph A. McLean Letters, Harrisburg Civil War Round Table Collection.
David Nichol Letter to parents, August 17, 1862, Harrisburg Civil War
Round Table Collection.
William H. Tallman Memoir, Harrisburg Civil War Round Table
Collection.
John D. Vautier Diary, Eighty-eighth Pennsylvania Infantry Collection.
John Viles Letters, Civil War Miscellaneous Collection.
Albert Weiser Letter to George Miller, August 24, 1862, George Miller
Collection.
University of Georgia. Hargrett Rare Book and Manuscript Library. Athens,
Georgia.
Francis Solomon Johnson Letter to Emily Hutchings, MS 243, Special
Collections.
Shepard Green Pryor Letters.
University of Michigan. William L. Clements Library. Ann Arbor, Michigan.
William J. Seymour Memoir, James S. Schoff Collection.
University of North Carolina. Southern Historical Collection. Chapel Hill,
North Carolina.

Joseph Franklin Kauffman Diary.
Virginia Historical Society. Richmond, Virginia.
James M. Binford Letter.
Gwathmey Family Papers.
George K. Harlow Papers.
Ambrose Powell Hill Letter to J. E. B. Stuart, November 14, 1862.
Lee Camp Soldiers' Home Ledger Book.
Pegram-Johnson-McIntosh Papers.
Georgia Callis West Papers.
Allen W. Wright, "The 42nd Virginia Infantry."
Virginia State Archives. Richmond, Virginia.
S. Bassett French Papers.
Henry H. Roach Letters.
Rosters of Virginia Units, Department of Military Affairs Papers.
John D. Summers Diary.
Western Reserve Historical Society. Cleveland, Ohio.
Levi F. Bauder Letter, William P. Palmer Collection.
West Virginia University Library, West Virginia and Regional History Collection. Morgantown, West Virginia.
William B. Curtis Papers.
Roy Bird Cook Papers.
T. H. McBee Letter to Zadoc McBee, August 14, 1862.
H. E. Matheny Collection.
George P. Wallace Letters.

Published Primary Sources

A., C. W. "The Battle of Cedar Run." August 14, 1862. *Columbus* (Ga.) *Daily Enquirer*, August 23, 1862.
Adjutant and Inspector-General's Office, Confederate States Army. *General Orders from Adjutant and Inspector-General's Office, Confederate States Army, from January 1862, to December, 1863*. Columbia, S.C., 1864.
Allan, William. *The Army of Northern Virginia in 1862*. Boston, Mass., 1892.
————. "Lee's Campaign against Pope in 1862." *Magazine of American History* 12 (1884): 126–47.
————. "Pope's Campaign Again." *Magazine of American History* 16 (1886): 483–89.
Anderson, Thomas M. "Civil War Recollections of the Twelfth Infantry." *Journal of the Military Service Institution* 41 (1907): 379–93.
Andrews, George L. "The Battle of Cedar Mountain." In Military Historical Society of Massachusetts, *Papers of the Military Historical Society of Massachusetts*. 12 vols. (Boston, Mass.: 1881–1912), 2:389–440.
Andrews, R. Snowden. *Richard Snowden Andrews, Lieutenant-Colonel Command-*

ing the First Maryland Artillery (Andrews' Battalion) Confederate States Army: A Memoir. Baltimore, Md., 1910.

Bartlett, Napier. Military Record of Louisiana. New Orleans, La., 1875.

Bates, Aaron P. Letter published in Second Annual Report of the State Historian of the State of New York. Albany, N.Y., 1897.

Beaudry, Louis N. Historic Records of the Fifth New York Cavalry. Albany, N.Y., 1865.

Benson, Berry G. Berry Benson's Civil War Book: Memoirs of a Confederate Scout and Sharpshooter. Athens, Ga., 1962.

Blackford, Charles M. Letters from Lee's Army. New York, N.Y., 1947.

Blackford, William W. War Years with Jeb Stuart. New York, N.Y., 1945.

Bliss, George N. Reminiscences of Service in the First Rhode Island Cavalry. Providence, R.I., 1878.

Blue, John. "Reminiscences." In an unidentified printed format (apparently an early twentieth-century newspaper) in the Civil War Times Illustrated Collection, U.S. Army Military History Institute, Carlisle Barracks, Pa.

Botsford, T. F. Memories of the War of Secession. Montgomery, Ala., 1911.

_____. A Sketch of the 47th Alabama Regiment Volunteers, C.S.A. Montgomery, Ala., 1909.

Boyce, Charles W. A Brief History of the Twenty-eighth Regiment New York State Volunteers. Buffalo, N.Y., 1896.

Boyle, John R. Soldiers True, the Story of the One Hundred and Eleventh Regiment Pennsylvania Veteran Volunteers. New York, N.Y., 1903.

Boyles, J. R. Reminiscences of the Civil War. Columbia, S.C., 1890.

Bradwell, I. G. "From Cold Harbor to Cedar Mountain." Confederate Veteran 29 (1921): 222–25.

Broaddus, W. F. Diary. Virginia Baptist Register, no. 21 (1982).

Brooks, Ulysses R. Stories of the Confederacy. Columbia, S.C., 1912.

Brown, Edmund R. The Twenty-seventh Indiana Volunteer Infantry in the War. Monticello, Inc., 1899.

Brunson, Joseph W. Pee Dee Light Artillery. University, Ala., 1983.

Bryant, Edwin E. History of the Third Regiment of Wisconsin Veteran Volunteer Infantry. Madison, Wisc., 1891.

Buck, Samuel D. "Gen. Joseph [sic] A. Walker." Confederate Veteran 10 (1902): 34–36.

_____. With the Old Confeds. Baltimore, Md., 1925.

Burton, J. Q. Forty-seventh Regiment Alabama Volunteers, C.S.A. N.p., n.d.

C. "From Jackson's Army." Columbus (Ga.) Daily Sun, August 28, 1862.

Cable, George W. "The Gentler Side of Two Great Southerners." Century 47 (1893–94): 292–94.

Caldwell, James Fitz James. The History of a Brigade of South Carolinians Known First as "Gregg's," and Subsequently as "McGowan's Brigade." Philadelphia, Pa., 1866.

Cammack, John H. Personal Recollections. Huntington, W.Va., 1920.

"Carleton" [pseud.]. *Stories of Our Soldiers.* Boston, Mass., 1893.

Casler, John O. *Four Years in the Stonewall Brigade.* Guthrie, Okla., 1893.

Chamberlayne, John Hampden. *Ham Chamberlayne, Virginian.* Richmond, Va., 1932.

Chapman, Almeron. "The Battle of Cedar Mountain." *National Tribune,* October 3, 1901.

Childs, Henry T. "Cedar Run Battle as I Saw It." *Confederate Veteran* 28 (1920): 24.

Clark, Walter. *Histories of the Several Regiments and Battalions from North Carolina in the Great War.* 5 vols. Raleigh and Goldsboro, N.C., 1901.

The Confederate States Almanac and Repository of Useful Knowledge for 1862. Vicksburg, Miss., 1861.

Conwell, Russell H. *Magnolia Journey.* University, Ala., 1974.

Cook, Benjamin F. *History of the Twelfth Massachusetts Volunteers.* Boston, Mass., 1882.

Cooke, John Esten. *Stonewall Jackson, a Military Biography.* New York, N.Y., 1866.

———. *Stonewall Jackson and the Old Stonewall Brigade.* Charlottesville, Va., 1954.

Dabney, Robert L. *Life and Campaigns of Lieut.-Gen. Thomas J. Jackson.* New York, N.Y., 1866.

Davidson, Charles Andrew. "Major Charles A. Davidson: Letters of a Virginia Soldier." Edited by Charles W. Turner. *Civil War History* 22 (1976): 16–40.

Davidson, J. Wood. "Horrors of the Battlefield." *Confederate Veteran* 15 (1907): 305–7.

Davis, Charles E. *Three Years in the Army.* Boston, Mass., 1894.

Denison, Frederic. *The Battle of Cedar Mountain.* Providence, R.I., 1881.

———. *Sabres and Spurs: The First Regiment Rhode Island Cavalry in the Civil War.* Central Falls, R.I., 1876.

Douglas, Henry Kyd. *I Rode with Stonewall.* Chapel Hill, N.C., 1940.

Dwight, Wilder. *Life and Letters of Wilder Dwight.* Boston, Mass., 1868.

Early, Jubal A. *Lieutenant General Jubal Anderson Early C.S.A.: Autobiographical Sketch and Narrative of the War between the States.* Philadelphia, Pa., 1912.

Emerson, A. J. "A Boy in the Camp of Lee." *Confederate Veteran* 24 (1916): 405–6.

English Combatant. *Battlefields of the South.* New York: N.Y., 1864.

Evans, Clement A., ed. *Confederate Military History.* 13 vols. Atlanta, Ga., 1899.

Faulk, Phil R. "Battle of Cedar Mountain." *Philadelphia Weekly Times,* March 31, 1883.

Fleet, Betsy, and John D. P. Fuller, eds. *Green Mount: A Virginia Plantation Family during the Civil War.* Charlottesville, Va., 1962.

Fonerden, Clarence A. *A Brief History of the Military Career of Carpenter's Battery.* New Market, Va., 1911.

Forbes, Edwin. *Thirty Years After: An Artist's Story of the Great War*. 2 vols. New York, N.Y., 1890.

Fourteenth Regiment Georgia Infantry. Unidentified newspaper account by a member of the regiment in a Georgia paper dated August 21, 1862, copy in the M. J. Solomons Scrapbook at Duke University (#4950).

Freeman, Douglas Southall. *Lee's Dispatches*. New York, N.Y., 1915.

———. *Lee's Lieutenants*. 3 vols. New York, N.Y., 1942–44.

French, S. Bassett. *Centennial Tales: Memoirs of Colonel Chester S. Bassett French, Extra Aide-de-Camp to Generals Lee and Jackson*. New York, N.Y., 1962.

Fulton, William F. *Family Record and War Reminiscences*. N.p., n.d.

Gache, Pere Louis-Hippolyte. *A Frenchman, a Chaplain, a Rebel*. Chicago, Ill., 1981.

"Gamma Sigma" [pseud.]. Letter to *Raleigh State Journal*, September 8, 1862, printed September 20, 1862.

"Georgians at the Battle of Cedar Run." *Augusta Daily Constitutionalist*, August 22, 1862.

Gilmor, Harry. *Four Years in the Saddle*. New York, N.Y., 1866.

Gordon, George H. *Brook Farm to Cedar Mountain*. Boston, Mass., 1883.

———. *History of the Campaign of the Army of Virginia, under John Pope, from Cedar Mountain to Alexandria, 1862*. Boston, Mass., 1880.

Gould, John M. *History of the First-Tenth-Twenty-ninth Maine Regiments*. Portland, Me., 1871.

Graham, C. R. *Tales of the Civil War*. Boston, Mass., 1896.

Grimsley, Daniel A. *Battles in Culpeper County, Virginia*. Culpeper, Va., 1900.

H., C. M. (Fifth Alabama Battalion). Letter in *Columbus* (Ga.) *Daily Enquirer*, August 26, 1862.

Hallum, John. *Reminiscences of the Civil War*. Little Rock, Ark., 1903.

Hamlin, Percy G., ed. *The Making of a Soldier*. Richmond, Va., 1935.

Handerson, Henry E. *Yankee in Gray*. Cleveland, Ohio, 1962.

Harvey, Charles M. "Cedar Mountain." *Richmond Times-Dispatch*, August 25, 1912, and rejoinder, October 6, 1912.

Haupt, Herman. *Reminiscences of General Herman Haupt*. Milwaukee, Wisc., 1901.

Hendricks, James M. "Pegram at Cedar Mountain." *Confederate Veteran* 27 (1919): 448–49.

Hetland, Anthony A. "Battle of Cedar Run." *Countryman* (Putnam County, Ga.), August 23, 1862.

Hickerson, Thomas F., ed. *Echoes of Happy Valley*. Chapel Hill, N.C., 1962.

Hinkley, Julian W. *A Narrative of Service with the Third Wisconsin Infantry*. Madison, Wisc., 1912.

"An Historic Flag, How It Was Lost and Recovered." Newspaper clipping from the *Dayton* (Ohio) *Journal*, n.d., in James Garver Collection, United States Army Military History Institute, Carlisle Barracks, Pa.

Horton, Charles P., et al. "The Campaign of General Pope in Virginia." In

Military Historical Society of Massachusetts, *Papers of the Military Historical Society of Massachusetts.* 12 vols. (Boston, Mass., 1881–1912), 2:31–53.

Hotchkiss, Jedediah. *Make Me a Map of the Valley.* Dallas, Tex., 1973.

Hough, Franklin B. *History of Duryee's Brigade during the Campaign in Virginia under Gen. Pope.* Albany, N.Y., 1864.

Howard, McHenry. *Recollections of a Maryland Confederate Soldier and Staff Officer under Johnston, Jackson, and Lee.* Baltimore, Md., 1914.

Hudson, L. E. "Battle of Cedar Mountain." *Richmond Times-Dispatch,* October 6, 1912.

Huffman, James. *Ups and Downs of a Confederate Soldier.* New York, N.Y., 1940.

Humphreys, David. *Heroes and Spies of the Civil War.* New York, N.Y., 1903.

Jackson, Mary Anna. *Memoirs of Stonewall Jackson.* Louisville, Ky., 1895.

Jaques, John Wesley. *Three Years' Campaign of the Ninth N.Y.S.M.* New York, N.Y., 1865.

Jones, Benjamin W. *Under the Stars and Bars.* Richmond, Va., 1909.

Jones, John B. *A Rebel War Clerk's Diary.* 2 vols. Philadelphia, Pa., 1866.

Jones, John William, ed. *Army of Northern Virginia Memorial Volume.* Richmond, Va., 1880.

Lee, Alfred E. "Cedar Mountain." *Magazine of American History* 16 (1886): 159–67.

Lee, Susan P. *Memoirs of William Nelson Pendleton.* Philadelphia, Pa., 1893.

Lindsley, John B. *The Military Annals of Tennessee.* Nashville, Tenn., 1886.

Lloyd, William Penn. *An Address on the Occasion of the Meeting of the "Blue" and the "Gray" on the Battlefield of Cedar Mountain, Va., August 9th, 1902.* Mechanicsburg, Pa., 1902?

———. *History of the First Reg't. Pennsylvania Reserve Cavalry.* Philadelphia, Pa., 1864.

Lyon, James S. *War Sketches from Cedar Mountain to Bull Run.* Buffalo, N.Y., 1882.

McClendon, William A. *Recollections of War Times by an Old Veteran.* Montgomery, Ala., 1909.

McClenthen, Charles S. *A Sketch of the Campaign in Virginia and Maryland from Cedar Mountain to Antietam.* Syracuse, N.Y., 1862.

McDonald, William N. *A History of the Laurel Brigade.* Baltimore, Md., 1907.

McGuire, Hunter H. *Address of Dr. Hunter McGuire . . . on 23d day of June, 1897.* Lynchburg, Va., 1897.

———. *Stonewall Jackson.* Richmond, Va., 1897.

Marvin, Edwin E. *The Fifth Regiment, Connecticut Volunteers.* Hartford, Conn., 1889.

"Massanutten" [pseud.]. "Battle of Cedar Run." *Richmond Dispatch,* August 18, 1862.

Maxson, William P. *Camp Fires of the Twenty-third.* New York, 1863.

Military Historical Society of Massachusetts. *Papers of the Military Historical Society of Massachusetts.* 12 vols. Boston, Mass., 1881–1912.

Miller, Robert H. "Letters of Lieutenant Robert H. Miller to His Family." Edited by Forrest P. Connor. *Virginia Magazine of History and Biography* 70 (1962): 62–91.

Moore, Edward A. *The Story of a Cannoneer under Stonewall Jackson*. New York, N.Y., 1907.

Moore, Frank, ed. *The Rebellion Record*. 11 vols. New York, N.Y., 1861–68.

Morse, Charles F. *Letters Written during the Civil War*. Boston, Mass., 1898.

Myers, Franklin M. *The Comanches: A History of White's Battalion, Virginia Cavalry*. Baltimore, Md., 1871.

Neese, George M. *Three Years in the Confederate Horse Artillery*. New York, N.Y., 1911.

Newman, Mark. Letter dated August 10, 1862, in *Augusta Daily Constitutionalist*, August 19, 1862.

Nineteenth Georgia "Participant." Unidentified contemporary Georgia newspaper, copy in the M. J. Solomons Scrapbook, Duke University (#4950).

Nisbet, James Cooper. *Four Years on the Firing Line*. Chattanooga, Tenn., 1915?

Noyes, George F. *The Bivouac and the Battle-field*. New York, N.Y., 1863.

Oates, William C. *The War between the Union and the Confederacy*. New York, N.Y., 1905.

O'Ferrall, Charles T. *Forty Years of Active Service*. New York, N.Y., 1904.

P., C. J. "From the 2d Georgia Battalion." *Columbus* (Ga.) *Daily Sun*, September 13, 1862.

Patrick, Marsena R. *Inside Lincoln's Army*. Edited by David S. Sparks. New York, N.Y., 1964.

Pender, William Dorsey. *The General to His Lady: The Civil War Letters of William Dorsey Pender to Fanny Pender*. Edited by William W. Hassler. Chapel Hill, N.C., 1965.

Player, Samuel T. Report of Cedar Mountain in *Sandersville* (Ga.) *Central Georgian*, August 27, 1862.

Poague, William T. *Gunner with Stonewall*. Edited by Monroe F. Cockrell. Jackson, Tenn., 1957.

[Prince, General]. "The Way Prince Was Captured." *Columbus* (Ga.) *Daily Sun*, August 22, 1862.

Pyne, Henry R. *The History of the First New Jersey Cavalry*. Trenton, N.J., 1871.

Quint, Alonzo H. *The Potomac and the Rapidan*. Boston, Mass., 1864.

––––––. *The Record of the Second Massachusetts Infantry*. Boston, Mass., 1867.

"Reunion on Battlefield." *Fredericksburg Free Lance*, August 13, 1912.

Rogers, Matthew Robert. Letter dated August 13, 1862, in *Augusta Daily Constitutionalist*, August 20, 1862, and *Columbus* (Ga.) *Daily Enquirer*, August 20, 1862.

Roll of Honor, No. XV. Washington, D.C., 1868.

Roll of Honor, No. XXVI. Washington, D.C., 1871.

[Roosevelt, Theodore]. "On Field of Battle: Visit to Cedar Mountain by President Roosevelt." *Washington Post*, November 3, 1902.

Saunders, Joseph H. Account of Cedar Mountain and Chancellorsville in an unidentified but evidently contemporary newspaper, clipping owned by a brigade descendant, copy in author's possession.

SeCheverall, John H. *Journal History of the Twenty-ninth Ohio Veteran Volunteers.* Cleveland, Ohio, 1883.

Sheeran, James B. *Confederate Chaplain: A War Journal.* Milwaukee, Wisc., 1960.

Slaughter, Philip. *A Sketch of the Life of Randolph Fairfax.* Richmond, Va., 1864.

————. *Views from Cedar Mountain.* New York, N.Y., 1884.

Small, Abner R. *The Road to Richmond.* Berkeley, Calif., 1939.

Stearns, Austin C. *Three Years with Company K.* Rutherford, N.J., 1976.

Stevens, John W. *Reminiscences of the Civil War.* Hillsboro, Tex., 1902.

Strother, David Hunter. *A Virginia Yankee in the Civil War.* Chapel Hill, N.C., 1961.

Taylor, Richard. *Destruction and Reconstruction.* New York, N.Y., 1879.

Thomas, Henry W. *History of the Doles-Cook Brigade.* Atlanta, Ga., 1903.

Tobie, Edward P. *History of the First Maine Cavalry, 1861–1865.* Boston, Mass., 1887.

Townsend, George A. *Campaigns of a Non-Combatant.* New York, N.Y., 1866.

Trimble, Isaac R. "The Civil War Diary of General Isaac Ridgeway Trimble." *Maryland Historical Magazine* 17 (1922): 1–20.

Tripp, Harrison A. Account of Cedar Mountain in an unidentified newspaper clipping, copy in Container 70, Hotchkiss Papers, Library of Congress.

————. "The Charge of Cedar Mountain." *Grand Army Scout and Soldiers Mail* 5, no. 38 (1886).

"The Twelth [*sic*] Georgia Again." *Columbus Daily Sun*, August 23, 1862.

U.S. Congress. *Report of the Joint Committee on the Conduct of the War.* 9 serials in 3 vols. Washington, D.C., 1863–66.

U.S. War Department. *War of the Rebellion: A Compilation of the Official Records of the Union and Confederate Armies.* 128 vols. Washington, D.C., 1880–1901.

West, John C. *A Texan in Search of a Fight.* Waco, Tex., 1901.

"What a Woman Saw at Cedar Mountain." *Richmond Times-Dispatch*, August 27, 1911.

White, William S. *Sketches of the Life of Captain Hugh A. White, of the Stonewall Brigade.* Columbia, S.C., 1864.

Whitman, George Washington. *Civil War Letters of George Washington Whitman.* Durham, N.C., 1975.

Williams, Alpheus S. *From the Cannon's Mouth.* Detroit, Mich., 1959.

Wilson, Lawrence. "Cedar Mountain: Blue and Gray Unite to Mark Positions on This Famous Battlefield." *National Tribune*, August 22, 1901.

Wood, George L. *The Seventh [Ohio] Regiment, a Record.* New York, N.Y., 1865.
Wood, James Harvey. *The War.* Cumberland, Md., 1910.
Worsham, John H. *One of Jackson's Foot Cavalry.* New York, N.Y., 1912.
Yeary, Mamie. *Reminiscences of the Boys in Gray.* Dallas, Tex., 1912.

Periodicals

Augusta (Ga.) *Daily Constitutionalist,* 1862.
Blue & Gray, 1986.
Century, 1893–94.
Civil War History, 1976.
Columbus (Ga.) *Daily Enquirer,* 1862.
Columbus (Ga.) *Daily Sun,* 1862.
Confederate Veteran, 1893–1932.
Connecticut Historical Society Bulletin, 1983.
Culpeper (Va.) *Exponent,* 1900.
Current Medical Digest, 1961.
Dayton (Ohio) *Journal,* undated clipping.
Fredericksburg Free Lance, 1912.
Grand Army Scout and Soldiers Mail, 1884, 1886.
Journal of the Military Service Institution, 1907.
Land We Love, 1866–69.
Magazine of American History, 1884, 1886.
Maryland Historical Magazine, 1922.
National Tribune, 1901, 1903.
New York Times, 1862.
Philadelphia Weekly Times, 1883.
Raleigh State Journal, 1862.
Richmond Dispatch, 1862.
Richmond Times, 1899, 1902.
Richmond Times-Dispatch, 1903, 1904, 1911, 1912.
Sandersville Central Georgian, 1862.
Southern Historical Society Papers, 1876–1959.
Staunton (Va.) *Vindicator,* 1896.
Virginia Baptist Register, 1982.
Virginia Magazine of History and Biography, 1962.
Washington Post, 1902.
Washington Star, 1933.
Yankee, 1982.

Secondary Sources

Allan, Elizabeth Randolph Preston. *A March Past*. Richmond, Va., 1938.

[Andrews, R. Snowden]. "A Desperate Wound . . . How He Impressed the Germans—His Wound Acted as a Magic Talisman." Unidentified newspaper clipping (ca. 1880s) in the Jedediah Hotchkiss Papers, Library of Congress, Roll 59, Frame 303, microfilm.

Bigelow, John. *The Campaign of Chancellorsville*. New Haven, Conn., 1910.

Birdsong, James C. *Brief Sketches of the North Carolina State Troops in the War between the States*. Raleigh, N.C., 1894.

Booth, Andrew B. *Records of Louisiana Confederate Soldiers*. 4 vols. New Orleans, La., 1920.

Brown, Riley S. *Stringfellow of the Fourth*. New York, N.Y., 1960.

Bruce, Philip A., ed. *History of Virginia*. 6 vols. Chicago, Ill., 1924.

Buckley, William. *Buckley's History of the Great Reunion of the North and South*. Staunton, Va., 1923.

Calfee, Berkeley G. *Confederate History of Culpeper County*. Culpeper, Va., 1948.

Chambers, Lenoir. *Stonewall Jackson*. 2 vols. New York, N.Y., 1959.

Chapla, John D. *42nd Virginia Infantry*. Lynchburg, Va., 1984.

"Confederate Museum." *Staunton Vindicator*, July 24, 1896.

Cook, Roy Bird. *Lewis County in the Civil War*. Charleston, W.Va., 1924.

Davis, Julia. *Mount Up*. New York, N.Y., 1967.

Dew, Charles B. *Ironmaker to the Confederacy: Joseph R. Anderson and the Tredegar Iron Works*. New Haven, Conn., 1966.

Driver, Robert J., Jr. *52nd Virginia Infantry*. Lynchburg, Va., 1986.

Folsom, James M. *Heroes and Martyrs of Georgia*. Macon, Ga., 1864.

Gilbert, John W. "Cedar Mountain." *Grand Army Scout and Soldiers Mail* 3, no. 49 (1884).

Goldsborough, William W. *The Maryland Line in the Confederate Army, 1861–1865*. Baltimore, Md., 1900.

Green, Bennett W. *Word-book of Virginia Folk-speech*. Richmond, Va., 1899.

Hamlin, Percy G. *"Old Bald Head."* Strasburg, Va., 1940.

Harris, Malcolm H. *History of Louisa County, Virginia*. Richmond, Va., 1936.

Hawkins, W. S. "Col. George W. Curtis." *Confederate Veteran* 11 (1903): 466.

Heitman, Francis B. *Historical Register and Dictionary of the United States Army*. 2 vols. Washington, D.C., 1903.

Henderson, George Francis Robert. *Stonewall Jackson and the American Civil War*. 2 vols. London, 1898.

Henderson, Lillian, comp. *Roster of the Confederate Soldiers of Georgia*. 6 vols. Hapeville, Ga., 1959–64.

Hodges, Elizabeth M. *C. B. Fleet: The Man and the Company*. Lynchburg?, Va., 1986?

Johnson, John Lipscomb. *The University Memorial*. Baltimore, Md., 1871.

Johnson, Thomas C. *The Life and Letters of Robert Lewis Dabney.* Richmond, Va., 1903.

Jordan, Weymouth T., Jr. *North Carolina Troops.* 11 vols. Raleigh, N.C., 1966–87.

Koontz, Amos R. "Disembowelment in the Field with Cure: The Amazing Feat of a Confederate Surgeon." *Current Medical Digest* 27 (1961): 50–52.

Krick, Robert K. "The Army of Northern Virginia's Most Notorious Court Martial." *Blue & Gray* 3 (June–July 1986): 27–32.

_____. *Lee's Colonels: A Biographical Register of the Field Officers of the Army of Northern Virginia.* Dayton, Ohio, 1984.

_____. *Maxcy Gregg.* Kent, Ohio, 1973.

Mahon, John K., and Romana Danysh. *Army Lineage Series, Infantry, Part I: Regular Army.* Washington, D.C., 1972.

Odell, William S. "Pegram's Strategy at Cedar Mountain." *Confederate Veteran* 26 (1918): 488.

Powell, Nora, and Watts Powell. *Historical and Genealogical Collections of Dooley County, Georgia.* 3 vols. Vienna, Ga., 1975.

Powell, Walter L. "Heaven Alone Can Soothe Hearts." *Connecticut Historical Society Bulletin* 48 (1983): 52–71.

Rankin, Thomas M. *23rd Virginia Infantry.* Lynchburg, Va., 1985.

_____. *37th Virginia Infantry.* Lynchburg, Va., 1987.

Reed, I. Richard. *100 Years Ago Today: Niagara County in the Civil War.* Lockport, N.Y., 1966.

Reidenbaugh, Lowell. *33rd Virginia Infantry.* Lynchburg, Va., 1987.

Richey, Homer, ed. *Memorial History of the John Bowie Strange Camp, United Confederate Veterans.* Charlottesville, Va., 1920.

Salley, Alexander S. *South Carolina Troops in Confederate Service.* 3 vols. Columbia, S.C., 1913–30.

Sanford, David. *"God Our Refuge in Trouble," a Sermon Preached August 24, 1862, at West Medway, in the Church of Rev. Dr. Ide, Occasioned by the Deaths of his Youngest Son, Mr. George H. Ide, Aged 26, and Mr. Herman S. Sparrow . . . Aged 21, Who Fell When Fighting in Defence of Their Country, at Cedar Mountain, Va., Aug. 9, 1862. . . .* Holliston, Mass., 1862.

Schenck, Martin. *Up Came Hill.* Harrisburg, Pa., 1958.

Scott, William W. *A History of Orange County, Virginia.* Richmond, Va., 1909.

"Souvenir of a Gallant Soldier." Unidentified newspaper article in Jedediah Hotchkiss Papers, Library of Congress, Roll 58, Frame 793, microfilm.

Squires, Charles H. *The 28th Regiment, N.Y. Vols., 1st Brig., 1st Div., 12th Army Corps, At the Battle of Cedar Mountain, Va., Aug. 9th, 1862.* Lockport, N.Y., n.d.

Steele, Matthew Forney. *American Campaigns.* 2 vols. Washington, D.C., 1909.

Strickler, Harry M. *A Short History of Page County.* Richmond, Va., 1952.

Tyler, Lyon G., ed. *Encyclopedia of Virginia Biography.* 5 vols. New York, N.Y., 1915.

Vandiver, Frank E. *Mighty Stonewall*. New York, N.Y., 1957.

Walker, Charles D. *Memorial, Virginia Military Institute*. Philadelphia, Pa., 1875.

Wallace, Lee A., Jr. *A Guide to Virginia Military Organizations, 1861–1865*. Lynchburg, Va., 1986.

[Winder, Charles S.]. "Local Matters: Gen. Charles Sidney Winder." *Richmond Dispatch*, August 18, 1862.

Wise, Jennings Cropper. *The Long Arm of Lee: Or, the History of the Artillery of the Army of Northern Virginia*. 2 vols. Lynchburg, Va., 1915.

[Wright, Marcus J.]. *List of Staff Officers of the Confederate States Army*. Washington, D.C., 1891.

INDEX

459